PERSONAL NAMES IN PALMYRENE INSCRIPTIONS

PERSONAL NAMES IN PALMYRENE INSCRIPTIONS

BY

JÜRGEN KURT STARK

OXFORD
AT THE CLARENDON PRESS
1971

Oxford University Press, Ely House, London W. 1

GLASGOW NEW YORK TORONTO MELBOURNE WELLINGTON
CAPE TOWN SALISBURY IBADAN NAIROBI DAR ES SALAAM LUSAKA ADDIS ABABA
BOMBAY CALCUTTA MADRAS KARACHI LAHORE DACCA
KUALA LUMPUR SINGAPORE HONG KONG TOKYO

PRINTED IN GREAT BRITAIN
AT THE UNIVERSITY PRESS, OXFORD
BY VIVIAN RIDLER
PRINTER TO THE UNIVERSITY

Sh

TO MY PARENTS

PREFACE

THE present book represents in a slightly expanded form my thesis submitted to The Johns Hopkins University, Baltimore, Maryland, in 1968 in partial fulfilment of the requirements for the degree of Doctor of Philosophy. To Professor D. R. Hillers I owe the deepest gratitude and respect for supervising this thesis and for directing my studies in Semitic philology. His abilities as a scholar and teacher, together with his humanity, will always be remembered. Thanks also are due to Professor H. B. Huffmon, who has read the entire manuscript and made valuable criticisms and suggestions. Professor G. Krotkoff was an irreplaceable guide in questions pertaining to Arabic. Professor J. H. Oliver was helpful with regard to the Greek and Latin names. None of these, however, is responsible for any shortcomings that remain.

Heartfelt thanks are due to Mr. and Mrs. Eugene B. Skarie for their constant encouragement during the writing of the dissertation, for their ever-ready help, and for all that they have taught me. I am grateful also to Mrs. Mary E. Pike, who generously consented to read the entire manuscript with a view to improving the English.

J. K. STARK

Trinity College, Dublin
October 1969

CONTENTS

LIST OF ABBREVIATIONS

AAS	*Annales archéologiques de Syrie.*
AfO	*Archiv für Orientforschung.*
'Afrique'	J.-B. Chabot, 'Nouvelle inscription palmyrénienne d'Afrique', *CRAIBL* (1932), 265–9.
AHw	W. von Soden, ed., *Akkadisches Handwörterbuch, Unter Benutzung des lexikalischen Nachlasses von Bruno Meissner (1868–1947)* (Wiesbaden, 1959–).
Ana. Bollandiana	*Analecta Bollandiana.*
Ana. Stud.	*Anatolian Studies.*
ANET	J. B. Pritchard, *Ancient Near Eastern Texts relating to the Old Testament*, 2nd edn. (Princeton, 1955).
ANG	J. J. Stamm, *Die akkadische Namengebung* (*MVÄG*, 44; Leipzig, 1939).
AnOr	*Analecta Orientalia.*
APN	K. L. Tallquist, *Assyrian Personal Names* (*Acta Societatis Scientiarum Fennicae*, xliii/l; Helsingfors, 1914).
APNMT	H. B. Huffmon, *Amorite Personal Names in the Mari Texts: A Structural and Lexical Study* (Baltimore, 1965).
ARM V	G. Dossin, ed., *Archives royales de Mari, V: Lettres* (TCL, xxvi; Paris, 1951).
ASD	W. Cureton, *Ancient Syriac Documents* (London and Edinburgh, 1864).
BA	Biblical Aramaic.
BAH	Bibliothèque archéologique et historique.
BANE	*The Bible and the Ancient Near East* (*Essays in Honor of William Foxwell Albright*), ed. G. E. Wright (Garden City, 1961).
BASOR	*Bulletin of the American Schools of Oriental Research.*
'Bas-relief'	J. Starcky, 'Bas-relief palmyrénien inédit, dédié aux génies Šalman et 'RGY'', *Semitica*, 3 (1950), 45–52.
Ben-Hayyim	Z. Ben-Hayyim, 'Palmyrene Inscriptions', *BJPES*, 13 (1947), 141–8.
Beth Sheʿarim	B. Mazar (Maisler), *Beth Sheʿarim.* Report on the Excavations during 1936–40. Vol. I: *The Catacombs I–IV* (Jerusalem, 1957).
BEUP	A. T. Clay, *Business Documents of Murashu Sons of Nippur* ('The Babylonian Expedition of the University of Pennsylvania', Series A, vol. x) (Philadelphia, 1904).
'Bilingue'	G. Levi della Vida, 'Une bilingue gréco-palmyrénienne à Cos', in *Mélanges syriens offerts à M. René Dussaud* (BAH, xxx; Paris, 1939), ii. 883–6.
BJPES	*Bulletin of the Jewish Palestine Exploration Society.*

BMAP	E. G. Kraeling, *The Brooklyn Museum Aramaic Papyri* (New Haven, 1953).
BMB	*Bulletin du Musée de Beyrouth.*
BO	J. S. Assemanus, *Bibliotheca Orientalis*, 4 vols. (Rome, 1719–28).
BSOAS	*Bulletin of the School of Oriental and African Studies.*
C	*Corpus Inscriptionum Semiticarum, pars secunda, tomus tertius*, Fasc. I (Paris, 1926); tabulae (Paris, 1951); Fasc. II (Paris, 1947); tabulae (Paris, 1954).
CaA	J. Cantineau, 'Inscriptions palmyréniennes', *RA*, 27 (1930), 27–51, nos. 1–36; and also separately Damascus, 1930, nos. 1–105.
CaB	J. Cantineau, 'Textes funéraires palmyréniennes', *RB*, 39 (1930), 520–49.
CaC	J. Cantineau, 'Textes palmyréniens provenant de la fouille du temple de Bēl', *Syria*, 12 (1931), 116–41.
CaD	J. Cantineau, 'Tadmorea', *Syria*, 14 (1933), 169–202 (nos. 1–16); *Syria*, 17 (1936), 267–82, 346–55 (nos. 17–27); *Syria*, 19 (1938), 72–82, 153–71 (nos. 28–46).
CaE	J. Cantineau, 'Un Restitutor Orientis dans les inscriptions de Palmyre', *Journal asiatique*, 222 (1933), 217–33.
CAD	A. L. Oppenheim, *et al.* (eds.), *The Assyrian Dictionary of the Oriental Institute of the University of Chicago* (Chicago, 1956–).
CIS	See under *C*.
CRAIBL	*Comptes rendus des séances de l'Académie des Inscriptions et Belles-Lettres.*
CT	*Cuneiform Texts from Babylonian Tablets in the British Museum* (London, 1896 ff.).
'Dédicace'	J. Starcky, 'Autour d'une dédicace palmyrénienne à Šadrafa et à Duʿanat', *Syria*, 26 (1949), 43–85.
Dura, Final Report V	C. Bradford Welles *et al.* (eds.), *The Excavations at Dura-Europos, Final Report V, Part I, The Parchments and Papyri* (New Haven, 1959).
'Euphrate'	J. Starcky, 'Une inscription palmyrénienne trouvée près de l'Euphrate', *Syria*, 40 (1963), 47–55.
f	Feminine name.
'Fouilles'	R. du Mesnil du Buisson, 'Première campagne de fouilles à Palmyre', *CRAIBL* (1966), 158–90.
GLECS	*Groupe linguistique d'études chamito-sémitiques. Comptes rendus.*
'Grave-Relief'	H. Ingholt, 'The oldest known Grave-Relief from Palmyra', *Acta Archaeologica*, 1 (1930), 191–4.
GVG	C. Brockelmann, *Grundriss der vergleichenden Grammatik der semitischen Sprachen*, 2 vols. (Berlin, 1908–13).
'Hatra'	A. Caquot, 'Nouvelles inscriptions araméennes de Hatra', *Syria*, 29 (1952), 89–118 (nos. 1–27); *Syria*, 30 (1953), 234–46 (nos. 28–42); *Syria*, 32 (1955), 49–69, 261–72 (nos. 43–78); *Syria*, 40 (1963), 1–16 (nos. 79–105); *Syria*, 41 (1964), 251–72

	(nos. 106–206); J. Teixidor, *Sumer*, 20 (1964), 77–80 (nos. 207–13).
HUCA	*Hebrew Union College Annual.*
'Hypogée'	S. Abdul-Hak, 'L'hypogée de Tai à Palmyre', *AAS*, 2 (1952), 193–251.
IEJ	*Israel Exploration Journal.*
ILS	H. Dessau, *Inscriptiones Latinae Selectae*, 3 vols. (Berlin, 1892–1916).
Ingh. A	H. Ingholt, 'Inscriptions and Sculptures from Palmyra', *Berytus*, 3 (1936), 83–127.
Ingh. B	H. Ingholt, 'Inscriptions and Sculptures from Palmyra—II', *Berytus*, 5 (1938), 93–140.
Ingh. C	H. Ingholt, 'Quelques fresques récemment découvertes à Palmyre', *Acta Archaeologica*, 3 (1932), 1–20.
Ingh. D	H. Ingholt, 'Palmyrene Sculptures in Beirut', *Berytus*, 1 (1934), 32–43.
Ingh. E	H. Ingholt, 'Five dated Tombs from Palmyra', *Berytus*, 2 (1935), 57–120.
Ingh. 'Quatre'	H. Ingholt, 'Quatre bustes palmyréniens', *Syria*, 11 (1930), 242–4.
Ingh. 'Th.'	H. Ingholt, 'Un nouveau thiase à Palmyre', *Syria*, 7 (1926), 128–41.
'Inscriptions'	J. Starcky, 'Deux inscriptions palmyréniennes', *MUSJ*, 38 (1961), 121–39.
Inv.	J. Cantineau, *Inventaire des inscriptions de Palmyre*. Fasc. 1–9, Damascus, 1930–6; fasc. 10 by J. Starcky, Damascus, 1949; fasc. 11 by J. Teixidor, Beirut, 1965.
'IP'	A. Bounni, 'Inscriptions palmyréniennes inédites', *AAS*, 11 (1961), 145–62.
IPN	M. Noth, *Die israelitischen Personennamen im Rahmen der gemeinsemitischen Namengebung* (Stuttgart, 1928).
'Iraq'	J. Teixidor, 'Three inscriptions in the Iraq Museum', *Sumer*, 18 (1962), 63–5.
JAOS	*Journal of the American Oriental Society.*
JBL	*Journal of Biblical Literature.*
JPOS	*Journal of the Palestine Oriental Society.*
JSOR	*Journal of the Society of Oriental Research.*
JSS	*Journal of Semitic Studies.*
KAI	H. Donner and W. Röllig, *Kanaanäische und Aramäische Inschriften*, 3 vols. (Wiesbaden, 1962–4).
'La Susiane'	J. Cantineau, 'La Susiane dans une inscription palmyrénienne', in *Mélanges syriens offerts à M. René Dussaud* (BAH, xxx; Paris, 1939), i, 277–9.
m	Masculine name.
'Malkû'	H. Ingholt, 'Palmyrene Inscription from the Tomb of Malkû', *MUSJ*, 38 (1962), 101–19.
MDOG	*Mitteilungen der Deutschen Orient-Gesellschaft.*
Michalowski	*Mélanges offerts à K. Michalowski* (Warsaw, 1966).

Misc. Ubach	*Miscellanea Biblica B. Ubach*, edited by Dom. Romualdo Diaz (Scripta et Documenta, 1; Montserrat, 1953).
'Monuments'	J. Teixidor, 'Monuments palmyréniens divers', *MUSJ*, 42 (1966), 175–9.
MRS	Mission de Ras Shamra.
MUSJ	*Mélanges de l'Université Saint Joseph.*
MVÄG	*Mitteilungen der Vorderasiatisch-aegyptischen Gesellschaft.*
NBN	K. Tallquist, *Neubabylonisches Namenbuch* (*Acta Societatis Scientiarum Fennicae*, xxxii/2; Helsingfors, 1905).
'Note'	A. Bounni, 'Note sur un nouveau bas-relief palmyrénien', *AAS*, 15 (1965), 87–98.
OSA	Old South Arabic.
Pal.	K. Michalowski, *Palmyre. Fouilles polonaises* 1959–64, 5 vols. (Warsaw and Paris, 1960–6).
Palmyrene	J. Ingholt, *Palmyrene and Gandharan Sculpture* (Yale University Art Gallery, 1954).
PEQ	*Palestine Exploration Quarterly.*
PNO	D. Schlumberger, *La Palmyrène du Nord-Ouest* (BAH, xlix; Paris, 1951).
PRU II	Ch. Virolleaud, *Le Palais royal d'Ugarit, II: Textes en cunéiformes alphabétiques des Archives Est, Ouest et Centrales* (MRS, vii; Paris, 1957).
PRU III	J. Nougayrol, *Le Palais royal d'Ugarit, III: Textes accadiens et hourrites des Archives Est, Ouest et Centrales* (MRS, vi; Paris, 1955), 2 vols.
PRU IV	J. Nougayrol, *Le Palais royal d'Ugarit, IV: Textes accadiens des Archives Sud* (MRS, ix; Paris, 1956), 2 vols.
PRU V	Ch. Virolleaud, *Le Palais royal d'Ugarit, V: Textes en cunéiformes alphabétiques des Archives Sud, Sud-Ouest et du Petit Palais* (MRS, xi; Paris, 1965).
PS	H. Ingholt, *Studier over Palmyrensk Skulptur* (Copenhagen, 1928).
PS	Proto-Semitic.
RA	*Revue d'assyriologie et d'archéologie orientale.*
RAO	Ch. Clermont-Ganneau, *Recueil d'archéologie orientale*, 8 vols. (Paris, 1888–1924).
RB	*Revue biblique.*
RES	*Répertoire d'épigraphie sémitique.*
RES	*Revue des études sémitiques.*
Rev. arch.	*Revue archéologique.*
RHR	*Revue de l'histoire des religions.*
RTP	H. Ingholt, H. Seyrig, and J. Starcky, *Recueil des Tessères de Palmyre* (BAH, lviii; Paris, 1955).
SBAW	*Sitzungsberichte der königlich preussischen Akademie der Wissenschaften zu Berlin.*
'Sculptures'	J. Sabeh, 'Sculptures palmyréniennes inédites du Musée de Damas', *AAS*, 3 (1953), 17–26.
StaA	J. Starcky, 'Trois inscriptions palmyréniennes', *MUSJ*, 28 (1949–50), 45–58.

StaB	J. Starcky and D. Al-Hassani, 'Autels palmyréniens découverts près de la source Efca', *AAS*, 3 (1953), 145–64; 7 (1957), 95–122.
StaC	J. Starcky, 'Inscriptions palmyréniennes conservées au Musée de Beyrouth', *BMB*, 12 (1955), 29–44.
StaD	J. Starcky, 'Inscriptions archaïques de Palmyre', in *Studi orientalistici in onore di G. Levi della Vida*, ii. 509–28 (Rome, 1956).
StaE	J. Starcky, 'Relief palmyrénien dédié au dieu Ilahay', in *Mélanges bibliques A. Robert*, 370–80 (without date).
StaF	J. Starcky, 'Les inscriptions', *Syria*, 26 (1949), 35–41.
Studi Semitici	S. Moscati, ed., *Le antiche divinità semitiche* (Studi Semitici, 1; Rome, 1958).
SWAW	*Sitzungsberichte der kaiserlichen Akademie der Wissenschaften zu Wien, Phil.-hist. Klasse.*
TCL	Museé du Louvre, Départment des Antiquités Orientales, Textes Cunéiformes.
'Tessera'	J. Walker, 'A Palmyrene Tessera', in *Studi orientalistici in onore di G. Levi della Vida*, ii. 601–2 (Rome, 1956).
'Tessères'	Ch. Dunant, 'Nouvelles tessères de Palmyre', *Syria*, 36 (1959), 102–10.
Thes. Syr.	R. Payne-Smith, *Thesaurus Syriacus* (Oxford, 1879–97).
'Trilingue'	M. Rodinson, 'Une inscription trilingue de Palmyre', *Syria*, 27 (1950), 137–42.
'ÜOSP'	Th. Nöldeke, 'Über Orthographie und Sprache der Palmyrener', *ZDMG*, 24 (1870), 85–109.
UT	C. H. Gordon, *Ugaritic Textbook* (*AnOr*, 38; Rome, 1965).
VT	*Vetus Testamentum.*
Wadd.	W. H. Waddington, *Recueil des inscriptions grecques et latines de la Syrie*, 1870.
'Wadi Hauran'	F. Safar, 'Inscriptions from Wadi Hauran', *Sumer*, 20 (1964), 9–27.
WO	*Die Welt des Orients.*
Wuthnow	H. Wuthnow, 'Eine palmyrenische Büste', in *Orientalistische Studien Enno Littmann . . . überreicht*, 63–9 (Leiden, 1935).
WVDOG	Wissenschaftliche Veröffentlichungen der Deutschen Orient-Gesellschaft.
WZKM	*Wiener Zeitschrift für die Kunde des Morgenlandes.*
ZA	*Zeitschrift für Assyriologie und verwandte Gebiete.*
ZAW	*Zeitschrift für die alttestamentliche Wissenschaft.*
ZDMG	*Zeitschrift der Deutschen morgenländischen Gesellschaft.*
ZDPV	*Zeitschrift des Deutschen Palästina-Vereins.*
ZS	*Zeitschrift für Semitistik und verwandte Gebiete.*

TRANSLITERATION OF BIBLICAL HEBREW

CONSONANTS

א = ʾ	ז = z	מ = m	ק = q
ב = b	ח = ḥ	נ = n	ר = r
ג = g	ט = ṭ	ס = s	שׂ = ś
ד = d	י = y	ע = ʿ	שׁ = š
ה = h	כ = k	פ = p	ת = t
ו = w	ל = l	צ = ṣ	

Note. The presence or absence of *dageš lene* in the *begadkepat* letters is not shown. Consonants with *dageš forte* are written double.

VOWELS (shown as preceded by *b*)

בָה, בָהּ = bāh	בִי = bî	בִֽ = bī	בִ = bi
בוֹ = bô	בָֽ = bā	בַ = ba	בֲ = bᵃ
בוּ = bû	בֹ = bō	בָ = bo	בְ = bᵉ
בֵי = bê	בֻֽ = bū	בֻ = bu	
בֶי = bè	בֵ = bē	בֶ = be	

בֶה = beh (although *h* is merely a *mater lectionis* here).

TRANSLITERATION OF GREEK

ᾳ = ą	θ = th	ω = ō
η = ē	υ = y	ῳ = ō$_i$
ῃ = ę	φ = ph	῾ = ʿ
	ψ = ps	

TRANSLITERATION OF ARABIC

ء = ʾ	د = d	ض = ḍ	ك = k
ب = b	ذ = ḏ	ط = ṭ	ل = l
ت = t	ر = r	ظ = ẓ	م = m
ث = ṯ	ز = z	ع = ʿ	ن = n
ج = j	س = s	غ = ǵ	ه = h
ح = ḥ	ش = š	ف = f	و = w
خ = ḫ	ص = ṣ	ق = q	ى = y

INTRODUCTION

I. *Previous Studies of Palmyrene Names.* The study of Palmyrene personal names is relatively young. Apart from individual treatments of the inscriptions, the first work that methodically collected all the names attested up to that time was E. Ledrain's *Dictionnaire des noms propres palmyréniens* (1887, 60 pp.; not accessible to me), the bulk of which was incorporated into M. Lidzbarski's *Handbuch der nordsemitischen Epigraphik* (1898). The next work dealing with Palmyrene personal names was W. Goldmann's Breslau dissertation, *Die palmyrenischen Personennamen* (1935, 40 pp.). This study confines itself to a structural grouping of the names, giving only occasionally an interpretation. Its usefulness is marred by the many incorrect readings which are incorporated. This, however, is not the fault of the author, who had to rely on transcriptions and could only seldom consult a photograph to verify the reading. (The plates to the *Corpus Inscriptionum Semiticarum, pars secunda, tomus tertius*, fasc. I, only came out as late as 1951.) Secondly, the book is in many respects incomplete and outdated with regard to the material, because of the many inscriptions that have been brought to light since 1935 as a result of excavations or publications of sculptures found in museums and private collections.

The first person to deal with the names from a structural and lexical point of view was A. Caquot in 'Remarques linguistiques sur les inscriptions des tessères de Palmyre', in *Recueil des tessères de Palmyre* (1955), and in his article in *Syria* (1962), 'Sur l'onomastique religieuse de Palmyre'. Although Caquot's studies are limited in scope—they deal with only about one-tenth of the material found in this study—they are extremely useful.

The latest work which draws upon the Palmyrene personal names is H. Schult's *Vergleichende Studien zur Alttestamentlichen Namenkunde* (Diss. Bonn, 1967), but his treatment of the Palmyrene material is very superficial with regard to grammar and lexicon, and a great number of misreadings have been incorporated owing to his use of secondary sources.

II. *Methodological Considerations and Possible Results.* The present study is part of a full-scale treatment of Semitic names in Palmyrene inscriptions, most of which are honorific or sepulchral and consist mainly of long lists of genealogies, thus leaving us with less information than the number of inscriptions would suggest. Among possible outcomes of such an investigation are (1) a fuller knowledge as to which language or languages were spoken at Palmyra, (2) more light on the Palmyrene pantheon about which relatively little is known, (3) more information about Palmyrene Aramaic, the dialect in which the inscriptions were written, and (4) an understanding of the ethnic composition of the population at Palmyra and the changes that may have taken place in it in the course of time.

My aim was to provide a thorough grammatical and lexical analysis, for only when these two requirements are fulfilled can relatively reliable conclusions be drawn for the areas named above.

In treating Semitic names I have not been selective, confining my analysis to names with Aramaic elements, but have been concerned with all the Semitic names. The reason for this is that the language situation at Palmyra is very complex, and I have preferred not to anticipate any possible results of this study.

However, the general picture that I have formed of Palmyrene has to some extent influenced my analysis of the individual names. A statistical survey of the names given in the Main List would show that more than half of them can be best explained through Arabic or can have a possible Arabic etymology. When one further considers that names like ḤYRN, MQYMW, MLKW, which lexically require an Arabic explanation, are attested with far greater frequency than other names, the balance weighs even more in favour of Arabic. For this reason I have in many cases given preference to the Arabic etymology of a name, but without omitting reference to a possible Aramaic interpretation.

This preliminary survey might affect the question about the language spoken at Palmyra, just as a similar investigation did for Nabataean. In regard to Nabataean it had generally been assumed that the language of Petra was Aramaic. But Th. Nöldeke discovered that the personal names occurring in the Nabataean inscriptions were practically all Arabic, a fact that led him to the conclusion that the scribes and people were Arabs using Aramaic in their inscriptions.[1] The answer for Palmyra does not seem to be as clear cut as it is for Petra, but already one can say that the Arabic stratum within the population of Palmyra must have been considerable.

For comparative material I have relied on a number of studies. For the Israelite personal names I consulted M. Noth's study. For the Akkadian onomasticon the works by K. Tallquist, A. Clay, and J. J. Stamm have been used. For South Semitic G. Ryckmans's collection of names has been consulted. H. Huffmon's book on Amorite personal names in the Mari texts was a mine of information for Amorite specifically and for North-west Semitic names in general.[2]

[1] Rosenthal, *Aramaistische Forschung*, 89.

[2] For full information on the works cited in the Introduction consult the bibliography.

I. MAIN

THE list of names is arranged as follows:

The first entry gives the personal names f
order of the North-west Semitic alphabet.
masculine names (*m*). It is assumed that in th
is given.

The entries immediately after the names
arranged in two classes, (1) dated (according
inscriptions. References are usually given by
of articles published in journals and *Festschri*
Square brackets within the text reference refer
year date. Round brackets indicate a scribal m
been corrected by the present writer.

Wherever possible the reading of the names ha
of the inscription. This could not be done in all c
graph could be obtained, sometimes because th
made any verification impossible. In many instanc
was gained by consulting a photograph (see Appe
The siglum *ILS* refers to Dessau, *Inscriptiones*

'B' (*m*) **1.** *502*, *C* 4174[2]—šmʿwn br 'B' br ḥnyn'. *526*, Ingh. E (Malê) p. 77, 111[1]—ywlys 'wrlys ḥyrn wywlys 'wrlys 'B' bny ywlys 'wrlys mqy br yrḥy. *568*, *PNO* 20—šmʿwn br 'B'. **2.** *C* 4180 A[3]—šmʿwn br 'B' 'brm'. *C* 4182—šmʿwn br 'B'. *PNO* 76 B—lšmš 'B'.

'BB (*m*) **1.** *425*, *C* 4374[5]—'l' brt yrḥy 'BB. *425*, *C* 4374 *bis*[3]—'l' brt yrḥy 'BB. **2.** *RTP* 697b—'BB ḥyrn mlkw. CaD 25[7]—. . .]ql br 'BB tymʿm[d . . .

'BB' (*f*) **2.** *C* 4436[1]—['B]B' brt tymy br bny. *C* 4462[1]—'BB' brt ḥyrn br khyly. *C* 4474[1]—'BB' brt whblt.

'BGL (*m*) **1.** *510*, *PNO* 3 A—'BGL br šʿrw. *510*, *PNO* 3 B—'BGL br šʿrw. *564*, *PNO* 15[1]—'BGL br [. . . . **2.** *PNO* 2 *ter*[2]—'BGL. *PNO* 2 *ter*[6]—'BGL. *PNO* 2 *ter*[10]—'BGL.

'BGR (*m*) **1.** *395*, CaD 29[1]—'BGR br pṭrqls dy mtqrh ʿstwrg' br lqyšw. [*4*]*47*, *Inv. X*, 81[3, 4]—mrqs 'lpys 'BGR br / ḥyrn 'BGR. [*452*], *Inv. X*, 99—'BGR br tymr[ṣw]. *466*, *C* 3928[2]—mrqs 'l[p]y[s] yr[ḥy br ḥyrn br '](b)gr. *467*, CaD 28 B[2]—[mr]qs 'lpys yrḥy b[r ḥyr]n 'BGR. *468*, *C* 3960[2]—mrqs 'lps yrḥy br ḥyrn 'BGR. [*468*], *Inv. X*, 90[2]—mrqws 'lpys yrḥy br ḥyrn 'BGR. [*46*]*8*, *Inv. X*, 77[1]—[mrqs 'lpys yrḥy br

ḥyrn] 'B
'lpys yrḥy
mrq[s 'lps
28 A[2]—m
CaD 28
'lpys mrqs
4199[11]—šy
E (Malkû)
br ʿnn. **2.**
ḥyrn. 'Iraq
zbdʿth. 'Eu
br zbdbwl.
[']BGR [ty]
'lpys [y]rḥy b

'BDY (*m*) **2.**

'BYHN (*m*)
zbdbwl br 'B
mkn' rb'. *42*
šm[ʿ]wn br 'BY
(Malkû) p. 101,
2. CaB 2 B[1]—
2 B[2]—. . .ty]mr
šmʿwn. *PNO* 5

'BYḤY (*m*) **2.**
mqy. Ingh. B, P

'BYN (*m*) **2.** *PN*
hrmy.

'BYN' (*f*) **2.** *PS*
yrḥy.

'BYʿ (*m*) **2.** *C*

'BYŠY (*f*) **2.**
zbdbl br m
'BYŠY.

'BLʿLY (*m*) **2**
638b—'BLʿL

'BMRT (*m*)

'BN' (*f*) **1.**
šlmn br šlm
'BN' brt šm
'BN'.

'BNYT (*m*)
mlkw br bl
bis[3]—ymlkw
'BNYT br

'BRWQ (*m*
tymrṣw 'B
ḥbn. *C* 45
ḥbn. *Inv.*
gḥynt.

'BRYKW

'BRM' (*m*
'BRM'.

'GDM (*m*
tymḥ' br
CaB 4 A
br ʿbdʿth
br 'lkdry
'GDM.

'GYʿ (*m*)
'GYʿ.

'GRP' (
VIII[2]—y
hlydyrs
p. 106[5]
ḥry hlyd
'GRP'.
br ['G
p. 129[2]

'GT' (
'GT'.

'GTG

'GTW
p. 104
grmn'

'GTP
ywlys
hlydw

'GT
VIII
hlyd

'D' (
rb'l.

'DB
wyr
bwl

4432—'ʿqb br 'BYʿ.

Inv. VIII, 12^{1}—'BYŠY brt
kw. *Inv. VIII*, 92—. . .]

. *RTP* 610b—'BLʿLY. *RTP*
Y mqymw tybwl.

. *C* 3991^{2}—whblt br 'BMRT.

507, *C* 4354^{1}—[']BN' brt
br tymrṣw. *530*, *C* 4306^{1}—
wn šqn. **2.** *Inv. VIII*, 27^{1}—

1. [*3*?]*42*, 'Dédicace' p. 44, 1—
ʿ]qb br 'BNYT. *394*, *C* 4123
br mqymw 'qlyš br mlkw
lʿqb br myk' br mt'.

) **1.** *345*, *C* 3980^{6}—yrḥbwl' br
WQ. **2.** *C* 4571 A^{2}—'BRWQ
71 B^{3}—ʿg' wšlmt bn[y] 'BRWQ
VIII, 25^{2}—'BRWQ br brʿth

(*m*) **2.** *RTP* 303a—'BRYKW.

) **2.** *C* 4180 A^{4}—šmʿwn br 'b'

) **1.** *378*, CaB 4 A^{2}—ydyʿbl br
ydyʿbl br ʿbdʿth 'GDM. *378*,
—ʿgylw wtymḥ' wʿty bny ḥyrn
'GDM. *502*, CaB 4 B^{2}—'lkdrys
br 'plnys nbwzbd br tym'' br

2. StaF p. 36, 1—ḥgwg' [br]

n) **1.** *525*, Ingh. E (Malkû) p. 99,
wlys 'wrlys 'GRP' br 'gtps br ḥry
rḥbwl' br ḥyrn bwn'. *525*, 'Malkû'
—ywlys 'wrlys 'GRP' br 'gtpws br
wrs yrḥbwl'. *525*, 'Malkû' p. 106^{7}—
547, *C* 4209—ywlys 'wrlys tydrws
P' br mrql']. *555*, Ingh. 'Th.'
—yrḥy 'GRP' yrḥy ydyʿbl ʿg' yʿt.

n) **2.** *RTP* 704b—mlkw mqymw

S (*m*) **1.** [*445*], *C* 3912^{2}—'GTGLS.

N' (*m*) **1.** *578*, Ingh. E (Malkû)
XII^{7}—ywly' 'wrly' 'GTWN' br bs'

WS (*m*) **1.** *525*, 'Malkû' p. 106^{5}—
'wrlys 'grp' br 'GTPWS br ḥry
rs yrḥbwl'.

S (*m*) **1.** *525*, Ingh. E (Malkû) p. 99,
—ywlys 'wrlys 'grp' br 'GTPS br ḥry
rs yrḥbwl' br ḥyrn bwn'.

n) **1.** *490*, CaD 8^{4}—ʿzyzw br 'D' br

(*m*) **1.** *426*, CaD 21^{2}—ʿwydw wmlkw
bwl[' wḥggw bny] bwlm' br ʿwydy br
' 'DB.

'DWN' see 'RWN'.

'DWNH (*m*) **2.** *Pal. 62*: 4^{3}—nḥ' br lšmš br 'DWNH.

'DYNT (*m*) **1.** *5*[*3*]*8*, *C* 4023^{2}—'DYNT. *563*, *C* 3944^{2}—spṭmyws ḥyrn br 'DYNT. *569*, *C* 3945^{1}—spṭmyws 'DYNT. *5*[*7*]*3* or *5*[*7*]*8*, *PNO* 21 A—'DYNT. *582*, *C* 3946^{1}—spṭmyws 'DY[NT]. **2.** *C* 3971^{4}—spṭymyws whblt 'tndr[ws] br spṭ[ymy]ws ['DYNT]. *C* 4202—'DYNT br ḥyrn whblt nṣwr. *C* 4594 A^{2}—ʿty brt 'DYNT. *RTP* 485a—ḥyrn 'DYN[T]. *RTP* 736a—ḥyrn 'DYNT. *RTP* 736b—whblt 'DYNT. *RTP* 746b—ḥyrn 'DY[NT]. *RTP* 807a—['DY]NT. CaC 17^{1}—'DYNT br ḥyrn whblt. *Pal. 62*: 6^{2}—yrḥy br 'DYNT br yrḥy. *Pal. 62*: 7^{3}—ʿsty' brt 'DYNT [br] yrḥy. *Inv. VIII*, 26^{4}—blḥzy br tymn' whby 'DY[NT].

'DRYNWS (*m*) **1.** *547*, *C* 4209—ywlys 'wrlys mrwn' br ml' dy [mtqr' mzbn]' br 'DRYNWS.

'HWD (*m*) **2.** *Inv. X*, 63^{2}—'lhbl br 'lhbl br zbdbwl 'HWD. *Inv. XI*, 98^{2}—rpbwl br 'HWD.

[']WṬYK/Q['] (*m*) **2.** *RTP* 425b—[']WṬYK['] or [']WṬYQ['].

'WṬK' (*m*) **1.** *502*, StaB p. 146, A 1172^{3}—mqymw br 'WṬK'. *541*, *Pal. 59*: 9 B^{4}—ywly' 'wrly' tym' wlšmš bny 'WṬK'. **2.** *C* 4103—'WṬK'. *C* 4211^{1}—ywlys 'wrlys 'WṬK' ḥgy. *C* 4357^{3}—zbyd' br 'WṬK' dy bwrp' 'kldy. *C* 4385^{1}—'WṬK' br ḥry mlkws'. *PNO* 50—'WṬK'.

'WYR see 'YYR.

'WR[2. CaA 57^{2}—. . .]l br yrḥy żẇ br ydyʿ br 'WR[. . . .

'WR (*m*) **1.** *544*, *C* 4031^{2}—ywl 'WR ḥlpwn' br ''ylmy zbyd' 'qwpʿ.

'WRLY' (*m*/*f*) **1.** *538*, *C* 4204^{2}—ywly' 'WRLY' šlmn wškny bny yrḥy šlmn br yd'. *541*, *Pal. 59*: 9 B^{1}—ywly' ['WR]LY'. *541*, *Pal. 59*: 9 B^{4}—ywly' 'WRLY' tym' wlšmš bny 'wṭk'. *543*, *Inv. IV*, 13^{2,3}—[ywly' 'WRLY' t]ym' brt ḥry 'WRLY' 'qm' brt 'nṭ[y]k[s ḥlypy]. *545*, *C* 4206^{1}—ywl' 'WRLY' ʿg' wšlm' [. . . nb]wmr bny ḥlh. *549*, Ingh. E (Malê) p. 88, IX^{3}—'WRLY' ṣmy brt lšmš. *550*, Ingh. B, p. 124, II^{3}—ywly' 'WRLY' šlmt brt ʿbdʿstwr br yrḥbwl'. *550*, Ingh. B, p. 124, II^{5}—ywly' 'WRLY' mlkw br ʿgylw br šlmn. *552*, *C* 4175^{2}—ywly' 'WRLY' btmlkw brt zbdbwl br šʿdy. *552*, CaD 36 C^{3}—ywly' 'WRLY' ḥyrn wmlwk' bny grmn'. *574*, Ingh. E (Naṣrallat) p. 110, II^{2}—ywly' 'WRLY' 'mt' brt bwlḥzy mqymw. *576*, Ingh. E (Naṣrallat) p. 112, III^{8}—ywly' 'WRLY' 'mt' brt bwlḥzy mqymw. *578*, Ingh. E (Malkû) p. 104, XII^{7}—ywly' 'WRLY' 'gtwn' br bs' grmn'. **2.** CaB 2 B^{1}—ywly' 'WRLY'

'byhn. CaB 2 B^{2}—ywly' 'WRLY' tymrṣ[w]. *Inv. VIII*, 58^{1}—ywly' 'WRLY' nwry wzbdbwl. w[ʿgylw] bny mq[y....] ḥbzy. *Inv. X*, 49—[']WRLY'.

'WRLYS (*m*) **1.** *525*, Ingh. E (Malkû) p. 97, VI^{1}—ywlys 'WRLYS nwrbl wml' bny mlkw rb' br mlkw mlkw nwrbl. *525*, Ingh. E (Malkû) p. 98, VII^{1}—ywlys 'WRLYS nwrbl wml' [bny] mlkw rb' br mlkw br mlkw br nwrbl. *525*, Ingh. E (Malkû) p. 98, VII^{2}—ywlys 'WRLYS ʿgylw br 'prhṭ br ḥry zbdbwl br mlkw 'swyt. *525*, Ingh. E (Malkû) p. 99, VIII^{1}—ywlys 'WRLYS nwrbl wml' bny mlkw rb' br mlkw br mlkw br nwrbl. *525*, Ingh. E (Malkû) p. 99, VIII^{2}—ywlys 'WRLYS 'grp' br 'gtps br ḥry hlydyrs yrḥbwl' br ḥyrn bwn'. *525*, 'Malkû' p. 106^{2,3}—ywlys 'WRLYS ydyʿbl dy mtqr' mzbn' br ywlys / 'WRLYS 'nynws. *525*, 'Malkû' p. 106^{3}—ywlys br 'WRLYS ʿgylw br 'prhṭ br ḥry zbdbwl. *525*, 'Malkû' p. 106^{5}—ywlys 'WRLYS 'grp' br 'gtpws br ḥry hlydwrs yrḥbwl'. *525*, 'Malkû' p. 106^{12}—ywlys 'WRLYS nš' br brʿth. *525*, 'Malkû' p. 106^{13}—ywlys 'WRLYS yrḥbwl' br mlkw. *526*, Ingh. E (Malê) p. 77, III^{1}—ywlys 'WRLYS ml' br ḥyrn br ssn. *526*, Ingh. E (Malê) p. 77, III^{1,2}—ywlys 'WRLYS ḥyrn wywlys 'WRLYS 'b' / bny ywlys 'WRLYS mqy br yrḥy. *529*, *C* 4302^{2}—[ywlys] 'WR[LYS] rp[bwl b]r ʿtʿqb [br] rpbwl br ʿtʿ[qb] dy mtqr' nb[wzbd]. *535*, Ingh. E (Malê) p. 78, IV^{1}—ywlyws 'WRLYS ml' br ḥyrn br ssn. *535*, Ingh. E (Malê) p. 78, IV^{1}—ywlys 'WRLYS ʿbsy br ḥnyn' br ḥnyn' br ʿg' yrq. *538*, *C* 4204^{3}—ywlys 'WRLYS yrḥbwl' br mqymw npry. *539*, Ingh. B p. 110, III^{2}—'WRLYS wrdn br ḥry 'nṭykys rpbwl br ʿtʿqb. *539*, Ingh. B p. 110, III^{3}—'WRLYS mlkw br šlmn bn'. *540*, Ingh. E (ʿAtenatan) p. 60, II^{1}—ywlys 'WRLYS mqy br zbdbwl mqy dwḥy. *543*, CaA 40^{5}—ywlys 'WRLYS hrms br ḥry 'WRL[YS]. *545*, *C* 4206^{1}—[ywl]ys 'WRLYS bwlm' br zbdbwl br bwlm' nyny'. *545*, *C* 4206^{3}—ywlys 'WRLYS bwlm' br zbdbwl b[r bwlm' nyny' .... b]rt [n]b[w]d' br tym' br nbwmw'. *545*, Ingh. E (Malê) p. 82, V^{1}—ywlys 'WRLYS ml' br ḥyrn br ml' ḥyrn ssn. *545*, Ingh. E (Malê) p. 82, V^{2}—ywlys 'WRLYS šyby br hrms mrq'. *546*, Ingh. E (Malê) p. 84, VI^{1}—ywlys 'WRLYS ml' br 'WRLYS ḥyrn br ml' ḥyrn ssn. *546*, Ingh. E (Malê) p. 84, VI^{2}—ywlys 'WRLYS ḥlpt' br mqymw zbd'. *546*, Ingh. E (Malê) p. 84, VII^{3}—ywlys 'WRLYS ml' br ḥyrn ml'. *546*, Ingh. E (Malê) p. 84, VII^{5}—ywlys 'WRLYS zbdbwl br zbdbwl khylw. *547*, *C* 4209—ywlys 'WRLYS mrwn' br ml' dy [mtqr' mzbn]' br 'drynws. *547*, *C* 4209—[ywlys 'WRLYS zbyd'] br ʿštwr zbyd'. *547*, *C* 4209—ywlys 'WRLYS tydrws br ['grp' br mrql']. *548*, Ingh. E (Malê) p. 86, VIII^{1}—ywlys 'WRLYS ḥyrn br mqy yrḥy. *548*, Ingh. E (Malê) p. 86, VIII^{3}—ywlys 'WRLYS 'sy [.] br ḥnyn' šmʿwn. *549*, Ingh. E (Malê) p. 88, IX^{2}—'WRLYS ḥyrn br mqy br yrḥy. *550*, Ingh. B p. 124, II^{4}—lwqys 'WRLYS brsmy'. *552*, *C* 4175^{4}—ywlys 'WRLYS ml' br ydʿw br ydyʿbl. *552*, Ingh. E (Malkû) p. 100, IX^{2}—ywlys 'WRLYS ʿg' br rwḥbl. *552*, Ingh. E (Malkû) p. 100, IX^{3}—ywlys 'WRLYS lmlk' br šlmn gpn. *552*, CaD 36 C^{4}—ywlys 'WRLYS typyls br tymrṣw [z]byd'. *554*, *C* 3932^{1}—ywlys 'WRLYS zbdl' br mlkw br mlkw nšwm. *558*, *C* 3933^{1}—ywlys 'WRLYS zbyd' br mqymw br zbyd' ʿštwr byd'. *563*, *C* 3944^{3}—'WRLYS plynws br mry' plyn' rʿy. *566*, *C* 3934^{1}—ywlys 'WRLYS ʿg' dy mtqr' slwqws br ʿzyzw ʿzyzw š'yl'. *569*, *C* 3936^{1}—ywlys 'WRLYS šlmlt br ml' ʿbdy. *570*, *C* 3937^{1}—'WRLYS [w]rwd. *574*, *C* 3939^{3}—ywlys 'W(R)LYS nbwzbd br šʿdw ḥyr'. *574*, Ingh. E (Naṣrallat) p. 110, II^{1}—ywlys 'WRLYS ydyʿbl br ʿbdšmy' br mlk'. *575*, *C* 3940^{3}—ywlys 'WRLYS spṭmyws yd' br 'lks[nd]rws ḥyrn srykw. [*576*], *C* 3941^{3}—[ywlys 'WRLYS spṭmy]ws ml[kw br mlwk' nšwm]. *576*, Ingh. E (Naṣrallat) p. 112, III^{1}—ywlys 'WRLYS ydyʿbl br ʿbšmy' mlk'. *578*, *C* 3943^{3}—ywlys 'WRLYS šlm' br qsyn' br mʿny. **2.** *Inv. X*, 115^{1}—ywlys 'WRLYS mlkw br wsḥw br mlkw br wsḥw nbwl'. *C* 4211^{1}—ywlys 'WRLYS 'wṭk' ḥgy. *PNO* 12—...]s 'WRLYS. *Inv. IX*, 30^{1}—[ywlys] 'WRLYS [nbwmy br tymšm]š bwn' [šby]. *Inv. X*, 126^{1}—ywlys 'WRLYS lšmš br tymw.

'WŠY (*m*) **1.** *360*, CaC 11^{3,4}—'WŠY br khylw w'WŠY [....]' bny ḥyrn br 'WŠY. *368*, *C* 4119^{3}—ʿgylw br 'WŠY br khylw. [*3*]*94*, *C* 3969^{1}—ʿt'm b[rt....] 'WŠY. *435*, *PS* 33^{2,3}—tmlk brt 'WŠY / br 'WŠY. [*5*]*63*, *C* 4363^{4,5}—šlwm brt 'WŠY / 'WŠY. **2.** *C* 4361^{3}—ʿwtn br lšmš 'WŠY. *C* 4362^{3}—ʿgylw br 'WŠY.

'WTQ' (*m*) **2.** *PNO* 38^{2}—šlmt w'WTQ' wmqymw.

'ZMR (*m*) **2.** *Inv. VIII*, 31^{4}—yrḥbwl' br tym' br 'ZMR.

'ZRZYRT (*m*) **1.** *5*[*64*], *C* 4213—...] br tym' 'ZRZYRT.

'Ḥ' (*f*) **1.** *460*, *PS* 39^{1}—'Ḥ' brt zbdlh br''. *461*, *C* 4254^{2}—'Ḥ' brt ḥlpt' br br'' zbdʿth. *480*, *C* 4255^{2}—hdyrt 'Ḥ' brt bwlḥ' br br'' br zbdʿth. **2.** *C* 4366—'Ḥ' [br]t zbdbw[l]. *C* 4440^{3}—'Ḥ' brt bwrp'. *C* 4516 A^{4}—'Ḥ' brt nš'. Ingh. B p. 135, IV F^{1}—'Ḥ' brt ʿg'.

'ḤY' (*m*) **2.** *PNO* 17^{2}—bwlm' br 'ḤY'. *Michalowski*, p. 314—'ḤY' br ḥry khyl[w].

'ḤYB (*m*) **2.** CaA 79^{6}—tyks' brt nṣry br lšmš 'ḤYB.

'ḤYBL (*m*) **2.** *Inv. IV*, 15b—'ḤYBL br mqymw.

'ḤYNY (*m*) **2.** 'Sculptures' p. 22, Pl. II^{1}—'ḤYNY br ḥtry.

’ḤYRY (*m*) **2.** *RTP* 40a—bryky šk‘t’ ’ḤYRY.

’ḤYTWR (*m*) **1.** *445, C* 4281^{5}—‘tntn gwry br bwrp’ ‘tntn ’ḤYTWR. **2.** *C* 4279^{4}—mlkw br bwrp’ ’ḤYTWR. *C* 4280^{3}—‘tntn br mlkw ’ḤYTWR. *C* 4282^{4}—whblt br bwlḥ’ br bwrp’ ’ḤYTWR. *C* 4285^{5}—[b]wlḥ’ [br] ‘tntn [bw]lḥ’ ’ḤYTWR. *C* 4287^{4}—ḥgt brt bwlḥ’ ‘tntn ’ḤYTWR.

’ḤLT (*m*) **2.** *PNO* 76 A^{1}—’ḤLT m‘n br zbyd’.

’ḤMR (*m*) **2.** CaC 6^{2}—ns’ br ḥl’ br ns’ ’ḤMR.

’ḤPLY (*m*) **1.** *451, C* 3927^{1}—’ḤPLY br ḥyrn šb’ br ḥyrn bwn’ š[’]t.

’ḤT’ (*f*) **2.** 4542^{1}—’ḤT’ brt šl’. *Inv. VIII,* 130^{2}—’ḤT’ brt ‘qyb’.

’ḤTY see BR ’ḤTY.

’ṬYK’ (*m*) **2.** *Inv. IX,* 4 A—’ṬYK’.

’ṬNYNYS (*m*) **2.** *Inv. X,* 102^{2}—’ṬNYNYS.

’YD‘N (*m*) **1.** *307,* CaD 17^{3}—‘gylw br ’YD‘N. **2.** *C* 4581^{2}—mlkt brt ’YD‘N. CaA 78^{3}—‘l’ brt ’YD‘N br yrḥy mqy. *Inv. VIII,* 33^{2}—tymrṣw ’YD‘N br lšmš br šwḥbw.

’YWN[**2.** *Inv. XI,* 80^{3}—bwln’ ’YWN[. . . .

’YWR see ’YYR.

’YYR (*m*) **2.** *RTP* 884a—‘bd’ ’YYR.

’YŠ’ (*m*) **1.** *373, Pal. 63*: 3^{2}—zbdlh dy mtqr’ sḥlph br šm‘wn br ’YŠ’. *3[87],* CaA 6^{1}—zb[d]lh br šmšgrm ’YŠ’.

’YTYBL (*m*) **1.** *500+?, C* 4197^{2}—ml’ br ‘g’ br ml’ br ‘gylw ’YT[YB]L. *500+?, C* 4197^{3}—‘g’ br šlm’ šmšgrm br br[.]š ‘g’ br ’YTYBL. **2.** *Inv. VIII,* 4^{2,4}—’YTYBL / br tym’ br / ’YTYBL br / ‘gylw. *Inv. VIII,* 51^{2}—’YTYBL br zbd’. *Inv. VIII,* 54^{4}—’mt’ brt ’YTYBL. *Inv. XI,* 82^{3}—’YTYBL.

’KLB (*m*) **1.** *500, Pal. 62*: 19^{3}—’lhbl br br‘th mqymw ’KLB. **2.** *Inv. XI,* 28^{3}—zbyd’ [br] šg’ ’KLB.

’KLDY (*m*) **2.** *C* 4357^{5}—zbyd’ br ’wṭk’ dy bwrp’ ’KLDY. *C* 4358 B^{3}—blšwr br ḥyr’ ’KLDY. *C* 4359^{3}—mqymw br ḥyr’ ’KLDY. ‘Sculptures’ p. 24, Pl. II^{2}—blšwr br ḥyr’ ’KLDY. ‘Sculptures’ p. 24, Pl. II^{2}—mqymw br ḥyr’ ’KLDY.

’KNBY (*m*) **1.** *425, C* 3986^{3}—nbwzbd wyrḥbwl’ bny brnbw br nbwzbd br zbdl’ ’KNBY.

’KNT (*m*) **2.** *Inv. VIII,* 22^{2}—zbdbwl br brwq’ br ’KNT.

’KRN (*m*) **2.** *C* 4391^{3}—mrty brt šlmlt ’KRN.

’LH (*m*) **2.** *C* 4083^{3}—šlm[t bt] ’LH.

’LHBL (*m*) **1.** *414, C* 4134^{1,2}—’LHBL wm‘ny wškyy / wmlkw bny whblt br m‘ny ’LHBL. *419, Inv. X,* 129^{2}—g’ys ywlys ḥyrn br ’LHBL. *47[5],* CaB 3^{1}—’LHBL br mlkw br zbdbwl brt’. *500, Pal. 62*: 19^{2}—’LHBL br br‘th mqymw ’klb. *505,* Ingh. B p. 95, II^{5}—šlmn br qlybw br ’LHBL. *505, PNO* 37^{2}—’LHBL wrb’l [w]mhrw bny bwly. *554, C* 4305^{1}—’LHBL br tym’ br ḥyrn. **2.** *C* 3962^{3}—’LHB[L br mlkw. . . . *C* 4082^{3}—[’]L[HB]L b[r. . . . *C* 4137^{1}—’LHBL br škyy br whblt. *C* 4138^{2}—m‘ny br ’LHBL br whblt. *C* 4140^{1,2}—’LHBL br / m‘ny br ’LHBL. *C* 4141^{2}—whblt br ’LHBL br whblt. *C* 4143^{2}—bl‘qb br ’LHBL br whblt. *C* 4145^{2}—’mt’ brt ’LHBL br whblt. *C* 4148^{3}—bl[‘qb] br ’LHBL whblt. *C* 4151^{2}—’LHBL br whblt. *C* 4154^{2}—hdyrt brt ’LHBL br whblt br m‘ny. *C* 4155^{2}—šgl brt ’LHBL br whblt. *C* 4157^{1}—bl‘qb br ’LHBL br whblt br m‘ny. *C* 4223—’LHBL. *C* 4296 A^{2}—mrty brt ’LHBL br mrywn. *C* 4296 B^{4}—mrywn br ’LHBL. *C* 4297^{3}—ḥyr[n] br mry[wn] br ’[LHBL]. *C* 4298^{4}—mrywn br ’LHBL. *C* 4299^{2}—mrywn br ’LH[B]L ḥyrn. *C* 4381^{2}—yrḥy br ’LHBL. *C* 4402—bgdn br ’LHBL br mlkw. *PS* 193—mqymw br ’LHBL br ḥyrn. CaA 33^{1}—mlkw br myd/rn ’LHBL. CaA 33^{2,3}—’LHBL wwhblt br / m‘ny br ’LHBL. Ingh. A p. 99, 7^{3}—’qmt brt [ml’ br ’]LHBL. *Inv. VIII,* 123^{2}—. . .] ’LH[BL] ṣ‘dy. *Inv. X,* 63^{1}—’LHBL br ’LHBL br zbdbwl ’hwd.

’LHW (*m*) **1.** *345, C* 3980^{6}—zbdbwl br ydy‘bl ’LHW. *373, Pal. 63*: 3^{6}—ḥlypy br yrḥy ’LHW. *409,* ‘Wadi Hauran’ 1^{6}—b‘ly ml’ ’LHW/Y.

’LHMNSB[**2.** *PNO* 52^{1}—’LHMNSB[. . . .

’LHŠ’ (*m*) **1.** *390, C* 4121—bny w’LHŠ’ w’r’wm bny tymš’ br bny dy mtqrh ’rwn’. **2.** *C* 4187^{1}—mqymw wtymš[’ wzbyd’ bny ’LHŠ]’ br ṣ‘dy br ’LHŠ’. *C* 4187^{1}—’LHŠ’ w‘gylw wṣ[‘dy bny m]qymw. *C* 4187^{2}—’LHŠ’ br [tymš’]. *C* 4188^{1,3}—’LHŠ’ / rb’ br mqymw / zbyd’ ’LHŠ’ / ṣ‘dy. *C* 4189^{2}—mqymw br ’LHŠ’ br mqymw ṣ‘dy. *C* 4191^{2}—’LHŠ’ br tymš’. *C* 4191^{6}—’LHŠ’ br tymš’ br šmšgrm [ḥ]bzy. *RTP* 725a—’LHŠ’ tymš’. *RTP* 775a—zb[d]’ ’LHŠ’ ṣ‘dy. CaA 68 A^{2}—tymṣ’ br ’LHŠ’ ‘gylw. CaA 68 B^{1}—tymṣ’ br ’LHŠ’. ‘Tessères’ 24b—’LHŠ’ tymš’. *Inv. VIII,* 127^{1,3}—’LHŠ’ br / mqymw br / ’LHŠ’ ṣ‘dy. *Inv. IX,* 4 B—’LHŠ’ br dynys.

’LWR (*m*) **2.** *PNO* 78^{5}—nḥšṭb ’LWR.

’LṬY (*m*) **1.** *525, Inv. X,* 119^{3}—tym’ br ḥlpt’ br‘th ’LṬY.

’LYS (*m*) **1.** *449,* CaB 8^{1,2}—pplys ’LYS tybwl / wpplys ’LYS yrḥbwl’ bny mlkw tybwl ṣm’. **2.** CaB 2 B^{2}—[ty]mrṣw br pplws ’LYS ’byhn br šm‘wn.

'LKDRYS (*m*) **1.** *502*, CaB 4 B^{1}—'LKDRYS br 'LKDRYS br 'plnys nbwzbd br tym'' br 'gdm.

'LKSDRS (*m*) **1.** *448*, *C* 3913 I^{2}—'LKSDRS br 'LKSDRS br plpṭr.

'LKSNDRWS (*m*) **1.** *554*, *C* 3932^{3}—'LKSNDRWS. *575*, *C* 3940^{4}—ywlys 'wrlys spṭmyws yd' br 'LKS[ND]RWS ḥyrn srykw. **2.** CaC 18^{1}—'LKSNDRWS.

'LKSNDRS (*m*) **1.** [*4*]*51*, *Inv. X*, 112^{2}—. . .] br 'LKSNDRS.

'[L]'' (*m*) **2.** *C* 4433^{3}—'ty brt '[L]''.

'LPY (*m*) **1.** *530*, *C* 4018^{5}—mqy (son of) yrḥy br zbyd['] 'LPY. **2.** *C* 3961^{1}—. . .] 'LPY br yrḥy br [. . . .

'LPYS (*m*) **1.** [*4*]*47*, *Inv. X*, 81^{3}—mrqs 'LPYS 'bgr br ḥyrn 'bgr. *466*, *C* 3928^{1}—mrqs 'L[P]Y[S] yr[ḥy br ḥyrn br '](b)gr. *467*, CaD 28 B^{1}—[mr]qs 'LPYS yrḥy b[r ḥyr]n 'bgr. [*46*]*8*, *Inv. X*, 77^{1}—[mrqs 'LPYS yrḥy br ḥyrn] 'bgr. [*468*], *Inv. X*, 90^{1}—mrqws 'LPYS yrḥy br ḥyrn 'bgr. [*468*], *Inv. X*, 96^{1}—[mrqs 'LPYS yrḥy br ḥyrn 'bgr]. *470*, CaD 28 A^{1}—mrqs 'LPYS yrḥy br ḥyrn 'bgr. *470*, CaD 28 C^{1}—'LPYS mrqs yrḥy br ḥyrn 'bgr. **2.** *Inv. X*, 91—['LPYS]. *Inv. X*, 128^{3}—mrq[s] 'LPYS [y]rḥy br ḥyr[n 'bgr].

'LPS (*m*) **1.** *468*, *C* 3960^{1}—mrqs 'LPS yrḥy br ḥyrn 'bgr. [*469*], CaA 8^{1}—mrq[s 'LPS yrḥy b]r ḥ[yrn 'bgr].

'LQM' (*m*) **2.** *C* 4515^{1}—'LQM' br šm'wn br hn'y.

'LQMS (*m*) **1.** *448*, *C* 3913 II^{78}—'LQMS.

'M' (*f*) **2.** *Inv. XI*, 50^{1}—brt' brt 'M'.

[']MBW (*f*) **2.** *Inv. VIII*, 149^{1}—[']MBW brt š'dy.

'MBY (*m*/*f*) **1.** *446*, *C* 4248^{1}—'MBY brt br'' zbd'th. *480*, CaC 8^{3}—'MBY brt bgrn br mlkw. **2.** Ingh. A p. 96, 5 A^{2}—. . .]' brt mqy ['MBY]. Ingh. A p. 96, 5 B^{2}—hgr brt mqy 'MBY. *C* 4553^{1}—'MBY brt ṣpr'. Ingh. D p. 40, Pl. X^{1}—'MBY brt 'gylw. *PS* 356—'MBY brt tybwl twry. 'Hypogée' p. 235, Pl. V^{2}—'MBY brt ml'.

'MBKR' (*m*) **1.** *458*, *PNO* 55 A—wrdn / brwq' / mhrdt / 'MBKR'.

'MBT' (*f*) **2.** *PS* 3^{2}—'MBT'.

'MDBW (*m*/*f*) **1.** *527*, *PNO* 61^{3}—bwn' br 'MDBW. *550*, Ingh. B p. 124, II^{4}—'MDBW brt ḥry lwqys 'wrlys brsmy'.

'MDY (*m*) **1.** *497*, Ingh. B p. 106, I^{1}—lšmš br lšmš br tym' w'MDY br ydy'bl.

'MW (*f*) **1.** *578*, Ingh. E (Malkû) p. 102, XI^{6}—'MW brt bs' š'rwn'. *578*, Ingh. E (Malkû) p. 104, XII^{6}—'MW brt bs' š'rwn'.

'MWN (*m*) **2.** *PS* 244 A—'MWN br nš' 'g' šlm'.

'MY' (*f*) **2.** *C* 4594 A^{4}—'MY'.

'MYN (*m*) **2.** *RTP* 718b—ydy 'MYN. 'Wadi Hauran' 3^{2}—'nš (?) br 'MYN.

'MYT (*f*) **2.** *C* 4428^{1}—'MYT brt yrḥy. StaC p. 35, 5—'MYT brt zbd't'.

'MLYWS (*m*) **1.** *474*, *Inv. X*, 29^{1}—mrqs 'MLYWS mrqynws 'sqlpyd'.

'MṢR (*m*) **2.** *C* 4062^{5}—'bydw 'sty br gwr' br nšm 'MṢR.

'MRY (*m*) **2.** *RTP* 37b—'bd[y/'] 'MRY mqymw 'g'. *Journal asiatique*, 12 (1918), 282 no. VII—'MRY br 'g' br 'bdy.

'MRS' (*m*) **2.** *Inv. IV*, 24—tymlt 'wydlt 'MRS'.

'MRŠ' (*m*) **1.** *412*, CaB 13 A^{3}—ydy'bl br 'MRŠ'. *450*, *C* 3931^{2}—bryky br 'MRŠ' br yrḥbwl'. **2.** *C* 3975^{1}—rb'l br 'MRŠ'. *C* 4437^{4}—'mt' brt mqy brt 'MRŠ'.

'MŠ' (*m*) **2.** *Beth She'arim*, i, p. 135—tm' 'MŠ'.

'MŠY (*m*) **2.** *Inv. VIII*, 17^{3}—mlkw br tym[. . . .] br 'MŠY.

'MŠ[MŠ] (*f*) **2.** CaA 21^{2}—'MŠ[MŠ].

'MT' (*f*) **1.** *574*, Ingh. E (Naṣrallat) p. 110, II^{2}—ywly' 'wrly' 'MT' brt bwlḥzy mqymw. *576*, Ingh. E (Naṣrallat) p. 112, III^{8}—ywly' 'wrly' 'MT' brt bwlḥzy mqymw. **2.** *C* 4145^{1}—'MT' brt 'lhbl br whblt. *C* 4153^{1}—'MT' brt škyy br whblt. *C* 4233—'M[T'] brt br'th. *C* 4368^{3}—'bs' [b]r šlwm [w]'MT'. *C* 4437^{2}—'MT' brt mqy brt 'mrš'. *C* 4523^{1}—'MT' brt whblt. *C* 4599^{1}—[']MT['] brt [ty]rdt. Ingh. B p. 102, III C—'MT'. *Inv. VIII*, 54^{2}—'MT' brt 'ytybl. *Inv. VIII*, 98^{1}—'MT' br[t. . . . *Inv. VIII*, 173^{1}—'MT' brt m'ny.

'MTBL (*f*) **1.** [*5*]*61*, StaC p. 36, 6—'MTBL brt bgrt. **2.** *C* 4081^{2}—hrms w'MTBL.

'MTB'[L] (*f*) **2.** Ben-Hayyim p. 145—[.]ḥ' 'MTB'[L] brt sryk'.

'MTḤ' (*f*) **1.** [*3*]*84*, *C* 4193^{2}— 'MTḤ' brt bwn'. **2.** *C* 4151^{1}—'MTḤ' brt bl'qb br nš'. *C* 4546—'MTḤ' brt zbyd'.

'MTLT (*f*) **2.** *C* 4367^{1}— 'MTLT brt mzbn'. *C* 4609^{1}—'MTLT brt ḥyr'.

'MTŠLM' (*f*) **1.** *497*, Ingh. E (Malkû) p. 91, II^{2}—rwḥbl br ḥry 'MTŠLM' bt ḥry šgl brt zbyd'.

'N' (*m*/*f*) **2.** *C* 4376^{4}—'N' brt d/rzyṣyḥ. *PS* 210—'N'. Ingh. B p. 135, IV A^{1}—'N' btmrṣw. Ingh. B p. 135, IV B^{1}—'N' bt tymrṣw. Ingh. B p. 135, IV B^{2}—'gylw br 'N'.

’NBT (*m*) **2.** *C* 3905^{2}—ḥbyby br mlkw ’NBT.

’NṬYWKWS (*m*) **2.** *C* 3971^{7}—’NṬYWKWS.

’NṬYKYS (*m*) **1.** *539*, Ingh. B p. 110, III^{2}—’NṬYKYS rpbwl br ‘t‘qb

’NṬYKS (*m*) **1.** *497*, Ingh. B p. 106, I^{2}—’NṬYKS rpbwl br ’NṬYKS ‘t‘qb br rpbwl. *543*, *Inv. IV*, 13^{3}—[ywly’ ’wrly’ t]ym’ brt ḥry ’wrly’ ’qm’ brt ’NṬ[Y]K[S ḥlypy].

’NṬWNYS (*m*) **1.** *485*, *Inv. X*, 113^{1}—(l)wqys ’NṬWNYS qlsṭrṭs.

’NYNWS (*m*) **1.** *525*, ‘Malkû’ p. 106^{3}—ywlys ’wrlys ydy‘bl dy mtqr’ mzbn’ br ywlys ’wrlys ’NYNWS.

’N‘M (*m*) **1.** *573*, *PNO* 57—’N‘M wb‘ly.

’NQY (*m*) **1.** *447*, *C* 3968^{3}—. . .] wmlkw br ‘wyd’ ’NQY br ‘g’ br [. . . . **2.** *RTP* 819b—zbd‘th mtn’ ’NQY.

’NŠ (?) (*m*) **1.** ‘Wadi Hauran’ 3^{1}—’NŠ(?) br ’myn.

’SDY (*m*) **2.** *PNO* 2—ḥnyn’ ‘gylw ’SDY. *PNO 2 bis*—. . . ‘gy]lw ’SDY.

’SWYT (*m*) **1.** *525*, Ingh. E (Malkû) p. 98, VII^{2}—ywlys ’wrlys ‘gylw br ’prhṭ br ḥry zbdbwl br mlkw ’SWYT.

’SṬ[Ṭ] (*m*) **2.** *C* 4068^{2}—’SṬ[Ṭ].

’SY[.] (*m*) **1.** *548*, Ingh. E (Malê) p. 86, VIII^{4}—ywlys ’wrlys ’SY[.] br ḥnyn’ šm‘wn.

’SY‘ see **’BY‘**.

’SPDYN (*m*) **1.** *500+?*, *C* 4054^{2}—’SPDYN.

’SPDY[S] (*m*) **1.** *369*, *C* 4235^{2}—[lwqy]ws ’SPDY[S] krystws.

[’]SPYDN (*m*) **1.** *570*, *C* 4049^{2}—[’]SPYDN [b]r [. . . .

’SQLPYD’ (*m*) **1.** *474*, *Inv. X*, 29^{2}—mrqs ’mlyws mrqynws ’SQLPYD’.

’STR (*f*) **2.** *Beth She‘arim*, i, p. 141 no. 126—’STR.

’‘B (*m*) CaA 36^{4}—yrḥbwl’ br mlkw ’‘B.

’‘BY (*m*) **1.** *377*, ‘Grave-Relief’ p. 192—br‘th br ḥnbl ’‘BY. *392*, *Inv. X*, 131^{2}—mlkw br lšmš br ḥnbl br br‘th ’‘BY. *400*, ‘Fouilles’ p. 170^{1}—yrḥbwl’ br mlkw br lšmš br ḥnbl ’‘BY. *400*, ‘Fouilles’ p. 172^{4}—[yrḥbwl’ br mlkw br] lšmš br ḥ[nbl ’‘BY]. *400+?*, *C* 3988^{2}—mlkw br ‘g’ ’‘[BY]. *400+?*, *C* 3963^{1}—tymrṣw br [l]šmš br mlkw ’‘B[Y]. *[4]58*, *C* 4458—. . .] mlkw br lšmš br ḥnbl ’‘BY. **2.** *C* 3990^{3}—ḥyr[n] br blḥzy br blḥ’ [m]qy [’‘B]Y. *C* 4456^{4}—mzbn’ br mlkw tymrṣw ’‘BY. *C* 4457^{4}—tymrṣw br mlkw br tymrṣw ’‘BY. *RTP* 31a—šlmn yrḥbwl’ mlkw ’‘B[Y]. *RTP* 34a—šlmn yrḥbwl’ mlkw ’‘BY. *RTP* 763a—yrḥbwl’ mlkw ’‘BY. *RTP* 770a—[m]lkw ḥyrn ’‘B[Y].

’‘WY (*m*) **2.** *RTP* 908a—’‘WY.

’‘WYD (*m*) **2.** *C* 4318^{5}—mlkw br zbdbwl br mlkw ’‘WYD. *C* 4319^{5}—‘gylw br mqymw br mlkw ’‘WYD. *C* 4320^{5}—r‘th brt mqymw ’‘WYD. *C* 4321^{3}—ḥb’ brt mqymw ’‘WYD.

’‘Y[**2.** *Inv. VIII*, 101^{1}—’‘Y[. . .

’‘YLM (*m*) **1.** *546*, *Inv. XI*, 1^{4}—yrḥbwl’ wbrḥwm ’‘YLM w’qm’ [w]’t‘m.

’‘YLMY (*m*) **1.** *399*, CaB 6 A^{1}—blḥzy br nwry br zbdbwl ’‘YLMY. *399*, CaB 6 A^{1}—’‘YLMY wnrglzbd w‘gylw. *399*, CaB 6 A^{3}—’‘YLMY. *450*, *C* 3930^{2}—’‘YLMY br ḥyrn br mqymw br ḥyrn mt’. *460*, *C* 4168^{3}—’‘YLMY wzbyd’ bny ḥyrn br mqymw br ḥyrn. *542*, *C* 4243^{3}—zbyd’ br mqymw br ḥyrn ’‘YLM[Y]. *544*, *C* 4031^{3}—ywl ’wr ḥlpwn’ br ’‘YLMY zbyd’ ‘qwp‘. **2.** *C* 4461^{4}—‘yt’ brt ’‘YLMY yrḥy. *RTP* 318 *bis* b—’‘YLMY sqḥ’. ‘Note’ p. 90^{1}—’‘YLMY. Ingh. ‘Quatre’ p. 242, Pl. XL^{1}—šgl brt whblt ’‘YLMY blḥzy. CaA 15^{1}—’‘YLMY br zbyd’ ḥyrn.

’‘PY (*m*) **1.** *537*, StaB p. 153, A 1205^{2}—zbyd’ br whblt byd’ ’‘PY.

’‘RY see BR ’‘RY.

[’PW . .] (*m*) **1.** *[49]6*, *C* 4196—[‘wyd’ br yrḥy br ml’ br ’PW . .].

’PWQḤ (*m*) **2.** *C* 4084^{5}—dwr’ br zbdbwl mlk’ ’tndwr’ ’PWQḤ.

’PYN (*m*) **1.** *484*, *C* 4003^{1}—. . .]’ br zbyd’ ’PYN.

’PLY (*m*) **2.** CaA 66—. . .]ydn br ’PLY. *RTP* 439b—’PLY klb’. *Inv. XI*, 97^{4}—’PLY.

’PLNYS (*m*) **1.** *502*, CaB 4 B^{1}—’lkdrys br ’lkdrys br ’PLNYS nbwzbd br tym’‘ br ’gdm. **2.** *Inv. VIII*, 183 A^{2}—’PLNYS.

’PRHṬ (*m*) **1.** *525*, ‘Malkû’ p. 106^{4}—ywlys br ’wrlys ‘gylw br ’PRHṬ br ḥry zbdbwl. *525*, Ingh. E (Malkû) p. 98, VII^{2}—ywlys ’wrlys ‘gylw br ’PRHṬ br ḥry zbdbwl br mlkw ’swyt. **2.** *C* 4239—’PRHṬ. ‘Malkû’ p. 104, line 13—’PRHṬ br ‘gylw.

’ṢWLY (*m*) **1.** *410*, Ingh. B p. 120, I^{2}—‘bd‘stwr br nwrbl br khylw br ‘tnwry ’ṢWLY.

’ṢYD/RNY (*m*) **2.** *Inv. VIII*, 11^{3}—tm’ brt ‘g’ ’ṢYD/RNY.

’ṢR‘ (*m*) **2.** *PNO* 47 A^{4}—lšmš br mqymy ’ṢR‘. *Inv. VIII*, 9^{4}—zbdb(w)l br mtn’ br zbdlh br bl‘qb dy mtqrh ’ṢR‘. *Inv. VIII*, 27^{3}—zbyd’ ’ṢR‘.

’Q[. .]WN 2. *RTP* 345b—’Q[. .]WN.

’QWP‘ (*m*) **1.** *515*, *C* 4198 B^{2}—. . .l]šmš br [’]QWP[‘]. *544*, *C* 4031^{4}—ywl ’wr ḥlpwn’ br ’‘ylmy zbyd’ ’QWP‘.

’QZMN (*m*) **2.** ‘Iraq’ p. 63^{7}, Pl. 5—mlkw br nbwl’ br ’QZMN.

’QYḤ (*m*) **1.** *420*, *C* 3917^{1}—’QYḤ br [n‘]ry br ’QYḤ. **2.** *C* 4615—’QYḤ.

’QLYŠ (*m*) **1.** *3[94]*, *C* 4123—ymlkw br mqymw dy mtqrh ’QLYŠ br mlkw br bl‘qb. *394*, *C* 4123 *bis*^{2}—ymlkw br mqymw ’QLYŠ br mlkw ’bnyt br bl‘qb br myk’ br mt’. **2.** *RTP* 761a—ymlkw mqymw ’QLYŠ.

’QM’ (*f*) **1.** *543*, *Inv. IV*, 13^{3}—[ywly’ ’wrly’ t]ym’ brt ḥry ’wrly’ ’QM’ brt ’nṭ[y]k[s ḥlypy]. *546*, *Inv. XI*, 1^{4}—yrḥbwl’ wbrḥwm ’‘ylm w’QM’ [w]’t‘m. [*563*], *C* 4212^{2}—’QM’ brt blṭy. **2.** *C* 4237 B^{1}—’QM’ bt bwlm’. *C* 4287^{5}—’QM’ brt dynys ṣ‘dy. *C* 4336^{1}—’QM’ brt zbdbwl br ‘g’. *C* 4338^{1}—’QM’ brt ḥbzy. *C* 4339^{3}—[l]wy’ bt [ḥ]ry ’QM[’ ḥbz]y. *C* 4346^{1}—’QM’ brt ‘gylw. *C* 4466^{1}—’QM’ brt mqymw. *C* 4472^{1}—’QM’ brt ‘(g)’ br [mt]ny. *C* 4482^{3}—‘bd[’] br ḥr’ ’QM’. *C* 4518 A^{1}—’QM’ brt mlkw br dynys. *C* 4570^{1}—’QM’ brt mqy. *C* 4573 B—’QM’. *C* 4606^{1}—’QM’ brt mtny br ḥyrn. CaD 36 E^{1}—[’]QM’ [wn]yny bny [nb]wm’. *PS* 394—’QM’ brt ḥ[. . . . *Inv. VIII*, 185 A^{1}—’QM’ brt ‘g’.

’QML (*m*) **1.** [*454*], *C* 4167—lšmš br nwrbl br mqymw br ‘gylw ’QML. **2.** *C* 4220^{2}—šlm’ brt ’QM[L br] šdy. CaD 25^{5}—. . .]lw br nwrbl ’QML bw [. . . . CaD 38^{3}—‘rwn’ [. . . .] bny š‘dy [. . .’]QML. *Inv. VIII*, 67^{3}—[’]QML.

’QMT (*m/f*) **1.** *497*, Ingh. E (Malkû) p. 91, II^{1}—nwrbl w’QMT ḥb’ bny mlkw rb’ br mlkw mlkw nwrbl. *497*, Ingh. E (Malkû) p. 93, III^{1}—nwrbl w’QMT ḥb’ bny mlkw rb’ br mlkw mlkw nwrbl. *505*, Ingh. B p. 95, II^{3}—’QMT bt yrḥy br mqymw. **2.** *C* 4190^{4}—’QMT. *C* 4200^{1}—’QMT brt ḥggw zbyd’ m‘n. *C* 4464^{2}—’QMT brt blḥzy nwry. *C* 4516 B^{1}—’QMT. *C* 4574^{1}—’QMT brt yrḥy šg’. *C* 4584^{1}—’QMT brt ydy. *C* 4605^{1}—’QMT brt zbd‘th. Ingh. E (Malê) p. 81, F—’QMT brt š‘dy. Ingh. A p. 99, A 7^{2}—’QMT brt [ml’ br ’]lhbl. ‘IP’ p. 156, 14 A^{1}—’QMT [b]rt ḥyrn br bnr. CaB 11^{6}—’QMT brt tym’. CaD 24^{2}—whby br nwrbl br ’QMT. StaB p. 97, A 1185^{1}—’QMT. *Inv. VIII*, 52—’QMT brt šm[. . . . *Inv. VIII*, 195 B—’QM[T]. *Inv. XI*, 92^{2}—š’yl’ b[r n]wrbl br ’QMT.

’QT[.] 2. *RTP* 212a—mqym[w] ’QT[.].

’R’WM (*m*) **1.** *390*, *C* 4121—bny w’lhš’ w’R’WM bny tymš’ br bny dy mtqrh ’rwn’.

’R’Š (*m*) **1.** *425*, *C* 4159^{3}—zbd‘th br ’t‘qb br zbd‘th br sry br zbd‘th br mlkw dy mtqr’ ’R’Š. *425*, *C* 4159^{5}—mqymw br zbd’ br mqymw br ‘t‘qb br mqymw br mlkw dy mtqr’ ’R’Š. **2.** *C* 4219^{3}—pṣy’l br šdy br rpbwl ’R’Š. *C* 4222—. . .] brt [š]dy ’R’Š. *C* 4225^{2}—rpbwl br ‘t‘qb br zbd zbd‘th ’R’Š. CaA 35^{3}—‘t‘qb wrpbwl wšdy bny br‘th br ‘t‘qb br zbd‘th ‘R‘Š.

’RB see ’DB.

’RBZ (*m*) **2.** CaC 18^{4}—’RBZ.

’RHDWN (*m*) **2.** *RTP* 682b—‘bdšlm ’RHDWN.

’RWN’ (*m*) **1.** *390*, *C* 4121—bny w’lhš’ w’r’wm bny tymš’ br bny dy mtqrh ’RWN’. **2.** CaD 38^{1}—’RWN’ [. . . .] bny š‘dy br [. . .’]qml. *Inv. VIII*, 67^{2}—’RWN’ br š‘dy br [. . . .

’RṬBN (*m*) **1.** *447*, *C* 3968^{4}—. . .] nṣryḥby br ‘g’ nṣryḥby ’RṬBN.

’RSṬYDS (*m*) **2.** *C* 4401^{1}—mrqws ywlyws mksmws ’RSṬYDS.

’RQṬWS (*m*) **1.** *476*, *Inv. XI*, 5^{4}—td’l brt ḥry bss br m‘n[w] br ’RQṬWS.

’RT (*f*) **2.** *C* 3907^{6}—brll bt bkrw bt bbt bt ’ḥth d’RT.

’ŠD (*m*) **2.** *C* 4476 A^{3}—. . .]t brt ’ŠD. *C* 4477^{3}—mlkw br ’ŠD. *C* 4478 A^{4}—šlmt brt ’ŠD.

’ŠDW (*m*) **2.** *Inv. VIII*, 175^{2}—’ŠDW br pṣy’l.

’ŠM (*m*) **2.** *RTP* 537a—‘gylw ‘gylw ’ŠM.

’Š‘[.]R (*m*) **2.** *C* 4467^{3}—mlkw br yrḥy ’Š‘[.]R.

’Š‘D (*m*) **2.** StaD p. 516, 3^{2}—mqym br zbdbwl ’Š‘D.

’Š‘‘ (*m*) **2.** *RTP* 480b—sṭm ḥyrn ’Š‘‘.

’ŠQR’ (*m*) **2.** *RTP* 181b—‘lyš’ ’ŠQR’. *RTP* 420b—‘gylw ’ŠQR’.

’TNDWR’ (*m*) **2.** *C* 4084^{5}—dwr’ br zbdbwl mlk’ ’TNDWR’ ’pwqḥ.

’TNDR[WS] (*m*) **2.** *C* 3971^{2}—spṭymyws whblt ’TNDR[WS] br spṭ[ymy]ws [’dynt].

’T‘M (*m*) **1.** *546*, *Inv. XI*, 1^{5}—yrḥbwl’ wbrḥwm ’‘ylm w’qm’ [w]’T‘M.

’T‘M[1. *551*, *Pal. 60*: 10^{1}—’T‘M[. . . .

’T‘MN (*m*) **2.** *C* 4081^{4}—tymrṣw w’T‘MN wyml’.

’T‘QB (*m*) **1.** *425*, *C* 4159^{2}—zbd‘th br ’T‘QB br zbd‘th br sry br zbd‘th br mlkw dy mtqr’ ’r’š. *583*, CaA 31^{4}—. . .] š‘‘ br ’T‘QB š‘‘. *583*, CaA 31^{5}—’T‘QB br yrḥy. **2.** *C* 4432^{2}—’T‘QB br ’by‘. ‘IP’ p. 160, 19^{3}—b‘‘ brt ’T‘QB btḥwml. Ingh. B, Pl. XLI^{5}—kytwt mzbn’ ’T‘QB.

'TPNY (*m*) **1.** *433*, *C* 4158^{2}—bltyḥn brt 'TPNY br mlkw 'tršwry. *473*, *C* 3956^{1}—ḥlypy br 'TPNY br ḥlypy. **2.** *C* 4080^{6}—mw'[l' br] 'TPNY br mrql'. *C* 4135^{1}—'TPNY br [m]'ny br whblt. *C* 4152^{1}—bltyḥn brt 'TPNY. CaC 12^{2}—lšmš br ḥlypy br 'TPNY. *Pal. 59*: 15^{2}—bltyḥn brt 'TPNY.

BBT (*f*) **2.** *C* 3907^{4}—brll bt bkrw bt BBT bt 'ḥth d'rt.

BGY (*m*) **1.** *502*, CaB 4 B^{2}—BGY br 'zyzw br mlkw.

BGDN (*m*) **2.** *C* 4076^{3}—gdy' b[r] ḥ[yrn B]GDN. *C* 4340^{4}—šlmt bt ḥry BGDN. *C* 4402—BGDN br 'lhbl br mlkw. *C* 4454—...']wyd' BGDN. *C* 4455^{3}—'ty brt rb'l br ḥyrn BG[DN]. *PS* 141—zbdlh br BGDN. *PS* 210—mzbn' br yrḥbwl' rpbwl BGDN. *PS* 395—'tdn brt BGDN.

BGRN (*m*) **1.** *42*[*9*], *Inv. VIII*, 78—[BGR]N br zbd'th. *480*, CaC 8^{3}—'mby brt BGRN br mlkw.

BGRT (*m*) **1.** [*5*]*61*, StaC p. 36, 6—'mtbl brt BGRT.

BGŠ (*m*) **2.** *C* 4395^{3}—ml' br mqymw BGŠ.

BGŠW (*m*) **1.** *439*, CaC 9^{1}—ḥb' br BGŠW br zbdbwl. *444*, *RTP* 32a—BGŠW ḥm'. *447*, *C* 3968^{5}—rb'l br ḥyrn BGŠW. **2.** CaC 10^{1,2}—BGŠW br ḥb[' br] / BGŠW. *Inv. VII*, 14—BGŠW br šḥrw ḥnyny.

BWṬ' (*m*) **1.** *527*, *C* 4017^{3}—BWṬ' br šmšgrm.

BWṬN (*m*) **1.** *559*, *C* 4043^{2}—ml' br BWṬN.

BWṬTN (*m*) **2.** *PNO* 66—BWṬTN 'ttn.

BWKY (*m*) **2.** *Pal. 61*: 15 B^{2}—BWKY.

B[WL]BRK (*m*) **1.** *391*, *C* 4122^{2}—mlkw br mqymw br B[WL]BRK ḥwml.

BWLZBD (*m*) **2.** *Inv. XI*, 49^{3}—...] br BWLZBD.

BWLḤ' (*m*) **1.** *333*, *C* 3915^{1}—ḥšš br nš' br BWLḤ' ḥšš *336*, CaC 4^{2}—mlkw br nš' br BWLḤ' dy mtqr' ḥšš. *336*, CaC 5^{2}—[ml]kw br nš' br BWLḤ' ḥšš. [*3*]*94*, *C* 3969^{2}—BWLḤ' [.... *415*, *Inv. VIII*, 59^{2}—BWLḤ' wmqymy wḥyrn wlšmš wb'l[y] bny whby br bwlḥzy. *437*, *C* 4247^{2}—hd' brt BWLḤ' br zbdl'. [*4*]*50*, *C* 4257^{3}—rm' br zbdlh br BWLḤ'. *480*, *C* 4255^{3}—hdyrt 'ḥ' brt BWLḤ' br br'' br zbd'th. *482*, CaB 14^{2}—šlm' brt BWLḤ' br bwrp'. *500*, *C* 4195^{4}—bwn' br BWLḤ' br bwn' br yqrwr. *516*, StaB p. 111, A 1169^{1}—BWLḤ' br ḥyrn br 't'qb ḥwml. *516*, StaB p. 111, A 1169^{8}—BWLḤ'. *516*, StaB p. 111, A 1169^{1} face droite—BWLḤ'. *550*, Ingh. B p. 124, II^{7}—m'yn' brt bwn' br BWLḤ'. **2.** *C* 4282^{2}—whblt br BWLḤ' br bwrp' 'ḥytwr. *C* 4283^{2}—'tntn br BWLḤ'. *C* 4285^{2,4}—[B]WLḤ' / [br] 'tntn / [BW]LḤ' / 'ḥytwr. *C* 4286^{2}—bwrp' br BWLḤ' 't(n)tn. *C* 4287^{2}—ḥgt brt BWLḤ' 't(n)tn 'ḥytwr. *C* 4400—[BW]LḤ' [br] mlkw. *C* 4488^{4}—...m]qymw [b]r BWLḤ' qwpyn. *RTP* 33a—BWLḤ' br ḥyrn. *RTP* 33b—BWLḤ'. *RTP* 64b—tym'md BWLḤ'. *RTP* 235b—BWLḤ'. *RTP* 280b—BWLḤ'. *RTP* 383b—BWLḤ' šlm'. *RTP* 804a—B[W]LḤ' or B[W]LM' ḥyrn. Ingh. D, Pl. IX^{2}—bwrp' br 'tntn BWLḤ'. Ingh. D, Pl. IX^{2}—BWLḤ' kldy'. 'Monuments' 3—tym'md BWLḤ'.

BWLḤZY (*m*) **1.** *415*, *Inv. VIII*, 59^{3}—bwlḥ' wmqymy wḥyrn wlšmš wb'l[y] bny whby br BWLḤZY. *574*, Ingh. E (Naṣrallat) p. 110, II^{2}—ywly' 'wrly' 'mt' brt BWLḤZY mqymw. *576*, Ingh. E (Naṣrallat) p. 112, III^{8}—ywly' 'wrly' 'mt' brt BWLḤZY mqymw. **2.** *RTP* 277b—BWLḤZY. *Inv. VIII*, 133^{3}—mšk[w] br BWLḤZY.

BWLY (*m*) **1.** *466*, Ingh. D, Pl. X^{2}—whb' 'bd'' BWLY. *474*, StaB p. 102, A 1167^{1}—BWLY br zbyd' br ḥyrn br mqymw mt'. *505*, *PNO* 37^{3}—'lhbl wrb'l [w]mhrw bny BWLY. **2.** *C* 4533—BWLY br 'gylw. Ingh. 'Quatre' p. 242, Pl. XL^{2}—whblt br blnwry dy mtqrh BWLY br bwš'. StaB p. 101, A 1168^{1}—BWL[Y] br zbyd' br ḥyrn br mq[ymw mt'].

BWLY' (*f*) **2.** *Inv. XI*, 57—BWLY' 'mt. 'Hypogée' p. 234, Pl. II^{2}—BWLY' brt 'g' br bwrp'.

BWLYD' (*m*) **2.** *RTP* 36a—BWLYD' mhrdt.

BWLM' (*m*) **1.** *426*, CaD 21^{2}—'wydw wmlkw wyrḥbwl[' wḥggw bny] BWLM' br 'wydy br BWLM' 'db. *545*, *C* 4206^{1}—[ywl]ys 'wrlys BWLM' br zbdbwl br BWLM' nyny'. *545*, *C* 4206^{3}—ywlys 'wrlys BWLM' br zbdbwl b[r BWLM' nyny'....b]rt [n]b[w]d' br tym' br nbwmw'. **2.** *C* 4237 B^{2}—'qm' bt BWLM'. *PNO* 17^{1}—BWLM' br 'ḥy'. *RTP* 804a—B[W]LM' or B[W]LḤ' ḥyrn.

BWLN' (*m*) **2.** *C* 3976^{2}—BWLN' br 'zyzw br 'zyzw br š'yl'. 'IP' p. 161, 21—B[W]LN' br[.... *Inv. XI*, 80^{3}—BWLN' 'ywn[....

BWLNWR (*m*) **1.** *504*, *C* 4199^{6}—zbyd' br m'n br BWLNWR (nwr)'th.

[B]WL'' (*f*) **2.** *C* 4394 A^{2}—[B]WL'' bt [']qyb'.

[BWL]Q' (*m*) **1.** *470*, CaC 14^{3}—rp'l br [BWL]Q' br nwrbl.

BWN' (*m*) **1.** *363*, 'Trilingue' p. 137^{2}—ḥyrn br BWN' br rb'l br BWN' br 'tntn br tymy. *363*, 'Trilingue' p. 138^{4}—BWN'. *371*, *Inv. IX*, 20^{2}—ḥyrn br BWN' br rb'l br BWN' br 'tntn dy [mt]qr' br š't. *380*, CaD 7 A^{1}—BWN' br rb'[.... [*3*]*84*, *C* 4193^{2}—

'mtḥ' brt BWN'. *385*, CaD 2^{1}—ḥ[y]rn br BWN[' dy mtqr' rb'l]. *406*, *C* 4130^{4}—mtny br nwrbl br mlkw br tymḥ' br mtny br BWN' br mtny dy mtqrh mhwy. *426*, *C* 4129 A^{4}—b'ltg' w'lyš' bny BWN' br šby. *426*, *C* 4129 B^{2}—'lyš' wb'ltg' bny BWN' br šby br blšwr br ḥyrn. *426*, *C* 4161^{1}—nš' wBW[N' bn]y nš' br tym[']. *448*, *C* 3913 $I^{1,2}$—BWN' br BWN' br ḥyrn. *451*, *C* 3927^{2}—'ḥply br ḥyrn šb' br ḥyrn BWN' š[']t. *500*, *C* $4195^{4,5}$—BWN' br bwlḥ' / br BWN' yqrwr. *525*, Ingh. E (Malkû) p. 99, VIII^{2}—hlydyrs yrḥbwl' br ḥyrn BWN'. *527*, *PNO* 61^{2}—BWN' br 'mdbw. *527*, *Inv. XI*, 16^{3}—BWN' 'g' gbyns. *550*, Ingh. B p. 124, II^{5}—BWN' br rb'l. *550*, Ingh. B p. 124, II^{7}—m'yn' brt BWN' br bwlḥ'. **2.** *RTP* 463a—BW[N]' br ḥyrn. *RTP* 477b—'gylw BWN'. *RTP* 752b—sṭm BWN' blty. *RTP* 795a—BWN'. *RTP* 881b—BWN'. *RTP* 906b—BWN'. *C* 4233—BWN'. *C* 4333 B^{1}—BWN'. *C* $4334^{2,5}$—mtn' br / br BWN' / br yrḥbwl' / šlmwy br / BWN'. *C* 4420^{2}—ydy'bl br BWN' br 'bd'stwr. *C* 4475^{2}—'g' br BWN'. *C* 4479 A^{2}—yrḥy br BWN'. *C* 4479 B—m'ynt brt BWN'. *C* 4512 A^{3}—ḥb' br[t] BWN'. *C* 4512 B^{4}—mrthwn brt [ḥ]lyp' BWN'. *C* 4535 A^{3}—sbbw br yrḥ[y] BWN'. CaD 36 D^{2}—BWN' br tymrṣw. *Inv. VIII*, 76^{1}—[BWN']. *Inv. VIII*, $190^{1,2}$—BWN' / br BWN'. *Inv. IX*, 30^{2}—[ywlys] 'wrlys [nbwmy br tymšm]š BWN' [šby. . . .

BWNWR (*m*) **2.** *RTP* 7b—BWNWR.

BWR[**2.** *RTP* 485b—BWR[. . . .

BWR' (*m*) **2.** *RTP* 793a—BWR'. *RTP* 795b—BWR'. *RTP* 813b—BWR'. *RTP* 909a—BWR'.

BWRP' (*m*) **1.** *329 Pal. 63*: 2^{4}—'gylw br ydy'bl br BWRP'. *348*, CaD 33^{3}—mlkw [wz]bd'[th. . . . .]bny tym'md b[r] BWRP' zg[wg]. *390*, *Inv. XI*, 81^{6}—BWRP'. *400+?*, 'Hypogée' p. 199, line 1—. . b]r BWRP' qsm'. *430*, CaB 7^{1}—šm'wn br BWRP' br 'gylw mṭn. *430*, *C* 4163^{2}—br'' wBWRP' bny rb'l br br''. *445*, *C* 4281^{4}—'tntn gwry br BWRP' 'tntn 'ḥytwr. *471*, CaB 1 A^{1}—tymrṣw br BWRP' br mlkw br 'šylt. *482*, CaB 14^{2}—šlm' brt bwlḥ' br BWRP'. *482*, CaB 14^{2}—'gylw br BWR[P]'. *490*, *C* 4006^{4}—BWRP'. *500*, *C* 4292^{3}—ḥyrn br BWRP' br ḥyrn br tybwl. *551*, *C* 4037^{1}—BWRP' br ḥ[lpt]' [br. . . . **2.** *C* 4279^{3}—mlkw br BWRP' 'ḥytwr. *C* 4282^{3}—whblt br bwlḥ' br BWRP' 'ḥytwr. *C* 4286^{1}—BWRP' br bwlḥ' 't(n)tn. *C* 4290^{2}—šlm' brt BWRP'. *C* 4357^{4}—zbyd' br 'wṭk' dy BWRP' 'kldy. *C* 4388^{3}—ḥnt' brt BWRP'. *C* 4438^{2}—hgr brt BWRP' br 'tyk'. *C* 4440^{4}—'ḥ' brt BWRP'. *C* 4494^{1}—BWRP' br mlkw. *C* 4547^{3}—šgl brt BWRP'. *C* 4567^{2}—m'n' br ḥry BWRP' br mrql'. *C* 4575^{3}—zbdbwl br zbdlh br BWRP' br zbdlh. *C* 4576^{3}—zbdlh br BWRP'. *C* 4577^{3}—whblt br BWRP'. *C* 4597^{1}—BWRP' 'g' zbyd' myṭq'. *C* 4618—ml[k]' br yrḥbwl' br BWRP' br ml[k]w. *RTP* 60b—'gylw BWRP' qšṭ'. *RTP* 103b—'tnwry BWRP'. *RTP* 257b—BWRP'. *RTP* 274b—yrḥy br BWRP'. *RTP* 419b—zbdl[h] or zbdb[wl] BWR[P']. *RTP* 640b—yrḥy zbd'th [B]WRP'. *RTP* 699b—BWRP'. *RTP* 754b—mlkw br BWRP'. *RTP* 756b—BWRP'. *RTP* 858a—BWRP'. *RTP* 990a—blkz or blsz tym'md BWRP'. Ingh. D pl. IX^{2}—BWRP' br 'tntn bwlḥ'. *Inv. X*, 130^{1}—g'ys [lqn]ys plwynws br BWRP'. *Inv. XI*, 98—BWRP' 'gylw. StaC 4, p. 34—zbdbwl br BWRP'. 'Tessères' 13b—'tnwry BWRP'. *Syria* 23 (1942–3), 80^{3}—mlkw br šm'wn BWRP'. 'Hypogée' p. 199, line 8—BWRP' br 'gylw br BWRP' qs[m'. . . . 'Hypogée' p. 223, Pl. II^{1}—q/mbwrm brt BWRP' / ṭ'y br BWRP'. 'Hypogée' p. 225, Pl. III^{1}—'g' br BWRP'. 'Hypogée' p. 226, Pl. IV^{1}—. . .]br BWRP' ṭ'y. 'Hypogée' p. 228, Pl. IV^{2}—BWRP' br 'g'. 'Hypogée' p. 234, Pl. II^{2}—ml' br 'g' BWRP'. 'Hypogée' p. 234, Pl. II^{2}—bwly' brt 'g' br BWRP'. 'Hypogée' p. 238, Pl. VII^{1}—BWRP' br mqymw br ṭ'y. 'Hypogée' p. 241, Pl. X^{1}—. . .]BWRP' ṭ'y.

BWŠ' (*m*) **1.** (*399*), CaB 6 B^{4}—whblt br blnwry BWŠ'. **2.** *C* 4579^{1}—BWŠ' br tym'. Ingh. 'Quatre' p. 242, Pl. XL^{2}—whblt br blnwry dy mtqrh bwly br BWŠ'. Ingh. 'Quatre' p. 243, Pl. XLI^{2}—ḥyrn br ndb'l BWŠ'.

BZY (*m*) **2.** *Inv. VIII*, 24^{2}—mlkw br tymn' BZY.

BYD' (*m*) **1.** *537*, StaB p. 153, A 1205^{2}—zbyd' br whblt BYD' ''py. *550*, CaA 32^{2}—br'th br zbyd' br[. . . . .]' BYD'. *558*, *C* 3933^{3}—ywlys 'wrlys zbyd' br mqymw br zbyd' 'štwr BYD'. **2.** *C* 4548^{2}—ḥrt' brt BYD'. *RTP* 436b—BYD' br b[. . . . *RTP* 759a—BYD'. 'Monuments' 5—zbd'th br zbyd' BYD'.

BYDN (*m*) **2.** *Inv. VIII*, 136^{3}—'ly br tymlt br BYDN.

BYLY see KYLY.

BKRW (*f*). **2.** *C* 3907^{2}—brll bt BKRW bt bbt bt 'ḥth d'rt.

BL[**1.** *38*[.], CaD 34^{1}—wBL[. . . .] ḥm'. **2.** CaD 25^{4}—. . .]br khylw br BL[. . . . *Pal. 61*: 8—BL[. . . . *RTP* 996b—BL[. . . .

BLBW (*m*) **2.** *PNO* 53—BLBW gwb'.

BLḤ' (*m*) **2.** *C* 3990^{2}—ḥyr[n] br blḥzy br BLḤ' [m]qy [''b]y. *C* 4559^{2}—BL[Ḥ'] br nš' ḥšš. *C* 4560^{2}—nš' br BLḤ' ḥšš. *RTP* 44b—BLḤ['].

BLḤZY (*m*) **1.** *399*, CaB 6 A^{1}—BLḤZY br nwry br zbdbwl ''ylmy. *430*, *Inv. VIII*, 62^{2}—ḥlyšy br bryky br BLḤZY. *461*, *PNO* 51—BLḤZY. **2.** *C* 3990^{2}—ḥyr[n] br BLḤZY br blḥ' [m]qy [''b]y. *C* 4464^{3}—

'qmt brt BLḤZY nwry. *RTP* 261b—BLḤZY šlmn. *RTP* 337a—BLḤZY gnb'. *RTP* 388a—BLḤZY. *RTP* 388b—BLḤZY. *RTP* 887b—rpb[w]l BLḤZY. Ingh. 'Quatre' p. 242, Pl. XL^{1}—šgl brt whblt ''ylmy BLḤZY. *Inv. VIII*, 26^{2}—BLḤZY br tymn' whby 'dy[nt]. *Inv. VIII*, 98^{2}—'mt' br[t....] BLḤZY.

BLḤY (*f*) **1.** *457*, *C* 3911^{10}—BLḤY brt ‘mrw.

BLṬY (*m*) **1.** [*563*], *C* 4212^{2}—'qm' brt BLṬY.

BLY (*m*) **1.** *499*, Ingh. E (Malkû) p. 95, IV—š‘rn' br BLY. *525*, Ingh. E (Malkû) p. 97, VI^{1}—bs' wrysq' bny š‘rn' BLY. **2.** *RTP* 720b—BLY zbyd' mlkw nṣrlt. *RTP* 746a—BLY whblt.

BLY' (*f*) **2.** *C* 4537 B^{1}—BLY'.

BLYD‘ (*m*) **1.** *426*, *C* 3995^{2,3}—BLYD‘ w‘tnwry wm‘nw [bny] / tym‘md br BLYD‘. *474*, *Inv. X*, 29^{4}—nš' br BLYD‘. *514*, *C* 3970^{1}—šlm' br mlkw br BLYD‘. *516*, StaB p. 111, A 1169^{6}—t[y]m‘ br[....] tym‘ BLYD[‘]. *C* 4440^{1}—BLYD‘ br ‘tyk'. *C* 4509^{4}—ḥbyby br mlkw BLY[D‘]. *RTP* 556b—BLYD‘. *RTP* 810a—brykw BLYD‘. *Inv. X*, 56—[š‘d]w br BL[YD‘].

BLYD‘W (*m*) **2.** CaA 75^{1}—BLYD‘W br mqymw br mlkw.

BLYHB (*m*) **2.** 'Iraq' p. 63^{5}, Pl. 5—tymy br tymy br BLYHB.

BLKZ (*m*) **2.** *RTP* 990a—BLKZ or BLSZ tym‘md bwrp'.

BLM' (*m*) **2.** CaD 25^{6}—...b]l‘qb ḥmnwn BLM'[.... *RTP* 130a—gd BLM'.

BLNWR (*m*) **2.** *RTP* 272b—BLNWR mqmw ḥyrn mly.

BLNWRY (*m*) **1.** (*399*), CaB 6 B^{4}—whblt br BLNWRY bwš'. **2.** *RTP* 182b—šky[bl] wšlmn wBLN[WR]Y [w]mqymw. *RTP* 219a—blty BLNWRY. Ingh. 'Quatre' p. 242, Pl. XL^{2}—whblt br BLNWRY dy mtqrh bwly br bwš'. *Inv. VIII*, 69^{2}—BLNWR[Y].

BLSZ see BLKZ.

BL‘QB (*m*) **1.** [*3*?]*42*, 'Dédicace' p. 44, 1—mlkw br BL[‘]QB br 'bnyt. [*3*?]*42*, 'Dédicace' p. 44, 3—BL‘QB br / ḥyrn BL‘QB. [*3*?]*42*, 'Dédicace' p. 45, 4—BL‘QB br / mlkw br BL‘QB. [*3*?]*42*, 'Dédicace' p. 45, 6—mlkw br BL‘QB br m[yk'.... *3*[*94*], *C* 4123—ymlkw br mqymw dy mtqrh 'qlyš br mlkw br BL‘QB. *394*, *C* 4123 *bis*^{3}—ymlkw br mqymw 'qlyš br mlkw 'bnyt br BL‘QB br myk' br mt'. *443*, *C* 3973^{8}—zbyd' br [š]m‘wn br BL‘QB. *570*, *C* 3937^{3}—BL‘QB br ḥrš'. **2.** *C* 4143^{1}—BL‘QB br 'lhbl br whblt. *C* 4148^{2}—BL[‘QB] br 'lhbl whblt. *C* 4151^{1}—'mtḥ' brt BL‘QB br nš'. *C* 4157^{1}—BL‘QB br 'lhbl br whblt br m‘ny. *C* 4353 A^{3}—rbt br BL‘QB. *RTP* 877a—BL‘QB. CaD 25^{6}—...B]L‘QB ḥmnwn blm' [.... *Inv. VIII*, 9^{3}—zbdb(w)l br mtn' br zbdlh br BL‘QB dy mtqrh 'ṣr‘. *Inv. XI*, 65^{2}—whblt br BL‘QB br [n]š'. *Inv. XI*, 97^{6}—...[br BL‘Q[B....

BLŠWR (*m*) **1.** *426*, *C* 4129 B^{3}—'lyš' wb‘ltg' bny bwn' br šby br BLŠWR br ḥyrn. [*469*], CaA 8^{3}—BL[ŠWR br yrḥy br tym']. **2.** *C* 4358 A^{3}—bt‘g' brt ḥyr' BLŠWR. *C* 4358 B^{1}—BLŠWR br ḥyr' 'kldy. *C* 4621^{4}—bt‘g' brt ḥyr' BLŠWR. 'Sculptures' p. 24, Pl. II^{2}—BLŠWR br ḥyr' 'kldy. *Inv. VIII*, 6^{2}—yrḥy br BLŠWR.

BLŠWRY (*m*) **1.** *336*, *Inv. IV*, 26 B—BLŠWRY br ḥggw. *345*, *C* 4114^{2}—ḥyrn br BLŠWRY br gdrṣw dy mtqrh br b‘'. *345*, *C* 4114^{5}—BLŠWRY. *363*, 'Trilingue' p. 138^{4}—b‘ltg' brt BLŠWRY. *394*, *C* 4124^{2}—šby wnbwzbd wt[ymy wnbwl'] bny BLŠWRY br ḥyrn br BLŠWRY br gdrṣw [....b‘']. **2.** *C* 3929^{1,2}—[BLŠ]WRY / br ḥggw br BLŠWRY b‘'. *C* 4125^{1}—[B]LŠWRY br šby br BLŠWRY. *C* 4126—...ḥ]yr[n] br BLŠWRY. *C* 4127 A—...]šby br BLŠWRY. *C* 4128^{3,5}—...]br š[by] / br BLŠ[WRY] / br ḥyrn / BLŠWRY. 'Büste' p. 313^{5}—tymy br BLŠWRY tymy. Ingh. B p. 137, line 18—mqymw br BLŠWRY.

BLT' (*m*/*f*) **1.** *4*[..], *Pal. 59*: 6^{1}—BLT'. **2.** *C* 4405 B—BLT'. *C* 4610^{2}—ḥyrn br BLT' br ḥyrn.

BLTY (*f*) **2.** *RTP* 674b—BLTY wydy. *RTP* 752b—sṭm bwn' BLTY.

BLTYḤN (*f*) **1.** *433*, *C* 4158^{2}—BLTYḤN brt 'tpny br mlkw ‘tršwry. **2.** *C* 4152^{1}—BLTYḤN brt 'tpny. *Pal. 59*: 15^{2}—BLTYḤN brt 'tpny. *Pal. 59*: 16^{1}—BLTYḤN.

BN' (*m*) **1.** *539*, Ingh. B p. 110, III^{4}—'wrlys mlkw br šlmn BN'. **2.** 'Inscriptions' p. 125, Pl. II—yrḥbwl' br [..]b' BN' (?).

BNWR (*m*) **1.** *466*, *C* 4251^{1}—BNWR br br‘' zbd‘th. *497*, Ingh. E (Bar‘â) p. 115^{2}—br‘' br BNWR br br‘' zbd‘th tšbb. **2.** *C* 4253^{2}—zbd‘th br BNWR br‘'.

BNWRY (*m*) **2.** *C* 4252 A^{4}—BNWRY br br‘'. *C* 4518 A^{2}—BNWRY.

BNY (*m*) **1.** *390*, *C* 4121—BNY w'lhš' w'r'wm bny tymš' br BNY dy mtqrh 'rwn'. **2.** *C* 4434^{1}—BNY br ḥyrn. *C* 4435^{1}—BNY br tymy. *C* 4436^{3}—[‘g]b' br tymy br BN[Y]. *C* 4586—BNY br ydy. *PS* 104—BNY br mrd. *Inv. X*, 16—...lt br] BNY. *Inv. XI*, 93—BNY.

BNR (*m*) **2.** 'IP' p. 156, 14 A^{4}—'qmt [b]rt ḥyrn br BNR.

BNR' (*m*) **2.** *C* 4331^{2}—BNR'.

BS' (*m*) **1.** *525*, Ingh. E (Malkû) p. 97, VI^{1}—BS' wrysq' bny š'rn' bly. *578*, Ingh. E (Malkû) p. 102, XI^{7}—'mw brt BS' š'rwn'. *578*, Ingh. E (Malkû) p. 104, XII^{6}—'mw brt BS' š'rwn'. *578*, Ingh. E (Malkû) p. 104, XII^{7}—ywly' 'wrly' 'gtwn' br BS' grmn'. **2.** Ingh. B p. 101, III A—BS' ṅqb'. *Inv. XI*, 32^{5}—. . .]br BS' nhtwm'.

BSM (*m*) **1.** *516*, *C* 4013^{3}—hrms BSM [b]r ḥry mlkw br whb'.

BSS (*m*) **1.** *476*, *Inv. XI*, 5^{3}—BSS br m'n[w] br 'rqṭws.

B'' (*m*/*f*) **1.** *394*, *C* 4124^{3}—šby wnbwzbd wt[ymy wnbwl'] bny blšwry br ḥyrn br blšwry br gdrṣw [. . . . B'']. **2.** *C* 3929^{2}—[blš]wry br ḥggw br blšwry B''. 'IP' p. 160, 19^{2}—B'' brt 't'qb btḥwml.

B'LW (*m*) **2.** 'Inscriptions' p. 125, Pl. II—B'LW.

B'LY (*m*) **1.** *409*, 'Wadi Hauran' 1^{6}—B'LY ml' 'lhy/w. *415*, *Inv. VIII*, 59^{2}—bwlḥ' wmqymy wḥyrn wlšmš wB'L[Y] bny whby br bwlḥzy. *[4]25*, *C* 3974^{1}—B'LY br yrḥbwl'. *497*, Ingh. E (Malkû) p. 93, III^{1}—B'LY br dywn mlkw. *499*, Ingh. E (Malkû) p. 95, IV—B'LY br dywn br mlkw. *501*, *Pal. 60*: 11^{3}—brny br B'LY. *573*, *PNO* 57—'n'm wB'LY. *574*, *C* 4051^{1}—B'LY. *578*, Ingh. E (Malkû) p. 104, XII^{8}—B'LY br 'bdy 'dwn. **2.** *C* 4105—B'LY. *Inv. VIII*, 137^{6}—B'LY. *Inv. XI*, 22^{4}—mzbn' br B'LY. *PNO* 5—B'LY.

B'LTG' (*m*/*f*) **1.** *363*, 'Trilingue' p. 138^{4}—B'LTG' brt blšwry. *426*, *C* 4129 A^{2}—B'LTG' w'lyš' bny bwn' br šby. *426*, *C* 4129 B^{2}—'lyš' wB'LTG' bny bwn' br šby br blšwr br ḥyrn. *579*, *C* 4053^{2}—B'LTG' bt 'g'. **2.** *C* 4296 A^{4}—B'LT[G]' brt 'wyd' b[r] tymrṣw. *C* 4417^{3}—B'LTG['] brt yrḥbw[l']. *C* 4419^{1}—B'LTG' brt 'bd'stwr nwrbl. Ingh. B p. 135, IV C^{1}—B'LTG' br 'g'. 'Monuments' 7—B'LTG' brt mqymw. *Pal. 60*: 5 A^{1}—[B'L]TG' [b]rt [']bgr [ty]mrṣw.

B'ŠMN (*m*) **2.** *Inv. VIII*, 162^{1}—B'ŠMN br ty[. . . .

BPNY' (*m*) **2.** *RTP* 933b—zmry BPNY'.

BQY (*m*) **2.** *C* 4517^{2}—kd/rnny brt mlkw BQY.

BR 'ḤTY (*m*) **1.** *[4]40*, 'Iraq' p. 64^{5}, Pl. 10—'g' br ml' br 'gylw br tybwl dy mtqrh BR 'ḤTY.

BR ''RY (*m*) **2.** *Inv. XI*, 88^{2}—mlkw br 'gylw dy [mt]qrh BR ''RY.

BR B'' (*m*) **1.** *345*, *C* 4114^{3}—ḥyrn br blšwry br gdrṣw dy mtqrh BR B''.

BR DKT' (*m*) **2.** Ingh. A p. 88, 2^{2}—ḥdwdn BR DKT' br ḥry btprmwn.

BR ZBYDY (*m*) **1.** *350*, CaD 31^{3}—mqymw br khylw br zbdbl [dy] mtqrh BR ZBYDY.

BR 'BDBL (*m*) **1.** *396*, *C* 3978^{5}—lšmš wzbyd' bny mlkw br ydy'bl br nš' dy mtqr' BR 'BDBL.

BR 'ZWLT (*m*) **2.** 'Wadi Hauran' 10^{4}—yrḥbwl' br lšmš br mqymw dy mtqr' BR 'ZWLT.

BR Š'T (*m*) **1.** *371*, *Inv. IX*, 20^{3}—ḥyrn br bwn' br rb'l br bwn' br 'tntn dy [mt]qr' BR Š'T.

BR[.]Š (*m*) **1.** *500+?*, *C* 4197^{2}—'g' br šlm' šmšgrm br BR[.]Š 'g' 'ytybl.

BR' (*m*) **1.** *502*, *C* 4173^{1}—zbdbwl br kptwt br BR'. **2.** *RTP* 189b—yrḥy BR'. *Inv. XI*, 78^{2}—[z]bdbwl BR'.

BR'T' (*m*) **2.** *PNO* 4—m'ny BR'T'.

[B]R'TY (*m*) **2.** *PNO* 26—[B]R'TY.

BRBRS (*m*) **1.** *448*, *C* 3913 II^{121}—BRBRS.

BRDWNY (*m*) **2.** Ingh. B p. 134, line 30—BRDWNY.

BRH' (*m*) **2.** *PNO* 41^{2}—BRH' br 'g'.

BRWQ' (*m*) **1.** *458*, *PNO* 55 A—wrdn / BRWQ' / mhrdt / 'mbkr'. *458*, *PNO* 55 C—wrdn wBRWQ' w'mbkr'. **2.** *C* 4311 B^{1}—BRWQ' br ns' 'lbn. *C* 4312^{3}—ydy'bl br mzbn' BRWQ'. *RTP* 220b—BRWQ['] mq[y]. *Inv. VIII*, 22^{1}—zbdbwl br BRWQ' br 'knt.

BRḤWM (*m*) **1.** *546*, *Inv. XI*, 1^{3}—yrḥbwl' wBRḤWM ''ylm w'qm' [w]'t'm.

BRY (*m*) **2.** *Inv. VIII*, 48^{2}—mqymw BRY.

BRYK (*m*) **2.** StaF p. 40, 7—BRYK. *RTP* 554b—BRYK tymy.

BRYKW (*m*) **1.** *409*, 'Wadi Hauran' 8^{9}—rb'l br tym' BRYKW. **2.** *RTP* 810a—BRYKW blyd'. *RTP* 200b—BRYK[W/Y].

BRYKY (*m*) **1.** *[4]19*, CaD 36 A^{3}—yrḥy br B[R]YKY br [ty]mrṣw. *[4]19*, CaD 36 A^{6}—[BRYKY]. *430*, *Inv. VIII*, 62^{2}—ḥlyšy br BRYKY br blḥzy. *441*, *PS* 3^{1}—BRYKY br tym' br ml' gyr'. *450*, *C* 3931^{2}—BRYKY br 'mrš' br yrḥbwl'. *530*, StaB p. 152, A 1207^{4}—tymrṣw br BRYKY. *544*, CaB 10 A^{1}—lšmš br 'stwrg' [b]r lš[mš] br [B]RYKY br lqy šlmn. *[563]*, CaA 39^{6}—BRYKY br [. . . . **2.** *C* 4240^{2}—whblt br BRYKY br zbdbwl. *C* 4534^{2}—tymrṣw br BRYKY. *RTP* 40a—BRYKY šk't' 'ḥyry. *RTP* 200b—BRYK[Y/W]. *RTP* 360b—BRYKY. *RTP* 730a—mlkw BRYK[Y]. *RTP* 730b—mlkw BRYKY. 'IP' p. 156, 14 B^{3}—nbwzbd BRYKY. 'IP' p. 157, 15^{2}—BRYKY br nbwzbd br [. . . . 'IP' p. 157, 16 A^{1}—. . .] brt BRYKY br nbwzbd br nbwzbd. 'IP' p. 157, 16 B^{2}—ḥn' brt BRYKY nbwzbd.

‘IP’ p. 158, 17^{2}—mzbw brt BRYKY br mqyn’. StaC p. 41, 10—tym[’ . . . . B]RYKY w[. . . . CaD 36 G^{3}—nṣ’ brt yrḥy br BRYKY. *Pal. 61*: 10—BRYKY br p[. . . . *Inv. VIII*, 10^{2}—mtny br BRYKY bt’. *Inv. XI*, 25^{2}—ḥyrn br BRYKY br ḥyrn.

BRYQY (*m*) **2.** *RTP* 547b—BRYQY yrḥbwl.

BR[K/P]’ (*m*) **2.** *C* 4245 B^{1}—BR[K/P]’ br zbyd’ mqymw.

BRKY (*m*) **1.** *328*, *C* 3925^{2}—‘zyzw br ydy‘bl BRKY.

BRLL (*f*) **2.** *C* 3907^{2}—BRLL bt bkrw bt bbt bt ’ḥth d’rt.

BRM[**2.** *Inv. VIII*, 170^{1}—BRM[. . . .

BRNBW (*m*) **1.** *425*, *C* 3986^{2}—nbwzbd wyrḥbwl’ bny BRNBW br nbwzbd br zbdl’ ’knby. **2.** *C* 4231 A^{2,3}—br‘th / br BRNBW br / BRNBW. *C* 4231 B^{2}—br‘th br BRNBW. *C* 4231 C^{1}—BRNBW br BRNBW. *C* 4231 D^{2}—nbwgdy br BRNBW. *RTP* 72a—BRNBW. *RTP* 296a—br‘th BRNBW. *Pal. 61*: 7^{1,2}—BRNB[W br] / BRNBW. StaF 4, p. 38—br‘’ zbd‘th wBRNBW wzdql. StaF 4, p. 38—BRNBW. *PS* 203—BRNBW br br‘th br BRNBW. *Inv. IV*, 15 A—ḥggw BRNBW br‘th. *Inv. IV*, 15 C—mqymw br BRNBW br‘th.

BRNY (*m*) **1.** *501*, *Pal. 60*: 11^{3}—BRNY br b‘ly. **2.** *C* 4542^{2}—BRNY. StaF 5, p. 39—BRNY.

BRS (*m*) **2.** *RTP* 700b—lqnys BRS. *RTP* 776a—lqnys BRS. *RTP* 835a—lqnys BR[S].

BRSMY’ (*m*) **1.** *532*, *Inv. XI*, 14^{4}—. . .] BRSMY’. *550*, Ingh. B p. 124, II^{4}—lwqys ’wrlys BRSMY’.

BR‘’ (*m*) **1.** *430*, *C* 4163^{2,3}—BR‘’ wbwrp’ / bny rb’l br BR‘’. *437*, *C* 4247^{4}—BR‘’ br zbd‘t’. [*4*]*45*, *C* 4246^{1,4}—BR‘’ br / zbd‘th / br zbd‘th / BR‘’. *446*, *C* 4248^{2}—’mby brt BR‘’ zbd‘th. *457*, *C* 4249^{2}—šlm[t] brt BR‘’ zbd‘th. *460*, *PS* 39^{3}—’ḥ’ brt zbdlh BR‘’. *461*, *C* 4254^{4}—’ḥ’ brt ḥlpt’ br BR‘’ zbd‘th. *466*, *C* 4251^{2}—bnwr br BR‘’ zbd‘th. *480*, *C* 4255^{4}—hdyrt ’ḥ’ brt bwlḥ’ br BR‘’ br zbd‘th. *487*, *C* 4250^{3}—zbdlh br BR‘’ br zbd‘th. *497*, Ingh. E (Bar‘â) p. 115^{2}—BR‘’ br bnwr br BR‘’ zbd‘th tšbb. **2.** *C* 4252 A^{5}—bnwry br BR‘’. *C* 4253^{3}—zbd‘th br bnwr BR‘’. *C* 4524^{10}—m‘ny br BR‘’. *PS* 209—m‘n br BR‘’. *PS* 288—mzbn’ br BR‘’ br zbd‘th. StaF 4, p. 38—BR‘’ zbd‘th wbrnbw wzdql. Ingh. B p. 114, line 24—tymn’ BR‘’. Ingh. B Pl. XLII^{1}—sry BR‘’ sry.

BR‘Y (*m*) **1.** *43*[*7*], CaD 30^{2}—mlkw br mqymw [br ḥyrn br] BR‘Y.

BR‘T’ (*m*) **2.** *C* 3901—rgyn’ bt ḥry BR‘T’. *Inv. VIII*, 107^{4}—šb’ brt ‘ttn BR‘T’.

BR‘TH (*m*) **1.** *377*, ‘Grave-Relief’ p. 192—BR‘TH br ḥnbl ’‘by. *392*, *Inv. X*, 131^{2}—mlkw br lšmš br ḥnbl br BR‘TH ’‘by. *449*, *C* 4165^{2}—ḥdw[dn] br ṣpry BR‘TH. *490*, CaA 41^{3,4}—[ṣ‘dw br BR‘TH / br ṣ‘dw br] BR[‘TH]. *500*, *Pal. 62*: 19^{2}—’lhbl br BR‘TH mqymw ’klb. *525*, ‘Malkû’ p. 106^{12}—ywlys ’wrlys nš’ br BR‘TH. *525*, *Inv. X*, 119^{3}—tym’ br ḥlpt’ BR‘TH ’lṭy. *54*[.], *C* 3957^{3}—BR‘TH br lšmš mlkw. *550*, CaA 32^{1}—BR‘TH br zbyd’ br [. . . .]’ byd’. **2.** *C* 4090^{2}—zbd[bw]l [br B]R‘TH. *C* 4231 A^{1}—BR‘TH br brnbw br brnbw. *C* 4231 B^{1}—BR‘TH br brnbw. *C* 4233—’m[t’] brt BR‘TH. *C* 4449^{2}—ḥsd brt BR‘TH ḥggw. *C* 4473^{2}—ḥgwg’ br BR‘TH. *C* 4489^{2}—[BR]‘TH [b]r [m]lkw. *C* 4552—mlkw b[r] zb’ BR[‘TH]. *RTP* 296a—BR‘TH brnbw. *RTP* 302b—yrḥbwl’ br mtn’ BR‘TH. *RTP* 555b—BR‘TH. *RTP* 669b—BR‘TH zbd[’]. *RTP* 993b—ḥld’ or ḥṭr’ BR‘TH. *RTP* 996a—‘t‘qb BR‘TH. CaA 35^{2}—‘t‘qb wrpbwl wšdy bny BR‘TH br ‘t‘qb br zbd‘th ’r’š. *PS* 203—brnbw br BR‘TH br brnbw. *Pal. 62*: 21^{2}—BR‘TH b[r. . . . *Inv. IV*, 15 A—ḥggw brnbw BR‘TH. *Inv. IV*, 15 C—mqymw br brnbw BR‘TH. *Inv. VIII*, 25^{3}—’brwq br BR‘TH gḥynt. *Inv. VIII*, 28^{2}—nbwyd‘ br [B]R‘TH nbwyd‘. *Inv. XI*, 73^{2}—BR‘TH br[. . . .

BRP’ (*m*) **1.** *430*, CaB 7^{2}—BRP’ wmlkw. *437*, *C* 3996^{6}—nrqys br ḥry ml’ BRP’. **2.** *C* 4520^{2}—dyny br BRP’. *RTP* 10b—nš’ BRP’. *C* 4245 B^{1}—BR[P/K]’ br zbyd’ mqymw.

BRQ (*m*) **1.** *447*, *C* 3999^{2}—šlmn br nš’ br ḥyr’ BRQ.

BRŠGL (*m*) **2.** *RTP* 903b—BRŠGL.

BRŠMŠ (*m*) **1.** *457*, *C* 3911^{6}—zbdbwl w‘tnwr wmlkw w‘mrw wydy‘bl bny BRŠMŠ br zbdbwl. *5*[*3*]*8*, *C* 4023^{1}—BRŠMŠ. **2.** *C* 4450^{3}—‘qrbn brh dBRŠMŠ. ‘Hypogée’ p. 222, Pl. I^{2}—ḥyrn br BRŠMŠ.

BRŠ‘D (*m*) **2.** *C* 4215^{2}—[BRŠ‘D]. *C* 4544—BRŠ‘D br [š]lṭ’.

BRT’ (*m*/*f*) **1.** *47*[*5*], CaB 3^{1}—’lhbl br mlkw br zbdbwl BRT’. **2.** *Inv. XI*, 50^{1}—BRT’ brt ’m’.

BRTW **2.** *Pal. 61*: 2—BRTẆ.

BŠR’ (*m*) **2.** *RTP* 643b—mlkw ḥyrn BŠR’.

BT’ (*f*) **2.** *Inv. VIII*, 10^{3}—mtny bryky BT’.

BTWHBY (*f*) **2.** *C* 4380—BTWHBY bt ‘dn.

BTZBY (*f*) **1.** *582*, *C* 3947^{1}—spṭmy’ BTZBY. **2.** *C* 3971^{5}—spṭymy’ BTZBY.

BTZBYD’ (*f*) **1.** *541*, *C* 4027^{2}—BTZBYD’ brt gdrṣw.

BTḤBY (*f*) **1.** *538*, *C* 4244 A^{2}—BTḤBY brt zbyd’.

BTḤW (*f*) **2.** *C* 4518 C^{1}—BTḤW.

BTḤWML (*f*) **2.** 'IP' p. 160, 19^{4}—b'' brt 't'qb BTḤWML.

BTḤYRN (*f*) **2.** *C* 4568 A^{2}—BTḤYRN brt ml'.

BTY (*m/f*) **2.** *C* 4383^{1}—BTY brt yrḥy br yrḥy. *C* 4384^{1}—BTY brt yrḥy. Ingh. B p. 135, IV E^{1}—BTY br 'g'.

BTML' (*f*) **2.** *Pal. 63*: 8—BTML' brt mtn'.

BTMLKW (*f*) **1.** *552*, *C* 4175^{2}—ywly' 'wrly' BTMLKW brt zbdbwl br š'dy. **2.** *C* 4176 B^{1}—BTMLKW bt zbdbwl br zbdbwl br ṣ'dy. *C* 4176 C—BTMLKW bt zbdbwl br zbdbwl br ṣ'dy. *C* 4184^{1}—BTMLKW bt zbdbwl br zbdbwl br ṣ'dy. *C* 4413 A^{1}—BTMLKW bt ml'. *Beth She'arim*, i, p. 138 no. 83—BTMLKW. *Beth She'arim*, i, p. 138 no. 86—BTMLKW.

BT'' (*f*) **2.** *C* 4178—BT'' brt ml'. *C* 4179^{1}—B[T]'' brt šm'wn. *C* 4416^{1}—BT'' brt qrd'.

BT'G' (*f*) **2.** *C* 4358 A^{1}—BT'G' brt ḥyr' blšwr. *C* 4621^{1}—BT'G' brt ḥyr' blšwr.

BT'TY (*f*) **2.** *C* 4431^{1}—BT'TY brt yrḥy br ḥyrn.

BTPRMWN (*f*) **2.** Ingh. A p. 88, 2^{4}—ḥdwdn br dkt' br ḥry BTPRMWN.

BTŠMY' (*f*) **2.** Ingh. B Pl. XLVIII^{2}—BTŠMY' brt ns'. Ingh. E (Malê) p. 80 E—BTŠMY' brt 'bsy.

[BT]ŠTG' (*f*) **2.** *C* 4448^{1}—[BT]ŠTG' b[r]t yml'.

G'YS (*m*) **1.** *419*, *Inv. X*, 129^{1}—G'YS ywlys ḥyrn br 'lhbl. **2.** *Inv. X*, 130^{1}—G'YS [lqn]ys plwynws br bwrp'.

GBYNS (*m*) **1.** *527*, *Inv. XI*, 16^{3}—bwn' 'g' GBYNS.

GBL (*f*) **2.** *C* 4593^{1}—GBL brt tybwl.

GBR' (*m*) **2.** *RTP* 507a—'bdy br mk GBR'.

GD' (*m*) **1.** *409*, 'Wadi Hauran' 1^{5}—GD'. *500+?*, *Inv. XI*, 9^{3}—gdy' b[r yr]ḥy [br] GD'. *500*, *C* 3981^{2}—zbdbwl wmqymw bny GD' br mqymw rp'l. *525*, 'Monuments' 1^{1}—GD' br mškw. *525*, 'Monuments' 1^{3}—GD' br mškw. *550*, *C* 4035^{2}—GD' br ḥly'. *550*, *Inv. XI*, 15^{2}—GD' br ḥlp'. **2.** *C* 4107^{2}—GD' br. *Inv. VIII*, 35^{2}—GD' br tymy.

GDY' (*m*) **1.** *367*, *C* 4116^{2}—'t'qb br GDY' br 't'qb. *367*, *C* 4116^{6}—GDY'. *500+?*, *Inv. XI*, 9^{2}—GDY' b[r yr]ḥy [br] gd'. **2.** *C* 4076^{2}—GDY' b[r] ḥ[yrn b]gdn. *C* 4089^{3}—šm'wn br [G]DY'. *C* 4117^{3}—'qyb' br 't'qb GDY'. *C* 4118^{2}—mqymw br GDY' 't'qb [z]bd' [r]b'. *C* 4376^{4}—GDY'. *C* 4529^{1}—GDY' br tybwl nwr'th. *Inv. VIII*, 95^{4}—'t'qb mqymw GDY'. *Inv. XI*, 67^{2}—... w]zbdbwl wnwrbl wGDY' wtybw[l....

GDYBWL (*m*) **2.** *C* 4231 E^{3}—'tm' [bt] mqymw GDYBWL.

GDYLT (*m*) **2.** *C* 4092^{2}—n'm br GDYLT.

GDYMY see GRYMY.

[GDN]BW (*m*) *Journal asiatique*, 12 (1918), 282 no. vi. 2—...']štwr [GDN]BW

GDRṢW (*m*) **1.** *345*, *C* 4114^{3}—ḥyrn br blšwry br GDRṢW dy mtqrh br b''. *394*, *C* 4124^{2}—šby wnbwzbd wt[ymy wnbwl'] bny blšwry br ḥyrn br blšwry br GDRṢW [....b'']. *541*, *C* 4027^{3}—btzbyd' brt GDRṢW. **2.** *C* 4313^{2}—n'm[y] bt GD[R]ṢW. *C* 4316^{1}—GDRṢW br ml' br ḥnyn'. *C* 4317^{3}—mlkw br GDRṢW ḥnyn'. *PS* 174—zbdbl br GDRṢW.

GWB' (*m*) **2.** *PNO* 53—blbw GWB'.

GWR' (*m*) **2.** *C* 3906^{1}—GWR' ydy. *C* 4062^{4}—'bydw 'sty br GWR' br nšm 'msr. *C* 4348^{4}—whblt br ml' br whblt GWR'. *C* 4349^{5}—yrḥbwl' br whblt [GW]R'.

GWRY (*m*) **1.** *445*, *C* 4281^{3}—'tntn GWRY br bwrp' 'tntn 'ḥytwr.

GWRNY (*m*) *[46]8*, *Inv. X*, 77^{2}—[tym' br] tymrṣw lšmš GWRNY. *522*, *Inv. X*, 53^{3}—ymlkw br whblt GWRNY.

GḤYNT (*m*) **2.** *Inv. VIII*, 25^{4}—'brwq br br'th GḤYNT.

GY (*m*) **1.** *539*, *C* 4024^{3}—mqymw br GY.

GYR' (*m*) **1.** *441*, *PS* 3^{1}—bryky br tym' br ml' br GYR'.

GYN' (*m*) **2.** *C* 4587—yrḥy br GYN'.

GYNWS (*m*) **2.** *RTP* 381b—šmšgrm br nwrbl GYNWS.

GYS (*m*) **1.** *448*, *C* 3913 II^{74}—GYS. **2.** *C* 4211^{2}—[GYS yw]ly[s hrmys].

GL' (*m*) **2.** *Inv. XI*, 42^{2}—'bnrgl br ḥry lšmš br ḥyrn GL'.

GL[Y]Ḥ[**2.** *Pal. 62*: 11^{2}—...]brt GL[Y]Ḥ[....

GLNWS (*m*) **1.** *485*, *Inv. X*, 113^{3}—GLNWS.

GML' (*m*) **1.** *425*, *C* 3994 A^{5}—mqy[mw] br yrḥbwl' GML'. *425*, *C* 3994 B^{5}—mq[ymw] br yrḥbwl' GML'. *425*, *C* 3994 C^{5}—mqymw br yrḥbwl' GML'. **2.** *C* 4058^{4}—[mqy]mw br yrḥbwl' br [GML'].

GMLY' (*m*) **1.** *471*, StaA 1^{6}—GMLY'.

GMLT (*f*) **2.** *Inv. XI*, 62^{1}—GMLT brt ngmw.

GMR' (*m*) **2.** *RTP* 673b—zbd' GMR'.

GNB' (*m*) **2.** *RTP* 337a—blḥzy GNB'.

G'L (*m*) **2.** *Inv. VIII*, 99^{3}—wrwd br G'L.

G'LW/Y (*m*) **2.** *Inv. XI*, 55^{5}—ml' br šm'wn br mlkw G'LW/Y.

GPN (*m*) **1.** *552*, Ingh. E (Malkû) p. 100, IX^{4}—ywlys 'wrlys lmlk' br šlmn GPN.

GRB' (*m*) **1.** *504*, *C* 3948^{2}—tymrṣw br tym' br mqymw GRB'. *522*, *C* 3949^{I}—[ydy br tymrṣw br tym' GR]B'. **2.** *C* 4524^{5}—mrthwn brt tymrṣw br ydy GRB'.

GRYMY (*m*) **1.** *269*, StaD p. 514, 2^{3}—GRYMY br nbwzbd. *553*, *C* 4460^{6}—ḥlypt brt 'ttn br GRYMY. **2.** *RTP* 298b—GRYMY. *RTP* 308b—GRYMY nbwl'. CaA 84^{2}—GRYMY pg'.

GRMY (*m*) **2.** *PNO* 52^{2}—GRMY.

GRMN' (*m*) **1.** *552*, CaD 36 C^{4}—ywly' 'wrly' ḥyrn wmlwk' bny GRMN'. *578*, Ingh. E (Malkû) p. 104, XII^{7}—ywly' 'wrly' 'gtwn' br bs' GRMN'.

GRMNQWS (*m*) **1.** *448*, *C* 3913, II^{103}—GRMNQWS.

GRMNQS (*m*) **2.** CaC 18^{3}—GRMNQS.

GTMY (*f*) **2.** *C* 4604 A^{I}—GTMY brt m'n. *C* 4604 B^{3}—m'n br GTMY brt m'n.

DBḤ (*m*) **1.** *505*, Ingh. B p. 95, II^{5}—tymw br DBḤ br ḥmyn.

DDYWN (*m*) **1.** *578*, Ingh. E (Malkû) p. 102, XI^{6}—DDYWN br ḥby br dygns.

DWḤY (*m*) **1.** *540*, Ingh. E ('Atenatan) p. 60, II^{I}—ywlys 'wrlys mqy br zbdbwl mqy DWḤY.

DWMNYN' (*f*) **1.** *532*, *C* 4020 A^{2}—DWMNYN' brt [y]dy'bl br yrḥy. **2.** *C* 4020 B^{3}—DWMNY[N' br]t ydy'bl.

DWR' (*m*) **2.** *C* 4084^{3}—DWR' br zbdbwl mlk' 'tndwr' 'pwqḥ.

[D]WRN 2. *Beth She'arim*, i, p. 141, no. 130—[D]WRN.

DZYṢYḤ (*m*) **2.** *C* 4376^{2}—'n' brt DZYṢYḤ or RZYṢYḤ.

DYGNS (*m*) **1.** *578*, Ingh. E (Malkû) p. 102, XI^{6}—ddywn br ḥby br DYGNS.

DYWDY (*m*) **2.** *Pal. 59*: 15^{I}—zbd' br mqymw br DYWDY.

DYWN (*m*) **1.** *497*, Ingh. E (Malkû) p. 93, III^{I}—b'ly br DYWN mlkw. *499*, Ingh. E (Malkû) p. 95, IV—b'ly br DYWN br mlkw.

DYN' (*m*) **2.** *Inv. XI*, 80^{2}—'lyš' wDYN' [....

DYNY (*m*) **1.** *445*, CaC 13^{2}—ml['] br DYNY. *574*, *C* 4052^{3}—....D]YNY br [.... **2.** *C* 4519^{2}—zbyd' br DYNY br ml'. *C* 4520^{I}—DYNY br brp'. *RTP* 111a—tymrṣw DYNY. 'Tessères' 2b—tymrṣw DYNY.

DYNYS (*m*) **1.** *458*, 'IP' p. 147, 1^{I}—šlmlt br mlkw br DYNYS. *458*, 'IP' p. 147, I^{3}—zbd'th br ḥnbl br DYNYS. **2.** *C* 4287^{6}—'qm' brt DYNYS ṣ'dy. *C* 4518 A^{2}—'qm' brt mlkw br DYNYS. *RTP* 250b—DYNYS ydy'bl šlm'. 'IP' p. 150, 2^{2}—šlml[t br mlkw] br DY[NYS]. 'IP' p. 152, 4^{2}—mlkw br DYNYS ḥnbl. 'IP' p. 152, 5^{2}—šlmlt br mlkw DYNYS. 'IP' p. 153, 8^{3}—[zb]d'[t]h [b]r ḥnbl DYNYS. 'IP' p. 155, 11^{I}—DYNYS br zbd'th ḥnbl. 'IP' p. 155, 12^{3}—zbd'th br DYNYS zbd'th. 'IP' p. 156, 13^{4}—mrty brt tymrṣw DYNYS. 'IP' p. 162, 23 D—[DY]NYS. *Inv. IX*, 4 B—'lhš' br DYNYS.

[DY]NS (*m*) **2.** 'IP' p. 153, 7^{2}—ml[kw DY]NS.

DK' (*m*) **1.** *494* or *493*, *Inv. X*, 4^{2}—yrḥy br mq[y]mw br zbd'th DK'. *543*, *C* 4030^{5}—ḥggw br yhyb' br yrḥy DK'. *572*, *C* 4050^{4}—[ḥ]ggw br yhyb' yrḥy DK'.

DKRY (*m*) **2.** *PNO* 77 A^{I}—DKRY 'byn br hrmy.

DKT' see BR DKT'.

DMY see RMY.

DMS (*m*) **1.** *529*, StaB p. 149, A 1172^{3}—mlk wDMS.

DN[2. CaA 81^{5}—syg' brt mlkw DN[....

DNY (*m*) **2.** *C* 4002$^{3, 4}$—...] DNY w[']lyw 'štw[rg]' / br DNY[.... *RTP* 329b—DNY 'bd'.

D'' see R''.

D'T' see R'T'.

DRM (*f*) **2.** *PS* 493—DRM brt zbd'.

HGY (*f*) **1.** *523*, *C* 4469^{I}—HGY brt tymw. **2.** *C* 4470 A^{I}—HGY brt ḥdwdn. *Inv. VIII*, 156 A—HGY brt yrḥbwl'.

HGR (*f*) **2.** *C* 4438^{I}—HGR brt bwrp' br 'tyk'. *C* 4443^{I}—HGR bt ml'. *C* 4444^{I}—HGR bt zbyd' br 'tyk'. 'Büste' p. 313^{I}—HGR brt zbyd' br ml'. Ingh. A p. 96, 5 B^{I}—HGR brt mqy 'mby.

HD' (*f*) **1.** *437*, *C* 4247^{I}—HD' brt bwlḥ' br zbdl'. **2.** *C* 4190^{I}—[H]D' brt mqymw br ṣ'dy.

HDYR' (*f*) **2.** *C* 4080^{3}—...] HDYR' brt [.... *C* 4501^{3}—HDYR'. *C* 4502^{2}—HDYR'.

HDYRT (*f*) **1.** *480*, *C* 4255^{1}—HDYRT 'ḥ' brt bwlḥ' br br''. **2.** *C* 4147^{1}—HDYRT brt m'ny br whblt. *C* 4154^{1}—HDYRT brt 'lhbl br whblt br m'ny.

HD/RMW (*m*) **1.** *420+?*, *Pal. 63*: 5^{2}—...] br HD/RMW [...

HDRYN[WS] (*m*) **1.** [*4*]*42*, *C* 3959^{3}—HDRYN[WS].

HLDRS (*m*) **2.** *RTP* 251b—HLDRS.

HLYDWRS (*m*) **1.** *525*, 'Malkû' p. 106^{6}—ywlys 'wrlys 'grp' br 'gtpws br ḥry HLYDWRS yrḥbwl'.

HLYDYRS (*m*) **1.** *525*, Ingh. E (Malkû) p. 99, VIII^{2}—HLYDYRS yrḥbwl' br ḥyrn bwn'.

HLYDRWS (*m*) **1.** *504*, CaB 13 B^{1}—ydy'bl br HLYDRWS [lš]mš br ydy'bl.

HN'Y (*m*) **2.** *C* 4515^{5}—'lqm' br šm'wn br HN'Y.

HRMZ (*m*) **2.** *C* 4074^{2}—[r]mlh' wHRMZ.

HRMZD (*m*) **2.** CaA 18 B—....] HRMZD [....

HRMY (*m*) **2.** *PNO* 77 A^{3}—dkry 'byn br HRMY.

[HRMYS] **2.** *C* 4211^{3}—[gys yw]ly[s HRMYS].

HRMS (*m*) **1.** *472*, *C* 4001^{9}—H[R]MS. *516*, *C* 4013^{3}—HRMS bsm [b]r ḥry mlkw br whb'. *543*, CaA 40^{5}—ywlys 'wrlys HRMS br ḥry 'wrl[ys]. *545*, Ingh. E (Malê) p. 82, V^{2}—ywlys 'wrlys šyby br HRMS mrq'. *560*, Ingh. E (Malkû) p. 101, X^{2}—mlkw br HRMS 'byhn. **2.** *C* 4081^{2}—HRMS w'mtbl. *PNO* 48^{1}—HRMS. *PNO* 59—HRMS. *PNO* 72^{2}—HRMS br ydy.

HRMSYN' (*m*) **1.** *524*, *C* 4016^{3}—rdwn br HRMSYN'.

HRQL' (*m*) **2.** *Inv. XI*, 44^{2}—HRQL' b[r....

HRQLYD' (*m*) **2.** *C* 4514^{1}—HRQLYD' br sbyn'.

WHB' (*m*) **1.** *466*, Ingh. D Pl. X^{2}—whb' 'bd'' bwly. *502*, *C* 4008^{1}—WH[B'] br mlkw ml'. *516*, *C* 4013^{4}—hrms bsm [b]r ḥry mlkw br WHB'. **2.** *C* 4327^{2}—zbd'th br WHB' br zbd'th. *C* 4327^{4}—WHB'. *C* 4328^{6}—WHB'. *C* 4329 A^{8}—WHB'. *C* 4329 B^{5}—WHB'. *C* 4330^{4}—[']g' [br] zbd'th WHB'. *C* 4343^{3}—[']lyy brt WHB' 'štwr. *Inv. XI*, 36^{4}—...] WHB'.

WHBY (*m*) **1.** *345*, *C* 3980^{3}—[WH]BY br 'tnwry 'wdw. *415*, *Inv. VIII*, 59^{3}—bwlḥ' wmqymy wḥyrn wlšmš wb'l[y] bny WHBY br bwlḥzy. *497*, Ingh. E (Malkû) p. 91, II^{2}—ḥnt' WHBY ḥlpt'. *507*, *C* 4354^{10}—...] br 'gy[lw] WHBY. **2.** *RTP* 370b—WHBY wmqymw wlšmš. CaD 24^{1}—WHBY br nwrbl br 'qmt. 'IP' p. 160, 20^{3}—m'n br WHBY. *Inv. VIII*, 26^{3}—blḥzy br tymn' WHBY 'dy[nt]. *Inv. VIII*, 50 A^{1}—WHBY '[...]t'bny. *Inv. VIII*, 138^{7}—WHBY br rmy. *Inv. VIII*, 180^{1}—šky br WHBY br ml'. *Inv. XI*, 77^{4}—ḥggw rb'n qymy wWHBY wzbdbwl.

WHBLT (*m*) **1.** (*399*), CaB 6 B^{4}—WHBLT br blnwry bwš'. *400+?*, *C* 3988^{2}—'y[t' brt m]lkw br whblt br 'rgn. *412*, CaB 13 A^{1,2}—ydy'bl br WHBLT / wWHBLT br 'wydlt bny ydy'bl br 'mrš'. *414*, *C* 4134^{2}—'lhbl wm'ny wškyy wmlkw bny WHBLT br m'ny 'lhbl. [*4*]*32*, *C* 3921^{1}—mlkw br WHBLT br m'ny. *433*, *C* 4158^{1}—m'ny br WHBLT m'ny. [*4*]*34*, *Pal. 63*: 14^{5}—...ṣl]mlt br WHBLT [br.... [*4*]*90*, *C* 3954^{1}—mrty brt yd[' br WHBLT] br šm'wn. *522*, *Inv. X*, 53^{3}—ymlkw br WHBLT gwrny. *522*, *Inv. X*, 53^{4}—WHBLT. *537*, StaB p. 153, A 1205^{1}—zbyd' br WHBLT byd' ''py. [*5*]*40*, *C* 4026^{3}—t[ymrṣw b]r WHBLT br tymrṣ[w]. *542*, *C* 4028^{4}—WHBLT br srykw. *547*, *Pal. 61*: 11^{3} WHBLT br tymrṣw br mlkw. *575*, *C* 4048^{4}—šbty brt WHBLT. **2.** *C* 3971^{2}—spṭymyws WHBLT 'tndr[ws] br spṭ[ymy]ws ['dynt]. *C* 3991^{1}—WHBLT br 'bmrt. *C* 4063^{4}—mktš br WHBLT br [.... *C* 4135^{2}—'tpny br [m]'ny br WHBLT. *C* 4136^{1,2}—WHBLT br / škyy br WHBLT. *C* 4137^{2}—'lhbl br škyy br WHBLT. *C* 4138^{2}—m'ny br 'lhbl br WHBLT. *C* 4139^{2}—m'ny ṭly' br WHBLT br [m'n]y. *C* 4141^{1,2}—WHBLT br / 'lhbl br WHBLT. *C* 4142^{1,2}—WHBLT br / mlkw br WHBLT. *C* 4143^{2}—bl'qb br 'lhbl br WHBLT. *C* 4144^{1,2}—WHBLT br / m'ny br WHBLT. *C* 4145^{2}—'mt' brt 'lhbl br WHBLT. *C* 4145^{4}—škyy br WHBLT. *C* 4146^{3}—mlkw br WHBLT. *C* 4147^{2}—hdyrt brt m'ny br WHBLT. *C* 4148^{2}—šgl brt šky[y br] WHBLT. *C* 4148^{3}—bl['qb] br 'lhbl WHBLT. *C* 4149^{2}—WHBLT br m'ny. *C* 4150—...]mt brt WHBLT br m'ny. *C* 4151^{2}—'lhbl br WHBLT. *C* 4152^{2}—m'ny br WHBLT. *C* 4153^{3}—'mt' brt škyy br WHBLT. *C* 4153^{5}—WHBLT br m'ny. *C* 4154^{3}—hdyrt brt 'lhbl br WHBLT br m'ny. *C* 4155^{3}—šgl brt 'lhbl br WHBLT. *C* 4155^{4,6}—WHBLT / br mlkw / br WHBLT. *C* 4156^{2}—šgl brt mlkw br WHBLT br m'ny. *C* 4157^{2}—bl'qb br 'lhbl br WHBLT br m'ny. *C* 4202—'dynt br ḥyrn WHBLT nṣwr. *C* 4232 A^{2}—mlkw br ḥg[g]w WHBLT. *C* 4232 B^{3}—pṣy'l br ḥggw br ml' WHBLT. *C* 4240^{1}—WHBLT br bryky br zbdbwl. *C* 4282^{1}—WHBLT br bwlḥ' br bwrp' 'ḥytwr. *C* 4348^{1,3}—WHBLT / br ml' / br WHBLT / gwr'. *C* 4349^{4}—yrḥbwl' br WHBLT [gw]r'. *C* 4369 A^{2}—tymḥ' br WHBLT br tym'. *C* 4474^{3}—'bb' brt WHBLT. *C* 4523^{3}—'mt' brt WHBLT. *C* 4577^{2}—WHBLT br bwrp'. *C* 4591

A—mlkw wyrḥy bny ymlkw br WHBLT. *C* 4591 B—mlkw wyrḥy bny ymlkw br WHBLT. *C* 4600^{2}—WHBLT br rmy br rp’l. *RTP* 84b—‘bdy WHBLT. *RTP* 118b—mlkw WHBLT. *RTP* 120b—WHBLT. *RTP* 341b—‘wyd’ wWHBLT. *RTP* 376b—škyy br W[HB]LT. *RTP* 696b—WHBLT šm‘[wn]. *RTP* 724a—WHBLT br šm‘wn. *RTP* 736b—WHBLT ’dynt. *RTP* 746a—bly WHBLT. *RTP* 765a—WHBLT mlkw. *RTP* 765b—WHBLT br mlkw rpnw. *RTP* 787a—WHBLT ḥyrn. *RTP* 787b—WHBLT ḥyrn. *RTP* 825a—škyy br WHBLT. *PS* 148—WHBLT br ymlkw br WHBLT. Ingh. ‘Quatre’ p. 242, Pl. XL^{1}—šgl brt WHBLT ’‘ylmy blḥzy. Ingh. ‘Quatre’ p. 242, Pl. XL^{2}—WHBLT br blnwry dy mtqrh bwly br bwš’. Ingh. ‘Quatre’ p. 243, Pl. XLI^{1}—WHBLT br WHBLT. *PNO* 70—[W]HBLT br rb’l. *Pal. 60*: 12^{3}—[W]HBLT. CaA 33^{2}—’lhbl wWHBLT br m‘ny br ’lhbl. CaC 17^{1}—’dynt br ḥyrn WHBLT [. . . . *Inv. VIII*, 39^{1}—WHBLT br ‘t‘qb br ḥšy. *Inv. VIII*, 66^{1}—. . .]br mqymw br WHBL[T] br [. . . . *Inv. VIII*, 165^{1}—WHBLT br ‘gylw br yrḥbwl’. *Inv. X*, 3—WHBLT. *Inv. XI*, 65^{1}—WHBLT br bl‘qb br [n]š’. ‘Hypogée’ p. 221, Pl. I^{1}—nbwl’ b[r] WHBLT b[r] ṭ‘y.

WLY (*m*) **2.** *Inv. VIII*, 168^{3}—zbd’ br ml’ br WLY.

WSḤW (*m*) **2.** *Inv. X*, 115^{1}—ywlys ’wrlys mlkw br WSḤW br mlkw br WSḤW nbwl’.

W‘D (*m*) **2.** *RTP* 148a—W‘D or W‘R.

W‘R (*m*) **2.** *RTP* 148a—W‘R or W‘D.

WRDN (*m*) **1.** *497*, Ingh. B p. 106, I^{2}—WRDN br ḥry ’nṭyks rpbwl br ’nṭyks ‘t‘qb br rpbwl. *539*, Ingh. B p. 110, III^{2}—’wrlys WRDN br ḥry ’nṭykys rpbwl br ‘t‘qb. **2.** *PNO* 55 A—WRDN / brwq’ / mhrdt / ’mbkr’. *PNO* 55 C—WRDN wbrwq’ w‘mbkr’.

WRWD (*m*) **1.** [*449*], *Inv. X*, 114^{8}—WRWD. *570*, *C* 3937^{1}—’wrlys [W]RWD. *573*, *C* 3938^{2}—sptmyws WRWD. *574*, *C* 3939^{1}—sptmys WRWD. *575*, *C* 3940^{1}—sptmyws WRWD. [*576*,] *C* 3941^{1}—spt[myws WRW]D. *578*, *C* 3943^{1}—sptmyws WRWD. *583*, CaA 31^{8}—‘gylw br WRWD. **2.** *C* 4105 *ter*—. . .] WRWD. ‘La Susiane’ p. 278^{3}—WRWD. Ingh. A p. 94, 4—WRWD. CaD 36 F^{1}—WRWD. *Inv. VIII*, 99^{1}—WRWD br g‘l.

WRTN (*m*) **2.** *PNO* 35 A^{2}—šm‘wn br m‘n br WRTN. *PNO* 35 B^{2}—šm‘wn br m‘n br WRTN.

ZB 2. *RTP* 734a—ZB ty. *RTP* 734b—ZB ml.

ZB’ (*m*) **2.** *C* 4552—mlkw b[r] ZB’ br[‘th]. *Inv. VIII*, 23^{2}—rmy br tymn’ br ZB’. *Inv. VIII*, 116^{2}—šlmt brt ZB’.

ZBD (*m*) **2.** *C* 4670^{3}—zby br zbd’ ZBD. *C* 4225^{2}—rpbwl br ‘t‘qb br ZBD zbd‘th ’r’š. *C* 4476 B—. . .br] ZBD [. . . . ‘Note’ p. 90^{2}—tym’ br ZBD [. . . .

ZBD’ (*m*) **1.** *425*, *C* 4159^{4}—mqymw br ZBD’ br mqymw br ‘t‘qb br mqymw br mlkw dy mtqr’ ’r’š. *450*, *Inv. XI*, 4^{3}—ZBD[’]. *452*, *Inv. VIII*, 2^{5}—ZBD’ br tym’ br ḥlpt’. *459*, ‘Sculptures’ p. 19, Pl. I^{2}—mqymw br nwrbl br ZBD’. *459*, ‘Sculptures’ p. 19, Pl. I^{2}—mqymw br nwrbl br ZBD’. *462*, *C* 4268^{2}—n‘my brt ZBD’ br tym’ br ḥlpt’. *500+?*, *Inv. XI*, 8^{4}—. . .] br ZB[D]’. *501*, *C* 4007^{3}—ydy‘bl br ZB[D]’ lšmš myšn. *503*, *C* 4009^{4}—[ḥl]pwn’ br ZBD’. *517*, StaB p. 148, A 1179^{4}—tymrṣw [b]r ḥyrn ZBD’. *546*, Ingh. E (Malê) p. 84, VI^{2}—ywlys ’wrlys ḥlpt’ br mqymw ZBD’. *548*, Ingh. E (Malê) p. 86, VIII^{15}—ḥlpt’ br mqymw ZBD’. *579*, *C* 4053^{1}—ZB[D’] br ḥl’. *582*, *C* 3946^{3}—sptmy’ ZBD’. *582*, *C* 3947^{2}—sptmyw’ ZBD’. **2.** *C* 4070^{3}—zby br ZBD’ zbd. *C* 4118^{4}—mqymw br gdy’ ‘t‘qb [Z]BD’ [r]b’. *C* 4259 A^{4}—zbdbwl br mqymw br nwrbl br ZBD’ [b]r ‘bdy [zbd]bwl. *C* 4351^{2}—šlmlt br ZBD’. *C* 4564^{2}—. . .]br [Z/‘]BD’ br yrḥy. *C* 4595$^{1, 2}$—pzl br ZBD’ / br ZBD’ pzl. *RTP* 227b—yrḥy b[r] ZBD’. *RTP* 468b—ZBD’ br mqym[w]. *RTP* 669b—br‘th ZBD[’]. *RTP* 673b—ZBD’ gmr’. *RTP* 715b—ZBD’ ydy‘bl. *RTP* 775a—ZB[D]’ ’lhš’ ṣ‘dy. *RTP* 778b—nšwm br [ZB]D’ br mlkw nšwm. *RTP* 837b—nšwm br ZBD’ br mlkw nšwm. *RTP* 1056a—ZBD’. *PS* 493—drm brt ZBD’. Ingh. B p. 137, line 10—ZBD’ rp[. .] mqymw. Ingh. B p. 137, line 13—ZB[D’]. Ingh. B p. 137, line 16—ZBD’. ‘IP’ p. 158, 17 A$^{4, 6}$—ZBD’ / br ‘zyzw br / br ZBD’. *Pal. 59*: 15^{1}—ZBD’ br mqymw br dywdy. *Pal. 59*: 17^{1}—ZBD’ br ‘g’. *Pal. 61*: 6^{1}—ZBD’ br nš’. CaA 85 B^{3}—mqymw br ‘gylw br ZBD’. *Inv. VI*, 4^{4}—ZBD’ [. . . . *Inv. VIII*, 51^{4}—’ytybl br ZBD’. *Inv. VIII*, 138^{4}—ḥg’ brt ZBD’ br m‘ny. *Inv. VIII*, 168^{2}—ZBD’ br ml’ br wly. *Inv. IX*, 5 A—ZBD’ [br] ‘dl b(r) ZBD[’]. *Inv. XI*, 27^{3}—ZBD’ br ḥyrn. *Inv. XI*, 61—ZBD’ [br ḥ]yrn mlk’l. *Inv. XI*, 79^{2}—ymlkw br ZB[D’].

ZBDBW (*m*) **1.** *390*, *Inv. XI*, 81^{5}—. . .]rb’ br ZBDBW ‘rym’.

ZBDBWL (*m*) **1.** [*3*]*08*, C 4112^{3}—ZBDBWL br[. . . .]br ‘tršwry. *340*, *C* 3922^{2}—‘gylw br tymy b[r] ZBDBWL. *345*, *C* 3980^{6}—ZBDBWL br ydy‘bl ’lhw. *345*, *C* 3980^{7}—‘gylw br nwry ZBDB(W)L. *362* or *382*, CaA 34$^{2, 3}$—ZBDBWL br ’byhn / br ZBDBWL br lšmš br mkn’ rb’. *3*[*92*], CaA 7^{1}—ZBDBWL [br] ‘g[ylw] br [’mt] br[. . . . *399*, CaB 6 A^{1}—blḥzy br nwry br ZBDBWL ’‘ylmy. *400*, ‘Fouilles’ p. 170^{1}—mqymw br mqymw br ZBDBWL ‘rym’. *400*, ‘Fouilles’ p. 172^{2}—[m]q[ymw br mqymw br ZBDBWL] ‘rym[’]. *439*, CaC 9^{2}—ḥb’ br bgšw br ZBDBWL. *444*, *C* 3998 A^{2}—[ZBDBWL] br yrḥbwl’ br lšmšy [ḥyrn]. *445*, Ingh. B p. 94, I³—ZBDBWL br mqymw. *457*, *C* 3911⁴,⁷—ZBDBWL / w'tnwr wmlkw w'mrw / wydy'bl bny bršmš / br ZBDBWL. *472*, *C* 4171¹—ḥdwdn br šlmn br ZBDBWL. *47[5]*, CaB 3¹—'lhbl br mlkw br ZBDBWL brt'. *480*, CaC 8¹—tm' brt nbwzbd br ZBDBWL šm'wn. *484*, *C* 4261²—š'd'l br ZBDBWL br mqymw. *484*, *C* 4261 *bis*³—š'd'l br ZBDBWL br mqymw. *486*, *C* 3914²—yrḥbwl' [br] 'g' w'wyd' br ḥdwdn bny yrḥbwl' br ḥdwdn br ZBDBWL br ḥdw[dn] prmwn. *500*, *C* 3981¹—ZBDBWL wmqymw bny gd' br mqymw rp'l. *502*, *C* 4173¹—ZBDBWL br kptwt br br'. *502*, *C* 4173³—ZBDBWL. *504*, *C* 3948⁵—ydy [wZ]BDBWL. [5]*24*, *PNO* 13¹—ZBDBWL br 'šr'. *525*, Ingh. E (Malkû) p. 98, VII²—ZBDBWL br mlkw 'swyt. *525*, 'Malkû' p. 106⁴—ywlys br 'wrlys 'gylw br 'prhṭ br ḥry ZBDBWL. *525*, *Inv. XI*, 12³—['g]ylw br ZBDBWL br [. . . . *533*, *C* 4021²—mrywn br ZBDBWL br mlkw. *540*, Ingh. E ('Atenatan) p. 60, II¹—ywlys 'wrlys mqy br ZBDBWL mqy dwḥy. *545*, *C* 4206¹—[ywl]ys 'wrlys bwlm' br ZBDBWL br bwlm' nyny'. *545*, *C* 4206³—ywlys 'wrlys bwlm' br ZBDBWL b[r bwlm' nyny' . . . . . b]rt [n]b[w]d' br tym' br nbwmw'. *546*, Ingh. E (Malê) p. 84, VII⁵,⁶—ywlys 'wrlys ZBDBWL br / ZBDBWL khylw. *551*, *C* 4036 A²,³—ZBDBWL br mlkw / ZBDBWL. *552*, *C* 4175³—ywly' 'wrly' btmlkw brt ZBDBWL br š'dy. **2.** *C* 3961²—[ZB]DBWL. *C* 3979—. . . br Z]BDBWL. *C* 3998 B²,³—ZBDBWL br / [ZBDBWL]. *C* 3998 B⁵—ZBDBWL br ZBDBWL. *C* 4036 B¹—mlkw br ZBDBWL br mlkw. *C* 4078³—mqymw br ZBD[B]WL b[r] ḥbry. *C* 4079³—[']g' br ZBDBWL br [. . . . *C* 4084⁴—dwr' br ZBDBWL mlk' 'tndwr' 'pwqḥ. *C* 4090¹—ZBD[BW]L [br b]r'th [. . . . *C* 4176 B¹,²—btmlkw bt ZBDBWL / br ZBDBWL br ṣ'dy. *C* 4176 C¹,²—btmlkw bt ZBDBWL / br ZBDBWL br ṣ'dy. *C* 4184¹,²—btmlkw bt ZBDBWL / br ZBDBWL br ṣ'dy. *C* 4240³—whblt br bryky br ZBDBWL. *C* 4259 A¹,⁶—ZBDBWL / br mqymw / br nwrbl / br zbd' / [b]r 'bdy / [ZBD]BWL. *C* 4260³—'lyt brt ZBDBWL. *C* 4262⁶—ZBDB[WL]. *C* 4318³—mlkw br ZBDBWL br mlkw ''wyd. *C* 4336²—'qm' brt ZBDBWL br 'g'. *C* 4341³—'tš' brt ZBDB(W)L. *C* 4366—'ḥ' [b]rt ZBDB[WL]. *C* 4372 A²—tymrṣ[w] br ZBDBWL. *C* 4372 B¹—ZBDBWL br mlk'l rmy. *C* 4372 C²—mlk'l br ZBDBWL. *C* 4396¹—ZBDBWL br šm'wn. *C* 4412³—'lyt brt ZBDBW[L]. *C* 4465²—ZBDBWL br ḥyrn nwry. *C* 4470 B¹—ZBDBWL br šlmn. *C* 4525—ḥyr' br ZBDBWL ḥyr'. *C* 4575¹—ZBDBWL br zbdlh br bwrp' br zbdlh. *C* 4605⁵—ZBDBWL. *RTP* 137b—ZBDBWL. *RTP* 186b—ZBDBWL. *RTP* 295b—ZBDBWL nbwzbd. *RTP* 299b—ZBDBWL ['gy]lw. *RTP* 311a—ZBDBWL. *RTP* 407b—sṭm br ZBDBWL zbd'th. *RTP* 419b—ZBDB[WL] or zbdl[h] bwr[p']. *RTP* 802b—ZBDBWL. *RTP* 995a—mlkw ZBDBWL. *RTP* 1045a—ZBDBWL. 'Tessères' 25b—ZBDBWL zbyd'. 'Euphrate' p. 47²—'bgr br šlmn br ZBDBWL. 'Monuments' 2—[ZB]DBWL. Ingh. E ('Atenatan) p. 64, III¹—mqy br ZBDBWL. StaC 4, p. 34—ZBDBWL br bwrp'. StaD p. 516, 3²—mqym br ZBDBWL 'š'd. *PS* 205—ZBDBWL br yrḥy. CaD 12 B³—mqym[w] br ZBDB[WL] br 'rym[']. CaD 12 B⁶—ZBDBWL. *Journal asiatique*, 12 (1918), 294 no. xvii—'lyt brt ZBDBWL. *Inv. VIII*, 9¹—ZBDB(W)L br mtn' br zbdlh br bl'qb dy mtqrh 'ṣr'. *Inv. VIII*, 22¹—ZBDBWL br brwq' br 'knt. *Inv. VIII*, 58¹—ywly' 'wrly' nwry wZBDBWL w['gylw] bny mq[y. . . .] ḥbzy. *Inv. VIII*, 77¹—. . .]' br ZBDB[WL]. *Inv. VIII*, 121³—tymrṣw br ZBDBWL. *Inv. X*, 63²—'lhbl br 'lhbl br ZBDBWL 'hwd. *Inv. XI*, 36³—ZBDBWL br [. . . . *Inv. XI*, 67²—. . . w]ZBDBWL wnwrbl wgdy' wtybw[l. . . . *Inv. XI*, 77⁵—ḥggw rb'n qymy wwhby wZBDBWL. *Inv. XI*, 78²—[Z]BDBWL br'. *Inv. XI*, 82²—. . .] br ZBDBWL [. . . . *Inv. XI*, 82⁴—nš' br ZBDBWL [. . . . Ben-Hayyim p. 143—ZBDBWL br mlk'l rmy. Ben-Hayyim p. 144—tymrṣw br ZBDBWL.

ZBDBWL' (*m*) **1.** *409*, 'Wadi Hauran' 5⁵—'bdy br ZBDBWL' šm['wn].

ZBDBL (*m*) **1.** *350*, CaD 31²—mqymw br khylw br ZBDBL [dy] mtqrh br zbydy. *440*, *C* 3997²—zbyd['] br ZBDBL ydy'bl. **2.** *C* 4392²—ZBDBL b[r] mqymw ḥb'. *C* 4499—. . .]t [br ZB]DBL or [br NW]RBL. *RTP* 110b—'tnwry ZB[DB]L. *RTP* 223b—tym'md ZBDBL. *RTP* 995b—'tnwry ZBDBL. StaF 2, p. 36—rp'l br twp' ZBDBL. *PS* 174—ZBDBL br gdrṣw. *Inv. VIII*, 12¹—'byšy brt ZBDBL br mlkw. *Inv. VIII*, 73²—. . .] br ZBDBL [. . . .

ZBDH (*m*) **1.** *468*, StaE p. 373—ZBDH.

ZBDY (*m*) **1.** *378*, *C* 3983¹—ZBDY br zbdnbw qḥzn.

ZBDL' (*m*) **1.** *397*, *Inv. X*, 127¹—yrḥy br ZBDL' qr[. . . . *425*, *C* 3986³—nbwzbd wyrḥbwl' bny brnbw br nbwzbd br ZBDL' 'knby. *437*, *C* 4247³—hd' brt bwlḥ' br ZBDL'. *466*, *C* 3928⁵—[zbd']t' br ZBDL' ydy. *493*, *C* 4192—zbd'th br ZBDL' br ydy. *554*, *C* 3932¹—ywlys 'wrlys ZBDL' br mlkw br mlkw nšwm. **2.** *RTP* 473b—ḥggw [Z]BDL'. 'Hypogée' p. 245, Pl. XII¹—ZBDL' br zbyd' ZBDL' ṭ'y.

ZBDLH (*m*) **1.** *314*, *C* 3992²—ZBDLH br mqym[w] ṭm[ys]. *345*, *C* 3980³—ḥggw br ZBDLH kmr'. *373*, *Pal. 63*: 3¹—ZBDLH dy mtqr' sḥlph br šm'wn br 'yš'. *387*, CaA 6¹—ZB[D]LH br šmšgrm 'yš'. [4]*50*, *C* 4257²—rm' br ZBDLH br bwlḥ'. *460*, *PS* 39²—'ḥ' brt ZBDLH br''. [*468*], *Inv. X*, 90³—ydy br ZBDL[H] ydy. *487*, *C* 4250²—ZBDLH br br'' br zbd'th.

2. *C* 4480^{3}—ḥgt brt yrḥy br ZBDLH krḥ. *C* $4575^{2,4}$—zbdbwl br / ZBDLH br / bwrp' br / ZBDLH. *C* 4576^{2}—ZBDLH br bwrp'. *RTP* 395b—mqymw 'lg' ZBDLH mšy. *RTP* 419b—ZBDL[H] or zbdb[wl] bwr[p']. *RTP* 830a—ZBDLH br zbd'th myk'. *RTP* 830b—ZBDLH zbd'th myk'. *PS* 141—ZBDLH br bgdn. StaD p. 516, 3^{1}—tbr' br ZBDLH. CaA 77^{3}—. . . br l]wy br ZBDL[H]. *Inv. VIII*, 9^{3}—zbdb(w)l br mtn' br ZBDLH br bl'qb dy mtqrh 'ṣr'. *Inv. VIII*, 125^{1}—[Z]BDLH. *Inv. XI*, 97^{5}—ZBDLH br [. . . .

ZBDNBW (*m*) **1.** *378*, *C* 3983^{1}—zbdy br ZBDNBW qḥzn.

ZBD'Y (*m*) **2.** *PNO* 47 A^{2}—'wyd' br ZBD'Y. *Inv. VIII*, 7^{2}—mlkw br ZBD'Y.

ZBD'T' (*m*) **1.** *437*, *C* 4247^{5}—br'' br ZBD'T'. *466*, *C* 3928^{5}—[ZBD']T' br zbdl' ydy. *504*, CaB 13 B^{3}—[m]zbn' wyrḥy wZBD'T' bny 'wydlt. **2.** *C* 4329 A^{5}—yrḥbwl' br ZBD'T'. *C* 4329 B^{3}—mqy[mw] br ZBD'T[']. *C* 4531^{2}—yrḥy br ZBD'T' pzg'. *C* 4617^{1}—ZBD'T' br ymlkw nš'. StaC 5, p. 35—'myt brt ZBD'T'.

ZBD'TH (*m*) **1.** *348*, CaD 33^{2}—mlkw [wZ]BD'[TH. . . .]bny tym'md b[r] bwrp' zg[wg]. *366*, *C* 3972^{2}—'tntn br ZBD'TH tšbb. *410*, Ingh. E ('Atenatan) p. 59, I^{1}—'tntn br ZBD'TH br ydy br tymy. *423*, *C* 3993^{3}—[ḥl]d' br ZBD'TH br ḥld'. *425*, *C* $4159^{2,3}$—ZBD'TH br 't'qb br ZBD'TH br sry br / ZBD'TH br mlkw dy mtqr' 'r'š. *42[9]*, *Inv. VIII*, 78—. . . bgr]n br ZBD'TH [. . . . [*4*]*45*, *C* $4246^{2,3}$—br'' br / ZBD'TH / br ZBD'TH br''. *446*, *C* 4248^{3}—'mby brt br'' ZBD'TH. *457*, *C* 4249^{3}—šlm[t] brt br'' ZBD'TH. *458*, 'IP' p. 146, 1^{3}—ZBD'TH br ḥnbl br dynys. *461*, *C* 4254^{5}—'ḥ' brt ḥlpt' br br'' ZBD'TH. *466*, *C* 4251^{3}—bnwr br br'' ZBD'TH. *480*, *C* 4255^{5}—hdyrt 'ḥ' brt bwlḥ' br br'' br ZBD'TH. *487*, *C* 4250^{4}—zbdlh br br'' br ZBD'TH. *492*, *C* 4194^{4}—sry br ZBD'TH br 't'qb. *493*, *C* 4192—ZBD'TH br zbdl' br ydy. *493*, *Inv. XI*, 6^{3}—ZBD'TH br [. . . . *494* or *493*, *Inv. X*, 4^{2}—yrḥy br mq[y]mw br ZBD'TH dk'. *497*, Ingh. E (Bar'â) p. 115^{2}—br'' br bnwr br br'' ZBD'TH tšbb. [*563*], *C* 4212^{2}—. . .] mqymw brt ZBD'TH **2.** *C* 4224^{3}—[t]m' brt 't'qb [ZBD]'TH ['t]'qb. *C* 4225^{2}—rpbwl br 't'qb br zbd ZBD'TH 'r'š. *C* 4253^{1}—ZBD'TH br bnwr br''. *C* $4327^{1,3}$—ZBD'TH / br whb' / br ZBD'TH. *C* $4328^{3,4}$—ZBD'TH / br ZBD'TH. *C* 4330^{3}—[']g' [br] ZBD'TH whb'. *C* 4418^{3}—'bd'stwr br ZBD'TH. *C* 4516 A^{2}—'tntn br ZBD'TH. *C* 4563^{1}—[Z]BD'TH br m'ny. *C* $4603^{3,4}$—ydy'bl br ZBD'TH / ZBD'TH br ydy'bl. *C* 4605^{3}—'qmt brt ZBD'TH. *RTP* 78b—ZBD'TH mtn'. *RTP* 287b—ZBD'TH mtn'. *RTP* 305b—mtn' ZBD'TH. *RTP* 407b—sṭm br zbdbwl ZBD'TH. *RTP* 451b—tymy br ZBD'TH. *RTP* 640b—yrḥy ZBD'TH [b]wrp'. *RTP* 819b—ZBD'TH mtn' 'nqy. *RTP* 830a—zbdlh br ZBD'TH myk'. *RTP* 830b—zbdlh ZBD'TH myk'. *RTP* 836b—ZBD'TH mtn'. 'IP' p. 151, 3^{2}—ZBD'TH. 'IP' p. 153, 8^{1}—[ZB]D'[T]H [b]r ḥnbl dynys. 'IP' p. 154, 9^{2}—ḥnbl br ZBD'TH br ḥnbl. 'IP' p. 154, 10^{2}—yrḥy br ZBD'TH ḥnbl. 'IP' p. 155, 11^{2}—dynys br ZBD'TH ḥnbl. 'IP' p. 155, $12^{2,4}$—ZBD'TH / br dynys / ZBD'TH. 'Iraq' p. 63^{9}, Pl. 8—'bgr br ml' br ZBD'TH. 'Monuments' 5—ZBD'TH br zbyd' byd'. *PS* 192—yrḥy br ZBD'TH pg'. *PS* 209—m'n br br'' br ZBD'TH. Ingh. A, p. 97, 6—. . .] wkhylw wZBD'TH bny mlkw br ḥyrn. Ingh. B p. 137, line 29—ZBD'TH. CaA 35^{3}—'t'qb wrpbwl wšdy bny br'th br 't'qb br ZBD'TH 'r'š. CaB 11^{2}—tyms' br ZBD'TH qys'. CaB 11^{3}—ZBD'TH. CaD 9^{2}—ZBD'TH. StaC p. 31, 1—ZBD'TH. StaF p. 38, 4—br'' ZBD'TH wbrnbw wzdql. *Inv. VIII*, 1^{1}—[ZBD]'TH br [']tntn. 'Wadi Hauran' $12^{1,3}$—ZBD'TH [br] / [ḥ]dydw / [ZBD]'TH br yrḥy br šdd'.

ZBWD (*m*) **1.** *560*, *C* 4045^{3}—. . .]' br ZBWD. **2.** *C* 4096^{1}—ZBWD.

ZBWDW (*m*) **1.** *568*, *Inv. XI*, 19^{3}—. . .] br ZBWDW 'b'.

ZBY (*m*) **1.** *555*, Ingh. 'Th.' p. 129^{8}—ZBY br š'd'. *5*[*7*]*3* or *5*[*7*]*8*, *PNO* 21 B—blb[.]y br ZBY s[. . . . *582*, *C* 3946^{3}—ZBY. *582*, *C* 3947^{3}—ZBY. **2.** *C* 4070^{2}—ZBY br zbd' zbd. *Pal. 61*: 9—ZBY br mlkw.

ZBYD' (*m*) **1.** *396*, *C* 3978^{3}—lšmš wZBYD' bny mlkw br ydy'bl br nš' dy mtqr' br 'bdbl. *400+?*, CaD 7 B^{1}—. . .] br yrḥbwl' br ZBYD' br tymy. *409*, 'Wadi Hauran' I^{2}—ZBYD' br ḥwml. *409*, 'Wadi Hauran' 2^{2}—ḥyrn br šm'wn br ZBYD'. *409*, 'Wadi Hauran' 5^{2}—ZBYD' br ḥwml. *409*, 'Wadi Hauran' 8^{6}—ZBYD' br tym'md mškw. *425*, *C* 3994 A^{3}—ZBYD['] br tym'md mškw. *425*, *C* 3994 B^{3}—ZBY[D'] br tym'md mškw. *425*, *C* 3994 C^{3}—ZBYD' br tym'md mškw. *428*, *C* 3919^{1}—ZBYD' br š'dw tymšmš. *440*, *C* 4164—mqymw br ZBYD' br yrḥy. *440*, *C* 3997^{1}—ZBYD['] br zbdbl ydy'bl. *443*, *C* 3973^{7}—ZBYD' br [š]m'wn br bl'qb. *448*, *C* 3913 I^{3}—ZBYD' br nš'. *448*, *Inv. XI*, 2^{3}—ZBYD'. *460*, *C* 4168^{3}—''ylmy wZBYD' bny ḥyrn br mqymw br ḥyrn mt'. *461*, *C* 4170—ZBYD' br mqymw ZBYD' [. . . . *462*, *C* $4268^{6,8}$—ḥlpt' br ZBYD' br / tym' ḥlpt' / ZBYD'. *474*, StaB p. 102, A 1167^{1}—bwly br ZBYD' br ḥyrn br mqymw mt'. *484*, *C* 4003^{1}—. . .]' br ZBYD' 'pyn. *497*, Ingh. E (Malkû) p. 91, II^{2}—šgl brt ZBYD'. *500+?*, *Inv. XI*, 23^{3}—'l' brt ZBYD' br 't'y rp'. *504*, *C* 4199^{6}—ZBYD' br m'n br bwlnwr (nwr)'th. *515*, *C* 4198 B^{2}—[ZBY]D['] br šlmny br 'bšlm'. *523*, *C* 4201^{2}—ZBYD' [wš]mw'l bny lwy br y'qwb br šmw'l. *530*, *C* 4018^{4}—mqy (son of) yrḥy br ZBYD['] 'lpy. *537*, StaB p. 153, A 1205^{1}—ZBYD' br whblt byd' ''py. *538*,

C 4244 A^{3}—btḥby brt ZBYD'. *542*, *C* 4243^{1}—ZBYD' br mqymw br ḥyrn ''ylm[y]. *544*, *C* 4031^{4}—ywl 'wr ḥlpwn' br ''ylmy ZBYD' 'qwp'. *547*, *C* 4033$^{4, 5}$—ZBYD' br mlkw / ZBYD' 'b'. *547*, *C* 4209—[ywlys 'wrlys ZBYD'] br 'štwr ZBYD'. *550*, CaA 32^{1}—br'th br ZBYD' br [. . . .]' byd'. *552*, CaD 36 C^{5}—ywlys 'wrlys typyls br tymrṣw [Z]BYD'. *558*, *C* 3933^{2}—ywlys 'wrlys ZBYD' br mqymw br ZBYD' 'štwr byd'. **2.** *C* 4073^{3}—sy'n' br ZB[Y]D'. *C* 4098^{2}—ḥyr' [b]r ZBYD'. *C* 4169—. . .] br ZBYD' br ḥyrn mt'. *C* 4187^{1}—mqymw wtymš[' wZBYD' bny 'lhš]' br ṣ'dy br 'lhš'. *C* 4187^{2}—[mqymw b]r ZBYD'. *C* 4188^{3}—'lhš' rb' br mqymw ZBYD' 'lhš' ṣ'dy. *C* 4200^{2}—'qmt brt ḥggw ZBYD' m'n. *C* 4245 A^{1}—mqy br ZBYD' mqymw. *C* 4245 B^{1}—br[k/p]' br ZBYD' mqymw. *C* 4252 A^{2}—tdmr brt ZBYD'. *C* 4252 B^{1}—ZBYD' *C* 4266^{1}—ZBYD' br tym' br ḥlpt'. *C* 4357^{1}—ZBYD' br 'wṭk' dy bwrp' 'kldy. *C* 4382—tm' brt ZBYD[']. *C* 4404—ZBYD' / br nṣr' br / mlk' ZBYD'. *C* 4421 B^{2}—ḥg' brt ZBYD'. *C* 4444^{2}—hgr bt ZBYD' br 'tyk'. *C* 4519^{1}—ZBYD' br dyny br ml'. *C* 4532^{5}—mlkw wZBYD'. *C* 4545—tym' br ZBYD'. C 4546—'mtḥ' brt ZBYD'. *C* 4551—mtny br ZBYD'. *C* 4582^{1}—ZBYD' [br] ḥlypt. *C* 4597^{2}—bwrp' 'g' ZBYD' myṭq'. *C* 4601^{2}—šm'w[n] br ZBYD' mw'l'. *RTP* 179b—mqymw tymrṣw wtymrṣw nš' wZBYD' [. . .]w. *RTP* 293a—ZBYD' 'lg. *RTP* 312b—[Z]BYD'. *RTP* 375b—[mq]ymw ZBYD' ḥy[. . . . *RTP* 406b—ZBYD' br [. . . . *RTP* 441b—yrḥbwl' ZBYD'. *RTP* 580b—m[q]ymw ZBYD'. *RTP* 581b—ZBYD'. *RTP* 626a—ZBYD'. *RTP* 659b—ZBYD'. *RTP* 720b—bly ZBYD' mlkw nṣrlt. *RTP* 745b—rb'l. ZBYD'. *RTP* 792a—ZBYD'. *RTP* 805a—ZBYD'. *RTP* 822a—nbwzbd br ZBYD'. *RTP* 997a—ZBYD' 'štwr. 'Tessères' 25b—zbdbwl ZBYD'. 'Büste' p. 313^{2}—hgr brt ZBYD' br ml'. 'Monuments' 5—zbd'th br ZBYD' byd'. CaA 15^{1}—''ylmy br ZBYD' ḥyrn. CaA 17—ZBYD'. CaA 26^{3}—ZBY[D'] br mqy[mw]. Ingh. D Pl. X^{1}—ZBYD' br ydy'bl. StaB p. 101, A 1168^{1}—bwl[y] br ZBYD' br ḥyrn br mq[ymw mt']. *PNO* 59—ZBYD' mhrdt. *PNO* 75^{2}—ZBYD' b[r. . . . *PNO* 76 A^{4}—'ḥlt m'n br ZBYD'. *Inv. VIII*, 27^{2}—ZBYD' 'ṣr'. *Inv. X*, 130^{3}—[ZBYD' w'bdy w']bd'štwr bny n[š' 't']qb. *Inv. XI*, 28^{2}—ZBYD' [br] šg' 'klb. *Inv. XI*, 34$^{2, 3}$—ZB[YD' br] / ZBYD' br ZB[YD']. *Inv. XI*, 67^{1}—ZBYD'. 'Hypogée' p. 245, Pl. XII^{1}—zbdl' br ZBYD' zbdl' ṭ'y. 'Wadi Hauran' 3^{6}—ZBYD' ḥwml. 'Wadi Hauran' 9$^{1, 3}$—ZBYD' / tym'md / ZBYD' / mškw. 'Wadi Hauran' 11^{7}—ḥby br ZBYD' ḥby. *Pal. 63*: 7^{2}—. . .] br ZBYD'.

ZBYDY see BR ZBYDY.

ZBKN' (*m*) **2.** *PNO* 34—ZBKN'.

ZGWG (*m*) **1.** *348*, CaD 33^{3}—mlkw [wz]bd'[th. . . .]bny tym'md b[r] bwrp' ZG[WG]. **2.** *C* 4522^{3}—[n]by brt yrḥy **br** ZGWG.

ZDQL (*m*) **2.** StaF 4, p. 38—br'' zbd'th wbrnbw wZDQL.

ZWZY (*m*) **1.** *552*, StaB p. 158, A 1174^{5}—mlk' w't'y bny ḥggw br mlky ZWZY.

ZWR (*m*) **1.** *513*, *C* 4294^{3}—'g' br tybwl ZWR. **2.** *C* 4295^{3}—[']g' br mlkw 'g' ZWR.

ZWRW (*m*) **2.** *C* 4293^{5}—mlkw br 'g' tybwl ZWRW.

ZKY' (*m*) **1.** *503*, *PNO* 39^{1}—tym' br ZKY'.

ZKN' see Lexicon.

ZMRY (*m*) **2.** *RTP* 933b—ZMRY bpny'.

Z'MW (*m*) **1.** *458*, *PNO* 55 D^{2}—Z'MW br ḥyrn br šḥr'.

Z'QW see Z'MW.

ZQ' (*m*) **1.** *441*, *Inv. IV*, 4 B—ZQ'.

ZRZYRT (*m*) **1.** *475*, *Inv. X*, 24^{1}—ḥ[d]wdn br ḥggw lš[mš]' ZRZYRT.

Ḥ[**1.** *493*, *Inv. XI*, 6^{2}—krsm' br Ḥ[. . . .

ḤB' (*m*/*f*) **1.** *439*, CaC 9^{1}—ḤB' br bgšw **br** zbdbwl. *497*, Ingh. E (Malkû) p. 91, II^{1}—nwrbl w'qmt ḤB' bny mlkw rb' br mlkw mlkw nwrbl. *497*, Ingh. E (Malkû) p. 93, III^{1}—nwrbl w'qmt ḤB' bny mlkw rb' br mlkw mlkw nwrbl. *551*, StaB p. 154, A 1204^{9}—ḤB'. **2.** *C* 4315^{1}—ḤB' bt ḥnyn'. *C* 4321^{1}—ḤB' brt mqymw ''wyd. *C* 4373 B^{1}—ḤB' br[t] 't'qb tym'. *C* 4392^{4}—zbdbl b[r] mqymw ḤB'. *C* 4443^{3}—ḤB' bt mlwk'. *C* 4512 A^{2}—ḤB' br[t] bwn'. *C* 4513 A^{1}—ḤB' brt ml'. *C* 4513 B^{1}—ḤB' brt ml'. *C* 4538^{2}—ḤB' brt 'g' yrḥy. *C* 4548^{3}—šgl bt ḤB'. *RTP* 812b—ḤB'. *RTP* 951b—ḤB'. CaC 10^{1}—bgšw br ḤB[' br] bgšw. *PS* 443—ḤB'. *Inv. VIII*, 183 B^{1}—. . .]t ḤB' [. . . .

ḤBBT (*f*) **2.** *C* 4399^{1}—ḤBBT brt mlkw.

ḤBWḂ **2.** *Inv. VIII*, 152^{3}—. . .] ḤBWḂ [. . . .

ḤBWL' (*m*) **2.** 4355^{2}—y(d)y'bl br ḤBWL'. *PS* 149—mlkw nš' br ḤBWL'.

ḤBZY (*m*) **2.** *C* 4191^{9}—'lhš' br tymš' br šmšgrm [Ḥ]BZY. *C* 4338^{3}—'qm' brt ḤBZY. *C* 4339^{4}—[l]wy' bt [ḥ]ry 'qm[' ḤBZ]Y. *Inv. VIII*, 58^{2}—ywly' 'wrly' nwry wzbdbwl w['gylw] bny mq[y. . . .] ḤBZY.

ḤBY (*m*) **1.** *578*, Ingh. E (Malkû) p. 102, XI^{6}—ddywn br ḤBY br dygns. **2.** *C* 4230^{1}—ḤBY br 'wyd'. 'Wadi Hauran' 11$^{6, 8}$—ḤBY br / zbyd' / ḤBY.

ḤBYB' (*m*) **2.** StaC 3, p. 34—ḤBYB' br šlmn.

ḤBYBY (*m*) **1.** *468*, *C* 3960^{4}—ḤBYBY br yrḥy br ḥyrn. **2.** *C* 3905^{1}—ḤBYBY br mlkw 'nbt. *C* 4309^{1}—ḤBYBY br nš' ‘lbn. *C* 4310 A^{1,2}—ḤBYBY / br ḤBYBY nš'. *C* 4310 B—ḤBYBY br ḤBYBY. *C* 4311 A^{1,2}—ḤBYBY br / ḤBYBY ns'. *C* 4509^{2}—ḤBYBY br mlkw bly[d‘]. *RTP* 171b—tymrṣ[w] ḤBYBY. *PS* 167—ḤBYBY r[b'] br yrḥbwl' br nwrbl. *Inv. VIII*, 110^{1}—ḤBYBY mqymy br ‘lyy.

ḤBN (*m*) **2.** *C* 4571 A^{2}—'brwq ḤBN. *C* 4571 B^{3}—‘g' wšlmt bn[y] 'brwq ḤBN.

ḤBRY (*m*) **2.** *C* 4078^{4}—mqymw br zbd[b]wl b[r] ḤBRY.

ḤBT' (*m*/*f*) **1.** *452*, *Inv. VIII*, 2^{1}—ḤBT' brt ḥlpt' br ḥlp[...] br tymrṣw. (*536*), *PNO* 73^{1}—ḤBT' wḥgt.

ḤG' (*f*) **1.** *525*, *Inv. X*, 119^{1}—ḤG'. **2.** *C* 4421 B^{1}—ḤG' brt zbyd'. *Inv. VIII*, 138^{2}—ḤG' brt zbd' br m‘ny.

ḤGGW (*m*) **1.** *320*, *Inv. IV*, 26 A—mqymw br [ḤG]GW. *336*, *Inv. IV*, 26 B—blšwry br ḤGGW. *345*, *C* 3980^{3}—ḤGGW br zbdlh kmr'. *409*, ‘Wadi Hauran' 5^{4}—ḤGGW br nš' ḥrš'. *409*, ‘Wadi Hauran' 8^{5}—tymrṣw wḤGGW bny tym' šwyr'. *4[23]*. *Inv. X*, 69^{1}—ḤGGW br yrḥy br ‘g' ydy‘bl. *426*, CaD 21^{1}—‘wydw wmlkw wyrḥbwl[' wḤGGW bny] bwlm' br ‘wydy br bwlm' 'db. *473*, *C* 3956^{2}—ḥlypy [b]r ḤGGW br mlkw. *475*, *Inv. X*, 24^{1}—ḥ[d]wdn br ḤGGW lš[mš]' zrzyrt. *543*, *C* 4030^{3}—ḤGGW br yhyb' br yrḥy dk'. *552*, StaB p. 158, A 1174^{4}—mlk' w‘t‘y bny ḤGGW br mlky zwzy. *572*, *C* 4050^{3}—[Ḥ]GGW br yhyb' yrḥy dk'. **2.** *C* 3929^{2}—[blš]wry br ḤGGW br blšwry b‘'. *C* 4200^{2}—'qmt brt ḤGGW zbyd' m‘n. *C* 4232 A^{2}—mlkw br ḤG[G]W whblt. *C* 4232 B^{2}—pṣy'l br ḤGGW br ml' whblt. *C* 4232 C^{2}—pṣ' brt nš' ḤGGW. *C* 4232 D—ḤGGW [br ml]'. *C* 4232 E^{2}—p[ṣ]' b[t] ḥg[gw]. *C* 4299^{5}—ḤGGW. *C* 4449^{3}—ḥsd brt br‘th ḤGGW. *C* 4468^{1}—ḤGGW br ‘g' br ydy‘b[l]. *C* 4501^{1}—mlkw br ḤGGW br mlkw. *C* 4502^{2}—tym' br mlkw br ḤGGW. *C* 4503^{3}—tbnn brt ḤGGW mlkw. *C* 4504^{2}—mlkw br ḤGGW. *RTP* 239b—ḤGGW. *RTP* 315b—mlkw ḤGGW. *RTP* 336a—šl' or šp' ḤGGW. *RTP* 473b—ḤGGW [z]bdl'. *Inv. IV*, 15 A—ḤGGW brnbw br‘th. *Inv. VIII*, 152^{1}—ḤGGW br [.... *Inv. XI*, 77^{3}—ḤGGW rb'n qymy wwhby wzbdbwl.

ḤGWG' (*m*) **2.** *C* 4473^{1}—ḤGWG' br br‘th. StaF p. 36, 1—ḤGWG' [br] 'gy‘.

ḤGWR (*m*) **1.** *548*, Ingh. D, Pl. IX^{1}—ḤGWR br mlkw mlkbl.

ḤGY (*m*) **1.** *461*, *C* 3967^{2}—[Ḥ]GY br ‘g' ḤGY. *500+?*, *Pal. 62*: 9^{2}—...] ḤGY [.... **2.** *C* 4211^{1}—ywlys 'wrlys 'wṭk' ḤGY. *RTP* 727b—ḤGY. *Inv. VIII*, 108^{2}—ḤGY br yrḥy br ‘g' ydy‘bl.

ḤGT (*m*/*f*) **1.** (*536*), *PNO* 73^{1}—ḥbt' wḤGT. **2.** *C* 4287^{1}—ḤGT brt bwlḥ' ‘tntn 'ḥytwr. *C* 4480^{1}—ḤGT brt yrḥy br zbdlh krḥ. *Pal. 60*: 5 B^{1}—ḤGT brt ‘gylw ‘mr. *Pal. 61*: 17^{1}—[Ḥ]GT brt yrḥyw br nbwd'.

ḤD' (*m*) **1.** *524*, *Inv. XI*, 11^{4}—‘gy[lw br] tymrṣw b[r] ḤD'.† **2.** *RTP* 840b—ḤD'.

ḤDWDN (*m*) **1.** *[3]84*, *C* 4193^{2}—‘gylw br ‘g' br mqymw br ḤDWDN. *449*, *C* 4165^{1}—ḤDW[DN] br ṣpry br‘th. *[468]*, *Inv. X*, 96^{3}—ḥnynw br [ḤDWDN]. *470*, CaD 28 C^{3}—ḤDWDN br ḤDWDN prmwn. *472*, *C* 4171^{1}—ḤDWDN br šlmn br zbdbwl. *475*, *Inv. X*, 24^{1}—Ḥ[D]WDN br ḥggw lš[mš]' zrzyrt. *475*, *Inv. X*, 24^{2}—ḤDWDN. *486*, *C* 3914^{2}—yrḥbwl' [br] ‘g' w‘wyd' br ḤDWDN bny yrḥbwl' br ḤDWDN br zbdbwl br ḤDW[DN] prmwn. *583*, CaA 31^{1}—ḤDWDN br ‘gylw mqy. **2.** *C* 4061^{4}—mrwn' [b]r ḤDWDN br [mr]wn'. *C* 4183—mlkw ḤDWDN. *C* 4425^{2}—ḤDWDN br mzbn'. *C* 4470 A^{3}—hgy brt ḤDWDN. *RTP* 290b—nbwlh ḤDWDN. *RTP* 486a—ḤDWDN. *RTP* 486b—[ḤD]WDN mq[y]. *RTP* 490a—ḤDWDN mqy. *RTP* 490b—ḤDWDN. *RTP* 491a—ḤDWDN mqy. *RTP* 491b—ḤDWDN. *RTP* 492a—ḤDWDN mqy. *RTP* 495a—ḤDWDN mqy. *RTP* 753b—ḤDWDN. *RTP* 851b—ḤDWDN ‘wyd' [ḤDWD]N. Ingh. A p. 88, 2^{1}—ḤDWDN br dkt' br ḥry bt prmwn. CaA 10^{2}—[m‘ny br] ‘mt br ḤDW[DN pr]mw[n]. CaC 17^{3}—‘gylw b[r....]ny ḤDWDN.

[Ḥ]DYDW (*m*) **2.** ‘Wadi Hauran' 12^{2}—zbd‘th [br Ḥ]DYDW [zbd]‘th br yrḥy br šdd'.

ḤWML (*m*) **1.** *391*, *C* 4122^{2}—mlkw br mqymw br b[wl]brk ḤWML. *409*, ‘Wadi Hauran' 1^{3}—zbyd' br ḤWML. *409*, ‘Wadi Hauran' 5^{2}—zbyd' br ḤWML. *480*, *C* 4236—yrḥy br mlkw br yrḥy ḤWML. *516*, StaB p. 111, A 1169^{2}—bwlḥ' br ḥyrn br ‘t‘qb ḤWML. **2.** ‘Wadi Hauran' 3^{6}—zbyd' ḤWML.

ḤṬR' (*m*) **2.** *RTP* 993b—ḤṬR' or ḥld' br‘th.

ḤṬRY (*m*) **1.** *486*, StaA p. 52, 2^{5}—šl' brt ḤṬRY. **2.** *C* 4483^{2}—šl' brt ḤṬRY br yrḥy. *C* 4484^{1}—ḤṬRY br yrḥy br ḥlpt'. *C* 4485^{5}—ḤṬRY br yrḥy. ‘Sculptures' p. 22, Pl. II^{1}—'ḥyny br ḤṬRY.

ḤYNY (*m*) **2.** *RTP* 183b—rbw ḤYNY.

ḤYQ[**1.** *552*, *C* 4039^{4}—yrḥb[wl' br yr]ḥbwl' ḤYQ[....

ḤYR' (*m*) **1.** *447*, *C* 3999^{2}—šlmn br nš' br ḤYR' brq. *574*, *C* 3939^{3}—ywlys 'wrlys

† This reading from Starcky, review of *Inv. XI*, in *RB*, 73 (1966), 615.

nbwzbd br šʿdw ḤYR'. **2.** *C* 4077^{3}—ʿgylw br ḤYR[']. *C* 4098^{1}—ḤYR' [b]r zbyd'. *C* 4358 A^{3}—btʿg' brt ḤYR' blšwr. *C* 4358 B^{2}—blšwr br ḤYR' 'kldy. *C* 4359^{2}—mqymw br ḤYR' 'kldy. *C* 4525—ḤYR' br zbdbwl ḤYR'. *C* 4609^{3}—'mtlt brt ḤYR'. *C* 4621^{3}—btʿg' brt ḤYR' blšwr. *C* 4623^{2}—ḤYR' br ḥyrn br ḥyrn ʿgylw. *RTP* 424a—ḤYR'. *RTP* 550a—ḤYR' šʿdw. *RTP* 550b—ḤYR' šʿdw. *RTP* 783b—ḤYR' yrḥy ʿmrt. *RTP* 910b—ḤYR'. 'Sculptures' p. 24, Pl. II^{2}—blšwr br ḤYR' 'kldy. 'Sculptures' p. 24, Pl. II^{2}—mqymw br ḤYR' 'kldy. *Palmyrene* no. 12—ḤYR' br mlkw. Ingh. B, Pl. XLIX^{2}—ḤYR' br ʿwydlt br mqymw ʿlbn.

ḤYRY (*m*) **2.** *RTP* 222b—ḤYRY mlkw.

ḤYRN (*m*) **1.** *304*, *C* 4109 A^{4}—khylw wḤYRN. *304*, *C* 4109 B^{3}—khylw wḤYRN. [*3*?]*42*, 'Dédicace' p. 44, 3—blʿqb br ḤYRN blʿqb. *345*, *C* 4114^{2}—ḤYRN br blšwry br gdrṣw dy mtqrh br bʿ'. *345*, *C* 4114^{5}—ḤYRN. *360*, CaC 11^{4}—'wšy br khylw w'wšy[....]' bny ḤYRN br 'wšy. *363*, 'Trilingue' p. 137^{2}—ḤYRN br bwn' br rb'l br bwn' br ʿtntn br tymy. *371*, *Inv. IX*, 20^{2}—ḤYRN br bwn' br rb'l br bwn' br ʿtntn dy [mt]qr' br šʿt. *378*, CaB 4 A^{3}—ʿgylw wtymḥ' wʿty bny ḤYRN br ʿbdʿth 'gdm. *385*, CaD 2^{1}—Ḥ[Y]RN br bwn[' dy mtqr' rb'l]. *393*, *C* 4197^{1}—...] br ḤYRN br mlkw. *394*, *C* 4124^{2}—šby wnbwzbd wt[ymy wnbwl'] bny blšwry br ḤYRN br blšwry br gdrṣw[....bʿ']. *400+?*, *Inv. XI*, 56^{3}—...] br ḤYRN. *409*, 'Wadi Hauran' 2^{1}—ḤYRN br šmʿwn br zbyd'. *415*, *Inv. VIII*, 59^{2}—bwlḥ' wmqymy wḤYRN wlšmš wbʿl[y] bny whby br bwlḥzy. *419*, *Inv. X*, 129^{1}—g'ys ywlys ḤYRN br 'lhbl. *426*, *C* 4129 B^{3}—ʿlyš' wbʿltg' bny bwn' br šby br blšwr br ḤYRN. *43[7]*, CaD 30^{2}—mlkw br mqymw [br ḤYRN br] brʿy. *444*, *C* 3998 A^{3}—[zbdbwl] br yrḥbwl' br lšmšy [ḤYRN]. *447*, *C* 3968^{5}—rb'l br ḤYRN bgšw. [*4*]*47*, *Inv. X*, 81^{4}—mrqs 'lpys 'bgr br ḤYRN 'bgr. *448*, *C* 3913 I^{2}—bwn' br bwn' br ḤYRN. *449*, CaB 8^{1}—ḤYRN br nš' tybwl ṣm'. *450*, *C* 3930^{2}—ʿ'ylmy br ḤYRN br mqymw br ḤYRN mt'. *450*, *C* 3930^{3}—ḤYRN. *451*, *C* 3927^{1,2}—'ḥply br ḤYRN šb' br / ḤYRN bwn' š[ʿ]t. *458*, *PNO* 55 D^{3}—zʿmw br ḤYRN br šḥr'. *460*, *C* 4168^{3}—ʿ'ylmy wzbyd' bny ḤYRN br mqymw br ḤYRN mt'. *466*, *C* 3928^{1}—mrqs 'l[p]y[s] yr[ḥy br ḤYRN br ']bgr. *467*, CaD 28 B^{2}—[mr]qs 'lpys yrḥy b[r ḤYR]N 'bgr. *468*, *C* 3960^{2}—mrqs 'lps yrḥy br ḤYRN 'bgr. *468*, *C* 3960^{3} ḤYRN br yrḥy br tym'. *468*, *C* 3960^{5}—ḥbyby br yrḥy br ḤYRN. [*46*]*8*, *Inv. X*, 77^{1}—[mrqs 'lpys yrḥy br ḤYRN] 'bgr. [*468*], *Inv. X*, 90^{1}—mrqws 'lpys yrḥy br ḤYRN 'bgr. [*468*], *Inv. X*, 96^{1}—[mrqs 'lpys yrḥy br ḤYRN 'bgr]. [*469*], CaA 8^{2}—mrq[s 'lps yrḥy b]r Ḥ[YRN 'bgr]. *470*, CaD 28 A^{1}—mrqs 'lpys yrḥy br ḤYRN 'bgr. *470*, CaD 28 C^{2}—'lpys mrqs yrḥy br ḤYRN 'bgr. *474*, StaB p. 102, A 1167^{2}—bwly br zbyd' br ḤYRN br mqymw mt'. *488*, *C* 4004^{1}—ḤYRN br [m]qy[mw] br yrḥy. *490*, *C* 3950^{1}—yd' br šrykw br ḤY[RN] b[r] ʿlyn' ṣpr'. *490*, *C* 3951^{1}—ʿlyn' br ḤYRN br [ʿ]lyn' ṣ[pr']. *490*, *C* 3952^{1}—šrykw br ḤYRN br ʿlyn' ṣpr'. *490*, *C* 3953^{1,2}—ḤYRN br šrykw br / ḤYRN br ʿlyn' ṣpr'. *495*, *C* 4507—ḤYRN. *500*, *C* 4292^{1,4}—ḤYRN / br bwrp' / br ḤYRN / tybwl. *504*, Ingh. E (Malê) p. 76, II^{1}—ml' br ḤYRN br ssn. *516*, StaB p. 111, A 1169^{1}—bwlḥ' br ḤYRN br ʿtʿqb ḥwml. *516*, StaB p. 111, A 1169^{7}—ḤYRN b[r] mqym[w]. *517*, StaB p. 148, A 1179^{4}—tymrṣw [b]r ḤYRN zbd'. *525*, Ingh. E (Malkû) p. 99, VIII^{2}—hlydyrs yrḥbwl' br ḤYRN bwn'. *526*, Ingh. E (Malê) p. 77, III^{1}—ywlys 'wrlys ml' br ḤYRN br ssn. *526*, Ingh. E (Malê) p. 77, III^{1}—ywlys 'wrlys ḤYRN wywlys 'wrlys 'b' bny ywlys 'wrlys mqy br yrḥy. *530*, *C* 4306^{1,2}—Ḥ[YR]N br tym' / br ḤYRN twp' *530*, *Inv. XI*, 13^{4}—[Ḥ]YRN. *535*, Ingh. E (Malê) p. 78, IV^{1}—ywlyws 'wrlys ml' br ḤYRN br ssn. *542*, *C* 4243^{3}—zbyd' br mqymw br ḤYRN ʿ'ylm[y]. *545*, *C* 4308^{2}—šmʿwn br ḤYRN. *545*, Ingh. E (Malê p. 82, V^{2}—ywlys 'wrlys ml' br ḤYRN br ml' ḤYRN ssn. *546*, Ingh. E (Malê) p. 84, VI^{1,2}—ywlys 'wrlys ml' br 'wrlys ḤYRN / br ml' ḤYRN ssn. *546*, Ingh. E (Malê) p. 84, VII^{3}—ywlys 'wrlys ml' br ḤYRN ml'. *547*, *C* 4032^{4}—[Ḥ]YRN. *548*, Ingh. E (Malê) p. 86, VIII^{2}—ywlys 'wrlys ḤYRN br mqy yrḥy. *548*, Ingh. E (Malê) p. 86, VIII^{13}—ḤYRN. *549*, Ingh. E (Malê) p. 88, IX^{2}—'wrlys ḤYRN br mqy br yrḥy. *552*, *C* 4307^{2}—mzbt' brt ḤYRN tym'. *552*, CaD 36 C^{3}—ywly' 'wrly' ḤYRN wmlwk' bny grmn'. *554*, *C* 4305^{3}—'lhbl br tym' br ḤYRN. *554*, *C* 4305^{6}—ḤYRN. *555*, StaB p. 159, A 1176^{3}—ḤYRN br yml' mqymw. *563*, *C* 3944^{1}—spṭmyws ḤYRN br 'dynt. *563*, StaB p. 97, line 6—[q]ryn br ḤYRN br yrḥbwl'. *575*, *C* 3940^{4}—ywlys 'wrlys spṭmyws yd' br 'lks[nd]rws ḤYRN srykw. **2.** *C* 3907^{9}—ḤYRN. *C* 3990^{1}—ḤYR[N] br blḥzy br blḥ' [m]qy [ʿ'b]y. *C* 4066^{3,4}—[ḤYRN] br srykw / ḤY[RN]. *C* 4076^{3}—gdy' b[r] Ḥ[YRN b]gdn. *C* 4111^{2}—khylw wḤYRN bny ʿtntn. *C* 4126—...Ḥ]YR[N] br blšwry. *C* 4128^{4}—...] br š[by] br blš[wry] br ḤYRN blšwry. *C* 4169—...] br zbyd' br ḤYRN mt'. *C* 4202—'dynt br ḤYRN whblt nṣwr. *C* 4234—šḥrw br ḤYRN. *C* 4290^{3}—ḤYRN br tybwl. *C* 4291^{2}—rʿt' brt ḤYRN tybwl. *C* 4297^{1}—ḤYR[N] br mry[wn] br '[lhbl]. *C* 4299^{3}—mrywn br 'lh[b]l ḤYRN. *C* 4350^{2}—ʿg' br ḤYRN [br] ʿg'. *C* 4360^{1}—ḤYRN br šlmn br ʿg'. *C* 4413 B^{1}—ḤYRN br qrd'. *C* 4414^{1}—ḤYRN br qrd' br ydy. *C* 4415^{2}—ḤYRN b[r] qrd'. *C* 4431^{4}—btʿty brt yrḥy br ḤYRN. *C* 4434^{2}—bny br ḤYRN. *C* 4455^{3}—ʿty brt rb'l br ḤYRN bg[dn]. *C* 4458 *bis*—...] šmʿwn br ḤYRN prdšy. *C* 4462^{1}—'bb' brt ḤYRN br khyly. *C* 4465^{3}—zbdbwl br ḤYRN nwry. *C* 4596^{5}—ʿtntn br kyly br mškw b[r] ʿtd/rt br ḤYRN. *C* 4606[4]—'qm' brt mtny br ḤYRN. *C* 4608[2]—šmʿwn br ḤYRN. *C* 4610[1, 2]—ḤYRN br blt' / br ḤYRN. *C* 4623[3, 4]—ḥyr' br / ḤYRN br / ḤYRN br / ʿgylw. *RTP* 12b—šmʿwn br ḤYRN. *RTP* 27b—ḤYRN ʿtnwry ṣlmy. *RTP* 33a—bwlḥ' br ḤYRN. *RTP* 38b—ydʿw tybwl ḤYRN ṣt'. *RTP* 156b—ḥrwṣ ḤYRN. *RTP* 267b—ḤYRN yrḥy. *RTP* 272b—blnwr mqmw ḤYRN mly. *RTP* 291b—ḤYRN ydʿw. *RTP* 361b—ḤY(RN). *RTP* 375b—[mq]ymw zbyd' ḤY[RN]. *RTP* 463a—bw[n]' br ḤYRN. *RTP* 465a—mlkw ḤYRN. *RTP* 480a—ḤYRN. *RTP* 480b—sṭm ḤYRN 'š''. *RTP* 482b—ḤYRN mlkw. *RTP* 485a—ḤYRN 'dyn[t]. *RTP* 488b—[m]tn' [ḤY]RN. *RTP* 576b—mqymw ḤYRN. *RTP* 592b—ḤY(RN). *RTP* 630b—šlmlt mlkw ḤYRN mʿnw. *RTP* 643b—mlkw ḤYRN bšr'. *RTP* 646b—ḤYR[N]. *RTP* 661a—mlkw br ḤYRN br ql[..]'. *RTP* 666b—ḤYRN ʿgyl'. *RTP* 697b—'bb ḤYRN mlkw. *RTP* 729a—mlkw ḤYRN. *RTP* 736a—ḤYRN 'dynt. *RTP* 741a—ḤY(RN) šr(ykw). *RTP* 741b—ḤYRN šrykw. *RTP* 742a—ḤYRN šrykw. *RTP* 746b—ḤYRN 'dy[nt]. *RTP* 756a—ṭʿqb ḤYR[N]. *RTP* 762a—ḤYRN. *RTP* 770a—[m]lkw ḤYRN ''b[y]. *RTP* 787a—whblt ḤYRN. *RTP* 787b—whblt ḤYRN. *RTP* 796a—ḤY[RN]. *RTP* 799a—ḤY(RN) ʿgy(lw). *RTP* 804a—b[w]lḥ' or b[w]lm' ḤYRN. *RTP* 870a—ḤYR[N]. *RTP* 871b—ḤYRN šrykw. *RTP* 954b—tybwl ḤYRN mndrs. *RTP* 957b—ḤYRN. *RTP* 986a—ḤYRN. 'Bilingue' p. 885[1]—[rb]'l br ḤYRN. 'Iraq' p. 63[3], Pl. 8—'bgr br ḤYRN. Ingh. 'Quatre' p. 243, Pl. XLI[2]—ḤYRN br ndb'l bwš'. *PS* 193—mqymw br 'lhbl br ḤYRN [.... *PS* 201—ḤYR[N] br m[q]y[mw] br '[.... *PS* 371—ml' ḤYRN smy'. Ingh. A p. 97, 6—...] wkhylw wzbdʿth bny mlkw br ḤYRN. Ingh. C p. 2, Fig. 1—ḤYRN br ydy br ḤYRN ḥnt'. Ingh. C, Pl. II—ḤYRN br tymrṣw. 'IP' p. 156, 14 A[3]—'qmt [b]rt ḤYRN br bnr. CaA 15[2]—''ylmy br zbyd' ḤYRN. CaA 18 B—ḤYRN. CaA 20—ḤYRN. CaA 26[2]—ty[m'] brt ḤYRN. CaA 83[2]—yrḥy br ḤYRN. CaA 85 A—ḤYRN. CaB 12 B[1]—ḤYRN. CaC 17[1]—'dynt br ḤYRN whblt. CaD 32[1]—mlkw br ḤYRN [br ʿ]gyl[w]. StaB p. 101, A 1168[1]—bwl[y] br zbyd' br ḤYRN br mq[ymw mt']. *PNO* 43[3]—nbwzbd br ṣʿdy br mqymw ḤYRN. *PNO* 65—ʿnbw br ḤYRN. *Inv. VIII*, 8[1]—ḤYRN b[r] yrḥy. *Inv. VIII*, 74[2]—...] ḤYRN [.... *Inv. VIII*, 94[3]—[ʿ]gylw br yrḥy br ḥry ḤY[RN]. *Inv. VIII*, 97[1]—ḤYRN br škyb[l.... *Inv. VIII*, 101[3]—ḤYRN. *Inv. VIII*, 103[1]—ḤYRN br mqymw mlkw. *Inv. VIII*, 106[2]—ḤYRN [.... *Inv. VIII*, 124[1]—ḤYRN br mqym[w] br mlkw mqym[w]. *Inv. VIII*, 129[2]—...] ḤYRN q[.... *Inv. VIII*, 132[1]—ḤYRN br ydy [.... *Inv. VIII*, 174[1]—ḤYRN br yrḥbwl[']. *Inv. IX*, 18—...] br ḤYR[N .... *Inv. X*, 128[3]—mrq[s] 'lpys [y]rḥy br ḤYR[N 'bgr]. *Inv. XI*, 25[2]—ḤYRN br bryky br ḤYRN. *Inv. XI*, 27[3]—zbd' br ḤYRN. *Inv. XI*, 42[2]—lšmš br ḤYRN gl'. *Inv. XI*, 59[2]—ʿtnwry br ḤYRN br ʿtnwry. *Inv. XI*, 61[2]—zbd' [br Ḥ]YRN mlk'l. *Inv. XI*, 72—ḤYRN br ydy. *Inv. XI*, 75[2]—ʿgylw br ḤYRN. *Inv. XI*, 95—mlkw ḤYRN. 'Hypogée' p. 222, Pl. I[2]—ḤYRN br bršmš. 'Wadi Hauran' 11[3]—lšmš br ḤYRN br lšmš br tybwl škybl.

ḤKYM (*m*) **2.** *RTP* 225a—ḤKYM.

ḤKYŠW (*m*) **1.** *3[6]2*, *C* 3923[2]—mqymw br ʿgylw pṣy'[l] br tymy dy mtqrh ḤKYŠW.

ḤL' (*m*) **1.** *[4]53*, *C* 3916[1]—ns' br ḤL' br ns' br ḤL' br rp'l br ʿbsy. *461*, *Inv. X*, 124[2]—(n)š' br ḤL' br nš' ḤL'. *530*, CaD 22[2]—ʿtnwry br tym'' ḤL' b[r] ʿtnwry. *548*, *C* 4210[1]—ḤL' br nbwzbd br kyly. *579*, *C* 4053[2]—zb[d'] br ḤL'. **2.** *C* 4342[4]—ml' br ml' br ḤL'. CaA 37—ydy br mqymw br ydy br rmw br ḤL'. CaC 6[1]—ns' br ḤL' br ns' 'ḥmr. *Inv. VIII*, 15[4]—šbty brt ʿnny br mqymy ḤL'. *Inv. VIII*, 166[2]—mzbt['] bt ḤL'. *Inv. VIII*, 184[2]—mlkw ḤL'.

ḤLD' (*m*) **1.** *423*, *C* 3993[3]—[ḤL]D' br zbdʿth br ḤLD'. **2.** *RTP* 993b—ḤLD' or ḥṭr' brʿth.

ḤLH (*m*) **1.** *545*, *C* 4206[2]—ywl' 'wrly' ʿg' wšlm'[....nb]wmr bny ḤLH.

ḤLY' (*m*) **1.** *550*, *C* 4035[3]—gd' br ḤLY'.

ḤLYW (*f*) **2.** *C* 4442[2]—ḤLYW brt [m]lwk['] ʿtyk'.

ḤLYP' (*m*) **2.** *C* 4512 B[3]—mrthwn brt [Ḥ]LYP' bwn'. *C* 4530[3]—syʿt brt ḤLYP'.

ḤLYPY (*m*) **1.** *373*, *Pal.* 63: 3[6]—ḤLYPY br yrḥy 'lhw. *473*, *C* 3956[1]—ḤLYPY br 'tpny br ḤLYPY. *473*, *C* 3956[2]—ḤLYPY [b]r ḥggw br mlkw. *543*, *Inv. IV*, 13[3]—[t]ym' brt ḥry 'wrly' 'qm' brt 'nṭ[y]k[s ḤLYPY]. *547*, *C* 3902[1]—yrḥy br ḤLYPY br yrḥy br lšmš šʿdw. *54[.]*, *C* 3957[2]—mlkw br mqym[w] br mʿyty br ḤLYPY. **2.** *C* 4347[2]—mqymw br ḤLYPY. CaC 12[2]—lšmš br ḤLYPY br 'tpny. 'IP' p. 161, 22[4]—[ḤL]YPY.

ḤLYPT (*f*) **1.** *553*, *C* 4460[2]—ḤLYPT brt ʿttn br grymy. **2.** *C* 4582[3]—zbyd' [br] ḤLYPT.

ḤLYŠW (*m*) *Journal asiatique*, 12 (1918), 295 no. xviii.—**2.** ḤLYŠW br [t]ymḥ'.

ḤLYŠY (*m*) **1.** *430*, *Inv. VIII*, 62[1]—ḤLYŠY br bryky br blḥzy.

ḤLKŠ (*m*) **1.** *315*, CaD 12 A[2]—[m]lkw br ḤLKŠ qrqpn.

ḤLP' (*m*) **1.** *515*, *C* 4198 B[1]—qwp' ḤLP' br ṣpry br [.... *550*, *Inv. XI*, 15[3]—gd' br ḤLP'. **2.** *C* 4289[2]—ḥlpw brt ḤLP' [br] lšmš [tybwl] rb'.

ḤLPW (*f*) **2.** *C* 4289^{1}—ḤLPW brt ḥlp' [br] lšmš [tybwl] rb'.

ḤLPWN' (*m*) **1.** *503, C* 4009^{3}—[ḤL]PWN' br zbd'. *544, C* 4031^{3}—ywl 'wr ḤLPWN' br ''ylmy zbyd' 'qwp'.

ḤLPT' (*m*) **1.** *450, C* 4166^{3}—m'ytw br ḤLPT' br m[. . . . *452, Inv. VIII,* 2^{2}—ḥbt' brt ḤLPT' br ḥlp[. . . .] br tymrṣw. *452, Inv. VIII,* 2^{6}—zbd' br tym' br ḤLPT'. *461, C* 4254^{3}—'ḥ' brt ḤLPT' br br'' zbd'th. *462, C* 4268^{4}—n'my brt zbd' br tym' br ḤLPT'. *462, C* 4268^{5,7}—ḤLPT' / br zbyd' br / tym' ḤLPT' / zbyd'. *486,* StaA p. 52, 2^{3,4}—[y]rḥy br ḤLPT' br yrḥy/br ḤLPT'. *497,* Ingh. E (Malkû) p. 91, II^{2}—ḥnt' whby ḤLPT'. *525, Inv. X,* 119^{3}—tym' br ḤLPT' br'th 'lṭy. *525, Inv. X,* 119^{2}—ḤLPT'. *525, Inv. X,* 119^{2}—ḤLPT'. *546,* Ingh. E (Malê) p. 84, VI^{2}—ywlys 'wrlys ḤLPT' br mqymw zbd'. *546,* Ingh. E (Malê) p. 84, VII^{9}—ḤLPT'. *548,* Ingh. E (Malê) p. 86, VIII^{14}—ḤLPT' br mqymw zbd'. *551, C* 4037^{2}—bwrp' br Ḥ[LPT]' [br. . . . **2.** *C* 4265^{2}—tym' br ḤLPT' br tym'. *C* 4266^{3}—zbyd' br tym' br ḤLPT'. *C* 4267^{1,3}—ḤLPT' / br tym' / ḤLPT'. *C* 4272^{2}—š'yl' br ḤLPT' qwqḥ. *C* 4273^{2}—nš' br ḤLPT' qwqḥ. *C* 4274^{3}—nš' br qwqḥ ḤLPT'. *C* 4277^{2,4}—tym' / br ḤLPT' / br tymrṣw / br ḤLPT' / br šm'wn dy mtqrh qwqḥ rb'. *C* 4278^{3}—tm' brt ḤLPT'. *C* 4427^{1}—ḤLPT' br mzbn'. *C* 4483^{6}—yrḥy b[r] ḤLPT'. *C* 4484^{3}—ḥtry br yrḥy br ḤLPT'. *Inv. VIII,* 134^{4}—ḤLPT['']. *Inv. VIII,* 198^{2,4}—Ḥ[L]PT' / br qwq' / ḤLPT'.

ḤM' (*m*) **1.** *444, RTP* 32a—bgšw ḤM'. **2.** *RTP* 17b—mlkw šm'wn ḤM'.

ḤMY (*m*) **2.** *RTP* 469b—ḤMY.

ḤMYN (*m*) **1.** *505,* Ingh. B p. 95, II^{5}—tymw br dbḥ br ḤMYN.

ḤMNWN (*m*) **2.** CaD 25^{6}—. . . b]l'qb ḤMNWN blm' [. . . .

ḤN' (*f*) **2.** *C* 4493^{1}—ḤN' brt mqymw br [tyb]wl. 'IP' p. 157, 16 B^{1}—ḤN' brt bryky nbwzbd. *Inv. VIII,* 134^{1}—ḤN' brt yrḥy.

ḤNBL (*m*) **1.** *377,* 'Grave-Relief' p. 192—br'th br ḤNBL ''by. *392, Inv. X,* 131^{2}—mlkw br lšmš br ḤNBL br br'th ''by. *400,* 'Fouilles' p. 170^{1}—yrḥbwl' br mlkw br lšmš br ḤNBL ''by. *400,* 'Fouilles' p. 172^{4}—[yrḥbwl' br mlkw br] lšmš br Ḥ[NBL ''by]. *[4]58, C* 4458—. . .] mlkw br lšmš br ḤNBL ''by. *458,* 'IP' p. 147, 1^{2}—ḤNBL br šlmlt br mlkw. *458,* 'IP' p. 147, I^{3}—zbd'th br ḤNBL br dynys. **2.** *C* 4615—ml' br ḤNBL. 'IP' p. 152, 4^{2}—mlkw br dynys ḤNBL. 'IP' p. 153, 8^{2}—[zb]d'[t]h [b]r ḤNBL dynys. 'IP' p. 154, 9^{1,3}—ḤNBL / br zbd'th / br ḤNBL. 'IP' p. 154, 10^{3}—yrḥy br zbd'th ḤNBL. 'IP' p. 155, 11^{3}—dynys br zbd'th ḤNBL. *Inv. XI,* 97^{2}—ḤNB[L].

ḤNYN' (*m*) **1.** *502, C* 4174^{2}—šm'wn br 'b' br ḤNYN'. *535,* Ingh. E (Malê) p. 78, IV^{1}—ywlys 'wrlys 'bsy br ḤNYN' br ḤNYN' br 'g' yrq. *548,* Ingh. E (Malê) p. 86, VIII^{4}—ywlys 'wrlys 'sy[.] br ḤNYN' šm'wn. **2.** *C* 4276^{3}—ṣpr' brt ḤNYN' qwqḥ. *C* 4313^{4}—ḤNYN' [y]rḥy. *C* 4314^{4}—yrḥy br ḤNYN'. *C* 4315^{2}—ḥb' bt ḤNYN'. *C* 4316^{4}—gdrṣw br ml' br ḤNYN'. *C* 4317^{4}—mlkw br gdrṣw ḤNYN'. *C* 4557^{2,3}—ḤNYN' / br ḤNYN' / 'g' yrq. *RTP* 382a—ḤNYN'. Ingh. E (Malê) p. 79 A—'bsy br ḤNYN' ḤNYN' yrq. Ingh. E (Malê) p. 79 B—ḤNYN' br ḤNYN' 'g' yrq. Ingh. E (Malê) p. 80 D—ḤNYN' br ḤNYN' ḤNYN' yrq. Ingh. E (Malê) p. 81 G—š'dy br ḤNYN' ḤNYN' yrq. Ingh. E (Malê) p. 82 H—š'dy br 'bsy br ḤNYN' yrq. Ingh. E (Malê) p. 82 I—šl' brt ḤNYN' ḤNYN' yrq. *PNO* 2—ḤNYN' 'gylw 'sdy. *PNO* 7 A—'g[' b]r ḤNYN' br 'gy[lw]. *PNO* 7 C—mq[y] ḤNYN'. *Inv. VIII,* 119^{2}—ḤNYN' br 'gylw nbwl'.

ḤNYNW (*m*) **1.** *[468], Inv. X,* 96^{3}—ḤNYNW br [ḥdwdn].

ḤNYNY (*m*) **2.** *Inv. VII,* 14—bgšw br šḥrw ḤNYNY.

ḤNT (*f*) **1.** *435* or *436,* CaB 9^{3}—ḤNT.

ḤNT' (*m/f*) **1.** *490, C* 4006^{2}—Ḥ[NT]' brt ['w]yd. *497,* Ingh. E (Malkû) p. 91, II^{1}—ḤNT' whby ḥlpt'. **2.** *C* 4388^{1}—ḤNT' brt bwrp'. Ingh. C p. 2, Fig. 1—ḥyrn br ydy br ḥyrn ḤNT'.

ḤSD (*f*) **2.** *C* 4449^{1}—ḤSD brt br'th ḥggw.

ḤSS (*m*) **1.** *551, C* 4038^{3}—š'dw br mlkw ḤSS.

ḤPRY (*m*) **1.** *505,* Ingh. B p. 95, II^{3}—mqymw br lšmš br ḤPRY.

ḤPRTM (*m*) **2.** *RTP* 625b—[ml]kw ḤPRTM.

ḤR' (*f*) **2.** *C* 4615—ḤR'.

ḤRWṢ (*m*) **2.** *RTP* 156b—ḤRWṢ ḥyrn.

ḤRŠ' (*m*) **1.** *409,* 'Wadi Hauran' 5^{4}—ḥggw br nš' ḤRŠ'. *570, C* 3937^{3}—bl'qb br ḤRŠ'. **2.** *C* 4131^{2}—tm' brt ḤRŠ'.

ḤRŠW (*m*) **1.** *435* or *436,* CaB 9^{1}—lšmšw br mqymw br ḤRŠW.

ḤRT' (*f*) **2.** *C* 4326^{1}—[ḤR]T' brt 'gylw šlmwy. *C* 4394 B^{2}—ḤRT' bt 'g'. *C* 4548^{1}—ḤRT' brt byd'.

ḤŠY (*m*) **2.** *Inv. VIII,* 39^{2}—whblt br 't'qb br ḤŠY.

ḤŠŠ (*m*) **1.** *333, C* 3915^{1}—ḤŠŠ br nš' br bwlḥ' ḤŠŠ. *336,* CaC 4^{2}—mlkw br nš' br bwlḥ' dy mtqr' ḤŠŠ. *336,* CaC 5^{2}—[ml]kw br nš' br bwlḥ' ḤŠŠ. **2.** *C* 4559^{4}—bl[ḥ'] br nš' ḤŠŠ. *C* 4560^{3}—nš' br blḥ' ḤŠŠ.

ḤTY (*m*) **1.** *345*, *C* 3980^{5}—mlkw br yrḥbwl' ḤTY. **2.** *RTP* 88b—ḤTY (?).

ṬBRYS (*m*) **2.** *C* 3903^{2}—ṬBRYS qlwdys plqs. *Inv. X*, 128^{1}—ṬBRYS qlwdys py[....

ṬYṬWYLW (*m*) **1.** *562*, StaB p. 160, A 1177^{4}—n'ry br mqymw ṬYṬWYLW.

ṬYMWN (*m*) **1.** *378*, CaB 4 A^{2}—myš' brt tymš' br ydy'bl ṬYMWN.

ṬMYS (*m*) **1.** *314*, *C* 3992^{2}—zbdlh br mqym[w] ṬM[YS]. **2.** *C* 4408—ksp' brt ṬM(Y)S. *C* 4409^{4}—mr' bt yrḥb(w)l' ṬMYS br ydy'bl.

ṬMS (*m*) **2.** *C* 4410—...]bwl ṬMS.

Ṭ'Y (*m*) **2.** 'Hypogée' p. 210, line 8—ydy'bl Ṭ'Y br mqymw. 'Hypogée' p. 221, Pl. I^{1}—nbwl' b[r] whblt b[r] Ṭ'Y. 'Hypogée' p. 223, Pl. II^{1}—q/mbwrm brt bwrp'; Ṭ'Y br bwrp'. 'Hypogée' p. 226, Pl. IV^{1}—...] br bwrp' Ṭ'Y. 'Hypogée' p. 229, Pl. V^{1}—mqymw br Ṭ'Y. 'Hypogée' p. 237, Pl. VI^{1}—Ṭ'Y br mqymw br Ṭ'Y. 'Hypogée p. 238, Pl. VII^{1}—bwrp' br mqymw br Ṭ'Y. 'Hypogée' p. 240, Pl. IX^{2}—nbwl' br m'nw Ṭ'Y. 'Hypogée' p. 241, Pl. X^{1}—...] bwrp' Ṭ'Y. 'Hypogée' p. 242, Pl. X^{2}—Ṭ'Y br mqymw. 'Hypogée' p. 242, Pl. XI^{1}—mqymw br yrḥbwl' Ṭ'Y. 'Hypogée' p. 245, Pl. XII^{1}—zbdl' br zbyd' zbdl' Ṭ'Y.

YD/R[**2.** *Inv. VIII*, 79^{1}—...]t lšmš br YD/R [.... *Inv. VIII*, 115^{2}—...] mzbt' br YD/R[....

YD' (*m*) **1.** *490*, *C* 3950^{1}—YD' br šrykw br ḥy[rn] b[r] 'lyn' ṣpr'. [*4*]*90*, *C* 3954^{1}—mrty brt YD[' br whblt] br šm'wn. *530*, *Inv. XI*, 13^{5}—YD' br m'y'. *538*, *C* 4204^{3}—ywly' 'wrly' šlmn wškny bny yrḥy šlmn br YD'. *539*, *C* 4025^{2}—YD'. *575*, *C* 3940^{3}—ywlys 'wrlys spṭmyws YD' br 'lks[nd]rws ḥyrn srykw.

YD/RBW (*m*) **2.** *C* 4491^{2}—ydy'bl br YD/RBW.

YDY[**2.** CaA 61^{2}—yrḥy br YDY[.... *Inv. VIII*, 132^{2}—ḥyrn br YDY[.... *Inv. XI*, 94^{2}—...] br YDY[....

YDY (*m*) **1.** *335*, *Inv. IX*, 7^{2}—[YD]Y br mlkw br 'gylw br 'bd'stwr br 'tz'. *335*, *Inv. IX*, 7^{3}—'gylw wYDY. *410*, Ingh. E ('Atenatan) p. 59, I^{2}—'tntn br zbd'th br YDY br tymy. *466*, *C* 3928^{5}—[zbd']t' br zbdl' YDY. [*468*], *Inv. X*, 90$^{3,\,4}$—YDY br zbdl[h] / YDY. *482*, CaB 14^{3}—YDY br kyly. *493*, *C* 4192—zbd'th br zbdl' br YDY. *500+?*, *Inv. XI*, 23$^{4,\,5}$—YDY / br tymrṣw YDY. *500+?*, *C* 4056^{3}—YDY br ḥ[.... *504*, *C* 3948^{4}—YDY [wz]bdbwl. *522*, *C* 3949^{1}—[YDY br tymrṣw br tym' gr]b'. **2.** *C* 3906^{1}—gwr' YDY. *C* 4414^{3}—ḥyrn br qrd' br YDY. *C* 4446^{2}—mlkw br YDY br ptyḥb. *C* 4447^{2}—yd'w br mlkw br YDY. *C* 4524^{4}—mrthwn brt tymrṣw br YDY grb'. *C* 4584^{3}—'qmt brt YDY. *C* 4585—šgl brt YDY. *C* 4586—bny br YDY. *RTP* 283b—mlkw br Y[DY]. *RTP* 363b—mqymw br YDY. *RTP* 660b—mqymw br YDY. *RTP* 674b—blty wYDY. *RTP* 718b—YDY 'myn. *RTP* 987a—YDY mtny. CaA 37—YDY br mqymw br YDY br rmw br ḥl'. *PNO* 72^{3}—hrms br YDY. *Inv. VIII*, 18^{2}—tbll brt YDY. *Inv. VIII*, 183 B^{2}—...] YDY. *Inv. XI*, 72—ḥyrn br YDY [.... Ingh. C p. 2, Fig. 1—ḥyrn br YDY br ḥyrn ḥnt'. 'Afrique' p. 266 A^{2}—yrḥbwl' YDY.

YDY' (*m*) **2.** CaA 57^{2}—...]l br yrḥy żẘ br YDY' br 'wr[.... Ingh. B p. 137, line 21—YDY'. Ingh. B p. 137, line 29—YDY'.

YDY'BL (*m*) **1.** *328*, *C* 3925^{2}—'zyzw br YDY'BL brky. *328*, *C* 3925^{3}—YDY['BL]. *329*, *Pal. 63*: 2^{3}—'gylw br YDY'BL br bwrp'. *330*, *C* 3924^{2}—YDY'BL br 'zyzw br YDY'[BL]. *330* (?), CaD 6$^{2,\,3}$—Y[DY'BL] / br n'b' br YDY'[BL]. *345*, *C* 3980^{6}—zbdbwl br YDY'BL 'lhw. *37*[*5*], *C* 3966^{3}—...b]r YDY'BL. *378*, CaB 4 A^{1}—YDY'BL br tymḥ' br YDY'BL br 'bd'th 'gdm. *378*, CaB 4 A^{2}—myš' brt tymš' br YDY'BL ṭymwn. *396*, *C* 3978^{4}—lšmš wzbyd' bny mlkw br YDY'BL br nš' dy mtqr' br 'bdbl. *400+?*, *Inv. XI*, 56^{3}—YDY'BL b[.... *412*, CaB 13 A$^{1,\,3}$—YDY'BL br whblt / wwhblt br 'wydlt bny / YDY'BL br 'mrš'. *4*[*23*], *Inv. X*, 69^{1}—ḥggw br yrḥy br 'g' YDY'BL. *439*, *C* 3920^{2}—tym' br lšmšy br 'g' YDY'BL. *440*, *C* 3997^{2}—zbyd['] br zbdbl YDY'BL. *453*, *C* 4561$^{2,\,4}$—YDY'BL / br 't'qb / YDY'BL / 't'qb 'qby. *457*, *C* 3911^{6}—zbdbwl w'tnwr wmlkw w'mrw wYDY'BL bny bršmš br zbdbwl. *468*, *C* 4616$^{3,\,5}$—'t'qb / br YDY'BL / br 't'qb / YDY'BL / 'qby. [*4*]*73*, *C* 4562^{3}—[tym]rṣw rb' br 't'qb br YDY'BL br 't'qb 'qby. *497*, Ingh. B p. 106, I^{1}—lšmš br lšmš br tym' w'mdy br YDY'BL. *501*, *C* 4007^{3}—YDY'BL br zb[d]' lšmš myšn. *504*, CaB 13 B$^{1,\,2}$—YDY'BL br hlydrws / [lš]mš br YDY'BL. *525*, 'Malkû' p. 106^{2}—ywlys 'wrlys YDY'BL dy mtqr' mzbn' br ywlys 'wrlys 'nynws. *532*, *C* 4020 A^{3}—dwmnyn' brt [Y]DY'BL br yrḥy. *552*, *C* 4175^{4}—ywlys 'wrlys ml' br yd'w br YDY'BL. *555*, Ingh. 'Th.' p. 129^{3}—yrḥy 'grp' yrḥy YDY'BL 'g' y't. *574*, Ingh. E (Naṣrallat) p. 110, II^{1}—ywlys 'wrlys YDY'BL br 'bdšmy' br mlk'. *576*, Ingh. E (Naṣrallat) p. 112, III^{1}—ywlys 'wrlys YDY'BL br 'bšmy' mlk'. **2.** *C* 4020 B^{3}—dwmny[n' br]t YDY'BL. *C* 4177 B—ml' br yd'w YDY'BL. *C* 4177 C—...y]d'w YDY'BL. *C* 4181 C—ml' br yd'w YDY'BL. *C* 4312^{1}—YDY'BL br mzbn' brwq'. *C* 4322^{5}—yrḥy br yrḥy br yrḥy YDY'BL y't. *C* 4324^{2}—[YDY']BL br 'g' y'tw. *C* 4346^{3}—YDY'BL br yrḥy. *C* 4352 A—...] br YDY'BL. *C* 4352 B^{3}—'t[....] brt YDY'BL. *C* 4355^{1}—Y(D)Y'BL br ḥbwl'. *C* 4364^{2}—yrḥy br Y(D)Y'BL br šm'wn 'rgn. *C* 4409^{5}—mr' bt yrḥb(w)l' ṭmys br YDYʿBL. *C* 4420^{1}—YDYʿBL br bwn' br ʿbdʿstwr. *C* 4463^{3}—nby brt khyly br YDYʿBL. *C* 4468^{3}—ḥggw br ʿg' br YDYʿB[L]. *C* 4491^{1}—YDYʿBL br yd/rbw. *C* 4555^{1}—[YDY]ʿBL br [m]qymw klb[y]. *C* 4556^{3}—mlkw [br] pṣy'l [YDY]ʿBL. *C* 4603^{1}—YDYʿBL br zbdʿth. *C* 4603^{5}—zbdʿth br YDYʿBL. Ingh. D Pl. X^{1}—zbyd' br YDYʿBL. *Inv. VIII*, 47^{1}—Y[D]Yʿ[BL] br tm' tymn'. *Inv. VIII*, 108^{5} ḥgy br yrḥy br ʿg' YDYʿBL. *Inv. XI*, 30^{4}—yrḥbwl' [br] YDYʿBL. *RTP* 6b—YDYʿBL. *RTP* 19b—lšmš YDYʿBL. *RTP* 250b—dynys YDYʿBL šlm'. *RTP* 715b—zbd' YDYʿBL. 'Hypogée' p. 210, line 7—YDYʿBL ṭʿy br mqymw.

YDYʿT (*f*) **2.** *C* 4304^{1}—YDYʿT brt syʿn'. *PS* 419—YDYʿT brt syʿwn' br tym['].

YDʿW (*m*) **1.** *552*, *C* 4175^{4}—ywlys 'wrlys ml' br YDʿW br ydyʿbl. **2.** *C* 4060$^{2, 3}$—YDʿW br / [ʿg]ylw br YDʿW. *C* 4177 B—ml' br YDʿW ydyʿbl. *C* 4177 C—. . . Y]DʿW ydyʿbl. *C* 4181 C—ml' br YDʿW ydyʿbl. *C* 4447^{1}—YDʿW br mlkw br ydy. *RTP* 38b—YDʿW tybwl ḥyrn ṣt'. *RTP* 291b—ḥyrn YDʿW. *RTP* 633b—YDʿW ʿbdy. *Inv. VII*, 10—šlmlt br YDʿW br šlmlt.

YDʿY (*m*) **2.** CaD 5^{1}—rb'l br ʿwyd' br YDʿY.

YDʿNW (*m*) **2.** *RTP* 802a—YDʿNW.

YHYB' (*m*) **1.** *543*, *C* 4030^{4}—ḥggw br YHYB' br yrḥy dk'. *555*, StaB p. 160, A 1206^{4}—ml' br [Y]HYB' ʿnn. *572*, *C* 4050^{3}—[ḥ]ggw br YHYB' yrḥy dk'. **2.** *RTP* 552b—YHYB'. *RTP* 798a—YHYB'. *RTP* 813a—YHYB'.

YWL (*m*) **1.** *544*, *C* 4031^{2}—YWL 'wr ḥlpwn' br ''ylmy zbyd' 'qwpʿ.

YWL' (*m*) **1.** *545*, *C* 4206^{1}—YWL' 'wrly' ʿg' wšlm'[. . . nb]wmr bny ḥlh.

YWLY' (*m*/*f*) **1.** *538*, *C* 4204^{2}—YWLY' 'wrly' šlmn wškny bny yrḥy šlmn br yd'. *541*, *Pal. 59*: 9 B^{3}—YWLY' 'wrly' tym' wlšmš bny 'wṭk'. *550*, Ingh. B p. 124, II^{3}—YWLY' 'wrly' šlmt brt ʿbdʿstwr br yrḥbwl'. *550*, Ingh. B p. 124, II^{5}—YWLY' 'wrly' mlkw br ʿgylw br šlmn. *552*, *C* 4175^{2}—YWLY' 'wrly' btmlkw brt zbdbwl br šʿdy. *552*, CaD 36 C^{3}—YWLY' 'wrly' ḥyrn wmlwk' bny grmn'. *574*, Ingh. E (Naṣrallat) p. 110, II^{2}—YWLY' 'wrly' 'mt' brt bwlḥzy mqymw. *576*, Ingh. E (Naṣrallat) p. 112, III^{7}—YWLY' 'wrly' 'mt' brt bwlḥzy mqymw. *578*, Ingh. E (Malkû) p. 104, XII^{6}—YWLY' 'wrly' 'gtwn' br bs' grmn'. **2.** CaB 2 B^{1}—YWLY' 'wrly' 'byhn. CaB 2 B^{2}—YWLY' 'wrly' tymrṣ[w]. *Inv. VIII*, 58^{1}—YWLY' 'wrly' nwry wzbdbwl w[ʿgylw] bny mq[y. . . .] ḥbzy.

YWLYWS (*m*) **1.** *535*, Ingh. E (Malê) p. 78, IV^{1}—YWLYWS 'wrlys ml' br ḥyrn br ssn. **2.** *C* 4401^{1}—mrqws YWLYWS mksmws 'rsṭyds.

YWLYS (*m*) **1.** *419*, *Inv. X*, 129^{1}—g'ys YWLYS ḥyrn br 'lhbl. [*4*]*47*, *Inv. X*, 81^{1}—YWLYS mksms. *525*, Ingh. E (Malkû) p. 97, VI^{1}—YWLYS 'wrlys nwrbl wml' bny mlkw rb' br mlkw mlkw nwrbl. *525*, Ingh. E (Malkû) p. 98, VII^{1}—YWLYS 'wrlys nwrbl wml' [bny] mlkw rb' br mlkw br mlkw br nwrbl. *525*, Ingh. E (Malkû) p. 98, VII^{2}—YWLYS 'wrlys ʿgylw br 'prhṭ br ḥry zbdbwl br mlkw 'swyt. *525*, Ingh. E (Malkû) p. 99, VIII^{1}—YWLYS 'wrlys nwrbl wml' bny mlkw rb' br mlkw br mlkw br nwrbl. *525*, Ingh. E (Malkû) p. 99, VIII^{2}—YWLYS 'wrlys 'grp' br 'gtps br ḥry hlydyrs yrḥbwl' br ḥyrn bwn'. *525*, 'Malkû' p. 106^{2}—YWLYS 'wrlys ydyʿbl dy mtqr' mzbn' br YWLYS 'wrlys 'nynws. *525*, 'Malkû' p. 106^{3}—YWLYS br 'wrlys ʿgylw br 'prhṭ br ḥry zbdbwl. *525*, 'Malkû' p. 106^{5}—YWLYS 'wrlys 'grp' br 'gtpws br ḥry hlydwrs yrḥbwl'. *525*, 'Malkû' p. 106^{12}—YWLYS 'wrlys nš' br brʿth. *525*, 'Malkû' p. 106^{13}—YWLYS 'wrlys yrḥbwl' br mlkw. *526*, Ingh. E (Malê) p. 77, III^{1}—YWLYS 'wrlys ml' br ḥyrn br ssn. *526*, Ingh. E (Malê) p. 77, III$^{1, 2}$—YWLYS 'wrlys ḥyrn wYWLYS 'wrlys 'b' / bny YWLYS 'wrlys mqy br yrḥy. *529*, *C* 4203^{2}—[YWLYS] 'wr[lys] rp[bwl b]r ʿtʿqb [br] rpbwl br ʿtʿ[qb] dy mtqr' nb[wzbd]. *535*, Ingh. E (Malê) p. 78, IV^{1}—YWLYS 'wrlys ʿbsy br ḥnyn' br ḥnyn' br ʿg' yrq. *538*, *C* 4204^{3}—YWLYS 'wrlys yrḥbwl' br mqymw npry. *540*, Ingh. E ('Atenatan) p. 60, II^{1}—YWLYS 'wrlys mqy br zbdbwl mqy dwḥy. *543*, CaA 40^{5}—YWLYS 'wrlys hrms br ḥry 'wrl[ys . . . . *545*, *C* 4206^{1}—[YWL]YS 'wrlys bwlm' br zbdbwl br bwlm' nyny'. *545*, *C* 4206^{3}—YWLYS 'wrlys bwlm' br zbdbwl b[r bwlm' nyny' . . . . b]rt [n]b[w]d' br tym' br nbwmw'. *545*, Ingh. E (Malê) p. 82, V^{1}—YWLYS 'wrlys ml' br ḥyrn br ml' ḥyrn ssn. *545*, Ingh. E (Malê) p. 82, V^{2}—YWLYS 'wrlys šyby br hrms mrq'. *546*, Ingh. E (Malê) p. 84, VI^{1}—YWLYS 'wrlys ml' br 'wrlys ḥyrn br ml' ḥyrn ssn. *546*, Ingh. E (Malê) p. 84, VI^{2}—YWLYS 'wrlys ḥlpt' br mqymw zbd'. *546*, Ingh. E (Malê) p. 84, VII^{2}—YWLYS 'wrlys ml' br ḥyrn ml'. *546*, Ingh. E (Malê) p. 84, VII^{4}—YWLYS 'wrlys zbdbwl br zbdbwl khylw. *547*, *C* 4209—YWLYS 'wrlys mrwn' br ml' dy [mtqr' mzbn]' br 'drynws. *547*, *C* 4209—[YWLYS 'wrlys zbyd'] br ʿštwr zbyd'. *547*, *C* 4209—YWLYS 'wrlys tydrws br ['grp' br mrql']. *548*, Ingh. E (Malê) p. 86, VIII^{1}—YWLYS 'wrlys ḥyrn br mqy yrḥy. *548*, Ingh. E (Malê) p. 86, VIII^{3}—YWLYS 'wrlys 'sy[.] br ḥnyn' šmʿwn. *552*, *C* 4175^{3}—YWLYS 'wrlys ml' br ydʿw br ydyʿbl. *552*, Ingh. E (Malkû) p. 100, IX^{2}—YWLYS 'wrlys ʿg' br rwḥbl. *552*, Ingh. E (Malkû) p. 100, IX^{3}—YWLYS 'wrlys lmlk' br šlmn gpn. *552*, CaD 36 C^{4}—YWLYS 'wrlys typyls br tymrṣw [z]byd'. *554*, *C* 3932^{1}—

YWLYS 'wrlys zbdl' br mlkw br mlkw nšwm. *554*, *C* 3932^{7}—YWLYS [prysqws]. *558*, *C* 3933^{1}—YWLYS 'wrlys zbyd' br mqymw br zbyd' 'štwr byd'. *566*, *C* 3934^{1}—YWLYS 'wrlys 'g' dy mtqr' slwqws br 'zyzw 'zyzw š'yl'. *569*, *C* 3936^{1}—YWLYS 'wrlys šlmlt br ml' 'bdy. *574*, *C* 3939^{3}—YWLYS 'w(r)lys **nb**wzbd br š'dw ḥyr'. *574*, Ingh. E (Naṣrallat) p. 110, II^{1}—YWLYS 'wrlys ydy'bl br 'bdšmy' br mlk'. *575*, *C* 3940^{2}—YWLYS 'wrlys spṭmyws yd' br 'lks[nd]rws ḥyrn srykw. *576*, Ingh. E (Naṣrallat) p. 112, III^{1}—YWLYS 'wrlys ydy'bl br 'bšmy' mlk'. [*576*], *C* 3941^{3}—[YWLYS 'wrlys spṭmy]ws ml[kw br mlwk' nšwm]. *578*, *C* 3943^{3}—YWLYS 'wrlys šlm' br qsyn' br m'ny. **2.** *C* 4211^{1}—YWLYS 'wrlys 'wṭk' ḥgy. *C* 4211^{3}—[gys YW]LY[S hrmys]. *Inv. IX*, 30^{1}—[YWLYS] 'wrlys [nbwmy br tymšm]š bwn' [šby.... *Inv. X*, 115^{1}—YWLYS 'wrlys mlkw br wsḥw br mlkw br wsḥw nbwl'. *Inv. X*, 126^{1}—YWLYS 'wrlys lšmš br tymw.

YM[2. *Inv. VIII*, 170^{2}—...] brt YM[....

YML' (*m*) **1.** *547*, *C* 4032^{3}—mqym[w] br YML'. *551*, StaB p. 156, A 1175^{4}—yrḥbwl' br mqymw YML'. *555*, StaB p. 159, A 1176^{3}—ḥyrn br YML' mqymw. **2.** *C* 4081^{4}—tymrṣw w't'mn wYML'. *C* 4448^{3}—[bt]štg' b[r]t YML'. *C* 4485^{3}—r't' brt YML[']. *C* 4589—YML' br tymlt br ymlkw kwmy. *C* 4602^{1,3}—YML' br / yrḥy br / YML'. *C* 4622^{4}—'td/rn brt YML'.

YMLKW (*m*) **1.** [*2*]*89*, StaD p. 512, 1^{4}—mqy[mw....] br YMLKW. *3*[*94*], *C* 4123—YMLKW br mqymw dy mtqrh 'qlyš br mlkw br bl'qb. *394*, *C* 4123 *bis*^{2}—YMLKW br mqymw 'qlyš br mlkw 'bnyt br bl'qb br myk' br mt'. *522*, *Inv. X*, 53^{3}—YMLKW br whblt gwrny. **2.** *C* 4445^{5}—khylw br mškw br YMLK[W]. *C* 4589—yml' br tymlt br YMLKW kwmy. *C* 4590—lšmš br tymlt br YMLKW kwmy. *C* 4591 A—mlkw wyrḥy bny YMLKW br whblt. *C* 4591 B—mlkw wyrḥy bny YMLKW br whblt. *C* 4617^{2}—zbd't' br YMLKW nš'. *RTP* 197b—tymrṣw wYMLKW wš'dy. *RTP* 761a—YMLKW mqymw 'qlyš. *PS* 148—whblt br YMLKW br whblt. *Inv. VIII*, 29^{2}—tymlt br YMLKW. *Inv. XI*, 79^{2}—YMLKW br zb[d'....

Y'QWB (*m*) **1.** *523*, *C* 4201^{2}—zbyd' [wš]mw'l bny lwy br Y'QWB br šmw'l. *542*, *C* 4029^{3}—kyly br Y'QWB tymrṣw. **2.** *RTP* 994a—Y'QWB.

Y'T (*m*) **1.** (*536*), *PNO* 73^{2}—[r]b'l br yrḥy Y'T. *555*, Ingh. 'Th.' p. 129^{3}—yrḥy 'grp' yrḥy ydy'bl 'g' Y'T. **2.** *C* 4322^{6}—yrḥy br yrḥy br yrḥy ydy'bl Y'T. *C* 4323^{4}—'g' br yrḥy Y'T. *C* 4325^{6}—yrḥy br 'g' Y'T. *C* 4326^{6}—rb'l yrḥy Y'T. *Inv. XI*, 69—...] 'gylw br Y'T br y[....

Y'TW (*m*) **2.** *C* 4324^{4}—[ydy']bl br 'g' Y'TW.

YQRWR (*m*) **1.** *500*, *C* 4195^{5}—bwn' br bwlḥ' br bwn' br YQRWR.

YR/D[2. *Inv. VIII*, 79^{1}—...]t lšmš br YR/D[.... *Inv. VIII*, 115^{2}—...] mzbt' br YR/D[....

YR/DBW (*m*) **2.** *C* 4491^{2}—ydy'bl br YR/DBW.

YRḤ[2. *Inv. VIII*, 43^{2}—...] br YRḤ[....

YRḤBWL' (*m*) **1.** *345*, *C* 3980^{5}—mlkw br YRḤBWL' ḥty. *345*, *C* 3980^{5}—YRḤBWL' br tymrṣw 'brwq. *37*[*5*], *C* 3966^{2}—šlmlt br [YRḤBW]L' br nwrbl. *400+?*, CaD 7 B^{1}—...] br YRḤBWL' br zbyd' br tymy. *400*, 'Fouilles' p. 170^{1}—YRḤBWL' br mlkw br lšmš br ḥnbl ''by. *400*, 'Fouilles' p. 172^{3}—[YRḤBWL' br mlkw br] lšmš br ḥ[nbl ''by]. [*4*]*25*, *C* 3974^{2}—b'ly br YRḤBWL'. *425*, *C* 3986^{2}—nbwzbd wYRḤBWL' bny brnbw br nbwzbd br zbdl' 'knby. *425*, *C* 3994 A^{5}—mqy[mw] br YRḤBWL' gml'. *425*, *C* 3994 B^{5}—mq[ymw] br YRḤBWL' gml'. *425*, *C* 3994 C^{5}—mqymw br YRḤBWL' gml'. *426*, CaD 21^{1}—'wydw wmlkw wYRḤBWL[' wḥggw bny] bwlm' br 'wydy br bwlm' 'db. *444*, *C* 3998 A^{2}—[zbdbwl] br YRḤBWL' br lšmšy [ḥyrn]. *447*, *C* 3968^{2}—YRḤBWL' br [.... [*449*], *Inv. X*, 114^{1}—YRḤBWL' br lšmš [.... *449*, CaB 8^{2}—pplys 'lys tybwl wpplys 'lys YRḤBWL' bny mlkw tybwl ṣm'. *450*, *C* 3931^{3}—bryky br 'mrš' br YRḤBWL'. *458*, *PNO* 55 B—mqymw YRḤBWL'. *46*[.], CaD 11^{4}—YRḤB[WL' br ml]kw br 'g'. *467*, *C* 4241^{3}—'m[rt] br lšmš br YRḤBWL[']. *483*, CaD 20^{2}—...YR]ḤBWL' [.... *486*, *C* 3914^{1,2}—YRḤBWL' [br] / 'g' w'wyd' br ḥdwdn bny YRḤBWL' br ḥdwdn br zbdbwl br ḥdw[dn] prmwn. *522*, *Inv. X*, 53^{1}—YRḤBWL' br mqymw br šrykw. *525*, Ingh. E (Malkû) p. 99, VIII^{2}—ywlys 'wrlys 'grp' br 'gtps br ḥry hlydyrs YRḤBWL' br ḥyrn bwn'. *525*, 'Malkû' p. 106^{6}—ywlys 'wrlys 'grp' br 'gtpws br ḥry hlydwrs YRḤBWL'. *525*, 'Malkû' p. 106^{13}—ywlys 'wrlys YRḤBWL' br mlkw. *538*, *C* 4204^{3}—ywlys 'wrlys YRḤBWL' br mqymw npry. *546*, *Inv. XI*, 1^{2}—YRḤBWL' wbrḥwm ''ylm w'qm' [w]'t'm. *550*, Ingh. B p. 124, II^{4}—ywly' 'wrly' šlmt brt 'bd'stwr br YRḤBWL'. *551*, StaB p. 156, A 1175^{3}—YRḤBWL' br mqymw yml'. *552*, *C* 4039^{3,4}—YRḤB[WL' br / YR]ḤBWL' ḥyq[.... *555*, Ingh. 'Th.' p. 129^{9}—YRḤBWL'. *562*, Ingh. B p. 104^{2}—YRḤBWL' br sbyn' br tym'. *563*, StaB p. 97, line 7—[q]ryn br ḥyrn br YRḤBWL'. *574*, *Inv. XI*, 20^{4}—[Y]RḤBWL' br YRḤBWL' 'rg'. *585*, Ingh. E (Malkû) p. 106, XIII^{6}—tm' brt 'bd'swdr br YRḤBWL'. **2.** *C* 4058^{3}—[mqy]mw br YRḤBWL' br [gml']. *C* 4072^{3}—[m]lkw wYRḤB[WL']. *C* 4086^{4}—sbyns br YRḤBWL' yrḥy. *C* 4215^{2}—[YRḤBWL']. *C* 4238^{1}—mrthwn [br]t lšmš br YRḤBWL' škybl. *C* 4242^{4}—lšm[š] br YRḤBWL[']. *C* 4329 A^{2}—YRḤBWL' br zbd't'. *C* 4333

A^{1}—YRḤBWL’ br mlkw. *C* 4334^{3}—mtn’ br br bwn’ br YRḤBWL’ šlmwy br bwn’. *C* 4335^{5}—mrt’ brt mlkw YRḤBWL’. *C* 4336^{4}—YRḤBWL’ br lšmšy br tym’. *C* 4337^{1}—YRḤBWL’ br rb’l šlm’. *C* 4349^{2}—YRḤBWL’ br whblt [gw]r’. *C* 4356^{1}—[m‘]ny br [YR]ḤBWL’ [.... *C* 4398^{2}—YRḤ(B)WL’ br šm‘wn. *C* 4398 *bis*—YRḤBWL’ br šm‘wn. *C* 4405 A^{1}—YRḤBWL’ br ml’. *C* 4406—YRḤBWL’ br ml’. *C* 4407—...brt] YRḤBWL’ br ml’. *C* 4409^{3}—mr’ bt YRḤB(W)L’ ṭmys br ydy‘bl. *C* 4411^{2}—’lyt [bt] YRḤB[WL’]. *C* 4411^{4}—YRḤB[WL’] nš’ ‘g’. *C* 4417^{5}—b‘ltg[’] brt YRḤBW[L’]. *C* 4421 A^{2}—šlmt brt ‘bd‘stwr YRḤBWL’. *C* 4422^{2}—‘bd‘stwr br YRḤBWL’. *C* 4535 B^{1}—YRḤBWL’ br tm’. *C* 4618—ml[k]’ br YRḤBWL’ br bwrp’ br ml[k]w. ‘Inscriptions’ p. 125, Pl. II—YRḤBWL’ br [..]b’ bn’ (?). Ingh. D, Pl. VIII^{2}—YRḤBWL’ br nš’ ‘g’ šlm’. Ingh. E (Malê) p. 79 C—mrty brt YRḤBWL’. *PS* 167—ḥbyby r[b’] br YRḤBWL’ br nwrbl. *PS* 210—mzbn’ br YRḤBWL’ rpbwl bgdn. CaA 36^{4}—YRḤBWL’ br mlkw ’‘b. CaA 82^{2}—m‘ny br YRḤBWL’. CaD 25^{11}—YRḤBWL’. *Pal. 61*: 20—...] brt YRḤB[WL’]. *PNO* 79^{4}—mry’ br YRḤBWL[’]. *Inv. VIII*, 31^{2}—YRḤBWL’ br tym’ br ’zmr. *Inv. VIII*, 115^{1}—...YR]ḤBWL’ šwyr’ [.... *Inv. VIII*, 156 A^{3}—hgy brt YRḤBWL’. *Inv. VIII*, 156 B^{1}—...YRḤB]WL’ [.... *Inv. VIII*, 165^{3}—whblt br ‘gylw br YRḤBWL’. *Inv. VIII*, 174^{3}—ḥyrn br YRḤBWL[’]. *Inv. VIII*, 176^{3}—...YR]ḤBWL’ [.... *Inv. VIII*, 191^{3}—...YR]ḤBWL’ [.... *Inv. XI*, 30^{3}—YRḤBWL’ [br] ydy‘bl. *Inv. XI*, 64—‘bdbl [Y]RḤBWL’. *RTP* 15b—YRḤBWL’. *RTP* 15b—YRḤBWL’ br šby. *RTP* 22b—YRḤBWL’ br šby. *RTP* 31a—šlmn YRḤBWL’ mlkw ’‘b[y]. *RTP* 34a—šlmn YRḤBWL’ mlkw ’‘by. *RTP* 35a—YRḤBWL’ lrmn. *RTP* 35b—YRḤBWL’. *RTP* 188b—šby YRḤBWL’ mqymw tymrṣw. *RTP* 289a—YRḤBWL’. *RTP* 302b—YRḤBWL’ br mtn’ br‘th. *RTP* 421b—YRḤBWL’ ‘wydw. *RTP* 441b—YRḤBWL’ zbyd’. *RTP* 763a—YRḤBWL’ mlkw ’‘by. *Journal asiatique*, 12 (1918), 281 no. v—r‘t’ brt ‘gylw br YRḤBWL’. ‘Hypogée’ p. 242, Pl. XI^{1}—mqymw br YRḤBWL’ ṭ‘y. ‘Afrique’ p. 266 A^{2}—YRḤBWL’ ydy. ‘Wadi Hauran’ 10^{1}—YRḤBWL’ br lšmš br mqymw dy mtqr’ br ‘zwlt. Ben-Hayyim p. 146, V^{4}—YRḤBWL’ br tybwl.

YRḤY (*m*) **1.** *373*, *Pal. 63*: 3^{6}—ḥlypy br YRḤY ’lhw. *378*, CaA 30^{1}—YRḤY br lšmš br r‘y. *397*, *Inv. X*, 127^{1}—YRḤY br zbdl’ qr[.... *400+?*, *Pal. 63*: 4^{2}—YRḤY [.... *409*, ‘Wadi Hauran’ 5^{8}—nbwl’ YRḤY [.... *[4]19*, CaD 36 A^{3}—YRḤY br b[r]yky br [ty]mrṣw. *4[23]*, *Inv. X*, 69^{1}—ḥggw br YRḤY br ‘g’ ydy‘bl. *[4]25*, *C* 3974^{4}—YRḤY. *425*, *C* 3994 A^{5}—YRḤ[Y] br nwrbl šgry. *425*, *C* 3994 B^{5}—YR[ḤY] br nwrbl šgry. *425*, *C* 3994 C^{5}—YRḤY br nwrbl šgry. *425*, *C* 4374^{4}—’l’ brt YRḤY ’bb. *425*, *C* 4374 *bis*^{3}—’l’ brt YRḤY ’bb. *440*, *C* 4164—mqymw br zbyd’ br YRḤY. *[4]42*, *C* 3959^{2}—[ml’] br YRḤY l[šmš] r‘y. *[442]*, *Inv. X*, 38—YRḤY br nbwzbd br [.... *445*, Ingh. B p. 94, I^{1}—YRḤY br mqymw. *466*, *C* 3928^{1}—mrqs ’l[p]y[s] YR[ḤY br ḥyrn br ’](b)gr. *467*, CaD 28 B^{1}—[mr]qs ’lpys YRḤY b[r ḥyr]n ’bgr. *468*, *C* 3960^{2}—mrqs ’lps YRḤY br ḥyrn ’bgr. *468*, *C* 3960^{3}—ḥyrn br YRḤY br tym’. *468*, *C* 3960^{5}—ḥbyby br YRḤY br ḥyrn. *[46]8*, *Inv. X*, 77^{1}—[mrqs ’lpys YRḤY br ḥyrn] ’bgr. *[468]*, *Inv. X*, 90^{1}—mrqws ’lpys YRḤY br ḥyrn ’bgr. *[468]*, *Inv. X*, 96^{1}—[mrqs ’lpys YRḤY br ḥyrn ’bgr]. *[469]*, CaA 8^{1}—mrq[s ’lps YRḤY b]r ḥ[yrn ’bgr]. *[469]*, CaA 8^{3}—bl[šwr br YRḤY br tym’]. *470*, CaD 28 A^{1}—mrqs ’lpys YRḤY br ḥyrn ’bgr. *470*, CaD 28 C^{1}—’lpys mrqs YRḤY br ḥyrn ’bgr. *470*, *Pal. 60*: 4$^{1, 3}$—YRḤY / br ‘gylw / [b]r YRḤY. *480*, *C* 4236—YRḤY br mlkw br YRḤY ḥwml. *486*, StaA p. 52, 2^{3}—[Y]RḤY br ḥlpt’ br YRḤY br ḥlpt’. *487*, *Inv. VIII*, 114^{2}—šgl brt ḥry YRḤY. *488*, *C* 4004^{2}—ḥyrn br [m]qy[mw] br YRḤY. *494* or *493*, *Inv. X*, 4^{1}—YRḤY br mq[y]mw br zbd‘th dk’. *[49]6*, *C* 4196—[‘wyd’ br YRḤY br ml’ br ’pw...]. *500+?*, *Inv. XI*, 9^{3}—gdy’ b[r YR]ḤY [br] gd’. *500+?*, *PNO* 31^{1}—YRḤ[Y br] yrḥyb[wl’]. *504*, CaB 13 B^{3}—[m]zbn’ wYRḤY wzbd‘t’ bny ‘wydlt. *505*, Ingh. B p. 95, II^{3}—’qmt bt YRḤY br mqymw. *526*, Ingh. E (Malê) p. 77, III^{2}—ywlys ’wrlys ḥyrn wywlys ’wrlys ’b’ bny ywlys ’wrlys mqy br YRḤY. *530*, *C* 4018^{4}—mqy (son of) YRḤY br zbyd[’] ’lpy. *532*, *C* 4020 A^{3}—dwmnyn’ brt [y]dy‘bl br YRḤY. *(536)*, *PNO* 73^{2}—[r]b’l br YRḤY y‘t. *(536)*, *PNO* 73^{3}—‘g[’] br YRḤ[Y]. *538*, *C* 4204^{3}—ywly’ ’wrly’ šlmn wškny bny YRḤY šlmn br yd’. *539*, *C* 4025^{2}—YRḤY. *539*, StaF p. 40, 2—mlkw br YRḤY. *542*, StaB p. 154, A 1208^{1}—[YR]ḤY. *543*, *C* 4030^{4}—ḥggw br yhyb’ br YRḤY dk’. *547*, *C* 3902$^{1, 2}$—YRḤY br ḥlypy br / YRḤY br lšmš š‘dw. *548*, Ingh. E (Malê) p. 86, VIII^{2}—ywlys ’wrlys ḥyrn br mqy YRḤY. *549*, Ingh. E (Malê) p. 88, IX^{3}—’wrlys ḥyrn br mqy br YRḤY. *550*, *C* 4034^{4}—mzbn’ b[r] YRḤY kyly. *551*, StaB p. 154, A 1204^{6}—YRḤY br šlmw. *552*, *C* 4039^{5}—YRḤY. *555*, Ingh. ‘Th.’ p. 129^{2}—YRḤY ’grp’ YRḤY ydy‘bl ‘g’ y‘t. *562*, StaB p. 164, A 1178^{3}—YRḤY br ‘gylw br skyy. *572*, *C* 4050^{3}—[ḥ]ggw br yhyb’ YRḤY dk’. *575*, *C* 4048^{1}—YRḤY br nbwd‘ br mqy. *583*, CaA 31^{3}—...] ml’ br YRḤY ml’. *583*, CaA 31^{5}—’t‘qb br YRḤY. **2.** *C* 3961^{1}—...br] ’py br YRḤY br [.... *C* 4086^{5}—sbyns br yrḥbwl’ YRḤY. *C* 4091^{1}—YRḤY br [.... *C* 4207—YRḤY br nš’ mky. *C* 4208—YRḤY mky. *C* 4234—šlmt brt YRḤY. *C* 4283^{5}—YRḤY. *C* 4284^{5}—YRḤY. *C* 4313^{5}—ḥnyn’ [Y]RḤY. *C* 4314^{2}—YRḤY br ḥnyn’. *C* 4322$^{2, 3, 4}$—YRḤY / br YRḤY / br YRḤY / ydy‘bl y‘t. *C* 4323^{3}—‘g’ br YRḤY y'ṯ. *C* 4325^{4}—YRḤY br 'g' y'ṯ. *C* 4326^{5}—rb'l YRḤY y'ṯ. *C* 4346^{4}—ydy'bl br YRḤY. *C* 4364^{1}—YRḤY br y(d)y'bl br šm'wn 'rgn. *C* 4381^{1}—YRḤY br 'lhbl. *C* 4383^{2,3}—bty brt / YRḤY br / YRḤY. *C* 4384^{2}—bty brt YRḤY. *C* 4428^{3}—'myt brt YRḤY. *C* 4429^{2}—mrty brt YRḤY. *C* 4430^{3}—'gylw br YRḤY. *C* 4431^{3}—bt'ty brt YRḤY br ḥyrn. *C* 4461^{5}—'yt' brt ''ylmy YRḤY. *C* 4467^{2}—mlkw br YRḤY 'š'[..]r. *C* 4471^{1}—YRḤY br mtny br 'g'. *C* 4479 A^{1}—YRḤY br bwn'. *C* 4480^{2}—ḥgt brt YRḤY br zbdlh krḥ. *C* 4481^{1}—...YRḤ]Y kr[ḥ] br nṣr'. *C* 4483^{3}—šl' brt ḥṭry br YRḤY. *C* 4483^{5}—YRḤY b[r] ḥlpt'. *C* 4484^{2}—ḥṭry br YRḤY br ḥlpt'. *C* 4485^{6}—ḥṭry br YRḤY. *C* 4522^{2}—[n]by brt YRḤY br zgwg. *C* 4531^{1}—YRḤY br zbd't' pzg'. *C* 4532^{2}—lwy' brt YRḤY br 'gyly. *C* 4535 A^{2}—sbbw br YRḤ[Y] bwn'. *C* 4537 A^{1}—YRḤY br 'g'. *C* 4538^{4}—ḥb' brt 'g' YRḤY. *C* 4539^{3}—'[ty] b[rt] YR[ḤY]. *C* 4543^{1}—YRḤY br sbn'. *C* 4558^{1}—YRḤY br nš' [br m]q[y]m[w]. *C* 4564^{3}—...] br [z/']bd' br YRḤY. *C* 4574^{2}—'qmt brt YRḤY šg'. *C* 4587—YRḤY br gyn'. *C* 4591 A—mlkw wYRḤY bny ymlkw br whblt. *C* 4591 B—mlkw wYRḤY bny ymlkw br whblt. *C* 4594 B—YRḤY. *C* 4598^{5}—tyrdt YRḤY. *C* 4602^{2}—yml' br YRḤY br yml'. *C* 4607—[Y]RḤY br / [YR]ḤY. *C* 4607. YRḤY / YRḤY. *C* 4624—YRḤY br šlmn. 'Iraq' p. 63^{6}, Pl. 8—YRḤY br tymrṣw br šṭ'. 'Euphrate' p. 47^{5}—YRḤY. *PS* 192—YRḤY br zbd'th pg'. *PS* 205—zbdbwl br YRḤY. *PS* 371—'byn' brt tyrdt br YRḤY. Ingh. D Pl. IX^{2}—'l' brt YRḤY. 'IP' p. 154, 10^{1}—YRḤY br zbd'th ḥnbl. CaA 25^{3}—[m]'ny br YRḤY [.... CaA 57^{1}—...]l br YRḤY żẇ br ydy' br 'wr[.... CaA 61^{2}—YRḤY br ydy[.... CaA 76^{2}—'wydlt [b]r YRḤY nṣr'. CaA 78^{4}—'l' brt 'yd'n br YRḤY mqy. CaA 83^{1}—YRḤY brt ḥyrn. CaD 36 G^{2}—nṣ' brt YRḤY br bryky. *Pal. 62*: 6^{1,3}—YRḤY br / 'dynt / br YRḤY. *Pal. 62*: 7^{4}—'sty' brt 'dynt [br] YRḤY. StaC p. 38, 8—'t'm brt tly' br (Y)RḤY. *PNO* 33—YRḤY. *PNO* 67—lšmš br šky YRḤY. *Inv. VIII*, 6^{1}—YRḤY br blšwr. *Inv. VIII*, 8^{2}—ḥyrn b[r] YRḤY. *Inv. VIII*, 19^{2}—'wydlt [b]r YRḤY nṣr'. *Inv. VIII*, 37^{3}—mqy[mw] YRḤY. *Inv. VIII*, 64^{3}—'tšb' bt YRḤY mlkw. *Inv. VIII*, 94^{2}—[']gylw br YRḤY br ḥry ḥy[rn]. *Inv. VIII*, 108^{3}—ḥgy br YRḤY br 'g' ydy'bl. *Inv. VIII*, 134^{3}—ḥn' brt YRḤY. *Inv. X*, 128^{3}—mrq[s] 'lpys [Y]RḤY br ḥyr[n 'bgr]. *Inv. XI*, 33^{2}—šm'wn br [Y]RḤY šm'[wn]. *Inv. XI*, 39^{2}—mzbn' br Y[RḤ]Y [b]r šm'wn. *Inv. XI*, 48^{2}—YRḤY b[r.... *Inv. XI*, 50^{2}—mlkw br YRḤY sg'. *Inv. XI*, 53—YRḤY br šḥry. *RTP* 11b—YRḤY. *RTP* 88a—YRḤY. *RTP* 189b—YRḤY br'. *RTP* 217b—YRḤY klb'. *RTP* 227b—YRḤY b[r] zbd'. *RTP* 267b—ḥyrn YRḤY. *RTP* 274b—YRḤY br bwrp'. *RTP* 316b—t[yml]t br YRḤY. *RTP* 429a—YRḤY 'g'. *RTP* 429b—YRḤY 'g'. *RTP* 489b—YRḤY. *RTP* 493a—'b' YRḤY. *RTP* 493b—mzbn' YRḤY. *RTP* 551a—YRḤY. *RTP* 557b—YRḤY byly or kyly. *RTP* 575b—YRḤY lšmš. *RTP* 613b—YRḤY b[.... *RTP* 640b—YRḤY zbd'th [b]wrp'. *RTP* 715a—YRḤY 'b'. *RTP* 779a—rpbwl YRḤY. *RTP* 783b—ḥyr' YRḤY 'mrt. *RTP* 797a—YRḤY. *RTP* 797b—YRḤY. *RTP* 798b—YRḤY. *RTP* 978a—YRḤY 'bšy. *RTP* 983a—YRḤY. *RTP* 991b—YR(ḤY). 'Wadi Hauran' 3^{5}—qwp' br šrykw YRḤY. 'Wadi Hauran' 12^{3}—zbd'th [br ḥ]dydw [zbd]'th br YRḤY br šdd'. *Michalowski*, p. 314—YRḤY.

YRḤYB[WL'] (*m*) **1.** *500+?*, *PNO* 31^{2}—yrḥ[y br] YRḤYB[WL'] or YRḤY b[r....

YRḤYW (*m*) **2.** *Pal. 61*: 17^{3}—[ḥ]gt brt YRḤYW br nbwd'.

YRQ (*m*) **1.** *535*, Ingh. E (Malê) p. 78, IV^{1}—ywlys 'wrlys 'bsy br ḥnyn' br ḥnyn' br 'g' YRQ. **2.** *C* 4557^{4}—ḥnyn' br ḥnyn' 'g' YRQ. Ingh. E (Malê) p. 79 A—'bsy br ḥnyn' ḥnyn' YRQ. Ingh. E (Malê) p. 79 B—ḥnyn' br ḥnyn' 'g' YRQ. Ingh. E (Malê) p. 80 D—ḥnyn' br ḥnyn' ḥnyn' YRQ. Ingh. E (Malê) p. 81 G—š'dy br ḥnyn' ḥnyn' YRQ. Ingh. E (Malê) p. 82 H—š'dy br 'bsy br ḥnyn' YRQ. Ingh. E (Malê) p. 82 I—šl' brt ḥnyn' ḥnyn' YRQ.

YTM' (*m*) **1.** *471*, StaA p. 46, 1^{4}—'bnrgl br ḥr' mqy br YTM'.

KD/RNNY (*f*) **2.** *C* 4517^{1}—KD/RNNY brt mlkw bqy.

KHYLW (*m*) **1.** *304*, *C* 4109 A^{2}—'tntn br KHYLW. *304*, *C* 4109 A^{4}—KHYLW wḥyrn. *304*, *C* 4109 B^{2}—'tn[tn] br KHYLW. *304*, *C* 4109 B^{3}—KHYLW wḥyrn. *350*, CaD 31^{2}—mqymw br KHYLW br zbdbl [dy] mtqrh br zbydy. *360*, CaC 11^{3}—'wšy br KHYLW w'wšy[....]' bny ḥyrn br 'wšy. *368*, *C* 4119^{4}—'gylw br 'wšy br KHYLW. *410*, Ingh. B p. 120, I^{2}—'bd'stwr br nwrbl br KHYLW br 'tnwry 'ṣwly. *[43]3*, *Inv. X* 54^{1,2}—[m]lkw br KHYLW qymw / [br nwrbl br KHY]LW. *546*, Ingh. E (Malê) p. 84, VII^{6}—ywlys 'wrlys zbdbwl br zbdbwl KHYLW. **2.** *C* 4110^{2}—'bdbl KHYLW. *C* 4111^{1}—KHYLW wḥyrn bny 'tntn. *C* 4233—KHYLW. *C* 4445^{2}—KHYLW br mškw br ymlk[w]. *RTP* 191b—KHYLW nbwzbd. CaD 25^{4}—...] br KHYLW br bl[.... Ingh. A p. 97, 6—...] wKHYLW wzbd'th bny mlkw br ḥyrn. *Michalowski*, p. 314—'ḥy' br ḥry KHYL[W].

KHYLY (*m*) **2.** *C* 4462^{2}—'bb' brt ḥyrn br KHYLY. *C* 4463^{2}—nby brt KHYLY br ydy'bl. *Pal. 61*: 14^{4}—pplys '[....] mšy br KHYLY.

KWMY (*m*) **2.** *C* 4588—KWMY br šlmlt. *C* 4589—yml' br tymlt br ymlkw KWMY. *C* 4590—lšmš br tymlt br ymlkw KWMY.

KYLY (*m*) **1.** *482*, CaB 14^3—ydy br KYLY. [*4/5*]*92*, *C* 4527^6—ʿty brt ʿtšwr br klby br lšmš br KYLY. *542*, *C* 4029^3—KYLY br yʿqwb tymrṣw. *548*, *C* 4210^2—ḥl’ br nbwzbd br KYLY. *550*, *C* 4034^4—mzbn’ b[r] yrḥy KYLY. **2.** *C* 4101^3—ʿb’ br [KY]LY b[r ʿ]b’. *C* 4596^2—ʿtntn br KYLY br mškw b[r] ʿtd/rt br ḥyrn. *RTP* 557b—yrḥy KYLY.

KYLYWN (*m*) **1.** *581*, *PNO* 14^3—ʿgylw KYLYWN.

KYTWT (*m*) **1.** *3*[*52*], *C* 4115^{1,2}—KYTWT / br tymrṣw br KYTWT br tymḥ’ rb’. *352*, *C* 4115 *bis*^{2}—KYTWT br [tymr]ṣw. **2.** *C* 4075^{4,5}—KYTWT br / KYT[W]T. *RTP* 709a—ʿgylw KYTWT. Ingh. B Pl. XLI^5—KYTWT mzbn’ ’tʿqb.

KLB’ (*m*) **2.** *RTP* 217b—yrḥy KLB’. *RTP* 439b—’ply KLB’.

KLBY (*m*) **1.** [*4/5*]*92*, *C* 4527^4—ʿty brt ʿtšwr br KLBY br lšmš br kyly. **2.** *C* 4555^2—[ydy]ʿbl br [m]qymw KLB[Y].

KMR’ (*m*) **1.** *345*, *C* 3980^3—ḥggw br zbdlh KMR’. **2.** *C* 3929^3—š[m]rp’ wKMR’.

KSP’ (*f*) **2.** *C* 4408^1—KSP’ brt ṭm(y)s.

KʿB[W] (*m*) **2.** *Inv. VIII*, 36^1—rmy br KʿB[W] nwrbl.

KPTWT (*m*) **1.** *502*, *C* 4173^1—zbdbwl br KPTWT br br’. *536*, CaD 4^1—KPTWT br šlwm [. . . . **2.** *RTP* 731a—ʿgylw KPTWT. *RTP* 731b—šmʿwn KPTWT. *RTP* 850b—KP[TWT]. *RTP* 864b—KPTWT.

KRḤ (*m*) **2.** *C* 4480^4—ḥgt brt yrḥy br zbdlh KRḤ. *C* 4481^2—[yrḥ]y KR[Ḥ] br nṣr’.

KRYSTWS (*m*) **1.** *369*, *C* 4235^2—[lwqy]ws ’spdy[s] KRYSTWS.

KRM see DRM.

KR/DNNY (*f*) **2.** *C* 4517^1—KR/DNNY brt mlkw bqy.

KRSM’ (*m*) **1.** *493*, *Inv. XI*, 6^2—KRSM’ br ḥ[. . . .

LWY (*m*) **1.** *523*, *C* 4201^2—zbyd’ [wš]mw’l bny LWY br yʿqwb br šmw’l. *523*, *C* 4201^2—LWY. **2.** CaA 77^3—. . . L]WY br zbdl[h. . . .

LWY’ (*f*) **1.** *546*, *C* 4301 A^1—LWY’. **2.** *C* 4339^2—[L]WY’ bt [ḥ]ry ’qm[’ ḥbz]y. *C* 4532^1—LWY’ brt yrḥy br ʿgyly.

[LWQY]WS (*m*) **1.** *369*, *C* 4235^1—[LWQY]WS ’spdy[s] krystws.

LWQYS (*m*) **1.** *485*, *Inv. X*, 113^1—(L)WQYS ’nṭwnys qlsṭrṭs. *550*, Ingh. B p. 124, II^4—LWQYS ’wrlys brsmy’. **2.** *Inv. XI*, 46^2—LWQYS. *Inv. XI*, 46^3—[LW]QYS.

LWQL’ (*f*) **2.** *C* 4401^4—LWQL’.

LMLK’ (*m*) **1.** *552*, Ingh. E (Malkû) p. 100, IX^3—ywlys ’wrlys LMLK’ br šlmn gpn.

LQY (*m*) **1.** *544*, CaB 10 A^1—lšmš br ’stwrg’ [b]r lš[mš] br [b]ryky br LQY šlmn.

LQYŠW (*m*) **1.** *395*, CaD 29^2—’bgr br pṭrqls dy mtqrh ’stwrg’ br LQYŠW.

LQNYS (*m*) **2.** *RTP* 700b—LQNYS brs. *RTP* 776a—LQNYS brs. *RTP* 835a—LQNYS br[s]. *Inv. X*, 130^1—g’ys [LQN]YS plwynws br bwrp’.

LRMN (*m*) **2.** *RTP* 35a—yrḥbwl’ LRMN.

LŠMŠ (*m*) **1.** *352*, *C* 4115 *bis*^{4}—LŠMŠ. *357*, CaD 1^2—LŠMŠ br tybwl br škybl. *362* or *382*, CaA 34^3—zbdbwl br ’byhn br zbdbwl br LŠMŠ br mkn’ rb’. *378*, CaA 30^1—yrḥy br LŠMŠ br rʿy. *392*, *Inv. X*, 131^1—mlkw br LŠMŠ br ḥnbl br brʿth ’ʿby. *396*, *C* 3978^3—LŠMŠ wzbyd’ bny mlkw br ydyʿbl br nš’ dy mtqr’ br ʿbdbl. *400+?*, *C* 3963^1—tymrṣw br [L]ŠMŠ br mlkw ’ʿb[y]. *400*, ‘Fouilles’ p. 170^1—yrḥbwl’ br mlkw br LŠMŠ br ḥnbl ’ʿby. *400*, ‘Fouilles’ p. 172^4—[yrḥbwl’ br mlkw br] LŠMŠ br ḥ[nbl ’ʿby]. *415*, *Inv. VIII*, 59^2—bwlḥ’ wmqymy wḥyrn wLŠMŠ wbʿl[y] bny whby br bwlḥzy. *437*, *C* 3996^4—prn(k) br ḥry LŠMŠ br šmšgrm. *440*, *C* 3955^2—[. . . . br LŠMŠ]. *440*, *C* 3955^4—LŠMŠ. [*4*]*42*, *C* 3959^2—[ml’] br yrḥy L[ŠMŠ] rʿy. [*449*], *Inv. X*, 114^1—yrḥbwl’ br LŠMŠ [. . . . [*454*], *C* 4167—LŠMŠ br nwrbl br mqymw br ʿgylw ’qml. [*4*]*58*, *C* 4458—. . .] mlkw br LŠMŠ br ḥnbl ’ʿby. *467*, *C* 4241^2—’m[rt] br LŠMŠ br yrḥbwl[’]. [*46*]*8*, *Inv. X*, 77^2—[tym’ br] tymrṣw LŠMŠ grny. *483*, CaD 20^3—. . .] LŠMŠ [. . . . *492*, *C* 4194^{2,3}—LŠMŠ / br LŠMŠ br tym’. [*4/5*]*92*, *C* 4527^5—ʿty brt ʿtšwr br klby br LŠMŠ br kyly. *497*, Ingh. B p. 106, I^1—LŠMŠ br LŠMŠ br tym’ w’mdy br ydyʿbl. *500*, *C* 4195^2—LŠMŠ br LŠMŠ br tym’. *500+?*, *C* 4056^4—LŠMŠ br š[. . . . *500+?*, *C* 4198 A^2—LŠMŠ br qm[. . . . *501*, *C* 4007^3—ydyʿbl br zb[d]’ LŠMŠ myšn. *504*, *C* 4199^3—pṣy’l br ’stwrg’ br ʿwyd br LŠMŠ br LŠMŠ. *504*, *C* 4199^{13}—šgl brt LŠMŠ br ’štwrg’ br pṣy’l. *504*, CaB 13 B^2—ydyʿbl br hlydrws [LŠ]MŠ br ydyʿbl. *505*, Ingh. B p. 95, II^2—mqymw br LŠMŠ br ḥpry. *515*, *C* 4198 B^2—[L]ŠMŠ br [’]qwp[ʿ]. *516*, *Inv. XI*, 10^3—mlkw br LŠMŠ. *54*[.], *C* 3957^3—brʿth br LŠMŠ mlkw. *541*, *Pal. 59*: 9 B^4—ywly’ ’wrly’ tym’ wLŠMŠ bny ’wṭk’. *544*, CaB 10 A^1—LŠMŠ br ’stwrg’ [b]r LŠ[MŠ] br [b]ryky br lqy šlmn. *544*, CaB 10 A^2—LŠMŠ br ’st[wrg]’ [br] lšmš. *547*, *C* 3902^2—yrḥy br ḥlypy br yrḥy br LŠMŠ š'dw. *549*, Ingh. E (Malê) p. 88, IX^{4}—'wrly' ṣmy brt LŠMŠ. *563*, StaB p. 97, line 7—[LŠ]MŠ qryn. *564*, *C* 4046^{5}—mqy br LŠMŠ. [*5*]*67*, *C* 4047^{3}—LŠMŠ. *567*, StaB p. 96, A 1173^{4}—LŠMŠ br qrynw br ml'. **2.** *C* 3904^{1}—[mqy br ml' LŠM]Š. *C* 4057^{4}—sws' br [L]ŠMŠ br 'gylw [br ty]m'. *C* 4238^{1}—mrthwn [br]t LŠMŠ br yrḥbwl' škybl. *C* 4242^{2}—LŠM[Š] br yrḥbwl[']. *C* 4288^{2}—tybwl br LŠMŠ tybwl rb'. *C* 4289^{3}—ḥlpw brt ḥlp' [br] LŠMŠ [tybwl] rb'. *C* 4325^{2}—. . .LŠM]Š [. . . . *C* 4361^{2}—'wtn br LŠMŠ 'wšy. *C* 4478 B^{1}—LŠMŠ b[r] š'd. *C* 4493^{2}—LŠMŠ škybl. *C* 4590—LŠMŠ br tymlt br ymlkw kwmy. *RTP* 19b—LŠMŠ ydy'bl. *RTP* 102b—[LŠ]MŠ [ty]mrṣw. *RTP* 195b—LŠMŠ tymrṣw. *RTP* 243a—LŠMŠ. *RTP* 362b—LŠMŠ mqymw. *RTP* 370b—whby wmqymw wLŠMŠ. *RTP* 386b—LŠMŠ. *RTP* 575b—yrḥy LŠMŠ. *RTP* 579a—LŠMŠ mqy. *RTP* 656b—[LŠM]Š ['g]ylw. *RTP* 716a—LŠMŠ. Ingh. B, Pl. XLII^{2}—LŠMŠ br rmy rp'l. CaA 62 G—. . .] LŠM[Š. . . . CaA 79^{5}—tyks' brt nṣry br LŠMŠ 'ḥyb. CaC 12^{1}—LŠMŠ br ḥlypy br 'tpny. CaD 24$^{2\,bis}$— LŠMŠ. CaD 25^{3}—. . .]š 'gylw br L[ŠMŠ. . . . *Pal. 62*: 4^{2}—nḥ' br LŠMŠ br 'dwnh. *PNO* 47 A^{3}—LŠMŠ br mqymy 'ṣr'. *PNO* 67—LŠMŠ br šky yrḥy. *PNO* 76 B—LŠMŠ 'b'. *Inv. VIII*, 33^{2}—tymrṣw 'yd'n br LŠMŠ br šwḥbw. *Inv. VIII*, 79^{1}—. . .]t LŠMŠ br yd[. . . . *Inv. VIII*, 157^{3}—ntny br šlmlt br LŠMŠ. *Inv. X*, 126^{2}—ywlys 'wrlys LŠMŠ br tymw. *Inv. XI*, 42^{2}—'bnrgl br ḥry LŠMŠ br ḥyrn gl'. *Inv. XI*, 52^{4}—šlmt brt tymw LŠMŠ. 'Wadi Hauran' 10^{2}—yrḥbwl' br LŠMŠ br mqymw dy mtqr' br 'zwlt. 'Wadi Hauran' 11^{2,4}—LŠMŠ br / ḥyrn br / LŠMŠ br tybwl škybl.

LŠ[MŠ]' (*m*) **1.** *475*, *Inv. X*, 24^{1}—ḥ[d]wdn br ḥggw LŠ[MŠ]' zrzyrt.

LŠMŠW (*m*) **1.** *435* or *436*, CaB 9^{1}—LŠMŠW br mqymw br ḥršw.

LŠMŠY (*m*) **1.** *439*, *C* 3920^{2}—tym' br LŠMŠY br 'g' ydy'bl. *444*, *C* 3998 A^{2}—[zbdbwl] br yrḥbwl' br LŠMŠY [ḥyrn]. *448*, *Inv. XI*, 2^{2,3}—LŠMŠY br tym' / LŠMŠY. **2.** *C* 3904^{1}—š'dw br tym' LŠMŠY. *C* 4336^{5}—yrḥbwl' br LŠMŠY br tym'.

M/QBWRM (*f*) **2.** 'Hypogée' p. 223, Pl. II^{1}—M/QBWRM brt bwrp'.

MHWY (*m*) **1.** *406*, *C* 4130^{5}—mtny br nwrbl br mlkw br tymḥ' br mtny br bwn' br mtny dy mtqrh MHWY. **2.** *C* 4131^{5}—mtny br nwrbl MHWY. *C* 4132^{3}—tm' brt tymy MHWY.

MHR (*m*) **2.** 'Iraq' p. 63^{10}, Pl. 5—MHR br 'tš't.

MHRDD (*m*) **1.** *583*, CaA 31^{7}—'gylw br MHRDD.

MHRDT (*m*) **1.** *458*, *PNO* 55 A—wrdn / brwq' / MHRDT / 'mbkr'. *471*, StaA p. 46, I^{5}—MHRDT. **2.** *RTP* 36a—bwlyd' MHRDT. *RTP* 567a—MHRDT. *PNO* 59—zbyd' MHRDT.

MHRW (*m*) **1.** *505*, *PNO* 37^{4}—'lhbl wrb'l [w]MHRW bny bwly.

MW'L' (*m*) **2.** *C* 4080^{5}—MW'[L' br] 'tpny br mrql'. *C* 4601^{3}—šm'w[n] br zbyd' MW'L'.

MWDL' (*f*) **2.** 'Hypogée' p. 239, Pl. VIII^{2}—. . .] rt' bt MWDL' bt mqymw.

MWS' (*m*) **2.** Ingh. B p. 135, IV D^{1}—MWS' br 'g'.

MZB' (*f*) **2.** *C* 4067^{1}—MZB' brt mzbn'.

MZBW (*f*) **2.** 'IP' p. 158, 17 A^{1}—MZBW brt bryky br mqyn'.

MZBN' (*m*) **1.** *504*, CaB 13 B^{3}—[M]ZBN' wyrḥy wzbd't' bny 'wydlt. *50*[*4*], CaC 3^{3}—MZBN'. *525*, 'Malkû' p. 106^{2}—ywlys 'wrlys ydy'bl dy mtqr' MZBN' br ywlys 'wrlys 'nynws. *547*, *C* 4209—ywlys 'wrlys mrwn' br ml' dy [mtqr' MZBN]' br 'drynws. *550*, *C* 4034^{3}—MZBN' b[r] yrḥy kyly. **2.** *C* 4067^{1}—mzb' brt MZBN'. *C* 4312^{2}—ydy'bl br MZBN' brwq'. *C* 4367^{2}—'mtlt brt MZBN'. *C* 4425^{3}—ḥdwdn br MZBN'. *C* 4426^{3}—[t]ym' br [M]ZBN'. *C* 4427^{2}—ḥlpt' br MZBN'. *C* 4456^{1}—MZBN' br mlkw tymrṣw ''by. *RTP* 493b—MZBN' yrḥy. *RTP* 739b—MZBN' tymrṣ[w]. *RTP* 743a—MZBN' wtymrṣ(w). *RTP* 855b—MZBN' nwrbl. *RTP* 912b—MZBN' ṣlm'. *PS* 210—MZBN' br yrḥbwl' rpbwl bgdn. *PS* 288—MZBN' br br''. *Pal. 60*: 7^{1}—MZBN' br nš'. Ingh. B, Pl. XLI^{5}—kytwt MZBN' 't'qb. *Inv. XI*, 22^{3}—MZBN' br b'ly. *Inv. XI*, 39^{2}—MZBN' br y[rḥ]y [b]r šm'wn.

MZBT' (*m/f*) **1.** *552*, *C* 4307^{1}—MZBT' brt ḥyrn tym'. **2.** *C* 4270^{1}—MZBT' brt tym'. StaC p. 38, 7—MZB[T'] brt mlkw. *Inv. VIII*, 115^{2}—. . .] MZBT' br yd/r[. . . . *Inv. VIII*, 166^{1}—MZBT['] bt ḥl'.

M/QZY (*m*) **2.** *Inv. VIII*, 73^{5}—. . .b]r M/QZY.

MḤLMW (*m*) **2.** *PNO* 74, line 6—MḤLMW br ryṣw.

MḤRBZN (*m*) **2.** CaD 35^{1}—MḤRBZN.

MṬN (*m*) **1.** *430*, CaB 7^{2}—šm'wn br bwrp' br 'gylw MṬN.

M/QYD/RL' (*m*) **2.** 'IP' p. 159, 17 B—M/QYD/RL'.

MYD/RN (*m*) **2.** CaA 33^{1}—mlkw br MYD/RN 'lbhl.

MYṬQ' (*m*) **2.** *C* 4597^{3}—bwrp' 'g' zbyd' MYṬQ'.

MYK’ (*m*) **1.** *[3?]42*, ‘Dédicace’ p. 45, 6—mlkw br bl‘qb br M[YK’.... *394*, *C* 4123 *bis*^{3}—ymlkw br mqymw ’qlyš br mlkw ’bnyt br bl‘qb br MYK’ br mt’. **2.** *RTP* 830a—zbdlh br zbd‘th MYK’. *RTP* 830b—zbdlh zbd‘th MYK’.

MYR/DN (*m*) **2.** CaA 33^{1}—mlkw br MYR/DN ’lhbl.

MYŠ’ (*f*) **1.** *352*, *C* 4115 *bis*^{3}—MYŠ’ brt [.... *378*, CaB 4 A^{2}—MYŠ’ brt tymš’ br ydy‘bl ṭymwn. *378*, CaB 4 A^{3}—MYŠ’.

MYŠN (*m*) **1.** *501*, *C* 4007^{4}—ydy‘bl br zb[d]’ lšmš MYŠN.

MYT’ (*m*) **2.** *RTP* 720a—sṭm[’] MYT’.

MK (*m*) **2.** *RTP* 507a—‘bdy br MK gbr’ ṭb’.

MKBL (*m*) **2.** *RTP* 70b—MKB[L] ‘gylw. *PS* 232—MKBL.

MKY (*m/f*) **1.** *518*, *C* 4014^{3}—MKY brt ‘g’. **2.** *C* 4207—yrḥy br nš’ MKY. *C* 4208—yrḥy MKY. *C* 4492^{3}—mlkw br ml’ br MKY. *Inv. VIII*, 5^{1}—MKY brt tymw ‘lyb‘l. *Inv. VIII*, 177^{2}—mqymw b[r] MKY br mqymw. *Inv. XI*, 63^{3}—šlmt brt MKY.

MKN’ (*m*) **1.** *362* or *382*, CaA 34^{3}—zbdbwl br ’byhn br zbdbwl br lšmš br MKN’ rb’.

MKSMWS (*m*) **2.** *C* 3908^{4}—MKSMWS. *C* 4401^{1}—mrqws ywlyws MKSMWS ’rsṭyds.

MKSMS (*m*) **1.** [*4*]*47*, *Inv. X*, 81^{1}—ywlys MKSMS. **2.** *Inv. VIII*, 135^{2}—...] MKSM[S....

MK‘’ (*m*) **1.** *468*, StaE p. 373—MK‘’.

MKŠM (*m*) **2.** *Pal. 60*: 13^{2}—MKŠM.

MKTŠ (*m*) **2.** *C* 4063^{3}—MKTŠ br whblt br [....

ML 2. *RTP* 734b—ML(KW) or ML(’) or ML(Y).

ML’ (*m*) **1.** *409*, ‘Wadi Hauran’ 1^{6}—b‘ly ML’ ’lhw/y. *420+?*, *Pal. 63*: 5^{2}—...]ML’. *422*, *Inv. X*, 62^{1}—ML’ br tym[.... *437*, *C* 3996^{5}—nrqys br ḥry ML’ brp’. [*4*]*40*, ‘Iraq’ p. 64^{2}, Pl. 10—‘g’ br ML’ br ‘gylw br tybwl dy mtqrh br ’ḥty. *441*, *PS* 3^{1}—bryky br tym’ br ML’ br gyr’. [*4*]*42*, *C* 3959^{1}—[ML’] br yrḥy l[šmš] r‘y. *445*, CaC 13^{1}—ML[’] br dyny. *454*, CaD 27^{1}—ML’ br ṣ‘dy br ML’. *464*, *Michalowski*, p. 318^{1}—ML’ br[.... *472*, *C* 4171^{1}—n‘m‘yn wML’ wṣ‘dy bny ṣ‘dy br ML’. *472*, *C* 4172^{1}—n‘m‘yn wML’ wṣ‘dy bny ṣ‘dy br ML’ br ṣ‘dy. [*49*]*6*, *C* 4196—[‘wyd’ br yrḥy br ML’ br ’pw....]. *500+?*, *C* 4197^{2}—ML’ br ‘g’ br ML’ br ‘gylw ’yt[yb]l. *502*, *C* 4008^{2}—wh[b’] br mlkw ML’. *502*, *C* 4173^{3}—n‘m‘yn wML’ wṣ‘dy bny ṣ‘dy. *504*, Ingh. E (Malê) p. 76, II^{1}—ML’ br ḥyrn br ssn. *518*, *C* 4014^{4}—ML’ br mlkw. *525*, Ingh. E (Malkû) p. 97, VI^{1}—ywlys ’wrlys nwrbl wML’ bny mlkw rb’ br mlkw mlkw nwrbl. *525*, Ingh. E (Malkû) p. 98, VII^{1}—ywlys ’wrlys nwrbl wML’ [bny] mlkw rb’ br mlkw br mlkw br nwrbl. *525*, Ingh. E (Malkû) p. 99, VIII^{1}—ywlys ’wrlys nwrbl wML’ bny mlkw rb’ br mlkw br mlkw br nwrbl. *526*, Ingh. E (Malê) p. 77, III^{1}—ywlys ’wrlys ML’ br ḥyrn br ssn. *529*, StaB p. 151, A 1209^{4}—ML’ br ‘g’ ns’ rb’. *535*, Ingh. E (Malê) p. 78, IV^{1}—ywlyws ’wrlys ML’ br ḥyrn br ssn. *545*, Ingh. E (Malê) p. 82, V$^{1, 2}$—ywlys ’wrlys ML’ br / ḥyrn br ML’ ḥyrn ssn. *546*, Ingh. E (Malê) p. 84, VI$^{1, 2}$—ywlys ’wrlys ML’ br ’wrlys ḥyrn / br ML’ ḥyrn ssn. *546*, Ingh. E (Malê) p. 84, VII$^{3, 4}$—ywlys ’wrlys ML’ br ḥyrn / ML’. *547*, *C* 4209—ywlys ’wrlys mrwn’ br ML’ dy [mtqr’ mzbn]’ br ’drynws. *552*, *C* 4175^{4}—ywlys ’wrlys ML’ br yd‘w br ydy‘bl. *555*, StaB p. 160, A 1206^{3}—ML’ br [y]hyb’ ‘nn. *559*, *C* 4043^{2}—ML’ br bwṭn. [*563*], *C* 4212^{2}—rmnws br ML[’]. *567*, StaB p. 96, A 1173^{5}—lšmš br qrynw br ML’. *569*, *C* 3936^{2}—ywlys ’wrlys šlmlt br ML’ ‘bdy. *583*, CaA 31^{3}—...] ML’ br yrḥy ML’. **2.** *C* 3904^{1}—[mqy br ML’ lšm]š. *C* 4071^{2}—ML’ br šm‘wn. *C* 4177 B—ML’ br yd‘w ydy‘bl. *C* 4178—bt‘’ brt ML’. *C* 4181 C—ML’ br yd‘w ydy‘bl. *C* 4232 B^{2}—pṣy’l br ḥggw br ML’ whblt. *C* 4232 D—ḥggw [br ML]’. *C* 4269^{3}—tym’ br ML’ tym’. *C* 4271^{2}—ML’ br tym’. *C* 4316^{2}—gdrṣw br ML’ br ḥnyn’. *C* 4342$^{2, 3}$—ML’ br / ML’ br / ḥl’. *C* 4348^{2}—whblt br ML’ br whblt gwr’. *C* 4395^{1}—ML’ br mqymw bgš. *C* 4405 A^{2}—yrḥbwl’ br ML’. *C* 4406—yrḥbwl’ br ML’. *C* 4407—...brt] yrḥbwl’ br ML’. *C* 4413 A^{2}—btmlkw bt ML’. *C* 4443^{2}—hgr bt ML’. *C* 4487—ML’ br nš’. *C* 4492^{2}—mlkw br ML’ br mky. *C* 4496^{2}—qbwd’ brt ML’ mtny. *C* 4510^{4}—tymš’ br ML’. *C* 4513 A^{2}—ḥb’ brt ML’. *C* 4513 B^{2}—ḥb’ brt ML’. *C* 4519^{3}—zbyd’ br dyny br ML’. *C* 4568 A^{4}—btḥyrn brt ML’. *C* 4573 A—ML’ br tybwl br ML’. *C* 4615—ML’ br ḥnbl. *RTP* 210b—mqymw ML’. *RTP* 412b—ML’ š[..] [...]by. *RTP* 432a—mqymw wML’. *RTP* 535b—ML’. *RTP* 899a—ML’. ‘Büste’ p. 313^{3}—hgr brt zbyd’ br ML’. ‘Iraq’ p. 63^{9}, Pl. 8—’bgr br ML’ br zbd‘th. *PS* 100—[.]qynt br ML’ [.... *PS* 284—sgn’ br ML’ br tym’. *PS* 329—ML’. *PS* 371—ML’ ḥyrn smy’. *PS* 371—ML’ ML’. Ingh. A p. 99, 7^{3}—’qmt brt [ML’ br ’l]hbl. *Inv. VIII*, 167^{1}—...]l ML’ b[r.... *Inv. VIII*, 168^{3}—zbd’ br ML’ br wly. *Inv. VIII*, 180^{1}—šky br whby br ML’. *Inv. XI*, 55^{2}—ML’ br šm‘wn br mlkw g‘lw/y. ‘Hypogée’ p. 234, Pl. II^{2}—ML’ br ‘g’ bwrp’. ‘Hypogée’ p. 235, Pl. V^{2}—’mby brt ML’. *Pal. 63*: 9^{2}—tm’ brt ML’ br [....

MLWK’ (*m*) **1.** *552*, CaD 36 C^{3}—ywly’ ’wrly’ ḥyrn wMLWK’ bny grmn’. [*576*], *C* 3941^{4}—[ywlys ’wrlys spṭmy]ws ml[kw br MLWK’ nšwm]. **2.** *C* 4441^{2}—nwrbl br MLWK’ ‘tyk’. *C* 4442^{4}—ḥlyw brt

[M]LWK['] ʿtyk'. *C* 4443^{4}—ḥb' bt MLWK'. *C* 4506—MLWK' mqyḥy. *C* 4619—[M]L[W]K'. Ingh. B p. 102, III B—MLWK'.

MLY (*m*) **2.** *C* 4389^{3}—ʿtʿqb mlkw MLY. *C* 4495^{3}—šgl brt ʿttn MLY. *RTP* 272b—blnwr mqmw ḥyrn MLY.

MLK (*m*) **1.** *529*, StaB p. 149, A 1172^{3}—MLK wdms.

MLK' (*m*) **1.** *42[2]*, *C* 3984^{2,3}—MLK' / br tym' br MLK' t[ym]'. *552*, StaB p. 158, A 1174^{3}—MLK' wʿtʿy bny ḥggw br mlky zwzy. *574*, Ingh. E (Naṣrallat) p. 110, II^{1}—ywlys 'wrlys ydyʿbl br ʿbdšmy' br MLK'. *576*, Ingh. E (Naṣrallat) p. 112, III^{2}—ywlys 'wrlys ydyʿbl br ʿbšmy' MLK'. **2.** *C* 4084^{4}—dwr' br zbdbwl MLK' 'tndwr' 'pwqḥ. *C* 4377—MLK' br [. . . . *C* 4404—zbyd' br nṣr' br MLK' zbyd'. *C* 4618—ML[K]' br yrḥbwl' br bwrp' br ml[k]w.

MLK'L (*m*) **1.** *430*, *RTP* 691b—MLK'L **2.** *RTP* 391b—MLK'L [. .]bds or brs. *C* 4372 B^{2}—zbdbwl br MLK'L rmy. *C* 4372 C^{1}—MLK'L br zbdbwl. Ben-Hayyim p. 143—zbdbwl br MLK'L rmy. *Inv. XI*, 61^{2}—zbd' [br ḥ]yrn MLK'L.

MLKBL (*m*) **1.** *548*, Ingh. D, Pl. IX^{1}—ḥgwr br mlkw MLKBL.

MLKW (*m*) **1.** *315*, CaD 12 A^{2}—[M]LKW br ḥlkš qrqpn. *335*, *Inv. IX*, 7^{2}—[yd]y br MLKW br ʿgylw br ʿbdʿstwr br ʿtz'. *336*, CaC 4^{1}—MLKW br nš' br bwlḥ' dy mtqr' ḥšš. *336*, CaC 5^{2}—[ML]KW br nš' br bwlḥ' ḥšš. [*3*?]*42*, 'Dédicace' p. 44, 1—MLKW br bl[ʿ]qb br 'bynt. [*3*?]*42*, 'Dédicace' p. 45, 4—blʿqb br MLKW br blʿqb. [*3*?]*42*, 'Dédicace' p. 45, 5—mqym[w] br MLKW. [*3*?]*42*, 'Dédicace' p. 45, 6—MLKW br blʿqb br m[yk'. . . . *345*, *C* 3980^{4}—[n]bwzbd br MLKW mtn'. *345*, *C* 3980^{5}—MLKW br yrḥbwl' ḥty. *345*, *C* 3980^{7}—MLKW br mqymw tymʿmd. *348*, CaD 33^{2}—MLKW [wz]bdʿ[th. . . .] bny tymʿmd b[r] bwrp' zg[wg]. *390*, *Inv. XI*, 81^{6}—MLKW. *391*, *C* 4122^{2}—MLKW br mqymw br b[wl]brk ḥwml. *392*, *Inv. X*, 131^{1}—MLKW br lšmš br ḥnbl br brʿth ''by. *393*, *C* 4197^{1}—. . .] br ḥyrn br MLKW. *3[94]*, *C* 4123—ymlkw br mqymw dy mtqrh 'qlyš br MLKW br blʿqb. *394*, *C* 4123 *bis*^{2}—ymlkw br mqymw 'qlyš br MLKW 'bnyt br blʿqb br myk' br mt'. *396*, *C* 3978^{4}—lšmš wzbyd' bny MLKW br ydyʿbl br nš' dy mtqr' br ʿbdbl. *400+?*, *C* 3963^{1}—tymrṣw br [l]šmš br MLKW ''b[y]. *400*, 'Fouilles' p. 170^{1}—yrḥbwl' br MLKW br lšmš br ḥnbl ''by. *400*, 'Fouilles' p. 172^{3}—[yrḥbwl' br MLKW br] lšmš br ḥ[nbl ''by]. *400+?*, *Inv. XI*, 56^{1}—. . .]y br MLKW br [. . . . *400+?*, *C* 3988^{2}—ʿy[t' brt M]LKW br whblt br ʿrgn. *400+?*, *C* 3988^{2}—MLKW br ʿg' ''[by]. *406*, *C* 4130^{1}—mtny br nwrbl br MLKW br tymḥ'. *406*, *C* 4130^{4}—mtny br nwrbl br MLKW br tymḥ' br mtny br bwn' br mtny dy mtqrh mhwy. *414*, *C* 4134^{2}—'lhbl wmʿny wškyy wMLKW bny whblt br mʿny 'lhbl. *425*, *C* 3994 A^{6}—ʿnnw br ML[KW] ʿnnw. *425*, *C* 3994 B^{7}—ʿnny [br] MLKW ʿnny. *425*, *C* 3994 C^{7}—ʿnnw br MLKW ʿnnw. *425*, *C* 4159^{3}—zbdʿth br 'tʿqb br zbdʿth br sry br zbdʿth br MLKW dy mtqr' 'r'š. *425*, *C* 4159^{5}—mqymw br zbd' br mqymw br ʿtʿqb br mqymw br MLKW dy mtqr' 'r'š. *426*, CaD 21^{1}—ʿwydw wMLKW wyrḥbwl[' wḥggw bny] bwlm' br ʿwydy br bwlm' 'db. [*4*]*30*, *C* 3982^{1}—. . .]' br MLKW [ʿš]twrg'. *430*, CaB 7^{2}—brp' wMLKW. *430*, *Inv. X*, 106^{1}—. . .] br MLKW nšwm. [*4*]*32*, *C* 3921^{1}—MLKW br whblt br mʿny. *432*, Ingh. E (Malkû) p. 90, I^{1,2}—MLKW br / MLKW br [nw]rbl. *433*, *C* 4158^{2}—bltyḥn brt 'tpny br MLKW ʿtršwry. [*43*]*3*, *Inv. X*, 54^{1}—[M]LKW br khylw qymw [br nwrbl br khy]lw. *43*[*7*], CaD 30^{1}—MLKW br mqymw [br ḥyrn br] brʿy. *443*, *C* 3987^{1}—ʿgylw br MLKW [b]r mqymw qšṭy. *447*, *C* 3968^{3}—. . .] wMLKW br ʿwyd' 'nqy br ʿg' br [. . . . *448*, *C* 3913 I^{3}—MLKW br ʿlyy br mqymw. *449*, CaB 8^{2}—pplys 'lys tybwl wpplys 'lys yrḥbwl' bny MLKW tybwl ṣm'. [*4*]*51*, *Inv. X*, 112^{4}—[MLKW br ʿzyzw]. *453*, Ingh. E (Naṣrallat) p. 109, 1^{3}—nṣrlt br MLKW br nṣrlt. [*454*], *C* 4167—MLKW. *457*, *C* 3911^{5}—zbdbwl wʿtnwr wMLKW wʿmrw wydyʿbl bny bršmš br zbdbwl. [*4*]*58*, *C* 4458—. . .] MLKW br lšmš br ḥnbl ''by. *458*, 'IP' p. 147, 1^{1}—šlmlt br MLKW br dynys. *458*, 'IP' p. 147, 1^{2}—šlmlt br MLKW. *458*, 'IP' p. 147, 1^{2}—ḥnbl br šlmlt br MLKW. *46*[.], CaD 11^{5}—yrḥb[wl' br ML]KW br ʿg'. *461*, *C* 3967^{1}—MLKW br [šʿd]y ʿty. *471*, CaB 1 A^{1}—tymrṣw br bwrp' br MLKW br ʿšylt. *473*, *C* 3956^{2}—ḥlypy [b]r ḥggw br MLKW. *47*[*5*], CaB 3^{1}—'lhbl br MLKW br zbdbwl brt'. *480*, *C* 4236—yrḥy br MLKW br yrḥy ḥwml. *480*, CaA 8^{4}—'mby brt bgrn br MLKW. *482*, CaB 14^{3}—MLKW br mqymw br ʿg'. *482*, CaB 14^{6}—MLKW. *482*, CaB 14^{7}—MLKW. *492*, *C* 4256—šlmt wnbwl' bny MLKW br nbwl'. *497*, Ingh. E (Malkû) p. 91, II^{1}—nwrbl w'qmt ḥb' bny MLKW rb' br MLKW MLKW nwrbl. *497*, Ingh. E (Malkû) p. 93, III^{1}—nwrbl w'qmt ḥb' bny MLKW rb' br MLKW MLKW nwrbl. *497*, Ingh. E (Malkû) p. 93, III^{1}—bʿly br dywn MLKW. *498*, *C* 4549^{4}—. . .]' br [ty]mḥ' br MLKW. *499*, Ingh. E (Malkû) p. 95, IV—bʿly br dywn br MLKW. *502*, CaB 4 B^{2}—bgy br ʿzyzw br MLKW. *502*, *C* 4008^{2}—wh[b'] br MLKW ml'. *502*, *C* 4173^{1}—nrqys br ḥry ʿgylw br MLKW. *512*, *C* 4439^{2}—ʿtyk' br MLKW. *514*, *C* 3970^{1}—šlm' br MLKW br blyd'. *516*, *C* 4013^{4}—hrms bsm [b]r ḥry MLKW br whb'. *516*, *Inv. XI*, 10^{3}—MLKW br lšmš. *518*, *C* 4014^{5}—ml' br MLKW. *520+?*, 'Inscriptions' p. 133, Pl. I—MLKW br mrbn'. *525*, 'Malkû' p. 106^{13}—ywlys 'wrlys yrḥbwl' br MLKW. *525*

'Monuments' 1^{8}—MLKW rbḥ. *525*, Ingh. E (Malkû) p. 97, VI^{1}—ywlys 'wrlys nwrbl wml' bny MLKW rb' br MLKW MLKW nwrbl. *525*, Ingh. E (Malkû) p. 98, VII^{1}—ywlys 'wrlys nwrbl wml' [bny] MLKW rb' br MLKW br MLKW br nwrbl. *525*, Ingh. E (Malkû) p. 98, VII^{2}—ywlys 'wrlys 'gylw br 'prhṭ br ḥry zbdbwl br MLKW 'swyt. *525*, Ingh. E (Malkû) p. 99, VIII^{1}—ywlys 'wrlys nwrbl wml' bny MLKW rb' br MLKW br MLKW br nwrbl. *533*, *C* 4021^{2}—mrywn br zbdbwl br MLKW. *539*, StaF p. 40, 2—MLKW br yrḥy. *539*, Ingh. B p. 110, III^{4}—'wrlys MLKW br šlmn bn'. *54*[.], *C* 3957^{1}—MLKW br mqym[w] br m'yty br ḥlypy. *54*[.], *C* 3957^{3}—br'th br lšmš MLKW. *546*, *C* 3989^{2}—m'ny br MLKW r[b]' br m'ny r'wm'. *547*, *Pal. 61*: 11^{4}—whblt br tymrṣw br MLKW. *547*, *C* 4033^{4}—zbyd' br MLKW zbyd' 'b'. *548*, Ingh. D Pl. IX^{1}—ḥgwr br MLKW mlkbl. *550*, Ingh. B p. 124, II^{5}—ywly' 'wrly' MLKW br 'gylw br šlmn. *551*, *C* 4036 A^{2}—zbdbwl br MLKW zbdbwl. *551*, *C* 4038^{3}—š'dw br MLKW ḥss. *554*, *C* 3932^{1}—ywlys 'wrlys zbdl' br MLKW br MLKW nšwm. *560*, Ingh. E (Malkû) p. 101, X^{2}—MLKW br hrms 'byhn. *570*, *C* 4049^{3}—. . . M]LKW br n[s']. [*576*], *C* 3941^{4}—[ywlys 'wrlys spṭmy]ws ML[KW br mlwk' nšwm]. **2.** *C* 3905^{2}—ḥbyby br MLKW 'nbt. *C* 3926^{1}—MLKW br m[. . . . *C* 3962^{3}—'lhb[l br MLKW. . . *C* 3964^{1}—m'ny br MLKW [br. . . . *C* 3965^{1}—'zyzy br ML[KW. . . . *C* 4036 B^{1,2}—MLKW br zbdbwl / br MLKW. *C* 4072^{3}—[M]LKW wyrḥb[wl']. *C* 4142^{2}—whblt br MLKW br whblt. *C* 4146^{2}—MLKW br whblt. *C* 4155^{5}—whblt br MLKW br whblt. *C* 4156^{1}—šgl brt MLKW br whblt br m'ny. *C* 4183—MLKW ḥdwdn. *C* 4232 A^{1}—MLKW br ḥg[g]w whblt. *C* 4233—MLKW. *C* 4237 A^{1}—MLKW br MLKW mqymw. *C* 4238^{2}—ML[K]W rb' br ['n]nw mqym[w]. *C* 4279^{2}—MLKW br bwrp' 'ḥytwr. *C* 4280^{2}—'tntn br MLKW 'ḥytwr. *C* 4293^{2}—MLKW br 'g' tybwl zwrw. *C* 4293 B—MLKW. *C* 4295^{2}—[']g' br MLKW 'g' zwr. *C* 4317^{2}—MLKW br gdrṣw ḥnyn'. *C* 4318^{2,4}—MLKW br / zbdbwl / br MLKW / ''wyd. *C* 4319^{4}—'gylw br mqymw br MLKW ''wyd. *C* 4332^{2}—'gylw br MLKW br mqym[w]. *C* 4333 A^{2}—yrḥbwl' br MLKW. *C* 4335^{4}—mrt' brt MLKW yrḥbwl'. *C* 4370^{2,3}—MLKW b[r] / MLKW / š'dy. *C* 4389^{2}—'t'qb MLKW mly. *C* 4390^{1}—MLKW br 'ty'qb. *C* 4399^{2}—ḥbbt brt MLKW. *C* 4400—[bw]lḥ' [br] MLKW. *C* 4402—bgdn br 'lhbl br MLKW. *C* 4403^{2}—nṣr' br MLKW br nṣr'. *C* 4446^{1}—MLKW br ydy br ptyḥb. *C* 4447^{2}—yd'w br MLKW br ydy. *C* 4451^{2,3}—MLKW / br MLKW. *C* 4456^{2}—mzbn' br MLKW tymrṣw ''by. *C* 4457^{2}—tymrṣw br MLKW br tymrṣw ''by. *C* 4459—MLKW. *C* 4467^{1}—MLKW br yrḥy 'š'[. .]r. *C* 4477^{2}—MLKW br 'šd. *C* 4486—MLKW br tm'. *C* 4489^{4}—[br]'th [b]r [M]LKW. *C* 4492^{1}—MLKW br ml' br mky. *C* 4494^{2}—bwrp' br MLKW. *C* 4501^{1,2}—MLKW br ḥggw br / MLKW. *C* 4502^{1}—tym' br MLKW br ḥggw. *C* 4503^{4}—tbnn brt ḥggw MLKW. *C* 4504^{1}—MLKW br ḥggw. *C* 4508^{3}—tm' brt šmšgrm br MLKW br nšwm. *C* 4509^{3}—ḥbyby br MLKW bly[d']. *C* 4511^{3}—tym' br MLKW [. . . . *C* 4517^{2}—kd/rnny brt MLKW bqy. *C* 4518 A^{2}—'qm' brt MLKW br dynys. *C* 4518 A^{3}—MLKW. *C* 4532^{4}—MLKW wzbyd'. *C* 4552—MLKW b[r] zb' br['th]. *C* 4556^{1}—MLKW [br] pṣy'l [ydy]'bl. *C* 4579^{4}—šlm' brt MLKW. *C* 4591 A—MLKW wyrḥy bny ymlkw br whblt. *C* 4591 B—MLKW wyrḥy bny ymlkw br whblt. *C* 4618—ml[k]' br yrḥbwl' br bwrp' br ML[K]W. *RTP* 17b—MLKW šm'wn ḥm'. *RTP* 31a—šlmn yrḥbwl' MLKW ''b[y]. *RTP* 34a—šlmn yrḥbwl' MLKW ''by. *RTP* 118b—MLKW whblt. *RTP* 222b—ḥyry MLKW. *RTP* 234b—MLKW br pg'. *RTP* 236a—[M]LKW. *RTP* 283b—MLKW br ydy. *RTP* 315b—MLKW ḥggw. *RTP* 322b—MLKW šm'wn. *RTP* 328b—MLKW [ty]my'm[d]. *RTP* 351b—'lyš' MLKW. *RTP* 465a—MLKW ḥyrn. *RTP* 469a—MLKW br [']tntn. *RTP* 482b—ḥyrn MLKW. *RTP* 548b—MLKW. *RTP* 561a—MLKW. *RTP* 625b—[ML]KW ḥprtm. *RTP* 630b—šlmlt MLKW ḥyrn m'nw. *RTP* 641b—ršy br MLKW. *RTP* 643b—MLKW ḥyrn bšr'. *RTP* 661a—MLKW br ḥyrn br ql[. .]'. *RTP* 697b—'bb ḥyrn MLKW. *RTP* 704b—MLKW mqymw 'gt'. *RTP* 720b—bly zbyd' MLKW nṣrlt. *RTP* 729a—MLKW ḥyrn. *RTP* 730a—MLKW bryk[y]. *RTP* 730b—MLKW bryky. *RTP* 754b—MLKW br bwrp'. *RTP* 763a—yrḥbwl' MLKW ''by. *RTP* 764a—[M]LKW [br] t[y]m'. *RTP* 764b—MLKW br tym' br 'šylt'. *RTP* 765a—whblt MLKW. *RTP* 765b—whblt br MLKW rpnw. *RTP* 766b—[ML]KW br mq[y]m[w] [.]š[. .]. *RTP* 770a—[M]LKW ḥyrn ''b[y]. *RTP* 773a—nšwm MLKW nšwm. *RTP* 774a—[n]šwm MLKW. *RTP* 778b—nšwm br [zb]d' br MLKW nšwm. *RTP* 821a—šlm' MLK[W]. *RTP* 831a—MLKW 'tnw(ry). *RTP* 837b—nšwm br zbd' br MLKW nšwm. *RTP* 838b—MLKW w't'qb. *RTP* 853b—MLKW. *RTP* 874a—ML[K]W. *RTP* 964b—MLKW nš'. *RTP* 992a—MLKW tymy. *RTP* 995a—MLKW zbdbwl. 'Tessera' p. 601—MLKW w't'qb. *Syria* 23 (1942–3), 80^{1}—MLKW br šm'wn bwrp'. 'Iraq' p. 63^{7}, Pl. 8—MLKW br nbwl' br 'qzmn. Ingh. A p. 97, 6—. . .] wkhylw wzbd'th bny MLKW br ḥyrn. Ingh. B, Pl. XLI^{1}—MLKW šlmn. 'IP' p. 150, 2^{1}—šlml[t br MLKW] br dy[nys]. 'IP' p. 150, 2^{3}—MLKW. 'IP' p. 152, 4^{1}—MLKW br dynys ḥnbl. 'IP' p. 152, 5^{2}—šlmlt br MLKW dynys. 'IP' p. 153, 7^{1}—ML[KW dy]ns. *Pal. 59*: 5^{1}—[M]LKW br [n]bwzbd br mqymw nḥwr. *Pal. 61*: 9—zby br MLKW. *Pal. 61*: 15 A^{1}—[M]LKW. *Pal. 62*: 13—MLKW b[r. . . . StaC p. 38, 7—mzb[t'] brt MLKW. *PS* 143—MLKW.

PS 149—MLKW nš' br ḥbwl'. *PS* 232—MLKW br ḥ[.... *PS* 262—MLKW br mqymw. *Palmyrene* no. 12—ḥyr' br MLKW. CaA 33^{1}—MLKW br myd/rn 'lhbl. CaA 36^{4}—yrḥbwl' br MLKW ''b. CaA 58^{2}—...] wMLKW br [.... CaA 59^{5}—ML[KW.... CaA 62^{1}—...] br 'gylw br MLKW [.... CaA 75^{4}—blyd'w br mqymw br MLKW [.... CaA 81^{4}—syg' brt MLKW dn[.... CaB 2 B^{1}—MLKW. CaB 2 B^{3}—...] br 'wyd' br MLKW. CaD 32^{1}—MLKW br ḥyrn [br ']gyl[w]. *Inv. VIII*, 7^{1}—MLKW br zbd'y rb'. *Inv. VIII*, 12^{2}—'byšy brt zbdbl br MLKW. *Inv. VIII*, 17^{2}—MLKW br tym[.... *Inv. VIII*, 24^{1}—MLKW br tymn' bzy. *Inv. VIII*, 32^{2}—MLKW br mtny pyl'. *Inv. VIII*, 64^{4}—'tšb' bt yrḥy MLKW. *Inv. VIII*, 73^{3}—MLKW b[r.... *Inv. VIII*, 73^{4}—...ML]KW br mqym[w.... *Inv. VIII*, 96^{6}—mqymt br MLKW. *Inv. VIII*, 98^{3}—MLKW [.... *Inv. VIII*, 103^{3}—ḥyrn br mqymw MLKW. *Inv. VIII*, 104^{1}—MLKW br nḥšṭb. *Inv. VIII*, 106^{3}—...] br MLK[W.... *Inv. VIII*, 118^{3}—MLKW. *Inv. VIII*, 124^{2}—...] br MLKW mqym[w .... *Inv. VIII*, 129^{1}—MLKW br [.... *Inv. VIII*, 184^{1}—MLKW ḥl'. *Inv. VIII*, 196—...] MLKW. *Inv. X*, 57—...]' br tymrṣw br MLKW [.... *Inv. X*, 115^{1}—ywlys 'wrlys MLKW br wsḥw br MLKW br wsḥw nbwl'. *Inv. XI*, 48^{3}—...] MLKW b[r.... *Inv. XI*, 50^{2}—MLKW br yrḥy sg'. *Inv. XI*, 55^{4}—ml' br šm'wn br MLKW g'lw/y. *Inv. XI*, 66^{4}—MLK[W] š[.... *Inv. XI*, 75—MLKW.† *Inv. XI*, 88^{1}—MLKW br 'gylw dy [m]tqrh br ''ry. *Inv. XI*, 95—MLKW ḥyrn. Wuthnow p. 64—MLKW br MLKW š'd. Ben-Hayyim p. 142—mqymw br MLKW br nṣr'. Ben-Hayyim p. 146, IV—MLKW br 'tyk'. *Michalowski*, p. 460, line 9—nwrbl br MLKW. *Michalowski*, p. 464, line 11—[M]LKW [br nwr]bl. *Michalowski*, p. 465, line 30—MLKW br MLKW br nwrbl.

MLKWS' (*m*) **1.** *555*, Ingh. 'Th.' p. 129^{7}—prṭnks wMLKWS'. **2.** *C* 4385^{2}—'wṭk' br ḥry MLKWS'. *RTP* 551b—MLKWS'.

MLKY (*m*) **1.** *552*, StaB p. 158, A 1174^{4}—mlk' w't'y bny ḥggw br MLKY zwzy.

MLKT (*f*) **2.** *C* 4581^{1}—MLKT brt 'yd'n.

MND/RYMN' 2. *RTP* 23b—MND/RYMN' or MND/RMN'.

MNDRS (*m*) **2.** *RTP* 595b—mqymw [M]NDR[S]. *RTP* 954b—tybwl ḥyrn MNDRS.

M/QN'[2. 'IP' p. 151, 3^{3}—mqymw M/QN'[....

M'ZYN (*m*) **2.** 'Iraq' p. 63^{8}, Pl. 8—mqymw M'ZYN.

† This reading from Starcky, review of *Inv. XI*, in *RB*, 73 (1966), 616.

M'Y' (*m*) **1.** *530*, *Inv. XI*, 13^{5}—yd' br M'Y'.

M'YN' (*f*) **1.** *550*, Ingh. B p. 124, II^{7}—M'YN' brt bwn' br bwlḥ'.

M'YNT (*f*) **2.** *C* 4479 B^{1}—M'YNT brt bwn'.

M'YR' (*m*) **1.** *458*, *PNO* 55 D^{6}—M'YR'.

M'YTW (*m*) **1.** *450*, *C* 4166^{2}—M'YTW br ḥlpt' br m[....

M'YTY (*m*) **1.** *443*, *C* 3973^{5}—M'YTY w'bdw. *54*[.], *C* 3957^{2}—mlkw br mqym[w] br M'YTY br ḥlypy.

M'N (*m*) **1.** *504*, *C* 4199^{6}—zbyd' br M'N br bwlnwr (nwr)'th. **2.** *C* 4200^{3}—'qmt brt ḥggw zbyd' M'N. *C* 4604 A^{3}—gtmy brt M'N. *C* 4604 $B^{1,5}$—M'N / br / gtmy / brt / M'N. *PS* 209—M'N br br'' br zbd'th. 'IP' p. 160, 20^{2}—M'N br whby. *PNO* 35 A^{2}—šm'wn br M'N br wrtn. *PNO* 35 B^{2}—šm'wn br M'N br wrtn. *PNO* 76 A^{3}—'ḥlt M'N br zbyd'.

M'N[2. *RTP* 508b—mqy M'N['/W/Y].

M'N' (*m*) **2.** *C* 4567^{1}—M'N' br ḥry bwrp' br mrql'.

M'NW (*m*) **1.** *426*, *C* 3995^{2}—blyd' w'tnwry wM'NW [bny] tym'md br blyd'. *476*, *Inv. XI*, 5^{3}—td'l brt ḥry bss br M'N[W] br 'rqṭws. **2.** *RTP* 630b—šlmlt mlkw ḥyrn M'NW. 'Monuments' 6—M'NW br mqymw. *Inv. VIII*, 96^{2}—[mq]ymt brt M'NW br mqymw. 'Hypogée' p. 240, Pl. IX^{2}—nbwl' br M'NW ṭ'y.

M'NY (*m*) **1.** *414*, *C* $4134^{1,2}$—'lhbl wM'NY wškyy / wmlkw bny whblt br M'NY 'lhbl. [*4*]*32*, *C* 3921^{1}—mlkw br whblt br M'NY. *433*, *C* 4158^{1}—M'NY br whblt M'NY. *546*, *C* 3989^{2}—M'NY br mlkw r[b]' br M'NY r'wm'. *578*, *C* 3943^{4}—ywlys 'wrlys šlm' br qsyn' br M'NY. **2.** *C* 3964^{1}—M'NY br mlkw [br.... *C* 4135^{2}—'tpny br [M]'NY br whblt. *C* 4138^{1}—M'NY br 'lhbl br whblt. *C* $4139^{1,2}$—M'NY ṭly' / br whblt br [M'N]Y. *C* 4140^{2}—'lhbl br M'NY br 'lhbl. *C* 4144^{2}—whblt br M'NY br whblt. *C* 4146^{2}—'ty brt šlmlt br M'NY. *C* 4147^{1}—hdyrt brt M'NY br whblt. *C* 4149^{2}—whblt br M'NY. *C* 4150—...]mt brt whblt br M'NY. *C* 4152^{2}—M'NY br whblt. *C* 4153^{7}—whblt br M'NY. *C* 4154^{4}—hydrt brt 'lhbl br whblt br M'NY. *C* 4156^{2}—šgl brt mlkw br whblt br M'NY. *C* 4157^{2}—bl'qb br 'lhbl br whblt br M'NY. *C* 4215^{2}—[M'NY]. *C* 4356^{1}—[M']NY br [yr]ḥbwl'. *C* 4452^{3}—šlmlt b[r] M'NY. *C* 4521^{3}—'ty brt M'NY. *C* 4524^{8}—M'NY br br''. *C* 4563^{2}—[z]bd'th br M'NY. *RTP* 719b—M'NY. *RTP* 812a—M'NY. Ingh. A p. 96, 5 B^{2}—M'NY. CaA 10^{2}—[M'NY br] 'mt br ḥdw[dn pr]mw[n]. CaA 25^{3}—[M]'NY br yrḥy [.... CaA 33^{3}—whblt br M'NY br 'lhbl. CaA 64^{2}—...M']NY mq[ymw.... CaA 82^{1}—M'NY br yrḥbwl'. *Inv. VIII*, 124^{5}—...] M'NY [.... *Inv. VIII*, 138^{5}—ḥg' brt zbd' br M'NY. *Inv. VIII*, 173^{3}—'mt' brt M'NY. *Inv. X*, 93—...] M'NY. *PNO* 4—M'NY br't'.

MPL[YS] (*m*) **1.** *426*, *C* 4160^{2}—šm'wn br pyl' br šm'wn MPL[YS].

MQ[2. *Inv. VIII*, 105^{2}—...] br MQ[....

MQWL' (*m*) **1.** [*5*]*50*, *C* 4094^{2}—slwq['] br MQWL' [br] tydwr' br [....

MQY (*m/f*) **1.** *447*, *C* 3968^{5}—...] MQY. *466*, *PNO* 6 A—MQY br 'zyzw. *471*, StaA p. 46, 1^{3}—'bnrgl br ḥr' MQY br ytm'. *510*, *Inv. X*, 44^{2}—'gylw br MQY 'gylw šwyr'. *526*, Ingh. E (Malê) p. 77, III^{2}—ywlys 'wrlys ḥyrn wywlys 'wrlys 'b' bny ywlys 'wrlys MQY br yrḥy. *530*, *C* 4018^{2}—MQY (son of) yrḥy br zbyd['] 'lpy. *540*, Ingh. E ('Atenatan) p. 60, II^{1}—ywlys 'wrlys MQY br zbdbwl MQY dwḥy. *548*, Ingh. E (Malê) p. 86, VIII^{2}—ywlys 'wrlys ḥyrn br MQY yrḥy. *549*, Ingh. E (Malê) p. 88, IX^{2}—'wrlys ḥyrn br MQY br yrḥy. *564*, *C* 4046^{5}—MQY br lšmš. *575*, *C* 4048^{2}—yrḥy br nbwd' br MQY. *583*, CaA 31^{2}—ḥdwdn br 'gylw MQY. **2.** *C* 3904^{1}—[MQY br ml' lšm]š. *C* 3910—...] MQY. *C* 3990^{3}—ḥyr[n] br blḥzy br blḥ' [M]QY [''b]y. *C* 4064^{3}—...] br MQY. *C* 4069^{2}—M[QY]. *C* 4080^{7}—rwḥ' bt MQY. *C* 4245 A^{1}—MQY br zbyd' mqymw. *C* 4353 B—MQY. *C* 4422^{3}—MQY. *C* 4437^{3}—'mt' brt MQY brt 'mrš'. *C* 4505—mqyḥy br MQY. *C* 4540^{1}—MQY br šmšgrm. *C* 4570^{2}—'qm' brt MQY. *C* 4592^{3}—'zyz br 'byḥy MQY. *RTP* 220b—brwq['] MQ[Y]. *RTP* 396b—MQY 'lg. *RTP* 486b—[ḥd]wdn MQ[Y]. *RTP* 490a—ḥdwdn MQY. *RTP* 491a—ḥdwdn MQY. *RTP* 492a—ḥdwdn MQY. *RTP* 495a—ḥdwdn MQY. *RTP* 508b—MQY m'n['/w/y]. *RTP* 579a—lšmš MQY. *PS* 307—nš' MQY nš'. Ingh. A p. 96, 5 A^{1}—...]' brt MQY ['mby]. Ingh. A p. 96, 5 B^{1}—hgr brt MQY 'mby. Ingh. B, Pl. XLI^{3}—šky br MQY. Ingh. B p. 137, line 21—MQY. Ingh. E ('Atenatan) p. 64, III^{1}—MQY br zbdbwl. CaA 78^{5}—'l' brt 'yd'n br yrḥy MQY. *PNO* 7 C—MQ[Y] ḥnyn'. *PNO* 76 C—MQY [.... *Inv. VIII*, 58^{1}—ywly' 'wrly' nwry wzbdbwl w['gylw] bny MQ[Y....] ḥbzy. *Inv. VIII*, 58^{2}—MQY. *Inv. VIII*, 135^{1}—MQY n[.... *Inv. VIII*, 137$^{1, 3}$—MQY / br š'dy / br MQY.

MQYḤY (*m*) **2.** *C* 4505—MQYḤY br mqy. *C* 4506—mlwk' MQYḤY.

MQYM (*m*) **2.** *Inv. XI*, 41—'gylw br MQYM. StaD p. 516, 3^{2}—MQYM br zbdbwl 'š'd.

MQYMW (*m/f*) **1.** [*2*]*89*, StaD p. 512, 1^{3}—MQY[MW....]br ymlkw. *314*, *C* 3992^{2}—zbdlh br MQYM[W] ṭm[ys]. *320*, *Inv. IV*, 26 A^{1}—MQYMW br [ḥg]gw. [*3*?]*42*, 'Dédicace' p. 45, 5—MQYM[W] br mlkw. *345*, *C* 3980^{7}—mlkw br MQYMW tym'md. *350*, CaD 31^{2}—MQYMW br khylw br zbdbl [dy] mtqrh br zbydy. *3*[*6*]*2*, *C* 3923^{1}—MQYMW br 'gylw br pṣy'[l] br tymy dy mtqrh ḥkyšw. [*3*]*84*, *C* 4193^{1}—'gylw br 'g' br MQYMW br ḥdwdn. *390*, *Inv. XI*, 81^{2}—MQYMW br MQYM[W.... *390*, *Inv. XI*, 81^{3}—MQYMW. *391*, *C* 4122^{2}—mlkw br MQYMW br b[wl]brk ḥwml. *3*[*94*], *C* 4123—ymlkw br MQYMW dy mtqrh 'qlyš br mlkw br bl'qb. *394*, *C* 4123 *bis*^{2}—ymlkw br MQYMW 'qlyš br mlkw 'bnyt br bl'qb br myk' br mt'. *400*, 'Fouilles' p. 170^{1}—MQYMW br MQYMW br zbdbwl 'rym'. *400*, 'Fouilles' p. 172^{2}—[M]Q[YMW br MQYMW br zbdbwl] 'rym[']. *425*, *C* 3994 A^{4}—MQY[MW] br yrḥbwl' gml'. *425*, *C* 3994 B^{4}—MQ[YMW] br yrḥbwl' gml'. *425*, *C* 3994 C^{4}—MQYMW br yrḥbwl' gml'. *425*, *C* 4159$^{3, 4}$—MQYMW / br zbd' br MQYMW br 't'qb br MQYMW br / mlkw dy mtqr' 'r'š. *435* or *436*, CaB 9^{1}—lšmšw br MQYMW br ḥršw. *43*[*7*], CaD 30^{1}—mlkw br MQYMW [br ḥyrn br] br'y. *440*, *C* 4164—MQYMW br zbyd' br yrḥy. *443*, *C* 3987^{2}—'gylw br mlkw [b]r MQYMW qšṭy. *445*, Ingh. B p. 94, I^{1}—yrḥy br MQYMW. *445*, Ingh. B p. 94, I^{2}—'tnwry br MQYMW. *445*, Ingh. B p. 94, I^{3}—zbdbwl br MQYMW. *448*, *C* 3913 I^{3}—mlkw br 'lyy br MQYMW. *450*, *C* 3930^{2}—''ylmy br ḥyrn br MQYMW br ḥyrn mt'. *450*, *C* 3931^{3}—MQYM[W]. [*454*], *C* 4167—lšmš br nwrbl br MQYMW br 'gylw 'qml. *457*, *C* 4258^{3}—MQYMW br nwrbl. *458*, *PNO* 55 B—MQYMW yrḥbwl'. *459*, 'Sculptures' p. 19, Pl. I^{2}—MQYMW br nwrbl br zbd'. *459*, 'Sculptures' p. 19, Pl. I^{2}—MQYMW br nwrbl br zbd'. *460*, *C* 4168^{3}—''ylmy wzbyd' bny ḥyrn br MQYMW br ḥyrn mt'. *461*, *C* 3909^{2}—MQYMW br šm'wn. *461*, *C* 4170—zbyd' br MQYMW zbyd' [.... *474*, StaB p. 102, A 1167^{2}—bwly br zbyd' br ḥyrn br MQYMW mt'. *482*, CaB 14^{3}—mlkw br MQYMW br 'g'. *484*, *C* 4261^{3}—š'd'l br zbdbwl br MQYMW. *484*, *C* 4261 *bis*^{4}—š'd'l br zbdbwl br MQYMW. *488*, *C* 4004^{2}—ḥyrn br [M]QY[MW] br yrḥy. *492*, *C* 4263^{3}—nwrbl br MQYMW nwrbl. *494* or *493*, *Inv. X*, 4^{1}—yrḥy br MQ[Y]MW br zbd'th dk'. *494* or *493*, *Inv. X*, 4^{3}—MQYMW. *500*, *C* 3981$^{2, 3}$—zbdbwl / wMQYMW bny gd' br / MQYMW rp'l. *500*, *Pal. 62*: 19^{2}—'lhbl br br'th MQYMW 'klb. *502*, StaB. p. 146, A 1171^{2}—MQYMW br 'wṭk'. *504*, *C* 3948^{1}—tymrṣw br tym' br MQYMW grb'. *505*, Ingh. B p. 95, II^{2}—MQYMW br lšmš br ḥpry. *505*, Ingh. B p. 95, II^{4}—'qmt bt yrḥy br MQYMW. *516*, StaB p. 111, A 1169^{7}—ḥyrn b[r] MQYM[W]. *522*, *Inv. X*, 53^{2}—yrḥbwl' br MQYMW br šrykw. *538*, *C* 4204^{4}—ywlys 'wrlys yrḥbwl' br MQYMW npry. *539*, *C* 4024^{3}—MQYMW br gy. *54*[.], *C* 3957^{1}—mlkw br MQYM[W] br m'yty br ḥlypy. *542*, *C* 4243^{2}—zbyd' br MQYMW br ḥyrn ''ylm[y]. *546*, Ingh. E (Malê) p. 84, VI^{2}—ywlys 'wrlys ḥlpt' br MQYMW zbd'. *547*, *C* 4032²—MQYM[W] br yml'. *548*, Ingh. E (Malê) p. 86, VIII¹⁴—ḥlpt' br MQYMW zbd'. *551*, StaB p. 156, A 1175⁴—yrḥbwl' br MQYMW yml'. *555*, StaB p. 159, A 1176⁴—ḥyrn br yml' MQYMW. *558*, *C* 3933²—ywlys 'wrlys zbyd' br MQYMW br zbyd' 'štwr byd'. *562*, StaB p. 160, A 1177³—n'ry br MQYMW ṭyṭwylw. [*563*], *C* 4212²—. . .] MQYMW brt zbd'th. *574*, Ingh. E (Naṣrallat) p. 110, II²—ywly' 'wrly' 'mt' brt bwlḥzy MQYMW. *576*, Ingh. E (Naṣrallat) p. 112, III⁹—ywly' 'wrly' 'mt' brt bwlḥzy MQYMW. **2.** *C* 4058³—[MQY]MW br yrḥbwl' br [gml']. *C* 4078³—MQYMW br zbd[b]wl b[r] ḥbry. *C* 4118¹—MQYMW br gdy' 't'qb [z]bd' [r]b'. *C* 4187¹—MQYMW wtymš[' wzbyd' bny 'lhš]' br ṣ'dy br 'lhš'. *C* 4187²—'lhš' w'gylw wṣ['dy bny M]QYMW. *C* 4187²—[MQYMW b]r zbyd'. *C* 4188²—'lhš' rb' br MQYMW zbyd' 'lhš' ṣ'dy. *C* 4189¹, ³—MQYMW / br 'lhš' / br MQYMW / ṣ'dy. *C* 4190²—[h]d' brt MQYMW br ṣ'dy. *C* 4231 E²—'tm' [bt] MQYMW gdybwl. *C* 4237 A²—mlkw br mlkw MQYMW. *C* 4238³—ml[k]w rb' br ['n]nw MQYM[W]. *C* 4245 A²—mqy br zbyd' MQYMW. *C* 4245 B²—br[k]' br zbyd' MQYMW. *C* 4259²—zbdbwl br MQYMW br nwrbl br zbd' [b]r 'bdy [zbd]bwl. *C* 4259 C—MQYMW. *C* 4262³—tdm[r] brt MQYMW br nwrb[l]. *C* 4264¹, ³—MQYMW / br n(w)rbl / br M[Q]YMW. *C* 4319³—'gylw br MQYMW br mlkw ''wyd. *C* 4320⁴—r'th brt MQYMW ''wyd. *C* 4321²—ḥb' brt MQYMW ''wyd. *C* 4329 B²—MQY[MW] br zbd't[']. *C* 4332³—'gylw br mlkw br MQYM[W]. *C* 4345³—šgl brt [']tnwry br MQYMW. *C* 4347¹—MQYMW br ḥlypy. *C* 4359¹—MQYMW br ḥyr' 'kldy. *C* 4373 A³—s[. . .] brt MQYMW. *C* 4392³—zbdbl b[r] MQYMW ḥb'. *C* 4395²—ml' br MQYMW bgš. *C* 4424³—[']ty b[t MQY]MW [nwr]bl. *C* 4466³—'qm' brt MQYMW. *C* 4486—MQYMW br tm'. *C* 4488³—. . .M]QYMW [b]r bwlḥ' qwpyn. *C* 4488⁶—MQYMW. *C* 4493¹—ḥn' brt MQYMW br [tyb]wl. *C* 4555²—[ydy]'bl br [M]QYMW klb[y]. *C* 4569¹—MQYMW br tymrṣw tym''. *C* 4572³—r't' brt MQYMW. *C* 4580², ³—MQYMW / br MQYMW. *C* 4583¹—MQYMW br 't'qb. 'Sculptures' p. 24, Pl. II²—MQYMW br ḥyr' 'kldy. 'Iraq' p. 63⁸, Pl. 8—MQYMW m'zyn. *PS* 193—MQYMW br 'lhbl br ḥyrn [. . . . *PS* 201—ḥyr[n] br M[Q]Y[MW] br '[. . . . *PS* 262—mlkw br MQYMW. 'Monuments' 6—m'nw br MQYMW. 'Monuments' 7—b'ltg' brt MQYMW. Ingh. B p. 137, line 10—zbd' rp[. .] MQYMW. Ingh. B p. 137, line 18—MQYMW br blšwry. Ingh. B, Pl. XLIX²—ḥyr' br 'wydlt br MQYMW 'lbn. CaA 16—MQYMW b[r. . . . CaA 26⁴—zby[d'] br MQY[MW]. CaA 36¹, ²—MQYMW br / MQYMW 'rym'. CaA 36³—MQYMW br MQYMW 'rym'. CaA 37—ydy br MQYMW br ydy br rmw br ḥl'. CaA 46²—. . .M]QYMW br [. . . . CaA 64³—. . . m']ny MQ[YMW. . . . CaA 75³—blyd'w br MQYMW br mlkw. CaA 85 B¹—MQYMW br 'gylw br zbd'. CaD 12 B³—MQYM[W] br zbdb[wl] br 'rym[']. *Pal. 59*: 5³—[m]lkw br [n]bwzbd br MQYMW nḥwr. *Pal. 59*: 15¹—zbd' br MQYMW br dywdy. *Pal. 62*: 20³—. . .n]bwzbd MQYM[W]. StaB p. 101, A 1168²—bwl[y] br zbyd' br ḥyrn br MQ[YMW mt']. StaC p. 33, 2—MQYMW br š'dy [. . . . *PNO* 38³—šlmt w'wtq' wMQYMW. *PNO* 43³—nbwzbd br ṣ'dy br MQYMW ḥyrn. 'IP' p. 151, 3³—. . .] MQYMW m/qn'[. . . . *Inv. IV*, 15 B—'ḥybl br MQYMW. *Inv. IV*, 15 C—MQYMW br brnbw br'th. *Inv. VIII*, 21²—tym[. . .] MQYMW tymy. *Inv. VIII*, 30—MQYMW br [. . . . *Inv. VIII*, 34—MQYMW br mrqy. *Inv. VIII*, 37²—MQY[MW] yrḥy. *Inv. VIII*, 41³—. . .M]QYMW. *Inv. VIII*, 42¹—'mt br MQ[YMW]. *Inv. VIII*, 48¹—MQYMW bry. *Inv. VIII*, 66¹—. . .] br MQYMW br whbl[t] br [. . . . *Inv. VIII*, 73⁴—. . .ml]kw br MQYM[W . . . . *Inv. VIII*, 95³—'t'qb MQYMW gdy'. *Inv. VIII*, 96³—[mq]ymt brt m'nw br MQYMW. *Inv. VIII*, 103²—ḥyrn br MQYMW mlkw. *Inv. VIII*, 124¹—ḥyrn br MQYM[W. . . . *Inv. VIII*, 124²—. . .] br mlkw MQYM[W. . . . *Inv. VIII*, 127²—'lhš' br MQYMW br 'lhš' ṣ'dy. *Inv. VIII*, 131¹, ³—MQYM[W] / br / MQYM[W]. *Inv. VIII*, 176⁴—. . .M]QYMW. *Inv. VIII*, 177¹, ³—MQYMW b[r] / mky br / MQYMW. *Inv. VIII*, 179²—'gylw br MQYMW br rpbwl br nṣrlt. *Inv. XI*, 54¹—[M]QYMW br 'lybwl br tymr[ṣw]. *Inv. XI*, 85¹—. . .]bwl bny MQYMW br tybwl dy [mt]qrh [. . . . *RTP* 37b—'bd['/y] 'mry MQYMW 'g'. *RTP* 76b—MQYMW. *RTP* 82b—MQYMW šg'w. *RTP* 179b—MQYMW tymrṣw wtymrṣw nš' wzbyd' [. . .]w. *RTP* 182b—šky[bl] wšlmn wbln[wr]y [w]MQYMW. *RTP* 188b—šby yrḥbwl' MQYMW tymrṣw. *RTP* 204b—MQYMW š'ydn. *RTP* 210b—MQYMW ml'. *RTP* 212a—MQYM[W] 'qt[.]. *RTP* 242b—MQYMW. *RTP* 306b—nbwzbd MQYMW. *RTP* 311b—MQYM[W]. *RTP* 330a—MQYMW. *RTP* 339b—tymrṣw MQYMW. *RTP* 362b—lšmš MQYMW. *RTP* 363b—MQYMW br ydy. *RTP* 370b—whby wMQYMW wlšmš. *RTP* 375b—[MQ]YMW zbyd' ḥy[rn]. *RTP* 378a—MQYMW 'gy[lw]. *RTP* 395b—MQYMW 'lg' zbdlh mšy. *RTP* 432a—MQYMW wml'. *RTP* 468b—zbd' br MQYM[W]. *RTP* 523a—MQYMW. *RTP* 576b—MQYMW ḥyrn. *RTP* 580b—M[Q]YMW zbyd'. *RTP* 590a—[M]QYMW. *RTP* 595b—MQYMW [m]ndr[s]. *RTP* 627b—MQYMW. *RTP* 638b—'bl'ly MQYMW tybwl. *RTP* 651a—MQYMW. *RTP* 660b—MQYMW br ydy. *RTP* 704b—mlkw MQYMW 'gt'. *RTP* 761a—ymlkw MQYMW 'qlyš. *RTP* 766b—[ml]kw br MQ[Y]M[W] [.]š[. .]. *RTP* 979a—

MQYMW 'stwrg'. 'Hypogée' p. 210, line 8—ydy'bl ṭ'y br MQYMW. 'Hypogée' p. 229, Pl. V^{1}—MQYMW br ṭ'y. 'Hypogée' p. 237, Pl. VI^{1}—ṭ'y br MQYMW br ṭ'y. 'Hypogée' p. 238, Pl. VII^{1}—bwrp' br MQYMW br ṭ'y. 'Hypogée' p. 239, Pl. VIII^{2}—rt' bt mwdl' bt MQYMW. 'Hypogée' p. 242, Pl. X^{2}—ṭ'y br MQYMW. 'Hypogée' p. 242, Pl. XI^{1}—MQYMW br yrḥbwl' ṭ'y. 'Wadi Hauran' 10^{2}—yrḥbwl' br lšmš br MQYMW dy mtqr' br 'zwlt. Ben-Hayyim p. 142—MQYMW br mlkw br nṣr'.

MQYMY (*m*) **1.** *415*, *Inv. VIII*, 59^{2}—bwlḥ' wMQYMY wḥyrn wlšmš wb'l[y] bny whby br bwlḥzy. **2.** *Inv. VIII*, 3^{2}—tmh brt MQYMY br šgdy. *Inv. VIII*, 15^{4}—šbty brt 'nny br MQYMY ḥl'. *Inv. VIII*, 110^{2}—ḥbyby MQYMY br 'lyy. *PNO* 47 A^{4}—lšmš br MQYMY 'ṣr'.

MQYMT (*m/f*) **2.** *Inv. VIII*, 96^{1}—[MQ]YMT brt m'nw br mqymw. *Inv. VIII*, 96^{5}—MQYMT br mlkw.

MQYN' (*m*) **2.** 'IP' p. 158, 17 A^{3}—mzbw brt bryky br MQYN'.

MQMW (*m*) **2.** *RTP* 272b—blnwr MQMW ḥyrn mly.

MR' (*f*) **2.** *C* 4409^{2}—MR' bt yrḥb(w)l' ṭmys br ydy'bl.

MRBN' (*m*) **1.** *520+?*, 'Inscriptions' p. 133, Pl. I—mlkw br MRBN'.

MRD (*m*) **2.** *PS* 104—bny br MRD.

MRH (*f*) **2.** *C* 4550^{3}—'bd' br MRH.

MRWN' (*m*) **1.** *547*, *C* 4209—ywlys 'wrlys MRWN' br ml' dy [mtqr' mzbn]' br 'drynws. **2.** *C* 4061$^{3, 5}$—MRWN' / [b]r ḥdwdn br / [MR]WN'.

MRY' (*m*) **1.** *563*, *C* 3944^{4}—'wrlys plynws br MRY' plyn' r'y. **2.** *Inv. XI*, 38^{4}—šlmn br MRY'. *PNO* 79^{2}—MRY' br yrḥbwl['].

MRYWN (*m*) **1.** *533*, *C* 4021^{2}—MRYWN br zbdbwl br mlkw. **2.** *C* 4296 A^{3}—mrty brt 'lhbl br MRYWN. *C* 4296 B^{2}—MRYWN br 'lhbl. *C* 4297^{2}—ḥyr[n] br MRY[WN] br '[lhbl]. *C* 4298^{2}—MRYWN br 'lhbl. *C* 4299^{1}—MRYWN br 'lh[b]l ḥyrn. *Inv. XI*, 94^{1}—. . .] br MRYWN [. . . .

MRYM (*f*) **1.** *5[3]8*, *C* 4023^{3}—MRYM.

MRYNS (*m*) **1.** *448*, *C* 3913 II^{65}—MRYNS.

MRN' (*m*) **2.** *RTP* 914a—MRN'.

MRQ' (*m*) **1.** *545*, Ingh. E (Malê) p. 82, V^{2}—ywlys 'wrlys šyby br hrms MRQ'.

MRQWS (*m*) **1.** *[468]*, *Inv. X*, 90^{1}—MRQWS 'lpys yrḥy br ḥyrn 'bgr. **2.** *C* 4401^{1}—MRQWS ywlyws mksmws 'rsṭyds.

MRQY (*m*) **2.** *Inv. VIII*, 34—mqymw br MRQY.

MRQYNWS (*m*) **1.** *474*, *Inv. X*, 29^{1}—mrqs 'mlyws MRQYNWS 'sqlpyd'.

MRQL' (*m*) **1.** *547*, *C* 4209—ywlys 'wrlys tydrws br ['grp' br MRQL']. **2.** *C* 4080^{4}—MRQL'. *C* 4080^{6}—mw'[l' br] 'tpny br MRQL'. *C* 4080^{8}—MRQL' b[r. . . . *C* 4565^{3}—qlsṭ' br šlm[n] dy MRQL'. *C* 4566^{3}—nrq(y)s br šlmn MRQL'. *C* 4567^{3}—m'n' br ḥry bwrp' br MRQL'.

MRQS (*m*) **1.** *[4]47*, *Inv. X*, 81^{3}—MRQS 'lpys 'bgr br ḥyrn 'bgr. *466*, *C* 3928^{1}—MRQS 'l[p]y[s] yr[ḥy br ḥyrn br '](b)gr. *467*, CaD 28 B^{1}—[MR]QS 'lpys yrḥy b[r ḥyr]n 'bgr. *468*, *C* 3960^{1}—MRQS 'lps yrḥy br ḥyrn 'bgr. *[46]8*, *Inv. X*, 77^{1}—[MRQS 'lpys yrḥy br ḥyrn] 'bgr. *[468]*, *Inv. X*, 96^{1}—[MRQS 'lpys yrḥy br ḥyrn 'bgr]. *[469]*, CaA 8^{1}—MRQ[S 'lps yrḥy b]r ḥ[yrn 'bgr]. *470*, CaD 28 A^{1}—MRQS 'lpys yrḥy br ḥyrn 'bgr. *470*, CaD 28 C^{1}—'lpys MRQS yrḥy br ḥyrn 'bgr. *474*, *Inv. X*, 29^{1}—MRQS 'mlyws mrqynws 'sqlpyd'. **2.** *Inv. X*, 128^{3}—MRQ[S] 'lpys [y]rḥy br ḥyr[n 'bgr].

MRT' (*f*) **2.** *C* 4335^{2}—MRT' brt mlkw yrḥbwl'.

MRTHWN (*f*) **2.** *C* 4238^{1}—MRTHWN [br]t lšmš br yrḥbwl' škybl. *C* 4512 B^{1}—MRTHWN brt [ḥ]lyp' bwn'. *C* 4524^{1}—MRTHWN brt tymrṣw br ydy grb'.

MRTY (*f*) **1.** *[4]27* or *[5]27*, *C* 4554^{1}—MRTY brt tymrṣ[w]. *[4]90*, *C* 3954^{1}—MRTY brt yd[' br whblt] br šm'wn. **2.** *C* 4296 A^{1}—MRTY brt 'lhbl br mrywn. *C* 4391^{1}—MRTY brt šlmlt 'krn. *C* 4429^{1}—MRTY brt yrḥy. Ingh. B p. 135, line 7—MRTY 'gylw. Ingh. E (Malê) p. 79 C—MRTY brt yrḥbwl'. 'IP' p. 156, 13^{1}—MRTY brt tymrṣw dynys.

MRTYN' (*m*) **2.** *Inv. XI*, 44^{3}—MRTYN'.

MŠY (*m*) **2.** *RTP* 395b—mqymw 'lg' zbdlh MŠY. *Pal. 61*: 14^{4}—pplys '[. . . .] MŠY br khyly.

MŠKW (*m*) **1.** *409*, 'Wadi Hauran' 8^{7}—zbyd' br tym'md MŠKW. *425*, *C* 3994 A^{4}—zbyd['] br tym'md MŠKW. *425*, *C* 3994 B^{4}—zby[d'] br tym'md MŠKW. *425*, *C* 3994 C^{4}—zbyd' br tym'md MŠKW. *525*, 'Monuments' 1^{1}—gd' br MŠKW. *525*, 'Monuments' 1^{3}—gd' br MŠKW. **2.** *C* 4445^{4}—khylw br MŠKW br ymlk[w]. *C* 4596^{3}—'tntn br kyly br MŠKW b[r] 'td/rt br ḥyrn. *RTP* 335b—'gylw wMŠKW. *Inv. VIII*, 133^{1}—MŠK[W] br bwlḥzy. *Inv. VIII*, 170^{3}—. . .] MŠKW ḥ[. . . . 'Wadi Hauran' 9^{4}—zbyd' tym'md zbyd' MŠKW.

MŠLM (*m*) **2.** *C* 3907^{7}—MŠLM br 'wb.

MT’ (*m*) **1.** [*3*?]*42*, ‘Dédicace’ p. 44, 2—‘th [brt] nš’ br MT’. *394*, *C* 4123 *bis*^{3}—ymlkw br mqymw ’qlyš br mlkw ’bnyt br bl‘qb br myk’ br MT’. *450*, *C* 3930^{2}—’‘ylmy br ḥyrn br mqymw br ḥyrn MT’. *460*, *C* 4168^{3}—’‘ylmy wzbyd’ bny ḥyrn br mqymw br ḥyrn MT’. *474*, StaB p. 102, A 1167^{2}—bwly br zbyd’ br ḥyrn br mqymw MT’. **2.** *C* 4169—. . .] br zbyd’ br ḥyrn MT’. StaB p. 101, A 1168^{2}—bwl[y] br zbyd’ br ḥyrn br mq[ymw MT’].

MTBWL (*m*) **2.** *C* 4375—MTBWL. *Inv. XI*, 76^{2}—MTBWL br m[. . .† ‘Jewellery’ p. 185—sym’ brt MTB(W)L.

MTN’ (*m*) **1.** *345*, *C* 3980^{4}—[n]bwzbd br mlkw MTN’. **2.** *C* 4334^{1}—MTN’ br br bwn’ br yrḥbwl’ šlmwy br bwn’. *RTP* 78b—zbd‘th MTN’. *RTP* 287b—zbd‘th MTN’. *RTP* 302b—yrḥbwl’ br MTN’ br‘th. *RTP* 305b—MTN’ zbd‘th. *RTP* 488b—[M]TN’ [ḥy]rn. *RTP* 819b—zbd‘th MTN’ ’nqy. *RTP* 836b—zbd‘th MTN’. *Inv. VIII*, 9^{2}—zbdb(w)l br MTN’ br zbdlh br bl‘qb dy mtqrh ’ṣr‘. *Pal. 63*: 8—btml’ brt MTN’.

MTNW (*m*) **2.** *C* 4205—‘g’ br MTNW.

MTNY (*m*) **1.** *406*, *C* 4130^{1}—MTNY br nwrbl br mlkw br tymḥ’. *406*, *C* 4130$^{3, 4, 5}$—MTNY br / nwrbl br mlkw br tymḥ’ br MTNY br bwn’ br / MTNY dy mtqrh mhwy. **2.** *C* 4131^{3}—MTNY br nwrbl mhwy. *C* 4133^{4}—nwrbl br tym[y] MTNY. *C* 4471^{2}—yrḥy br MTNY br ‘g’. *C* 4472^{3}—’qm’ brt ‘(g)’ br [MT]NY. *C* 4496^{3}—qbwd’ brt ml’ MTNY. *C* 4551—MTNY br zbyd’. *C* 4606^{3}—’qm’ brt MTNY br ḥyrn. *RTP* 321b—MTNY. *RTP* 987a—ydy MTNY. *Inv. VIII*, 10^{1}—MTNY br bryky bt’. *Inv. VIII*, 20—. . .] MTNY [. . . . *Inv. VIII*, 32^{3}—mlkw br MTNY pyl’. *PS* 124—‘g’ br MTNY.

N’RY (*m*) **1.** *562*, StaB p. 160, A 1177^{3}—N’RY br mqymw ṭyṭwylw.

NBW[**2.** *RTP* 780a—NBW[. . . .

NBWGDY (*m*) **2.** *C* 4231 D^{1}—NBWGDY br brnbw.

NBWD’ (*m*) **1.** *545*, *C* 4206^{4}—ywlys ’wrlys bwlm’ br zbdbwl b[r bwlm’ nyny’ . . . .b]rt [N]B[W]D’ br tym’ br nbwmw’. **2.** *Pal. 61*: 17^{5}—[ḥ]gt brt yrḥyw br NBWD’.

NBWD‘ (*m*) **1.** *575*, *C* 4048^{2}—yrḥy br NBWD‘ br mqy.

NBWZ’ (*m*) **1.** *457*, *C* 4249^{6}—nbwl’ NBWZ’. *518*, *C* 4015^{2}—[N]BWZ’ br nš’. *545*, *Pal. 63*: 6^{1}—tymrṣw br NBWZ’.

NBWZBD (*m*) **1.** *269*, StaD p. 514, 2^{4}—grymy br NBWZBD. *345*, *C* 3980^{4}—[N]BWZBD br mlkw mtn’. *394*, *C* 4124^{1}—šby wNBWZBD wt[ymy wnbwl’] bny blšwry br ḥyrn br blšwry br gdrṣw[. . . .b‘’]. *425*, *C* 3986$^{2, 3}$—NBWZBD wyrḥbwl’ bny brnbw / br NBWZBD br zbdl’ ’knby. [*442*], *Inv. X*, 38—yrḥy br NBWZBD br [. . . . *480*, CaC 8^{1}—tm’ brt NBWZBD br zbdbwl šm‘wn. *502*, CaB 4 B^{1}—’lkdrys br ’lkdrys br ’plnys NBWZBD br tym‘’ br ’gdm. *525*, *PNO* 16^{2}—NBWZBD nḥy. *529*, *C* 4203^{2}—[ywlys] ’wr[lys] rp[bwl b]r ‘t‘qb [br] rpbwl br ‘t‘[qb] dy mtqr’ NB[WZBD]. *548*, *C* 4210^{2}—ḥl’ br NBWZBD br kyly. *574*, *C* 3939^{3}—ywlys ’w(r)lys NBWZBD br š‘dw ḥyr’. **2.** *RTP* 191b—khylw NBWZBD. *RTP* 295b—zbdbwl NBWZBD. *RTP* 306b—NBWZBD mqymw. *RTP* 398b—NBWZBD šlmlt. *RTP* 749b—qrynw br NBWZBD. *RTP* 818b—q[ry]nw NBWZBD. *RTP* 822a—NBWZBD br zbyd’. ‘IP’ p. 156, 14 B^{2}—NBWZBD bryky. ‘IP’ p. 157, 15^{3}—bryky br NBWZBD br [. . . . ‘IP’ p. 157, 16 A$^{2, 3}$—. . .]brt bryky / br NBWZBD / br NBWZBD. ‘IP’ p. 157, 16 B^{3}—ḥn’ brt bryky NBWZBD. *Pal. 59*: 5^{2}—[m]lkw br [N]BWZBD br mqymw nḥwr. *Pal. 62*: 20^{3}—. . .N]BWZBD mqym[w]. *PNO* 43^{2}—NBWZBD br ṣ‘dy br mqymw ḥyrn. *Inv. VIII*, 155$^{1, 2, 3}$—NBWZBD / br NBWZBD / br NBWZBD.

NBWYD‘ (*m*) *Inv.* **2.** *VIII*, 28$^{1, 2}$—NBWYD‘ br / [b]r‘th NBWYD‘.

NBWL’ (*m*) **1.** *394*, *C* 4124^{1}—šby wnbwzbd wt[ymy wNBWL’] bny blšwry br ḥyrn br blšwry br gdrṣw[. . . .b‘’]. *409*, ‘Wadi Hauran’ 5^{8}—NBWL’ yrḥy [. . . . *457*, *C* 4249^{5}—NBWL’ nbwz’. *492*, *C* 4256A—šlmt wNBWL’ bny mlkw br NBWL’. **2.** *RTP* 308b—grymy NBWL’. ‘Iraq’ p. 63^{7}, Pl. 8—mlkw br NBWL’ br ’qzmn. *Inv. VIII*, 119^{4}—ḥnyn’ br ‘gylw NBWL’. *Inv. X*, 115^{1}—ywlys ’wrlys mlkw br wsḥw br mlkw br wsḥw NBWL’. ‘Hypogée’ p. 221, Pl. I^{1}—NBWL’ b[r] whblt[b]r ṭ‘y. ‘Hypogée’ p. 240, Pl. IX^{2}—NBWL’ br m‘nw ṭ‘y.

NBWLH (*m*) **2.** *RTP* 290b—NBWLH ḥdwdn.

[NB]WM’ (*m*) **2.** CaD 36 E^{3}—[’]qm’ [wn]yny bny [NB]WM’.

NBWMW’ (*m*) **1.** *545*, *C* 4206^{4}—ywlys ’wrlys bwlm’ br zbdbwl b[r bwlm’ nyny’ . . . .b]rt [n]b[w]d’ br tym’ br NBWMW’.

[NBWMY] (*m*) **2.** *Inv. IX*, 30^{2}—[ywlys] ’wrlys [NBWMY br tymšm]š bwn’ [šby. . . .

[NB]WMR (*m*) **1.** *545*, *C* 4206^{2}—ywl’ ’wrly’ ‘g’ wšlm’ [. . . .NB]WMR bny ḥlh. *545*, *Pal. 63*: 6^{1}—šlmlt br NBWMR.

NBWŠY (*f*) **1.** *441*, *PS* 3^{2}—NBWŠY.

NBY (*f*) **1.** *406*, *C* 4130^{2}—NBY. *406*, *C* 4130^{6}—NBY. **2.** *C* 4463^{1}—NBY brt khyly br ydy‘bl. *C* 4522^{1}—[N]BY brt yrḥy br zgwg.

† This reading from Starcky, review of *Inv. XI*, in *RB*, 73 (1966), 616.

NGMW (*m*) **2.** *Inv. XI*, 62^{3}—gmlt brt NGMW.

NDB'L (*m*) **2.** Ingh. 'Quatre' p. 243, Pl. XLI^{2}—ḥyrn br NDB'L bwš'.

NHR' (*f*) **1.** *[5]38*, *C* 4300^{1}—NHR' bt šlmn.

NHTWM' (*m*) **2.** *Inv. XI*, 32^{5}—. . .] br bs' NHTWM'.

NWRBL (*m*) **1.** *37[5]*, *C* 3966^{2}—šlmlt br [yrḥbw]l' br NWRBL. *406*, *C* 4130^{1}—mtny br NWRBL br mlkw br tymḥ'. *406*, *C* 4130^{2} —NWRBL. *406*, *C* 4130^{4}—mtny br NWRBL br mlkw br tymḥ' br mtny br bwn' br mtny dy mtqrh mhwy. *406*, *C* 4130^{5}—NWRBL. *410*, Ingh. B p. 120, I^{1}—'bd'stwr br NWRBL br khylw br 'tnwry 'ṣwly. *425*, *C* 3994 A^{6}—yrḥ[y] br NWRBL šgry. *425*, *C* 3994 B^{6}—yr[ḥy] br NWRBL šgry. *425*, *C* 3994 C^{6}—yrḥy br NWRBL šgry. *429*, CaB 2 A^{1}—'b[yhn br šm']wn br 'byhn br NWRBL. *432*, Ingh. E (Malkû) p. 90, I^{2}—mlkw br mlkw br [NW]RBL. *[43]3*, *Inv. X*, 54^{2}—[m]lkw br khylw qymw [br NWRBL br khy]lw. *[454]*, *C* 4167—lšmš br NWRBL br mqymw br 'gylw 'qml. *457*, *C* 4258^{4}—mqymw br NWRBL. *459*, 'Sculptures' p. 19, Pl. I^{2}—mqymw br NWRBL br zbd'. *459*, 'Sculptures' p. 19, Pl. I^{2}—mqymw br NWRBL br zbd'. *470*, CaC 14^{3}—rp'l br [bwl]q' br NWRBL. *492*, *C* 4263^{2,3}—NWRBL br / mqymw NWRBL. *497*, Ingh. E (Malkû) p. 91, II^{1}—NWRBL w'qmt ḥb' bny mlkw rb' br mlkw mlkw NWRBL. *497*, Ingh. E (Malkû) p. 93, III^{1} —NWRBL w'qmt ḥb' bny mlkw rb' br mlkw mlkw NWRBL. *525*, Ingh. E (Malkû) p. 97, VI^{1}—ywlys 'wrlys NWRBL wml' bny mlkw rb' br mlkw mlkw NWRBL. *525*, Ingh. E (Malkû) p. 98, VII^{1}—ywlys 'wrlys NWRBL wml' [bny] mlkw rb' br mlkw br mlkw br NWRBL. *525*, Ingh. E (Malkû) p. 99, VIII^{1}—ywlys 'wrlys NWRBL wml' bny mlkw rb' br mlkw br mlkw br NWRBL. **2.** *C* 4131^{4}—mtny br NWRBL mhwy. *C* 4133^{2}—NWRBL br tym[y] mtny. *C* 4218^{1} —šmšgrm br NWRBL. *C* 4259 A^{3}—zbdbwl br mqymw br NWRBL br zbd' [b]r 'bdy [zbd]bwl. *C* 4262^{4}—tdm[r] brt mqymw br NWRB[L]. *C* 4264^{2}—mqymw br N(W)RBL br m[q]ymw. *C* 4419^{3}—b'ltg' brt 'bd'stwr NWRBL. *C* 4424^{4}—[']ty b[t mqy]mw [NWR]BL. *C* 4441^{1}—NWRBL br mlwk' 'tyk'. *C* 4499—. . .]t [br NW]RBL or [br zb]dbl. *C* 4541^{3}—nn' brt NWRBL. *RTP* 381b—šmšgrm br NWRBL gynws. *RTP* 767a—šmšgrm NWRBL. *RTP* 855b—mzbn' NWRBL. *PS* 167—ḥbyby r[b'] br yrḥbwl' br NWRBL. CaA 46^{3} —N]WRBL [. . . . CaD 24^{1}—whby br NWRBL br 'qmt. CaD 25^{5}—. . .]lw br NWRBL 'qml bw [. . . . *Pal. 61*: 3^{1,3} —NWRBL / br nšm / br NWRBL. *Inv. VIII*, 36^{2}—rmy br k'b[w] NWRBL. *Inv. VIII*, 143^{1}—NWRB[L. . . . *Inv. XI*, 67^{2}— . . .w]zbdbwl wNWRBL wgdy' wtybw[l. . . *Inv. XI*, 92^{1}—š'yl' b[r N]WRBL br 'qmt. *Michalowski*, p. 460, line 9—NWRBL br mlkw. *Michalowski*, p. 464, line 11—[m]lkw [BR NWR]BL. *Michalowski*, p. 465, line 30—mlkw br mlkw br NWRBL. 'IP' p. 162, 23 C—NW[RBL]?

NWRY (*m*) **1.** *345*, *C* 3980^{7}—'gylw br NWRY zbdb(w)l. *399*, CaB 6 A^{1}—blḥzy br NWRY br zbdbwl ''ylmy. **2.** *C* 4464^{4}—'qmt brt blḥzy NWRY. *C* 4465^{3}—zbdbwl br ḥyrn NWRY. *Inv. VIII*, 58^{1}—ywly' 'wrly' NWRY wzbdbwl w['gylw] bny mq[y. . . .]ḥbzy.

NWR'TH (*m*) **1.** *504*, *C* 4199^{6}—zbyd' br m'n br bwlnwr (NWR)'TH. **2.** *C* 4529^{3}—gdy' br tybwl NWR'TH.

NḤ' (*m/f*) **2.** CaD 36 D^{1}—NḤ' brt typyls. *Pal. 62*: 4^{1}—NḤ' br lšmš br 'dwnh.

NḤWR (*m*) **2.** *Pal. 59*: 5^{3}—[m]lkw br [n]bwzbd br mqymw NḤWR.

NḤY (*m*) **1.** *525*, *PNO* 16^{3}—nbwzbd NḤY.

NḤY'ZYZ (*m*) **1.** *556*, *C* 4041^{3}—NḤY'ZYZ [']rby.

NḤŠṬB (*m*) **1.** *497*, Ingh. E (Malkû) p. 91, II^{1}—NḤŠṬB br ḥry ḥnt' whby ḥlpt'. **2.** *PNO* 45^{3}—NḤŠṬB. *PNO* 78^{4}—NḤŠṬB 'lwr. *Inv. VIII*, 104^{2}—mlkw br NḤŠṬB.

[N]YNY (*m*) **2.** CaD 36 E^{2}—[']qm' [wN]YNY bny [nb]wm'.

NYNY' (*m*) **1.** *545*, *C* 4206^{1}—. . .ywl]ys 'wrlys bwlm' br zbdbwl br bwlm' NYNY'. *545*, *C* 4206^{3}—ywlys 'wrlys bwlm' br zbdbwl b[r bwlm' NYNY' . . . . b]rt [n]b[w]d' br tym' br nbwmw'.

NYQ' (*f*) **2.** *C* 4085^{4}—nšry wNYQ'.

NN' (*f*) **2.** *C* 4541^{1}—NN' brt nwrbl.

NS' (*m*) **1.** *[4]53*, *C* 3916^{1}—NS' br ḥl' br NS' br ḥl' br rp'l br 'bsy. *529*, StaB p. 151, A 1209^{5}—ml' br 'g' NS' rb'. *570*, *C* 4049^{3}— . . .m]lkw br N[S']. **2.** *C* 4059^{3,4}—NS' b[r / N]S' [br r]p[']l. *C* 4311 A^{3}—ḥbyby br ḥbyby NS'. *C* 4311 B^{2}—brwq' br NS' 'lbn. Ingh. B p. 116, Fig. 1—NS'. Ingh. B, Pl. XLVIII^{2}—btšmy' brt NS'. CaC 6^{1,2}—NS' br ḥl' / br NS' 'ḥmr.

N'B' (*m*) **1.** *330* (?), CaD 6^{3}—y[dy'bl] br N'B' br ydy'[bl]. **2.** *Inv. VIII*, 143^{2}— . . .] N'B' br n[. . . .

[N]'YM (*m*) **2.** *RTP* 684b—[N]'YM.

N'M (*m/f*) **2.** *C* 4092^{2}—N'M br gdylt. *Palmyrene* no. 12—N'M. CaA 80^{2}—N'M brt rmy br rp'l.

N'MY (*f*) **1.** *462*, *C* 4268^{1}—N'MY brt zbd' br tym' br ḥlpt'. **2.** *C* 4313^{1}—N'M[Y] bt gd[r]ṣw.

N'M'YN (*m*) **1.** *472*, *C* 4171^{1}—N'M'YN wml' wṣ'dy bny ṣ'dy br ml'. *472*, *C* 4172^{1}—N'M'YN wml' wṣ'dy bny ṣ'dy br ml' br ṣ'dy. *502*, *C* 4173^{3}—N'M'YN wml' wṣ'dy bny ṣ'dy.

[N']RY (*m*) **1.** *420*, *C* 3917^{1}—'qyḥ br [N']RY br 'qyḥ.

NPDY see NPRY.

NPRY (*m*) **1.** *538*, *C* 4204^{4}—ywlys 'wrlys yrḥbwl' br mqymw NPRY. **2.** 'Bas-relief' p. 47—šlmn br šm'wn NPRY. 'Bas-relief' p. 47—šm'wn NPRY.

NṢ' (*f*) **2.** CaD 36 G^{1}—NṢ' brt yrḥy bryky.

NṢWR (*m*) **2.** *C* 4202—'dynt br ḥyrn whblt NṢWR.

NṢR' (*m*) **2.** *C* 4403^{1,3}—NṢR' br / mlkw br / NṢR'. *C* 4404—zbyd' br NṢR' br mlk' zbyd'. *C* 4481^{3}—...yrḥ]y kr[ḥ] br NṢR'. CaA 76^{2}—'wydlt [b]r yrḥy NṢR'. *Inv. VIII*, 19^{2}—'wydlt [b]r yrḥy NṢR'. Ben-Hayyim p. 142—mqymw br mlkw br NṢR'.

NṢRY (*m*) **2.** CaA 79^{4}—tyks' brt NṢRY br lšmš 'ḥyb.

NṢRYḤBY (*m*) **1.** *447*, *C* 3968^{4}—...] NṢRYḤBY br 'g' NṢRYḤBY 'rṭbn.

NṢRLT (*m*) **1.** *453*, Ingh. E (Naṣrallat) p. 109, I^{3}—NṢRLT br mlkw br NṢRLT. **2.** *RTP* 720b—bly zbyd' mlkw NṢRLT. *Inv. VIII*, 179^{4}—'gylw br mqymw br rpbwl br NṢRLT.

NQB' (*m*) **2.** Ingh. B p. 101, III A—bs' NQB'.

NRGLZBD (*m*) **1.** *399*, CaB 6 A^{1}—''ylmy wNRGLZBD w'gylw.

NRQYS (*m*) **1.** *437*, *C* 3996^{5}—NRQYS br ḥry ml' brp'. *502*, *C* 4173^{1}—NRQYS br ḥry 'gylw br mlkw. *502*, *C* 4174^{1}—NRQYS br ḥry 'gylw. *583*, CaA 31^{7}—NRQYS. **2.** *C* 4185—NRQYS 'gylw. *C* 4566^{1}—NRQ(Y)S br šlmn mrql'.

NŠ' (*m*) **1.** *333*, *C* 3915^{1}—ḥšš br NŠ' br bwlḥ' ḥšš. *336*, CaC 4^{2}—mlkw br NŠ' br bwlḥ' dy mtqr' ḥšš. *336*, CaC 5^{2}—[ml]kw br NŠ' br bwlḥ' ḥšš. [*3*?]*42*, 'Dédicace' p. 44, 2—'th [brt] NŠ' br mt'. *396*, *C* 3978^{4}—lšmš wzbyd' bny mlkw br ydy'bl br NŠ' dy mtqr' br 'bdbl. *409*, 'Wadi Hauran' 5^{4}—ḥggw br NŠ' ḥrš'. *426*, *C* 4161^{1,2}—NŠ' wbw[n' bn]y / NŠ' br tym[']. *447*, *C* 3999^{1}—šlmn br NŠ' br ḥyr' brq. *448*, *C* 3913 I^{3}—zbyd' br NŠ'. *449*, CaB 8^{1}—ḥyrn br NŠ' tybwl ṣm'. *461*, *Inv. X*, 124^{2}—(N)Š' br ḥl' br NŠ' ḥl'. *474*, *Inv. X*, 29^{4}—NŠ' br blyd'. *525*, 'Malkû' p. 106^{12}—ywlys 'wrlys NŠ' br br'th. *527*, *C* 3908 *bis*^{2}—rp'l br NŠ' [t]y[m]y. *578*, *C* 4015^{2}—[n]bwz' br NŠ'. **2.** *C* 4151^{1}—'mtḥ' brt bl'qb br NŠ'. *C* 4207—yrḥy br NŠ' mky. *C* 4215^{2}—['gylw br šlmlt br NŠ']. *C* 4215^{2}—[NŠ']. *C* 4232 C^{2}—pṣ' brt NŠ' ḥggw. *C* 4273^{1}—NŠ' br ḥlpt' qwqḥ. *C* 4274^{1}—NŠ' br qwqḥ ḥlpt'. *C* 4309^{2}—ḥbyby br NŠ' 'lbn. *C* 4310 A^{3}—ḥbyby br ḥbyby NŠ'. *C* 4411^{5}—yrḥb[wl'] NŠ' 'g'. *C* 4423^{2,4}—NŠ' br / 'g' / NŠ'. *C* 4487—ml' br NŠ'. *C* 4516 A^{4}—'ḥ' brt NŠ'. *C* 4558^{2}—yrḥy br NŠ' [br m]q[y]m[w]. *C* 4559^{3}—bl[ḥ'] br NŠ' ḥšš. *C* 4560^{1}—NŠ' br blḥ' ḥšš. *C* 4617^{3}—zbd't' br ymlkw NŠ'. *RTP* 10b—NŠ' brp'. *RTP* 179b—mqymw tymrṣw wtymrṣw NŠ' wzbyd' [...]w. *RTP* 687a—NŠ'. *RTP* 687b—NŠ'. *RTP* 964b—mlkw NŠ'. Ingh. D, Pl. VIII^{2}—yrḥbwl' br NŠ' 'g' šlm'. *PS* 149—mlkw NŠ' br ḥbwl'. *PS* 244 A—'mwn br NŠ' 'g' šlm'. *PS* 307—NŠ' mqy NŠ'. CaC 7^{1}—tym'md br NŠ' br [.... *Pal. 60*: 7^{1}—mzbn' br NŠ'. *Pal. 61*: 6^{2}—zbd' br NŠ'. *Inv. VIII*, 125^{2}—[z]bdlh NŠ[']. *Inv. VIII*, 171 A^{1}—NŠ' br tym'. *Inv. X*, 130^{4}—[zbyd' w'bdy w']bd'stwr bny N[Š' 't']qb. *Inv. XI*, 65^{3}—whblt br bl'qb br [N]Š'. *Inv. XI*, 82^{4}—NŠ' br zbdbwl.

NŠWM (*m*) **1.** *430*, *Inv. X*, 106^{1}—...] br mlkw NŠWM. *554*, *C* 3932^{2}—ywlys 'wrlys zbdl' br mlkw br mlkw NŠWM. [*576*], *C* 3941^{4}—[ywlys 'wrlys spṭmy]ws ml[kw br mlwk' NŠWM]. **2.** *C* 4508^{4}—tm' brt šmšgrm br mlkw br NŠWM. *RTP* 773a—NŠWM mlkw NŠWM. *RTP* 774a—[N]ŠWM mlkw. *RTP* 778b—NŠWM br [zb]d' br mlkw NŠWM. *RTP* 837b—NŠWM br zbd' br mlkw NŠWM.

NŠM (*m*) **2.** *C* 4062^{4}—'bydw 'sty br gwr' br NŠM 'mṣr. *Pal. 61*: 3^{2}—nwrbl br NŠM br nwrbl.

NŠRY (*m*) **2.** *C* 4085^{4}—NŠRY wnyq'. *Inv. VIII*, 16^{2}—NŠRY br šmy.

NTNY (*m*) **2.** *Inv. VIII*, 157^{1}—NTNY br šlmlt br lšmš.

SB' (*m*) **1.** *531*, *C* 4019^{4}—...] br SB'.

SBBW (*m*) **2.** *C* 4535 A^{1}—SBBW br yrḥ[y] bwn'.

SBYN' (*m*) **1.** *562*, Ingh. B p. 104^{2}—yrḥbwl' br SBYN' br tym'. **2.** *C* 4514^{2}—hrqlyd' br SBYN'.

SBYNS (*m*) **2.** *C* 4086^{3}—SBYNS br yrḥbwl' yrḥy.

SBN' (*m*) **2.** *C* 4543^{2}—yrḥy br SBN'.

SG' (*m*) **2.** *Inv. XI*, 50^{2}—mlkw br yrḥy SG'.

SGN' (*m*) **2.** *PS* 284—SGN' br ml' br tym'.

SWS' (*m*) **2.** *C* 4057^{3}—SWS' br [l]šmš br 'gylw [br ty]m'.

SḤLPH **1.** *373*, *Pal. 63*: 3^{2}—zbdlh dy mtqr' SḤLPH br šm'wn br 'yš'.

SṬṬYLS (*m*) **1.** *448*, *C* 3913 II^{104}—SṬṬYLS.

SṬM (*m*) **2.** *RTP* 407b—SṬM br zbdbwl zbd'th. *RTP* 480b—SṬM ḥyrn 'š''. *RTP* 752b—SṬM bwn' blty. *RTP* 997b—SṬM.

SṬM' (*m*) **2.** *RTP* 249a—SṬM[']. *RTP* 525b—SṬM'. *RTP* 720a—SṬM['] myt'.

SYG' (*f*) **2.** CaA 81^{2}—SYG' brt mlkw dn[. . . .

SYWD/R' (*m*) **2.** *Inv. XI*, 31^{3}—. . .] br SYWD/R'.

SYM' (*f*) **2.** 'Jewellery' p. 185—SYM' brt mtb(w)l.

SY'WN' (*m*) **1.** [5]*38*, *C* 4300^{3}—SY'WN'. *546*, *C* 4301 A^{2}—SY'WN' br šlmn. *552*, *C* 4302^{1}—SY'WN' br šlmn. **2.** *C* 4303^{2}—'g' br SY'WN' br tym'. *PS* 419—ydy't brt SY'WN' br tym['].

SY'N' (*m*) **2.** *C* 4073^{3}—SY'N' br zb[y]d'. *C* 4304^{2}—ydy't brt SY'N'.

SY'T (*f*) **2.** *C* 4530^{1}—SY'T brt ḥlyp'.

SKYY (*m*) **1.** *562*, StaB p. 164, A 1178^{4}—yrḥy br 'gylw br SKYY.

SLWQ' (*m*) **1.** [5]*50*, *C* 4094^{1}—SLWQ['] br mqwl' [br] tydwr' br [. . . . *575*, *C* 4048^{3}—qwšy brt SLWQ'.

SLWQWS (*m*) **1.** *566*, *C* 3934^{2}—ywlys 'wrlys 'g' dy mtqr' SLWQWS br 'zyzw 'zyzw š'yl'. *570*, *C* 3935^{1}—S[LWQWS] 'g' br 'zyzw 'z[yzw b]r š'yl'.

SLWQS (*m*) **1.** *562*, Ingh. B p. 104^{1}—SLWQS br typyls br SLWQS.

SMY' (*m*) **2.** *PS* 371—ml' ḥyrn SMY'.

SSN (*m*) **1.** *504*, Ingh. E (Malê) p. 76, II^{1}—ml' br ḥyrn br SSN. *526*, Ingh. E (Malê) p. 77, III^{1}—ywlys 'wrlys ml' br ḥyrn br SSN. *535*, Ingh. E (Malê) p. 78, IV^{1}—ywlyws 'wrlys ml' br ḥyrn br SSN. *545*, Ingh. E (Malê) p. 82, V^{2}—ywlys 'wrlys ml' br ḥyrn br ml' ḥyrn SSN. *546*, Ingh. E (Malê) p. 84, VI^{2}—ywlys 'wrlys ml' br 'wrlys ḥyrn br ml' ḥyrn SSN.

SPṬYMY' (*f*) **2.** *C* 3971^{5}—SPṬYMY' btzby.

SPṬYMYWS (*m*) **2.** *C* 3971$^{1, 4}$—SPṬYMYWS whblt 'tndr[ws] br SPṬ[YMY]WS ['dynt].

SPṬMY' (*m*/*f*) **1.** *582*, *C* 3946^{2}—SPṬMY' zbd'. *582*, *C* 3947^{1}—SPṬMY' btzby.

SPṬMYW' (*m*) **1.** *582*, *C* 3947^{2}—SPṬMYW' zbd'.

SPṬMYWS (*m*) **1.** *563*, *C* 3944^{1}—SPṬMYWS ḥyrn br 'dynt. *569*, *C* 3945^{1}—SPṬMYWS 'dynt. *573*, *C* 3938^{1}—SPṬMYWS wrwd. *575*, *C* 3940^{1}—SPṬMYWS wrwd. *575*, *C* 3940^{3}—ywlys 'wrlys SPṬMYWS yd' br 'lks[nd]rws ḥyrn srykw. [*576*], *C* 3941^{1}—SPṬ[MYWS wrw]d. [*576*], *C* 3941^{3}—[ywlys 'wrlys SPṬMY]WS ml[kw br mlwk' nšwm]. *578*, *C* 3943^{1}—SPṬMYWS wrwd. *582*, *C* 3946^{1}—SPṬMYWS 'dy[nt].

SPṬMYS (*m*) **1.** *574*, *C* 3939^{1}—SPṬMYS wrwd.

SPR (*m*) **2.** *Inv. XI*, 91—SPR.

SQḤ' (*m*) **2.** *RTP* 318 *bis* b—''ylmy SQḤ'.

SR' (*f*) **1.** [5]*58*, *C* 4042^{3}—SR'.

SRY (*m*) **1.** *425*, *C* 4159^{2}—zbd'th br 't'qb br zbd'th br SRY br zbd'th br mlkw dy mtqr' 'r'š. *492*, *C* 4194^{4}—SRY br zbd'th br 't'qb. **2.** Ingh. B p. 114, line 29—SRY wtymn'. Ingh. B, Pl. XLII^{1}—SRY br'' SRY.

SRYK' (*m*) **2.** Ben-Hayyim p. 145—[.]ḥ' 'mtb'[l] brt SRYK'.

SRYKW (*m*) **1.** *542*, *C* 4028^{5}—whblt br SRYKW. *575*, *C* 3940^{4}—ywlys 'wrlys spṭmyws yd' br 'lks[nd]rws ḥyrn SRYKW. **2.** *C* 4066^{3}—[ḥyrn] br SRYKW ḥy[rn]. *C* 4068^{3}—SRYKW.

'B' (*m*) **1.** *547*, *C* 4033^{5}—zbyd' br mlkw zbyd' 'B'. *568*, *Inv. XI*, 19^{3}—. . .] br zbwdw br 'B'. **2.** *C* 4101$^{2, 4}$—'B' / br [ky]ly b[r / ']B'. *RTP* 493a—'B' yrḥy. *RTP* 715a—yrḥy 'B'.

'BD' (*m*) **1.** *504*, Ingh. E (Malê) p. 76, II^{1}—tybwl br 'BD' br tybwl. **2.** *C* 4288^{7}—'zyz br tybwl dy mtqr' [']BD'. *C* 4482^{1}—'BD['/y] br ḥr' 'qm'. *C* 4550^{1}—'BD' br mrh. *C* 4564^{2}—. . .] br ['/z]BD' br yrḥy. *C* 4598^{2}—šlmt 'BD' 't'y šydn. *RTP* 37b—'BD['/y] 'mry mqymw 'g'. *RTP* 329b—dny 'BD'. *RTP* 344a—'BD' or 'mr'. *RTP* 884a—'BD' 'yyr. *RTP* 891b—'BD' br tym'.

'BDBL see BR 'BDBL.

'BDBL (*m*) **1.** *550*, *PNO* 42^{2}—'BDBL. **2.** *C* 4110^{1}—'BDBL khylw. *Inv. XI*, 64^{1}—'BDBL [y]rḥbwl'.

'BDW (*m*) **1.** *443*, *C* 3973^{6}—m'yty w'BDW.

'BDY (*m*) **1.** *409*, 'Wadi Hauran' 5^{5}—'BDY br zbdbwl' šm['wn]. [5]*52*, *C* 4040^{2}—[t]lymy br 'BDY [. . . . *569*, *C* 3936^{2}—ywlys 'wrlys šlmlt br ml' 'BDY. *578*, Ingh. E (Malkû) p. 104, XII^{8}—b'ly br 'BDY 'dwn. **2.** *C* 4259 A^{5}—zbdbwl br mqymw br nwrbl br zbd' [b]r 'BDY [zbd]bwl. *RTP* 84b—'BDY whblt. *RTP* 507a—'BDY br mk gbr'. *RTP* 633b—yd'w 'BDY. *Journal asiatique*, 12 (1918), 282 no. vii—'mry br 'g' br 'BDY.

Inv. X, 130^{3}—[zbyd' w'BDY w']bd'stwr bny n[š' 't']qb.

'BDLT (*m*) **1.** *560*, *C* 4044^{3}—'gylw br 'BDLT br 'rby.

'BD'' (*m*) **1.** *466*, Ingh. D, Pl. X^{2}—whb' 'BD'' bwly.

'BD'SWDR (*m*) **1.** *585*, Ingh. E (Malkû) p. 106, XIII^{5}—tm' brt 'BD'SWDR br yrḥbwl'.

'BD'STWR (*m*) **1.** *335*, *Inv. IX*, 7^{2}—[yd]y br mlkw br 'gylw br 'BD'STWR br 'tz'. *410*, Ingh. B p. 120, I^{1}—'BD'STWR br nwrbl br khylw br 'tnwry 'ṣwly. *550*, Ingh. B p. 124, II^{3}—ywly' 'wrly' šlmt brt 'BD'STWR br yrḥbwl'. **2.** *C* 4418^{1}—'BD'STWR br zbd'th. *C* 4419^{2}—b'ltg' brt 'BD'STWR nwrbl. *C* 4420^{3}—ydy'bl br bwn' br 'BD'STWR. *C* 4421 A^{1}—šlmt brt 'BD'STWR yrḥbwl'. *C* 4422^{1}—'BD'STWR br yrḥbwl'. *Inv. X*, 130^{4}—[zbyd' w'bdy w']BD'STWR bny n[š' 't']qb.

'BD'T' (*m*) **2.** *C* 4536^{1}—'BD'T' br šlmn.

'BD'TH (*m*) **1.** *378*, CaB 4 A^{1}—ydy'bl br tymḥ' br ydy'bl br 'BD'TH 'gdm. *378*, CaB 4 A^{3}—ḥyrn br 'BD'TH 'gdm.

'BDṢYD/R' (*m*) **1.** *472*, *C* 4172^{1}—'BDṢYD/R' br ḥry 't'qb br rpbwl.

'BDŠLM' (*m*) **2.** *RTP* 682b—'BDŠLM' 'rhdwn.

'BDŠMY' (*m*) **1.** *574*, Ingh. E (Naṣrallat) p. 110, II^{1}—ywlys 'wrlys ydy'bl br 'BDŠMY' br mlk'.

'BYDW (*m*) **1.** *443*, *C* 3973^{1}—'BYDW br 'nmw [br] š'dlt. **2.** *C* 4062^{3}—'BYDW 'sty br gwr' br nšm 'mṣr.

'BNY (*m*) **1.** *450*, *Inv. XI*, 4^{2}—'BNY.

'BNRGL (*m*) **1.** *454*, *C* 4000^{3}—'BNRGL br ḥry tym' br 'nn. *471*, StaA p. 46, I^{2}—'BNRGL br ḥr' mqy br ytm'. *535* or *536*, StaB p. 152, A 1184^{3}—...]m br 'BNRGL. **2.** *Inv. XI*, 42^{1}—'BNRGL br ḥry lšmš br ḥyrn gl'.

'BS' (*m*) **2.** *C* 4368^{1}—'BS' [b]r šlwm [w]'mt'.

'BSY (*m*) **1.** *[4]53*, *C* 3916^{2}—ns' br ḥl' br ns' br ḥl' br rp'l br 'BSY. *535*, Ingh. E (Malê) p. 78, IV^{1}—ywlys 'wrlys 'BSY br ḥnyn' br ḥnyn' br 'g' yrq. **2.** Ingh. E (Malê) p. 79 A—'BSY br ḥnyn' ḥnyn' yrq. Ingh. E (Malê) p. 79 C—'BSY. Ingh. E (Malê) p. 80 E—btšmy' brt 'BSY. Ingh. E (Malê) p. 82 H—š'dy br 'BSY br ḥnyn' yrq.

'BŠY (*m*) **1.** *450*, *Inv. XI*, 3^{3}—'BŠY. **2.** *RTP* 978a—yrḥy 'BŠY. 'Hypogée' p. 224, Pl. II^{1}—'BŠY brt 'wydlt.

'BŠLM' (*m*) **1.** *515*, *C* 4198 B^{2}—[zby]d['] br šlmny br 'BŠLM'.

'BŠMY' (*m*) **1.** *576*, Ingh. E (Naṣrallat) p. 112, III^{2}—ywlys 'wrlys ydy'bl br 'BŠMY' mlk'.

'G[2. *Inv. VIII*, 154^{1}—...] br 'G[....

'G' (*m*) **1.** *[3]84*, *C* 4193^{1}—'gylw br 'G' br mqymw br ḥdwdn. *[3]84*, *C* 4193^{3}—'G'. *400+?*, *C* 3988^{2}—mlkw br 'G' '[by]. *[4]23*, *Inv. X*, 69^{1}—ḥggw br yrḥy br 'G' ydy'bl. *430*, *Inv. VIII*, 62^{3}—š'd br 'G' br 'wydy. *439*, *C* 3920^{2}—tym' br lšmšy br 'G' ydy'bl. *[4]40*, 'Iraq' p. 64^{1}, Pl. 10—'G' br ml' br 'gylw br tybwl dy mtqrh br 'ḥty. *447*, *C* 3968^{3}—...] wmlkw br 'wyd' 'nqy br 'G' br [.... *447*, *C* 3968^{4}—...] nṣryḥby br 'G' nṣryḥby 'rṭbn. *46*[.], CaD 11^{5}—yrḥb[wl' br ml]kw br 'G' [.... *461*, *C* 3967^{2}—[ḥ]gy br 'G' ḥgy. *482*, CaB 14^{3}—mlkw br mqymw br 'G'. *486*, *C* 3914^{2}—yrḥbwl' [br] 'G' w'wyd' br ḥdwdn bny yrḥbwl' br ḥdwdn br zbdbwl br ḥdw[dn] prmwn. *500+?*, *C* 4197^{2}—ml' br 'G' br ml' br 'gylw 'yt[yb]l. *500+?*, *C* 4197^{2}—'G' br šlm' šmšgrm br br[.]š 'G' br 'ytybl. *513*, *C* 4294^{1}—'G' br tybwl zwr. *518*, *C* 4014^{4}—mky brt 'G'. *524*, Ingh. E (Malkû) p. 96, V^{2}—'G'. *527*, *Inv. XI*, 16^{3}—bwn' 'G' gbyns. *529*, StaB p. 151, A 1209^{5}—ml' br 'G' ns' rb'. *535*, Ingh. E (Malê) p. 78, IV^{1}—ywlys 'wrlys 'bsy br ḥnyn' br ḥnyn' br 'G' yrq. (*536*), *PNO* 73^{3}—'G['] br yrḥ[y]. *545*, *C* 4206^{1}—ywl' 'wrly' 'G' wšlm' [...nb]wmr bny ḥlh. *552*, Ingh. E (Malkû) p. 100, IX^{2}—ywlys 'wrlys 'G' br rwḥbl. *555*, Ingh. 'Th.' p. 129^{3}—yrḥy 'grp' yrḥy ydy'bl 'G' y't. *560*, Ingh. E (Malkû) p. 101, X^{2}—'G' br rwḥbl. *566*, *C* 3934^{2}—ywlys 'wrlys 'G' dy mtqr' slwqws br 'zyzw 'zyzw s'yl'. *570*, *C* 3935^{1}—s[lwqws] 'G' br 'zyzw 'z[yzw b]r š'yl'. *579*, *C* 4053^{3}—b'ltg' bt 'G'. **2.** *C* 4079^{3}—[']G' br zbdbwl br [.... *C* 4205—'G' br mtnw. *C* 4293 A^{3}—mlkw br 'G' tybwl zwrw. *C* 4295$^{1, 2}$—[']G' br / mlkw 'G' / zwr. *C* 4303^{1}—'G' br sy'wn' br tym'. *C* 4323^{2}—'G' br yrḥy y't. *C* 4323—'G'. *C* 4324^{3}—[ydy']bl br 'G' y'tw. *C* 4325^{5}—yrḥy br 'G' y't. *C* 4330^{2}—[']G' [br] zbd'th whb'. *C* 4336^{3}—'qm' brt zbdbwl br 'G'. *C* 4350$^{1, 3}$—'G' / br ḥyrn / [br] 'G'. *C* 4360^{3}—ḥyrn br šlmn br 'G'. *C* 4394 B^{3}—ḥrt' bt 'G'. *C* 4411^{6}—yrḥb[wl'] nš' 'G'. *C* 4423^{3}—nš' br 'G' nš'. *C* 4468^{2}—ḥggw br 'G' br ydy'b[l]. *C* 4471^{3}—yrḥy br mtny br 'G'. *C* 4472^{2}—'qm' brt '(G)' br [mt]ny. *C* 4475^{1}—'G' br bwn'. *C* 4537 A^{2}—yrḥy br 'G'. *C* 4538^{3}—ḥb' brt 'G' yrḥy. *C* 4557^{4}—ḥnyn' br ḥnyn' 'G' yrq. *C* 4571 A^{2}—['G]' wšlmt. *C* 4571 B^{1}—'G' wšlmt bn[y] 'brwq ḥbn. *C* 4597^{2}—bwrp' 'G' zbyd' myṭq'. *RTP* 13b—...]d/rw br 'G[']. *RTP* 37b—'bd['/y] 'mry mqymw 'G'. *RTP* 429a—yrḥy 'G'. *RTP* 429b—yrḥy 'G'. *RTP* 474b—'G' 'G'. *RTP* 562b—'G'. *RTP* 591b—'G'. *RTP* 622b—'G'. *RTP* 650b—'G' 'w[.]. *RTP* 893a—'G'. *RTP* 899b—'G'. 'Tessères' 14a—'G' šm'wn. *PS* 124—'G' br mtny. *PS* 244 A—’mwn br nš’ ‘G’ šlm’. Ingh. B, Pl. XLIV^{1}—šlm brt ‘G’. Ingh. B p. 135, IV C^{2}—b‘ltg’ br ‘G’. Ingh. B p. 135, IV D^{2}—mws’ br ‘G’. Ingh. B p. 135, IV E^{2}—bty br ‘G’. Ingh. B p. 135, IV F^{2}—’ḥ’ brt ‘G’. Ingh. D, Pl. VIII^{2}—yrḥbwl’ br nš’ ‘G’ šlm’. Ingh. E (Malê) p. 79 B—ḥnyn’ br ḥnyn’ ‘G’ yrq. ‘IP’ p. 159, 18^{2}—‘t‘m brt ‘G’ šryky. *Pal. 59*: 17^{2}—zbd’ br ‘G’. *PNO* 7 A^{1}—‘G[’ b]r ḥnyn’ br ‘gy[lw]. *PNO* 7 B—qryn ‘G’. *PNO* 41^{2}—brh’ br ‘G’. *Inv. VIII*, 11^{2}—tm’ brt ‘G’ ’ṣyd/rny. *Inv. VIII*, 108^{4}—ḥgy br yrḥy br ‘G’ ydy‘bl. *Inv. VIII*, 185 A^{3}—’qm’ brt ‘G’. *Journal asiatique*, 12 (1918), 282 no. vii—’mry br ‘G’ br ‘bdy. ‘Hypogée’ p. 234, Pl. II^{2}—ml’ br ‘G’ bwrp’. ‘Hypogée’ p. 234, Pl. II^{2}—bwly’ brt ‘G’ br bwrp’. ‘Hypogée’ p. 225, Pl. III^{1}—‘G’ br bwrp’. ‘Hypogée’ p. 228, Pl. IV^{2}—bwrp’ br ‘G’. Ben-Hayyim p. 146, V^{2}—‘ty brt ‘G’ br tybwl.

[‘G]B’ 2. *C* 4436^{1}—see [’B]B’.

‘GY (*m*) **2.** *Pal. 60*: 13^{3}—‘GY or ‘gyz.

‘GYZ (*m*) **2.** *Pal. 60*: 13^{3}—‘GYZ or ‘gy.

‘GYL’ (*m*) **2.** *RTP* 666b—ḥyrn ‘GYL’.

‘GYLW (*m*) **1.** *307*, CaD 17^{3}—‘GYLW br ’yd‘n. *315*, CaD 12 A^{2}—‘GYLW br [. . . . *329*, *Pal. 63*: 2^{3}—‘GYLW br ydy‘bl br bwrp’. *335*, *Inv. IX*, 7^{2}—[yd]y br mlkw br ‘GYLW br ‘bd‘stwr br ‘tz’. *335*, *Inv. IX*, 7^{3}—‘GYLW wydy. *340*, *C* 3922^{1}—‘GYLW br tymy b[r] zbdbwl. *345*, *C* 3980^{4}—tymw br ‘GYLW rbbt. *345*, *C* 3980^{6}—‘GYLW br nwry zbdb(w)l. *3[6]2*, *C* 3923^{1}—mqymw br ‘GYLW br pṣy’[l] br tymy dy mtqrh ḥkyšw. *368*, *C* 4119^{3}—‘GYLW br ’wšy br khylw. *378*, CaB 4 A^{3}—‘GYLW wtymḥ’ w‘ty bny ḥyrn br ‘bd‘th ’gdm. *[3]84*, *C* 4193^{1}—‘GYLW br ‘g’ br mqymw br ḥdwdn. *3[92]*, CaA 7^{2}—zbdbwl [br] ‘G[YLW] br [‘mt] br [. . . . *399*, CaB 6 A^{2}—’‘ylmy wnrglzbd w‘GYLW. *430*, CaB 7^{1}—šm‘wn br bwrp’ br ‘GYLW mtn. *443*, *C* 3987^{1}—‘GYLW br mlkw [b]r mqymw qšṭy. *[4]40*, ‘Iraq’ p. 64^{3}, Pl. 10—‘g’ br ml’ br ‘GYLW br tybwl dy mtqrh br ’ḥty. *[454]*, *C* 4167—lšmš br nwrbl br mqymw br ‘GYLW ’qml. *470*, *Pal. 60*: 4^{2}—yrḥy br ‘GYLW [b]r yrḥy. *482*, CaB 14^{2}—‘GYLW br bwr[p]’. *482*, CaB 14^{7}—‘GYLW. *500+?*, C 4197^{2}—ml’ br ‘g’ br ml’ br ‘GYLW ’yt[yb]l. *502*, *C* 4173^{1}—nrqys br ḥry ‘GYLW br mlkw. *502*, *C* 4174^{1}—nrqys br ḥry ‘GYLW. *507*, *C* 4354^{9}—. . .] br ‘GY[LW] whby. *510*, *Inv. X*, 44^{2}—‘GYLW br mqy ‘GYLW šwyr’. *524*, *Inv. XI*, 11^{2}—‘GY[LW br] tymrṣw b[r] ḥd’. *525*, *Inv. XI*, 12^{3}—[‘G]YLW br zbdbwl br [. . . . *525*, Ingh. E (Malkû) p. 98, VII^{2}—ywlys ’wrlys ‘GYLW br ’prhṭ br ḥry zbdbwl br mlkw ’swyt. *525*, ‘Malkû’ p. 106^{4}—ywlys br ’wrlys ‘GYLW br ’prhṭ br ḥry zbdbwl. *550*, Ingh. B p. 124, II^{6}—ywly’ ’wrly’ mlkw br ‘GYLW br šlmn. *555*, Ingh. ‘Th.’ p. 129^{7}—‘GYLW. *560*, *C* 4044^{3}—‘GYLW br ‘bdlt br ‘rby. *562*, StaB p. 164, A 1178^{3}—yrḥy br ‘GYLW br skyy. *574*, *C* 4052^{6}—‘GYLW. *581*, *PNO* 14^{3}—‘GYLW kylywn. *583*, CaA 31^{2}—ḥdwdn br ‘GYLW mqy. *583*, CaA 31^{6}—. . .] ‘GYLW. *583*, CaA 31^{7}—‘GYLW br mhrdd. *583*, CaA 31^{8}—‘GYLW br wrwd. **2.** *C* 3990^{4}—[‘GY]LW. *C* 4057^{4}—sws’ br [l]šmš br ‘GYLW [br ty]m’. *C* 4060^{3}—yd‘w br [‘G]YLW br yd‘w. *C* 4077^{3}—‘GYLW br ḥyr[’]. *C* 4097^{2}—šlmn br ‘GYLW. *C* 4185—nrqys ‘GYLW. *C* 4187^{1}—’lhš’ w‘GYLW wṣ[‘dy bny m]qymw. *C* 4215^{2}—[‘GYLW br šlmlt br nš’]. *C* 4215^{2}—[‘GYLW]. *C* 4319^{2}—‘GYLW br mqymw br mlkw ’‘wyd. *C* 4326^{3}—[ḥr]t’ brt ‘GYLW šlmwy. *C* 4332^{1}—‘GYLW br mlkw br mqym[w]. *C* 4346^{2}—’qm’ brt ‘GYLW. *C* 4362^{1}—‘GYLW br ’wšy. *C* 4430^{1}—‘GYLW br yrḥy. *C* 4497^{2}—‘GYLW br ‘tnwry. *C* 4498—‘tnwry br ‘GYLW. *C* 4533—bwly br ‘GYLW. *C* 4623^{5}—ḥyr’ br ḥyrn br ḥyrn br ‘GYLW. ‘Malkû’ p. 104, line 13—’prhṭ br ‘GYLW. *Journal asiatique*, 12 (1918), 281 no. v—r‘t’ brt ‘GYLW br yrḥbwl’. Ingh. B p. 135, line 7—mrty ‘GYLW. Ingh. B p. 135, IV B^{2}—‘GYLW br ’n’. Ingh. D, Pl. X^{1}—’mby brt ‘GYLW. *PS* 225—‘GYLW. *RTP* 14b—‘GYLW tymḥ’. *RTP* 60b—‘GYLW bwrp’ qšṭ’. *RTP* 70b—mkb[l] ‘GYLW. *RTP* 178a—‘GYLW. *RTP* 233a—tymrṣw ‘GY[LW]. *RTP* 299b—zbdbwl [‘GY]LW. *RTP* 335b—‘GYLW wmškw. *RTP* 378a—mqymw ‘GY[LW]. *RTP* 420b—‘GYLW ’šqr’. *RTP* 477b—‘GYLW bwn’. *RTP* 516b—‘GYL[W]. *RTP* 537a—‘GYLW ‘GYLW ’šm. *RTP* 656b—[lšm]š [‘G]YLW. *RTP* 670b—‘tnw[r]y ‘GYLW. *RTP* 709a—‘GYLW kytwt. *RTP* 731a—‘GYLW kptwt. *RTP* 799a—ḥy(rn) ‘GY(LW). *RTP* 828a—[‘]GYL[W]. *RTP* 885b—‘GYLW. CaA 62^{1}—. . .] br ‘GYLW br mlkw [. . . . CaA 68 A^{3}—tymṣ’ br ’lhš’ ‘GYLW. CaA 85 B^{2}—mqymw br ‘GYLW br zbd’. CaC 17^{2}—‘GYLW b[r. . . .]ny ḥdwdn. CaD 25^{3}—. . .]š ‘GYLW br l[šmš]. CaD 32^{2}—mlkw br ḥyrn [br ‘]GYL[W]. CaD 37^{1}—‘GYLW. *Pal. 60*: 5 B^{3}—ḥgt brt ‘GYL[W] ‘mr. *PNO* 2—ḥnyn’ ‘GYLW ’sdy. *PNO* 2 *bis*—[‘GY]LW ’sdy. *PNO* 7 A^{2}—‘g[’ b]r ḥnyn’ br ‘GY[LW]. *Inv. VIII*, 4^{5}—’ytybl br tym’ br ’ytybl br ‘GYLW. *Inv. VIII*, 38^{2}—. . .] ‘GY[L]W [. . . . *Inv. VIII*, 50 B^{1}—‘GYL[W] b(r) tymn’. *Inv. VIII*, 58^{1}—ywly’ ’wrly’ nwry wzbdbwl w[‘GYLW] bny mq[y . . . .]ḥbzy. *Inv. VIII*, 94^{1}—[‘]GYLW br yrḥy br ḥry ḥy[rn]. *Inv. VIII*, 102^{1}—. . .‘]GYLW [. . . . *Inv. VIII*, 119^{3}—ḥnyn’ br ‘GYLW nbwl’. *Inv. VIII*, 165^{2}—whblt br ‘GYLW br yrḥbwl’. *Inv. VIII*, 179^{1}—‘GYLW br mqymw br rpbwl br nṣrlt. *Inv. X*, 94—‘GYL[W. . . . *Inv. XI*, 40^{4}—. . .‘G]YLW [. . . . *Inv. XI*, 41—‘GYLW br mqym. *Inv. XI*, 69—. . .] ‘GYLW br y‘t br y[. . . . *Inv. XI*, 75^{1}—‘GYLW br ḥyrn. *Inv. XI*, 88^{1}—mlkw br ‘GYLW dy [m]tqrh br ’’ry. *Inv. XI*, 98—

bwrp' ʿGYLW. 'Hypogée' p. 199, line 8—bwrp' br ʿGYLW br bwrp' qs[m'....

ʿGYLY (*m*) **2.** *C* 4532³—lwy' brt yrḥy br ʿGYLY.

ʿGLBWL' (*m*) **1.** *[3]94*, *C* 3969³—ʿGLBWL' [....

ʿD' (*f*) **1.** *562*, StaB p. 160, A 1177⁴—ʿD'.

ʿDWN (*m*) **1.** *578*, Ingh. E (Malkû) p. 104, XII⁸—bʿly br ʿbdy ʿDWN.

ʿDL (*m*) **2.** *Inv. IX*, 5 A²—zbd' [br] ʿDL b(r) zbd['].

ʿDN (*m*) **2.** *C* 4380—btwhby bt ʿDN.

ʿWB (*m*) **2.** *C* 3907⁸—mšlm br ʿWB.

ʿWD'L (*m*) **1.** *514*, *C* 4012³—...] ʿWD'L.

ʿWDW (*m*) **1.** *345*, *C* 3980³—[wh]by br ʿtnwry ʿWDW.

ʿWYD (*m*) **1.** *490*, *C* 4006³—ḥ[nt]' brt [ʿW]YD. *504*, *C* 4199²—pṣy'l br ʿstwrg' br ʿWYD br lšmš br lšmš. **2.** *RTP* 628a—ʿWYD.

ʿWYD' (*m*) **1.** *409*, 'Wadi Hauran' 5⁶—ʿWYD' d/r'[.... *447*, *C* 3968³—...]wmlkw br ʿWYD' 'nqy br ʿg' br [.... *486*, *C* 3914²—yrḥbwl' [br] ʿg' wʿWYD' br ḥdwdn bny yrḥbwl' br ḥdwdn br zbdbwl br ḥdw[dn] prmwn. *[49]6*, *C* 4196—[ʿWYD' br yrḥy br ml' br 'pw.... *551*, StaB p. 156, A 1175⁵—ʿWYD'. **2.** *C* 4227²—ʿty br ʿtntn ʿWYD' tybwl. *C* 4228²—ʿty br ʿ[tntn] ʿWYD'. *C* 4230¹—ḥby br ʿWYD'. *C* 4296 A⁵—bʿlt[g]' brt ʿWYD' b[r] tymrṣw. *C* 4454—[ʿ]WYD' bgdn. *RTP* 30a—ʿ[W]YD' br tymrṣw br ʿWYD'. *RTP* 341b—ʿWYD' wwhblt. *RTP* 424b—ʿWYD' bn[..]mn. *RTP* 851b—ḥdwdn ʿWYD' [ḥdwd]n. CaB 2 B³—...] br ʿWYD' br mlkw. CaD 5¹—rb'l br ʿWYD' br ydʿy. *PNO* 47 A¹—ʿWYD' br zbdʿy. *PNO* 47 C—ʿWYD'. *Pal. 63*: 10²—...(b)rt ʿWYD'.

ʿWYDW (*m*) **1.** *426*, CaD 21¹—ʿWYDW wmlkw wyrḥbwl[' wḥggw bny] bwlm' br ʿwydy br bwlm' 'db. **2.** *RTP* 421b—yrḥbwl' ʿWYDW.

ʿWYDY (*m*) **1.** *426*, CaD 21²—ʿwydw wmlkw wyrḥbwl[' wḥggw bny] bwlm' br ʿWYDY br bwlm' 'db. *430*, *Inv. VIII*, 62³—šʿd br ʿg' br ʿWYDY. **2.** *RTP* 494b—šʿdw ʿWYDY. *RTP* 760b—šlmlt br tym' ʿWYDY.

ʿWYDLT (*m*) **1.** *412*, CaB 13 A²—ydyʿbl br whblt wwhblt br ʿWYDLT bny ydyʿbl br 'mrš'. *504*, CaB 13 B³—[m]zbn' wyrḥy wzbdʿt' bny ʿWYDLT. **2.** CaA 76¹—ʿWYDLT [b]r yrḥy nṣr'. Ingh. B, Pl. XLIX²—ḥyr' br ʿWYDLT br mqymw ʿlbn. *Inv. IV*, 24²—tymlt ʿWYDLT 'mrsʿ. *Inv. VIII*, 19¹—ʿWYDLT [b]r yrḥy nṣr'. 'Hypogée' p. 224, Pl. II¹—ʿbšy brt ʿWYDLT.

ʿWYDT (*f*) **2.** *Inv. VIII*, 117¹—ʿWYDT.

ʿWMY (*m*) **2.** *RTP* 157b—ʿWMY.

ʿWTN (*m*) **2.** *C* 4361¹—ʿWTN br lšmš 'wšy.

ʿZWLT see BR ʿZWLT.

ʿZY (*m*) **2.** *RTP* 707a—ʿZ[Y]. *RTP* 708a—ʿZY. *RTP* 708b—ʿZY.

ʿZYZ (*m*) **2.** *C* 4288⁴—ʿZYZ br tybwl dy mtqr' [ʿ]bd'. *C* 4592¹—ʿZYZ br 'byḥy mqy.

ʿZYZW (*m*) **1.** *328*, *C* 3925²—ʿZYZW br ydyʿbl brky. *330*, *C* 3924²—ydyʿbl br ʿZYZW br ydyʿ[bl]. *[4]51*, *Inv. X*, 112⁴—[mlkw br ʿZYZW]. *466*, *PNO* 6 A—mqy br ʿZYZW. *490*, CaD 8⁴—ʿZYZW br ʿd' br rb'l. *502*, CaB 4 B²—bgy br ʿZYZW br mlkw. *566*, *C* 3934³—ywlys 'wrlys ʿg' dy mtqr' slwqws br ʿZYZW ʿZYZW š'yl'. *570*, *C* 3935²—s[lwqws] ʿG' br ʿZYZW ʿZ[YZW b]r š'yl'. **2.** *C* 3976³—bwln' br ʿZYZW br ʿZYZW br š'yl'. *RTP* 549b—ʿZYZW. Ingh. B, Pl. XLI²—ʿZYZW 'byḥy. 'IP' p. 158, 17 A⁵—zbd' br ʿZYZW br br zbd'. CaA 63²—...] br ʿZ[YZW.... *PNO* 10B—ʿZYZW.

ʿZYZY (*m*) **2.** *C* 3965¹—ʿZYZY br ml[kw....

ʿYT' (*f*) **1.** *400+?*, *C* 3988¹—ʿY[T' brt m]lkw br whblt br ʿrgn. **2.** *C* 4461²—ʿYT' brt 'ʿylmy yrḥy.

ʿ[K]T' (*f*) **2.** *C* 4365²—ʿ[K]T'.

ʿL' (*f*) **1.** *425*, *C* 4374²—ʿL' brt yrḥy 'bb. *425*, *C* 4374 *bis*²—ʿL' brt yrḥy 'bb. *500+?*, *Inv. XI*, 23³—ʿL' brt zbyd' br ʿtʿy rp'. **2.** Ingh. D, Pl. IX²—ʿL' brt yrḥy. CaA 78¹—ʿL' brt 'ydʿn br yrḥy mqy.

ʿLBN (*m*) **1.** *472*, *C* 4001⁶—...] ʿLBN m[.... **2.** *C* 4309³—ḥbyby br nš' ʿLBN. *C* 4311 B³—brwq' br ns' ʿLBN. Ingh. B, Pl. XLIX²—ḥyr' br ʿwydlt br mqymw ʿLBN.

ʿLG (*m*) **2.** *RTP* 293a—zbyd' ʿLG. *RTP* 396b—mqy ʿLG.

ʿLG' (*m*) **2.** *RTP* 395b—mqymw ʿLG' zbdlh mšy.

ʿLY (*m*) **2.** *Inv. VIII*, 136¹—ʿLY br tymlt br bydn.

ʿLYY (*m/f*) **1.** *448*, *C* 3913 I³—mlkw br ʿLYY br mqymw. **2.** *C* 4343²—[ʿ]LYY brt whb' ʿštwr. *Inv. VIII*, 110³—ḥbyby mqymy br ʿLYY.

ʿLYBWL (*m*) **2.** *Inv. XI*, 54¹—[m]qymw br ʿLYBWL br tymr[ṣw].

ʿLYBʿL (*m*) **2.** *Inv. VIII*, 5²—mky brt tymw ʿLYBʿL. *Inv. XI*, 63—ʿLYBʿL.

[ʿ]LYW (*m*) **2.** *C 4002*^{3}—. . .] dny w[ʿ]LYW bny ʿšt[rg]ʾ br dny [. . . .

ʿLYNʾ (*m*) **1.** *490*, *C* 3950^{2}—ydʾ br šrykw br ḥy[rn] b[r] ʿLYNʾ ṣprʾ. *490*, *C* 3951^{1}—ʿLYNʾ br ḥyrn br [ʿ]LYNʾ ṣ[prʾ]. *490*, *C* 3952^{1}—šrykw br ḥyrn br ʿLYNʾ ṣprʾ. *490*, *C* 3953^{2}—ḥyrn br šrykw br ḥyrn br ʿLYNʾ ṣprʾ.

ʿLYŠʾ (*m*) **1.** *426*, *C* 4129 A^{3}—bʿltgʾ wʿLYŠʾ bny bwnʾ br šby. *426*, *C* 4129 B^{2}—ʿLYŠʾ wbʿltgʾ bny bwnʾ br šby br blšwr br ḥyrn. *475*, *Inv. X*, 24^{2}—ʿLYŠʾ. **2.** *RTP* 181b—ʿLYŠʾ ʾšqrʾ. *RTP* 351b—ʿLYŠʾ mlkw. *Inv. VIII*, 53 B—ʿlyt brt ʿLYŠʾ. *Inv. XI*, 80^{2}—ʿLYŠʾ wdynʾ.

ʿLYT (*f*) **2.** *C* 4259 D—ʿLYT. *C* 4260^{1}—ʿLYT brt zbdbwl. *C* 4411^{1}—ʿLYT [bt] yrḥb[wlʾ]. *C* 4412^{1}—ʿLYT brt zbdbw[l]. *C* 4500^{3}—šʿdʾ brt ʿLYT. *Journal asiatique*, 12 (1918), 294 no. xvii—ʿLYT brt zbdbwl. *Inv. VIII*, 53 A^{1}—ʿLYT. *Inv. VIII*, 53 B—ʿLYT brt ʿlyšʾ.

ʿMBKRʾ (*m*) **1.** *458*, *PNO* 55 C—wrdn wbrwqʾ wʿMBKRʾ.

ʿMLʾ (*m*) **2.** *PNO* 30—ʿMLʾ.

ʿMR (*m*) **2.** *Pal. 60*: 5 B^{4}—ḥgt brt ʿgyl[w] ʿMR.

ʿMRʾ (*m*) **2.** *RTP* 344a—ʿMRʾ or ʿbdʾ.

ʿMRW (*m*) **1.** *457*, *C* 3911^{5}—zbdbwl wʿtnwry wmlkw wʿMRW wydyʿbl bny bršmš br zbdbwl. *457*, *C* 3911^{11}—blḥy brt ʿMRW.

ʿMRT (*m*) **1.** *467*, *C* 4241—ʿM[RT] br lšmš br yrḥbwl[ʾ]. **2.** *RTP* 783b—ḥyrʾ yrḥy ʿMRT.

ʿMT (*m*) **1.** *3[92]*, CaA 7^{2}—zbdbwl [br] ʿg[ylw] br [ʿMT] br [. . . . **2.** CaA 10^{2}—[mʿny br] ʿMT br ḥdw[dn pr]mw[n]. *RTP* 992b—ʿMT. *Inv. VIII*, 42^{1}—ʿMT br mq[ymw]. *Inv. XI*, 57—bwlyʾ ʿMT.

ʿNBW (*m*) **2.** *PNO* 65—ʿNBW br ḥyrn.

ʿNYNY (*m*) **2.** *RTP* 167a—ʿNYNY tymy.

ʿNMW (*m*) **1.** *443*, *C* 3973^{1}—ʿbydw br ʿNMW [br] šʿdlt.

ʿNN (*m*) **1.** *454*, *C* 4000^{4}—ʾbnrgl br ḥry tymʾ br ʿNN. *454*, *C* 4000^{6}—ʿNN. *555*, StaB p. 160, A 1206^{4}—mlʾ br [y]hybʾ ʿNN. *585*, Ingh. E (Malkû) p. 106, XIII^{7}—ʾbgr br tymʾ br ʿNN. **2.** *PNO* 47 B—ʿNN.

ʿNNW (*m*) **1.** *425*, *C* 3994 A^{6,7}—ʿNNW br ml[kw] / ʿNNW. *425*, *C* 3994 C^{6,7}—ʿNNW br / mlkw ʿNNW. *539*, StaF p. 40, 2—ʿNNW. **2.** *C* 4238^{2}—ml[k]w rbʾ br [ʿN]NW mqym[w]. *Inv. XI*, 37^{1}—ʿNNW. ʿWadi Hauranʾ 12^{5}—ʿNNW.

ʿNNY (*m*) **1.** *425*, *C* 3994 B^{6,7}—ʿNNY [br] / mlkw ʿNNY. **2.** *PNO* 72^{7}—ʿNNY br [. . . . *Inv. VIII*, 15^{3}—šbty brt ʿNNY br mqymy ḥlʾ.

ʿSTWRGʾ (*m*) **1.** *395*, CaD 29^{2}—ʾbgr br pṭrqls dy mtqrh ʿSTWRGʾ br lqyšw. *504*, *C* 4199^{2}—pṣyʾl br ʿSTWRGʾ br ʿwyd br lšmš br lšmš. *544*, CaB 10 A^{1}—lšmš br ʿSTWRGʾ [b]r lš[mš] br [b]ryky br lqy šlmn. *544*, CaB 10 A^{2}—lšmš br ʿST[WRG]ʾ [br] lšmš. **2.** *RTP* 979a—mqymw ʿSTWRGʾ. ʿAfriqueʾ p. 266 B^{2}—ʿSTWRGʾ.

ʿSTY (*m*) **2.** *C* 4062^{3}—ʿbydw ʿSTY br gwrʾ br nšm ʾmṣr.

ʿSTYʾ (*f*) **2.** *Pal. 62*: 7^{1}—ʿSTYʾ brt ʾdynt [br] yrḥy.

ʿQBY (*m*) **1.** *453*, *C* 4561^{6}—ydyʿbl br ʿtʿqb ydyʿbl ʿtʿqb ʿQBY. *468*, *C* 4616^{6}—ʿtʿqb br ydyʿbl br ʿtʿqb ydyʿbl ʿQBY. *[4]73*, *C* 4562^{5}—[tym]rṣw rbʾ br ʿtʿqb br ydyʿbl br ʿtʿqb ʿQBY.

ʿQYBʾ (*m*) **2.** *C* 4117^{1}—ʿQYBʾ br ʿtʿqb gdyʾ. *C* 4394 A^{3}—[b]wlʿʾ bt [ʿ]QYBʾ. *Inv. VIII*, 130^{3}—ʾḥtʾ brt ʿQYBʾ.

ʿQRBN (*m*) **2.** *C* 4450^{1}—ʿQRBN brh dbršmš.

ʿRBY (*m*) **1.** *556*, *C* 4041^{4}—nḥyʿzyz [ʿ]RBY. *560*, *C* 4044^{4}—ʿgylw br ʿbdlt br ʿRBY.

ʿRGʾ (*m*) **1.** *574*, *Inv. XI*, 20^{5}—[y]rḥbwlʾ br yrḥbwlʾ ʿRGʾ.

ʿRGN (*m*) **1.** *400 + ?*, *C* 3988^{2}—ʿy[tʾ brt m]lkw br whblt br ʿRGN. **2.** *C* 4364^{4}—yrḥy br y(d)yʿbl br šmʿwn ʿRGN.

ʿRYMʾ (*m*) **1.** *390*, *Inv. XI*, 81^{5}—. . .]rbʾ br zbdbw ʿRYMʾ. *400*, ʿFouillesʾ p. 170^{1}—mqymw br mqymw br zbdbwl ʿRYMʾ. *400*, ʿFouillesʾ p. 172^{3}—[m]q[ymw br mqymw br zbdbwl] ʿRYM[ʾ]. **2.** CaA 36^{2}—mqymw br mqymw ʿRYMʾ. CaA 36^{3}—mqymw br mqymw ʿRYMʾ. CaD 12 B^{4}—mqym[w] br zbdb[wl] br ʿRYM[ʾ].

ʿŠY (*m*) **2.** *C* 4099^{1}—ʿŠY.

ʿŠYLT (*m*) **1.** *471*, CaB 1 A^{1}—tymrṣw br bwrpʾ br mlkw br ʿŠYLT.

ʿŠYLTʾ (*m*) **2.** *RTP* 764b—mlkw br tymʾ br ʿŠYLTʾ.

ʿŠRʾ (*m*) **1.** *[5]24*, *PNO* 13^{2}—zbdbwl br ʿŠRʾ.

ʿŠTWR (*m*) **1.** *547*, *C* 4209—[ywlys ʾwrlys zbydʾ] br ʿŠTWR zbydʾ. *558*, *C* 3933^{2}—ywlys ʾwrlys zbydʾ br mqymw br zbydʾ ʿŠTWR bydʾ. **2.** *C* 4343^{4}—[ʿ]llyy brt whbʾ ʿŠTWR. *Journal asiatique*, 12 (1918), 282 no. vi—. . . ʿ]ŠTWR [gdn]bw. *RTP* 997a—zbydʾ ʿŠTWR.

‘ŠTWRG’ (*m*) **1.** [*4*]*30*, *C* 3982[1]—. . .]’ mlkw [‘Š]TWRG’. *504*, *C* 4199[13]—šgl brt lšmš ‘ŠTWRG’ br pṣy’l.

‘ŠT[RG]’ (*m*) **2.** *C* 4002[3]—. . .] dny w[‘]lyw bny ‘ŠT[RG]’ br dny [. . . .

‘T[**2.** *C* 4352 B[1]—‘T[. . . .] brt ydy‘bl.

‘T’ **2.** *Inv. VIII*, 107[4]—see BR‘T’.

‘T’M (*f*) **1.** [*3*]*94*, *C* 3969[1]—‘T’M b[rt. . . .] ’wšy. **2.** ‘IP’ p. 159, 18[1]—‘T’M brt ‘g’ šryky.

‘TD/RN (*f*) **2.** *C* 4622[2]—‘TD/RN brt yml’. *PS* 395—‘TD/RN brt bgdn.

‘TD/RT (*m*) **2.** *C* 4596[4]—‘tntn br kyly br mškw b[r] ‘TD/RT br ḥyrn.

‘TH (*f*) **1.** [*3*?]*42*, ‘Dédicace’ p. 44, 2—‘TH [brt] nš’ br mt’.

‘THZB[D] (*m*) **2.** ‘IP’ p. 153, 6[4]—[prštn]’ [br]t tymrṣw ‘THZB[D].

‘TW (*m*) **2.** *Michalowski*, p. 316, line 7—‘TW.

‘TZ’ (*m*) **1.** *335*, *Inv. IX*, 7[2]—[yd]y br mlkw br g‘ylw br ‘bd‘stwr br ‘TZ’.

‘TZBD (*m*) **1.** *458*, ‘IP’ p. 147, 1[3]—prštn’ brt tymrṣw br ‘TZBD.

‘TḤN (*m*). *Beth She‘arim*, I, p. 141 no. 132—‘TḤN. *Beth She‘arim*, I, p. 142 no. 133—‘TḤN.

‘TY (*m*/*f*) **1.** *378*, CaB 4 A[3]—‘gylw wtymḥ’ w‘TY bny ḥyrn br ‘bd‘th ’gdm. *461*, *C* 3967[1]—mlkw br [š‘d]y ‘TY. *466*, *PNO* 6 D—‘TY. [*4*]*92* or [*5*]*92*, *C* 4527[2]—‘TY brt ‘tšwr br klby br lšmš br kyly. *500*+?, *Pal. 62*: 9[1]—‘TY. *522*, *C* 4526[1]—‘TY brt ‘tšwr. **2.** *C* 4146[1]—‘TY brt šlmlt br m‘ny. *C* 4227[1]—‘TY br ‘tntn ‘wyd’ tybwl. *C* 4228[1]—‘TY br ‘[tntn] ‘wyd’. *C* 4284[1]—‘TY brt ‘tntn. *C* 4424[2]—[‘]TY b[t mqy]mw [nwr]bl. *C* 4433[1]—‘TY brt ’[l]‘’. *C* 4455[1]—‘TY brt rb’l br ḥyrn bg[dn]. *C* 4521[1]—‘TY brt m‘ny. *C* 4539[1]—‘[TY] b[rt] yr[ḥy]. *C* 4594 A[1]—‘TY brt ’dynt. Ben-Hayyim p. 146, V[1]—‘TY brt ‘g’ br tybwl.

‘TYK’ (*m*) **1.** *512*, *C* 4439[1]—‘TYK’ br mlkw. **2.** *C* 4438[3]—hgr brt bwrp’ br ‘TYK’. *C* 4440[2]—blyd‘ br ‘TYK’. *C* 4441[3]—nwrbl br mlwk’ ‘TYK’. *C* 4442[5]—ḥlyw brt [m]lwk[’] ‘TYK’. *C* 4444[3]—hgr bt zbyd’ br ‘TYK’. Ben-Hayyim p. 146, IV—mlkw br ‘TYK’.

‘TY‘QB (*m*) **2.** *C* 4390[3]—mlkw br ‘TY‘QB.

‘TM‘ (*f*) **2.** *C* 4231 E[1]—‘TM‘ [bt] mqymw gdybwl.

‘TNWR (*m*) **1.** *457*, *C* 3911[5]—zbdbwl w‘TNWR wmlkw w‘mrw wydy‘bl bny bršmš br zbdbwl.

‘TNWRY (*m*) **1.** *345*, *C* 3980[3]—[wh]by br ‘TNWRY ‘wdw. *410*, Ingh. B p. 121, I[2]—‘bd‘stwr br nwrbl br khylw br ‘TNWRY ’ṣwly. *426*, *C* 3995[2]—blyd‘ w‘TNWRY wm‘nw [bny] tym‘md br blyd‘. *445*, Ingh. B p. 94, I[2]—‘TNWRY br mqymw. *530*, CaD 22[2, 3]—‘TNWRY br tym‘’ ḥl’ b[r] / ‘TNWRY. **2.** *C* 4345[2]—šgl brt [‘]TNWRY br mqymw. *C* 4497[4]—‘gylw br ‘TNWRY. *C* 4498—‘TNWRY br ‘gylw. *RTP* 27b—ḥyrn ‘TNWRY ṣlmy. *RTP* 103b—‘TNWRY bwrp’. *RTP* 110b—‘TNWRY zb[db]l. *RTP* 670b—‘TNW[R]Y ‘gylw. *RTP* 831a—mlkw ‘TNW(RY). *RTP* 995b—‘TNWRY zbdbl. ‘Tessères’ 13b—‘TNWRY bwrp’. *Inv. XI*, 59[1, 3]—‘TNWRY / br ḥyrn / br ‘TNWRY.

‘TNTN (*m*) **1.** *304*, *C* 4109 A[2]—‘TNTN br khylw. *304*, *C* 4109 B[1]—‘TN[TN] br khylw. *363*, ‘Trilingue’ p. 137[2]—ḥyrn br bwn’ br rb’l br bwn’ br ‘TNTN br tymy. *366*, *C* 3972[2]—‘TNTN br zbd‘th tšbb. *371*, *Inv. IX*, 20[2]—ḥyrn br bwn’ br rb’l br bwn’ br ‘TNTN dy [mt]qr’ br š‘t. *410*, Ingh. E (‘Atenatan) p. 59, I[1]—‘TNTN br zbd‘th br ydy br tymy. *445*, *C* 4281[2, 5]—‘TNTN / gwry br / bwrp’ / ‘TNTN ’ḥytwr. **2.** *C* 4111[2]—khylw wḥyrn bny ‘TNTN. *C* 4227[1]—‘ty br ‘TNTN ‘wyd’ tybwl. *C* 4228[1]—‘ty br ‘[TNTN] ‘wyd’. *C* 4280[1]—‘TNTN br mlkw ’ḥytwr. *C* 4283[1]—‘TNTN br bwlḥ’. *C* 4284[2]—‘ty brt ‘TNTN. *C* 4285[3]—[b]wlḥ’ [br] ‘TNTN [bw]lḥ’ ’ḥytwr. *C* 4286[3]—bwrp’ br bwlḥ’ ‘T(N)TN. *C* 4287[3]—ḥgt brt bwlḥ’ ‘TNTN ’ḥytwr. *C* 4516 A[1]—‘TNTN br zbd‘th. *C* 4596[1]—‘TNTN br kyly br mškw b[r] ‘td/rt br ḥyrn. *RTP* 469a—mlkw br [‘]TNTN. Ingh. D, Pl. IX[2]—bwrp’ br ‘TNTN bwlḥ’. *Inv. VIII*, 1[2]—[zbd]‘th br [‘]TNTN.

‘T‘Y (*m*) **1.** *500*+?, *Inv. XI*, 23[3]—‘l’ brt zbyd’ br ‘T‘Y rp’. *552*, StaB p. 158, A 1174[3]—mlk’ w‘T‘Y bny ḥggw br mlky zwzy. **2.** *C* 4598[3]—šlmt ‘bd’ ‘T‘Y šydn.

‘T‘M (*f*) **2.** StaC p. 38, 8—‘T‘M brt tly’ (y)rḥy.

‘T‘QB (*m*) **1.** *367*, *C* 4116[2, 3]—‘T‘QB br gdy’ / br ‘T‘QB. *425*, *C* 4159[4]—mqymw br zbd’ br mqymw br ‘T‘QB br mqymw br mlkw dy mtqr’ ’r’š. *453*, *C* 4561[3, 5]—ydy‘bl / br ‘T‘QB / ydy‘bl / ‘T‘QB / ‘qby. *468*, *C* 4616[2, 4]—‘T‘QB / br ydy‘bl / br ‘T‘QB / ydy‘bl / ‘qby. *472*, *C* 4172[1]—‘bdṣyd/r’ br ḥry ‘T‘QB br rpbwl. [*4*]*73*, *C* 4562[2, 4]—[tym]rṣw rb’ br ‘T‘QB / br ydy‘bl / br ‘T‘QB / ‘qby. *492*, *C* 4194[5]—sry br zbd‘th br ‘T‘QB. *497*, Ingh. B p. 106, I[2]—’nṭyks rpbwl br ’nṭyks ‘T‘QB br rpbwl. *516*, StaB p. 111, A 1169[2]—bwlḥ’ br ḥyrn br ‘T‘QB ḥwml. *529*, *C* 4203[2]—[ywlys] ’wr[lys] rp[bwl b]r ‘T‘QB [br] rpbwl br ‘T‘[QB] dy mtqr’ nb[wzbd]. *539*, Ingh. B p. 110, III[3]—’wrlys wrdn br ḥry ’nṭykys rpbwl br ‘T‘QB. **2.** *C* 4117[2]—‘qyb’ br ‘T‘QB gdy’. *C* 4118[3]—mqymw br gdy’

'T'QB [z]bd' [r]b'. *C* 4224^{2,5}—[t]m' / brt 'T'QB / [zbd]'th / ['T]'QB. *C* 4225^{1}—rpbwl br 'T'QB br zbd zbd'th 'r'š. *C* 4287^{8}—'T'QB br šdy. *C* 4373 B^{2}—ḥb' br[t] 'T'QB. *C* 4389^{1}—'T'QB mlkw mly. *C* 4583^{2}—mqymw br 'T'QB. *RTP* 233b—'T'QB rb'. *RTP* 714a—'T'QB. *RTP* 756a—'T'QB ḥyr[n]. *RTP* 838b—mlkw w'T'QB. *RTP* 996a—'T'QB br'th. 'Tessera' p. 601—mlkw w'T'QB. CaA 35^{1,2}—'T'QB wrpbwl wšdy / bny br'th br 'T'QB br zbd'th 'r'š. CaB 11^{5}—'T'QB. Ingh. B, Pl. XLIX^{3}—...]b' br 'T'QB. *Inv. VIII*, 39^{1}—whblt br 'T'QB br ḥšy. *Inv. VIII*, 95^{1}—'T'QB mqymw gdy'. *Inv. X*, 130^{4}—[zbyd' w'bdy w']bd'stwr bny n[š' 'T']QB. *Inv. XI*, 49^{1}—...] 'T'QB br [....

'TR/DN (*f*) **2.** *C* 4622^{2}—'TR/DN brt yml'. *PS* 395—'TR/DN brt bgdn.

'TRŠWRY (*m*) **1.** *[3]08*, *C* 4112^{4}—zbdbwl br [....]h br 'TRŠWRY. *433*, *C* 4158^{3}—bltyḥn brt 'tpny br mlkw 'TRŠWRY.

'TR/DT (*m*) **2.** *C* 4596^{4}—'tntn br kyly br mškw b[r] 'TR/DT br ḥyrn.

'TŠ' (*f*) **2.** *C* 4341^{1}—'TŠ' brt zbdb(w)l.

'TŠB' (*f*) **2.** *Inv. VIII*, 64^{2}—'TŠB' bt yrḥy mlkw. *Inv. VIII*, 118^{1}—'TŠB'.

'TŠWR (*m*) **1.** *[4]92* or *[5]92*, *C* 4527^{3}—'ty brt 'TŠWR br klby br lšmš br kyly. *522*, *C* 4526^{3}—'ty brt 'TŠWR.

'TŠ'T (*m*) **2.** 'Iraq' p. 63^{10}, Pl. 5—mhr br 'TŠ'T.

'TTN (*m*) **1.** *524*, Ingh. E (Malkû) p. 96, V^{2}—'TTN. *553*, *C* 4460^{4}—ḥlypt brt 'TTN br grymy. **2.** *C* 4495^{2}—šgl brt 'TTN mly. StaC p. 31, 1—'TTN zbd'th. *PNO* 66—bwṭtn 'TTN. *Inv. VIII*, 107^{3}—šb' brt 'TTN br't' [....

PG' (*m*) **2.** CaA 84^{3}—grymy PG'. *RTP* 234b—mlkw br PG'. *PS* 192—yrḥy br zbd'th PG'.

PZG' (*m*) **2.** *C* 4531^{3}—yrḥy br zbd't' PZG'.

PZL (*m*) **2.** *C* 4595^{1,2}—PZL br zbd' / br zbd' PZL.

PṬRQLS (*m*) **1.** *395*, CaD 29^{1}—'bgr br PṬRQLS dy mtqrh 'stwrg' br lqyšw.

PY[2. *Inv. X*, 128^{1}—ṭbrys qlwdys PY[....

PYL' (*m*) **1.** *426*, *C* 4160^{1}—šm'wn br PYL' br šm'wn mpl[ys]. *426*, *C* 4160^{3}—PYL'. **2.** *Inv. VIII*, 32^{3}—mlkw br mtny PYL'.

PLWYN' (*m*) **2.** *RTP* 913b—PLWYN'.

PLWYNWS (*m*) **2.** *Inv. X*, 130^{1}—g'ys [lqn]ys PLWYNWS br bwrp'.

PLYN' (*m*) **1.** *563*, *C* 3944^{4}—'wrlys plynws br mry' PLYN' r'y. **2.** *RTP* 858b—PLYN'.

PLYNWS (*m*) **1.** *563*, *C* 3944^{4}—'wrlys PLYNWS br mry' plyn' r'y.

PLNS (*m*) **2.** *C* 4369 B^{1}—PLNS.

PLPṬR (*m*) **1.** *448*, *C* 3913 I^{2}—'lksdrs br 'lksdrs PLPṬR.

PLQS (*m*) **2.** *C* 3903^{2}—ṭbrys qlwdys PLQS.

P'L[2. *RTP* 518b—P'L[...] (pers. n.?).

PPLWS (*m*) **2.** CaB 2 B^{2}—...ty]mrṣw br PPLWS 'lys 'byhn br šm'wn.

PPLYS (*m*) **1.** *449*, CaB 8^{1,2}—PPLYS 'lys tybwl / wPPLYS 'lys yrḥbwl' bny mlkw tybwl ṣm'. **2.** *Pal. 61*: 14^{3}—PPLYS '[....] mšy br khyly.

PṢ' (*f*) **2.** *C* 4232 C^{1}—PṢ' brt nš' ḥggw. *C* 4232 E^{1}—P[Ṣ]' b[t] ḥg[gw].

PṢGW (*m*) **2.** *RTP* 464b—PṢGW.

PṢY' (*m*) **2.** *C* 4220^{5}—šlmy brt PṢY'.

PṢY'L (*m*) **1.** *3[6]2*, *C* 3923^{1}—mqymw br 'gylw br PṢY'[L] br tymy dy mtqrh ḥkyšw. *504*, *C* 4199^{2}—PṢY'L br 'stwrg' br 'wyd br lšmš br lšmš. *504*, *C* 4199^{14}—šgl brt lšmš br 'štwrg' br PṢY'L. **2.** *C* 4065^{3}—[PṢ]Y'L br zm[.... *C* 4088^{3}—PṢY'[L br ty]m['] b[r.... *C* 4219^{1}—PṢY'L br šdy br rpbwl 'r'š. *C* 4232 B^{1}—PṢY'L br ḥggw br ml' whblt. *C* 4556^{2}—mlkw [br] PṢY'L [ydy]'bl. *Inv. VIII*, 175^{3}—'šdw br PṢY'L.

PRDŠY (*m*) **2.** *C* 4458 *bis*—...] šm'wn br ḥyrn PRDŠY.

PRṬNKS (*m*) **1.** *555*, Ingh. 'Th.' p. 129^{7}—PRṬNKS wmlkws'. **2.** *C* 4401^{4}—PRṬNKS. *RTP* 806a—PRṬNKS.

[PRYSQWS] (*m*) **1.** *554*, *C* 3932^{7}—ywlys [PRYSQWS].

PRMWN (*m*) **1.** *470*, CaD 28 C^{3}—ḥdwdn br ḥdwdn PRMWN. *486*, *C* 3914^{3}—yrḥbwl' [br] 'g' w'wyd' br ḥdwdn bny yrḥbwl' br ḥdwdn br zbdbwl br ḥdw[dn] PRMWN. **2.** CaA 10^{2}—[m'ny br] 'mt ḥdw[dn PR]MW[N].

PRN(K) (*m*) **1.** *437*, *C* 3996^{3}—PRN(K) br ḥry lšmš br šmšgrm.

PRŠTN' (*f*) **1.** *458*, 'IP' p. 147, 1^{3}—PRŠTN' brt tymrṣw br 'tzbd. **2.** 'IP' p. 153, 6^{1}—[PRŠTN]' [br]t tymrṣw 'thzb[d].

PTYḤB (*m*) **2.** *C* 4446^{3}—mlkw br ydy br PTYḤB.

ṢLM' (*m*) **2.** *RTP* 912b—mzbn' ṢLM'.

ṢLMY (*m*) **2.** *RTP* 27b—ḥyrn 'tnwry ṢLMY.

[ṢL]MLT (*m*) **1.** *[4]34, Pal. 63*: 14^{5}—...ṢL]MLT br whblt [br....

ṢM’ (*m*) **1.** *449*, CaB 8^{1}—ḥyrn br nš’ tybwl ṢM’. *449*, CaB 8^{2}—pplys ’lys tybwl wpplys ’lys yrḥbwl’ bny mlkw tybwl ṢM’.

ṢMY (*f*) **1.** *549*, Ingh. E (Malê) p. 88, IX^{3}—’wrly’ ṢMY brt lšmš.

[Ṣ‘DW] (*m*) **1.** *490*, CaA 41^{3,4}—[Ṣ‘DW br br‘th / br Ṣ‘DW br] br‘[th].

Ṣ‘DY (*m*) **1.** *454*, CaD 27^{1}—ml’ br Ṣ‘DY br ml’. *472*, *C* 4171^{1}—n‘m‘yn wml’ wṢ‘DY bny Ṣ‘DY br ml’. *472*, *C* 4172^{1}—n‘m‘yn wml’ wṢ‘DY bny Ṣ‘DY br ml’ br Ṣ‘DY. *502*, *C* 4173^{3}—n‘m‘yn wml’ wṢ‘DY bny Ṣ‘DY. **2.** *C* 4176 B^{2}—btmlkw bt zbdbwl br zbdbwl br Ṣ‘DY. *C* 4176 C^{2}—btmlkw bt zbdbwl br zbdbwl br Ṣ‘DY. *C* 4184^{2}—btmlkw bt zbdbwl br zbdbwl br Ṣ‘DY. *C* 4187^{1}—mqymw wtymš[’ wzbyd’ bny ’lhš]’ br Ṣ‘DY br ’lhš’. *C* 4187^{2}—’lhš’ w‘gylw wṢ[‘DY bny m]qymw. *C* 4188^{4}—’lhš’ rb’ br mqymw zbyd’ ’lhš’ Ṣ‘DY. *C* 4189^{4}—mqymw br ’lhš’ br mqymw Ṣ‘DY. *C* 4190^{3}—hd’ brt mqymw br Ṣ‘DY. *C* 4287^{7}—’qm’ brt dynys Ṣ‘DY. *RTP* 775a—zb[d]’ ’lhš’ Ṣ‘DY. *PNO* 43^{2}—nbwzbd br Ṣ‘DY br mqymw ḥyrn. *Inv. VIII*, 123^{3}—...]’lh[bl] Ṣ‘DY. *Inv. VIII*, 127^{3}—’lhš’ br mqymw br ’lhš’ Ṣ‘DY.

ṢPR’ (*m/f*) **1.** *490*, *C* 3950^{2}—yd’ br šrykw br ḥy[rn] b[r] ‘lyn’ ṢPR’. *490*, *C* 3951^{2}—‘lyn’ br ḥyrn br [‘]lyn’ Ṣ[PR’]. *490*, *C* 3952^{2}—šrykw br ḥyrn br ‘lyn’ ṢPR’. *490*, *C* 3953^{2}—ḥyrn br šrykw br ḥyrn br ‘lyn’ ṢPR’. **2.** *C* 4276^{1}—ṢPR’ brt ḥnyn’ qwqḥ. *C* 4553^{3}—’mby brt ṢPR’.

ṢPRY (*m*) **1.** *449*, *C* 4165^{1}—ḥdw[dn] br ṢPRY br‘th. *515*, *C* 4198 B^{1}—qwp’ ḥlp’ br ṢPRY br [....

ṢT’ (*m*) **2.** *RTP* 38b—yd‘w tybwl ḥyrn ṢT’.

QBWD’ (*f*) **2.** *C* 4496^{1}—QBWD’ brt ml’ mtny.

Q/MBWRM (*f*) **2.** ‘Hypogée’ p. 223, Pl. II^{1}—Q/MBWRM brt bwrp’.

QWP’ (*m*) **1.** *515*, *C* 4198 B^{1}—QWP’ ḥlp’ br ṣpry br [.... **2.** ‘Wadi Hauran’ 3^{4}—QWP’ br šrykw yrḥy. ‘Wadi Hauran’ 6—QWP’ br šrykw.

QWPYN (*m*) **2.** *C* 4488^{5}—...m]qymw [b]r bwlḥ’ QWPYN.

QWQ’ (*m*) **2.** *Inv. VIII*, 198^{3}—ḥ[l]pt’ br QWQ’ ḥlpt’.

QWQḤ (*m*) **2.** *C* 4272^{3}—š’yl’ br ḥlpt’ QWQḤ. *C* 4273^{3}—nš’ br ḥlpt’ QWQḤ. *C* 4274^{2}—nš’ br QWQḤ ḥlpt’. *C* 4275^{1,3}—QWQḤ b[r] / šm‘wn / br QWQḤ. *C* 4276^{4}—ṣpr’ brt ḥnyn’ QWQḤ. *C* 4277^{7}—tym br ḥlpt’ br tymrṣw br ḥlpt’ br šm‘wn dy mtqrh QWQḤ rb’.

QWŠY (*f*) **1.** *575*, *C* 4048^{3}—QWŠY brt slwq’.

QZB[L] (*m*) **2.** *Pal. 59*: 7—QZB[L]. *Pal. 60*: 6^{3}—QZB(L).

Q/MZY (*m*) **2.** *Inv. VIII*, 73^{5}—...b]r Q/MZY.

QḤZN (*m*) **1.** *378*, *C* 3983^{1}—zbdy br zbdnbw QḤZN.

QYMW (*m*) **1.** *[43]3*, *Inv. X*, 54^{1}—[m]lkw br khylw QYMW [br nwrbl br khy]lw.

QYMY (*m*) **2.** *Inv. XI*, 77^{4}—ḥggw rb’n QYMY† wwhby wzbdbwl.

QYS’ (*m*) **2.** CaB 11^{2}—tyms’ br zbd‘th QYS’.

QL[..]’ **2.** *RTP* 661a—mlkw br ḥyrn br QL[..]’.

QLWDYS (*m*) **2.** *C* 3903^{2}—ṭbrys QLWDYS plqs. *Inv. X*, 128^{1}—ṭbrys QLWDYS py[....

QLYBW (*m*) **1.** *505*, Ingh. B p. 95, II^{4}—šlmn br QLYBW br ’lhbl.

QLSṬ’ (*m*) **2.** *C* 4565^{1}—QLSṬ’ br šlm[n] dy mrql’. *C* 4566^{6}—tym’ br QLSṬ’.

QLSṬRṬS (*m*) **1.** *485*, *Inv. X*, 113^{2}—(l)wqys ’nṭwnys QLSṬRṬS.

QLSTQS (*m*) **2.** *C* 3962^{1}—QLSTQS.

QLQYS (*m*) **1.** *448*, *C* 3913 II^{62}—QLQYS br ḥry qysr.

QM[**1.** *500+?*, *C* 4198 A^{2}—lšmš br QM[....

QML’ (*m*) **1.** *581*, *PNO* 14^{6}—QML’ tym’ š‘dw.

Q/MN‘[**2.** ‘IP’ p. 151, 3^{3}—mqymw Q/MN‘[....

QSYN’ (*m*) **1.** *578*, *C* 3943^{4}—ywlys ’wrlys šlm’ br QSYN’ br m‘ny. **2.** CaD 5^{2}—šlm’ br QSYN’.

QSM’ (*m*) **1.** *400+?*, ‘Hypogée’ p. 199, line 1—...b]r bwrp’ (?) QSM’. **2.** ‘Hypogée’ p. 199, line 8—bwrp’ br ‘gylw br bwrp’ QS[M’].

QSPRYNS (*m*) **1.** *4[52]*, *RTP* 785a—QSPRYNS.

QR[**1.** *397*, *Inv. X*, 127^{1}—yrḥy br zbdl’ QR[....

QRBLWN (*m*) **1.** *448*, *C* 3913 II^{121}—QRBLWN.

---

† This reading from Starcky, review of *Inv. XI*, in *RB*, 73 (1966), 616.

QRD’ (*m*) **2.** *C* 4413 B^{2}—ḥyrn br QRD’. *C* 4414^{2}—ḥyrn br QRD’ br ydy. *C* 4415^{3}—ḥyrn b[r] QRD’. *C* 4416^{3}—bt‘’ brt QRD’.

QRYN (*m*) **1.** *563*, StaB p. 97, line 6—[Q]RYN br ḥyrn br yrḥbwl’. *563*, StaB p. 97, line 7—[lš]mš QRYN. **2.** *PNO* 7 B—QRYN ‘g’.

QRYNW (*m*) **1.** *567*, StaB p. 96, A 1173^{5}—lšmš br QRYNW br ml’. **2.** *RTP* 749b—QRYNW br nbwzbd. *RTP* 818b—Q[RY]NW nbwzbd.

Q[R]SPYNWS (*m*) **1.** *554*, *C* 3932^{4}—Q[R]SPYNWS.

QRQPN (*m*) **1.** *315*, CaD 12 A^{2}—[m]lkw br ḥlkš QRQPN.

QŠṬ’ (*m*) **2.** *RTP* 60b—‘gylw bwrp’ QŠṬ’. *RTP* 78a—QŠṬ’. *RTP* 91b—QŠṬ’. *RTP* 94b—tymrṣw br šlmn QŠṬ’. *RTP* 142b—QŠṬ’.

QŠṬY (*m*) **1.** *443*, *C* 3987^{2}—‘gylw br mlkw [b]r mqymw QŠṬY.

QŠT’ (*m*) **2.** ‘*RTP*’ 942b—QŠT’. ‘Tessères’ 14b—QŠT’.

R’WM’ (*m*) **1.** *546*, *C* 3989^{3}—m‘ny br mlkw r[b]’ br m‘ny R’WM’.

RB’ (*m*) **1.** *390*, *Inv. XI*, 81^{5}—. . .]RB’ br zbdbw ‘rym’. **2.** *RTP* 184b—š‘wt or t[b]‘wt bny šlm RB’. *RTP* 233b—‘t‘qb RB’.

RB’[1. *380*, CaD 7 A^{1}—bwn’ br RB’[. . . .

RB’L (*m*) **1.** *363*, ‘Trilingue’ p. 137^{2}—ḥyrn br bwn’ br RB’L br bwn’ br ‘tntn br tymy. *371*, *Inv. IX*, 20^{2}—ḥyrn br bwn’ br RB’L br bwn’ br ‘tntn dy [mt]qr’ br š‘t. *[3]85*, CaD 2^{1}—ḥ[y]rn br bwn[’ dy mtqr’ RB’L]. *409*, ‘Wadi Hauran’ 8^{8}—RB’L br tym’ brykw. *430*, *C* 4163^{3}—br‘’ wbwrp’ bny RB’L br br‘’. *447*, *C* 3968^{5}—RB’L br ḥyrn bgšw. *490*, CaD 8^{5}—‘zyzw br ‘d’ br RB’L. *505*, *PNO* 37^{2}—’lhbl RB’L [w]mhrw bny bwly. (*536*), *PNO* 73^{2}—[R]B’L br yrḥy y‘t. *550*, Ingh. B p. 124, II^{5}—bwn’ br RB’L. **2.** *C* 3975^{1}—RB’L br ’mrš’. *C* 4326^{5}—RB’L yrḥy y‘t. *C* 4337^{2}—yrḥbwl’ br RB’L šlm’. *C* 4455^{2}—‘ty brt RB’L br ḥyrn bg[dn]. *RTP* 372b—RB’L. *RTP* 745b—RB’L zbyd’. *RTP* 901b—RB’L. *RTP* 911b—RB’L. ‘Bilingue’ p. 885^{1}—[RB]’L br ḥyrn. ‘Tessères’ 27b—R[B’]L. CaD 5^{1}—RB’L br ‘wyd’ br yd‘y. *PNO* 70—. . .] whblt br RB’L.

RB’N (*m*) **2.** *Inv. XI*, 77^{3}—ḥggw RB’N qymy wwhby wzbdbwl.

RBBT (*m*) **1.** *345*, *C* 3980^{4}—tymw br ‘gylw RBBT.

RBW (*m*) **2.** *RTP* 183b—RBW ḥyny.

RBWTY (*m*) **2.** *C* 4371^{2}—š[‘]d’ br rmy RBWTY.

RBḤ (*m*) **1.** *525*, ‘Monuments’ 1^{8}—mlkw RBḤ.

RBN (*m*) **2.** ‘Wadi Hauran’ 12^{5}—š‘dw br RBN.

RBN’ (*m*) **1.** *518*, *C* 4015^{4}—RBN’ wn[. . . .

RBT (*m*) **2.** *C* 3908^{2}—šrykw br RBT. *C* 4353 A^{1}—RBT br bl‘qb.

RGYN’ (*f*) **2.** *C* 3901—RGYN’ bt ḥry br‘t’.

RDWN (*m*) **1.** *524*, *C* 4016^{3}—RDWN br hrmsyn’.

RDM see KRM.

RWḤ’ (*f*) **2.** *C* 4080^{7}—RWḤ’ bt mqy.

RWḤBL (*m*) **1.** *497*, Ingh. E (Malkû) p. 91, II^{2}—RWḤBL br ḥry ’mtšlm’ bt ḥry šgl brt zbyd’. *552*, Ingh. E (Malkû) p. 100, IX^{2}—ywlys ’wrlys ‘g’ br RWḤBL. *560*, Ingh. E (Malkû) p. 101, X^{2}—‘g’ br RWḤBL.

RWMY (*f*) **2.** *C* 4587—RWMY.

RWṢY (*f*) **2.** *PNO* 74^{1}—RWṢY brt t(y)m‘md.

RZYṢYḤ 2. *C* 4376^{2}—’n’ brt RZYṢYḤ or dzyṣyḥ.

RḤ(. .) 2. *RTP* 991a—RḤ(. .) or rṣ(. .).

RYSQ’ (*m*) **1.** *525*, Ingh. E (Malkû) p. 97, VI^{1}—bs’ wRYSQ’ bny š‘rn’ bly.

RYṢW (*m*) **2.** *PNO* 74, line 7—mḥlmw br RYṢW.

RM’ (*m*/*f*) **1.** [*4*]*50*, *C* 4257^{1}—RM’ br zbdlh br bwlḥ’. **2.** *Inv. XI*, 21—RM’.

RMW (*m*) **2.** CaA 37—ydy br mqymw br ydy br RMW br ḥl’.

RMY (*m*) **2.** *C* 4371^{2}—š[‘]d’ br RMY rbwty. *C* 4372 B^{2}—zbdbwl br mlk’l RMY. *C* 4600^{3}—whblt br RMY br rp’l. Ingh. B, Pl. XLII^{2}—lšmš br RMY rp’l. CaA 80^{3}—n‘m brt RMY br rp’l. *Inv. VIII*, 23^{1}—RMY br tymn’ br zb’. *Inv. VIII*, 36^{1}—RMY br k‘b[w] nwrbl. *Inv. VIII*, 138^{8}—whby br RMY. Ben-Hayyim p. 143—zbdbwl br mlk’l RMY.

[R]MLH’ (*m*) **2.** *C* 4074^{2}—[R]MLH’ whrmz.

RMNWS (*m*) **1.** [*563*], *C* 4212^{2}—RMNWS br ml’ b[. . . .

RMŠ’ (*m*) **2.** *RTP* 461a—RMŠ’.

RSTQ’ (*m*) **2.** *C* 4379^{3}—rpbwl br RSTQ’ šdy.

R‘’ (*m*) **2.** *RTP* 892b—R‘’.

R‘Y (*m*) **1.** *378*, CaA 30^{1}—yrḥy br lšmš br R‘Y. [*4*]*42*, *C* 3959^{2}—[ml’] br yrḥy l[šmš] R‘Y. *563*, *C* 3944^{4}—’wrlys plynws br mry’ plyn’ R‘Y.

R‘T’ (*f*) **2.** *C* 4291^{1}—R‘T’ brt ḥyrn tybwl. *C* 4485^{1}—R‘T’ brt yml[’]. *C* 4572^{1}—R‘T’ brt mqymw. *Journal asiatique*, 12 (1918), 281 no. v—R‘T’ brt ‘gylw br yrḥbwl’.

R‘TH (*f*) **2.** *C* 4320^{2}—R‘TH brt mqymw ’‘wyd.

RP’ (*m*) **1.** *500+?*, *Inv. XI*, 23^{4}—‘l’ brt zbyd’ br ‘t‘y RP’. **2.** *Inv. XI*, 51—. . .] br RP’.

RP’L (*m*) **1.** [*4*]*53*, *C* 3916^{2}—ns’ br ḥl’ br ns’ br ḥl’ br RP’L br ‘bsy. *470*, CaC 14^{2}—RP’L br [bwl]q’ br nwrbl. *500*, *C* 3981^{3}—zbdbwl wmqymw bny gd’ br mqymw RP’L. *527*, *C* 3908 *bis*^{1}—RP’L br nš’ [t]y[m]y. **2.** *C* 4059^{4}—ns’ b[r n]s’ [br R]P[’]L. *C* 4080^{9}—RP’[L. . . . *C* 4600^{4}—whblt br rmy br RP’L. Ingh. B, Pl. XLII^{2}—lšmš br rmy RP’L. CaA 80^{4}—n‘m brt rmy br RP’L. StaF p. 36, 2—RP’L br twp’ zbdbl.

RPBWL (*m*) **1.** *472*, *C* 4172^{1}—‘bdṣyd/r’ br ḥry ‘t‘qb br RPBWL. *497*, Ingh. B p. 106, I^{2,3}—’nṭyks RPBWL br ’nṭyks ‘t‘qb / br RPBWL. *529*, *C* 4203^{2}—[ywlys] ’wr[lys] RP[BWL b]r ‘t‘qb [br] RPBWL br ‘t‘[qb] dy mtqr’ nb[wzbd]. *539*, Ingh. B p. 110, III^{3}—’nṭykys RPBWL br ‘t‘qb. **2.** *C* 4219^{3}—pṣy’l br šdy br RPBWL ’r’š. *C* 4225^{1}—RPBWL br ‘t‘qb br zbd zbd‘th ’r’š. *C* 4379^{1}—RPBWL br rstq’ šdy. *RTP* 505a—[. . .] RPBWL [. . .]. *RTP* 779a—RPBWL yrḥy. *RTP* 805b—RPB(WL). *RTP* 887b—RPB[W]L blḥzy. CaA 35^{1}—‘t‘qb wRPBWL wšdy bny br‘th br ‘t‘qb br zbd‘th ’r’š. *Inv. VIII*, 179^{3}—‘gylw br mqymw br RPBWL br nṣrlt. *Inv. XI*, 71^{1}—RPBWL [. . . . *Inv. XI*, 71^{2}—RP[BWL. . . . *Inv. XI*, 98^{1}—RPBWL br ’hwd. *PS* 210—mzbn’ br yrḥbwl’ RPBWL bgdn.

RPNW (*m*) **2.** *RTP* 765b—whblt br mlkw RPNW.

RṢ(. .) **2.** *RTP* 991a—RṢ(. .) or rḥ(. .).

RŠY (*m*) **2.** *RTP* 641b—RŠY br mlkw.

RT’ (*f*) **2.** ‘Hypogée’ p. 239, Pl. VIII^{2}—RT’ bt mwdl’ bt mqymw.

Š’YL’ (*m*) **1.** *566*, *C* 3934^{3}—ywlys ’wrlys ‘g’ dy mtqr’ slwqws br ‘zyzw ‘zyzw Š’YL’. *570*, *C* 3935^{2}—s[lwqws] ‘g’ br ‘zyzw ‘z[yzw b]r Š’YL’. **2.** *C* 3976^{3}—bwln’ br ‘zyzw br ‘zyzw br Š’YL’. *C* 4272^{1}—Š’YL’ br ḥlpt’ qwqḥ. *Inv. XI*, 92^{1}—Š’YL’ b[r n]wrbl br ’qmt.

ŠB’ (*m*/*f*) **1.** *451*, *C* 3927^{1}—’ḥply br ḥyrn ŠB’ br ḥyrn bwn’ š[‘]t. *435* or *436*, CaB 9^{3}—ŠB’. **2.** *Inv. VIII*, 107^{2}—ŠB’ brt ‘ttn br‘t’ [. . . .

ŠBY (*m*) **1.** *394*, *C* 4124^{1}—ŠBY wnbwzbd wt[ymy wnbwl’] bny blšwry br ḥyrn br blšwry br gdrṣw[. . . . b’‘]. *426*, *C* 4129 A^{5}—b‘ltg’ w‘lyš’ bny bwn’ br ŠBY. *426*, *C* 4129 B^{2}—‘lyš’ wb‘ltg’ bny bwn’ br ŠBY br blšwr br ḥyrn. **2.** *C* 4125^{1}—[b]lšwry br ŠBY br blšwry. *C* 4125^{2}—ŠBY. *C* 4127—. . .] ŠBY br blšwry. *C* 4128^{2}—. . .] br Š[BY] br blš[wry] br ḥyrn blšwry. *RTP* 15b—yrḥbwl’ br ŠBY. *RTP* 22b—yrḥbwl’ br ŠBY. *RTP* 188b—ŠBY yrḥbwl’ mqymw tymrṣw. *Inv. IX*, 30^{3}—[ywlys] ’wrlys [nbwmy br tymšm]š bwn’ [ŠBY. . . .

ŠBḤY (*f*) **2.** *C* 4382^{1}—ŠBḤY.

ŠB’‘ (*m*) **2.** *RTP* 758a—ŠB’‘.

ŠB‘T’ (*m*) **2.** *RTP* 292a—ŠB‘T’. ‘Tessères’ 5a—ŠB‘T’.

ŠBTY (*f*) **1.** *575*, *C* 4048^{4}—ŠBTY brt whblt. **2.** *Inv. VIII*, 15^{2}—ŠBTY brt ‘nny br mqymy ḥl’.

ŠG’ (*m*) **2.** *C* 4574^{3}—’qmt brt yrḥy ŠG’. *Inv. XI*, 28^{3}—zbyd’ [br] ŠG’ ’klb.

ŠGD’ see ŠGR’.

ŠGL (*f*) **1.** [*4*]*27* or [*5*]*27*, *C* 4554 A^{4}—ŠGL. *487*, *Inv. VIII*, 114^{1}—ŠGL brt ḥry yrḥy. *497*, Ingh. E (Malkû) p. 91, II^{2}—rwḥbl br ḥry ’mtšlm’ bt ḥry ŠGL brt zbyd’. *504*, *C* 4199^{12}—ŠGL brt lšmš br ‘štwrg’ br pṣy’l. **2.** *C* 4058^{4}—ŠGL. *C* 4148^{1}—ŠGL brt šky[y br] whblt. *C* 4149^{1}—ŠGL brt škyy br šlmn br tymr[ṣw] rb’. *C* 4155^{1}—ŠGL brt ’lhbl br whblt. *C* 4156^{1}—ŠGL brt mlkw br whblt br m‘ny. *C* 4345^{1}—ŠGL brt [‘]tnwry br mqymw. *C* 4495^{1}—ŠGL brt ‘ttn mly. *C* 4547^{2}—ŠGL brt bwrp’. *C* 4548^{2}—ŠGL bt ḥb’. *C* 4585—ŠGL brt ydy. Ingh. ‘Quatre’ p. 242, Pl. XL^{1}—ŠGL brt whblt ’‘ylmy blḥzy.

ŠG‘W (*m*) **2.** *RTP* 82b—mqymw ŠG‘W.

ŠGR’ (*m*) **2.** *Inv. XI*, 26^{1}—ŠGR’.

ŠGRY (*m*) **1.** *425*, *C* 3994 A^{6}—yrḥ[y] br nwrbl ŠGRY. *425*, *C* 3994 B^{6}—yr[ḥy] br nwrbl ŠGRY. *425*, *C* 3994 C^{6}—yrḥy br nwrbl ŠGRY. **2.** *Inv. VIII*, 3^{2}—tmh brt mqymw br ŠGRY.

ŠDD’ (*m*) **2.** ‘Wadi Hauran’ 12^{4}—zbd‘th [br ḥ]dydw [zbd]‘th br yrḥy br ŠDD’.

ŠDY (*m*) **2.** *C* 4219^{2}—pṣy’l br ŠDY br rpbwl ’r’š. *C* 4220^{3}—šlm’ brt ’qml [br] ŠDY. *C* 4222—. . .] brt [Š]DY ’r’š. *C* 4287^{9}—‘t‘qb br ŠDY. *C* 4378^{2}—. . .] br [. .]’ ŠDY. *C* 4379^{4}—rpbwl br rstq’ ŠDY. CaA 35^{1}—‘t‘qb wrpbwl wŠDY bny br‘th br ‘t‘qb br zbd‘th ’r’š.

ŠH(Y)MW (*m*) **1.** *490*, CaD 8^{3,4}—šlmt brt ŠH(Y)MW br / ŠH(Y)MW.

ŠWḤBW (*m*) **2.** *Inv. VIII*, 33^{3}—tymrṣw 'yd'n br lšmš br ŠWḤBW.

ŠWYR' (*m*) **1.** *409*, 'Wadi Hauran' 8^{6}—tymrṣw wḥggw bny tym' ŠWYR'. *464*, *Michalowski*, p. 318^{1}—...]br ŠWYD/R' br tym'. *510*, *Inv. X*, 44^{3}—'gylw br mqy 'gylw ŠWYR'. **2.** *Inv. VIII*, 115^{1}—...yr]ḥbwl' ŠWYR' [....

ŠWQN (*m*) **2.** *PNO* 52 *ter* A^{2}—...]by br ŠWQN [....

ŠḤR' (*m*) **1.** *458*, *PNO* 55 D^{3}—z'mw br ḥyrn br ŠḤR'.

ŠḤRW (*m*) **2.** *C* 4234—ŠḤRW br ḥyrn. *Inv. VII*, 14—bgšw br ŠḤRW ḥnyny.

ŠḤRY (*m*) **2.** *Inv. XI*, 53^{2}—yrḥy br ŠḤRY.

ŠṬ' (*m*) **2.** *C* 4544—brš'd br [Š]Ṭ'. 'Iraq' p. 63^{6}, Pl. 8—yrḥy br tymrṣw br ŠṬ'.

ŠYBY (*m*) **1.** *545*, Ingh. E (Malê) p. 82, V^{2}—ywlys 'wrlys ŠYBY br hrms mrq'.

ŠYDN (*m*) **2.** *C* 4598^{4}—šlmt 'bd' 't'y ŠYDN.

ŠY'N (*m*) **1.** *504*, *C* 4199^{10}—ŠY'N br tym' br 'bgr.

ŠYQN (*m*) **2.** *PNO* 19 A—ŠYQN šm'wn.

ŠYŠT' (*f*) **2.** 4462^{3}—ŠYŠT'.

ŠKY (*m*) **2.** *RTP* 854a—ŠKY. Ingh. B, Pl. XLI^{3}—ŠKY br mqy. *PNO* 67—lšmš br ŠKY yrḥy. *Inv. VIII*, 180^{1}—ŠKY br whby br ml'. *Inv. XI*, 60—...š]'dy br ŠKY.

ŠKYBL (*m*) **1.** *357*, CaD 1^{3}—lšmš br tybwl br ŠKYBL. **2.** *C* 4238^{2}—mrthwn [br]t lšmš br yrḥbwl' ŠKYBL. *C* 4493^{2}—lšmš ŠKYBL. *RTP* 182b—ŠKY[BL] wšlmn wbln[wr]y [w]mqymw. *Inv. VIII*, 97^{1}—ḥyrn br ŠKYB[L.... 'Wadi Hauran' 11^{5}—lšmš br ḥyrn br lšmš br tybwl ŠKYBL.

ŠKYY (*m*) **1.** *320*, *C* 4113^{5}—šlmn br tymrṣw br ŠKYY. *409*, 'Wadi Hauran' 5^{7}—ŠKYY br tlm[.... *414*, *C* 4134^{1}—'lhbl wm'ny wŠKYY wmlkw bny whblt br m'ny 'lhbl. **2.** *C* 4136^{2}—whblt br ŠKYY br whblt. *C* 4137^{2}—'lhbl br ŠKYY br whblt. *C* 4145^{3}—ŠKYY br whblt. *C* 4148^{1}—šgl brt ŠKY[Y br] whblt. *C* 4149^{1}—šgl brt ŠKYY br šlmn br tymr[ṣw] rb'. *C* 4153^{2}—'mt' brt ŠKYY br whblt. *RTP* 376b—ŠKYY br w[hb]lt. *RTP* 825a—ŠKYY br whblt.

ŠKNY (*m*) **1.** *538*, *C* 4204^{3}—ywly' 'wrly' šlmn wŠKNY bny yrḥy šlmn br yd'.

ŠK'T' (*m*) **2.** *RTP* 40a—bryky ŠK'T' 'ḥyry.

ŠL' (*f*) **1.** *486*, StaA p. 52, 2^{5}—ŠL' brt ḥṭry. **2.** *C* 4483^{1}—ŠL' brt ḥṭry br yrḥy. *C* 4542^{1}—'ḥt' brt ŠL'. *RTP* 336a—ŠL' or šp' ḥggw. Ingh. E (Malê) p. 82 I—ŠL' brt ḥnyn' ḥnyn' yrq.

ŠLWM (*m*/*f*) *536*, CaD 4^{1}—kptwt br ŠLWM. [*5*]*63*, *C* 4363^{2}—ŠLWM brt 'wšy 'wšy. **2.** *C* 4368^{2}—'bs' [b]r ŠLWM [w]'mt'. *Inv. XI*, 35^{4}—ŠLWM.

ŠLM (*f*) **2.** Ingh. B, Pl. XLIV^{1}—ŠLM brt 'g'.

ŠLM' (*m*/*f*) **1.** *482*, CaB 14^{2}—ŠLM' brt bwlḥ' br bwrp'. [*4*]*90*, *C* 4005^{2}—ŠLM'[.... *500*+ ?, *C* 4197^{2}—'g' br ŠLM' šmšgrm br br[.]š 'g' br 'ytybl. *514*, *C* 3970^{1}—ŠLM' br mlkw br blyd'. *545*, *C* 4206^{1}—ywl' 'wrly' 'g' wŠLM' [...nb]wmr bny ḥlh. *578*, *C* 3943^{3}—ywlys 'wrlys ŠLM' br qsyn' br m'ny. **2.** *C* 4215^{2}—[ŠLM']. *C* 4220^{1}—ŠLM' brt 'qml [br] šdy. *C* 4221—ŠLM'. *C* 4290^{1}—ŠLM' brt bwrp'. *C* 4337^{3}—yrḥbwl' br rb'l ŠLM'. *C* 4579^{3}—ŠLM' brt mlkw. *C* 4614^{2}—ŠLM'. *RTP* 150a—ŠLM'. *RTP* 185b—tym' ŠLM'. *RTP* 250b—dynys ydy'bl ŠLM'. *RTP* 383b—bwlḥ' ŠLM'. *RTP* 821a—ŠLM' mlk[w]. Ingh. D, Pl. VIII^{2}—yrḥbwl' br nš' 'g' ŠLM'. CaD 5^{2}—ŠLM' br qsyn'. StaF p. 39, 5—ŠLM'. *Inv. VIII*, 158—ŠLM' brt [.... *PS* 234—ŠLM' [.... *PS* 244 A—'mwn br nš' 'g' ŠLM'.

ŠLMW (*m*) **1.** *551*, StaB p. 154, A 1204^{6}—yrḥy br ŠLMW.

ŠLMWY (*m*) **2.** *C* 4326^{3}—[ḥrt]' brt 'gylw ŠLMWY. *C* 4334^{4}—mtn' br br bwn' br yrḥbwl' ŠLMWY br bwn'.

ŠLMY (*f*) **2.** *C* 4220^{4}—ŠLMY brt pṣy'. *C* 4283^{3}—ŠLMY.

ŠLMLT (*m*) **1.** *37*[*5*], *C* 3966^{1}—ŠLMLT br [yrḥbw]l' br nwrbl. *400*+ ?, CaA 74^{2}—ŠLMLT br tym'. *458*, 'IP' p. 147, 1^{1}—ŠLMLT br mlkw br dynys. *458*, 'IP' p. 147, 1^{2}—ŠLMLT br mlkw. *458*, 'IP' p. 147, 1^{2}—ḥnbl br ŠLMLT br mlkw. *545*, *Pal. 63*: 6^{1}—ŠLMLT br nbwmr. *569*, *C* 3936^{2}—ywlys 'wrlys ŠLMLT br ml' 'bdy. **2.** *C* 4146^{1}—'ty brt ŠLMLT br m'ny. *C* 4215^{2}—['gylw br ŠLMLT br nš']. *C* 4351^{1}—ŠLMLT br zbd'. *C* 4391^{2}—mrty brt ŠLMLT 'krn. *C* 4452^{2}—ŠLMLT b[r] m'ny. *C* 4588—kwmy br ŠLMLT. *RTP* 398b—nbwzbd ŠLMLT. *RTP* 630b—ŠLMLT mlkw ḥyrn m'nw. *RTP* 760a—[ŠL]M[LT]. *RTP* 760b—ŠLMLT br tym' 'wydy. 'IP' p. 150, 2^{1}—ŠLML[T br mlkw] br dy[nys]. 'IP' p. 152, 5^{1}—ŠLMLT br mlkw dynys. 'IP' p. 162, 23 B—[ŠL]MLT. *Inv. VII*, 10—ŠLMLT br yd'w br ŠLMLT. *Inv. VIII*, 157^{2}—ntny br ŠLMLT br lšmš.

ŠLMN (*m*) **1.** *320*, *C* 4113^{3}—ŠLMN br tymrṣw br škyy. *352*, *C* 4115 *bis*^{5}—ŠLMN. *404*, *Pal. 59*: 9 A^{2}—...] ŠLMN br tymḥ'.

447, *C* 3999¹—ŠLMN br nš' br ḥyr' brq. *472*, *C* 4171¹—ḥdwdn br ŠLMN br zbdbwl. *505*, Ingh. B p. 95, II⁴—ŠLMN br qlybw br 'lhbl. *507*, *C* 4354²,³—[']bn' brt / ŠLMN br / ŠLMN br tymrṣw. *538*, *C* 4204³—ywly' 'wrly' ŠLMN wškny bny yrḥy ŠLMN br yd'. [*5*]*38*, *C* 4300²—nhr' bt ŠLMN. *539*, Ingh. B p. 110, III⁴—'wrlys mlkw br ŠLMN bn'. *544*, CaB 10 A¹—lšmš br 'stwrg' [b]r lš[mš] br [b]ryky br lqy ŠLMN. *546*, *C* 4301 A³—sy'wn' br ŠLMN. *550*, Ingh. B p. 124, II⁶—ywly' 'wrly' mlkw br 'gylw br ŠLMN. *552*, *C* 4302²—sy'wn' br ŠLMN. *552*, Ingh. E (Malkû) p. 100, IX⁴—ywlys 'wrlys lmlk' br ŠLMN gpn. *581*, *PNO* 14²—ŠLMN. **2.** *C* 4097¹—ŠLMN br 'gylw. *C* 4149¹—šgl brt škyy br ŠLMN br tymr[ṣw] rb'. *C* 4301 B—ŠLMN. *C* 4360²—ḥyrn br ŠLMN br 'g'. *C* 4470 B²—zbdbwl br ŠLMN. *C* 4536²—'bd't' br ŠLMN. *C* 4565²—qlsṭ' br ŠLM[N] dy mrql'. *C* 4566²—nrq(y)s br ŠLMN mrql'. *C* 4624—yrḥy br ŠLMN. *RTP* 31a—ŠLMN yrḥbwl' mlkw ''b[y]. *RTP* 34a—ŠLMN yrḥbwl' mlkw ''by. *RTP* 34b—ŠLMN. *RTP* 94b—tymrṣw br ŠLMN qšṭ'. *RTP* 182b—šky[bl] wŠLMN wbln[wr]y [w]mqymw. *RTP* 261b—blḥzy ŠLMN. 'Bas-relief' p. 47—ŠLMN br šm'wn npry. 'Euphrate' p. 47²—'bgr br ŠLMN br zbdbwl. Ingh. B, Pl. XLI¹—mlkw ŠLMN. *Pal.* *59*: 12—. . .] ŠLMN [. . . . *Pal.* *60*: 14—ŠLMN [. . . . StaC p. 34, 3—ḥbyb' br ŠLMN. *PNO* 24—ŠLMN. *PNO* 45²—ŠL[MN. . . . *PNO* 56²—ŠLMN. *Inv.* *X*, 6—. . .] ŠLMN [. . . . *Inv.* *XI*, 38⁴—ŠLMN br mry'.

ŠLMN' (*m*) **2.** *C* 4417¹—ŠLMN'.

ŠLMN[Y] (*m*) **1.** *515*, *C* 4198 B²—[zby]d['] br ŠLMN[Y] br 'bšlm'.

ŠLMT (*f*) **1.** *457*, *C* 4249¹—ŠLM[T] brt br'' zbd'th. *470*, CaC 14¹—ŠLMT. *490*, CaD 8³—ŠLMT brt šh(y)mw br šh(y)mw. *492*, *C* 4256 A—ŠLMT wnbwl' bny mlkw br nbwl'. *495*, *C* 4507¹—ŠLMT. *495*, *C* 4507³—ŠLMT brt šmšgrm. *531*, *C* 4019⁶—ŠLMT. *532*, *Inv. XI*, 14⁶—ŠLMT. *550*, Ingh. B p. 124, II³—ywly' 'wrly' ŠLMT brt 'bd'stwr br yrḥbwl'. **2.** *C* 4083²—ŠLM[T bt] 'lh. *C* 4234—ŠLMT brt yrḥy. *C* 4340¹—ŠLMT bt ḥry bgdn. *C* 4365¹—ŠLMT. *C* 4393¹—[Š]LM[T] brt tym[']. *C* 4421 A¹—ŠLMT brt 'bd'stwr yrḥbwl'. *C* 4478 A²—ŠLMT brt 'šd. *C* 4528—ŠLMT brt tym'. *C* 4571 A³—['g]' wŠLMT. *C* 4571 B²—'g' wŠLMT bn[y] 'brwq ḥbn. *C* 4598¹—ŠLMT 'bd' 't'y šydn. *C* 4613¹—ŠLMT brt šrykw. CaB 11⁸—ŠLMT. *PS* 429—ŠLMT brt [. . . . *PNO* 38¹—ŠLMT w'wtq' wmqymw. *Inv.* *VIII*, 116¹—ŠLMT brt zb'. *Inv.* *XI*, 52¹—ŠLMT brt tymw lšmš. *Inv.* *XI*, 58¹—ŠLMT brt tym'. *Inv.* *XI*, 63¹—ŠLMT brt mky.

ŠM[2. *Inv.* *VIII*, 52—'qmt brt ŠM [. . . .

ŠMW'L (*m*) **1.** *523*, *C* 4201²—zbyd' [wŠ]MW'L bny lwy br y'qwb br ŠMW'L.

ŠMY (*m*) **2.** *Inv.* *VIII*, 16²—nšry br ŠMY.

ŠM'W' (*m*) **2.** *Inv.* *VIII*, 49²—. . .] br ŠM'W' br tdm(r)'.

ŠM'WN (*m*) **1.** *373*, *Pal.* *63*: 3²—zbdlh dy mtqr' sḥlph br ŠM'WN br 'yš'. *409*, 'Wadi Hauran' 2¹—ḥyrn br ŠM'WN br zbyd'. *409*, 'Wadi Hauran' 5⁵—'bdy br zbdbwl' ŠM['WN]. *426*, *C* 4160¹,²—ŠM'WN br pyl' / br ŠM'WN mpl[ys]. *429*, CaB 2 A¹—'b[yhn br ŠM']WN br 'byhn br nwrbl. *430*, CaB 7¹—ŠM'WN br bwrp' br 'gylw mtn. *443*, *C* 3973⁸—zbyd' br [Š]M'WN br bl'qb. *461*, *C* 3909³—mqymw br ŠM'WN. *480*, CaC 8²—tm' brt nbwzbd br zbdbwl ŠM'WN. [*4*]*90*, *C* 3954²—mrty brt yd[' br whblt] br ŠM'WN. *502*, *C* 4174²—ŠM'WN br 'b' br ḥnyn'. *530*, *C* 4306²—'bn' brt ŠM'WN šqn. *545*, *C* 4308¹—ŠM'WN br ḥyrn. *548*, Ingh. E (Malê) p. 86, VIII⁴—ywlys 'wrlys 'sy[.] br ḥnyn' ŠM'WN. *568*, *PNO* 20—ŠM'WN br 'b'. **2.** *C* 4071²—ml' br ŠM'WN. *C* 4089²—ŠM'WN br [g]dy'. *C* 4179³—b[t]'' brt ŠM'WN. *C* 4180 A²—ŠM'WN br 'b' 'brm'. *C* 4182—ŠM'WN br 'b'. *C* 4275²—qwqḥ b[r] ŠM'WN br qwqḥ. *C* 4277⁵—tym' br ḥlpt' br tymrṣw br ḥlpt' br ŠM'WN dy mtqrh qwqḥ rb'. *C* 4344—. . .b]r ŠM'W[N]. *C* 4364³—yrḥy br y(d)y'bl br ŠM'WN 'rgn. *C* 4396²—zbdbwl br ŠM'WN. *C* 4397³—tymḥ' br ŠM'WN. *C* 4398³—yrḥ(b)wl' br ŠM'WN. *C* 4398 *bis*—yrḥbwl' br ŠM'WN. *C* 4458 *bis*—. . .] ŠM'WN br ḥyrn prdšy. *C* 4515³—'lqm' br ŠM'WN br hn'y. *C* 4601¹—ŠM'W[N] br zbyd' mw'l'. *C* 4608¹—ŠM'WN br ḥyrn. *PS* 377—tm' brt ŠM'WN. CaB 2 B²—. . .ty]mrṣw br pplws 'lys 'byhn br ŠM'WN. *Syria* 23 (1942–3), 80²—mlkw br ŠM'WN bwrp'. *PNO* 19 A—šyqn ŠM'WN. *PNO* 35 A¹—ŠM'WN br m'n br wrtn. *PNO* 35 B¹—ŠM'WN br m'n br wrtn. *Inv.* *XI*, 33¹,²—ŠM'WN br / [y]rḥy ŠM'[WN]. *Inv.* *XI*, 39³—mzbn' br y[rḥ]y [b]r ŠM'WN. *Inv.* *XI*, 49²—. . .]wl ŠM'WN [. . . . *Inv.* *XI*, 55³—ml' br ŠM'WN br mlkw g'lw/y. *RTP* 12b—ŠM'WN br ḥyrn. *RTP* 17b—mlkw ŠM'WN ḥm'. *RTP* 322b—mlkw ŠM'WN. *RTP* 696b—whblt ŠM'[WN]. *RTP* 724a—whblt br ŠM'WN. *RTP* 731b—ŠM'WN kptwt. *RTP* 850a—ŠM'WN. *RTP* 864a—ŠM'WN. *RTP* 890b—ŠM'[W]N. 'Bas-relief' p. 47—šlmn br ŠM'WN npry. 'Bas-relief' p. 47—ŠM'WN npry. 'Tessères' 14a—'g' ŠM'WN.

ŠM'R' (*m*) **2.** *RTP* 585a—ŠM'R'.

ŠM'[R]Y (*m*) **2.** *RTP* 706b—ŠM'[R]Y.

Š[M]RP' (*m*) **2.** *C* 3929³—Š[M]RP' wkmr'.

ŠMŠGRM (*m*) **1.** *387*, CaA 6[1]—zb[d]lh br ŠMŠGRM 'yš'. *437*, *C* 3996[4]—prn(k) br ḥry lšmš br ŠMŠGRM. *495*, *C* 4507[4]—šlmt brt ŠMŠGRM. *500+?*, *C* 4197[2]—'g' br šlm' ŠMŠGRM br br[.]š 'g' br 'ytybl. *527*, *C* 4017[3]—bwṭ' br ŠMŠGRM. **2.** *C* 4191[8]—'lhš' br tymš' br ŠMŠGRM [ḥ]bzy. *C* 4218[1]—ŠMŠGRM br nwrbl. *C* 4508[2]—tm' brt ŠMŠGRM br mlkw br nšwm. *C* 4540[2]—mqy br ŠMŠGRM. *RTP* 381a—ŠMŠGRM. *RTP* 381b—ŠMŠGRM br nwrbl gynws. *RTP* 767a—ŠMŠGRM nwrbl. CaC 18[6]—...ŠM]ŠGRM.

ŠMŠRM' (*m*) **2.** *RTP* 151b—ŠMŠRM' (?).

Š'' (*m*) **1.** *583*, CaA 31[4]—...] Š'' br 't'qb Š''.

Š'D (*m*) **1.** *430*, *Inv. VIII*, 62[2]—Š'D br 'g' br 'wydy. **2.** *C* 4478 B—lšmš b[r] Š'D. Wuthnow p. 64—mlkw br mlkw Š'D.

Š'D' (*m*/*f*) **1.** *555*, Ingh. 'Th.' p. 129[8]—zby br Š'D'. **2.** *C* 4371[1]—Š[']D' br rmy rbwty. *C* 4500[1]—Š'D' brt 'lyt.

Š'D'L (*m*) **1.** *484*, *C* 4261[1]—Š'D'L br zbdbwl br mqymw. *484*, *C* 4261 *bis*[2]—Š'D'L br zbdbwl br mqymw.

Š'DW (*m*) **1.** *428*, *C* 3919[1]—zbyd' br Š'DW tymšmš. *439*, *C* 3920[3]—Š'DW. *510*, *PNO* 3 A+B—'bgl br Š'DW. *547*, *C* 3902[2]—yrḥy br ḥlypy br yrḥy br lšmš Š'DW. *551*, *C* 4038[3]—Š'DW br mlkw ḥss. *574*, *C* 3939[3]—ywlys 'w(r)lys nbwzbd br Š'DW ḥyr'. *581*, *PNO* 14[7]—qml' tym' Š'DW. **2.** *C* 3904[1]—Š'DW br tym' lšmšy. *RTP* 494b—Š'DW 'wydy. *RTP* 550a—ḥyr' Š'DW. *RTP* 550b—ḥyr' Š'DW. *Inv. X*, 56—...Š'D]W br bl[yd'.... 'Wadi Hauran' 12[4]—Š'DW br rbn.

Š'DY (*m*) **1.** *461*, *C* 3967[1]—mlkw br [Š'D]Y 'ty. *552*, *C* 4175[3]—ywly' 'wrly' btmlkw brt zbdbwl br Š'DY. **2.** *C* 4370[4]—mlkw b[r] mlkw Š'DY. *RTP* 197b—tymrṣw wymlkw wŠ'DY. *RTP* 533a—[Š]'DY. Ingh. E (Malê) p. 81 F—'qmt brt Š'DY. Ingh. E (Malê) p. 81 G—Š'DY br ḥnyn' ḥnyn' yrq. Ingh. E (Malê) p. 82 H—Š'DY br 'bsy br ḥnyn' yrq. CaD 38[2]—'rwn' [....] bny Š'DY br [...']qml. StaC p. 33, 2—mqymw br Š'DY. *Inv. VIII*, 45[2]—Š'DY br tym'. *Inv. VIII*, 67[2]—'rwn' br Š'DY br [.... *Inv. VIII*, 137[2]—mqy br Š'DY br mqy. *Inv. VIII*, 149[3]—...']mbw brt Š'DY. *Inv. XI*, 60—[Š]'DY br šky.

Š'DLT (*m*) **1.** *443*, *C* 3973[2]—'bydw br 'nmw [br] Š'DLT. *443*, *C* 3973[6]—Š'DLT.

Š'W[D]' (*m*) **1.** *54[.]*, CaB 10 B[3]—...] br Š'W[D]'.

Š'WT (*m*) **2.** *RTP* 184b—Š'WT or t[b]'wt bny šlm rb'.

Š'YDN (*m*) **2.** *RTP* 204b—mqymw Š'YDN.

Š'RWN' (*m*) **1.** *578*, Ingh. E (Malkû) p. 102, XI[7]—'mw brt bs' Š'RWN'. *578*, Ingh. E (Malkû) p. 104, XII[6]—'mw brt bs' Š'RWN'.

Š'RN' (*m*) **1.** *499*, Ingh. E (Malkû) p. 95, IV—Š'RN' br bly. *525*, Ingh. E (Malkû) p. 97, VI[1]—bs' wrysq' bny Š'RN' bly.

Š[']T (*m*) **1.** *451*, *C* 3927[2]—'ḥply br ḥyrn šb' br ḥyrn bwn' Š[']T.

Š'T see BR Š'T.

ŠP' (*m*) **2.** *RTP* 336a—šl' or ŠP' ḥggw.

ŠQN (*m*) **1.** *530*, *C* 4306[2]—'bn' brt šm'wn ŠQN.

ŠRYKW (*m*) **1.** *490*, *C* 3950[1]—yd' br ŠRYKW br ḥy[rn] b[r] 'lyn' ṣpr'. *490*, *C* 3950[3]—ŠRY[KW]. *490*, *C* 3952[1]—ŠRYKW br ḥyrn br 'lyn' ṣpr'. *490*, *C* 3953[1]—ḥyrn br ŠRYKW br ḥyrn br 'lyn' ṣpr'. *490*, *C* 3953[2]—[Š]RYKW. *[4]90*, *C* 3954[1]—ŠRYK[W]. *522*, *Inv. X*, 53[2]—yrḥbwl' br mqymw br ŠRYKW. **2.** *C* 3908[2]—ŠRYKW br rbt. *C* 4518 B[1]—ŠRYKW. *C* 4613[2]—šlmt brt ŠRYKW. *RTP* 741b—ḥyrn ŠRYKW. *RTP* 742a—ḥyrn ŠRYKW. *RTP* 870b—ŠRYK[W]. *RTP* 871b—ḥyrn ŠRYKW. 'Wadi Hauran' 3[4]—qwp' br ŠRYKW yrḥy. 'Wadi Hauran' 6—qwp' br ŠRYKW.

ŠRYKY (*m*) **2.** 'IP' p. 159, 18[3]—'t'm brt 'g' ŠRYKY.

TBLL (*f*) **2.** *Inv. VIII*, 18[1]—TBLL brt ydy.

TBNN (*f*) **2.** *C* 4503[1]—TBNN brt ḥggw mlkw.

TB'WT (*m*) **2.** *RTP* 174a—tym'md TB'WT. *RTP* 184b—T[B]'WT or š'wt bny šlm rb'.

TBR' (*m*) **2.** StaD p. 516, 3[1]—TBR' br zbdlh.

TD'L (*f*) **1.** *476*, *Inv. XI*, 5[2]—TD'L brt ḥry bss br m'n[w] br 'rqṭws.

TDMWR (*f*) **2.** *C* 4259 B—TDMWR. *C* 4262[1]—TDM[WR] brt mqymw br nwrb[l].

TDMR (*f*) **1.** *457*, *C* 4258[1]—TDMR. *459*, 'Sculptures' p. 19, Pl. I[2]—TDMR. **2.** *C* 4252 A[1]—TDMR brt zbyd'.

TDM(R)' (*m*) **2.** *Inv. VIII*, 49[3]—...] br šm'w' br TDM(R)' (?).

TDRŠ (*m*) **2.** *Beth She'arim*, i, p. 136—TDRŠ.

TW'L (*f*) **2.** *C* 4620[2]—TW'L brt tym'.

TWP' (*m*) **1.** *530*, *C* 4306^{2}—ḥ[yr]n br tym' br ḥyrn TWP'. StaF p. 36, 2—rp'l br TWP' zbdbl.

TWRY (*m*) **2.** *PS* 356—'mby brt tybwl TWRY.

TY(..) **2.** *RTP* 734a—zb TY(M') or TY(MY).

TY[**2.** *Inv. VIII*, 46^{1,2}—TY[....] br TY[....] tym[.... *Inv. VIII*, 162^{1}—b‘šmn br ty[....

TYBWL (*m*) **1.** *357*, CaD 1^{2}—lšmš br tybwl br škybl. [*4*]*40*, ‘Iraq' p. 64^{4}, Pl. 10—‘g' br ml' br ‘gylw br tybwl dy mtqrh br 'ḥty. *449*, CaB 8^{1}—ḥyrn br nš' TYBWL ṣm'. *449*, CaB 8^{1,2}—pplys 'lys TYBWL / wpplys 'lys yrḥbwl' bny mlkw TYBWL ṣm'. *500*, *C* 4292^{5}—ḥyrn br bwrp' br ḥyrn br TYBWL. *504*, Ingh. E (Malê) p. 76, II^{1}—TYBWL br ‘bd' br TYBWL. *513*, *C* 4294^{2}—‘g' br TYBWL zwr. *529*, *Inv. X*, 13^{1}—TYBWL br [.... **2.** *C* 4227^{2}—‘ty br ‘tntn ‘wyd' TYBWL. *C* 4288^{1,2}—TYBWL br / lšmš TYBWL rb'. *C* 4288^{5}—‘zyz br TYBWL dy mtqr' [‘]bd'. *C* 4289^{4}—ḥlpw brt ḥlp' [br] lšmš [TYBWL] rb'. *C* 4290^{4}—ḥyrn br TYBWL. *C* 4291^{3}—r‘t' brt ḥyrn TYBWL. *C* 4293 A^{4}—mlkw br ‘g' TYBWL zwrw. *C* 4493^{2}—ḥn' brt mqymw [TYB]WL. *C* 4529^{2}—gdy' br TYBWL nwr‘th. *C* 4573 A—ml' br TYBWL br ml'. *C* 4593^{2}—gbl brt TYBWL. *RTP* 38b—yd‘w TYBWL ḥyrn ṣt'. *RTP* 638b—'bl‘ly mqymw TYBWL. *RTP* 791a—TYBWL. *RTP* 954b—TYBWL ḥyrn mndrs. *PS* 356—'mby brt TYBWL twry. *Inv. XI*, 67^{2}—...w]zbdbwl wnwrbl wgdy' wTYBW[L.... *Inv. XI*, 85^{1}—...]bwl bny mqymw br TYBWL dy [mt]qrh [.... ‘Wadi Hauran' 11^{5}—lšmš br ḥyrn br lšmš br TYBWL škybl. Ben-Hayyim p. 146, V^{3}—‘ty brt ‘g' br TYBWL. Ben-Hayyim p. 146, V^{5}—yrḥbwl' br TYBWL.

TYDWR' (*m*) **1.** [*5*]*50*, *C* 4094^{3}—slwq['] br mqwl' [br] TYDWR' br [....

TYDRWS (*m*) **1.** *547*, *C* 4209—ywlys 'wrlys TYDRWS br ['grp' br mrql'].

TYKS' (*f*) **2.** CaA 79^{2}—TYKS' brt nṣry br lšmš 'ḥyb.

TYM[**1.** *422*, *Inv. X*, 62^{1}—ml' br TYM[.... **2.** *Inv. VIII*, 17^{2}—mlkw br TYM[.... *Inv. VIII*, 46^{3}—...] TYM[....

TYM' (*m/f*) **1.** *400+?*, CaA 74^{2}—šlmlt br TYM' [.... *409*, ‘Wadi Hauran' 8^{5}—tymrṣw wḥggw bny TYM' šwyr'. *409*, ‘Wadi Hauran' 8^{8}—rb'l br TYM' brykw. *42*[*2*], *C* 3984^{3}—mlk' br TYM' br mlk' T[YM]'. *426*, *C* 4161^{2}—nš' wbw[n' bn]y nš' br TYM[']. *439*, *C* 3920^{2}—TYM' br lšmšy br ‘g' ydy‘bl. *441*, *PS* 3^{1}—bryky br TYM' br ml' gyr'. *448*, *Inv. XI*, 2^{2}—lšmšy br TYM' lšmšy. *452*, *Inv. VIII*, 2^{5}—zbd' br TYM' br ḥlpt'. *454*, *C* 4000^{4}—‘bnrgl br ḥry TYM' br ‘nn. *462*, *C* 4268^{3}—n‘my brt zbd' br TYM' br ḥlpt'. *462*, *C* 4268^{7}—ḥlpt' br zbyd' br TYM' ḥlpt' zbyd'. *464*, *Michalowski*, p. 318^{1}—...] br šwyd/r' br TYM'. *468*, *C* 3960^{4}—ḥyrn br yrḥy br TYM'. [*46*]*8*, *Inv. X*, 77^{2}—[TYM' br] tymrṣw lšmš grny [.... [*469*], CaA 8^{3}—bl[šwr br yrḥy br TYM']. *492*, *C* 4194^{3}—lšmš br lšmš br TYM'. *497*, Ingh. B p. 106, I^{1}—lšmš br lšmš br TYM' w'mdy br ydy‘bl. *500*, *C* 4195^{3}—lšmš br lšmš br TYM'. *503*, *PNO* 39^{1}—TYM' br zky'. *504*, *C* 3948^{1}—tymrṣw br TYM' br mqymw grb'. *504*, *C* 4199^{10}—šy‘n br TYM' br 'bgr. *510*, *C* 4011^{3}—[T]YM' [.... *522*, *C* 3949^{1}—[ydy br tymrṣw br TYM' gr]b'. *525*, *Inv. X*, 119^{2}—TYM' br ḥlpt' br‘th 'lṭy. *525*, *Inv. X*, 119^{2}—ḥg' brth dy TYM'. *530*, *C* 4306^{1}—ḥ[yr]n br TYM' br ḥyrn twp'. *541*, *Pal. 59*: 9 B^{4}—ywly' 'wrly' TYM' wlšmš bny 'wṭk'. *543*, *Inv. IV*, 13^{3}—[T]YM' brt ḥry 'wrly' 'qm' brt 'nṭ[y]k[s ḥlypy]. *545*, *C* 4206^{4}—ywlys 'wrlys bwlm' br zbdbwl b[r bwlm' nyny' .... b]rt [n]b[w]d' br TYM' br nbwmw'. *552*, *C* 4307^{3}—mzbt' brt ḥyrn TYM'. *554*, *C* 4305^{2}—'lhbl br TYM' br ḥyrn. *562*, Ingh. B p. 104^{2}—yrḥbwl' br sbyn' br TYM'. *5*[*64*], *C* 4213—...] br TYM' 'zrzyrt. *581*, *PNO* 14^{7}—qml' TYM' š‘dw. *585*, Ingh. E (Malkû) p. 106, XIII^{7}—'bgr br TYM' br ‘nn. **2.** *C* 3904^{1}—š‘dw br TYM' lšmšy. *C* 4010^{5}—ydy br tymrṣw [TYM']. *C* 4057^{5}—sws' br [l]šmš br ‘gylw [br TY]M'. *C* 4088^{3}—pṣy‘[l br TY]M['] b[r.... *C* 4104—TYM' br [.... *C* 4265^{1,5}—TYM' / br ḥlp / t' / br / TYM'. *C* 4266^{2}—zbyd' br TYM' br ḥlpt'. *C* 4267^{2}—ḥlpt' br TYM' ḥlpt'. *C* 4269^{2,4}—TYM' / br ml' / TYM'. *C* 4270^{3}—mzbt' brt TYM'. *C* 4271^{3}—ml' br TYM'. *C* 4277^{1}—TYM' br ḥlpt' br tymrṣw br ḥlpt' br šm‘wn dy mtqrh qwqḥ rb'. *C* 4303^{3}—‘g' br sy‘wn' br TYM'. *C* 4336^{6}—yrḥbwl' br lšmšy br TYM'. *C* 4369 A^{3}—tymḥ' br whblt br TYM'. *C* 4373 B^{2}—TYM'. *C* 4393^{4}—[š]lm[t] brt TYM[']. *C* 4426^{1}—[T]YM' br [m]zbn'. *C* 4502^{1}—TYM' br mlkw br ḥggw. *C* 4511^{2}—TYM' br mlkw [.... *C* 4528—šlmt brt TYM'. *C* 4545—TYM' br zbyd'. *C* 4566^{5}—TYM' br qlsṭ'. *C* 4579^{2}—bwš' br TYM'. *C* 4620^{4}—tw'l brt TYM'. *PS* 284—sgn' br ml' br TYM'. *PS* 419—ydy‘t brt sy‘wn' br TYM[']. *RTP* 185b—TYM' šlm'. *RTP* 500a—TYM'. *RTP* 760b—šlmlt br TYM' ‘wydy. *RTP* 764a—[m]lkw [br] T[Y]M'. *RTP* 764b—mlkw br TYM' br ‘šylt'. *RTP* 891b—‘bd' br TYM'. ‘Tessères' 12b—TYM'. ‘Note' p. 90^{2}—TYM' br zbd[.... CaA 26^{1}—TY[M'] brt ḥyrn. CaB 11^{4}—TYM'. CaB 11^{7}—'qmt brt TYM'. StaC p. 41, 10—....] TYM['....br] bryky. *Inv. VI*, 4^{2}—...] TYM' b[r.... *Inv. VIII*, 4^{3}—'ytybl br TYM' br 'ytybl br ‘gylw. *Inv. VIII*, 31^{3}—yrḥbwl' br TYM' br 'zmr. *Inv. VIII*, 45^{3}—š‘dy br TYM'. *Inv. VIII*, 128^{2}—...T]YM' [.... *Inv. VIII*, 149^{5}—TYM'. *Inv. VIII*, 171 A^{1}—nš' br TYM'.

Inv. XI, 58^{3}—šlmt brt TYM’. *Pal. 63*: 13^{2}—. . .]TYM’ [. . . .

TYMW (*m*) **1.** *345*, *C* 3980^{4}—TYMW br ‘gylw rbbt. *505*, Ingh. B p. 95, II^{5}—TYMW br dbḥ br ḥmyn. *523*, *C* 4469^{2}—hgy brt TYMW. **2.** *Inv. VIII*, 5^{2}—mky brt TYMW ‘lyb‘l. *Inv. X*, 126^{2}—ywlys ’wrlys lšmš br TYMW. *Inv. XI*, 52^{3}—šlmt brt TYMW lšmš.

TYMḤ’ (*m*) **1.** *3[52]*, *C* 4115^{2}—kytwt br tymrṣw br kytwt br TYMḤ’ rb’. *378*, CaB 4 A^{1}—ydy‘bl br TYMḤ’ br ydy‘bl br ‘bd‘th ’gdm. *378*, CaB 4 A^{2}—TYMḤ’. *378*, CaB 4 A^{3}—‘gylw wTYMḤ’ w‘ty bny ḥyrn br ‘bd‘th ’gdm. *404*, *Pal. 59*: 9 A^{2}—. . .] šlmn br TYMḤ’. *406*, *C* 4130^{2}—mtny br nwrbl br mlkw br TYMḤ’. *406*, *C* 4130^{4}—mtny br nwrbl br mlkw br TYMḤ’ br mtny br bwn’ br mtny dy mtqrh mhwy. *498*, *C* 4549^{3}—. . .]’ br [TY]MḤ’ br mlkw. **2.** *C* 4369 A^{1}—TYMḤ’ br whblt br tym’. *C* 4397^{1}—TYMḤ’ br šm‘wn. *Journal asiatique*, 12 (1918), 295 no. xviii—ḥlyšw br [T]YMḤ’. *RTP* 14b—‘gylw TYMḤ’. CaA 23^{2}—. . .TY]MḤ’. ‘Wadi Hauran’ 3^{2}—TYMḤ’ br tymš’.

TYMY (*m*) **1.** *340*, *C* 3922^{1}—‘gylw br TYMY b[r] zbdbwl. *3[6]2*, *C* 3923^{2}—mqymw br ‘gylw br pṣy’[l] br TYMY dy mtqrh ḥkyšw. *363*, ‘Trilingue’ p. 137^{3}—ḥyrn br bwn’ br rb’l br bwn’ br ‘tntn br TYMY. *394*, *C* 4124^{1}—šby wnbwzbd wT[YMY wnbwl’] bny blšwry br ḥyrn br blšwry br gdrṣw[. . . .b‘’]. *400+?*, CaD 7 B^{1}—. . .] br yrḥbwl’ br zbyd’ br TYMY. *410*, Ingh. E (‘Atenatan) p. 59, I^{2}—‘tntn br zbd‘th br ydy br TYMY. *527*, *C* 3908 *bis*^{2}—rp’l br nš’ [T]Y[M]Y. *[5]52*, *C* 4040^{2}—. . .T]YMY br ‘bdy [. . . . **2.** *C* 4132^{2}—tm’ brt TYMY mhwy. *C* 4133^{3}—nwrbl br TYM[Y] mtny. *C* 4412^{5}—TYMY. *C* 4435^{2}—bny br TYMY. *C* 4436^{2}—[’b]b’ brt TYMY br bn[y]. *RTP* 59b—TYMY. *RTP* 167a—‘nyny TYMY. *RTP* 451b—TYMY br zbd‘th. *RTP* 554b—bryk TYMY. *RTP* 992a—mlkw TYMY. *Journal asiatique*, 12 (1918), 294 no. xvii—TYMY. ‘Büste’ p. 313^{4,6}—TYMY br / blšwry / TYMY. ‘Iraq’ p. 63^{5}, Pl. 5—TYMY br TYMY br blyhb. CaA 58^{1}—TYMY br [. . . . *Inv. VIII*, 14^{2}—. . .T]YMY br [. . . . *Inv. VIII*, 21^{1,3}—TYM[Y br] / mqymw / TYMY. *Inv. VIII*, 35^{3}—gd’ br TYMY.

[TY]MY‘M[D] (*m*) **2.** *RTP* 328b—mlkw [TY]MY‘M[D].

TYMLT (*m*) **2.** *C* 4589—yml’ br TYMLT br ymlkw kwmy. *C* 4590—lšmš br TYMLT br ymlkw kwmy. *Inv. IV*, 24^{1}—TYMLT ‘wydlt ’mrs‘. *Inv. VIII*, 29^{1}—TYMLT br ymlkw. *Inv. VIII*, 136^{2}—‘ly br TYMLT br bydn. *Inv. XI*, 28^{4}—TYMLT br [. . . . *Inv. XI*, 35^{1}—. . .] br TYMLT [. . . . *RTP* 316b—T[YML]T br yrḥy. *PNO* 54 A—TYMLT br tymrṣw.

TYMN’ (*m*) **2.** *Inv. VIII*, 23^{1}—rmy br TYMN’ br zb’. *Inv. VIII*, 24^{2}—mlkw br TYMN’ bzy. *Inv. VIII*, 26^{3}—blḥzy br TYMN’ whby ’dy[nt]. *Inv. VIII*, 47^{2}—y[d]y‘[bl] br tm’ TYMN’. *Inv. VIII*, 50 B^{2}—‘gyl[w] b(r) TYMN’. Ingh. B p. 114, line 24—TYMN’ br‘’. Ingh. B p. 114, line 29—sry wTYMN’. ‘IP’ p. 161, 22^{2}—[TY]MN’.

TYMS’ (*m*) **1.** *544*, CaB 10 A^{3}—TYMS’. **2.** CaB 11^{1}—TYMS’ br zbd‘th qys’. Ingh. B, Pl. XLVIII^{2}—TYMS’. CaA 23^{1}—. . .T]YMS’ [. . . .

TYM‘ (*m*) **1.** *516*, StaB p. 111, A 1169^{6}—T[Y]M‘ br [. . . .] TYM‘ blyd[‘].

TYM‘’ (*m*) **1.** *502*, CaB 4 B^{1}—’lkdrys br ’lkdrys br ’plnys nbwzbd br TYM‘’ br ’gdm. *530*, CaD 22^{2}—‘tnwry br TYM‘’ ḥl’ b[r] ‘tnwry. **2.** *C* 4569^{3}—mqymw br tymrṣw TYM‘’.

TYM‘MD (*m*) **1.** *345*, *C* 3980^{7}—mlkw br mqymw TYM‘MD. *348*, CaD 33^{3}—mlkw [wz]bd‘[th . . . .] bny TYM‘MD b[r] bwrp’ zg[wg]. *348*, CaD 33^{5}—TYM[‘MD]. *409*, ‘Wadi Hauran’ 8^{7}—zbyd’ br TYM‘MD mškw. *425*, *C* 3994 A^{4}—zbyd[’] br TYM‘MD mškw. *425*, *C* 3994 B^{4}—zby[d’] br TYM‘MD mškw. *425*, *C* 3994 C^{4}—zbyd’ br TYM‘MD mškw. *426*, *C* 3995^{3}—blyd‘ w‘tnwry wm‘nw [bny] TYM‘MD br blyd‘. **2.** *RTP* 64b—TYM‘MD bwlḥ’. *RTP* 174a—TYM‘MD tb‘wt. *RTP* 223b—TYM‘MD zbdbl. *RTP* 777a—TYM‘M[D]. *RTP* 990a—blkz or blsz TYM‘MD bwrp’. ‘Monuments’ 3—TYM‘MD bwlḥ’. CaC 7^{1}—TYM‘MD br nš’ br [. . . . CaD 25^{7}—. . .]ql br ’bb TYM‘M[D . . . . *Inv. XI*, 97^{7}—TYM‘MD br [. . . . ‘Wadi Hauran’ 9^{2}—zbyd’ TYM‘MD zbyd’ mškw. *PNO* 74^{2}—rwṣy T(Y)M‘MD.

TYMṢ’ (*m*) **2.** CaA 68 A^{1}—TYMṢ’ br ’lhš’ ‘gylw. CaA 68 B^{1}—TYMṢ’ br ’lhš’.

TYMRṢW (*m*) **1.** *320*, *C* 4113^{4}—šlmn br TYMRṢW br škyy. *345*, *C* 3980^{5}—yrḥbwl’ br TYMRṢW ’brwq. *3[52]*, *C* 4115^{2}—kytwt br TYMRṢW br kytwt br tymḥ’ rb’. *352*, *C* 4115 *bis*^{3}—kytwt br [TYMR]ṢW. *400+?*, *C* 3963^{1}—TYMRṢW br [l]šmš br mlkw ‘’b[y]. *409*, ‘Wadi Hauran’ 8^{4}—TYMRṢW wḥggw bny tym’ šwyr’. *[4]19*, CaD 36 A^{4}—yrḥy br b[r]yky br [TY]MRṢW. *[4]27* or *[5]27*, *C* 4554 A^{2}—mrty brt TYMRṢ[W]. *452*, *Inv. VIII*, 2^{4}—ḥbt’ brt ḥlpt’ br ḥlp[. . .] br TYMRṢW. *[452]*, *Inv. X*, 99—’bgr br TYMR[ṢW. . . . *458*, ‘IP’ p. 147, 1^{3}—prštn’ brt TYMRṢW br ‘tzbd. *[46]8*, *Inv. X*, 77^{2}—[tym’ br] TYMRṢW lšmš gwrny [. . . . *471*, CaB 1 A^{1}—TYMRṢW br bwrp’ br mlkw br ‘šylt. *[4]73*, *C* 4562^{1}—[TYM]RṢW rb’ br ‘t‘qb br ydy‘bl br ‘t‘qb ‘qby. *490*, *C* 4006^{3}—TYMRṢW. *500+?*, *Inv. XI*, 23^{5}—ydy br TYMRṢW ydy. *504*, *C* 3948^{1}—TYMRṢW br tym’ br mqymw grb'. *507*, *C* 4354^{4}—[']bn' brt šlmn br šlmn br TYMRṢW. *517*, StaB p. 148, A 1179^{3}—TYMRṢW [b]r ḥyrn zbd'. *522*, *C* 3949^{1}—[ydy br TYMRṢW br tym' gr]b'. *524*, *Inv. XI*, 11^{3}—'gy[lw br] TYMRṢW b[r] ḥd'. *530*, StaB p. 152, A 1207^{3}—TYMRṢW br bryky. [5]*40*, *C* 4026^{2,3}—T[YMRṢW / b]r whblt br TYMRṢ[W]. *542*, *C* 4029^{4}—kyly br y'qwb TYMRṢW. *547*, *Pal. 61*: 11^{3}—whblt br TYMRṢW br mlkw. *545*, *Pal. 63*: 6^{1}—TYMRṢW br nbwz'. *552*, CaD 36 C^{4}—ywlys 'wrlys typyls br TYMRṢW [z]byd'. **2.** *RTP* 30a—'[w]yd' br TYMRṢW br 'wyd'. *RTP* 94b—TYMRṢW br šlmn qšṭ'. *RTP* 102b—[lš]mš [TY]MRṢW. *RTP* 111a—TYMRṢW dyny. *RTP* 171b—TYMRṢ[W] ḥbyby. *RTP* 179b—mqymw TYMRṢW wTYMRṢW nš' wzbyd' [. . .]w. *RTP* 188b—šby yrḥbwl' mqymw TYMRṢW. *RTP* 195b—lšmš TYMRṢW. *RTP* 197b—TYMRṢW wymlkw wš'dy. *RTP* 233a—TYMRṢW 'gy[lw]. *RTP* 339b—TYMRṢW mqymw. *RTP* 739b—mzbn' TYMRṢ[W]. *RTP* 740b—[TY]MRṢ[W] br TYMRṢW. *RTP* 743a—mzbn' wTYMRṢ(W). *RTP* 743b—TYMRṢW TYMRṢW. *RTP* 889b—TYMRṢW. 'Tessères' 2b—TYMRṢW dyny. 'Iraq' p. 63^{6}, Pl. 8—yrḥy br TYMRṢW br šṭ'. *C* 4081^{3}—TYMRṢW w't'mn wyml'. *C* 4149^{1}—šgl brt škyy br šlmn br TYMR[ṢW] rb'. *C* 4277^{3}—tym' br ḥlpt' br TYMRṢW br ḥlpt' br šm'wn dy mtqrh qwqḥ rb'. *C* 4296 A^{6}—b'lt[g]' brt 'wyd' b[r] TYMRṢW. *C* 4372 A^{1}—TYMRṢ[W] br zbdbwl. *C* 4456^{3}—mzbn' br mlkw TYMRṢW ''by. *C* 4457^{1,3}—TYMRṢW / br mlkw / br TYMRṢW / ''by. *C* 4524^{3}—mrthwn brt TYMRṢW br ydy grb'. *C* 4534^{1}—TYMRṢW br bryky. *C* 4569^{2}—mqymw br TYMRṢW tym''. Ingh. C, Pl. II—ḥyrn br TYMRṢW. Ingh. B p. 135, IV B^{1}—'n' bt TYMRṢW. 'IP' p. 151, 3^{1}—TYMR[ṢW . . . . 'IP' p. 153, 6^{3}—[prštn]' [br]t TYMRṢW 'thzb[d]. 'IP' p. 156, 13^{3}—mrty brt TYMRṢW dynys. CaB 2 B^{2}—. . . TY]MRṢW br pplws 'lys 'byhn br šm'wn. CaB 2 B^{2}—ywly' 'wrly' TYMRṢ[W. . . . CaD 36 B^{1}—. . . TYM]RṢ[W. . . . CaD 36 D^{2}—bwn' br TYMRṢW. *Pal. 60*: 5 A^{4}—[b'l]tg' [b]rt [']bgr [TY]MRṢW. *PNO* 52 *bis*—TYMRṢW. *PNO* 54 A—tymlt br TYMRṢW. *Inv. VIII*, 33^{1}—TYMRṢW 'yd'n br lšmš br šwḥbw. *Inv. VIII*, 121^{1}—TYMRṢW br zbdbwl. *Inv. X*, 57—. . .]' br TYMRṢW br mlkw [. . . . *Inv. XI*, 54^{3}—[m]qymw br 'lybwl br TYMR[ṢW]. *Inv. XI*, 97^{3}—TYMRṢW [. . . . Ben-Hayyim p. 144—TYMRṢW br zbdbwl.

TYMŠ' (*m*) **1.** *378*, CaB 4 A^{2}—myš' brt TYMŠ' br ydy'bl ṭymwn. *390*, *C* 4121—bny w'lhš' w'r'wm bny TYMŠ' br bny dy mtqrh 'rwn'. **2.** *C* 4187^{1}—mqymw wTYMŠ[' wzbyd' bny 'lhš]' br ṣ'dy br 'lhš'. *C* 4187^{2}—'lhš' br [TYMŠ']. *C* 4191^{4}—'lhš' br TYMŠ'. *C* 4191^{7}—'lhš' br TYMŠ' br šmšgrm [ḥ]bzy. *C* 4510^{2}—TYMŠ' br ml'. *RTP* 725a—'lhš' TYMŠ'. 'Tessères' 24b—'lhš' TYMŠ'. 'Wadi Hauran' 3^{3}—tymḥ' br TYMŠ'.

TYMŠMŠ (*m*) **1.** *428*, *C* 3919^{2}—zbyd' br š'dw TYMŠMŠ. **2.** *Inv. IX*, 30^{2}—[ywlys] 'wrlys [nbwmy br TYMŠM]Š bwn' [šby. . . .

TYPYLS (*m*) **1.** *552*, CaD 36 C^{4}—ywlys 'wrlys TYPYLS br tymrṣw [z]byd'. *562*, Ingh. B p. 104^{1}—slwqs br TYPYLS br slwqs. **2.** CaD 36 D^{1}—nṣ' brt TYPYLS.

TYRDT (*m*) **2.** *C* 4598^{5}—TYRDT yrḥy. *C* 4599^{3}—[']mt['] brt [TY]RDT. *PS* 371—'byn' brt TYRDT br yrḥy.

TLY' (*m*) **2.** StaC p. 38, 8—'t'm brt TLY' br (y)rḥy.

TLM[**1.** *409*, 'Wadi Hauran' 5^{7}—škyy br TLM[. . . .

TM' (*m*/*f*) **1.** *480*, CaC 8^{1}—TM' brt nbwzbd br zbdbwl šm'wn. *585*, Ingh. E (Malkû) p. 106, XIII^{4}—TM' brt 'bd'swdr br yrḥbwl'. **2.** *C* 4131^{1}—TM' brt ḥrš'. *C* 4132^{1}—TM' brt tymy mhwy. *C* 4224^{1}—[T]M' brt 't'qb [zbd]'th ['t]'qb. *C* 4278^{1}—TM' brt ḥlpt'. *C* 4382—TM' brt zbyd[']. *C* 4486—mlkw br TM'. *C* 4486—mqymw br TM'. *C* 4508^{1}—TM' brt šmšgrm br mlkw br nšwm. *C* 4535 B^{2}—yrḥbwl' br TM'. *Beth She'arim*, i, p. 135—TM' 'mš'. *Inv. VIII*, 11^{2}—TM' brt 'g' 'ṣyd/rny. *Inv. VIII*, 47^{2}—y[d]y'[bl] br TM' tymn'. *PS* 377—TM' brt šm'wn. *Pal. 63*: 9^{1}—TM' brt ml' br [. . . .

TMH (*f*) **2.** *Inv. VIII*, 3^{1}—TMH brt mqymw br šgry.

TMLK (*f*) **1.** *435*, *PS* 33^{1}—TMLK brt 'wšy br 'wšy.

TMRṢW (*m*) **2.** Ingh. B p. 135, IV A^{1}—'n' bTMRṢW.

T'YD/R (*f*) **2.** *C* 4614^{1}—T'YD/R.

TQYM (*f*) **2.** *Inv. XI*, 24^{2}—TQYM.

TŠŠB (*m*) **1.** *366*, *C* 3972^{2}—'tntn br zbd'th TŠŠB. *497*, Ingh. E (Bar'â) p. 115^{2}—br'' br bnwr br br'' zbd'th TŠŠB.

List of Tribal Names

'NWBT **1.** *468*, *C* 3960^{5}—bny 'NWBT.

''LY **2.** *RTP* 98b—bny ''LY. *RTP* 109a—bny ''LY. *RTP* 503b—bny ''LY.

BWDL' **2.** *RTP* 92b—bny BWDL'.

BWLḤ' **2.** *RTP* 82a—bny BWLḤ'. *RTP* 718a—bny BWLḤ'.

BWL'' 2. *RTP* 83a—bny BWL''. *RTP* 107a—bny BWL[']'.

BWN' 2. *RTP* 135a—bny BWN'. *RTP* 993a—bny BWN'.

BWR' 2. *RTP* 62a—bny BWR'. *RTP* 64a—bny BWR'.

BḤR/D 2. *RTP* 106b—bny BḤR/D.

BLNWRY 2. *RTP* 272a—bny BLNWRY.

BRKYW 2. CaD 3[5]—. . .b]ny BRKYW.

GDYBWL 1. *350*, CaD 31[4]—bny [GD]YBWL. *363*, 'Trilingue' p. 138[5]—bny GDYBWL. *420*, *C* 3917[2]—bny GDYBWL.

GWG' 2. *RTP* 80a—bny GWG'. *RTP* 100a—bny GWG'.

GWGW 2. *RTP* 81a—bny GWGW.

ZBDBWL 1. *3[6]2*, *C* 3923[2]—bny ZB[DBWL]. *490*, *C* 3950[2]—bny ZBDB[WL]. *490*, *C* 3951[2]—bny [Z]BDBWL. *490*, *C* 3953[3]—bny [Z]BDBWL. **2.** *RTP* 138b—bny ZBDBWL. *RTP* 141a—bny ZBDBWL.

ZBWD 1. *335*, *Inv. IX*, 7[3]—bny ZBWD.

ZGWG 2. *Inv. XI*, 96—bny ZGWG.

ZMR' 1. *(3?)42*, 'Dédicace' p. 45, 6—bny ZMR'.

ḤṬRY 1. *440*, *C* 4164—bny ḤṬRY.

ḤKYM 2. *RTP* 364b—bny ḤKYM.

ḤL' 2. *RTP* 134b—bny ḤL'. *RTP* 195a—bny ḤL'.

ḤLH 1. *545*, *C* 4206[4]—bt ḤLH.

ḤNWD/R 2. *RTP* 97a—bny ḤNWD/R.

ḤŠŠ 1. *439*, CaC 9[3]—bny ḤŠŠ. **2.** *RTP* 93b—bny ḤŠŠ. *RTP* 457b—bny ḤŠŠ. CaC 10[2]—bny Ḥ[ŠŠ].

YDY'BL 1. *[4]42*, *C* 3959[7]—bny YDY'BL. **2.** *RTP* 95b—[b]n[y] YDY['B]L. *RTP* 124a—bny YDY'BL. *RTP* 586a—bny YDY'BL.

YŠW'L' 2. *RTP* 985a—bny YŠW'L'.

KHNBW 1. *269*, StaD p. 514, 2[5]—bny KHNBW. **2.** *Inv. XI*, 83[2]—bny KHNBW.

KMR' 1. *300+?*, *Inv. XI*, 86[2]—bny KMR'. *307*, CaD 17[3]—bny KMR'. *[3]08*, *C* 4112[5]—bny KMR'. *333*, *C* 3915[2]—bny KMR'. *336*, CaC 4[3]—bny KMR'. *336*, CaC 5[2]—bny KMR'. *340*, *C* 3922[2]—bny KMR'. *357*, CaD 1[3]—bny KMR'. *378*, CaB 4 A[4]—bny KMR'. *[3]94*, *C* 3969[4]—bny KMR'. **2.** *Inv. XI*, 85[2]—bny KMR'. *Inv. XI*, 90—bny KMR'.

KNBT 1. *345*, *C* 4114[4]—bny KNBT.

MGDT 1. *396*, *C* 3978[6]—bny MGDT. **2.** *RTP* 105b—bny MGDT.

MZY' 2. *RTP* 96b—bny MZY'.

MYT' 1. *304*, *C* 4109 A[5]—bny MYT'. *304*, *C* 4109 B[4]—bny MY[T']. *360*, CaC 11[5]—bny MYT'. *363*, 'Trilingue' p. 137[3]—bny MYT'. *367*, *C* 4116[4]—bny MYT'. *368*, *C* 4119[5]—bny MYT'. *371*, *Inv. IX*, 20[3]—bny MYT'. *380*, CaD 7 A[2]—bny MYT['. . . . *395*, CaD 29[3]—bny MYT'. **2.** CaD 9[3]—bny MYT'.

MKN' 2. 'Monuments' 4a—bny MKN'. 'Monuments' 4b—bny MKN'.

M'ZYN 1. *373*, *Pal. 63*: 3[3]—bny M'ZYN. *37[5]*, *C* 3966[4]—bn[y M]'ZYN. *378*, *C* 3983[1]—bny M'ZYN. *378*, CaA 30[1]—bny M'ZYN. *[3]92*, *C* 3958[2]—[bny] M'ZYN. *[3]92*, CaA 7[3]—bny M'ZYN. *393*, *C* 4197[1]—bny M'ZYN. **2.** CaD 24[2]—bny M'ZYN. *Inv. XI*, 88[2]—bny M'Z[YN]. *Inv. XI*, 92[2]—bny M'ZYN.

MŠKN' 1. *409*, 'Wadi Hauran' 5[3]—bny MŠKN'.

MTBWL 1. *320*, *C* 4113[6]—bny MTBWL. *328*, *C* 3925[3]—[b]ny MTBWL. *330*, *C* 3924[3]—bny MTBW[L]. *333*, *C* 3915[2]—bny MTBWL. *3[52]*, *C* 4115[3]—bny [MT]BWL. *362* or *382*, CaA 34[4]—bny MTBWL. *412*, CaB 13 A[3]—bny MTBWL. *471*, CaB 1 A[1]—bny MTBWL. **2.** *C* 3975[2]—bny MTBWL. *C* 4187[2]—[bny MTBW]L.

NWRBL 1. *373*, *Pal. 63*: 3[3]—bny (N)WRBL. **2.** *RTP* 123a—bny NWRBL. *RTP* 165b—bny NWRBL.

SKN' 2. *RTP* 96a—bny SKN'.

'BD[.] 2. *RTP* 176b—bny 'BD[.].

'GRWD 1. *392*, *Inv. X*, 131[3]—bny 'GRWD. **2.** *RTP* 99a—bny 'GRWD. CaD 12 B[5]—bn[y] 'GRWD. *Inv. XI*, 73[3]—bny 'GRWD.

'LYY 2. *RTP* 137a—bny 'LYY. *RTP* 295b—bny 'LYY. 'Tessères' 25b—bny 'LYY.

'ṢR 2. *RTP* 339a—bny 'ṢR.

'TR/D 1. *490*, CaA 41[4]—bny 'TR/D.

PṬRT' 1. *530*, CaD 22[4]—bny PṬRT'.

QṢMYT 2. *RTP* 106a—bny QṢMYT.

RB'L 2. *RTP* 276b—bny RB'L.

ŠZ' 2. *RTP* 977a—bny ŠZ'.

ŠLM 2. *RTP* 184b—bny ŠLM.

ŠMWN 2. *RTP* 79a—bny ŠMWN. *RTP* 128b—bny ŠMWN.

ŠM'D/R 2. CaC 7^{2}—bny ŠM'D/R.

ŠM'WN 2. *RTP* 252a—bny ŠM'WN.

Š'D' 1. *426*, CaD 21^{3}—bny Š'D'.

Š'DW 2. *RTP* 341a—bny Š'DW.

Š'DY 2. *RTP* 334a—bny Š'DY.

TYMY 2. *RTP* 108a—bny TYMY. *RTP* 262b—bny TYMY.

TYMRṢW 2. *RTP* 66a—bny TYMRṢW. *RTP* 77b—bny TYMRṢW. CaC 12^{3}—bny TYMRṢW.

List of Deities

'BGL 1. *464, Michalowski*, p. 318^{2}—lbl wlb'šmn [wl'glbwl wlmlk]bl wl'štrt wlnmsys wl'rṣw wl'BGL. *466, PNO* 6 B—'BGL gny'. *510, PNO* 3—'BGL 'lh'. [5]*24, PNO* 13^{2}—'BGL 'lh' ṭb' wskr'. *525, PNO* 16^{5}—'glbwl wmlkbl w'BGL gny'. *564, PNO* 15^{2}—'BGL 'lh'. *568, PNO* 20—'BGL 'lh' ṭb' wškr'. 5[7]*3* or 5[7]*8*, *PNO* 21 C—. . .']BGL 'lh' ṭb'. **2.** *PNO* 4—'BGL 'lh' ṭb' wskr'. *PNO* 5—'BGL gny' ṭb' wškr'. *PNO* 7 A^{2}—'BGL wm'n 'lhy' ṭby' wškry'. *PNO* 10 A—'BGL. *PNO* 11—'BGL. *PNO* 17^{3}—'BGL g[n]y'. *PNO* 23—'BGL gny' ṭb[']. *PNO* 26—'B[GL]. *PNO* 27—'BGL 'lh' ṭb'. *PNO* 29—'BGL '[lh']. *PNO* 33—'BGL 'lh' ṭb'. *PNO* 38^{5}—'BGL. *PNO* 68—[']BGL gn[y]' ṭb'.

'DGY' 2. 'Bas-relief' p. 47—šlmn w'DGY' or 'rgy' gny' ṭby' wškry'.

'[L]HY 1. *468*, StaE p. 373^{3}—'[L]HY 'lh' ṭb' wskr'.

'LQWNR' 1. *350*, CaD 31^{5}—'LQWNR' 'lh' ṭb'.

'LQNR' *RTP* 220a to 223a—'LQNR'.

'LT 1. *373, Pal. 63*: 3^{3}—'LT. *37*[5], *C* 3966^{4}—'LT. *440*, *C* 3955^{7}—šmš w'LT wrḥm 'lhy' ṭby'. **2.** *RTP* 123b—'LT. *RTP* 164a—'LT. *RTP* 165a—'LT. *RTP* 272a—mlkbl w'LT. CaD 5^{1}—'LT wrḥm. *PNO* 40^{3}—'LT.

'NHYT 2. *RTP* 166a—'NHYT. *RTP* 167a—'NHYT.

'RGY' 2. 'Bas-relief' p. 47—šlmn w'RGY' or 'dgy' gny' ṭby' wškry'.

'RṢW 1. [*4*]*25*, *C* 3974^{1}—'RṢW w'zyzw 'lhy' ṭby' wskry'. *464, Michalowski*, p. 318^{2}—lbl wlb'šmn [wl'glbwl wlmlk]bl wl'štrt wlnmsys wl'RṢW wl'bgl. *525*, 'Monuments' 1^{2}—bl w'RṢW. **2.** *C* 3975^{3}—[']RṢW [']lh'. *RTP* 169a to 170a—'RṢW. *RTP* 175b—'RṢW r'yy'. *RTP* 176b—r'y' 'RṢW. *RTP* 180b—'RṢW r[b']. *RTP* 183b—'RṢW. *RTP* 184a—'RṢW. *RTP* 186b—[']R]Ṣ[W]. *RTP* 187a—[']R[Ṣ]W. *RTP* 190a—rb' 'RṢW. *RTP* 192 to 195—'RṢW. *RTP* 196a—rb [']RṢW. *RTP* 753a—[']R]ṢW. 'Inscriptions' p. 125, Pl. II—gd' dy gny' w'RṢW wrḥm. *Michalowski*, p. 314—lbl wlyrḥbwl wl'glbwl wl'RṢW. *Inv. X*, 118—. . .] 'RṢW [. . . .

'RṢWBL 2. *RTP* 197a—'RṢWBL.

'ŠLM 1. *536*, CaD 4^{2}—. . .]w'd/rd/ryn w'šr w'ŠLM.

'ŠR 1. *466*, *PNO* 6 C—'ŠR gny' ṭb'. *536*, CaD 4^{2}—. . .]w'd/rd/ryn w'ŠR w'šlm. **2.** *Inv. XI*, 66^{1}—'ŠR gny'.

[']ŠT[R] 2. *RTP* 121b—[']ŠT[R].

'ŠTR' 1. *330*, CaD 6^{4}—'ŠTR'. **2.** CaC 12^{4}—'ŠTR'.

'ŠTRBD 2. *RTP* 198b—'ŠTRBD mlkt'. *RTP* 199a—'ŠTRBD.

BWL'STR 1. *360*, CaC 11^{5}—BW[L]'STR [wšdy'] 'lhy' ṭby'. *360*, CaC 11^{9}—[BW]L'STR wšdy'. **2.** CaD 32^{2}—BWL'STR 'lh'.

BYL 2. 'Bilingue' p. 885^{2}—BYL tdmry' wyrḥbl w'glbwl.

BL 1. *269*, StaD p. 514, 2^{3}—BL. *330*, *C* 3924^{5}—[BL]. *336*, CaC 4^{5}—BL. *357*, CaD 1^{4}—BL wyrḥbwl w'glbwl 'lhy'. *371*, *Inv. IX*, 20^{4}—BL. *428*, *C* 3919^{4}—BL. *464*, *Michalowski*, p. 318^{1}—lBL wlb'šmn [wl'glbwl wlmlk]bl wl'štrt wlnmsys wl'rṣw wl'bgl. *483*, CaD 20^{7}—BL. *486*, *C* 3914^{5}—BL. *525*, 'Monuments' 1^{2}—BL w'rṣw. *525*, 'Monuments' 1^{9}—BL 'lh' ṭb'. **2.** *C* 3904^{1}—[BL wyrḥbwl w'glbwl w'. . . .]. *C* 3977^{4}—BL. *RTP* 10a—BL 'lh'. *RTP* 11a to 29a—BL. *RTP* 36a—58a BL. *RTP* 59a—BL twr'. *RTP* 60a to 93a—BL. *RTP* 93a—BL w'bl'ly. *RTP* 94a to 115a—BL. *RTP* 117b—BL. *RTP* 122a to 124a—BL. *RTP* 125a—BL wbl'str. *RTP* 126a to 127a—BL. *RTP* 128a to 129a—BL blty. *RTP* 130a—BL gd blm'. *RTP* 131a—BL gd mšḥ'. *RTP* 132b—BL. *RTP* 133a—BL ḥrt'. *RTP* 134a—BL wḥrt' wnny. *RTP* 135a to 136a—BL. *RTP* 137a—BL wnbw. *RTP* 138a to 139a—BL šmš. *RTP* 140a to 141a—BL wšmš. *RTP* 142a—BL. *RTP* 143a—

brt BL. *RTP* 144a—brt BL. *RTP* 680b—gd‘t’ dy BL. *RTP* 1132a—BL. *Michalowski*, p. 313—‘strt ‘glbwl BL b‘lš[mn] yrḥbwl. *Michalowski*, p. 314—lBL wlyrḥbwl wl‘glbwl wl’rṣw. ‘Tessères’ 1a—BL. ‘Tessères’ 2b—BL. ‘Monuments’ 4a—BL. CaD 3^{4}—BL ’lh’ rb’. CaD 3^{6}—BL ’lh’. CaE p. 230^{6}——bt brt BL. StaD p. 516, 3^{3}—BL blḥmwn wmnwt. *Inv. XI*, 74^{1}—BL wy[rḥbwl] w‘glbwl.

BLḤMWN 1. *400*, ‘Fouilles’ p. 170^{1}—BLḤMWN. *400*, ‘Fouilles’ p. 172^{1}—[BLḤMWN]. **2.** ‘Fouilles’ p. 174^{2}—BLḤM[WN]. StaD p. 516, 3^{3}—bl BLḤMWN wmnwt. *RTP* 212a to 214a—BLḤMWN.

BLḤMN 2. *RTP* 215a—BLḤMN.

BL‘STR 2. *RTP* 125a—bl wBL‘STR. *RTP* 126b—[BL]‘STR. *RTP* 127b—BL‘STR nrgl. *RTP* 211a—B[L‘]STR.

BLTY 2. *RTP* 128a—bl BLTY. *RTP* 129a—bl BLTY. *RTP* 216a to 218a—BLTY. *RTP* 219a—BLTY blnwry. *RTP* 777a—[BL]TY.

B‘LŠMYN 2. *RTP* 209a—B‘LŠMYN mlkbl.

B‘LŠMN 1. *378*, *C* 3983^{1}—B‘LŠMN ’lh’ ṭb’. *378*, CaA 30^{1}—B‘LŠMN ’lh’ ṭb’ wškr’. *400*+?, *C* 3988^{1}—B‘LŠMN rb’ wrḥmn’. *425*, *C* 3986^{1}—B‘LŠMN mr’ ‘lm’. [*4*]*42*, *C* 3959^{6}—B‘LŠMN. *443*, *C* 3987^{1}—B‘LŠMN. [*445*] *C* 3912^{1}—B‘LŠMN mr’ ‘lm’. **2.** CaA 10^{1}—B‘LŠMN rb’ w[r]ḥmn’. *RTP* 203a to 208a—B‘LŠMN. ‘Monuments’ 4b—B‘LŠMN. *Michalowski*, p. 313—‘strt ‘glbwl bl B‘LŠ[MN] yrḥbwl. CaE p. 230^{5}—B‘LŠ[MN].

B‘ŠMN 1. *464*, *Michalowski*, p. 318^{1}—lbl wlB‘ŠMN [wl‘glbwl wlmlk]bl wl‘štrt wlnmsys wl’rṣw wl’bgl. *527*, *PNO* 61^{4}—B‘ŠMN ṭb’ wskr’. *539*, StaF p. 40, 2—B‘ŠMN.

BRT BL 1. [*2*]*89*, StaD p. 512, 1^{6}—BRT BL. **2.** *RTP* 143a to 144a—BRT BL.

GBR’ 2. *RTP* 507a—GBR’ rb’.

GD BLM’ 2. *RTP* 130a—bl GD BLM’.

GD MŠḤ’ 2. *RTP* 131a—bl GD MŠḤ’. *RTP* 132a—GD MŠḤ’.

GD N’WM 2. *PNO* 63—GD N’WM or gdn’.

GD ‘GRWD 2. *RTP* 213b—GD ‘GRWD. *RTP* 224b—GD ‘GRWD.

GD QRYT’ 1. *461*, *PNO* 51—GD QRYT’.

GD TDMR 2. CaD 18^{2}—[‘g]lbwl wGD TDMR.

GD TYMY 1. *451*, *C* 3927^{4}—mlkbl wGD TYMY w‘tr‘th ’lh[y’] ṭb[y’]. **2.** *RTP* 135b—mlkbl wGD TYMY. *RTP* 273a—mlkbl wGD TYMY. *RTP* 274a—mlkbl GD TYMY. *RTP* 275a—mlkbl GD TYMY. *RTP* 277a—mlkbl GD TYMY. *RTP* 279a—mlkbl wGD TYMY.

GD’ DY GNY’ 1. *550*, *PNO* 42^{4}—gdh dy qryt’ wGD’ DY GNY’. **2.** ‘Inscriptions’ p. 125, Pl. II—GD’ DY GNY’ w’rṣw wrḥm.

GD’ DY ‘YN’ 2. *C* 3976^{1}—GD’ DY ‘YN’.

GD’ DY QRT[’] 1. *520*+?, ‘Inscriptions’ p. 133, Pl. I—GD’ DY QRT[’].

GD’ ṬB’ 2. *RTP* 718a—GD’ ṬB’.

GDH DY QRYT’ 1. *550*, *PNO* 42^{3}—GDH DY QRYT’ wgd’ dy gny’.

GDH DY SY[WN] 1. *550*, *Inv. XI*, 15^{4}—GDH DY SY[WN].

GDN’ 2. *PNO* 63—GDN’ or gd n’wm.

GD‘T’ 2. *RTP* 680b—GD‘T’ dy bl.

GNY’ 2. *RTP* 225b—GNY’. *RTP* 226a—GNY’. *PNO* 43^{3}—GNY’ ’lh’ ṭb’ wškr’.

DDḤLWN 2. *RTP* 987a—DDḤLWN.

DWD/RḤLWN 2. *AAS*, 7 (1957), 81—DWD/RḤLWN.

D‘NT 1. (*3*?)*42*, ‘Dédicace’ p. 45, 6—šdrp’ wD‘NT ’lhy’ ṭb[y’]. **2.** *RTP* 329a—šdrp’ D‘NT.

ḤRT’ 1. *307*, CaD 17^{6}—ḤRT’ wnny wršp ’lhy’. **2.** *RTP* 133a—bl ḤRT’. *RTP* 134a—bl wḤRT’ wnny. *RTP* 238a—ḤRT’ nny. *RTP* 239a—ḤRT’. *RTP* 240a—ḤRT’ wnny. *RTP* 241a—ḤRT[’] nny. *RTP* 242a—ḤRT’ wnny. *Inv. XI*, 80^{5}—ḤR[T’].

YRḤBWL 1. *357*, CaD 1^{4}—bl wYRḤBWL w‘glbwl ’lhy’. *428*, *C* 3919^{3}—YRḤBWL ’lhy’. *520*+?, ‘Inscriptions’ p. 133, Pl. I—YRḤBWL. *554*, *C* 3932^{6}—YRḤBWL ’lh’. **2.** *C* 3904^{1}—[bl wYRḤBWL w‘glbwl w‘. . . .]. *RTP* 119b—YRḤBWL ‘glbwl. *RTP* 244a—YRḤBWL w‘glbwl. *RTP* 247a—YRḤBWL. *RTP* 547b—YRḤBWL (?). ‘Tessères’ 3b—YRḤBWL. ‘Tessères’ 26a—YRḤBWL w‘glbwl nbw. CaD 26^{9}—YRḤBW[L]. *PNO* 2 *ter*^{5}—YRḤBWL. *PNO* 52 *ter* A^{3}—YRḤ[BWL]. *PNO* 52 *ter* B^{4}—YRḤBWL. *Michalowski*, p. 313—‘strt ‘glbwl bl b‘lš[mn] YRḤBWL. *Michalowski*, p. 314—lbl wlYRḤBWL wl‘glbwl wl’rṣw. *Inv. XI*, 74^{1}—bl wY[RḤBWL] w‘glbwl.

YRḤBL 2. ‘Bilingue’ p. 885^{3}—byl tdmry’ wYRḤBL w‘glbwl.

YRḤYBWL 1. *516*, StaB p. 111, A 1169^{2}—YRḤYBWL ’lh’.

MLK' 1. *573, PNO* 57—MLK' ṭb' wškr'.

MLKBWL 2. 'Dédicace' p. 61—'glbwl wMLKBWL.

MLKBL 1. *345, C* 3980^{2}—'glbwl wMLKBL 'lh[y']. *348*, CaD 33^{4}—['glbwl w]MLKBL 'lhy' ṭby'. [*4*]*34, Pal. 63*: 14^{6}—'glbwl wMLKBL. *451, C* 3927^{4}—MLKB[L] wgd tymy w'tr'th 'lh[y'] ṭb[y']. *464, Michalowski*, p. 318^{2}—lbl wlb'šmn [wl'glbwl wlMLK]BL wl'štrt wlnmsys wl'rṣw wl'bgl. *500, C* 3981^{6}—'glbwl wMLKBL. *525, PNO* 16^{4}—'glbwl wMLKBL w'bgl gny'. *547, C* 3902^{1}—'glbwl wMLKBL. **2.** *C* 3903^{1}—MLKBL w'lhy tdmr. CaA 60^{2}—MLKBL. CaA 67—'glbwl wMLKBL. *Pal. 61*: 4—'glbwl wMLKBL. *Pal. 61*: 5^{1}—MLKBL 'gl(bwl). *Pal. 62*: 17—'glbwl wMLKBL. *PNO* 50—'glbwl w[M]LKBL. *PNO* 79^{5}—MLKBL. *RTP* 135b—MLKBL wgd tymy. *RTP* 155a—'glbwl ML[KB]L. *RTP* 156a—'glbwl MLKBL. *RTP* 157a—'glbwl MLKBL. *RTP* 158a—'glbwl wMLKBL. *RTP* 159b—MLKBL twr'. *RTP* 160a—'glbwl MLKBL. *RTP* 161a—'glbwl MLKBL. *RTP* 209a—b'lšmyn MLKBL. *RTP* 262a to 264a—MLKBL. *RTP* 270a—[M]LKBL. *RTP* 271a—MLKBL. *RTP* 272a—MLKBL w'lt. *RTP* 273a—MLKBL wgd tymy. *RTP* 274a to 277a—MLKBL gd tymy. *RTP* 279a—MLKBL wgd tymy. *Inv. XI*, 12^{6}—. . .] wMLKBL 'lhy'. *Inv. XI*, 33^{5}—'glbwl wMLKBL. *Inv. XI*, 73^{4}—['glbwl] wMLKBL 'lhy'.† *Inv. XI*, 79^{4}—'glbwl wM[LKBL]. *Inv. XI*, 80^{4}—['glbwl] wMLKBL. *Inv. XI*, 85^{2}—'glbwl wMLKBL.

MNWT 1. *400*, 'Fouilles' p. 170^{2}—MNWT. *400*, 'Fouilles' p. 172^{7}—MNWT. **2.** StaD p. 516, 3^{3}—bl blḥmwn wMNWT. *Inv. XI*, 46^{2}—MNWT. *RTP* 281a—MNWT.

MNP 2. *RTP* 219b—tmwz' wMNP.

M'N 2. *PNO* 7 A^{2}—'bgl wM'N 'lhy' ṭby' wškry'. *PNO* 35 A^{3}—M'N 'lh'. *PNO* 35 C—M'N wš'r 'lhy'.

M'NW 1. *505, PNO* 37^{4}—M'NW 'lh' ṭb' wskr'. **2.** *RTP* 153b—M'NW. *RTP* 248a—M'NW š'rw gny'. *RTP* 249a—M'NW. *RTP* 251a—M'NW. *RTP* 252a—M'NW t[w]r'.

NBW 2. *RTP* 119a—NBW. *RTP* 136b—NBW. *RTP* 137a—bl wNBW. *RTP* 137b—NBW. *RTP* 287a to 289a—NBW. *RTP* 290a—NB[W] or N(RG)L. *RTP* 291a to 300a—NBW. *RTP* 302a to 309a—NBW. 'Tessères' 5a—NBW. 'Tessères' 6b—NBW. 'Tessères' 25a—NBW. 'Tessères' 26a—yrḥbwl w'glbwl NBW.

NMSYS 1. *464, Michalowski*, p. 318^{2}—lbl wlb'šmn [wl'glbwl wlmlk]bl wl'štrt wlNMSYS wl'rṣw wl'bgl.

NNY 1. *307*, CaD 17^{6}—ḥrt' wNNY wršp 'lhy'. **2.** *RTP* 134a—bl wḥrt' wNNY. *RTP* 238a—ḥrt' NNY. *RTP* 239b—NNY. *RTP* 240a—ḥrt' wNNY. *RTP* 241a—ḥrt['] NNY. *RTP* 242a—ḥrt' wNNY. *RTP* 285a—NNY škny šy't bbl.

NRGL 2. *RTP* 127b—bl'str NRGL. *RTP* 227b—NRGL. *RTP* 290a—nb[w] or N(RG)L.

'GLBWL 1. *345, C* 3980^{2}—'GLBWL wmlkbl 'lh[y']. *348*, CaD 33^{4}—['GLBWL w]mlkbl 'lhy' ṭby'. *357*, CaD 1^{5}—bl wyrḥbwl w'GLBWL 'lhy'. *38*[.], CaD 34^{1}—'GLBW[L]. [*4*]*30, C* 3982—[']GLBWL. [*4*]*34, Pal. 63*: 14^{6}—'GLBWL wmlkbl. *447, C* 3968^{1}—'GLBWL. *464, Michalowski*, p. 318^{2}—lbl wlb'šmn [wl'GLBWL wlmlk]bl wl'štrt wlnmsys wl'rṣw wl'bgl. *500, C* 3981^{6}—'GLBWL wmlkbl. *525, PNO* 16^{3}—'GLBWL wmlkbl w'bgl gny'. *547, C* 3902^{1}—'GLBWL wmlkbl. **2.** *C* 3904^{1}—[bl wyrḥbwl w'GLBWL w'. . . .]. CaA 67—'GLBWL wmlkbl. CaD 18^{2}—['G]LBWL wgd tdmr. *PNO* 50—'GLBWL w[m]lkbl. *Pal. 61*: 4—'GLBWL wmlkbl. *Pal. 61*: 5^{2}—mlkbl 'GL(BWL). *Pal. 62*: 17—'GLBWL wmlkbl. *Inv. XI*, 33^{4}—'GLBWL wmlkbl. *Inv. XI*, 73^{3}—['GLBWL] wmlkbl 'lhy'.† *Inv. XI*, 74^{2}—bl w[yrḥbwl] w'GLBWL. *Inv. XI*, 79^{4}—'GLBWL wm[lkbl]. *Inv. XI*, 80^{3}—['GLBWL] wmlkbl. *Inv. XI*, 85^{2}—'GLBWL wmlkbl. *RTP* 119b—yrḥbwl 'GLBWL. *RTP* 122b—'GLBWL. *RTP* 145b—'GLBWL. *RTP* 146a—'GLBWL. *RTP* 149a—'GLBW[L]. *RTP* 149b—'GLBWL. *RTP* 150a—'GLBWL. *RTP* 153a to 154a—'GLBWL. *RTP* 155a—'GLBWL ml[kb]l. *RTP* 156a—'GLBWL mlkbl. *RTP* 157a—'GLBWL mlkbl. *RTP* 158a—'GLBWL wmlkbl. *RTP* 159a—'GLBWL twr'. *RTP* 160a to 161a—'GLBWL mlkbl. *RTP* 244a—yrḥbwl w'GLBWL. 'Bilingue' p. 885^{3}—byl tdmry' wyrḥbl w'GLBWL. *Michalowski*, p. 313—'strt 'GLBWL bl b'lš[mn] yrḥbwl. *Michalowski*, p. 314—lbl wlyrḥbwl wl'GLBWL wl'rṣw. 'Dédicace' p. 61—'GLBWL wmlkbwl. 'Tessères' 26a—yrḥbwl w'GLBWL nbw.

'D/RD/RYN(?) **1.** *536*, CaD 4^{2}—. . .] w'D/RD/RYN w'šr w'šlm.

'ZYZW 1. [*4*]*25, C* 3974^{1}—'rṣw w'ZYZW 'lhy' ṭby' wskry'. [*4*]*25, C* 3974^{2}—'ZYZW 'lh' ṭb' wrḥmn'.

'ŠTR 2. 'Tessères' 23b—'ŠTR.

† This reading from Starcky, review of *Inv. XI*, in *RB*, 73 (1966), 616.

'ŠTRT 1. *464, Michalowski,* p. 318[2]—lbl wlb'šmn [wl'glbwl wlmlk]bl wl'ŠTRT wlnmsys wl'rṣw wl'bgl. **2.** *RTP* 124b—'ŠTRT. *Michalowski,* p. 313—'ŠTRT 'glbwl bl b'lš[mn] yrḥbwl.

'ŠTR[T'] 1. *445,* CaC 13[2]—'ŠTR[T'] 'štr' ṭbt'.

'TR'TH 1. *451, C* 3927[4]—mlkb[l] wgd tymy w'TR'TH 'lh[y'] ṭb[y']. **2.** *RTP* 201a—'TR'TH.

Ṣ'B[W] 2. *C* 3991[3]—Ṣ'B[W] dy mqr' gd' [']nbt.

RḤM 1. *440, C* 3955[7]—šmš w'lt wRḤM 'lhy' ṭby'. **2.** 'Inscriptions' p. 125, Pl. II—gd' dy gny' w'rṣw wRḤM. CaD 5[1]—'lt wRḤM.

R'Y' 2. *RTP* 176b—R'Y' 'rṣw.

R'YY' 2. *RTP* 175b—'rṣw R'YY'.

RŠP 1. *307,* CaD 17[6]—ḥrt' wnny wRŠP 'lhy'.

ŠDY' 1. *360,* CaC 11[6]—bw[l]'str [wŠDY'] 'lhy' ṭby'. *360,* CaC 11[9]—[bw]l'str wŠDY'.

ŠDRP' 1. *(3?)42,* 'Dédicace' p. 45, 6—ŠDRP' wd'nt 'lhy' ṭb[y']. *366, C* 3972[3]—ŠDRP' 'lh' ṭb'. **2.** *RTP* 317a—ŠDRP'. *RTP* 321a—ŠDRP'. *RTP* 325a—ŠDRP' twr'. *RTP* 328b—ŠDRP'. *RTP* 329a—ŠDRP' d'nt. 'Dédicace' p. 68, Fig. 7—ŠDRP'.

ŠY''LQWM 1. *443, C* 3973[4]—ŠY''LQWM 'lh' ṭb' wškr'. *443, C* 3973[9]—ŠY''LQWM 'lh' ṭb'.

[ŠY]'LQWM 2. *RTP* 332b—[ŠY]'LQWM.

ŠKNY 2. *RTP* 285a—nny ŠKNY šy't bbl.

ŠLMN 2. 'Bas-relief' p. 47—ŠLMN w'r/dgy' gny' ṭby' wškry'. *PNO* 38[4]—ŠLMN w'bgl.

ŠLMT 2. CaD 35[1]—ŠLMT.

ŠMŠ 1. *396, C* 3978[6]—ŠMŠ 'lh. *440, C* 3955[6]—ŠMŠ w'lt wrḥm 'lhy' ṭby'. *490, C* 3951—ŠMŠ [']lh[']. **2.** *C* 3979—ŠMŠ 'lh' ṭb[']. *RTP* 138a to 141a—bl ŠMŠ. *RTP* 142b—ŠMŠ. *RTP* 333a—ŠMŠ šrn rb'. *RTP* 334a to 336a—ŠMŠ. *RTP* 337b—ŠMŠ. *RTP* 339a to 341a—ŠMŠ.

Š'R 2. *PNO* 35 C—m'n wŠ'R 'lhy'.

Š'RW 2. *RTP* 248a—m'nw Š'RW gny'. *RTP* 249b—[Š']RW. *RTP* 331a—Š'[R]W.

TMWZ' 2. *RTP* 218b—TMWZ'. *PRT* 219b—TMWZ' wmnp. *RTP* 342a—TMWZ'.

II. LEXICON

THIS lexical study is intended to explain as far as possible the elements occurring in Semitic personal names found in Palmyrene inscriptions. The Greek, Latin, and Persian names are included, but they have not been dealt with lexically, as this was not within the scope of the thesis. Only orthographic features in the transcription of foreign names into Palmyrene have been commented upon. However, references to works on Greek and Persian names are given under the individual names.

The interpretation of the Semitic names has to rely heavily on comparative material from languages spoken in areas neighbouring on Palmyra, languages about which we have more information from literary evidence than we have for Palmyrene Aramaic itself. This primarily concerns Arabic, Syriac, and other dialects of Aramaic. Only when these sources failed have other Semitic languages been drawn on for comparative evidence.

Whenever a name could be explained from either an Aramaic or an Arabic root, preference has in general been given to the latter, but without omitting reference to the Aramaic interpretation.

Explanations from the Arabic, however, are to be taken cautiously. There is a time span of about four hundred years between the latest Palmyrene inscription and the earliest Arabic literary evidence. It remains therefore always a matter of uncertainty whether an Arabic word was attested in pre-Islamic times and with the specific meaning it acquired later (on this see discussion under MŠLM). That the etymology of many names had early become unknown is seen by the fact that the Arabic lexicographer Ibn Doreid, writing in the ninth century A.D., was in many cases no longer aware of the original meaning of the early Arabic names which he treated (see *Abu Bekr Muhammed ben el-Hassan Ibn Doreid's genealogisch-etymologisches Handbuch*, ed. F. Wüstenfeld), and often cites all roots from which the name could possibly have been derived; e.g. see Ibn Doreid, 234^{11}, on the etymology of NPR.

The procedure adopted in the lexical part was to list first the structural type, grammatical form, and etymology, and thereafter reference was made to comparative evidence and the explanations of the names by other scholars.

Many of the lexical interpretations offered are tentative. This applies even to some cases where this is not specifically stated. The term 'uncertain' was used whenever the name was grammatically and etymologically of unusual obscurity. The word 'unexplained' indicates that I could find no explanation for the name with the sources I used.

The term proto-Arabic is used to designate Safaitic, Thamudic, and Lihyanite, and is not employed to refer to a reconstructed prototype of classical (northern) Arabic.

The names of tribes and deities have been listed separately at the end of Chapter I (Main List), but have not been dealt with in the lexical part.

The term 'genitive compound' has been employed throughout, following Noth's and Huffmon's use of the term for names like 'BDBL, 'servant of Bēl'. The term does not imply genitive case inflexion of the second element, but refers to the dependent relationship of the first element.

'B'. *One-word name.* 'Father'
'Ab is no longer used as a theophorous element at Palmyra; see Caquot, 'Onomastique', 236. Among the inscriptions from Hatra are two examples where 'b substitutes for a divine name—no. 107[2]: 'bgdy cf. nbwgdy; no. 106a: 'bšp'. This evidence, however, is insufficient to make any definite statements with regard to the existence of this type of name in the Palmyrene onomasticon as long as no clear structural examples can be found at Palmyra. On its use as divine epithet see Noth, 'Gemeinsemitische', 1–45; Huffmon, *APNMT*, 154. For its meaning see Nöldeke, *Beiträge*, 92. For further parallels see Ryckmans, i. 36, 'b; Cantineau, *Le Nabatéen*, ii. 55; 'Hatra', nos. 5[3], 107[1], 140[3], 176, 188[1], 'b'; Elephantine, *CIS*, ii. 122[1], 'bh; Aramaic inscription from the Wadi Ḥammâmât, in *RA*, 41 (1947), 106, 'b; *Thes. Syr.* 5; Talmudic name, see Jastrow, 2; Galling, 173[5]. Greek transcription: Abba, Wuthnow, 6.

'BB. *One-word name.* 'Ripening'
Act. part. masc.; see Rosenthal, *Sprache*, 67. Goldmann, *Personennamen*, 24, considers the name to be the reduplicated form of 'b. The explanation of the editor of the *Corpus* (*C* 4374), who attaches the word to the root 'bb (see Jastrow, 2) is preferable. Cf. the Amharic proper name abbaba, 'he has blossomed'. Greek transcription: Ababou, Wuthnow, 6.

'BB'. *One-word name.* 'Ripening'
Act. part. fem.; cf. masc. form 'BB. Aleph and He interchange in Palmyrene; see Rosenthal, *Sprache*, 21. For discussion see under 'BB.

'BGL. *One-word name.* 'Honoured'
Af'al form; cf. Arabic bajala. For names formed from the root BGL see Cantineau, *Le Nabatéen*, ii. 70; Littmann, *Safaitic Inscriptions*, 301b; Ryckmans, i. 48. The latter gives as the meaning of Arabic bajala, 'être gai, content'. See also Wüstenfeld, *Register*, 101.

'BGR. *One-word name.* 'Big-bellied'
Af'al form; Arabic: abjar. Goldmann, *Personennamen*, 29, considers the name Persian and translates 'Lahmer', following *Thes. Syr.* 7. For Abgar as a personal name see Ryckmans, i. 48; Cantineau, *Le Nabatéen*, ii. 70; Ibn Doreid, 208[10]. Greek transcription: Abgaros, Wuthnow, 7.

'BDY. *One-word name.* 'Wild animal'
Arabic: ābid. The root 'bd is found in many names; see Ryckmans, i. 39; Cantineau, *Le Nabatéen*, ii. 55, 'bdw (reading 'brw is possible); Wüstenfeld, *Register*, 37. Arabic abada means 'stay, linger'; ābid is a 'wild animal', so called because it endures for a long time. That 'bdy = 'bdy is impossible. The change '/' is not attested at Palmyra unless there are reasons for it, e.g. dissimilation; see Rosenthal, *Sprache*, 35. Caquot, *RTP*, 160, proposes to read 'bry and takes it as a hypocoristicon of *'b-'rṣw, 'Arṣû is (my) father'. This explanation is rather unlikely because a good interpretation of the name is possible.

'BYHN. *Uncertain*
According to the Greek transcription 'Obaianēs', attested from a bilingual text (*RB*, 39 [1930], 526), this name must be a diminutive of an Af'al form of an unknown Arabic root *bhn. For a discussion of this type and for further parallels see under ''YLM.

'BYḤY. *Nominal sentence with adjectival predicate.* 'My father is living'
Name of a bishop of Nicaea; see *Thes. Syr.* 12. See also Galling, 183[70]. For similar names see Noth, *IPN*, 70; *CIS*, ii. 123[2], 'byṭb; Stamm, *ANG*, 294–5. Ingholt, (*Berytus*, 5 [1938], 114), proposes 'byḥy = *'by-'ḥy, 'my father is my brother', describing the care that the son should give to the father, as if he were his brother. Structurally the name would be analogous to 'ḥy'b, 'my brother is (my) father'; see Cowley, *Papyri*, 2[2]. There are good semantic parallels for the first suggestion, and no structural alteration is involved.

'BYN. *One-word name.* 'Daddy'
The Arabic name ubay is well attested; see Ṭabari, *Index*, 11. Several meanings have been proposed for this name, but the most convincing interpretation is given by Littmann, *Safaitic Inscriptions*, Leyden, 1904, p. 128: 'b plus diminutive ending; he is followed in this by Ryckmans, i. 36. Nöldeke, *Beiträge*, 93, considers the form 'hebraisierend': 'b plus possessive-suffix. Cantineau, *Le Nabatéen*, ii. 55, compares Arabic abyan, 'more distinct'. Lidzbarski, *Ephemeris*, 2, 352, considers 'byn to be a diminutive to Arabic abān; see Ibn Doreid, 143[16].

'BYN'. *Uncertain*
Two interpretations for this name are possible: (1) To explain it in the same way as 'byn, with the help of the Arabic ubay—diminutive of 'b plus hypocoristic ending -ân. (2) As a shortened form of *'by-nbw, 'my father is Nabû'. But there are no clear attestations of this structural type at Palmyra; see Caquot, 'Onomastique', 240 n. 9.

'BY'. *One-word name.* 'White'
Arabic: abyaḍ. For parallels see Ryckmans, i. 51; Euting, *Nabatäische Inschriften*, 6[2], 'byṣ (reading 'byn possible, [so Cantineau, *Le Nabatéen*, ii. 55]). On the treatment of Arabic ḍ in Nabataean see Cantineau, *Le Nabatéen*, i. 42. Goldmann, *Personennamen*, 23, proposes 'by' = 'by'qb, Chabot in the *Corpus* (4432) 'by' = 'byd'. But both are anomalous abbreviations. The proposed reading 'sy' (*C* 4432) is semantically possible, but disputable on epigraphical grounds.

'BYŠY. *Uncertain*
Various explanations are possible. (1) On the problem of the O.T. 'ᵃbîšay see Noth, *IPN*, 40: Bauer, *ZAW*, 48 (1930), 77, translates 'der Vater existiert' and compares Akkadian names with ibašši. (2) It could be a shortened form of *'by-šmš, 'my father is Šamaš'. But there are no clear examples of this structural type at Palmyra: see Caquot, 'Onomastique', 240 n. 9. (3) It could be a shortened form of *'by-šwry, 'my father is my stronghold'. 'b in this case would serve as a theophorous element. But there are no clear examples for this at Palmyra, although names from Palmyra composed with šwr would favour this interpretation. Cf. blšwr, nbwšwry, ʿtršwry, etc.

'BLʿLY. *Nominal sentence.* 'My father is ʿAlî'
This name is difficult to interpret. Various explanations have been offered. (1) Lidzbarski, *Ephemeris*, 3, 153, divides the name into the following components: 'b+bl+ʿly, '(mein) Vater Bel (wacht) über mich'. As a structural parallel he cites 'bʿly (Ryckmans, i. 254), and for the orthography he compares Phoenician 'bʿl = *'bbʿl; see *CIS*, i. 1901. (2) Goldmann, *Personennamen*, 7 n. 1, rejects this explanation. Names composed of three elements do not exist at Palmyra. He proposes instead (ibid. 31): '+bl+ʿly, 'Bēl (wacht) über mich'. (3) Caquot, *RTP*, 158, compares the name with Palmyrene ʿlybʿl, and with Nabataean ʿly'l (Cantineau, *Le Nabatéen*, ii. 131). ʿly is not a preposition plus suffix, but the Arabic adjective ʿalî, 'high, elevated, noble'. His translation is 'Bêl est élevé'. The Aleph he interprets as Aleph prostheticum. (4) Nyberg in his 'Studien zum Religionskampf im Alten Testament', 337, interprets the name as 'Ab-la-ʿalî, 'der Vater ist fürwahr ʿAlî'. In ʿly he sees a divine name; on this see Pope, in *Wörterbuch*, 254–5; Dahood, 'The Divine Name ʿēlî in the Psalms', *Theological Studies*, 14 (1953), 452–7; Noth, *IPN*, 129, 146; Huffmon, *APNMT*, 194. The Lamed serves as asseverative particle. (Ugar. l [Gordon, *UT*, par. 9.16], Hebr. l [Brockelmann, *GVG*, ii. 110, par. 56b; Nötscher, 'Zum emphatischen Lamed', *VT*, 3 (1953), 372–80], Old Aram. l [Garbini, 'Aramaico', 256, par. 4e], Arab. la [Wright, i. 282–3], Amorite la [Huffmon, *APNMT*, 223].) Cf. also the Hatra evidence: šmšlṭb, 'Šamaš is surely good' ('Hatra', no. 30³).

Attestations for 'blʿly as deity: *RTP*, 93a: 'gn bl w'blʿly, 'hear, Bēl and 'blʿly'.

'BMRT. *Persian name?*
See Justi, *Namenbuch*, 502, Apanmart.

'BN'. *Uncertain*
Various interpretations are possible. (1) It could be a shortened form of *'b-nbw, 'Nabû is father'. There are no clear parallels for this type of name at Palmyra; see Caquot, 'Onomastique', 240 n. 9. (2) 'bn is attested in Min., Saf., Qat.; see Ryckmans, i. 39, who compares with it Arabic abana, 'reprimand'. (3) According to Littmann, *Safaitic Inscriptions*, 296a, 'bn is derived from the name of a mountain; so states already Ibn Doreid, 104¹². Abân is mentioned as the name of several Arabs by Wüstenfeld, *Register*, 1–2.

'BNYT. *Hypocoristicon.* 'N.N. has built'
The divine name at the beginning of the name is suppressed. On names with bnh see Noth, *IPN*, 172. A similar name was found at 'Hatra', no. 10²: šmšḥryt.

'BRWQ. *One-word name.* 'Morning star'
*brq, 'shine, lighten' (Common Semitic). It is difficult to explain the Aleph as a prosthetic syllable serving to avoid a consonant cluster. 'brwq is most likely a qātōl type noun and as such has a long vowel in the first syllable; see Brockelmann, *GVG*, i. 343, par. 128. The meaning and origin of the Aleph are obscure.

For parallels of names formed from brq see Ryckmans, i. 56, 288; Noth, *IPN*, 226; Huffmon, *APNMT*, 178.

'BRYKW. *Hypocoristicon.* 'Blessed by N.N.'
Aramaic pass. part. 'BRYKW is attested besides BRYKW. Cf. in Biblical Hebrew zᵉrôaʿ besides 'ezrōaʿ. BRK as an element in personal names is widely attested. For parallels see Noth, *IPN*, 183; Harris, *Grammar*, 91–2; Ryckmans, i. 55; Cantineau, *Le Nabatéen*, ii. 75; Cowley, *Papyri*, 280; 'Hatra', nos. 79⁵, 80², 81².

'BRM'. *Jewish name*
For discussion see Noth, *IPN*, 52, 77, 145. Greek transcriptions: Abramos, Abramēs, Wuthnow, 11.

'GDM. *One-word name.* 'The Amputee'
Aramaic, Syriac gᵉdam. The Greek transcription Aggodomou is attested from a bilingual text (*RB*, 39 [1930], 532). The name is formed with the prefix 'an-: 'anquṭul > 'aqquṭul. This structural type of name was first discussed by Cantineau in *RB*, 39 (1930), 535; see also Lecerf, 'Noms propres palmyréniens', *GLECS*, 1935, 29–30. This noun-type emphasizes physical peculiarities. See also under 'QLŠ and 'QML.

'GYʿ. *Reading uncertain*
No other attestation. The name cannot be the Afʿal form of Arabic jâʿa, 'be hungry', as Starcky, *Syria*, 26 (1949), 36, assumes. One would expect *'GWʿ.

The name remains unexplained.

'GRP'. *Latin name*
Agrippa; see *ILS*, 165b. See also Appendix IV, 2.1; 2.5; 2.18; 2.22.B.

'GT'. *Greek name*
Agathos; see Pape, 6. See also Appendix IV, 1.1; 1.8; 1.15; 1.22; 1.25.D. Cantineau's statement that 'les exemples extrêmement

rares, de -us, -os, transcrit par ' dans des noms propres, doivent être expliqués par des étymologies populaires: c'est ainsi que QSYN', Cassianus, peut avoir subi l'analogie des nombreux adjectifs en -ān' is complicating a relatively simple case (*Journal asiatique*, 222 [1933], 222). The Aramaic status emphaticus ending has replaced the Greek ending -os.

'GTGLS. *Greek name*
Agathangelos, Agathaggelos; see Pape, 5. See also Appendix IV, 1.1; 1.8; 1.15; 1.22; 1.23; 1.25.D. The vowel-less N in Greek words is usually assimilated; see Rosenthal, *Sprache*, 40.

'GTWN'. *Greek name*
Agathōn; see Pape, 6. See also Appendix IV, 1.1; 1.8; 1.15; 1.22; 1.25.F. The Aramaic status emphaticus ending is added.

'GTPWS. See under 'GTPS

'GTPS, 'GTPWS. *Greek name*
Agathopous; see Pape, 6. See also Appendix IV, 1.1; 1.6; 1.8; 1.18; 1.22; 1.25.G. Rosenthal's statement (*Sprache*, 20) that ū is always written with Waw has to be modified in view of the defective writing of 'GTPS. Cf. the Punic name N'MP'M' (Harris, *Grammar*, 124). The latinized form of this Punic name is Namphamo which was explained by St. Augustine as 'boni pedis hominem' (*Epis.* 44).

'D'. *Hypocoristicon* of Addu, Haddu
The name occurs at Hatra under the forms 'd' and 'dy (nos. 58[1]; 46, 56, 57[1]), and is well attested in Syriac; see *Thes. Syr.* 36, 'dy. The O.T. 'iddô is taken by Noth, *IPN*, 39 n. 3, as a hypocoristicon of 'ādôn. This is rather improbable because of the gemination of the second radical. For further parallels see Harris, *Grammar*, 73; Jastrow, 15. Hadad is attested in the onomasticon of Dura: Zebi[dadados], Ragēadadou (*Syria*, 5 [1924], 347; *Syria*, 4 [1923], 217, no. 31.) Greek transcriptions: Adda, Addaios, Addai; see Wuthnow, 12. The O.T. evidence and the Greek transcriptions assure the doubling of the second radical in 'D'. On the role of the god Hadad-Adad at Palmyra see Février, *Religion*, 244.

'DB. *One-word name.* 'Having much hair'
Af'al form. Arabic: adabb. The root DBB occurs as component element in Sabaean and Safaitic names. Opinions differ as to its meaning; see Ryckmans, i. 218; Littmann, *Safaitic Inscriptions*, 296b; Wüstenfeld, *Register*, 43.

'DWN'. See under 'RWN'.

'DWNH. *One-word name.* 'Lord'
Aram. 'ādôn. The spelling represents a variant of 'DWN'. The latter is found frequently in epigraphic Syriac; see Segal, *BSOAS*, 16 (1954), 17, no. 2[4], with further references.

'DYNT. *One-word name.* 'Ear' (dimin.)
Arabic uḏaina. Aram.: 'ôden. For parallels see Ryckmans, i. 41; Cantineau, *Le Nabatéen*, ii. 56; Littmann, *Safaitic Inscriptions*, 297a. Greek transcriptions: Odainathos, Odainatos; see Wuthnow, 87. Latin transcription: Odenatus. On the use of parts of the body as personal names see Nöldeke, *Beiträge*, 101.

'DRYNWS. *Latin name*
Hadrianus; see *ILS*, 200a. Also see Appendix IV, 2.6; 2.8; 2.10; 2.13; 2.19; 2.22.A; 2.23.D. The Greek spiritus asper and the Latin 'h' are usually transcribed as HE. On exceptions see Rosenthal, *Sprache*, 36. The spelling with Aleph in this case could be a scribal error.

'HWD. *One-word name.* 'Gentle'
Af'al form. Cf. Arabic hāda. For parallels see Ryckmans, i. 72, who gives as the meaning of hāda, 'chantonner'. Ahwad is attested as an Arabic name in Wüstenfeld, *Register*, 51. The interpretation given here is based on Ibn Doreid's explanation of the name (Ibn Doreid, 321[12]).

[']WṬYK/Q[']. *Greek name*
Eutychēs; see Pape, 427. See also Appendix IV, 1.2; 1.3; 1.9; 1.17; 1.19; 1.22; 1.25.A. The diphthong -eu is always transcribed as Waw; see Rosenthal, *Sprache*, 23. Y by itself is usually transcribed as Yodh; see Rosenthal, *Sprache*, 20. But cf. 'WṬK' where the Y seems to be unaccented and therefore short. The spelling with Qoph shows an assimilation of the Kaph to the preceding emphatic /ṭ/. The variants are: 'WṬK', 'WTQ',

'WṬK'. *Greek name*
Eutychēs; see Pape, 427. See also Appendix IV, 1.2; 1.3; 1.9; 1.17; 1.19; 1.22; 1.25.A. The Greek ending is replaced by the Aramaic status emphaticus ending. See also discussion under [']WṬYK/Q['].

'WYR. See under 'YYR.

'WR. *Latin name*
Short form for 'WRLYS (see below).

'WRLY'. *Latin name*
Aurelius, Aurelia; see *ILS*, 22 ff., 173b. See also Appendix IV, 2.9; 2.10; 2.17; 2.22.A. On the treatment of the diphthongs see Rosenthal, *Sprache*, 23; Cantineau, *Grammaire*, 49. Forms as 'WRLY' or YWLY' can be interpreted in three different ways. (1) They are feminine names with the Latin feminine ending -a transcribed by Aleph. (2) They are masculine names. The Latin ending -us is replaced by the Aramaic status emphaticus ending; see discussion under 'GT'. (3) They represent an Aramaic (Palmyrene) plural formation. This is always the case when 'WRLYS or

YWLYS form part of the name of two persons who are mentioned together. When the two persons' names are joined by Waw, then, for convenience sake, the Latin nomenclature belonging to both persons is only mentioned with the first person. For this reason 'WRLYS or YWLYS are put in the plural (Greek plural as in *C* 3947, or Aramaic plural as in *C* 4204); see Rosenthal, *Sprache*, 23; Cantineau, *Grammaire*, 50.

'WRLYS. *Latin name*
Aurelius; see also discussion under 'WRLY'.

'WŠY. *Hypocoristicon*. 'Gift of N.N.'
Arabic aws. For parallels see Cantineau, *Le Nabatéen*, ii. 57; Ryckmans, i. 41–2. Cf. the O.T. name yô'āš; see Noth, *IPN*, 171. 'WŠ came later to be used as a name for 'wolf'; see Nöldeke, *Beiträge*, 79. Greek transcription: Ausos; see Wuthnow, 30.

On the sibilant (palato-alveolar fricative) š: in the South Arabic languages PS š has already become s. The northern Arabic dialect which influenced Palmyrene had not yet undergone this development; see Rosenthal, *Sprache*, 39; Cantineau, *Le Nabatéen*, i. 43–4; Brockelmann, *GVG*, i. 129–30; Beeston, 'Arabian Sibilants', 222–33, esp. 227; 'Phonology', 1–26.

'WTQ'. *Greek name*
Eutykēs; see Pape, 427. See also Appendix IV, 1.3; 1.9; 1.17; 1.19; 1.22; 1.25.A. One would expect *'WṬQ'. It is probably a case of dissimilation because of the following emphatic; cf. QLSTQS, Celesticus (?) (*C* 3962); see Rosenthal, *Sprache*, 36. See also discussion under [']WṬYK/Q['].

'ZMR. *One-word name*. 'Beardless'
Af'al form; cf. Arabic zamara. For parallels see Ryckmans, i. 85; Littmann, *Safaitic Inscriptions*, 313b; cf. the Talmudic name Zimra (Jastrow, 405). Greek transcription: Zomerou; see Wuthnow, 51.

'ZRZYRT. *One-word name*. 'Starling'
Hebr. zarzîr; Syr. zarzîrā'; Arab. zarzūr. The Aleph as Aleph prostheticum is difficult to explain. The ending -at cannot be the feminine ending as the name in question is masculine. On the use of birds' names as personal names see Nöldeke, *Beiträge*, 111; Noth, *IPN*, 230. See also under the variant ZRZYRT.

'Ḥ'. *One-word name*. 'Sister'
This is not the status emphaticus of 'ḥ, 'brother', but the status absolutus of 'ḥt', 'sister'. For a possible parallel see Cantineau, *Le Nabatéen*, ii. 60. On the use of family relationship names as personal names see Nöldeke, *Beiträge*, 92[2]. See also under 'ḤT'.

'ḤY'. *Hypocoristicon*. 'My brother is N.N.'
'ḥ does not serve as a theophorous element or a divine epithet at Palmyra (for possible exception see under TYMḤ'). For attestations consult Tallquist, *APN*, 17; Huffmon, *APNMT*, 160; Ryckmans, i. 37; Cantineau, *Le Nabatéen*, ii. 59; *Thes. Syr.* 114; Noth, *IPN*, 66–75. For structural parallels see under 'ḤYBL.

The origin of the Yodh which quite frequently appears between two name elements is still a matter of dispute. Noth, *IPN*, 33–6, argues in favour of an old case ending. It is unlikely that this is true for onomastica as late as the Palmyrene. One would tend to argue for the latter that the Yodh represents the suffix of the first person singular.

'ḤYB. *Unexplained*
It may be possible that the reading is wrong. But nothing definite can be said as no photograph of the inscription is available.

'ḤYBL. *Nominal sentence*. 'My brother is Bēl'
For parallels see Huffmon, *APNMT*, 160; Ugar., *PRU*, ii. 60, B[3]; *PRU*, iii. 238; Gröndahl, *Personennamen*, 91–2; Harris, *Grammar*, 75; Noth, *IPN*, 141–2. See also under: 'ḤY', 'ḤYRY, 'ḤYTWR, 'ḤYNY.

'ḤYNY. *Hypocoristicon*. 'My brother is Nabû'
*'ḥy-nbw.
For parallels and discussion see under 'ḤYBL.

'ḤYRY. *Hypocoristicon*. 'My brother is Arṣû'
*'ḥy-'rṣw.
For parallels and discussion see under 'ḤYBL. Another possible explanation would be that 'ḤYRY = 'ḤYRM. In this case 'ḥ would be a divine element. But there are no clear attestations for this type of name at Palmyra; see Caquot, 'Onomastique', 236.

'ḤYTWR. *Nominal sentence*. 'My brother is Ṯûr'
This name has been interpreted in various ways. (1) 'ḥ+ytwr, 'a brother has been added' (so Clermont-Ganneau, *RAO*, ii. 383). Ytr (pi) means 'add'. But what form would ytwr be? (2) Caquot, *Syria*, 39 (1962), 236 n. 3, wants to connect the name with Akkadian tāru, G itur, '(My) brother has returned'. Tāru is not attested in Aramaic, although tyr' < tayyāru occurs as epithet of the unknown god; see Rosenthal, *Sprache*, 89; Cantineau, *Grammaire*, 153. But the Akkadian influence at Palmyra is negligible. (3) The editor of the *Corpus* (*C* 4279) compares Syriac t[e]war, 'be amazed, shocked'. But this does not yield any satisfactory sense. (4) Goldmann, *Personennamen*, 20, takes twr as equivalent for the divine name. He thinks of the Apis bull. (5) Twr may be connected with the Sabaean god ṯwr (Ṯawr); see Ryckmans, i. 35. The name of a month is called Ḏu Ṯawr, 'of the Bull'. Ṯūr-Ba'al is attested as name of a deity; see Eissfeldt, *ZDMG*, 83 (1929), 28. This seems to be the

most acceptable explanation. For structural parallels see under 'ḤYBL.

'ḤLT. *Genitive compound.* 'The brother of Allat'
*'ḥ-'lt.
A nominal sentence, 'brother is Allat', is less likely, because Allat is a female deity. But cf. an example at Ugarit where the divine name is used as masculine and feminine: 'ṯtr'um, 'Aṯtar is mother'; 'ṯtr'b, 'Aṯtar is father'; see Virolleaud, *CRAIBL*, 1955, 79. See also Gröndahl, *Personennamen*, 86, and §§ 75, 141.

'ḤMR. *One-word name.* 'Ruddy'
Af'al form. Arabic: aḥmar. For parallels see Littmann, *Safaitic Inscriptions*, 315b. According to Cantineau's hand-copy of the inscription, the Resh is pointed. Otherwise the reading 'ḤMD (Arabic ḥamada, 'praise') would be possible. 'ḤMD is a very common name in islamic Arabic. For attestations see Littmann, *BSOAS*, 15 (1953), 18; Ryckmans, i. 93. Cf. the well-known name Muḥammad. Arabic aḥmad means 'commendable'.

'ḤPLY. *One-word name.* 'Generous'
Af'al form. Arabic: ḥafala. The formation of the name is analogous to ajnabī, 'foreign'. For names formed from this root see Cantineau, *Le Nabatéen*, ii. 98; Littmann, *Safaitic Inscriptions*, 316a. The Af'al form is augmented by the suffix Yodh; for parallels cf. the names from 'Hatra': 'nšb', 'dltw (nos. 45[2], 10). The Greek transcription Ao[ph]alein is attested from a bilingual inscription (*C* 3927).

'ḤT'. *One-word name.* 'Sister'
For attestations in other Semitic languages see Nöldeke, *Beiträge*, 92. See also under 'Ḥ'. Consult Albright, *Proto-Sinaitic*, 38; *IEJ*, 8 (1958), 228.

'ḤTY. See under BR 'ḤTY.

'ṬYK'. *Greek name*
Antiochos; see Pape, 98. See also Appendix IV, 1.2; 1.9; 1.12; 1.22; 1.23; 1.25.D. On the transliteration of dentals and velars see Rosenthal, *Sprache*, 36, 37. In the Tang-i Sarvak inscriptions (nos. 1 and 2) occurs the name 'ṭ/tyk'. This is probably the same name as here; see *BSOAS*, 27 (1964), 287.

'ṬNYNYS. *Latin name*
Antōninus; see *ILS*, 14 f., 169a. See also Appendix IV, 2.7; 2.11; 2.12; 2.18; 2.21; 2.22.A. The vowel-less N in Greek or Latin words is seldom written. For possible exceptions see Rosenthal, *Sprache*, 40.

'YD'N. *One-word name.* 'Saffron'
Arabic aida'. For attestations see Siggel, *Wörterbuch der Stoffe*, 18, 35. Greek transcription: Aidaanou, Wuthnow, 14. The name is augmented by the ending -ân; on this see under MYŠN.

'YWR. See under 'YYR.

'YYR. *One-word name.* 'Phallus' (dimin.)
Quṭail form. Arabic air. Caquot, *RTP*, 165, proposed to read 'YWR or 'WYR. Tentatively he linked the name with Arabic uwār, 'flame, fire'. But there are no semantic parallels to this name. The new reading, which is absolutely certain, has the support of semantic parallels. See Littmann, *Safaitic Inscriptions*, 227, no. 971, where he explains the Safaitic personal name kmr through the Arabic kamar, 'glans penis'. Van den Branden, *Histoire*, 59, refers to names with a similar meaning in Thamudic. See also Nöldeke, *Beiträge*, 102.

'YŠ'. *One-word name.* 'Reward'
Arabic âsa. For parallels see Ryckmans, i. 43; Littmann, *Safaitic Inscriptions*, 298a; Cantineau, *Le Nabatéen*, ii. 61. Iyās is mentioned in Wüstenfeld, *Register*, 245, as the name of several Arabs. Greek transcription: Iasou, Wuthnow, 57. The Aramaic status emphaticus ending is added to the name. On the change of Š to S see discussion under 'WŠY.

'YTYBL. *Verbal sentence with the perfect.*
Aphel perfect of 'TH. 'Bēl has brought (the child)'. Clermont-Ganneau's interpretation, 'Bēl exists' (Aram. 'yty), is less likely (*RAO*, ii. 191). The name is also found in Nabataean (Cantineau, *Le Nabatéen*, ii. 61) and at Dura, *Final Report V, Part I*, 62, Aethibelus.

'KLB. *One-word name.* 'Enraged'
Af'al form. Arabic: aklab. The name is attested in Nabataean; see Cantineau, *Le Nabatéen*, ii. 107; *Syria*, 35 (1958), 227. Greek transcription: Achlabou, *Syria*, 31 (1954), 212.

'KLDY. *One-word name.* 'The astrologer'
This is presumably the Arabic form of the Aramaic KLDY', 'the Chaldaean', which occurs in this form in one inscription; see *Berytus*, 1 (1934), 38, iv[7]; for discussion ibid. 39.

It is assumed that the L of the Arabic article is assimilated to the following velar. But as we do not know much about the form of the Arabic article in pre-Islamic times, the interpretation given remains somewhat doubtful. For evidence in support of the proposed explanation see Caskel, *Lihyan*, 68.

'KNBY. *One-word name.* 'Callous'
Af'al form; cf. Arabic kanaba. The name is not attested elsewhere. For an explanation of the grammatical form see discussion under 'ḤPLY.

'KNT. *One-word name.* 'Husky'
Af'al form; cf. Arabic kanata. The root is not attested in personal names anywhere else. For similar names see Noth, *IPN*, 229.

'KRN. *One-word name.* 'Ploughman'
Syriac 'akārā'. The name is attested in

Thamudic (Ryckmans, i. 44) and in Nabataean (Cantineau, *Le Nabatéen*, ii. 61). The form is augmented by the ending -ân; on this see under MYŠN.

'LH. *Hypocoristicon.* 'N.N. is god'
The nominal, possibly verbal, element is missing. The name is very frequent in Safaitic (Littmann, *Safaitic Inscriptions*, 298a). There are some occurrences of the name in Nabataean (Cantineau, *Le Nabatéen*, ii. 63). Greek transcription: Aleos, Wuthnow, 17. For a discussion of the structural type see under 'LHBL.

'LHBL. *Nominal sentence.* 'Bēl is god'
Names of the type: noun plus divine name are common throughout the Semitic onomasticon. For attestations see Tallquist, *APN*, 96a; Huffmon, *APNMT*, 163; *PRU*, v. 34, B[8]; 30, A[5]; Gröndahl, *Personennamen*, 95; Ryckmans, i. 218; Hatra, no. 10[1]; O.T., 'ēlîyyāhû; Cumont, *Fouilles de Doura-Europos*, 362, 6c.

'LHW. See under 'LH
This is a variant of 'LH to which the hypocoristic ending Waw has been added.

'LHMNSB[. *Unexplained*
The word division is completely uncertain. For a rather questionable interpretation see Caquot, 'Onomastique', 245.

'LHŠ'. *Hypocoristicon.* 'Šamaš is god'
*'lh-šmš.
For discussion and parallels see under 'LHBL.

'LWR. *Divine name used as personal name.* 'Iluwer'
For a discussion of this type of name and for parallels see under B'ŠMN. 'LWR as a god's name is mentioned on the Zakir-stela (*KAI*, 202, A[1], B[20]). There is only one attestation of 'LR(?) in south Arabic (Ryckmans, i. 44, 237). The god 'LWR is attested in Mari under the name Itur-Mer (Huffmon, *APNMT*, 271). Iluwer is probably a weather god and is to be identified with Adad; cf. the texts *CT* 29, 45, 18–24: ī-lu-me-er = ^{d}Adad; *CT* 25, 20, 7: ^{d}IM+ gloss ì-lì-me-er. The etymology of the name is unknown. A connection with Akkadian illūru is very uncertain; see von Soden, *AHw*, 373a.

'LṬY. *One-word name.* 'Toothless'
Arabic alaṭṭ (Wahrmund, i. 116). The Greek transcription Allataiou is attested from a bilingual text (*Inv. X*, 119). If the interpretation is right, it shows that one cannot rely too much on the Greek transcriptions of Semitic names. The ending Yodh is added to the name.

'LYS. *Latin name*
Aelius. See *ILS*, 3 ff., 164b. See also Appendix IV, 2.10; 2.16; 2.22.A. On the treatment of the diphthongs in Greek and Latin words in Palmyrene see Rosenthal, *Sprache*, 23; Cantineau, *Grammaire*, 50.

'LKDRYS. *Greek name*
Alexandros; see Pape, 55. See also Appendix IV, 1.4; 1.7; 1.22; 1.23; 1.25.D; 1.26 I, III. There are two scribal errors in the name. (1) The Samech is left out in the transcription of Greek ksi = ks in Palmyrene. (2) A Yodh is written for the expected Waw; cf. a similar mistake in WRḤY for YRḤY (Starcky, *BMB*, 12 [1955], 38, no. 8). See also under the variants: 'LKSDRS, 'LKSNDRWS, 'LKSNDRS.

'LKSDRS. *Greek name*
Alexandros; see Pape, 55. See also Appendix IV, 1.4; 1.7; 1.22; 1.23; 1.25. D. The vowelless N in Greek words is usually not written; see Rosenthal, *Sprache*, 40. For variants see under 'LKDRYS.

'LKSNDRWS. *Greek name*
For discussion and variants see under 'LKSDRS and 'LKDRYS.

'LKSNDRS. *Greek name*
For discussion and variants see under 'LKSDRS and 'LKDRYS.

'[L]''. *Hypocoristicon.* 'God has rewarded'
*'l-'qb.
The reading of the name is doubtful. The editor of the *Corpus* (*C* 4433) omits the second and third radical as being too uncertain. This etymology was first proposed by Goldmann, *Personennamen*, 23. For structural parallels see discussion under 'T'QB.

'LPY. *Uncertain*
The name could be derived from 'elep, 'neat'; cf. KLB'. The Greek transcription Alphaios which is usually related to ḤLPY could also be the transcription of 'LPY. The name is also found on an Aramaic ostracon from Elephantine (*Revue des Études sémitiques et Babyloniaca*, 1945, 67[4] and 73 n. 6); Dalman, *Handwörterbuch* 21, mentions a personal name 'LP'.

'LPYS, 'LPS. *Latin name*
Ulpius. See *ILS*, 157 ff. See also Appendix IV, 2.5; 2.10; 2.18; 2.22.A. Plene writing besides defective writing.

'LPS. See under 'LPYS.

'LQM'. *Greek name*
Alkimos; see Pape, 62. See also Appendix IV, 1.3; 1.16; 1.22; 1.25.D. The Greek ending -os is replaced by the Aramaic status emphaticus ending by analogy to the Aramaic noun; see discussion under 'GT'.

'LQMS. See under variant 'LQM'

'M', 'MW. *One-word name.* 'Mother'
For parallels see *Thes. Syr.* 222; Ryckmans, i. 37. For other occurrences see Nöldeke, *Beiträge*, 93.

[']MBW. *Hypocoristicon.* 'The mother of the father'
*'m-'bw.
Another likely restoration would be [ʿ]QBW or [N]QBW. For discussion see under 'MBY.

'MBY. *Hypocoristicon.* 'The mother of (my) father'
*'m-'by.
The name alludes to the resemblance of the child to the paternal grandmother. Structural parallels are existent; see Tallquist, *APN*, 241b, ᶠUmmi-a-bi-a; Du Mesnil du Buisson, *Inventaire*, 57; Cumont, *Fouilles de Doura-Europos*, 432, no. 98, Abe[mm]ous; Stamm, *ANG*, 302; Noth, *IPN*, 222. See also Nöldeke, *Beiträge*, 94–5.

'MBKR'. *Unexplained*
Caquot, *Syria*, 39 (1962), 236 n. 5, considers the name a variant of ʿMBKR', the former of which he explains as composed of the prefix 'n+bkr in analogy to the names of the type 'nqṭl > 'qqṭl (see Cantineau, *RB*, 39 [1930], 535). If Caquot's theory were right one would expect that 'nbkr > 'bbkr. The change ' to ʿ in ʿMBKR' is likewise difficult to account for. The explanation of 'm as 'mother' or of ʿm as 'paternal uncle' is equally unsatisfactory. Bkr, 'first-born', is well attested in the Semitic languages.

'MBT'. *Nominal sentence.* 'The mother is the daughter'
The name refers to the likeness of the daughter to the mother. For parallels to this kind of name see under 'MBY.

'MDBW. *Genitive compound.* 'The mother of his/her father'
The name calls to remembrance the paternal grandmother. Cf. the Jewish name 'bwdm', 'father of his mother', which Jastrow, 3, incorrectly identifies with the Greek name Eudēmos. For similar names in Syriac and in other Semitic languages see Nöldeke, *Beiträge*, 95–6; *Thes. Syr.* 114. For further parallels see Saqqara-stela (*KAI*, 267, 1^1); Stamm, *ANG*, 302. On the relative pronoun dᵉ instead of dî see Cantineau, *Grammaire*, 130; Rosenthal, *Sprache*, 51.

'MDY. *Unexplained*
'MD and 'MDW are attested in Lihyanite (Ryckmans, i. 44). Arabic amad, 'wrath, end, limit', is rather unsuitable as meaning for a personal name. No other occurrences of the name have been found so far.

'MW. See under 'M'

'MWN. *One-word name.* 'Faithful'
*'mn, 'be faithful'. Qātōl-type.
The name is attested in Hebrew; see Noth, *IPN*, 228. See also under 'MYN.

'MY'. *Unexplained*
Cf. the O.T. name 'āmî (Neh. 7^{59}) and the Jewish name ᶠ'myh (Greek: Ammia; *RES* 715). The meaning of those three names is not clear.

'MYN. *One-word name.* 'Faithful'
Arabic amîn. 'MYN could also represent the Arabic diminutive Umayn. For parallels see Cantineau, *Le Nabatéen*, ii. 64; Ryckmans, i. 45; Littmann, *Safaitic Inscriptions*, 298b. See also under 'MWN which represents the Aramaic form of the same root.

'MYT. *One-word name.* 'Maid' (dimin.)
Arabic Umayat. Quṭail-form. For attestations see Cantineau, *Le Nabatéen*, ii. 64; Ryckmans, i. 44. 'MYT occurs in north Arabic names frequently as masculine; see Bräu, 'Altnordarabischen', 107.

'MLYWS. *Latin name*
Aemilius, see *ILS*, 6 ff. See also Appendix IV, 2.10; 2.16; 2.22.A. On the treatment of diphthongs in Latin and Greek words in Palmyrene see Rosenthal, *Sprache*, 23; Cantineau, *Grammaire*, 50.

'MṢR. *Uncertain*
No other attestations of this name are known. The only possible root for this form is Arabic maṣara, 'cultivate, settle'. Is an Afʿal form with the meaning 'cultivator, settler' possible?

'MRY. *Hypocoristicon.* 'Man of N.N.'
*'mr plus divine name; cf. Arabic imra'.
This structural type: noun plus divine name is abundantly attested in Semitic onomastics. For parallels see Cantineau, *Le Nabatéen*, ii. 64; Ryckmans, i. 219; Lankester Harding, *Thamudic*, no. 51; Caskel, *Lihyan*, 149, mar'il, mar'-Lāh; Ammonite, *BASOR*, 160 (1960), 38–41, mr'l. Cf. the Amorite names with mutu (Huffmon, *APNMT*, 234) and the Assyrian names with aw/mil (Tallquist, *APN*, 21). On the O.T. 'îš see Noth, *IPN*, 138–9. See also Nöldeke, *Beiträge*, 103, with parallels from Ethiopic. For the O.T. mᵉtûšā'ēl see Tsevat, *VT*, 4 (1954), 41–9. For a discussion of Arabic imra' see Bräu, 'Altnordarabischen', 95–6. Greek transcriptions of this type of name are attested in Wuthnow, 20.
The possible explanation of 'MR as verbal form (Arabic, Aramaic, 'command, speak') is less likely in view of the supporting evidence for 'MR, 'man'. This latter explanation is undoubtedly true for the O.T. 'ᵃmaryâhû and similar names; see Noth, *IPN*, 173; Huffmon, *APNMT*, 168; Gröndahl, *Personennamen*, 99.

'MRSʿ. *Hypocoristicon.* 'Man of Saʿad'
*'mr-sʿd.
The absence of a hypocoristic ending is somewhat unusual. For discussion and parallels see under 'MRY.

'MRŠ'. *Hypocoristicon.* 'Man of Šamaš'
*'mr-šmš.
The Greek transcription Amrisamsou is

given in a bilingual text (*C* 3931). For discussion and parallels see under 'MRY.

'MŠ'. See under 'MŠY for discussion

'MŠY. *Uncertain*
The variant 'MŠ' is attested as name of a Palmyrene Jew from the necropolis of Beth She'arim (*JPOS*, 18 [1938], 46, Pl. VIII[2]). The name could be derived from the Aramaic 'emeš, 'evening, twilight'. But the Greek transcription Amasē is not in favour of this derivation (*JPOS*, 18 [1938], 46); but cf. Arabic ams, 'evening'. Mazar (*Beth She'arim*, i, p. 135) considers the name to be a shortened form of 'MTŠMŠ. Theoretically, this could be possible. It seems, however, less likely when it is seen that both 'MŠ' and 'MŠY seem to be masculine names. The father's name is usually given in the patronymic at Palmyra.

'MŠ[MŠ]. *Genitive compound.* 'Maid of Šamaš'
*'mt-šmš.
For the elision of a dental before a following sibilant see Cantineau, *Grammaire*, 39. The same name is found on a bilingual tomb inscription from Edessa (Urfa). The Greek transcription is Amassamsēs; see Sachau, 'Edessenische Inschriften', 145.

'MT'. *One-word name.* 'Maid'
For occurrences see Cantineau, *Le Nabatéen*, ii. 64; Ryckmans, i. 44; Gordon, *UT*, 2117: 49. 'MT in Safaitic is masculine. The Greek transcription Amathē is given in a bilingual text (*Berytus*, 2 [1935], 110). 'MT' could theoretically be a shortened form of 'MT plus divine name; on this see discussion under 'MTBL.

'MTBL. *Genitive compound.* 'Maid of Bēl'
Structural type: noun plus divine name. Parallels to this type are found in practically all Semitic languages; see Tallquist, *APN*, 22b; Ryckmans, i. 255; Cantineau, *Le Nabatéen*, ii. 64; Bräu, 'Altnordarabischen', 106; Harris, *Grammar*, 79; Sachau, 'Edessenische Inschriften', 145; Dura, *Final Report V, Part I*, 63.

'MTB'[L]. *Genitive compound.* 'Maid of Ba'al'
Phoenician name. For parallels and discussion see under 'MTBL.

'MTḤ'. *Hypocoristicon.* 'Maid of Ḥerta'
*'mt-ḥrt'.
The feminine name to the masculine TYMḤ' (see below). That 'MTḤ' = *'MT-'Ḥ' is less likely, as 'ḥ' in this case would serve as a theophorous element, but there are no sure attestations for this at Palmyra. As to the etymology of ḤRT', Caquot, *RTP*, 182, considers the name to be the Aramaic transcription of Akkadian ḫīrtu, 'spouse' (von Soden, *AHw*, 348a), which is an epithet of Ištar (Tallquist, *Götterepitheta*, 97).

'MTLT. *Genitive compound.* 'Maid of Allat'
*'mt-'lt.
For discussion and parallels see under 'MTBL.

'MTŠLM'. *Genitive compound.* 'Maid of Šalman'
*'mt-šlmn.
The reading 'MTŠLMN, which is still maintained by Caquot, *RTP*, 158, is wrong (see photograph). For parallels and discussion see under 'MTBL.

'N'. *Unexplained*
The name is found in Nabataean (*RES* 1471, *Corpus* 488 reads 'b') and in Aramaic (Cooke, *Textbook*, 345, perhaps name of a deity here; Driver, *Documents*, 35, no. 13[2]). The name is attested in epigraphic Syriac (Segal, *BSOAS*, 16 [1954], 20, no. 5[2]; 23, no. 8[3]). A Christian martyr is known by this name (Assemanus, *BO*, i. 190). 'N' is also found in the Peshiṭṭo (Gen. 36^{24}; 2 Sam. 3^{7}; the Hebrew text has 'ayyāh). The variant 'NY occurs frequently in Safaitic (Littmann, *Safaitic Inscriptions*, 299a). See also Galling, 173^{6}. 'NY is attested twice in the Peshiṭṭo (for references see *Thes. Syr.* 270).

'NBT. *One-word name.* 'Having pubic hair'
Af'al form; cf. Arabic nabata 'grow'. For attestations of the root see Ryckmans, i. 135. Nabt is listed in Wüstenfeld, *Register*, 330, as the name of several Arabs. Cf. also the O.T. name nābôt (Noth, *IPN*, 221).

'NṬYWKWS *Greek name*
Antiochos; see Pape, 98. See also Appendix IV, 1.2; 1.9; 1.12; 1.18; 1.22; 1.23; 1.25.D. The variants are 'NṬYKYS, 'NṬYKS, 'ṬYK'.

'NṬYKYS. See under 'NṬYWKWS
See also Appendix IV, 1.26.I.

'NṬYKS. See under 'NṬYWKWS

'NṬWNYS. *Latin name*
Antōnius; see *ILS*, 14 f., 169a. See also Appendix IV, 2.7; 2.10; 2.12; 2.18; 2.22.A. ō is spelled with and without mater lectionis; see Rosenthal, *Sprache*, 20.

'NYNWS. *Latin name*
See Appendix IV, 2.10; 2.18; 2.22.A. Derivative of Annius; see Ingholt, *MUSJ*, 38 (1962), 108–9, esp. 109 n. 2; *ILS*, 168a.

'N'M. *One-word name.* 'Tender'
Af'al form. Arabic an'am. For parallels see Littmann, *Safaitic Inscriptions*, 299a; Ryckmans, i. 142; Cantineau, *Le Nabatéen*, ii. 121; Wüstenfeld, *Register*, 81. The name is mentioned by Wellhausen, *Reste*, 19, as name of a tribe (An'um); see Littmann, *Nabataean Inscriptions*, 14. Greek transcription: Anamos, Wuthnow, 21.

'NQY. *One-word name.* 'Having thin fingers' Arabic anqā. This interpretation was first proposed by Lidzbarski, *Ephemeris*, 2, 300. See also Caquot, *RTP*, 169.

'NŠ. *Reading uncertain*
The name could be an Afʿal form.

'SDY. *Uncertain*
The name is probably a variant of 'ŠD (see below). On the change of the sibilants in Arabic see Starcky, *PNO*, 143, n. 1.

'SWYT. *Unexplained*
It is very unlikely that the form is Arabic.

'SṬ[Ṭ]. *Unexplained*
The name is most probably non-Semitic. Is it comparable to 'ŠṬṬ, 'ŠṬṬY ('Hatra', nos. 26^1, 94, 5^2)? The Hatra names are probably to be connected with Persian Aštāt, Aštād (Justi, *Namenbuch*, 47).

'SY[.]. *Name incomplete*
Ingholt, *Berytus*, 2 (1935), 87, suggests the reading 'S[DW], but the Yodh is clearly legible. It may be 'SY['], 'doctor', used as an appellative.

'SYʿ. See under 'BYʿ.

'SPDYN. See under [']SPYDN

'SPDY[S]. *Greek name*
Spedios; see Pape, 1433. See also Appendix IV, 1.6; 1.7; 1.12; 1.24; 1.25.D. The Aleph prostheticum serves to avoid a consonant cluster (Rosenthal, *Sprache*, 31).

[']SPYDN. *Greek name*
Spedianos; see Pape, 1433. See also Appendix IV, 1.6; 1.7; 1.12; 1.15; 1.24; 1.25.D. The Aleph prostheticum serves to avoid a consonant cluster (Rosenthal, *Sprache*, 31). The form is most likely a wrong spelling for 'SPDYN; cf. QLQYS for QYLQS.

'SQLPYD'. *Greek name*
Asklēpiadēs; see Pape, 158. See also Appendix IV, 1.3; 1.6; 1.7; 1.11; 1.12; 1.15; 1.22; 1.25.A. ē is never written with mater lectionis (Rosenthal, *Sprache*, 20). The Greek ending -ēs is regularly replaced by the Aramaic status emphaticus ending.

'STR. *Jewish name*
For discussion see Noth, *IPN*, 11.

'ʿB. *One-word name.* 'Having a fat nose' Arabic aʿabb. See also under 'ʿBY which is probably a variant of this.

'ʿBY. *One-word name.* 'Having a fat nose' Arabic aʿabb (Wahrmund, i. 90). Caquot, *RTP*, 169, follows Chabot (*C* 3963) and considers the name to be a hypocoristicon of a theophorous name with ʿbd-, 'servant of N.N.'. He mentions as support an undocumented Nabataean name ʿbyw. The explanation is unconvincing and the abbreviation would be unparalleled. Goldmann, *Personennamen*, 31, takes 'ʿBY to be a variant of ʿB' (see below) with Aleph prostheticum. The Greek transcription Aabei is found on a bilingual text (*C* 3964).

'ʿWY. *One-word name.* 'The Howler'
Afʿal form; cf. Arabic ʿawā (epithet of the jackal). The name cannot be derived from Aramaic ʿiwyā', 'serpent', which is just a laryngal confusion for ḥiwyā'. Jaussen et Savignac, *Mission en Arabie*, ii. 199, no. 256, compare Arabic ʿawā, Syriac ʿᵉwā', 'howl'. For another parallel see Cantineau, *Le Nabatéen*, ii. 128. On the use of animal names as personal names see Nöldeke, *Beiträge*, 86–7.

'ʿWD. *Hypocoristicon.* 'Protected by N.N.'
Arabic pass. part.; see Brockelmann, *GVG*, i. 354, par. 138 a–c. Arabic ʿawḏ.
The root is attested in Nabataean and proto-Arabic (Cantineau, *Le Nabatéen*, ii. 128; Ryckmans, i. 159–60; Littmann, *Safaitic Inscriptions*, 334b). The root occurs also at Hatra, no. 65^7, 127. Greek transcription: Aoueidos, Wuthnow, 24. For names of the type ʿwd plus divine name see under ʿWD'L.

'ʿYLM, 'ʿYLMY. *One-word name.* 'Aʿalam' (dimin.)
Diminituve of the Afʿal form. For grammatical parallels see Ṭabari, *Index*, 22, 46: uḥaimir, al'uʿaisir. A locality in Iraq is called uhaiḍir. Aʿalam is mentioned as a name in Wüstenfeld, *Register*, 56. It is important to understand that, once a diminutive is formed from a personal name, the meaning of the name as such is no longer of importance; e.g. a certain Ubayḍī from the tribe of the banū al abyaḍ is attested (*Diwan al Farazdaq*, Beyrouth, 1960, vol. 2, 233). Ubayḍī is not to be rendered 'the small white one' but 'the small Abyaḍ'.

'ʿYLMY. See under 'ʿYLM.

'ʿPY. *Uncertain*
It is tentatively proposed to derive the name from Arabic ʿāf, 'having long hair' (Lane, v. 2094). 'ʿPY would then have to be an Afʿal form.

'ʿRY. See under BR 'ʿRY

['PW..]. *Restoration uncertain*
The editor of the Corpus (*C* 4196) would like to restore 'PWṢ' based on the Greek transcription Aphphousos in this bilingual text. No comments can be made on a possible explanation of the name because the restoration is very uncertain.

'PWQḤ. *Uncertain*
The explanation of this name as an Itpoʿal form (Dalman, *Grammatik*, 103, 273) of pqḥ, 'open (the eye)' is impossible, because the structurally identical name 'QWPʿ cannot

be explained in that way, the root qpʿ being not attested in Aramaic, Syriac, or Hebrew. However, it is possible that these two names represent an unattested Afawʿal form. Classical Arabic has not preserved and not completely exhausted all possibilities for forming nouns. Sometimes the dialects preserve more ancient material. On the Fawʿal form in Arabic see Barth, *Nominalbildung*, 169, par. 116. Arabic faqaḥa, 'open (the eye), blossom'.

'PYN. *Greek name*
Appiōn; see Pape, 112. See also Appendix IV, 1.6; 1.12; 1.22; 1.25.F. ō is sometimes written defectively; see Rosenthal, *Sprache*, 20.

'PLY. *One-word name.* 'Young camel'
Arabic afīl. The name is comparable to Lihyanite 'PL (Ryckmans, i. 46).

'PLNYS. *Greek name*
Apollōnios; see Pape, 110. See also Appendix IV, 1.6; 1.12; 1.14; 1.18; 1.22; 1.25.D. ō is sometimes written defectively; see Rosenthal, *Sprache*, 20.

'PRHṬ. *Persian name*
Frahāta; see Justi, *Namenbuch*, 101–2. The Aleph prostheticum serves to avoid a consonant cluster (Rosenthal, *Sprache*, 31). The name occurs in the Dura onomasticon; see Dura, *Prel. Report V*, 234, no. 590; Dura, *Final Report V, Part I*, 65. Aphraat is attested as a Persian bishop's name (*Thes. Syr.* 350). The name is found at Aššur where it is probably the name of a Parthian king (W. Andrae, 'Aramäische Inschriften aus Assur und Hatra aus der Partherzeit', *MDOG*, 60 [1920], 12).

'ṢWLY. *One-word name.* 'Pure, noble, steadfast'
Arabic aṣīl. The Aramaic qāṭūl form replaces the qaṭīl form. 'ṢWL is found in Kraeling, *BMAP*, 7^{44}. Cf. also the O.T. name 'ǎṣalyāhû (Noth, *IPN*, 193).

'ṢYD/RNY. *Unexplained*
The reading or the word division could well be wrong.

'ṢRʿ. *One-word name.* 'Wrestler'
Afʿal form; cf. Arabic ṣaraʿ. The name is once attested in Safaitic as name of a tribe (Littmann, *Safaitic Inscriptions*, 300b). Ṣaraʿ is not attested in Arabic in the fourth form!

'QWPʿ. *Uncertain*
Arabic qafaʿ, 'have the toes, ears crippled'. For a discussion of the grammatical form see under 'PWQḤ.

'QZMN. *Unexplained*
The name seems to be non-Semitic.

'QYḤ. *Unexplained*
The Greek transcriptions Akkeos, Akkaeos are attested from a bilingual text (*C* 3917).

'QLYŠ. *One-word name.* 'The thin one'
Aramaic qālîš, 'thin, weak'. The name is formed with the prefix 'an: 'anqaṭîl > 'aqqaṭîl; for a discussion of this grammatical form see under 'GDM. The Greek transcription Akkaleisou is found on a bilingual inscription (*C* 4123).

'QM'. *Greek name*
Akmē; see Pape, 46. See also Appendix IV, 1.3; 1.22; 1.25.B. The Greek ending -ē is replaced by the Aramaic status emphaticus ending.

'QML. *One-word name.* 'The decayed one'
Syriac qᵉmal. The name is formed with the prefix 'an: 'anqiṭil > 'aqqiṭil; for a discussion of this grammatical form see under 'GDM. The Greek transcription Akkim[il]os is attested from a bilingual text (*C* 4167).

'QMT. *Uncertain*
Although the name has the feminine ending it occurs as masculine and feminine. The Greek transcription Akamathē is found in a bilingual text (*Berytus*, 3 [1936], 99). As the name is also met as masculine it can hardly be explained as the third person sing. of Arabic qāma IV, 'she has settled'.

'R'WM. *Uncertain*
The name is probably to be derived from Aramaic rûm, but the grammatical form is unclear. The origin of the Aleph at the beginning of the word is obscure; cf. the variant R'WM'. The spelling with Aleph within the word is strange but not uncommon. The same spelling is found in Nabataean names, e.g. BRY'Y and BRYW; PṢY'W and PṢYW (Littmann, *Nabataean Inscriptions*, xxv). In epigraphic Syriac the name 'RWM or 'DWM is found; see Sachau, 'Edessenische Inschriften', *ZDMG*, 36 (1882), 161.

'R'Š. *One-word name.* 'Large headed'
Afʿal form. Arabic aras. The name is attested in Safaitic (Littmann, *Safaitic Inscriptions*, 300b) and in Nabataean with the variant spelling 'RWS (Littmann, *Nabataean Inscriptions*, xvi, xxv). Cf. the O.T. name R'Š (Gen. 46^{21}; text usually considered corrupt). 'R'Š occurs only as surname at Palmyra.

'RB. See under 'DB

'RBZ. *Persian name*
Orobazos; see Justi, *Namenbuch*, 234 and 489. It is the name of a king of Characene; see Kirste, 'Orabazes', in *SWAW*, 182, 2. Abhandlung, 1917; Nodelman, 'A Preliminary History of Characene', *Berytus*, 13 (1960), 83–121.

'RHDWN. *Unexplained*
It is not very likely that 'RHDWN is a transcription of the Greek Rodōn (Pape, 1313) which is attested at Palmyra as

RDWN (see below). In order to explain the Aleph one would have to assume that the He has consonantal value and this is very unlikely; see Nöldeke, *Syrische Grammatik*, 26, par. 39.

'RWN'. *One-word name.* 'Calf'
Syriac 'arwānā'. On the name see Nöldeke, *Beiträge*, 83.

'RṬBN. *Persian name*
Artabanos; see Justi, *Namenbuch*, 31.

'RSṬYDS. *Greek name*
Aristeidēs; see Pape, 129. See also Appendix IV, 1.7; 1.9; 1.16; 1.22; 1.25.A. The diphthong -ei in Greek words is always written with Yodh; see Rosenthal, *Sprache*, 20.

'RQṬWS. *Greek name*
Arktos; see Pape, 139. See also Appendix IV, 1.3; 1.9; 1.22; 1.25.D.

'RT. *Unexplained*
The name is also attested from a Phoenician inscription (*CIS*, i. 713).

'ŠD. *One-word name.* 'Lion'
Arabic asad. The name occurs with final Waw in Nabataean (Cantineau, *Le Nabatéen*, ii. 68). The proto-Arabic form 'SD is widely attested (Ryckmans, i. 45; Littmann, *Safaitic Inscriptions*, 299b). Wüstenfeld, *Register*, lists several Arabs with the name Asad. See also Huffmon, *APNMT*, 169. Cf. the O.T. name layiš (1 Sam. 25[44]). 'ŠDW is also found as name of a deity (Littmann, *Nabataean Inscriptions*, 26); cf. the theophorous name 'Abd-al Asad (Wellhausen, *Reste*, 2). See also under ŠB''.

'ŠDW. See under 'ŠD
This form is regularly attested in Nabataean.

'ŠM. *One-word name.* 'Having a big nose'
Arabic ašamm (Wahrmund, i. 80). It is not very likely that the name is to be connected with north-west Semitic 'ŠM; see discussion on the latter in Lidzbarski, *Ephemeris*, 3, 260–5.

'Š'[.]R. *Unexplained*
See *Corpus* 4467.

'Š'D. *One-word name.* 'Happy'
Af'al form. Arabic as'ad. For attestations of the root see Cantineau, *Le Nabatéen*, ii. 152; Littmann, *Safaitic Inscriptions*, 332b; Lankester Harding, *Thamudic Inscriptions*, no. 53b; for parallels see Ryckmans, i. 153.

'Š''. *One-word name.* 'Smooth'
Aramaic še'a'. Aleph prostheticum is added to the name. There are no other attestations of the name. The divine name Š'Y'W is derived from the same root (Littmann, *Nabataean Inscriptions*, 82).

'ŠQR'. *One-word name.* 'Reddish'
Af'al form. Arabic ašqar. The Aramaic ending has been added. For attestations of the root see Cantineau, *Le Nabatéen*, ii. 153; Winnett, *Safaitic Inscriptions*, nos. 143, 865; Ryckmans, i. 212.

'TNDWR'. *Greek name*
Athēnodōros; see Pape, 25. See also Appendix IV, 1.7; 1.8; 1.18; 1.22; 1.25.D. ē is never written with Yodh; ō is usually written plene; see Rosenthal, *Sprache*, 20. The Aramaic status emphaticus ending has replaced the Greek ending -os. Variant: 'TNDR[WS].

'TNDR[WS]. See under 'TNDWR'

'T'M. *Nominal sentence*
Shortened form of 'T'MN (see below).

'T'MN. *Nominal sentence.* 'Athe is with us'
This structural type is rare in Semitic onomastics. There are only two examples attested so far: the O.T. 'immānû'ēl (Isa. 7[14]) and 'MNYH from the Jewish colony at Elephantine (Cowley, *Papyri*, 22[105]). Names of the type Nabu-ittiya (Tallquist, *APN*, 151a) refer only to the bearer of the name and not to the whole clan. There are four different forms of this name extant: (1) 'T'M, (2) 'T'M, (3) 'T'MN, (4) 'TM'. (1) and (2) are most probably shortened forms of (3). In (2) the dissimilation of ' to ' has not taken place. If (4) fits into this pattern, then it is probably an Arabized form. The Aramaic preposition 'm has been replaced by the corresponding Arabic form m'.

'T'QB. *Verbal sentence with the perfect.* 'Athe has protected'
*'qb, 'follow' (Aram., Arab.; cf. Eth., 'keep', guard').
Goldmann's suggestion that 'T'QB is a verbal sentence in the passive should be discarded (*Personennamen*, 16). The verbal form is the third pers. sing. masc. although 'TH is fem. See the discussion under BLTYḤN on this point. Noth, *IPN*, 46, holds the use of 'qb in south Arabic, Aramaic, and post-exilic Hebrew as characteristic of the proto-Aramaic stratum within the Semitic onomasticon.

For a discussion of the verbal root and for parallels see Noth, *IPN*, 177–8; Tallquist, *APN*, 25a; *NBN*, 10a; Ryckmans, i. 244; 'Hatra', nos. 10[1], 23[2], 35[3]; Cowley, *Papyri*, 22[20], 12[9]; Aššur, *MDOG*, 60 (1920), 'sr'[qb], nbw'qb, p. 37; Dura, *Final Report V, Part I*, 61, Bel-acabus. The Phoenician onomasticon uses šmr. For attestations see Harris, *Grammar*, 152. Akkadian uses naṣaru (Tallquist, *APN*, 297b). See also under: [B]WL'', [BWL]Q', BL'QB, 'QBY, 'QYB', 'TY'QB, 'T'Y, 'T'QB.

'TPNY. *Verbal sentence with the perfect.* 'Athe has turned'
Goldmann's suggestion that 'TPNY is a verbal sentence in the passive should be discarded (*Personennamen*, 16). Likewise the *Corpus*'s explanation (*C* 3956) to regard the Aleph as prefixed. PNY is attested in

Safaitic (Ryckmans, i. 179) with the meaning 'disappear'; cf. Arabic faniya. The name could mean that Athe has caused childlessness to disappear. Possible, but unlikely. A better interpretation is to understand PNY in the biblical sense 'turn'. For a discussion of this root see Noth, *IPN*, 199. On the religious use of pānāh in the O.T. cf. Ps. 102^{18}, 25^{16}.

BBT. *One-word name.* 'Pupil (of the eye)'
Aramaic bābāh. The name occurs as BBT' in a Nabataean contract; see Yadin, *IEJ*, 12 (1962), 244. The name is otherwise not attested.

BGY. *Uncertain*
The Greek transcription Baggaiọ, attested from a bilingual text (*RB*, 39 [1930], 532), would tend to favour an explanation from the Persian Bagōas, O.T. bigway, LXX Bagouai; see Justi, *Namenbuch*, 59.

BGDN. *One-word name.* 'Garment'
Arabic bijād; Aramaic, Hebrew beged. Occurs as a tribal name and as a personal name in Safaitic. For attestations see Ryckmans, i. 48; Littmann, *Safaitic Inscriptions*, 301b; Wüstenfeld, *Register*, 112. A derivation from the Persian bagadāna (Justi, *Namenbuch*, 487, 490) is rather unlikely. Persian names are extremely rare at Palmyra.

BGRN. *One-word name.* 'Navel'
Arabic bujra. For parallels see Ryckmans, i. 48; Cantineau, *Le Nabatéen*, ii. 70. The diminutive ending -ân is added. The Greek transcription Bogranēs is found on a bilingual text (*Inv. VIII*, 78).

BGRT. *One-word name.* 'Navel'
For parallels see Ryckmans, i. 48; Cantineau, *Le Nabatéen*, ii. 70. Greek transcriptions: Bagratos, Bagrathos, Wuthnow, 31. See also under BGRN, 'BGR.

BGŠ. *Uncertain*
No other attestations of this name are known. The form could be derived from Arabic bajasa, 'flow freely'. Lidzbarski, *Ephemeris*, 2, 300, thought that the name might refer metaphorically to the semen. It is more likely, however, that the name is derived from Arabic bujs, 'rain-cloud'. Caquot, *RTP*, 169, thinks of the Persian name Bagōsēs (Justi, *Namenbuch*, 60). The Greek transcription Bagesos (*Inv. III*, 2) does not favour this identification. Persian names at Palmyra are rare. Variant: BGŠW.

BGŠW. See under BGŠ

BWṬ. *Unexplained*
Cf. the Talmudic name Bûṭā' (Jastrow, 144). The editor of the *Corpus* (*C* 4017) says that BWṬ' in the Talmud renders the Greek name Battos (Pape, 202).

BWṬN. *One-word name.* 'Pistacia terebintha'
Aramaic buṭnā'. This interpretation was already proposed by Goldmann, *Personennamen*, 30. The practice of naming people after plants is common in the Semitic onomasticon. For similar names see Noth, *IPN*, 230.

BWṬTN. *Unexplained*
The name seems to be non-Semitic.

BWKY. *Unexplained*

B[WL]BRK. *Verbal sentence with the perfect.* 'Bôl has blessed'
*brk, 'bless' (Common Semitic).
Structural type: divine name plus verb; for type: verb plus divine name see under BRYK. For parallels and discussion see Tallquist, *APN*, 7a; Cantineau, *Le Nabatéen*, ii. 75 (reading uncertain); 'Hatra', nos. 79^5, 80^2, 81^2, 115, 147; Dura. *Prel. Report V*, 178, no. 505; Mouterde-Jalabert, *Inscriptions V*, 59, no. 2088; Harris, *Grammar*, 91.

BWLZBD. *Verbal sentence with the perfect.* 'Bôl has given'
Structural type: divine name plus verb; for type: verb plus divine name see under ZBDBWL. The verbal element is considered by Noth, *IPN*, 46, as characteristic of the proto-Aramaic stratum within the Semitic onomasticon. For discussion and attestations see Tallquist, *APN*, 100a; Clay, *BEUP*, x. 47a, Bêl-za-bad-du; Kraeling, *BMAP*, $8^{11,12}$; Noth, *IPN*, 47. See also under: NRGLZBD, NBWZBD, NBWZ', 'THZB[D], 'TZ', 'TZBD.

BWLḤ'. *Hypocoristicon.* 'Bôl has seen'
*bwl-ḥzh.
The interpretation is confirmed by the fact that a certain BLḤ' is the grandson of BWLḤZY (*Inv. VIII*, 59), hence papponymy. For the various interpretations that have been proposed for this name see Caquot, *RTP*, 170. Structural type: divine name plus verb; the type: verb plus divine name is not found at Palmyra among the names that are attested. For parallels and discussion see Noth, *IPN*, 198–9; cf. the names with r'y in proto-Arabic (Ryckmans, i. 248). See also under BLḤ', BWLḤZY, BLḤZY, BLḤY.

BWLḤZY. *Verbal sentence with the perfect.* 'Bôl has seen'
Goldmann, *Personennamen*, 9, explains the second element of the name as imperative (in the variant BLḤZY). This is rather unlikely. It would be the only example of this type at Palmyra. Caquot, *RTP*, 170, interprets the Yodh of ḥzy as a hypocoristic ending, which is not very likely. It is more probable that the spelling was influenced by the Arabic Lamedh Yodh verbs; for a similar case see 'TPNY. For discussion and parallels see BWLḤ'.

BWLY. *Hypocoristicon.* 'Bôl is my light'
*bwl-nwry.
For the interpretation of the name see *Syria*, 11 (1930), 242. The text of the inscription reads: BLNWRY dy mtqrh BWLY. For discussion and parallels see under BWLNWR.

BWLY'. *Hypocoristicon.* 'Bôl has known'
*bwl-yd'.
For parallels and discussion see under BWLYD'.

BWLYD'. *Verbal sentence with the perfect.* 'Bôl has known'
*yd', 'know' (Common Semitic). Structural type: divine name plus verb; for type: verb plus divine name see under YD'NW. On the variant spelling BWL/BL see Caquot, *RTP*, 154 n. 4. For parallels and discussion see Noth, *IPN*, 181; Ryckmans, i. 231; *Thes. Syr.* 467, BWLYD' (name of a Christian martyr). See also under: BWLY', BLYD', BLYD'W, NBWD', NBWD', NBWYD'.

BWLM'. *Hypocoristicon.* 'Bôl is (my) mother'
*bwl-'m.
The Greek transcription Bōlemmeou[s] from a bilingual text (*Syria*, 17 [1936], 346), supports the interpretation given. Ugarit offers another example where a deity occurs as masc. and fem.: 'ṯtr'ab and 'ṯtr'um (see Virolleaud, *CRAIBL*, 1955, 79). Šamaš was considered with the Assyrians masc., but at Ugarit the god is attested as of fem. gender (Šapaš); see Bottéro in *Studi Semitici*, i. 48. The maternal aspect of a deity is also mentioned in Isa. 66^{13} with regard to Yahweh. On this see also Dhorme, *RHR*, 105 (1932), 229–44.

BWLN'. *Hypocoristicon.* 'Bôl is (my) light'
*bwl-nwr.
Sachau, *ZDMG*, 35 (1881), 743, suggested that BWLN' is a shortened form for *BWL-LN'. This interpretation is impossible because the suffix of the first person plur. is -n in Palmyrene and Syriac and only BA has -n'. No parallel for this type of name is known to me. For parallels and discussion see under BWLNWR.

BWLNWR. *Nominal sentence.* 'Bôl is (my) light'
This is a corrected reading of BWLNWR'TH = BWLNWR (NWR)'TH. Case of haplography; see Seyrig, *Berytus*, 2 (1935), 47–8. Structural type: divine name plus noun; for type: noun plus divine name see under NWRBL. For parallels and discussion see Tallquist, *APN*, 177–8; Huffmon, *APNMT*, 243; Ammonite, 'dnnr, Albright in *Misc. Ubach*, 133; Cowley, *Papyri*, 6^{19}, 11^{12}; Segal, *Iraq*, 19 (1957), 140, ii^{2}; Galling, 174^{12}; Noth, *IPN*, 167–8. On the variant spelling BWL/BL see Caquot, *RTP*, 154 n. 4. See also under: BWLY, BWLN', BLNWR, BWN', BWNWR, BLNWRY, BN', BNWR, BNWRY, BNR, BNR', 'TNWR, 'TNWRY.

[B]WL''. *Hypocoristicon.* 'Bôl has protected'
*bwl-'qb.
Various suggestions as to its original form have been made. Clermont-Ganneau, *RAO*, vi. 113^{4}, BWL'' = *BWL'N'; Lidzbarski, *Ephemeris*, 2, 311, reconstructed *BWL'BD and *BWL'DR. None of the interpretations suggested occurs as a personal name. It is more likely therefore to restore the name to BWL'QB, whose second element is widely attested in the Palmyrene onomasticon. For parallels and discussion see under 'T'QB.

[BWL]Q'. *Hypocoristicon.* 'Bôl has protected'
*bwl-'qb.
The abbreviation is rather anomalous. For parallels and discussion see under 'T'QB. One might wonder whether [BWL]M' (see below) is not the more correct reading.

BWN'. *Hypocoristicon.* 'Bôl is (my) light'
*bwl-nwr.
This interpretation was already proposed by Goldmann, *Personennamen*, 18. Lidzbarski's restoration of BWN' to *BWL-N'['] should be discarded (*Handbuch*, 235). For discussion and parallels see under BWLNWR.

BWNWR. *Nominal sentence.* 'Bôl is (my) light'
The Lamedh is assimilated to the Nun; cf. the Greek transcription Bōnnouros. For parallels and discussion see BWLNWR.

BWR'. *Hypocoristicon.* 'Bôl has healed'
*bwl-rp'.
In *Inv. X*, 130, BWRP' is transcribed by Byrros which is undoubtedly the rendering for BWR'. On the method of transcribing Semitic names through Latin or Greek homonyms see Clermont-Ganneau, *RAO*, i. 186. For parallels and discussion see under BWRP'.

BWRP'. *Verbal sentence with the perfect.* 'Bôl has healed'
*rp', 'heal' (Heb., Phoen., Aram.; Arab., 'repair').
Structural type: divine name plus verb; for type: verb plus divine name see under RP'L. For discussion and parallels see Huffmon, *APNMT*, 263–4; Ryckmans, i. 249; van den Branden, *Inscriptions*, 315, ṣlmrf'; Nöldeke, *Beiträge*, 100. The Greek transcription Bōropha is given in a bilingual text (*RB*, 39 [1930], 523). The Greek transcription confirms that the verbal element is a finite verb form and not a participle. See also under BWR'.

BWŠ'. *Hypocoristicon.* 'Bôl has heard'
*bwl-šm'.
The labial is assimilated to the following

sibilant; cf. b'lšmn > b'šmn. This interpretation was proposed by Caquot, *RTP*, 161 n. 2. Structural type: divine name plus verb. For discussion and parallels see Noth, *IPN*, 185; Ryckmans, i. 239; Harris, *Grammar*, 151; Tallquist, *APN*, 308b.

BZY. *One-word name.* 'Falcon'
Arabic bāziyy. For similar names see Noth, *IPN*, 230.

BYD'. *Shortened form of* ZBYD' (*Aphaeresis*)
Lidzbarski, *Ephemeris*, 2, 9, suggested that the name is composed of the following elements: b+yd+divine name, 'in the hands of N.N.'. The Greek transcription Baida from a bilingual text does not favour Lidzbraski's view (*C* 3933). The proposed interpretation was already given by Goldmann, *Personennamen*, 23.

BYDN. *Unexplained*
It is conceivable that BYDN was formed from BYD' at a time when the etymology of the latter name had become unknown.

BYLY. See under KYLY.

BKRW. *One-word name.* 'Young camel'
Arabic bakr. For discussion and parallels see Cantineau, *Le Nabatéen*, ii. 71; *Thes. Syr.* 526, Bakrû (name of two kings of Edessa); Noth, *IPN*, 230. The name occurs frequently in Arabic. The variant BKRY is found in epigraphic Syriac (Segal, *BSOAS*, 22 [1959], 31, no. 4^3).

BLBW. *Nominal sentence.* 'Bēl is father'
*bl-'bw.
For parallels see Noth, *IPN*, 141–2, yô'āb; Tallquist, *APN*, 263b.

BLḤ'. *Hypocoristicon.* 'Bēl has seen'
*bl-ḥzh.
For discussion and parallels see under BWLḤ'.

BLḤZY. *Verbal sentence with the perfect.* 'Bēl has seen'
For discussion and parallels see under BWLḤZY.

BLḤY. *Hypocoristicon.* 'Bēl has seen'
*bl-ḥzh.
For discussion and parallels see under BWLḤZY. The name could also be understood as 'Bēl is living', but the variant BLḤ' makes this rather doubtful; see under 'BYḤY.

BLṬY. *Hypocoristicon*
Akkadian balāṭu, 'life' (*AHw*, 98b). The same name occurs on an Aramaic ostracon from Nippur (*RES* 957). Cureton, *Spicilegium Syriacum*, 25^{10}, mentions a man called BLṬ. For discussion and parallels see Tallquist, *APN*, 51a; Stamm, *ANG*, 188.

BLY. *Uncertain*
It could be a shortened form of a theophorous name, e.g. BLNWRY or BLYD'. A one-word name is also conceivable; see Cantineau, *Le Nabatéen*, ii. 71, BLY (is it a personal name or just the exclamation BLY?); Ryckmans, i. 287, 407; Wüstenfeld, *Register*, 106, mentions an Arab called Balī ben Amr. The name BLY is found on a mosaic from Edessa (*Syria*, 34 [1957], 321). It is also the name of a disciple of Ephraem the Syrian (Baumstark, *Geschichte*, 61).

BLY'. *Hypocoristicon.* 'Bēl has known'
*bl-yd'.
For discussion and parallels see under BWLYD'.

BLYD'. *Verbal sentence with the perfect.* 'Bēl has known'
For parallels and discussion see under BWLYD'.

BLYD'W. *Verbal sentence with the perfect.* 'Bēl has known'
The ending Waw is added to a verbal sentence. It is the only occurrence of such a grammatical form. The reading might well be wrong. The only comparable name would be LŠMŠ' where the hypocoristic ending has been added to the divine name plus preposition. For parallels and discussion see under BWLYD'.

BLYHB. *Verbal sentence with the perfect.* 'Bēl has given'
The Palmyrene personal names use various verbal stems to express the idea of giving: 'wš (see under 'WŠY); zbd (see under ZBDBWL); ntn (see under 'TNTN); whb (see under WHBLT); yhb. The least frequently used of these verbs is yhb. For parallels see 'Hatra', nos. 183, 152; Dura, *Final Report V, Part I*, 61, Belihabus, Nabouiaabos; a Greek transcription from Palmyra names Same(s)iaabos, *šmšyhb (*Syria*, 20 [1939], 317).

BLKZ. *Unexplained*
Another possible reading is BLSZ (see below).

BLM'. *Uncertain*
Various suggestions have been made. (1) Cantineau, *Syria*, 17 (1936), 351, considers it a defective writing for BWLM' (see above). This does not mean that the name is to be explained the way BWLM' is. Our third suggestion (see below) would be suitable for BWLM' in this case. (2) Caquot, *Syria*, 39 (1962), 241, considers the possibility of attaching the name to Thamudic blm (Ryckmans, i. 52 [Arabic balama, 'be carried away by passion']) or to Lihyanite blmt (Caskel, *Lihyan*, 144 [balamat, 'Frucht der Dornakazien']). The connection is too vague. (3) BLM'/ BWLM' could be a shortened form of *BLMR / BWLMR; cf. at Palmyra NBWM' pro *NBWMR (see below).

BLNWR. *Nominal sentence.* 'Bēl is (my) light'
For discussion and parallels see under BWLNWR.

BLNWRY. *Nominal sentence.* 'Bēl is my light'
For discussion and parallels see under BWLNWR.

BLSZ. *Unexplained*
Another possible reading is BLKZ.

BL'QB. *Verbal sentence with the perfect.* 'Bēl has protected'
For discussion and parallels see under 'T'QB.

BLŠWR. *Nominal sentence.* 'Bēl is (my) stronghold'
The same idea express the names formed in Akkadian with dūru and in Hebrew with mā'ôz and maḥseh. For discussion and parallels see Tallquist, *APN*, 279a; Cowley, *Papyri*, 8[27]; Galling, 178[41]; Kraeling, *BMAP*, 4[22], 2[15], 8[2]; Noth, *IPN*, 157–8. See also: BLŠWRY, NBWŠY, 'TRŠWRY, 'TŠWR, 'TŠ'.

BLŠWRY. *Nominal sentence.* 'Bēl is my stronghold'
For discussion and parallels see under BLŠWR.

BLT'. *Uncertain*
According to the editor of the *Corpus* (*C* 4405) the form is a hypocoristicon of a theophorous name, one of whose elements is the divine name Beltî, e.g. BLTYḤN. Variant: BLTY.

BLTY. *Uncertain*
The name is either a shortened form of BLTYḤN, or the divine name used as a personal name. For this latter interpretation see discussion under B'ŠMN. See also BLT'.

BLTYḤN. *Verbal sentence with the perfect.* 'Beltî is gracious'
*ḥnn, 'be gracious' (Common Semitic, except Eth.).
The gender of the verbal element is masculine although the deity is feminine. The verbal form of a sentence name tends to agree with the gender of the namebearer even though the subject of the verbal sentence is a female deity. For parallels from Akkadian see Edzard, 'Genuskongruenz', *ZA*, 55 (1963), 113–30. Structural type: divine name plus verb; for type: verb plus divine name see ḤNBL. For parallels and discussion see Huffmon, *APNMT*, 200; Ryckmans, i. 229–30; Diringer, *Iscrizioni*, 195; Harris, *Grammar*, 103; Noth, *IPN*, 187.

BN'. *Hypocoristicon.* 'Bôl is (my) light'
*bwl-nwr > bwn' > bn'.
Ingholt, *Berytus*, 5 (1938), 111 n. 9, says that the Latin transcription Bannae weighs in favour of Bôl as the first element and not Bēl, for which the Latin transcription should read *Bennae. For discussion and parallels see under BWLNWR.

BNWR. *Hypocoristicon.* 'Bôl is (my) light'
*bwl-nwr.
The Greek transcription Bōnnourou is attested from a bilingual text (*Berytus*, 2 [1935], 115). For discussion and parallels see BWLNWR.

BNWRY. *Hypocoristicon.* 'Bôl is (my) light'
For discussion and parallels see BWLNWR.

BNY. *Uncertain*
Various interpretations are possible. (1) The name could be a hypocoristicon of *bl-nwry, 'Bēl is my light'. (2) The form could be derived from *bny, 'build'. For discussion and possible parallels see Ryckmans, i. 52; Cantineau, *Le Nabatéen*, ii. 72; Noth, *IPN*, 172. (3) BNY could be an Arabic diminutive form (so Littmann, *Safaitic Inscriptions*, 302b). See also Nöldeke, *Beiträge*, 91. The Greek transcriptions Banios, Bennos, Bōneou (Wuthnow, 35, 37) do not help either. See also Starcky, *RB*, 61 (1954), 171.

BNR. *Hypocoristicon.* 'Bēl is my light'
*bl-nwry > bnwr > bnr.
For discussion and parallels see BWLNWR.

BNR'. *Hypocoristicon.* 'Bēl is my light'
The Aramaic status emphaticus ending is added to BNR (see above). For discussion and parallels see BWLNWR.

BS'. *One-word name.* 'Cat'
The name is to be connected with Safaitic BS (Ryckmans, i. 53), which is explained from the Arabic bass, 'cat'. The Aramaic status emphaticus ending is added to an Arabic word. For the Nabataean BSS (Cantineau, *Le Nabatéen*, ii. 72), the Aramaic bissā' (Dalman, *Handwörterbuch*, 59), and the Syriac basûs (*Thes. Syr.* 547) the Latin name Bassus was usually assumed to be the origin. It is more likely, however, that the names represent the Hellenized form of the Semitic word bass, 'cat', easily due to the homonym Bassus/Bassos (Wuthnow, 34); following Caquot, *RTP*, 167.

BSM. *One-word name.* 'Perfumist'
Aramaic bassām.

BSS. *One-word name*
The name represents the Hellenized form of BS (Arabic bass, 'cat'). For discussion see BS'.

B''. *Hypocoristicon.* 'Asked for'
The editor of the *Corpus* (*C* 4114) thinks of a hypocoristicon of a name composed with the divine name B'L. The present interpretation was suggested by D. R. Hillers. Cf. the O.T. name šā'ûl; for discussion see Noth, *IPN*, 136.

B'LW, B'LY. *Hypocoristicon*
Shortened form of a theophorous name with the divine name B'L. For discussion, parallels, and variants see Cantineau, *Le Nabatéen*, ii. 73; Ryckmans, i. 54; Diringer, *Iscrizioni*, 43; Harris, *Grammar*, 89; Noth, *IPN*, 119. The divine name B'L is found very rarely at Palmyra; cf. B'ŠMN, B'LTG'.

B'LY. See under B'LW

B'LTG'. *Hypocoristicon.* 'Ba'alat is (my) fortune'
*b'lt-gd.
Structural type: divine name plus noun; for type: noun plus divine name see GDYBWL. For parallels and discussion see Caskel, *Lihyan*, 152, ṣlmgd; Noth, *IPN*, 126. GD in these two structural types is not so much a deific name as an appellative. It is rather doubtful whether GD is a shortened form of GRM; cf. ŠMŠGRM. See also under: 'ŠTWRG', 'STWRG', NBWGDY.

B'ŠMN. *Divine name used as personal name*
The labial is assimilated to the following sibilant. The use of a divine name as a personal name is amply attested at Palmyra. For parallels from elsewhere see Tallquist, *APN*, 128, mardukā; Driver, *Documents*, Letter VI[1]; Noth, *IPN*, 63–4. BR B'ŠMN is found in Syriac (Sachau, *ZDMG*, 36 [1882], 146; Segal, *BSOAS*, 22 [1959], 38, no. 9 A[2], with further references). Bar Hebraeus, *BO*, ii. 399, interprets the name as meaning 'of the four names', 'rb' šmhyn, in order to avoid any pagan associations.

BPNY'. *Unexplained*
It is uncertain whether it is a personal name at all.

BQY. *One-word name.* 'Bottle'
Aramaic buqā'. For similar names and discussion see Noth, *IPN*, 226, 105.

BR 'ḤTY. *Genitive compound.* 'The son of 'ḤTY'
There are eight cases of this type of name at Palmyra: br plus qualifying element. In all instances we have a surname which is preceded by the introductory formula 'dy mtqr'/h'. There is only one exception where 'dy mtqr'/h' is omitted, probably on purpose. It is the name of a freedman where usually no patronymic is given and thus the surname could not be mistaken for the father's name: ḥdwdn *br dkt'* br ḥry btprmwn. The names will be left untranslated. Explanations of the second element will be found under their respective headings. For discussion of 'ḤTY see 'ḤT'.

BR ''RY. *Genitive compound.* 'The son of ''RY'
For discussion see BR 'ḤTY. The second element is difficult to explain, but it is most likely the divine name A'ra transformed into a personal name by adding the ending Yodh (nisbe). On the deity see Starcky, *Supp. au Dict. de la Bible*, vii. 988.

BR B''. *Genitive compound.* 'The son of B'''
For discussion see BR 'ḤTY.

BR DKT'. *Genitive compound.* 'The son of DKT''
DKT' is probably to be derived from the root dk', 'be pure', dkwt', 'purity, cleanness'. On the defective spelling of dkwt' see Cantineau, *Grammaire*, 115, par. d; Rosenthal, *Sprache*, 73, no. 2. For discussion see BR 'ḤTY.

BR ZBYDY. *Genitive compound.* 'The son of ZBYDY'
For discussion see BR 'ḤTY. On ZBYDY see under ZBYD'.

BR 'BDBL. *Genitive compound.* 'The son of 'BDBL'
For discussion see BR 'ḤTY.

BR 'ZWLT. *Genitive compound.* 'The son of 'ZWLT'
For discussion see BR 'ḤTY.

BR Š'T. *Genitive compound.* 'The son of Š'T'
For discussion see BR 'ḤTY.

BR'. *Uncertain*
The editor of the *Corpus* (*C* 4173) considers the possibility of an appellative BR', 'son' (Nöldeke, *Beiträge*, 91), or of a hypocoristicon of BR'T' (see below). Caquot, *RTP*, 171, proposes another possible interpretation: BR' is a shortened form of BRP' (see below). See variant BRY.

BR'T'. *Genitive compound.* 'Son of Athe'
For parallels and discussion see Tallquist, *APN*, 276a; Huffmon, *APNMT*, 175–6; Ryckmans, i. 221; van den Branden, *Inscriptions*, 363; Old Aramaic, BRHDD, BRRKB (*KAI*, 201[1], 215[1]); Ugaritic, *PRU*, iii. 195, B[17]; Gordon, *UT*, 306[7], 1036[15]; Harris, *Grammar*, 87; 'Hatra', nos. 13, 145, 212; Dura, *Final Report V, Part I*, 63[7]. In later Aramaic these formations abound; see Hatra and Dura. See also: [B]R'TY, BR'', BR'Y, BR'T', BR'TH, BRT'.

[B]R'TY. *Genitive compound.* 'Son of Athe'
For discussion and parallels see BR'T'.

BRBRS. *Greek name*
Barbaros; see Pape, 197. See also Appendix IV, 1.5; 1.15; 1.25.D.

BRDWNY. *Genitive compound.* 'Son of my lord'
*br-'dwny.
Ingholt, *Berytus*, 5 (1938), 134 n. 8, derives the name from the Arabic root brd, 'be cold.' See Ryckmans, i. 55, for Thamudic and Safaitic names from the same stem. The proposed interpretation is more likely.

Cf. the Greek transcription Baradōniou, Wuthnow, 33.

BRH'. *Nominal sentence.* 'A son is he'
Exclamation of the mother at the birth of her child. The proposed reading of the editors, BRHN, is wrong (see photograph).

BRWQ'. *One-word name.* 'Morning star'
The name occurs in the *Talmud* (Aboth, IV^{4}). Bārôqā' in Aramaic means 'morning star'. On the root brq see below. See also Caquot, *RTP*, 171.

BRḤWM. *Genitive compound.* 'Son of the Merciful One'
On the divine epithet raḥḥûm see Starcky, *AAS*, 3 (1953), 162. To invoke a deity without naming it goes back to Arabic influence; see Dussaud, *Pénétration*, 98.

BRY. *Uncertain*
For discussion see assumed variant BR'.

BRYK. *Hypocoristicon.* 'Blessed by N.N.'
Aramaic pass. part. The Greek transcription Bareichein, Wuthnow, 33, excludes a possible interpretation of the name as a Quṭail form (diminutive). For parallels and discussion see Noth, *IPN*, 183. Variants: BRYKW, BRYKY. See also BRKY.

BRYKW. See under BRYK

BRYKY. See under BRYK

BRYQY. *One-word name.* 'Shining'
Arabic barīq. The name could also be a diminutive form of barīq, namely burayq (= personal name cited in Lidzbarski, *Ephemeris*, 1, 335^{94}). For discussion see Caquot, *RTP*, 162, and BRQ (see below).

BR[K]'. *Hypocoristicon*
The other possible reading is BR[P]' (see below). For discussion and parallels see BRKY.

BRKY. *Hypocoristicon.* 'N.N. has blessed'
Structural type: verb plus divine name; for type: divine name plus verb see BWLBRK. For discussion and parallels see Littmann, *Safaitic Inscriptions*, 303b; Ryckmans, i. 259; Harris, *Grammar*, 91–2; Noth, *IPN*, 183; see also Job, 32^{2,6}. Wuthnow, 33, cites Barechbēlos.

BRLL. *Unexplained*
The name could be non-Semitic.

BRNBW. *Genitive compound.* 'Son of Nabû'
For discussion and parallels see BR'T'. BRNBW appears in the Hellenized form Barnabas in the N.T. (Acts 9^{27}, 13^{1}; see Bauer–Arndt–Gingrich, 133). For further discussion see *Syria*, 34 (1957), 320.

BRNY. *Hypocoristicon.* 'Son of Nabû'
*br-nbw.
For discussion see under BRNBW. Barna, Barnaios are found in Greek transcriptions (Wuthnow, 34). The name may be found in epigraphic Syriac; see Segal, *BSOAS*, 22 (1959), 36, no. 8^{4}.

BRS. *Latin name*
Burrus; see *ILS*, 176b. See also Appendix IV, 2.4; 2.22.A.

BRSMY'. *Genitive compound.* 'Son of Simia'
The explanation of the theophorous element is difficult. The name SMY' / ŠMY' is amply attested at Hatra (nos. 34^{4}, 35^{2}, 75, 81^{1}, 28^{2}, 36^{3}, etc.). In Syriac BRSMY', 'BSMY', and 'BSYMY' are found (*Thes. Syr.* 592, 2783). Ingholt, 'Parthian Sculptures from Hatra', *Memoirs of the Connecticut Academy*, xii (1954), 17–27 (not accessible), wants to see in SMY' / ŠMY' the divine name for heaven. For the rejection of this view see Caquot, *Syria*, 32 (1955), 67–8. Segal's suggestion, *BSOAS*, 16 (1954), 21, to interpret Samyā, the Blind One, as an epithet of Mars, as was done among the people of Harran, is too farfetched; see Chwolson, *Ssabier*, ii. 188. SMY' / ŠMY' has often been associated with the deity Simia, Sēmēion, mentioned in Lucian's *De Dea Syria*; see H. Stock, 'Studien zu Lukian's "De Dea Syria",' *Berytus*, 4 (1937), 16. The name of the deity requires an /i/ in the first syllable. As long as the Greek transcription cannot assure the phoneme /i/, another interpretation will have to be found for those names not with sēm-, sim-. Caquot (ibid., p. 68) considers some of the names in SMY' / ŠMY' abridged theophorous names of ŠMŠ augmented by the suffix -y', e.g. 'BDŠMY' with the Greek transcription Abisamaia. The /š/ in ŠMŠ is original, therefore names in SMY' should refer to the deity Simia, Sēmēion. For Greek transcriptions see Dura, *Final Report V, Part I*, 63^{7}, and Wuthnow, 34. For further discussion and parallels see BR'T'.

BR'', BR'Y. *Hypocoristicon.* 'Son of Athe'
*br-'th.
For discussion and parallels see BR'T'.

BR'Y. See under BR''.

BR'T'. *Genitive compound.* 'Son of Athe'
Aleph has replaced He in many instances in Palmyrene; see Rosenthal, *Sprache*, 22. BR'T' is also found in epigraphic Syriac; see Segal, *BSOAS*, 22 (1959), 32. For discussion and parallels see BR'T'.

BR'TH. *Genitive compound.* 'Son of Athe'
For discussion and parallels see BR'T'.

BRP'. *Verbal sentence with the perfect.* 'Bôl has healed'
This is probably a case of a defective writing for BWRP'. This interpretation is supported by the fact that BRP' is the grandson of a certain BWRP' in a funerary inscription

(*RB*, 39 [1930], 537, no. 7). For discussion and parallels see BWRP'.

BRQ. *One-word name.* 'Thunder'
*brq, 'lighten, shine' (Common Semitic).
For parallels and discussion see Huffmon, *APNMT*, 178; Ryckmans, i. 56, 288; Noth, *IPN*, 226. Cf. the name of Hamilkar Barkas, suffete of Carthage. BRQ is found in Cureton, *ASD*, 73[4]. BRQ' occurs in epigraphic Syriac (*BSOAS*, 22 [1959], 35, no. 7[5]). See also under 'BRWQ, BRWQ', BRYQY.

BRŠGL. *Genitive compound.* 'Son of Šegel'
On the deity see under ŠGL. For discussion and parallels see BR'T'.

BRŠMŠ. *Genitive compound.* 'Son of Šamaš'
The name is also attested in epigraphic Syriac (*BSOAS*, 22 [1959], 35, no. 7[4]), and at early Edessa (see Cureton, *ASD*, 18[20]). For discussion and parallels see BR'T'.

BRŠ'D. *Genitive compound.* 'Son of Ša'd'
On the deity see Höfner in *Wörterbuch*, 464. For discussion and parallels see BR'T'.

BRT'. *Hypocoristicon.* 'Son of Athe'
*br-'th.
Cantineau, *RB*, 39 (1930), 528, proposed two interpretations: (1) BRT' is a contracted form of *BR-RT'. The *Thes. Syr.* 3993, does not list the root *rr'* in the Pe'al, only two attestations in the Pa''el. The verb occurs mainly in the Aphel. (2) 'Son of T''. T' being the divine name attested at Sinai and found only in Nabataean inscriptions so far. The interpretation given above seems to be preferable. For discussion and parallels see BR'T'.

BRTW. *Uncertain*
The photograph is illegible and the Waw is marked by the editor as doubtful. Could BRT' (see above) be the correct reading?

BŠR'. *One-word name.* 'Bringer of good news'
*bśr, 'bring good news' (Common Semitic). BŠR is attested as personal name in Syriac and Thamudic (*Thes. Syr.* 623; Ryckmans, i. 57). Bašir and Bišr are listed as names of Arabs in Wüstenfeld, *Register*, 108, 112. BŠR is also a Sabaean deity (Ryckmans, i. 8). The Aramaic status emphaticus ending is added to an Arabic word. The form could also be a hypocoristicon; cf. the Neo-Punic name [f]BŠRBL, 'Ba('a)l has pronounced a good message' (*KAI*, 162[1]).

BT'. *One-word name.* 'Daughter'
Does the Aleph present the vocative ending (Greek -ē), or the status emphaticus ending? See variant BTY.

BTWHBY. *Genitive compound.* 'Daughter of WHBY'
Feminine names formed with BT as their first element are well attested at Palmyra (see Main List). The word BT in these cases does not imply an immediate physical relationship between the bearer of the name and the person mentioned in the second part of the name. (Names with a divine name as second element are excluded from the present discussion, as they form a special structural class by themselves.) The second name element, always a personal name, is probably to be understood as the ancestor par excellence of the family. Explanations of the second name elements will be found under their respective headings. The proper names will be left untranslated as in practically all cases no suitable meaning can be found when composed with BT.

BTZBY. *Genitive compound.* 'Daughter of ZBY'
For discussion see BTWHBY.

BTZBYD'. *Genitive compound.* 'Daughter of ZBYD''
For discussion see BTWHBY.

BTḤBY. *Genitive compound.* 'Daughter of ḤBY'
For discussion see BTWHBY. For the interpretation of ḤBY see ḤB'.

BTḤW. *Genitive compound.* 'Daughter of 'ḤW'
For discussion see BTWHBY. The interpretation is uncertain, but preferable to Nöldeke's suggestion (apud Mordtmann, *MVÄG*, 4 [1899], 8), that BTḤW is *BT'ḤWH, 'daughter of her brother', '. . . eine Kleine, die, nach dem Tode des Vaters geboren, von dem älteren Bruder in Obhut genommen wäre'. This interpretation is still upheld by Goldmann, *Personennamen*, 29.

BTḤWML. *Genitive compound.* 'Daughter of ḤWML'
For discussion see BTWHBY. It is very unusual to find a woman's name as last element in the patronymic. But BTḤWML can hardly have been a man's name.

BTḤYRN. *Genitive compound.* 'Daughter of ḤYRN'
For discussion see BTWHBY.

BTY. *One-word name.* 'My daughter'
On the name see Nöldeke, *Beiträge*, 91. Cf. the name BNYT, 'Töchterchen' (Arabic bunayyat); see Euting, *Nabatäische Inschriften*, 50, no. 13[2].

BTML'. *Genitive compound.* 'Daughter of ML''
For discussion see BTWHBY.

BTMLKW. *Genitive compound.* 'Daughter of MLKW'
For discussion see BTWHBY.

BT''. *Hypocoristicon.* 'Daughter of Athe'
*bt-'th.
For discussion and parallels see BT'TY.

BT'G'. *Genitive compound.* 'Daughter of 'G''
For discussion see BTWHBY.

BT''TY. *Genitive compound.* 'Daughter of Athe'
Structural type: noun plus divine name. For parallels and discussion see Huffmon, *APNMT*, 120, n. 10; Harris, *Grammar*, 89, 124, BTB'L, BTN'M; Cumont, *Fouilles de Doura-Europos*, 360, no. 5c; 437, no. 111; Caquot, 'Onomastique', 240. Names of the type: bt plus divine name, are less well attested than names of the type: br plus divine name.

BTPRMWN. *Genitive compound.* 'Daughter of PRMWN'
For discussion see BTWHBY.

BTŠMY'. *Genitive compound.* 'Daughter of Šamaš'
*bt-šmš.
For discussion and parallels see BRSMY' and Caquot, *Syria*, 32 (1955), 67.

[BT]ŠTG'. *Unexplained*
The restoration of [BT] is purely conjectural.

G'YS. *Latin name*
Gaius; see *ILS*, 71b, 197b. See also Appendix IV, 2.1; 2.8; 2.10; 2.22.A; 2.23.E. See also the variants GYS, GY.

GBYNS. *Latin name*
Gabinius; see *ILS*, 71b. See also Appendix IV, 2.1; 2.4; 2.10; 2.11; 2.13; 2.22.A.

GBL. *One-word name.* 'Big, stout'
Arabic jabal, 'mountain' (used metaphorically). For discussions and parallels see Ryckmans, i. 57; Cantineau, *Le Nabatéen*, ii. 76. It is the name of several Arabs and of an Arabic king mentioned in Bar Hebraeus's Chronicle (Wüstenfeld, *Register*, 173; *Thes. Syr.* 642). The name is also attested at 'Hatra', no. 30^{2}.

GBR'
The name is not so much a personal name as an appellative on this tessera; see Caquot, *RTP*, 142. For attestations of GBR as personal name see ibid., p. 142. n. 5. Further occurrences are found in the Kilamuwa inscription (*KAI*, $24^{2,15}$); Galling, 185^{88}. For Assyrian transcriptions of GBR see Tallquist, *APN*, 78a.

GD'. *Divine name used as personal name*
For discussion see B'ŠMN. For parallels see Cantineau, *Le Nabatéen*, ii. 76; Littmann, *Safaitic Inscriptions*, 304a; Harris, *Grammar*, 93; Galling, 185^{90}; 'Hatra', no. 107^{2}; Dura, *Final Report V*, *Part I*, 61^{2}; Noth, *IPN*, 126; Nöldeke, *Beiträge*, 94. Greek transcription: Gaddos, Wuthnow, 38.

GDY'. *Uncertain*
(1) The name could be a hypocoristicon. Structural type: noun plus divine name. For parallels and discussion see GDYBWL. (2) A one-word name is conceivable. Aramaic gᵉdî, 'kid, goat'. For parallels and discussion see Cantineau, *Le Nabatéen*, ii. 76; 'Hatra', no. 71; Jastrow, 211; Nöldeke, *Beiträge*, 82. Greek transcription: Gadias, Wuthnow, 38.

GDYBWL. *Nominal sentence.* 'My fortune is Bôl'
Structural type: noun plus divine name; for type: divine name plus noun see B'LTG'. For discussion and parallels see Littmann, *Safaitic Inscriptions*, 304a; *CIS*, ii. 76; Diringer, *Iscrizioni*, 220; Galling, 177^{30}, 184^{82}; Noth, *IPN*, 126; Caquot, 'Onomastique', 242. See also GDYLT, GDRṢW.

GDYLT. *Nominal sentence.* 'My fortune is Allat'
*gdy-'lt.
For parallels and discussion see GDYBWL.

GDYMY. See under GRYMY

[GDN]BW. *Nominal sentence.* '(My) fortune is Nabû'
For discussion and parallels see under GDYBWL.

GDRṢW. *Nominal sentence.* '(My) fortune is Arṣû'
*gdy-'rṣw.
Bräu, 'Altnordarabischen', 89, wants to take GD as an appellative, 'Glück von Arṣû'. Greek transcription: Gaddarsou, Wuthnow, 38.

GWB'. *Uncertain*
The name is most likely derived from Aramaic gôbā', 'locust'. Starcky, *PNO*, 163, thinks of Syriac gûbā', 'well, cistern', which, however, does not yield any satisfactory meaning.

GWR'. *One-word name.* 'Young lion'
Aramaic gûr. For discussion and more names see Nöldeke, *Beiträge*, 78; Dura, *Final Report V*, *Part I*, 62, Gores. Greek transcription: Goura, Wuthnow, 42.

GWRY. *One-word name.* 'My young lion'
Aramaic gûr plus personal suffix. For discussion see GWR'.

GWRNY. *Unexplained*
The Greek transcription Gouronnaiou is given in a bilingual text (*Inv. X*, 77). The name may be non-Semitic. See also *Inv. X*, 53, commentary.

GḤYNT. *Unexplained*
No photograph is available to verify the reading. G. Krotkoff informs me of an Egyptian name Zaki Ṭulaimāt. Thus the name could be vocalized Guḥaināt, but the meaning remains uncertain.

GY. See under G'YS

GYR'. *One-word name.* 'Lime'
Arabic, Aramaic gîr. For a parallel see Ryckmans, i. 60. No other occurrences are known.

GYN'. *Latin name*
See *ILS*, 197b. See also Appendix IV, 2.1; 2.8; 2.10; 2.22.A. Gaianus (derived from Gaius). The Aramaic status emphaticus ending has replaced the Latin ending -us. According to Starcky, *RTP*, 183, Addenda ad 166, GYNWS is a transcription of Arabic ǵayyân (Wuthnow, 39, 155). On the possibility of transcribing a Semitic name through a Greek or Latin homonym see Clermont-Ganneau, *RAO*, i. 186. See also the variant GYNWS.

GYNWS. See under GYN'

GYS. See under G'YS

GL'. *One-word name.* 'Great, outstanding'
Arabic jall. For parallels and discussion see Cantineau, *Le Nabatéen*, ii. 78; Littmann, *Safaitic Inscriptions*, 304b; Wüstenfeld, *Register*, 179. A derivation from Arabic jull, 'rose', is also conceivable.

GL[Y]Ḥ[
The reading is uncertain and the interpretation therefore impossible.

GLNWS. *Greek name*
Galēnos; see Pape, 239. See also Appendix IV, 1.1; 1.11; 1.15; 1.25.D.

GML'. *One-word name.* 'Camel'
Arabic jamal; Aramaic gāmāl. For parallels and discussion see Ryckmans, i. 61; Cantineau, *Le Nabatéen*, ii. 78; Littmann, *Safaitic Inscriptions*, 305a; Nöldeke, *Beiträge*, 82. In spite of the Greek transcription Gamēlos, Wuthnow, 39, a derivation from Arabic jamîl, 'beautiful', seems unlikely. Long î would have been written with Yodh; cf. 'MYN; but see also GHLT.

GMLY'. *Uncertain*
The name may be a shortened form of gamlî'ēl or of any other name with Aramaic g^{e}mal, 'give, requite', as first element. It is very unlikely that the form is the status emphaticus plur. (see Cantineau, *Le Nabatéen*, ii. 78).

GMLT. *One-word name.* 'Handsome'
Arabic jamîl. For parallels see Cantineau, *Le Nabatéen*, ii. 78; Littmann, *Safaitic Inscriptions*, 305a; Wüstenfeld, *Register*, 180. Greek transcriptions: Gomolathē, Gomollathē, Wuthnow, 41.

GMR'. *One-word name.* 'Charcoal'
Arabic jamra. The name is otherwise unattested. The O.T. name riṣpāh is comparable; see Noth, *IPN*, 232. GMR' could also be a shortened form of a theophorous name in which the divine element has been suppressed; cf. O.T. g^{e}maryāhû; for discussion see Noth, *IPN*, 175.

GNB'. *One-word name.* 'Side (of the body)'
Arabic janb. For parallels see Ryckmans, i. 62; Wüstenfeld, *Register*, 181, Janb, Jannāb. A derivation from the Aramaic gannāb, 'thief', is less likely (so Goldmann, *Personennamen*, 29). Caquot's explanation, *RTP*, 163, of the word as 'stranger' is inadmissible, as this is only a secondary derivation from janb, 'side' and therefore probably chronogically later than the Palmyrene name.

G'L. *One-word name.* 'Black beetle'
Arabic ju'l. For discussion and parallels see Ryckmans, i. 62; Littmann, *Safaitic Inscriptions*, 305b; Wüstenfeld, *Register*, 185; Noth, *IPN*, 230; Nöldeke, *Beiträge*, 88. Greek transcription: Gyalēs, Wuthnow, 42. Variant: G'LW/Y.

G'LW/Y
For discussion and parallels see G'L. The hypocoristic ending Waw, Yodh is extended to one-word names. Cf. also G'L' (*KAI*, 227, Vs.[5]), which is also a variant of the preceding name.

GPN. *One-word name.* 'Eyelid'
Arabic jafn. For parallels see Ryckmans, i. 62; Littmann, *Safaitic Inscriptions*, 305b. Cf. the Greek transcription Gophenathē, Wuthnow, 42. Ingholt, *Berytus*, 2 (1935), 101, derives the name from Syriac gûfnā', 'vine'. Both interpretations are possible. On the use of parts of the body as personal names see van den Branden, *Histoire*, 59.

GRB'. *Uncertain*
The name is either to be derived from the Aramaic garbā', 'bottle', see Noth, *IPN*, 226, or from the Aramaic, Syriac garbā', 'leprosy', see Goldmann, *Personennamen*, 30. Cf. 'Simon the Leper' in the N.T. (Mark 14[3]); in the Syriac Bible garbā'.

GRYMY. *One-word name.* 'Dry dates'
Arabic jarīm. For a different interpretation see Caquot, *RTP*, 171. On the proposed interpretation see Noth, *IPN*, 230, for semantic parallels.

GRMY. *Hypocoristicon.* 'N.N. has decided'
Syriac g^{e}ram, 'decide, determine'. Structural type: verb plus divine name; for type: divine name plus verb see under ŠMŠGRM. For parallels and discussion see Ryckmans, i. 63, 222 *bis*; Littmann, *Safaitic Inscriptions*, 305b, 306a; Cantineau, *Le Nabatéen*, ii. 79; Littmann, 'Nabataean', *BSOAS*, 15 (1953), 19–20; Wüstenfeld, *Register*, 183; 'Hatra', no. 193[3]. Cf. the O.T. tribal name garmî. On GRMW found in epigraphic Syriac, and for occurrences of GRMY in Syriac see *Syria*, 34 (1957), 321. Greek transcriptions: Garmos, Garmaios, Wuthnow, 39. See also: GRYMY, GRMN', ŠMŠGRM.

GRMN'. *Uncertain*
Two interpretations are possible: (1) The name is a shortened form of ***GRM-NBW**

For discussion and parallels see GRMY. (2) GRMN' is the Latin name Germanus, in which the Aramaic status emphaticus ending has replaced the Latin ending -us. This interpretation receives support from the Greek transcription Germanou found in a bilingual text (*Syria*, 19 [1938], 155). On the proposed reading GRMNWS, *Inv. VII*, 13[2], see the reading suggested by the editor of the *Corpus* (*C* 4212).

GRMNQWS. *Latin name*
Germanicus; see *ILS*, 199a. See also Appendix IV, 2.1; 2.2; 2.8; 2.22.A. Variant: GRMNQS.

GRMNQS. See under GRMNQWS

GTMY. *One-word name.* 'The lazy one'
Arabic juṯm. For another parallel see Ryckmans, i. 64. The hypocoristic ending Yodh is extended to one-word names.

DBḤ. *One-word name.* 'Sacrificer'
*ḏbḥ, 'sacrifice' (Common Semitic).
For parallels see Ryckmans, i. 68; 'Hatra', no. 47[2]. Cf. the Midianite king name zebaḥ mentioned in the O.T. The new edition of Koehler–Baumgartner explains the Midianite king's name as 'am Tage des Zebaḥ geboren'. This is somewhat unlikely as no feast of the name zebaḥ is known. Secondly one would expect the nisbe form *ZBḤY; cf. ŠBTY, ḤGY. See also Böhl, *Op. min.* 17–18.

DDYWN. *Uncertain*
This is probably the Semitic word dd, 'paternal uncle', augmented by the Greek ending iōn; cf. MLKYWN. For parallels to and discussion of dd see Ryckmans, i. 65; Littmann, *Safaitic Inscriptions*, 307a; Nöldeke, *Beiträge*, 96. Greek transcription: Dados, Wuthnow, 42.

DWḤY. *One-word name.* 'Corpulent'
Arabic dauḥ. No other occurrences of this name are attested so far.

DWMNYN'. *Latin name*
Domnina, Domneina. See also Appendix IV, 2.6; 2.11; 2.15; 2.22.B. ī, ei is always written with Yodh; see Rosenthal, *Sprache*, 20.

DWR'
Shortened form of 'TNDWR', name of the ancestor (*C* 4084).

[D]WRN. *Unexplained*

DZYṢYḤ. *Unexplained*
The reading RZYṢYḤ is possible. The name seems to be non-Semitic.

DYGNS. *Greek name*
Diogenēs; see Pape, 301. See Appendix IV, 1.1; 1.7; 1.12; 1.13; 1.18; 1.25.A.

DYWDY. *Genitive compound.* 'The one of Wadd'
Archaic demonstrative pronoun *ḏū, 'the one of' (Heb. zeh, Aram. dī, Arab. ḏū, Ugar. d). For discussion and parallels see Huffmon, *APNMT*, 186; Caquot, 'Onomastique', 238, no. 2; Moran, *BANE*, 61, with further parallels.

DYWN. *One-word name.* 'Judge'
Akkadian dayânū. On the change â > ô see Rosenthal, *Sprache*, 27. Nöldeke, *ÜOSP*, 94, still maintained: 'das ā ist allem Anschein nach nirgends zu ō geworden'. See also DYN', DYNY.

DYN'. *One-word name.* 'Judge'
For discussion and parallels see Noth, *IPN*, 10; Sachau, 'Edessenische Inschriften', *ZDMG*, 36 (1882), 161. Caquot, *RTP*, 171, ad DYNY, takes the form to be the Aramaic pass. part., 'judged', augmented by the ending Yodh.

DYNY. *One-word name.* 'Judged by N.N.'
Aramaic pass. part. For parallels and discussion see Cantineau, *Le Nabatéen*, ii. 82; Caquot, *RTP*, 171.

DYNYS. *Greek name*
Dionysios; see Pape, 307. See Appendix IV, 1.7; 1.12; 1.13; 1.18; 1.25.D. See bilingual text in *AAS*, 11 (1961), 146–7. For other proposed names of which DYNYS could be the transcription see *RTP*, 171.

[DY]NS. *Greek name*
Deinis; see Pape, 278. See Appendix IV, 1.7; 1.13; 1.25.H. If the name is a variant of DYNYS it is odd. ȳ is always written with Yodh (Rosenthal, *Sprache*, 20). The restoration may be wrong.

DK'. *One-word name.* 'Pure'
Aramaic dᵉkā'. For semantic parallels and discussion see Noth, *IPN*, 228; Ryckmans, i. 107.

DKRY. *Hypocoristicon.* 'N.N. has remembered'
*ḏkr, 'remember' (Common Semitic).
For discussion and parallels see Huffmon, *APNMT*, 187; Ryckmans, i. 69; Cantineau, *Le Nabatéen*, ii. 82; Noth, *IPN*, 186–7; Harris, *Grammar*, 99; Zakir-stela (*KAI*, 202, A[1,2]); Schottroff, '*Gedenken*', 78–83.

DKT'. See under BR DKT'

DMY. See under RMY

DMS. *Greek name*
Dēmas, see Pape, 288. See Appendix IV, 1.7; 1.11; 1.15; 1.25.C. DMS occurs on a Greek–Nabataean bilingual inscription; see *RB*, 6 (1909), 590. ē is never written with a mater lectionis (Rosenthal, *Sprache*, 20).

DNY. *Hypocoristicon.* 'N.N. has judged'
Chabot, *CIS*, ii. 4002[2], takes the name to be a variant of DYNY, DYNYS. More likely with Caquot, *RTP*, 171, the perfect of dān augmented by the hypocoristic ending Yodh. Cf. the O.T. name dānî'ēl.

D'T'. *One-word name.* 'Hate, wrath'
Arabic di'āt. There is no supporting evidence for the reading R'T'. For parallels on proposed explanation see Cantineau, *Le Nabatéen*, ii. 84; Caskel, *Lihyan*, 145; Ryckmans, i. 67; Hess, *Beduinennamen*, 22. Variant: D'TH.

DRM. *One-word name.* 'Slow-walker'
Arabic darama; act. part. I, dārim. For parallels see Ryckmans, i. 67; Littmann, *Safaitic Inscriptions*, 308a; Wüstenfeld, *Register*, 150. The name in our inscription is feminine, in the references quoted DRM is masculine.

The proposed reading KRM, (*Journal asiatique*, 12 [1918], 289), is very dubious for epigraphic reasons. KRMW, KRM are attested in Nabataean (Cantineau, *Le Nabatéen*, ii. 108; Littmann, 'Nabataean', *BSOAS*, 16 [1954], 234). Arabic karam, 'noble-mindedness'. The reading RDM has nothing in favour of it.

D''. See under R''

D'TH. See under D'T'

HGY. *Uncertain*
(1) Cantineau, *Le Nabatéen*, ii. 84, lists a Nabataean name HGW, which he derives from Arabic hajj, 'leave one's country, go into exile'. (2) Aramaic root h^{a}gā', 'speak, reason'. The name would be a hypocoristicon of a theophorous name. (3) Cf. the O.T. name hēgay (Esther $2^{8,15}$). Persian name. The O.T. name is masc. whereas our name is fem. There are probably no connections at all between these two names. (4) A derivation from Arabic hajī, 'prudent, noble', seems to be the best explanation for the name.

HGR. *One-word name.* 'Fugitive'
Arabic hajara; act. part. I hājir. For parallels and discussion see Cantineau, *Le Nabatéen*, ii. 84; Ryckmans, i. 71, 292; Littmann, *Safaitic Inscriptions*, 309a. Greek transcription: Agarē, Wuthnow, 11.

HD'. *Hypocoristicon.* 'May N.N. guide'
Syriac h^{e}dā'. Expressing a mother's wish that the god may lead her daughter. Chabot, *CIS*, ii. 4190, suggested that the name is a contracted form of HDYR'. This is less likely. For parallels to the proposed interpretation see Ryckmans, i. 72.

HDYR'. *One-word name.* 'She who is adorned'
Aramaic pass. part. fem. Variant: HDYRT. For parallels see Cantineau, *Le Nabatéen*, ii. 84.

HDYRT. See under HDYR'

HD/RMW. *Unexplained*
The reading of the name is very uncertain, and it is therefore impossible to give its etymology.

HDRYN[WS]. *Latin name*
See *ILS*, 200a. See Appendix IV, 2.6; 2.8; 2.10; 2.13; 2.19; 2.22.A; 2.23.D. Hadrianus. Latin 'h' is always transcribed as He (Rosenthal, *Sprache*, 36). For possible exception see variant 'DRYNWS.

HLDRS. *Greek name*
Hēliodōros; see Pape, 456. See Appendix IV, 1.7; 1.11; 1.12; 1.14; 1.18; 1.21; 1.25.D; 1.26.I, III. Hēlios is identified with the Palmyrene sungod Yarḥibôl. Thus Hēliodōros serves as a translation of Yarḥibôlā' and Lišamš (see *RB*, 39 [1930], 546–7, no. 13 B^{2}). Cf. *C* 3902 where Hēliodōros is used to translate Yarḥay, hypocoristicon of Yarḥibôlā'. The variants are HLYDWRS, HLYDYRS, HLYDRWS.

HLYDWRS. See under HLDRS

HLYDYRS. See under HLDRS

HLYDRWS. See under HLDRS

HN'Y. *One-word name.* 'Happy'
Arabic hāni'. For parallels see Cantineau, *Le Nabatéen*, ii. 87; Littmann, *Safaitic Inscriptions*, 310a; Wüstenfeld, *Register*, 204. HN'Y is mentioned by Ibn Doreid as name of several Arabs (*Ibn Doreid*, 218^{16}). Greek transcriptions: Aneos, Aniou, Wuthnow, 22, 23. The meaning 'servant', that Cantineau (op. cit.) prefers for HN'Y, is a secondary development and probably a euphemism for 'bd. (This information was supplied by G. Krotkoff.)

A connection with Aramaic h^{a}nā' 'please, profit' is possible, though less likely. In this case HN'Y would have to be a hypocoristicon.

HRMZ. *Persian name*
Hurmuz; see Justi, *Namenbuch*, 7. Cf. hôrmîz (Jastrow, 341). The variant HRMZD is attested.

HRMZD. See under HRMZ

HRMY. *Uncertain*
A derivation from Arabic harim, 'senile', is possible. For discussion and parallels see Ryckmans, i. 74; Littmann, *Safaitic Inscriptions*, 310a; Wüstenfeld, *Register*, 206. But it is more likely that HRMY is just a variant of HRMS; see Starcky, *PNO*, 173–4.

[HRMYS]. *Greek name*
Hermeias; see Pape, 382. See Appendix IV, 1.13; 1.21; 1.25.C.

HRMS. *Greek name*
Hermēs; see Pape, 382. See Appendix IV, 1.21; 1.25.A.

HRMSYN'. *Greek name*
Hermēsianos; see Pape, 384. See Appendix IV, 1.11; 1.12; 1.15; 1.21; 1.25.D. The Greek ending -os is replaced by the Aramaic status emphaticus ending.

HRQL'. *Greek name*
Hēraklēs; see Pape, 467. See Appendix IV, 1.11; 1.21; 1.25.A.

HRQLYD'. *Greek name*
Hērakleidēs; see Pape, 464. See Appendix IV, 1.11; 1.13; 1.21; 1.25.A.

WHB', WHBY. *Hypocoristicon*
Shortened form of WHBLT. For discussion and parallels see under WHBLT.

WHBY. See under WHB'

WHBLT. *Genitive compound.* 'Gift of Allat'
Arabic wahb. On the various possibilities of expressing 'give' in Palmyrene personal names see under BLYHB. For parallels and discussion see Ryckmans, i. 224; van den Branden, *Inscriptions*, 205, whbnhy; Cantineau, *Le Nabatéen*, ii. 89; Caquot, *RTP*, 172; Dura, *Final Report V, Part I*, 62, Vabalathus. The Greek transcription Ouaballathou is attested from a bilingual text (*C* 3921).

WLY. *One-word name.* 'Close friend (of god)'
Arabic walīy. For parallels see Ryckmans, i. 79; Littmann, *Safaitic Inscriptions*, 311b.

WSḤW. *One-word name.* 'Dirty, filthy'
Arabic wasiḫ. For a parallel see Ryckmans, i. 79. The Greek transcription Ouaseou is attested from a bilingual text (*Inv. X*, 115). The name is augmented by the ending Waw.

W'D. *One-word name.* 'He who promises'
Arabic act. part. I wāʿid. For parallels see Ryckmans, i. 80; Winnett, *Safaitic Inscriptions*, 206. Greek transcription: Oaedos, Wuthnow, 85. The other possible reading is W'R (see below).

W'R. *One-word name.* 'Rough, uneven terrain'
Arabic waʿr. For parallels see Ryckmans, i. 80; Littmann, *Safaitic Inscriptions*, 312a; Lankester Harding, *Thamudic Inscriptions*, no. 515. Greek transcription: Ouaros, Wuthnow, 92. The other possible reading is W'D (see above).

WRDN. *Persian name*
Wardān; see Justi, *Namenbuch*, 351. The word passed as a loan-word into Arabic. The meaning of the word in Persian and Arabic is 'rose'. For a very good discussion with further references to occurrences of the Persian word in other languages see Jeffery, *Foreign Vocabulary*, 287. See also Noth, *IPN*, 231. But his etymology for Hebrew YRD is wrong; see Kopf, *VT*, 8 (1958), 179.

WRWD. *Persian name*
Hurauda, Ouorōdēs; see Justi, *Namenbuch*, 133.

WRTN. *Unexplained*
Ingholt, *PNO*, 177, no. 5, suggested a connection with Safaitic WRŠ, which is rather unlikely. Could the name be a variant of WRDN?

ZB. Abbreviation of a name like ZBD' or ZBDY.

ZB'. *Hypocoristicon.* 'N.N. has given'
*zbd-bwl > zbd' > zb'.
For attestations see Dura, *Final Report V, Part I*, 62, Zebaios. For discussion and parallels see under ZBDBWL.

ZBD. *Hypocoristicon.* 'Gift of N.N.'
For discussion and parallels see Littmann, *Safaitic Inscriptions*, 312b; Ryckmans, i. 83. For the corresponding names in other languages see Cantineau, *Le Nabatéen*, ii. 89; 'Hatra', no. 23²; Noth, *IPN*, 170; Harris, *Grammar*, 108. Greek transcription: Zabdos, Wuthnow, 48.

ZBD'. *Hypocoristicon.* 'Gift of N.N.'
For discussion and parallels see ZBDBWL. Variants: ZBDH, ZBDY.

ZBDBW. *Hypocoristicon.* 'Gift of Bôl'
*zbd-bwl.
For discussion and parallels see ZBDBWL.

ZBDBWL. *Genitive compound.* 'Gift of Bôl'
Structural type: noun (construct) plus divine name; for type: divine name plus verb see BWLZBD. On the variant spelling BWL/BL see Caquot, *RTP*, 154, n. 4. For parallels see Dura, *Final Report V, Part I*, 62, Zabdibolus. See also the literature under ZBD. See also: ZBDBL, ZBDL', ZBDLH, ZBDNBW, ZBD'T', ZBD'TH.

ZBDBWL'. *Genitive compound.* 'Gift of Bôl'
The Aleph is added by analogy to YRḤBWL' and 'GLBWL'. For discussion see ZBDBWL.

ZBDBL. *Genitive compound.* 'Gift of Bēl'
Polybius, *Histories*, v. 79, mentions an Arabic prince Zabdibēlos who accompanied Antiochus III at the battle of Raphia. For discussion see ZBDBWL.

ZBDH. See under ZBD'

ZBDY. *Hypocoristicon.* 'Gift of N.N.'
For parallels see Littmann, *Safaitic Inscriptions*, 312b; Cantineau, *Le Nabatéen*, ii. 91; Cowley, *Papyri*, 65⁷; Kraeling, *BMAP*, 1¹¹; Matt. 4²¹. Greek transcription: Zabdaios, Wuthnow, 47. Dussaud, *Les Arabes en Syrie*, 99, takes the name without explicit basis to be an abbreviation of *ZBD'L. For discussion see ZBDBWL.

ZBDL'. *Hypocoristicon.* 'Gift of god'
*zbd-'lh.
Caquot, *RTP*, 172, restores *ZBD-'LT, but this seems less likely. Cf. the Greek name

Theodōros, Pape, 490. Greek transcription: Zabdila, Wuthnow, 48. Variant: ZBDLH. For discussion see ZBDBWL.

ZBDLH. See under ZBDL'

ZBDNBW. *Genitive compound.* 'Gift of Nabû'
For discussion see ZBDBWL. The Greek transcriptions with Zabd- as their first element favour an interpretation: noun (construct) plus divine name; rather than: verb plus divine name. For the latter construction the Greek transcription should have Zebad-.

ZBD'Y. *Hypocoristicon.* 'Gift of Athe'
*zbd-'th.
Cf. the variant form from Dura: ZBD'H (Du Mesnil du Buisson, *Inventaire*, no. 19^{2}). For discussion see ZBDBWL.

ZBD'T'. *Genitive compound.* 'Gift of Athe'
The name is attested at Dura, *Final Report V, Part I*, 62, Zabad-athēs, Zabda-athēs. For discussion see ZBDBWL. Variants: ZBD'Y, ZBD'TH.

ZBD'TH. See under ZBD'T'

ZBWD. *Hypocoristicon.* 'Given by N.N.'
Qaṭūl form; see Brockelmann, *GVG*, i. 357, par. 141. For parallels see Kraeling, *BMAP*, 1^{14}; Clay, *BEUP*, x. 66, Za-bu-du, Za-bu-da-a. Greek transcription: Zaboudos, Wuthnow, 48.

ZBWDW. *Hypocoristicon.* 'Given by N.N.'
On the grammatical form see ZBWD. For parallels and discussion see Cantineau, *Le Nabatéen*, ii. 91; Littmann, *Nabataean Inscriptions*, 1. Cf. also the alternative Aramaic form ZBYD'.

ZBY. *Hypocoristicon.* 'Gift of N.N.'
*zbd-bwl > zbdy > zby?
For discussion and parallels see Littmann, *Safaitic Inscriptions*, 312b; Ryckmans, i. 83, who derives the name from Arabic zabiy, 'burden'. See also Noth, *IPN*, 39, 47. The name is found in epigraphic Syriac (Segal, *BSOAS*, 16 [1954], 17, no. 1^{2}). Greek transcription: Zabbaios, Wuthnow, 47. See also ZBDBWL, ZBD'.

ZBYD'. *Hypocoristicon.* 'Given by N.N.'
Aramaic pass. part.
For attestations see Jastrow, 378; Dura, *Final Report V, Part I*, 62, Zebeidas, Zebidas. The Greek transcription Zebeidou is found in a bilingual text (*C* 3913 I^{3}). See also under YHYB'. Variant: ZBYDY. Nabataean and Hatra ZBYDW are diminutive forms of Arabic zubayd (Cantineau, *Le Nabatéen*, ii. 91; 'Hatra', no. 46; Wüstenfeld, *Register*, 474). Greek transcription: Zobaidos, Wuthnow, 50.

ZBYDY. See under ZBYD'

ZBKN'. *Uncertain*
There are no parallels to this reading anywhere. The reading ZBDN' seems possible according to the photograph. It would then be a hypocoristicon of a theophorous name: 'gift of Nabû'. For discussion see ZBDBWL.

ZGWG. *One-word name.* 'Glazier'
Qāṭōl type; cf. Aramaic, Syriac z^{e}gûgîtā' 'glass, crystal'. For semantic parallels see Noth, *IPN*, 231.

ZDQL. *Nominal sentence.* 'El is just'
The reading is not quite certain. On the dissimilation of the emphatics cf. krṣy < qrṣy (Carpentras-stela, *KAI*, 269^{2}); kyṣ' < qyṣ' (Brrkb inscription, *KAI*, 216^{19}). For discussion and parallels see Huffmon, *APNMT*, 256; Ryckmans, i. 182, 246, 269; Noth, *IPN*, 161–2, 189; Harris, *Grammar*, 140.

ZWZY. *Uncertain*
A derivation from Aramaic zûz, 'silver coin, money', may be possible. Cf. KSP' and ḤRWṢ in Palmyrene.

ZWR. *One-word name.* 'Throat'
Arabic zaur. On the use of parts of the body as personal names see Nöldeke, *Beiträge*, 101–3; van den Branden, *Histoire*, 59. Variant: ZWRW.

ZWRW. *One-word name.* 'Throat'
For discussion see ZWR. Ending Waw added (common in Nabataean).

ZKY'. *One-word name.* 'Pure, innocent'
*ḏ/zak, 'pure, innocent' (Heb. zkh, Aram. ḏ/zky, Arab. ḏ/zkw/y). For parallels see Huffmon, *APNMT*, 186; Cantineau, *Le Nabatéen*, ii. 92; Ryckmans, i. 69. Zaki is a common name in Egypt. Cf. the N.T. name Zakchaios (Luke 19^{2}).

ZKN'
This reading of the *Corpus* (*C* 4198 B^{2}) has no support from the original photograph published by Sobernheim in *MVÄG*, 10 (1905), 50, no. 42, Pl. XXIV, where clearly mn can be recognized where the *Corpus* reads ZKN'. Secondly, the standard phrase in legal texts is always: rḥq l ... mn, as in *CIS* 4174^{1,2}.

ZMRY. *One-word name.* 'Beardless, handsome'
Arabic zamīr. The root *zmr is attested in practically all Semitic languages. For a discussion and attestations see Starcky, *Syria*, 26 (1949), 49–51.

Z'MW. *One-word name.* 'Chief'
Arabic za'īm. For parallels see Littmann, *Safaitic Inscriptions*, 313b; Ryckmans, i. 86. The other proposed reading is Z'QW (see below).

Z'QW. *One-word name.* 'Crying'
Arabic za'īq. For another parallel found in Safaitic see Ryckmans, i. 86. The variant reading Z'MW (see above) seems preferable.

ZQ'. *One-word name.* 'Bottle'
Aramaic ziqqā', zîqā'. Cf. the Palmyrene name BQY. Most probably a surname in this inscription.

ZRZYRT. *One-word name.* 'Starling'
Hebrew zarzîr. For discussion see 'ZRZYRT.

ḤB'. *Hypocoristicon.* 'N.N. has loved'
*ḥbb plus divine name.
For parallels from other languages see Cantineau, *Le Nabatéen*, ii. 93; Ryckmans, i. 86; 'Hatra', nos. 153, 159, 169. The Greek transcription [A]bb[e]ous is found in a bilingual text (*Syria*, 12 [1931], 129, no. 10) and supports the proposed interpretation. Variant: ḤBY.

ḤBBT. *One-word name.* 'Sweetheart', 'darling'
Arabic ḥabība. For parallels see Cantineau, *Le Nabatéen*, ii. 93; Ryckmans, i. 86. Greek transcription: Ababathē, Abibathē, Wuthnow, 6. 9.

ḤBWḂ. *Uncertain*
The last letter is very doubtful. It could be a qaṭūl form of ḥbb; see Brockelmann, *GVG*, i. 357, par. 141.

ḤBWL'. *One-word name.* 'Crippled'
Qaṭṭūl form; cf. Arabic ḫabala. See Brockelmann, *GVG*, i. 363, par. 156.

ḤBZY. *One-word name.* 'Baker'
Arabic ḫabbāz. This interpretation was first proposed by Sachau in *ZDMG*, 35 (1881), 763, no. 3. For semantic parallels see Noth, *IPN*, 231.

ḤBY. See under ḤB'

ḤBYB'. *One-word name.* 'Beloved one'
Aramaic pass. part. or Arabic ḥabīb, 'friend'. For parallels see Cantineau, *Le Nabatéen*, ii. 93; Littmann, *Safaitic Inscriptions*, 313b; Ryckmans, i. 86; Wüstenfeld, *Register*, 191. Ḥabīb is a very common name in Arabic. Greek transcription: Abiba, Wuthnow, 9. Variant: ḤBYBY.

ḤBYBY. *One-word name*
For discussion see under ḤBYB'. The Latin transcription Habibi from a bilingual text (*C* 3905) could show that the Yodh does not represent the suffix of the first person sing., but stands for a hypocoristic ending or an Arabic nisbe. Unaccented long final vowels and diphthongs were dropped in later Aramaic. They were still written but no longer pronounced. The exact date when this process was completed is unknown. See Brockelmann, *Syrische Grammatik*, 45, par. 75; Rosenthal, *Sprache*, 44; Cantineau, *Grammaire*, 53.

ḤBN. *One-word name.* 'Dropsy'
Arabic ḥaban. For discussion as to its meaning see Littmann, *Safaitic Inscriptions*, 314a; 'Nabataean', *BSOAS*, 15 (1953), 21. For attestations see Wüstenfeld, *Register*, 191. See van den Branden, *Histoire*, 58, for names of diseases given to individuals.

ḤBRY. *Uncertain*
Two interpretations are possible: (1) To derive the name from Arabic ḥabr, 'joy'. For parallels see Ryckmans, i. 87. (2) To connect the name with Aramaic ḥābēr, 'friend, associate'. For parallels see Noth, *IPN*, 222. For an explanation of the ending Yodh see under ḤBYBY.

ḤBT'. *One-word name.* 'Grain, seed'
Arabic ḥabba. The name is not to be derived from Arabic ḥabba, 'love', which would make no sense. The grammatical form would be the third person sing. fem., 'she has loved'. It would be extremely difficult to explain the Aleph as being part of a verbal form. For parallels see Cantineau, *Le Nabatéen*, ii. 93; Ryckmans, i. 86. The Greek transcription Abbatha is attested from a bilingual text (*PNO*, 170, no. 73).

ḤG'. See under ḤGY

ḤGGW. *One-word name.* 'The pilgrim'
Arabic ḥajja. Qaṭṭāl form; see Brockelmann, *GVG*, i. 360, par. 149. See also Caquot, *RTP*, 172.

ḤGWG'. *One-word name.* 'Feasting'
Aramaic ḥ^{a}gag. Qaṭūl form; Brockelmann, *GVG*, i. 357. See also under ḤGGW, ḤGY, ḤG'.

ḤGWR. *One-word name.* 'The lame one'
Aramaic ḥāgar. Qaṭṭūl form. This form is often used in forming names which denote a physical peculiarity of a person; see Brockelmann, *GVG*, i. 363, par. 156; Barth, *Nominalbildung*, 196, par. 132.

ḤGY. *One-word name.* 'Born on a feast'
Jewish name. For parallels and discussion see Ryckmans, i. 88; Littmann, *Safaitic Inscriptions*, 314a; Cantineau, *Le Nabatéen*, ii. 93; Cowley, *Papyri*, 12^{5}, 28^{16}; Kraeling, *BMAP*, 5^{15}, 11^{13}; Nimrud Ostracon, *Iraq*, 19 (1957), 140, II^{3}; Harris, *Grammar*, 100; Noth, *IPN*, 222. Among Jewish exiles in Babylon we find Ḫa-ag-ga-a^{f}, Ḫa-ag-ta-a (Clay, *BEUP*, x. 50). Cf. the later Jewish name Yôm Ṭôb. Variant: ḤG'.

ḤGT. *Unexplained*
The name is most likely to be derived from the Arabic ḥajja, 'go on a pilgrimage'. But the grammatical form is uncertain.

ḤD'. *One-word name.* 'Cheek'
Arabic ḫadd. For parallels see Littmann, *Safaitic Inscriptions*, 314a; Ryckmans, i. 88, derives the word from Arabic ḥadd, 'sharpen, point'. Greek transcription: Addos, Wuthnow, 12. For a partial list of parts of the body used as personal names see van den Branden, *Histoire*, 59.

ḤDWDN. *Uncertain*
The Greek transcription Addoudanou, attested from a bilingual text (*C* 3914), would suggest a qaṭṭūl form. The name is probably to be derived from the Aramaic ḥādad, Arabic ḥadda, 'be sharp (intellect)'. See also Caquot, *RTP*, 172.

[Ḥ]DYDW. *One-word name.* 'Sharp (intellect)'
Arabic ḥadīd. Cf. also ḤDWDN.

ḤWML. *One-word name.* 'Black cloud'
Arabic ḥaumal. The name has not been found elsewhere.

ḤṬR'. *One-word name.* 'Branch (of a tree)'
Arabic ḫiṭr. The spelling with Aleph rejects the explanation of the name as gentilic, 'the man of Hatra'. For a parallel see Ryckmans, i. 90. See also Caquot, *RTP*, 156. Variant: ḤṬRY.

ḤṬRY. See under ḤṬR'

ḤYNY. *One-word name.* 'Living'
Arabic ḥayy. For parallels and discussion see Cantineau, *Le Nabatéen*, ii. 95; Littmann, *Safaitic Inscriptions*, 315a; Ryckmans, i. 91; Wüstenfeld, *Register*, 197, Ḥayyān; 'Hatra', nos. 149, 206; Kilamuwa inscription (*KAI*, 25[3]); Huffmon, *APNMT*, 191; Tallquist, *APN*, 83a.

ḤYR'. *One-word name.* 'Good, excellent'
Arabic ḫair. For parallels see Cantineau, *Le Nabatéen*, ii. 96; Littmann, *Nabataean Inscriptions*, 48, no. 54; 'Hatra', nos. 48[2], 52[1]. Greek transcriptions: Airou, Chairos, Wuthnow, 15, 119. Variants: ḤYRY, ḤYRN.

ḤYRY. *One-word name.* 'Good, excellent'
For discussion see under ḤYR'.

ḤYRN. *One-word name.* 'Good, excellent'
Suffix -ān added to the Arabic adjective ḫair. For discussion see under ḤYR'.

ḤKYM. *One-word name.* 'Wise man'
*ḥkm, 'be wise' (Common Semitic). Cf. Arabic ḥakīm. For parallels see Cantineau, *Le Nabatéen*, ii. 96; Littmann, *Safaitic Inscriptions*, 315a; Ryckmans, i. 91; Wüstenfeld, *Register*, 198, Ḥakīm; *Thes. Syr.* 1268; Dalman, *Handwörterbuch*, 146. Greek transcription: Achim, Wuthnow, 31. ḤKYM is attested as personal name and as tribal name.

ḤKYŠW. *One-word name.* 'Burrower' (dimin.)
Arabic ḥakaša (Barthélemy, i. 168). For a discussion and for further parallels of the quṭṭail form see Littmann, *Zeitschrift für Semitistik*, 4 (1926), 31 ff. The Greek transcription Ochchaisou is attested from a bilingual text (*C* 3923).

ḤL'. *One-word name.* 'Maternal uncle'
Arabic ḫāl. For parallels and discussion see Ryckmans, i. 102; Littmann, *Safaitic Inscriptions*, 317b; Nöldeke, *Beiträge*, 96, with a parallel from Syriac. Theoretically the name could be derived from Arabic ḫull, ḫill, 'friend', but all the transcriptions from bilingual texts have Ala (e.g. *C* 3916), which clearly supports the present interpretation. Variant: ḤLH.

ḤLD'. *One-word name.* 'Lasting'
Arabic ḫālid. For discussion and parallels see Cantineau, *Le Nabatéen*, ii. 96; Littmann, *Safaitic Inscriptions*, 317b; Ryckmans, i. 103; Wüstenfeld, *Register*, 124, Ḫālid; Noth, *IPN*, 230, with different explanation. Greek transcription: Aldē, Chaldē, Wuthnow, 17, 119. The Greek transcriptions favour a connection with Arabic ḫālid, 'lasting', amply attested as a personal name. But a derivation from Arabic ḫuld, 'mole', is also possible. On the question of derivation see Nöldeke, *Beiträge*, 80.

ḤLH. See under ḤL'

ḤLY'. *One-word name.* 'Fresh, juicy herbage'
Arabic ḫaliyy. For semantic parallels see Noth, *IPN*, 230. A derivation from Syriac ḥ[e]lî, 'be sweet', seems to me less likely. Variant: ḤLYW.

ḤLYW. See under ḤLY'

ḤLYP'. *One-word name.* 'Successor'
Arabic ḫalīfa. For discussion of this type of name see Nöldeke, *Beiträge*, 98. For parallels see Ryckmans, i. 104; Ṭabari, *Index*, 172. Greek transcription: Chalipos, Wuthnow, 119. See also under ḤLP', ḤLPT'.

ḤLYPY. *One-word name.* 'Successor'
For discussion see under ḤLYP'.

ḤLYPT. *One-word name.* 'Successor'
For discussion see under ḤLYP'.

ḤLYŠW. For discussion see under ḤLYŠY. Ingholt's suggestion ('Some Sculptures from the Tomb of Malkû at Palmyra', 461, n. 23) that the name be read ḤNYŠW cannot be accepted as long as there is no photograph from which to verify the reading. Moreover the present reading yields a satisfactory interpretation. Ingholt interprets his name as a quṭail form from the Arabic ḥanaš 'serpent'. For parallels see his article.

ḤLYŠY. *One-word name.* 'Saddle blanket' (dimin.)
Quṭail form. Arabic ḥils. For parallels see Ryckmans, i. 93; Hess, *Beduinennamen*, 19. Variant: ḤLYŠW.

ḤLKŠ. *Unexplained*
No photograph is available to verify the reading. The name seems to be non-Semitic.

ḤLP'. *One-word name.* 'Successor'
Arabic ḫalaf. For discussion and parallels see Cantineau, *Le Nabatéen*, ii. 96; Ryckmans, i. 104; Littmann, *Safaitic Inscriptions*,

317b; Nöldeke, *Beiträge*, 98. Greek transcription: Alaphos, Wuthnow, 16. On the various possibilities of transcribing names formed from this root see Littmann, *Nabataean Inscriptions*, 19, no. 19. See aslo ḤLYP', ḤLYPY, ḤLYPT, ḤLPW, ḤLPWN', ḤLPT'.

ḤLPW. *One-word name.* 'Successor'
For discussion see under the variant ḤLP'.

ḤLPWN'. *One-word name.* 'Successor' (dimin.)
Diminutive ending -ān added. For discussion see under ḤLP'. For parallels see Ryckmans, i. 104; Littmann, *Safaitic Inscriptions*, 317b. Greek transcription: Alaphōnas, Wuthnow, 17.

ḤLPT'. *One-word name.* 'Successor'
For parallels see Ryckmans, i. 104. Greek transcription: Chalaphatos, Wuthnow, 119. Names formed from the root ḥlp at Palmyra express the same idea for which the O.T. names use šlm, that of restitution for a lost child; see Noth, *IPN*, 174. For discussion see under ḤLP'.

ḤM'. *Hypocoristicon.* 'N.N. protects'
Arabic ḥamā. For discussion and parallels see Ryckmans, i. 94, 229; Littmann, *Safaitic Inscriptions*, 315a. Caquot's proposed second translation 'El is father-in-law' is uncertain (*RTP*, 163); see Caskel, *Lihyan*, 147; Ryckmans, i. 229. Goldmann's theory (*Personennamen*, 23), that ḤM' is an abbreviation through Aphaeresis of MNḤM' is without support. For a discussion on the possible connection with the O.T. name ḥammû'ēl, LXX Amouēl, see Noth, *IPN*, 79; Lewy, 'Sungod', 473; Praetorius, 'Eigennamen', 778. ḤM' occurs frequently in post-biblical times (Lidzbarski, *Ephemeris*, 3, 34, thinks the name is Jewish). See also Starcky, 'L'ostracon', 31, conv. 2. It is also possible that the name is to be derived from Arabic ḥummā, 'fever, heat'. An Arab called Ḥummā is mentioned in Wüstenfeld, *Register*, 235. See also van den Branden, *Histoire*, 58, on the various names of diseases used as personal names. It is unlikely that the verbal element is derived from Aramaic ḥᵃmā', 'see'. ḥᵃzā' was used in Palmyrene personal names to express the idea of seeing. Variant: ḤMY.

ḤMY. See under ḤM'

ḤMYN. *One-word name.* 'Warm'
Arabic ḥamiya. Qaṭlān form (ḥamyān). For discussion and parallels see Cantineau, *Le Nabatéen*, ii. 97; Littmann, *Safaitic Inscriptions*, 315b.

ḤMNWN. *One-word name.* 'Louse' (dimin.)
Arabic ḥamnān (Wahrmund, i. 547). For semantic parallels see Noth, *IPN*, 230.

ḤN'. *Hypocoristicon.* 'N.N. is gracious'
*ḥnn, 'be gracious' (Common Semitic, except Eth.).
Hypocoristica of the root *ḥnn are attested throughout the Semitic onomasticon. For parallels see Ryckmans, i. 95; 'Hatra', no. 125^{1}; Galling, 181^{58}, Cowley, *Papyri*, 2^{3}; Diringer, *Iscrizioni*, 45; Ugar., *PRU*, ii. 35 B^{9}. Cf. the N.T. name Ananias (Acts $5^{1,3}$). Greek transcription: Anneos, Wuthnow, 23. See also under ḤNBL.

ḤNBL. *Verbal sentence with the perfect.* 'Bēl is gracious'
Structural type: verb plus divine name; for type: divine name plus verb, see under BLTYḤN. For parallels and discussion see Littmann, *Safaitic Inscriptions*, 315b; Ryckmans, i. 229; Huffmon, *APNMT*, 200; Cantineau, *Le Nabatéen*, ii. 98; Diringer, *Iscrizioni*, 45; Harris, *Grammar*, 102–3; 'Hatra', no. 191; Noth, *IPN*, 187; Gordon, *UT*, 2084: 8, ḥn'il. Albright, *Proto-Sinaitic*, 40, yḥnb'l. See also ḤN', ḤNYN', ḤNYNW, ḤNYNY, ḤNT, ḤNT'.

ḤNYN'. *Hypocoristicon.* 'Favoured by N.N.'
Aramaic pass. part. The name is found at 'Hatra', no. 68^{2}, and is very frequent in post-biblical times (Jastrow, 483). The Greek transcription Ona[in]ou from a bilingual text (*Inv. X*, 96) would favour an interpretation of the name as a diminutive (quṭail form). Other Greek transcriptions favour either of the two interpretations: Onainos, Onēnos, Aninas, Aninos, Wuthnow, 89, 23. See also under ḤNBL. Variants: ḤNYNW, ḤNYNY.

ḤNYNW. See under ḤNYN'

ḤNYNY. See under ḤNYN'
The variants show that the endings Waw, Yodh, Aleph are used without apparent distinction.

ḤNT. *Hypocoristicon*
For discussion see under ḤNT'.

ḤNT'. *Hypocoristicon.* 'Athe is gracious'
*ḥnt-'t'.
The masc. verb on a fem. noun is strange. It can only be explained as analogy to the names with a masc. noun; see discussion under BLTYḤN. For discussion of this structural type see ḤNBL.

ḤSD. *One-word name.* 'Goodness, mercy'
For discussion and parallels see Huffmon, *APNMT*, 201; Ryckmans, i. 96; Noth, *IPN*, 183.

ḤSS. See under ḤŠŠ

ḤPRY. *Hypocoristicon.* 'N.N. has protected'
Arabic ḥafara. For parallels see Ryckmans, i. 97; Noth, *IPN*, 155; Diringer, *Iscrizioni*, 236.

ḤPRTM. *Unexplained*
The photograph is illegible. It might not be a personal name at all. The form has the appearance of being a finite verb.

ḤR'. *One-word name.* 'Noble, free-born'
*ḥrr, 'be free' (Common Semitic).
For parallels see Littmann, *Safaitic Inscriptions*, 316a; Cantineau, *Le Nabatéen*, ii. 99. Greek transcription: Ouros, Wuthnow, 93.

ḤRWṢ. *One-word name.* 'Gold'
Hebrew ḥārûṣ. For parallels see Noth, *IPN*, 223; Cowley, *Papyri*, 17[6]; Cantineau, *Le Nabatéen*, ii. 99; Harris, *Grammar*, 104; Tallquist, *APN*, 86b; Bresciani, *Hermopoli*, 419 *sub voce* ḤRWṢ. Cf. also Ryckmans, i. 99.

ḤRŠ'. *One-word name.* 'Mute, dumb'
Aramaic ḥaršā'. For discussion and a parallel see Noth, *IPN*, 228. The Greek transcription Arsa, found on a bilingual text (*C* 3937), argues against an identification with Nabataean ḤRŠW, which is derived from Arabic ḥirš (see Cantineau, *Le Nabatéen* ii. 100). Variant: ḤRŠW.

ḤRŠW. See under ḤRŠ'

ḤRT'. *Divine name used as personal name*
For discussion of this type of name see under B'ŠMN.

ḤŠY. *One-word name*
Arabic ḥašiya, 'breathe short, be asthmatic'. The grammatical form is unclear. ḤŠY occurs in the Birecik-inscription (*Syria*, 39 [1962], 97[8]). Otherwise no occurrences are found.

ḤŠŠ. *One-word name*
The meaning is uncertain. The name is either to be connected with Arabic ḫašaš, 'creeping things of the earth', or with Arabic ḫass, 'lettuce'. For parallels see Ryckmans, i. 107; Wüstenfeld, *Register*, 130, Ḫaššān; Cantineau, *Le Nabatéen*, ii. 101; see also Caquot, *RTP*, 173. It is not absolutely certain that ḤSS is an orthographic variant of ḤŠŠ. It might be derived from Arabic ḫass, 'lettuce'.

ḤTY. *One-word name.* 'Weak'
Arabic ḥatīt. This interpretation—proposed by Caquot, *RTP*, 163—is very tentative. For possible parallels see Cantineau, *Le Nabatéen*, ii. 101; Ryckmans, i. 107; Littmann, *Safaitic Inscriptions*, 318b; Noth, *IPN*, 227.

ṬBRYS. *Latin name*
Tiberius; see *ILS*, 141b. See Appendix IV, 2.4; 2.7; 2.10; 2.22.A.

ṬYṬWYLW. *Unexplained*
Starcky, *AAS*, 3 (1953), 161, thinks it is an incorrect writing for Titius.

ṬYMWN. *Greek name*
Teimōn, Timōn; see Pape, 1500, 1531. See Appendix IV, 1.9; 1.13; 1.25.F.

ṬMYS. *Greek name*
Tīmaios; see Pape, 1526. See Appendix IV, 1.9; 1.13; 1.20; 1.25.D. According to Rosenthal, *Sprache*, 20, ī is always written with Yodh. Thus we would have an exceptional spelling here. On the other hand, the identification with the Greek name Timaios may well be wrong. Other possible names would be Timios (Pape, 1528), Tamias (Pape, 1483). Cf. also ṬMS.

ṬMS. *Greek name*
See Appendix IV, 1.9; 1.25.D. For discussion and possible identifications see under ṬMYS. If ṬMS is the Greek name Timaios we would have a defective spelling for ī and ai.

Ṭ'Y. *Uncertain*
The name can be derived from the Arabic ṭaġa, 'immoderate', or from the Arabic ṭaġyā, 'young antelope'. Both interpretations involve the same Arabic root. For possible parallels see Ryckmans, i. 108; van den Branden, *Inscriptions*, 86; 'Hatra', no. 202[4].

YD'. *Hypocoristicon.* 'N.N. has known'
For discussion see under YD'NW. The Greek transcription Iadēs is attested from a bilingual text (*C* 3950).

YD/RBW. *Unexplained*
The easier reading is YDBW, which could be explained as a hypocoristicon of yd' plus divine name.

YDY. *Hypocoristicon.* 'N.N. has known'
*yd' plus divine name.
The Greek transcription Iaddaiou is attested from a bilingual text (*C* 3948). It is possible that YDY is a shortened form of ydy' plus divine name. On this see discussion under YDY'BL. For parallels and discussion see Noth, *IPN*, 181; Goldmann, *Personennamen*, 22.

YDY'. *Hypocoristicon.* 'Known by N.N.'
For discussion and parallels see YDY'BL.

YDY'BL. *Genitive compound.* 'Known by Bēl'
Aramaic pass. part. For discussion and parallels see Huffmon, *APNMT*, 209; Noth, *IPN*, 181. Cf. the Greek names Theognōstos (Pape, 488), Diognōstos (Pape, 302). See also under BWLYD' and YD'NW.

YDY'T. *Hypocoristicon.* 'Known by N.N.'
Aramaic pass. part. The corresponding fem. name to the masc. name YDY'BL.

YD'W. *Hypocoristicon.* 'N.N. has known'
For discussion and parallels see under YD'NW. Variant: YD'Y.

YD'Y. See under YD'W

YD'NW. *Hypocoristicon.* 'Nabû has known' *yd'-nbw.
Structural type: verb plus divine name; for type: divine name plus verb see under BWLYD'. In the verbal sentence names the order of subject and verb freely interchanges; for discussion see Goldmann, *Personennamen*, 10. For parallels see Dura, *Final Report V, Part I*, 62, Iadi-belus; Tallquist, *APN*, 90–1; Huffmon, *APNMT*, 209; Ryckmans, i. 231, 263; Littmann, *Safaitic Inscriptions*, 319b; Noth, *IPN*, 181; Harris, *Grammar*, 106.

YHYB'. *Hypocoristicon.* 'Given by N.N.'
Aramaic pass. part. yhb, which is only attested at Palmyra in this form, is relatively frequent at 'Hatra' (see nos. 23^2, 180 (?), 106b, 13^1). It is the name of an Edessenian bishop (*Thes. Syr.* 1567). Cf. the Latin name Donatus. Greek transcriptions: Eeibas, Iaeibas, Wuthnow, 145.

YWL. *Latin name*
Julius; shortened form.

YWL'. *Latin name*
Julius; see *ILS*, 77 ff., 206b. See Appendix IV, 2.22.B; 2.10. Defective spelling or scribal error for YWLY'. See also under YWLY'.

YWLY'. *Latin name*
Julius, Julia; see *ILS*, 77 ff., 206b. See Appendix IV, 2.22.B. On form see discussion under 'WRLY'.

YWLYWS. *Latin name*
Julius; see *ILS*, 77 ff., 206b. See Appendix IV, 2.10; 2.22.A. Unusual plene writing of ending -us. Variant: YWLYS.

YWLYS. See under YWLYWS

YML'. *Hypocoristicon*
Shortened form of YMLKW. The inscription *C* 4589, in which a certain YML' is the grandson of a YMLKW, supports the proposed interpretation (case of papponymy). For parallels and discussion see Noth, *IPN*, 28; Koehler, 'Nominalpräfix', 404–5. See also under YMLKW.

YMLKW. *Hypocoristicon.* 'N.N. shall cause to rule'
Third person sing. masc. causative. For discussion and parallels see Huffmon, *APNMT*, 230; Ryckmans, i. 127; Cantineau, *Le Nabatéen*, ii. 104; 'Hatra', nos. 110; 99, YMLYK; O.T. yamlēk (1 Chron. 4^{34}, text considered corrupt); Dura, *Final Report V, Part I*, 63, Iamlichus. Greek transcriptions: Iamblichos, Iammblichos, Wuthnow, 56. There are only a few examples of a verbal sentence with the imperfect at Palmyra. For a discussion see Caquot, *RTP*, 173.

Y'QWB. *Jewish name*
Jacob. For a discussion see Noth, *IPN*, 197.

Y'T. *Divine name used as personal name* *yǵṯ.
For discussion and parallels see Cantineau, *Le Nabatéen*, ii. 104; Ryckmans, i. 173; Bräu, Altnordarabischen', 104. Greek transcriptions: Iagouthos, Iaouthos, Wuthnow, 55, 56, 155. For discussion of the name type see under B'ŠMN. On the deity see Ryckmans, i. 16; *Religions*, 16. Variant: Y'TW.

Y'TW. *Divine name used as personal name*
Chabot, *CIS*, ii. 4324, considers the form to be a scribal mistake for Y'T. This is not necessarily so. The ending Waw could easily have been added later by analogy to hypocoristic names; cf. YRḤBWL', 'GLBWL'. For discussion see under Y'T.

YQRWR. *One-word name.* 'Frog'
Syriac yaqrûrā'. For discussion see Nöldeke, *Beiträge*, 87; *WZKM*, 4 (1890), 298, with parallels from Ethiopic and Arabic.

YR/DBW. See under YD/RBW

YRḤBWL'. *Divine name used as personal name*
The ending Aleph was added by analogy to other hypocoristic names. For a discussion of the name type see under B'ŠMN. The name is attested at Dura, *Final Report V, Part I*, 62, Iarhaboles. [YRḤB]WL' is found on a Nabataean inscription from Egypt (*BSOAS*, 16 [1954], 234). See also under Y'TW and 'GLBWL'.

YRḤY. *Hypocoristicon*
The name is most probably an abbreviated form of YRḤBWL' as the Greek translation Hēliodōros (*C* 3902) tends to show. The name is amply attested at Palmyra, but there are hardly any parallels in other languages. See Huffmon, *APNMT*, 214, for an unexplained parallel. The name occurs as YRḤW at Elephantine (Dupont-Sommer, 'L'ostracon', *RHR*, 128 [1944], 31). YRḤ'ZR is found in Ammonite (Albright, *Misc. Ubach*, 135). On the O.T. city name yᵉrīḥô see Astour, 'Benê-Iamina', *Semitica*, 9 (1959), 10–11; Vincent, 'Jéricho', *MUSJ*, 37 (1960–1), 85–90.

YRḤYB[WL']
This is undoubtedly an erroneous restoration. The better and more correct reading is YRḤY b[r... (already proposed by the editors).

YRḤYW. *Uncertain*
Two explanations are possible. Either YRḤY was not considered to be a hypocoristicon, but a divine name or a one-word name to which the hypocoristic ending Waw was added, or the Waw is a scribal error.

YRQ. *One-word name.* 'Pale, green, yellow'
Aramaic yāraq; *wrq, 'be green, yellow' (Common Semitic). For discussion and parallels see Noth, *IPN*, 225; Ryckmans,

i. 294, wrqn (ethnic name), 334, wrq (place name); Huffmon, *APNMT*, 215.

YTM'. *One-word name.* 'Orphan'
*ytm, 'orphan' (Common Semitic). For discussion and parallels see Ryckmans, i. 112; Noth, *IPN*, 231; Kraeling, *BMAP*, 4^{24}, 9^{24}; Cowley, *Papyri*, 11^{1}, 33^{4}; Galling, 178^{39a}. Cf. the O.T. name yitmāh (1 Chron. 11^{46}).

KD/RNNY. *Uncertain*
Various interpretations have been suggested. (1) Caquot, *Syria*, 39 (1962), 234, n. 3 thinks of an Akkadian name formation comparable to kidin-^{d}na-na-a (Tallquist, *APN*, 114b), 'protection from Nanā'. The divine name NNY is attested at Palmyra. (2) Cantineau, *Le Nabatéen*, ii. 108, lists KRNW (but reading uncertain; Corpus reads KRBW). K^{e}rān occurs as the name of an Edomite in the O.T. (Gen. 36^{26} = 1 Chron. 1^{41}). Ryckmans, i. 263, lists the Thamudic name KRNLB. The meaning of KRN in all these cases is unknown. One would have to assume a double hypocoristic ending -an, -ay for KRNNY, if it was to be derived from KRN. (3) In the Talmud, *Baba Bathra*, 91a, the legendary name of Abraham's grandmother is karn^{e}bô, 'lamb of Nebô'. Could KRNNY signify 'lamb of Nanai'?

KHYLW. *Uncertain*
The editor of the *Corpus* (*C* 4109) suggests the diminutive form of Arabic kahl, 'mature age'; see Cantineau, *Le Nabatéen*, ii. 106; Wüstenfeld, *Register*, 268, Kuhayl. Littmann, *Nabataean Inscriptions*, 50, no. 55, followed by Caquot, *RTP*, 174, opts for an interpretation of KHYLW as the Aramaic pass. part. of the verb k^{e}hal, 'be able'. The Greek transcription Cheilou, from a bilingual text (*Inv. X*, 54), tends to support this interpretation. Cf. also Cheeilos, Wuthnow, 120. Variant: KHYLY.

KHYLY. See under KHYLW

KWMY. *Uncertain*
For a parallel see Cantineau, *Le Nabatéen*, ii. 106. One might very tentatively propose to derive the name from Arabic kaum, 'heap, pile, hill' (Dozy, 2, 501). The meaning still remains uncertain.

KYLY. *One-word name.* 'Land-surveyor'
Syriac kayyālā'. Ingholt's suggestion (*Berytus*, 5 [1938], 115) that KYLY is a contraction of KHYLW/Y or of KLBW is without basis. Such an abbreviation would seem to be anomalous. For a parallel see *Thes. Syr.* 1723. For semantic parallels see Noth, *IPN*, 231. See also KYLYWN.

KYLYWN. *One-word name.* 'Land-surveyor' (dimin.)
Cf. KYLY to which the diminutive ending -ōn was added (Barth, *Nominalbildung*, 318, par. 194c; Brockelmann, *GVG*, i. 388, par. 210).

KYTWT. *Unexplained*
Various suggestions have been offered, but none of them is really convincing. Ingholt, *Berytus*, 5 (1938), 115, derives the name from the root ktt, which is found in Safaitic (Ryckmans, i. 116) and in Nabataean (*CIS*, ii. 311 B). But it is difficult to conceive what kind of noun formation this would be, were the name derived from ktt. Caquot, *RTP*, 174, thinks of an abstract ending -ūt added to an unattested root *kyt, *kwt.

KLB'. *One-word name.* 'Dog'
*kalb, 'dog' (Common Semitic).
For discussion and parallels see Huffmon, *APNMT*, 221; Ryckmans, i. 114; Cantineau, *Le Nabatéen*, ii. 107; Harris, *Grammar*, 111; Gordon, *UT*, Glossary no. 1233; Noth, *IPN*, 230; *Thes. Syr.* 1743, bar kalbā', name of an Edessene nobleman; Nöldeke, *Beiträge*, 79; Josephus, *Contra Apionem*, i. 157, Chelbēs. Greek transcriptions: Chalbas, Chalbēs, Wuthnow, 119. Variant: KLBY.

KLBY. See under KLB'

KMR'. *One-word name.* 'Priest'
For discussion and parallels see Cantineau, *Le Nabatéen*, ii. 107; *Thes. Syr.* 1759, Abû-l'Faraj bar kamār, name of a Syrian patriarch. The name is found in epigraphic Syriac (*BSOAS*, 20 [1957], 519). Bar Kamrā' occurs conjecturally in a contract from Edessa, dated 243 A.D., which was discovered at Dura-Europos (Torrey, *Zeitschrift für Semitistik*, 10 [1935], 36^{6}, 39). It is also possible that KMR' is the Arabic word kamar, 'glans penis', which occurs as personal name; see Littmann, *Safaitic Inscriptions*, 227, no. 971.

KSP'. *One-word name.* 'Silver'
For parallels see Tallquist, *APN*, 113a; Stamm, *ANG*, 301–2. For similar names see Noth, *IPN*, 223.

K'B[W]. *One-word name.* 'Heel'
Arabic ka'b. For parallels see Cantineau, *Le Nabatéen*, ii. 107; Ryckmans, i. 115. Wüstenfeld, *Register*, 261, mentions several Arabs with the name Ka'b.

KPTWT. *Uncertain*
The Greek transcription Chaphath[o]uthou (*RB*, 39 [1930], 544) tends to show that this is a qaṭal type noun with the abstract ending -ūt. The root is only attested in Aramaic and Syriac, kāpat, 'tie, knot'. The interpretation was proposed by Caquot, *RTP*, 174.

KRḤ. *Unexplained*
The reading KDḤ is possible. Lidzbarski, *Ephemeris*, 3, 144, cites the name Kaudaḥ given in Qāmûs, i. 243. But this would reflect a spelling *KWDḤ; cf. DWḤY, ZWR for spelling.

KRYSTWS. *Greek name*
Chrysanthos; see Pape, 1692. See Appendix

IV, 1.2; 1.8; 1.13; 1.15; 1.23; 1.24; 1.25.D. The vowel-less N in Greek words is usually left unexpressed; see Rosenthal, *Sprache*, 40.

KRM. See under DRM

KR/DNNY. See under KD/RNNY

KRSM'. *Unexplained*
The name seems to be non-Semitic

LWY. *Jewish name*
Levi. On this name and its etymology see Albright, *Archaeology and the Religion of Israel*, 204–5, no. 4. See also Huffmon, *APNMT*, 225 f.; de Vaux, *Ancient Israel*, 369–71.

LWY'. *Uncertain*
Goldmann, *Personennamen*, 26, following the *Corpus*, takes the name to be the fem. of LWY. It is more likely, however, that this is the Latin name Livia; see ILS, 91.

[LWQY]WS. *Latin name*
Lucius; see *ILS*, 92 f. See Appendix IV, 2.2; 2.10; 2.22.A. The restoration is based on the Greek text (bilingual inscription). Variant: LWQYS.

LWQYS. See under [LWQY]WS

LWQL'. *Latin name*
Lucilla; see *ILS*, 210a. See Appendix IV, 2.2; 2.22.B.

LMLK'. *Prepositional phrase.* 'Belonging to Malka'
For structural parallels see under LŠMŠ.

LQY. *Latin name*
Lucius; see *ILS*, 92b, 210a. See Appendix IV, 2.2; 2.10; 2.22.A. Cf. the variant LWQY (*KAI*, 118^2).

LQYŠW. *One-word name.* 'Ripening late'
Arabic liqqīs. The Greek transcription Lekeisou is attested from a bilingual text (*Syria*, 19 [1938], 76). No other occurrences of the name are known.

LQYNS. *Latin name*
Licinius; see *ILS*, 89 f. See Appendix IV, 2.2; 2.10; 2.14; 2.22.A.

LRMN. *Prepositional phrase.* 'Belonging to Ramman'
For structural parallels see under LŠMŠ. RMN is an Aramaean deity. 2 Kings 5^{18} alludes to a temple of Rimmôn at Damascus; cf. also the names Ṭab-rimmôn (1 Kings 15^{18}) and Hadad-rimmôn (Zech. 12^{11}). See also *CIS*, ii. 117, for the old Aramaic name RMNNTN. Rummān is a Sabaean deity (Höfner in *Wörterbuch*, 525; Ryckmans, i. 32).

LŠMŠ. *Prepositional phrase.* 'Belonging to Šamaš'
For parallels and discussion see Noth, *IPN*, 32, 153; Prov. 31^1, lᵉmû'ēl; Nöldeke, *Beiträge*, 104–5; Ryckmans, i. 243, L'LYN; 'Hatra', no. 22, LŠGL', no. 155, LṬWBN (uncertain whether this is a divine name); Huffmon, *APNMT*, 223, La-a-mu-ri-im. In south Arabic Lamedh plus personal name is also found; see Ryckmans, i. 264; Caskel, *Lihyan*, 149, LZDT; *Muséon*, 64 (1951), 90, B, LḪLD. See also LRMN, LMLK'.

LŠ[MŠ]'. *Prepositional phrase.* 'Belonging to Šamaš'
Generalized ending Aleph has been added. For discussion see under LŠMŠ. Variants: LŠMŠW, LŠMŠY.

LŠMŠW. See under LŠ[MŠ]'

LŠMŠY. See under LŠ[MŠ]'

M/QBWRM. *Unexplained*

MHWY. *Uncertain*
It could be a Parthian name, Māhūī; see Justi, *Namenbuch*, 187. A derivation from Arabic mahw, 'pearls', is also possible. For parallels and discussion see Littmann, *Safaitic Inscriptions*, 323a.

MHR. *One-word name.* 'Colt, foal'
Arabic muhr. Teixidor, *Sumer*, 18 (1962), 64, takes the name to be a hypocoristicon of MHRDT. For parallels to the proposed interpretation see Ryckmans, i. 124; Nöldeke, *Beiträge*, 81. See also Huffmon, *APNMT*, 229 f. Variant: MHRW.

MHRDD. *Persian name*
Mithradāta; see Justi, *Namenbuch*, 209. Variant: MHRDT.

MHRDT. *Persian name*
Variant of MHRDD (see above). Name of a king of Characene; see Nodelman, 'Preliminary', 121; *Inv. X*, 38.

MHRW. *One-word name.* 'Colt, foal'
Starcky, *PNO*, 155, takes the name to be a hypocoristicon of MHRDT. For proposed interpretation see parallels and discussion under MHR.

MW'L'. *One-word name.* 'Refuge'
Arabic wa'ala; act. part. IV; cf. Arabic mau'il. For parallels see Cantineau, *Le Nabatéen*, ii. 88; Ryckmans, i. 75;. Greek transcription: Mauelou, Wuthnow, 75. Cf. the Phoenician names with GR.

MWDL'. *Unexplained*
The form seems to require an explanation from the Arabic. The form is most likely the act. part. IV of a root wdl. Wahrmund, 2, 1171, mentions Arabic wadala, 'den Schlauch zum Buttern schütteln'. The meaning seems unsuitable for a personal name.

MWS'. *Jewish name*
Cf. the O.T. form mōšeh (Noth, *IPN*, 63). One would expect Š instead of S, but the pronunciation and orthography are probably

based on the Arabic mūsā. Greek transcriptions: Mousēs, Mousē, Mouses, Wuthnow, 79.

MZB'. *One-word name.* 'Sold'
Aramaic part. pa''el; cf. Aramaic z^eban. Shortened form of MZBT' or MZBN'. For discussion see under MZBN'. Variant: MZBW.

MZBW. See under MZB'

MZBN'. *One-word name.* 'Sold'
Aramaic z^eban; part. pa''el (passive). The Greek transcription Mezzab[anēs] from a bilingual text (*Inv. IX*, 26) supports the interpretation. Goldmann, *Personennamen*, 8, makes MZBN' a hypocoristicon of an unattested *MZBN'L, which seems very unlikely. Cf. the O.T. name mākîr (Noth, *IPN*, 232). There is no reason for claiming a Persian origin of MZBN' as Caquot, *RTP*, 174, tentatively does. See also: MZB', MZBW, MZBT'.

MZBT'. *One-word name.* 'Sold'
Aramaic z^eban; pass. part. pa''el. *mzbnt' > mzbtt'. The name occurs as masc. in *Inv. VIII*, 115². For discussion and parallels see under MZBN'.

M/QZY. *Unexplained*
Neither of the readings is attested anywhere. Cf. Samaria Ostracon no. 49, MZY, but the reading itself is doubtful.

MḤLMW. *One-word name.* 'Dreamy'
*ḥlm, 'dream' (Common Semitic, except Akk). Arabic act. part. II. The name is also attested in Lidzbarski, *Krugaufschriften*, 8, no. 14c. The name is frequent in Safaitic. See also Ibn Doreid 174, 215.

MḤRBZN. *Unexplained*
Probably a Persian name.

MṬN. *Unexplained*
No parallels anywhere.

M/QYD/RL'. *Unexplained*

MYD/RN. *Uncertain*
Ryckmans, i. 125, lists a Thamudic name MYD, which he explains from the Arabic root māda, 'feel giddy'. The reading MYRN is supported by parallels from Thamudic and Nabataean (Ryckmans, i. 126; Cantineau, *Le Nabatéen*, ii. 113). Arabic māra, 'supply, provide'. In both cases the name is augmented by the ending -ān.

MYṬQ'. *Unexplained*
The transcription does not correspond with the name Mētakos (Justi, *Namenbuch*, 204). ē is usually not written with Yodh; see Rosenthal, *Sprache*, 20.

MYK'. *Hypocoristicon.* 'Who is like El?'
Hebrew name. Shortened form of MYK'L. Interrogative sentence. For discussion and parallels see Noth, *IPN*, 144; Diringer, *Iscrizioni*, 190; Cowley, *Papyri*, 22⁶⁴; Kraeling, *BMAP*, 1^2,10. See also: MKBL.

MYR/DN. See under MYD/RN

MYŠ'. *One-word name.* 'Kind of tree'
Arabic mays. The exact species of the tree is unknown. Dalman, *Wörterbuch*, 235, says it is a celtis australis; Payne-Smith, *Thes. Syr.*, 2098, identifies the tree as quercus coccifera. For parallels see Cantineau, *Le Nabatéen*, ii. 113 (reading uncertain); Littmann, *Safaitic Inscriptions*, 324a. Aramaic status emphaticus ending has been added. see also MYŠN.

MYŠN. *One-word name.* 'Tree'
For discussion see under MYŠ'. On the ending -an see Littmann, *Pedersen Festschrift*, 194–5; Gómez, *Arabica*, 1 (1954), 129.

MYT'. *One-word name.* 'Tender'
Arabic mayyiṯ. The name occurs only once as a personal name, otherwise as a tribal name. Cantineau, *Syria*, 14 (1933), 187, explained the tribal name BNY MYT' as 'sons of death', understanding by this a corporation that was in charge of burying the dead. The attestation of MYT' as personal name invalidates Cantineau's theory. The tribe is probably named after the ancestor. The name is most likely to be derived from Arabic mayyiṯ, which occurs as a personal name in south Arabic (Ryckmans, i. 126). This interpretation was first suggested by Ingholt (see Caquot, *RTP*, 174). The Greek transcription Mithēnōn is attested from a bilingual text (*Inv. IX*, 20).

MK. *Uncertain*
It could be a one-word name derived from Aramaic māk, 'lowly, humble'. For semantic parallels see Noth, *IPN*, 228. Caquot, *RTP*, 156, considers MK to be an orthographic variant of MKY (see below). According to Littmann, *Safaitic Inscriptions*, 324a, MK is a hypocoristicon of MLK.

MKBL. *Interrogative sentence.* 'Who is like Bēl?'
Caquot, *RTP*, 175, following Ingholt, *Berytus*, 1 (1934), 38, takes MKBL to be the assimilated form of MLKBL, basing his conclusion on a Greek inscription from Syria, where the name Machchi[bē]los occurs. A better solution is to take MKBL as an assimilated form of *mn-k-bl, 'who is like Bēl?'. For parallels to the assimilation of N to K see Brockelmann, *GVG*, i. 175, pars. bb, dd, ee. This interpretation receives support from a name attested at 'Hatra' (no. 157), MKMRTN, 'who is like our lady?'. This name can hardly be interpreted in any other way. For parallels see Tallquist, *APN*, 124 f.; Bresciani, 'Hermopoli', 373¹⁴, MKBNT. See also under MYK' and the following names: MK, MKY, MKN', MK''.

MKY. *Hypocoristicon.* 'Who is like Bēl?' *mn-k-bl.
For parallels see Cowley, *Papyri*, 1[11]; Harris, *Grammar*, 117; Diringer, *Iscrizioni*, 141; Cantineau, *Le Nabatéen*, ii. 113 (reading uncertain). Noth, *IPN*, 232, proposes for the O.T. mākî that it is a hypocoristicon of mākîr. For further discussion see under MKBL.

MKN'. *Hypocoristicon.* 'Who is like Nabû?' *mn-k-nbw.
Cantineau, *Inscriptions palmyréniennes*, 26, thinks of a Persian etymology. For discussion see under MKBL.

MKSMWS, MKSMS, MKŠM. *Latin name*
Maximus; see *ILS*, 214 f. See Appendix IV, 2.3; 2.13; 2.22.A; 2.23.A. The ending is written plene in the first case, defectively in the second, and completely left out in the third instance. Latin X, Greek ksi is usually transcribed with KS, but there are two cases where KŠ is used: MKŠM and 'KŠDR' (*C* 4171[2]).

MK''. *Hypocoristicon.* 'Who is like Athe?' *mn-k-'th.
Starcky, *Mélanges A. Robert*, 374, interprets the name as a shortened form of *mlk-'qb/'n', 'Malka has protected/answered'. None of these names occur anywhere. In footnote 7 he mentions the possibility of the interpretation adopted here. For discussion and parallels see under MKBL.

MKŠM. See under MKSMWS.

MKTŠ. *Unexplained*
No parallels can be found.

ML
This is an abbreviation for one of the following names: ML', MLY, MLKW.

ML'. *Hypocoristicon*
Shortened form of MLKW. A certain ML' is the grandson of a MLKW, hence one may assume papponymy (*Inv. XI*, 55). The Greek transcription Malēs is attested from a bilingual text (*C* 3959). Variant: MLY. For discussion see under MLKW.

MLWK'. *One-word name.* 'Counsellor'
Aram., Syr. mālôkā'. The Greek transcription Malōchas is attested from a bilingual text (*C* 3914). Qātōl type noun (nomen agentis). A parallel, MLWKW (reading uncertain), is found in Nabataean (*BSOAS*, 15 [1953], 22).

MLY. *Hypocoristicon*
No Greek transcription is available. For discussion see under ML'.

MLK. *One-word name.* 'King'
*mlk, 'King' (Common Semitic).
For parallels and discussion see Ryckmans, i. 127; Cantineau, *Le Nabatéen*, ii. 114; Wüstenfeld, *Register*, 281–5, Mālik. Greek transcription: Malik, Malichos, Wuthnow, 70.

MLK'. *Hypocoristicon*
This is probably a shortened form of some name composed with mlk, 'king', such as MLK'L, MLKBL. On the other hand, it is quite conceivable that MLK' (and the variants MLKW/Y) was originally a name formed with the divine name MLK and whose second name element has been suppressed. See also Caquot, *RTP*, 175, under MLKW. The Greek and Latin renderings of the name are: Malichos, Malchos, and Malichus, Malchus; cf. John 18[10]. Variants: MLKW, MLKY.

MLK'L. *Nominal sentence.* 'El is king'
For discussion and parallels see Ryckmans, i. 234; Noth, *IPN*, 118, 140; Dura, *Final Report V, Part I*, 62, Malachelas.

MLKBL. *Nominal sentence.* 'Bēl is king'
For parallels see under MLK'L.

MLKW. *Hypocoristicon*
The name occurs at 'Hatra' as MLYKW (no. 146[2]). For discussion see under MLK'.

MLKWS'
To the Latin name Malchus, originally derived from the Semitic MLKW, is added the Aramaic status emphaticus ending. The interpretation was proposed by Euting, *SBAW*, 1887, 414–15, no. 106.

MLKY. *Hypocoristicon*
For discussion see under MLK'.

MLKT. *One-word name.* 'Queen'
For parallels see Ryckmans, i. 127; Littmann, *Safaitic Inscriptions*, 324b. Greek transcriptions: Malichathos, Malichathē, Wuthnow, 70.

MND/RYMN'. *Unexplained*
Probably non-Semitic.

MNDRS. *Greek name*
Menandros; see Pape, 895. See Appendix IV, 1.15; 1.23; 1.25.D. Caquot's other suggestion (*RTP*, 167) Mēnodōros (Pape, 916) is questionable. One would expect *MNDWRS, although it is true that ō is not always written with a vowel letter.

M/QN'[. *Unexplained*
The reading is incomplete.

M'ZYN. *One-word name.* 'Goat'
Arabic ma'z, ma'az. For parallels see Ryckmans, i. 130; Nöldeke, *Beiträge*, 82. On the ending -īn see Cantineau, *Arabe de Palmyre*, i. 189, d.

M'Y'. *One-word name.* 'Intestines, bowels'
Aramaic m^e'î, Arabic ma'y. See van den Branden, *Histoire*, 59, on the various names of the body used as personal names.

M'YN'. *One-word name.* 'Belly, womb'
Aramaic ma'yānā'. Ingholt's interpretation, *Berytus*, 5 (1938), 132, of M'YN' and M'YNT as being derived from Arabic ma'na,

'be keen, intent', cannot be upheld. The Arabic forms of this root suggest a borrowing from the Aramaic.

M'YNT. *One-word name.* 'Belly, womb'
For discussion see under M'YN'.

M'YR'. *One-word name.* 'Raider'
Arabic muġīr. For parallels see Cantineau, *Le Nabatéen*, ii. 117; Ryckmans, i. 174; 'Hatra', no. 191[1]. Greek transcription: Moairos, Mogeairou, Wuthnow, 77.

M'YTW. *One-word name.* 'Helper'
Arabic muġīṯ. For parallels see Cantineau, *Le Nabatéen*, ii. 117; Ryckmans, i. 173. Greek transcription: Moeithos, Mogitos, Wuthnow, 77. M'T' is found in epigraphic Syriac and could be a variant (*BSOAS*, 16 [1954], 20, no. 5[3]). No composite names with M'YT are attested anywhere. Variant: M'YTY.

M'YTY. See under M'YTW.

M'N. *Divine name used as personal name*
For parallels to this type of name see under B'ŠMN. The name is well known in Arabic; see Wüstenfeld, *Register*, 286. Found at Dura, *Final Report V*, *Part I*, 62, Mannas. Greek transcription: Manos, Wuthnow, 72.

M'N'. *Divine name used as personal name*
For parallels see 'Hatra', nos. 12, 43[2], 79[13]; Cantineau, *Le Nabatéen*, ii. 117. The name is found in epigraphic Syriac (*BSOAS*, 16 [1954], 19, no. 4[2], with further references). It is the name of two Syrian Christian theologians in the fifth century (Baumstark, *Geschichte*, 105).

M'NW. *Divine name used as personal name*
For parallels see 'Hatra', no. 189; Cantineau, *Le Nabatéen*, ii. 117; Ryckmans, i. 130. The name is found in epigraphic Syriac (*BSOAS*, 16 [1954], 20, no. 5[3]). It was the name of several kings of Edessa (*Thes. Syr.* 2186). Dio Cassius (Book 68, 22) mentions a Mannus as king of 'Arabia' during Trajan's time. The endings Waw, Yodh, Aleph, which are found with M'N, are extended by analogy to hypocoristic names. Variants: M'N', M'NY.

M'NY. *Divine name used as personal name*
For discussion and parallels see under M'NW.

MPL[YS]
The restoration of the last two letters is based on the Greek text of the inscription (*C* 4160). The Greek name reads Mophleou. The name is unexplained, and the restoration may well be wrong.

MQWL'
Chabot, *CIS*, ii. 4094[2], states that de Vogüé's copy reads MQWN', but that the better reading is MQWL'. (The reading cannot be verified, because the photograph is illegible.) Chabot's connection of the name with Greek Mikkylos, Makkalos is untenable for orthographic reasons. Y is always written with Yodh and never with Waw. The reading MQWN' on the other hand finds good correspondents in the Greek names Mēkōn (Pape, 913) and Mikōn (Pape, 924).

MQY. *Hypocoristicon*
Shortened form of MQYMW. In one of the inscriptions a certain MQY is the grandson of MQYMW (case of papponymy). The Greek transcription Makkai[ou] is attested from a bilingual text (*C* 3910). On the name type see Goldmann, *Personennamen*, 22.

MQYḤY. *Uncertain*
Lidzbarski, *Ephemeris*, 3, 142, explains the name as 'hartnäckiger Weigerer', citing Arabic muqīḥ. But his etymology of the word is obscure. However, there is an Arabic root qāḥa, 'suppurate', from which the name could be derived (Dozy, 2, 429; Barthélemy, iv. 694).

MQYM. *Hypocoristicon.* 'He who causes to arise'
Arabic act. part. IV. For discussion see under MQYMW.

MQYMW. *Hypocoristicon.* 'He who causes to arise'
Arabic act. part. IV. *qwm, 'rise' (Common Semitic, except Akk.). For discussion and parallels see Cantineau, *Le Nabatéen*, ii. 142; Ryckmans, i. 189, 247; 'Hatra', no. 60, MQYMŠMŠ; Huffmon, *APNMT*, 259. The name is found in epigraphic Syriac (*BSOAS*, 16 [1954], 29, no. 14[3]; Moritz, *Syrische Inschriften*, 167). The name occurs likewise in a Jewish inscription from *Beth She'arim*, i, p. 136 (MQYM). The Latin transcription Mocimus and the Greek transcription Mokeimos are attested from Dura, *Final Report V*, *Part I*, 63. See also MQYM, MQYMY, MQMW, MQYMT.

MQYMY. *Hypocoristicon*
For discussion see under variant MQYMW.

MQYMT. *Hypocoristicon*
The name occurs as masc. and fem. in the same inscription (*Inv. VIII*, 96[1,5]). For discussion see under MQYMW.

MQYN'. *Unexplained*
The Arabic verb qāna is only attested very late (Dozy, 2, 434) and most likely a secondary form in Arabic.

MQMW. *Hypocoristicon*
This is a defective writing for MQYMW or just a scribal error; cf. Safaitic MQM (Ryckmans, i. 189). In epigraphic Syriac the same form is found (Segal, *Ana. Studies*, 3 [1953], 104[13]). For discussion see under MQYMW.

MR'. *One-word name.* 'The bitter one'
Aramaic mar. For parallels see Littmann,

Safaitic Inscriptions, 326a; cf. Ruth 1[20]: qᵉre'nā lî mārā'. See also under MRH.

MRBN'. *Uncertain*
The form creates some difficulties. The Mem could be taken as dittography of the previous line. RBN' might then be a hypocoristicon of *RB-NBW, 'great is Nabû'. For parallels see under RB'L. If one retains the Mem one would have a form of the part. pa''el of rbh, mᵉrabbē, 'he who raises, rears', plus an unknown second element n'-, which might be a hypocoristic form for NBW: 'Nabû raises, rears'; cf. MQYMŠMŠ ('Hatra', no. 60). This last explanation was suggested by H. B. Huffmon.

MRD. *One-word name.* 'Rebel'
*mrd, 'rebel' (Heb., Aram., Syr., Arabic). Arabic act. part. I. For parallels see Ryckmans, i. 132.

MRH. *One-word name.* 'The bitter one'
For discussion see under MR'. Chabot, *CIS*, ii. 4550, takes the form to be masc. But it is hard to conceive what form this would be if it were masc. It is better to explain the name as fem. That the mother's name should be given in the genealogy is unusual, but seems not without parallels (cf. *C* 4582).

MRWN'. *One-word name.* 'Lord' (dimin.)
Aramaic mar. For names from the same root see Ryckmans, i. 132. For similar name forms see Goldmann, *Personennamen*, 26. The name is attested in epigraphic Syriac (*BSOAS*, 22 [1959], 39, no. 10[2], with further references). Greek transcription: Marōnas, Wuthnow, 73.

MRY'. *Uncertain*
The name is most probably a derivative of the word marā'; cf. the Syriac status emphaticus form māryā', 'the lord'. For discussion see Starcky, *PNO*, 174, no. 79.

MRYWN. *Greek name*
Mariōn; see Pape, 862. See Appendix IV, 1.16; 1.25.F. 'i' is sometimes written plene; see Rosenthal, *Sprache*, 15.

MRYM. *Jewish name*
O.T. miryām, N.T. Mariam. For discussion see Noth, *IPN*, 250. The name is frequent in Talmudic literature.

MRYNS. *Latin name*
Marinus; see *ILS*, 213a. See Appendix IV, 2.11; 2.13; 2.22.A.

MRN'. *One-word name.* 'Lord' (dimin.)
The name is augmented by the suffix -ān and the Aramaic status emphaticus ending (Goldmann, *Personennamen*, 26). It is possible that MRN' is a defective writing for MRWN'. For some examples where ō is written defectively see Cantineau, *Grammaire*, 57.

MRQ'. *Uncertain*
This is either the Latin name Marcus with the Aramaic status emphaticus ending, or the name is to be derived from the Aramaic root mrq, 'polish, clean', adjective mārqā', 'yellowish, pale'. For similar names see Noth, *IPN*, 225. See also under MRQY.

MRQWS, MRQS. *Latin name*
Marcus; see *ILS*, 97a, 213a. See Appendix IV, 2.2; 2.13; 2.22.A. See also under MRQ'.

MRQY. *Uncertain*
It could be a variant of MRQ', 'yellowish, pale'. In that case one would have to assume that the Aleph in MRQ' was not considered the status emphaticus ending.

MRQYNWS. *Latin name*
Marcianus; see *ILS*, 212 f. See Appendix IV, 2.2; 2.8; 2.10; 2.13; 2.22.A.

MRQL'. *Latin name*
Marcellus; see *ILS*, 212b. See Appendix IV, 2.2; 2.13; 2.22.A.

MRQS. See under MRQWS

MRT'. *One-word name.* 'Lady'
Aramaic mārtā'. For parallels see Ryckmans, i. 132; *Thes. Syr.* 2233. Greek transcription: Martha, Marthas, Marthe, Wuthnow, 72. Cf. the N.T. name Martha.

MRTHWN. *One-word name.* 'Their lady'
The masc. equivalent MRHWN is found at 'Hatra' (no. 43) and as name of a bishop, marhūn (*Thes. Syr.* 2220).

MRTY. *One-word name.* 'My lady'
For a parallel see Cantineau, *Le Nabatéen*, ii. 118.

MRTYN'. *Uncertain*
Perhaps the Syriac word martyānā', 'admonisher, monitor'.

MŠY. *One-word name.* 'Evening'
Arabic misy, musy. Cf. the O.T. name mûšî, mūšî. Contra Caquot's interpretation, *RTP*, 161, which is based on a wrong translation of the Arabic masā.

MŠKW. *Hypocoristicon.* 'N.N. has taken possession'
Aramaic mᵉšak. *mšk plus divine name. For parallels see Cantineau, *Le Nabatéen*, ii. 118; Ryckmans, i. 129; Littmann, *Safaitic Inscriptions*, 325a. Greek transcription: Masechos, Wuthnow, 74.

MŠLM. *One-word name*
Arabic act. part. II or IV (uncertain). For parallels see Cantineau, *Le Nabatéen*, ii. 151; Ryckmans, i. 150; Wüstenfeld, *Register*, 325 ff. Greek transcription: Moslemos, Wuthnow, 79. It is uncertain whether the name Muslim is already found in pre-Islamic times. If not, the name has to be read musallam, 'unimpaired'. Noth, *IPN*, 174, takes šlm to mean 'restore, repay' (in a

juridical sense). In view of the great influence that Arabic had at Palmyra, the name is best explained from the Arabic and not from the north-west Semitic. Ḥlp is used at Palmyra to express the idea of restitution (see under ḤLP').

MT'. *Hypocoristicon.* 'Gift of N.N.'
The name is probably a shortened form of MTBWL. The variant MTY is found in epigraphic Syriac (*BSOAS*, 16 [1954], 23, no. 7[1]). Cf. the N.T. name Maththaios (Luke 6[15]). Greek transcription: Maththa, Wuthnow, 69.

MTBWL. *Genitive compound.* 'Gift of Bôl'
For parallels and discussion see Noth, *IPN*, 170; Cowley, *Papyri*, 22[77]; Harris, *Grammar*, 108–9; Ugar., *PRU*, ii. 35[17], 72[11]; Gröndahl, *Personennamen*, 147. The name occurs as gentilic and as personal name. The Greek transcription Manth(a)bōleiō[n] is attested from a bilingual text (*C* 3925). See also MT', MTN', MTNY, MTNW.

MTN'. *Hypocoristicon.* 'Gift of N.N.'
It could be a shortened form of *mtnbw, 'gift of Nabû'. For discussion see under MTBWL. Variants: MTNY, MTNW.

MTNW. See under MTN'.

MTNY. See under MTN'

N'RY. *Divine name used as personal name*
According to Starcky, *AAS*, 3 (1953), 161, N'RY = N'RY with weakening of the pharyngal. But the examples that Starcky cites are due to dissimilation (Rosenthal, *Sprache*, 35). Starcky's explanation, however, receives some support from other inscriptional material. In Syriac inscriptions from the second and third century A.D. found at Sumatar we find 'BDNḤY (= 'BDNḤY) side by side with 'BDŠMŠ in the same inscription (*BSOAS*, 16 [1954], 29, no. 14[5,8]). In an Aramaic inscription 'BDNBW appears (*RES* 962, reading doubtful) and in Phoenician 'BDB'L (*RES* 902). The evidence, however, is not sufficient to establish Starcky's interpretation. Another possible explanation would be to consider N'RY to be a variant of NHRY. The change '/H, however, is only attested at the beginning of words (Rosenthal, *Sprache*, 35).

In Safaitic inscriptions a god Nâr, Nûr is attested (Ryckmans, i. 23; Höfner in *Wörterbuch*, 457; *CIS*, v. 743, 1970, N'R). N'RY then probably presents the Safaitic word nâr augmented by the ending Yodh. The spelling with Aleph is somewhat difficult, because long internal Aleph is never written. It would be an exception here.

NBWGDY. *Nominal sentence.* 'Nabû is my fortune'
For discussion and parallels see under B'LTG'.

NBWD'. *Hypocoristicon.* 'Nabû has known'
*nbw-yd'.
For discussion and parallels see under BWLYD'.

NBWD'. *Hypocoristicon.* 'Nabû has known'
*nbw-yd'.
For discussion and parallels see under BWLYD'.

NBWZ'. *Hypocoristicon.* 'Nabû has given'
*nbw-zbd.
For discussion and parallels see under BWLZBD.

NBWZBD. *Verbal sentence with the perfect.* 'Nabû has given'
For parallels see under BWLZBD.

NBWYD'. *Verbal sentence with the perfect.* 'Nabû has known'
For parallels and discussion see under BWLYD'.

NBWL'. *Hypocoristicon.* 'Nabû is god'
*nbw-'l.
For discussion and parallels see Tallquist, *APN*, 267a; Ryckmans, i. 224, WD'L; Cantineau, *Le Nabatéen*, ii. 117, *sub voce* M'NW; Noth, *IPN*, 140; *CIS*, ii. 154[5], NBW'LH, from Elephantine. The Greek transcription Neboulas is attested from a bilingual text (*C* 4124). Variant: NBWLH.

NBWLH. See under NBWL'

[NB]WM'. *Hypocoristicon.* 'Nabû is lord'
*nbw-mr.
For discussion and parallels see under [NB]WMR.

NBWMW'. *Unexplained*
This is probably a name composed of the divine name Nabû and an unknown second element MW', which can hardly be a verbal root. It is tempting to take NBWMW' as a shortened form of NBWMR with a double hypocoristic ending: Aleph, Waw.

[NBWMY]
For discussion see under [NB]WM'. The name is restored from the Greek transcription [N]e[b]oumaion (*Inv. IX*, 30).

[NB]WMR. *Nominal sentence.* 'Nabû is lord'
For parallels see Tallquist, *APN*, 7a, Adad-bēl, 146b, Nabū-bēl; Ugar., *PRU*, ii. 24[4a].

NBWŠY. *Hypocoristicon.* 'Nabû is (my) stronghold'
*nbw-šwr.
For discussion and parallels see under BLŠWR.

NBY. *Unexplained*

NGMW. *One-word name.* 'Star'
Arabic najm. For parallels see Cantineau, *Le Nabatéen*, ii. 120; Ryckmans, i. 136; Wüstenfeld, *Register*, 333, Najm. Najm is

the Arabic name for the Pleiades. The name 'Abd-Najm indicates that they were considered deities (Wüstenfeld, *Register*, 30). Greek transcription: Nagmos, Wuthnow, 80.

NDB'L. *Verbal sentence with the perfect.* 'God has granted'
For discussion and parallels see Tallquist, *APN*, 296a; Diringer, *Iscrizioni*, 189; Nimrud ostracon, *Iraq*, 19 (1957), 140, I[4]; Noth, *IPN*, 193.

NHR'. *One-word name.* 'Day, light'
Arabic nahār, Aram. nah^{a}rā'. For parallels see Ryckmans, i. 137; Wüstenfeld, *Register*, 333, Nahār; 'Hatra', nos. 139[1], 198[1], NYHR'. Greek transcription: Narou, Wuthnow, 81. NHR is a deity attested in Safaitic, and it is conceivable that NHR' represents the shortened form of a theophorous name; cf. the personal names NHRWHB, NHR'L, NHRBYT (Ryckmans, i. 236, 225, 221). On the deity see Höfner in *Wörterbuch*, 456; Ryckmans, i. 22.

NHTWM'. *Unexplained*
The reading of the second and third letter might well be wrong. The Waw can also be read as Yodh.

NWRBL. *Nominal sentence.* 'Bēl is light'
Structural type: noun plus divine name; for type: divine name plus noun see under BWLNWR. For discussion and parallels see Ryckmans, i. 236; Ugar., *PRU*, iii. 252; *PRU*, iv. 248, nuri(?)-^{il}nergal; Gröndahl, *Personennamen*, 165–6. Noth, *IPN*, 167–8; Phoenician, *CIS*, i. 1 (= *KAI*, 10[1]). See also NWRY, NWR'TH.

NWRY. *Hypocoristicon.* 'N.N. is light'
Nûrî is found as personal name in the *Talmud* (Erubin, iv. 5). For discussion and parallels see under NWRBL.

NWR'TH. *Nominal sentence.* 'Athe is light'
For discussion and parallels see under NWRBL.

NḤ'. See under NḤY.

NḤWR. *One-word name.* 'Snorer'
Aramaic, Syriac n^{e}ḥar. Arabic naḫar. Qātōl type noun (Brockelmann, *GVG*, i. 343, par. 128; Cantineau, *Grammaire*, 107–8). No parallels to the name. Cf. perhaps ḤŠY (see above).

NḤY. *Divine name used as personal name*
In Syriac inscriptions of the second and third century A.D. the names 'BDNḤY and 'MTNḤY occur (*BSOAS*, 16 [1954], 29, no. 14[5,12]). On the basis of these two names it seems clear that NḤY is a deity or a deified hero. Pseudo-Meliton mentions an Elamite goddess NḤ. (For a good discussion of the reading and the source see Leroy, *Syria*, 34 [1957], 324 ff.). Nuḥai, god of the Arabs, is mentioned in the Prism inscription of Esarhaddon (translated in *ANET*, 2nd edn., 1955, 291b; see also T. W. Rosmarin, *JSOR*, 16 [1932], 32). On the title BDR DNḤY see *Syria*, 39 (1962), 100–3. Starcky's interpretation, *PNO*, 150, no. 16, that NḤY is a shortened form of NḤŠṬB is to be abandoned.

NḤY'ZYZ. *Nominal sentence with adjectival predicate.* 'Naḥai is powerful'
Arabic 'azīz. On the god NḤY see above.

NḤŠṬB. *Nominal sentence.* 'Good fortune'
Syriac nēḥšā'. For other attestations see Ryckmans, i. 231, NḤSṬB; Caskel, *Lihyan*, 150, Naḥs-ṭāb; Dura, *Final Report V, Part I*, 64, Nahestabus; *Prel. Report, II*, 139, D 103, Naastabos; 'Hatra', no. 200[1], NḤ(Š)ṬB; *Thes. Syr. Supp.* 203b, N'SṬBWS; the name is found on a Nabataean inscription, *RB*, 42 (1933), 412, no. 3[3]; Old Aramaic NḤŠ(Ṭ)B, *CIS*, ii. 120; Clay, *BEUP*, X, 57, Na-ḫi-iš-ṭâbu. On NḤŠṬB as name of a deity see Höfner in *Wörterbuch*, 518; Jamme, 'Panthéon', 77. See also Eissfeldt, *JBL*, 82 (1963), 196–200.

[N]YNY. *Unexplained*
The name as restored by Cantineau cannot be explained. A more likely restoration would be [D]YNY (see above).

NYNY'. *One-word name.* 'Bishop's weed (ammi copticum)'
Aramaic nînyā'. Name of a plant. For semantic parallels see Noth, *IPN*, 230.

NYQ'. *Greek name*
Nikē; see Pape, 1002. See Appendix IV, 1.3; 1.13; 1.25.B.

NN'. *Divine name used as personal name*
The name is a variant of NNY. NN' is found in Old Aramaic (Lidzbarski, *Altaramäische*, 15, ii. 1[4]). NNY occurs as personal name at 'Hatra' (no. 4[1]) and in names from Dura; see *Final Report V, Part I*, 62. Sentence names with NNY as element are not attested at Palmyra.

NS'. See under NŠ'

N'B'. *One-word name.* 'Raven'
Syriac na'bā'. The name is otherwise unattested. Cf. the synonym 'RB. For discussion and parallels see Ryckmans, i. 176, 'RB; Nöldeke, *Beiträge*, 85.

[N]'YM. *One-word name.* 'Na'm' (dimin.)
*n'm, 'be pleasant, gracious' (Heb., Jew. Aram., Ugar., Arab., OSA).
Quṭail form. For parallels see Cantineau, *Le Nabatéen*, ii. 121; Wüstenfeld, *Register*, 338, Nu'aym. N'YM is considered by Ibn Doreid, 85[14], as either a diminutive of nu'm or of an'am; see under either of them. Greek transcription: Noaimath, Wuthnow, 83. See also under N'M.

N'M. *One-word name.* 'Happiness'
Arabic nu'm. For parallels and discussion see Huffmon, *APNMT*, 237; Ryckmans,

i. 142; Harris, *Grammar*, 124; Noth, *IPN*, 166; Gordon, *UT*, Glossary no. 1665; Albright, *Proto-Sinaitic*, 42; Gröndahl, *Personennamen*, 163. See also: 'N'M, N'YM, N'MY, N'M'YN.

N'MY. See under N'M. The name is most likely an orthographic variant of *N'MH; cf. 'TY pro 'TH.

N'M'YN. *Genitive compound.* 'Delight of the eye'
For parallels and discussion see Ryckmans i. 237; Diringer, *Iscrizioni*, 249; Galling, 180[53]; Harris, *Grammar*, 124; *PRU*, iv. 247, na'am-^{il}nergal; Gröndahl, *Personennamen*, 163. The parallels are all of the type: noun (construct) plus divine name. There are no attestations anywhere of the type: noun (construct) plus noun.

[N']RY. *Hypocoristicon.* 'Na'r is [my] fortune'
*n'r-gd.
For attestations see van den Branden, *Dédanites*, 58, no. 24; Caskel, *Lihyan*, 38–9. On the deity see Jamme, 'Panthéon', 142. The restoration of the name might not be correct. It is based on the Greek transcription of the name Noaraiou (bilingual text).

NPDY. *Uncertain.* NPDY is not attested as personal name. Nafida in Arabic means 'be exhausted'. See under NPRY.

NPRY. *Uncertain*
The name could be derived from Arabic nafr, 'person, individual'; see Ryckmans, i. 143; Littmann, *Safaitic Inscriptions*, 329a; see also Ibn Doreid, 234[11], who already at his time no longer knew the proper etymology of the name and thus only enumerates all possible roots from which the name could be derived.

NṢ'. *One-word name.* 'Hawk'
Aramaic nāṣā', naṣṣā'. No other attestations. See Nöldeke, *Beiträge*, 86.

NṢWR. *One-word name.* 'Chirper'
Aramaic n^{e}ṣar. On the grammatical form (qāṭōl type) see Brockelmann, *GVG*, i. 343, par. 128; Cantineau, *Grammaire*, 107–8. The Greek transcription Nasōrou is attested from a bilingual text (*C* 4202).

NṢR'. *Hypocoristicon*
Shortened form of NṢRLT. For parallels see 'Hatra', no. 67, NṢRW; Ryckmans, i. 143; Cantineau, *Le Nabatéen*, ii. 122. Greek transcription: Nasros, Wuthnow, 82. Variant: NṢRY. See also under NṢRLT.

NṢRY. See under NṢR'.

NṢRYḤBY. It seems that the name was wrongly divided and should most probably be read as two individual names: NṢRY (br) ḤBY. For discussion see under the individual names.

NṢRLT. *Genitive compound.* 'Help from Allat'
Arabic naṣr. For discussion and parallels see Littmann, *Safaitic Inscriptions*, 329b; Diringer, *Iscrizioni*, 259; Cantineau, *Le Nabatéen*, ii. 122. Cf. the Greek name from Syria: Nesrosa[m]sos (Mouterde, *Inscriptions*, v. no. 2385). The Greek transcription Nasrallathos is attested from a bilingual text (*Berytus*, 2 [1935], 109). The Greek transcription does not favour an interpretation of NṢRLT as a verbal sentence. It could also be a nominal sentence, but this type is practically non-existent in Arabic. See also Caquot, *RTP*, 176.

NQB'. *One-word name.* 'Leader, chief'
Arabic naqīb. For parallels see Ryckmans, i. 144; Wüstenfeld, *Register*, 330, Naqb. On the reading of the name see Ingholt, *Berytus*, 5 (1938), 101. In *Inv. VIII*, 149[1], a likely restoration would be [N]QBW. The reading [']MBW has been accepted in the Main List.

NRGLZBD. *Verbal sentence with the perfect.* 'Nergal has given'
For discussion and parallels see under BWLZBD.

NRQYS. *Greek name*
Narkaios; see Pape, 976. See Appendix IV, 1.20; 1.25.D.

NŠ'. *Hypocoristicon.* 'N.N. has lifted up'
*nś', 'raise, lift up (oneself)' (Common Semitic).
For parallels see Huffmon, *APNMT*, 239; 'Hatra', no. 30[10]; Phoenician, *CIS*, i. 1513, NSY. The Greek transcription Nesa is attested from a bilingual text (*C* 3915). The name is a shortened form of names like Nasaēlou, Naseathos, Wuthnow, 81, 82; Dura, *Final Report V, Part I*, 62, Nassibelus. The variant NS' suggests a PS form *nś'.

NŠWM. *One-word name.* 'Breather'
Aramaic n^{e}šam. On the grammatical form (qaṭṭūl type) see Brockelmann, *GVG*, i. 363, par. 156. The name probably refers to a respiratory disease. The Greek transcription Nassoumou is attested from a bilingual text (*Inv. III*, 8[7]). See also NŠM.

NŠM. Variant of NŠWM (see above).

NŠRY. *Hypocoristicon.* 'Našr has (given?)'
*nšr-verb.
For parallels see 'Hatra', nos. 91, 117, 101[1]; no. 4, NŠRYHB, no. 23[2], NŠR'QB. On the god NŠR see Ryckmans, i. 23; Höfner in *Wörterbuch*, 457; *CIS*, iv. 552[2], NSR. In the *Talmud* (Abodah Zarah 11b) the worship of the Arabian deity nišrā' is denounced. Likewise in the *Doctrine of Addai* (ed. Phillips, 24[18]). Jacob of Sarug connects the worship of the eagle with the Persians (Martin, *ZDMG*, 29 [1876], 111[77]).

NTNY. *Hypocoristicon.* 'N.N. has given' *ntn, 'give' (Heb., Aram.; cf. Ugar. Phoen. ytn; Akk. nadānu).
Structural type: verb plus divine name; for the more common type: divine name plus verb see under 'TNTN. For parallels and discussion see Ryckmans, i. 238; Diringer, *Iscrizioni*, 191; Noth, *IPN*, 170; 'Hatra', no. 113[2], NTWN'ŠR.

SB'. *Uncertain*
The name is attested in the Talmud (for references see Jastrow, 948). It is possibly derived from Aramaic sāb, 'grey, old', hence sābā', 'the grey-haired one'. (One-word name.)

SBBW. *Uncertain*
The name could be connected with Arabic sababu, 'rope, string'. Parallels are not attested and the reading of the name is not absolutely certain.

SBYN', SBYNS. *Latin name*
Sabinus; see *ILS*, 126a, 237a. See Appendix IV, 2.4; 2.11; 2.13; 2.22.A. The Aramaic status emphaticus ending has replaced the Latin ending -us in the first name.

SBYNS. See under SBYN'.

SBN'. *Uncertain*
This is definitely not the Latin name Sabinus (contra Chabot, *CIS*, ii. 4543[2]), because ī is always written with Yodh. The name is most likely (with Lidzbarski, *Ephemeris*, 1, 343) an augmented form of SB' (see above). Cf. a similar case in Mandaean: 'lima and 'limana, 'young man' (Drower–Macuch, *Dictionary*, 351).

SG'. *Uncertain*
The name could be connected with the Aramaic sîgā', 'twig'. In that case one would have to assume a defective spelling for SYG'. No other attestations are found.

SGN'. *Uncertain*
It could be an augmented form of SG' (see above). See also under SBN'. One might also compare the Aramaic signā', 'chief, ruler'. Cf. the name Signas attested at Dura (*Final Report V, Part I*, 63).

SWS'. *One-word name.* 'Horse'
Aramaic sûs. For discussion see Nöldeke, *Beiträge*, 81.

SḤLPH. *Unexplained*

SṬṬYLS. *Latin name*
Statilius; see *ILS*, 135 f. See Appendix IV, 2.7; 2.10; 2.13; 2.14; 2.20; 2.22.A.

SṬM. *Uncertain*
Caquot, *RTP*, 161, proposes to see in this name the Aramaic/Syriac s[e]ṭam, 'close, seal'. According to him these names express the same idea as the theophorous names with 'āḥaz in Hebrew (see Noth, *IPN*, 179). The deity takes possession of the man. It is hard to see any connection between these two verbs. It is more likely that s[e]ṭam, 'close, seal' is used in the sense of protection; cf. Huffmon, *APNMT*, 253, *sub voce* STR. Variant: SṬM'.

SṬM'. See under SṬM.

SYG'. *One-word name.* 'Twig'
Aramaic sîgā'. The interpretation is somewhat doubtful. For semantic parallels see Noth, *IPN*, 230–1. See also under SG', SGN'.

SYWD/R'. *Unexplained*
The name could be connected with Aramaic s[e]yûrā', 'spy', but this is very uncertain.

SYM'. *Uncertain*
It is possibly the Aramaic form of the Greek name Simē (Pape, 1392). Short 'i' is quite often written plene (Rosenthal, *Sprache*, 15). It is less likely that this is a spelling for the name of the goddess Simia. The theophorous names with Simia reveal only the spelling SMY', never *SYMY'. For discussion see under BRSMY'. The explanation as Greek name is most likely.

SY'WN'. *One-word name.* 'Follower' (dimin.)
Aramaic sî'ā'. For discussion and parallels of the corresponding Arabic root šay' see Ryckmans, i. 208; Caskel, *Lihyan*, 152; Noth, *IPN*, 252; Wüstenfeld, *Register*, 418, Šay'. The diminutive ending -ôn has been added (see Goldmann, *Personennamen*, 28).

SY'N'. *One-word name.* 'Follower' (dimin.)
Variant of SY'WN' (see above). The diminutive ending -ân has been added instead of -ôn; see Brockelmann, *GVG*, i. 394, par. 217.

SY'T. *One-word name*
The editor of the *Corpus* (*C* 4530) takes the name to be the fem. part. of sî'ā, 'help, assist'. Greek transcription: Siathēs, Wadd. 2161.

SKYY. *Hypocoristicon*
Shortened form of *SKYBL. For discussion and parallels see under the variant ŠKYBL.

SLWQ', SLWQWS, SLWQS. *Greek name*
Seleukos; see Pape, 1363. See Appendix IV, 1.3; 1.19; 1.25.D. Cf. the variants SLWK ('Hatra', no. 94); Birecik inscription SLW[K] (*Syria*, 39 [1962], 97[8]); s[e]lûk beside sēlēwqîyā' (*Thes. Syr.* 2642).

SLWQWS. See under SLWQ'

SLWQS. See under SLWQ'

SMY'. *Divine name used as personal name*
For a discussion of this type of name see under B'ŠMN. On the difficulties of interpretation concerning this name see BRSMY'.

SSN. *Uncertain*
Two interpretations are possible: (1) The name is derived from the Aramaic sāsā', 'moth', augmented by the suffix -ān. For semantic parallels see Noth, *IPN*, 230; Nöldeke, *Beiträge*, 88–90. (2) The name is Persian: it is that of the ancestor of the Sassanids (Justi, *Namenbuch*, 291).

SPṬYMY', SPṬMY'. *Latin name*
Septimia; see *ILS*, 131a. See Appendix IV, 2.5; 2.7; 2.10; 2.14; 2.22.B.

SPṬYMYWS, SPṬMYW', SPṬMYWS, SPṬMYS, SPṬMY'. *Latin name*
Septimius; see *ILS*, 130 f. See Appendix IV, 2.5; 2.7; 2.10; 2.14; 2.22.A. In nos. 2 and 5 the Aramaic status emphaticus ending has replaced the Latin ending -us.

SPṬMY'. See under SPṬYMY' and SPṬYMYWS

SPṬMYW'. See under SPṬYMYWS

SPṬMYWS. See under SPṬYMYWS

SPṬMYS. See under SPṬYMYWS

SPR. *One-word name*. 'Scribe'
The name occurs in the *Talmud* (Pesachim 52b) and in Syriac (*Thes. Syr.* 2710). It is attested at Dura (*Final Report VIII, Part I*, 263 A[7], SPRH; 277, no. 24, Barsaphara). The stone is in a bad condition and it may well be that SPR' was written. For semantic parallels see Noth, *IPN*, 231.

SQḤ'. *Unexplained*
It is not certain that this is a personal name at all. No photograph is supplied to verify the reading.

SR'. *One-word name*. 'Mistress'
Aramaic śārāh. The name occurs frequently in Syriac (*Thes. Syr.* 2724, sarā'). Cf. the O.T. name śārā, śāray.

SRY. *One-word name*. 'Noble, high-minded'
Arabic sarīy. Ingholt, *Berytus*, 5 (1938), 115, following Lidzbarski, *Ephemeris*, 2, 16, regards the name as a shortened form of SRYKW, which seems to me very unlikely. For discussion and parallels see Littmann, *Safaitic Inscriptions*, 333a.

SRYK'. For discussion and parallels see under ŠRYKW. SRYK' occurs as personal name on a Syriac seal; see *Iraq*, 29 (1967), 6. Variant: SRYKW.

SRYKW. See under SRYK'.

'B'. *One-word name*. 'Lizard'
Syriac 'abbā'. One parallel is found at 'Hatra' (no. 11). For parallels from Arabic see Nöldeke, *Beiträge*, 86–7. Caquot, *RTP*, 176, rejects this explanation and considers the name to be an abbreviation of a theophorous name having as first element 'bd, 'servant'. This is rather unlikely, since the name can perfectly well be explained without assuming any structural alterations.

'BD'. *Hypocoristicon*. 'Servant of N.N.'
*'bd, 'slave, servant' (Common Semitic, except Akk.).
For parallels see Ryckmans, i. 155; Cantineau, *Le Nabatéen*, ii. 125; Noth, *IPN*, 137; Harris, *Grammar*, 128; 'Hatra', no. 24[3]; *PRU*, ii. 46[48]; Gröndahl, *Personennamen*, 104–6. 'BD' occurs frequently as a name among Syrian Christians; for references see Segal, *BSOAS*, 20 (1957), 515. Variants: 'BDW, 'BDY.

'BDBL. *Genitive compound*. 'Servant of Bēl'
There are two groups of names in Palmyrene. The one formed with 'BD- plus divine name, the other with TYM- plus divine name. Bräu, 'Altnordarabischen', 99 f., differentiates the two groups for Arabic names, but his conclusions also apply for Palmyrene. 'BD is the person who fulfils the cultic obligations for the deity ('der 'BD ist also der "Gottesdiener"', ibid. 99). TYM denotes the servitude a man has towards the deity ('Vertragsverpflichtung', ibid. 100). For parallels and discussion see Tallquist, *APN*, 25–8; Ryckmans, i. 240 f., 267; Cantineau, *Le Nabatéen*, ii. 125–6; Harris, *Grammar*, 128–30; *PRU*, ii. 223; Gröndahl, *Personennamen*, 104–6; Noth, *IPN*, 137–8; Cowley, *Papyri*, 82[2]; Driver, *Documents*, Fragment 7[3]; Galling, 180[55, 57], 193[141]; Dura, *Final Report V*, *Part I*, 63. Only one Arabic theophorous name occurs in this structural type at Palmyra: 'BDLT. Names formed with 'BD are relatively rare in Palmyrene compared with other Semitic onomastica, e.g. Phoenician. Greek transcription: Abidbēlou, Wuthnow, 9. See also 'BD', 'BDW, 'BDY, 'BDLT, 'BD'', 'BD'STWR, 'BD'T', 'BD'TH, 'BDṢYD/R', 'BDŠLM', 'BDŠMY', 'BDNRGL, 'BŠLM', 'BŠMY'.

'BDW. See under 'BD'

'BDY. See under 'BD'.

'BDLT. *Genitive compound*. 'Servant of Allat'
*'bd-'lt.
The name is found in epigraphic Syriac (*BSOAS*, 22 [1959], 31[2]). It is also the name of a legendary chief of Edessa. For discussion and further parallels see 'BDBL.

'BD''. *Hypocoristicon*. 'Servant of Athe'
*'bd-'th.
For discussion and parallels see under 'BDBL.

'BD'SWDR. Scribal mistake for 'BD'STWR (see below).

'BD'STWR. *Genitive compound.* 'Servant of 'Aštar'
'STWR is undoubtedly the deity 'Aṯtar, 'Aštar. On the change of short a to ō see the names from 'Hatra': NRGWL (nos. 71, 81[3]); NTWN'ŠR (nos. 113[2], 114[2]). Note the variant spelling of the divine name in 'ŠTWRG' (see below). See also Cantineau, *Grammaire*, 51. The latter questions that 'STWR is a divine name for two reasons. (1) The name is given to men (see under 'ŠTWR, Main List) without a derivative suffix. This, however, is nothing unusual since there are many examples at Palmyra where the divine name is used as personal name without any modifications (for discussion and parallels see under B'ŠMN). (2) Why are there two divine names in 'ŠTWRG'? GD in this case is more an appellative than a divine name (for discussion see under B'LTG'). His suggestion that 'STWR might be a tribal ancestor is unfounded. The Greek transcription Abdaastō[ro]n is attested from a bilingual text (*Berytus*, 5 [1938], 121).

'BD'T'. *Genitive compound.* 'Servant of Athe'
The name occurs in epigraphic Syriac under the variant 'BD'T' (*BSOAS*, 16 [1954], 28, no. 13[1], with further references). For discussion and parallels see under 'BDBL.

'BD'TH. *Genitive compound.* 'Servant of Athe'
For discussion and parallels see under 'BD'T', 'BDBL.

'BDṢYD/R'. *Genitive compound*
The *Corpus* gives only a copy of the inscription and no photograph. According to the copy the Reš is clearly marked as such on the inscription (dotted). However, no attestations of a personal name from the root ṣyr, 'paint', can be found anywhere, whereas the reading ṣyd', 'hunter', as personal name is amply attested; see Cantineau, *Le Nabatéen*, ii. 140; Ryckmans, i. 183; Littmann, *Safaitic Inscriptions*, 340a; Wüstenfeld, *Register*, 146, Ṣaydā. It is tempting to accept ṢYD' as the more correct reading. The structural type 'bd plus personal name is otherwise unattested at Palmyra, but found in Nabataean (see Cantineau, *Le Nabatéen*, ii. 126). It is possible that ṢYD' could be the epithet of a god, 'servant of the hunter'. For possible parallels see 'Hatra', no. 77[1], 'BḤYRN; *PRU*, iii. 241, abdi-ia-qub-b[u?] (on this see Gröndahl, *Personennamen*, 104). There is no reason to connect ṢYD' with the Phoenician deity Ṣid (ṢD, always written defectively). The influence of Phoenician on the Palmyrene onomasticon is negligible. On Ṣid see Röllig in *Wörterbuch*, 310 f.; Harris, *Grammar*, 139–40.

'BDŠLM'. *Genitive compound.* 'Servant of Šalman'
The name occurs at Dura, *Final Report V, Part I*, 63, Abed-salman, Abed-salmas. See also under 'BŠLM'. For discussion and parallels see under 'BDBL.

'BDŠMY'. *Genitive compound.* 'Servant of Šamaš'
*'bd-šmš.
The Greek transcription Abisamaia is attested from a bilingual text (*Berytus*, 2 [1935], 110). The second element of the name has sometimes been associated with the goddess Simia. On this see discussion under BRSMY'. For parallels see 'Hatra', no. 35[2], 'BDŠMY'. 'BDŠMŠ is the name of a prince of Edessa (see *Syria*, 34 [1957], 322). See also under 'BŠMY'. For discussion and parallels see under 'BDBL.

'BYDW. *One-word name.* ''Abd' (dimin.)
Quṭail form. For parallels see Cantineau, *Le Nabatéen*, ii. 125; Ryckmans, i. 156; 'Hatra', no. 179; Wüstenfeld, *Register*, 342, 'Ubayd. Greek transcription: Obaidos, Wuthnow, 85.

'BNY. *One-word name.* 'Fat'
Arabic 'aban. For parallels see Ryckmans, i. 307; 'Hatra', no. 207, 'BN'. For semantic parallels see Noth, *IPN*, 226. The ending Yodh is added by analogy to other names. A derivation from Arabic ǵabn, 'fraud', seems less likely; but cf. Ryckmans, i. 173. Teixidor's suggestion, *Sumer*, 20 (1964), 78, to connect the name with Persian Aban (Justi, *Namenbuch*, 1) is doubtful. A Persian etymology of the name would require a more solid basis.

'BNRGL. *Genitive compound.* 'Servant of Nergal'
Assimilation of the dental to the nasal. For discussion and references see under 'BDBL.

'BS'. *One-word name.* 'Austere, severe'
Arabic 'ābis. For parallels see 'Hatra', nos. 13[1], 58[2]; Ryckmans, i. 156. The Greek transcription Abisseou is attested from a bilingual inscription (*C* 3916). Variant: 'BSY.

'BSY. See under 'BS'

'BŠY. *One-word name.* 'Severe, austere'
Arabic 'ābis. For parallels see Cantineau, *Le Nabatéen*, ii. 127; 'Hatra', no. 92; attested in Syriac (see *BSOAS*, 22 [1959], 32, and *Syria*, 34 [1957], 322, with further references). See also Nöldeke, *Beiträge*, 77. Arabic 'ābis is also employed as epithet for the lion, hence the meaning 'lion'. The name is a variant of 'BS'/Y; see Caquot, *RTP*, 153.

'BŠLM'. *Genitive compound.* 'Servant of Šalman'
On the assimilation of the dental to the following sibilant see 'MŠMŠ. The name is found in epigraphic Syriac (*BSOAS*, 22 [1959], 30, no. 3[1], with further references). It is a well-known name in the early history

of Edessa. For discussion and parallels see under ʿBDBL.

ʿBŠMYʾ. *Genitive compound.* 'Servant of Šamaš'
The same person's name is spelled ʿBDŠMYʾ (see above) in a different inscription (*Berytus*, 2 [1935], 110[1]). The Greek transcription Abisamaia—attested from a bilingual text—does not favour the interpretation 'servant of Heavens'. One would expect *Abisemaia. On this problem see discussion under BRSMYʾ. For discussion and parallels see under ʿBDBL.

ʿGʾ. *Uncertain*
The name is of unclear derivation, though most probably a shortened form of ʿGYLW which itself is most likely a hypocoristicon of ʿGLBWL. The basis for this interpretation is an inscription in which a certain ʿGʾ is the grandson of ʿGYLW; hence one may assume papponymy (*C* 4197[2]). The Greek transcription Oga is attested from a bilingual text (*Inv. X*, 69). See also Cantineau, *Journal asiatique*, 222 (1933), 220–1, on the transcription. For parallels see 'Hatra', nos. 5[4], 13[1], 48[2]; Dura, *Final Report V, Part I*, 64, Ogas.

[ʿG]Bʾ
The restoration [ʾB]Bʾ is more likely, especially since ʾBBʾ is attested several times as a fem. name. [ʿG]Bʾ as shortened form of ʿGLBWL would be a hapax, and this is less convincing.

ʿGY or ʿGYZ
The reading is uncertain. ʿGY could be taken as an otherwise unattested variant of ʿGʾ, or as a scribal error for ʿGʾ. There is a Syriac personal name ʿagay (*Thes. Syr.*, 2792) whose meaning, however, is unknown. Ryckmans, i. 157, lists a Safaitic name ʿGZ, of which ʿGYZ could be a variant. Arabic ʿajīz, 'impotent'. For semantic parallels see Noth, *IPN*, 227.

ʿGYZ. See under ʿGY

ʿGYLʾ. See under ʿGYLW

ʿGYLW. *One-word name.* 'Calf' (dimin.)
*ʿgl, 'calf' (Common Semitic). Quṭail form. For parallels and discussion see Ryckmans, i. 157; Littmann, *Safaitic Inscriptions*, 333b; Wüstenfeld, *Register*, 106[29]; Dura, *Final Report V, Part I*, 64, Ogelus; Noth, *IPN*, 230; Nöldeke, *Beiträge*, 83. The Greek transcription Ogēlou is attested from a bilingual text (*C* 3923). It seems safe to assume that ʿGYLW came at one stage to be considered as a shortened form of ʿGLBWL. This would explain the many occurrences of the name (so Lidzbarski, *Ephemeris*, 2, 283). Variants: ʿGYLʾ, ʿGYLW, ʿGYLY.

ʿGYLY. See under ʿGYLW

ʿGLBWLʾ. *Divine name used as personal name*
For this type of name see discussion under BʿŠMN. One of the legendary kings of Aksum was named Aglebul or Aglebu (Conti Rossini, *Storia d'Etiopia*, 145). Cf. also YRḤBWLʾ which is of the same type.

ʿDʾ. *Unexplained*
For parallels see 'Hatra', no. 27, ʿDʾ; Ryckmans, i. 157; cf. the O.T. names [f]ʿādā, [m]ʿiddō'. For a proposed, but unconvincing interpretation see Starcky, *AAS*, 3 (1953), 161.

ʿDWN. *One-word name.* 'Beast of prey'
Arabic ʿadawān; see Lane, v. 1980a. For parallels see Ryckmans, i. 157; Wüstenfeld, *Register*, 47, ʿAdwān (?). A derivation from Syriac ʿadēn, 'be pleasant', was proposed by Ingholt, *Berytus*, 2 (1935), 106. This would then be a qāṭōl type noun.

ʿDL. *One-word name.* 'Just, fair'
Arabic ʿādil. For parallels see Ryckmans, i. 157; Wüstenfeld, *Register*, 47, ʿAdl; Harris, *Grammar*, 131. Noth's interpretation (*IPN*, 231) of O.T. ʿadlay as 'Gartenkresse' is not convincing (based on Jewish–Aramaic ʿădāl, 'lepidium sativum'). Cf. also Ugar. ʿdl, Aistleitner, 2008; Gröndahl, *Personennamen*, 107.

ʿDN. *Unexplained*
Possibly derived from Aramaic ʿēden, 'pleasure'.

ʿWB. *Uncertain*
Probably to be connected with Aramaic ʿôb, 'bag'.

ʿWDʾL. *Genitive compound.* 'Protection of God'
Arabic ʿauḏ. For parallels see Ryckmans, i. 242. Greek transcription: Audēlou, Wuthnow, 28. See also: ʿWDW, ʿWYDʾ, ʿWYDW, ʿWYDY, ʿWYDLT, ʿWYDT.

ʿWDW. *Hypocoristicon.* 'Protection of N.N.'
For parallels see Cantineau, *Le Nabatéen*, ii. 128; Ryckmans, i. 159–60; 'Hatra', nos. 65[7], 127. See also under ʿWDʾL.

ʿWYD. *Hypocoristicon.* 'Refugee of N.N.'
Qaṭīl form; see Brockelmann, *GVG*, i. 354, par. 138. For parallels see Cantineau, *Le Nabatéen*, ii. 128. For discussion see under ʿWYDLT. Variants: ʿWYDʾ, ʿWYDW, ʿWYDY.

ʿWYDʾ. *Hypocoristicon.* 'Refugee of N.N.'
Attested at Dura, *Final Report V, Part I*, 62, Avidas. The name is well-known in the early history of Edessa. The fem. form is ʿWYTʾ with assimilation of d to t; cf. Hebrew ʾḤT: *ʾaḥadt > ʾaḥatt). The name occurs in epigraphic Syriac (*BSOAS*, 22 [1959], 26, C7, with further references). The unassimilated form ʿW(Y)DT is attested

from Assur. The reading, however, is not quite certain; see Andrae, 'Inschriften aus Assur', *MDOG*, 60 (1920), 36. See also under 'WYD.

'WYDW. See under 'WYD

'WYDY. See under 'WYD

'WYDLT. *Genitive compound.* 'Refugee of Allat'
A parallel is found at 'Hatra', no. 204[2], 'WYD'ŠR. The name is attested at Dura, *Final Report V, Part I*, 62, Avid-alathus. The Greek transcription Aoueidallathou occurs in a bilingual text (*RB*, 39 [1930], 546). See also under 'WD'L.

'WYDT. See under 'WYD'

'WMY. *One-word name.* 'Swimmer'
Arabic 'aum. For parallels see Cantineau, *Le Nabatéen*, ii. 128; Ryckmans, i. 160; Wüstenfeld, *Register*, 99, 'Awwām. Greek transcription: Aumos, Wuthnow, 29.

'WTN. *One-word name.* 'Helper'
Arabic ġauṯ. For parallels see Cantineau, *Le Nabatéen*, ii. 128; Ryckmans, i. 173; Wüstenfeld, *Register*, 171, Ġauṯ; Dura, *Final Report V, Part I*, 62, Authaeus. Greek transcription: Gautos, Authos, Wuthnow, 40, 29. On the suffix -ān see Brockelmann, *GVG*, 392, par. 215. This suffix usually expresses the result of an action (resultatives -ān); cf. Arabic sakara, 'get drunk', sakrān, 'drunk, intoxicated'; see also under MYŠN.

'ZWLT. *Uncertain*
It could be a genitive compound of the Arabic ġazw, 'raid', and the goddess Lât/Allat, 'raid of Allat'. The interpretation is highly questionable. No parallels otherwise.

'ZY. *Uncertain*
This is most likely a shortened form of 'ZYZW (see below). For parallels see Cantineau, *Le Nabatéen*, ii. 129; 'Hatra', no. 155, 'Z'; Cumont, *Fouilles de Doura-Europos*, 318[6], Azzaios. It is possible, that the name of the Arabic goddess al-'uzzā is used as a personal name; cf. the name 'bd-'l-'zy (Cantineau, *Le Nabatéen*, ii. 129). One would have to assume a shortened form (omission of the article). On the deity see Höfner, *Wörterbuch*, 475. Cf. also the O.T. name 'uzzî, which is formed from the same root; see Noth, *IPN*, 160; Harris, *Grammar*, 131.

'ZYZ. *One-word name.* 'Mighty, powerful'
Arabic 'azīz, Aram. 'azzîz. For parallels see Ryckmans, i. 161; Wüstenfeld, *Register*, 100, 'Azīz. For similar names see Noth, *IPN*, 225. Greek transcription: Azizos, Wuthnow, 13.

'ZYZW. *Divine name used as personal name*
For parallels see Cantineau, *Le Nabatéen*, ii. 129. For structural parallels see under B'ŠMN. Cf. the O.T. name 'Azîzā'. The name could also be interpreted as the Arabic adjective 'azīz (see above), augmented by the ending Waw. Variant: 'ZYZY.

'ZYZY. See under 'ZYZW

'YT'. *One-word name.* 'Rain'
Arabic ġaiṯ. For parallels see Cantineau, *Le Nabatéen*, ii. 130. Cf. the O.T. tribal name maṭrî. See also Ryckmans, i. 125, MṬR; Schult, *Vergleichende Studien*, 89. See also Aistleitner, 1120, ṯly; Gröndahl, *Personennamen*, 202. The Ugaritic name, however, is divine. It is also possible that the name is connected with Arabic 'aiṯ, 'create disaster', used as epithet for the lion. For parallels see Ryckmans, i. 163; Wüstenfeld, *Register*, 54, 'Ayṯ.

'[K]T'. *Unexplained*
The reading is not certain. '[P]T' has been suggested.

'L'. *One-word name.* 'August, Exalted'
Arabic 'alīy. *'ly, 'go up, rise' (Common Semitic). For parallels see Cantineau, *Le Nabatéen*, ii. 130; Ryckmans, i. 164; Wüstenfeld, *Register*, 58, 'Alī. Greek transcription: Aleios, Wuthnow, 17. Cf. the O.T. name 'ēlî (Noth, *IPN*, 146). Variant: 'LY.

'LBN. *One-word name.* 'Victor, conqueror'
Arabic ġālib. For parallels see Cantineau, *Le Nabatéen*, ii. 130; Ryckmans, i. 174; Wüstenfeld, *Register*, 169, Ġālib; Aistleitner, 2031, 'lby. Greek transcriptions: Albos, Alebou, Wuthnow, 17. A connection with Arabic 'alib, 'thick, coarse, rude', is less likely, but see Ryckmans, i. 163. On the ending -ān see under 'WTN+MYŠN. The O.T. name 'abî-'albôn is probably a corruption of 'abî-ba'al (see Koehler–Baumgartner, *Lexicon*) and not to be connected with our root.

'LG. *Uncertain*
The name could be explained by reference to Arabic 'ilāj, 'healing', or to Arabic 'alij, 'strong, sturdy'. Parallels to the first explanation: Littmann, *Safaitic Inscriptions*, 335a; Wüstenfeld, *Register*, 246, 'Ilāj; Cantineau, *Le Nabatéen*, ii. 130 (reading uncertain). It is not surprising that such an abstract name as 'healing' would be employed as a personal name. Cf. the name ġauṯ, 'help', which occurs as personal name in modern Arabic. Parallels to the second suggestion: Wüstenfeld, *Register*, 62, 'Alija. 'Alij does not primarily mean 'wild ass' (thus Caquot, *RTP*, 164), but is only an epithet of it. Variant: 'LG'.

'LG'. See under 'LG

'LY. See under 'L'.

'LYY. *One-word name.* ''Alī' (dimin.)
Quṭail form. The Greek transcription Olaious is found in a bilingual text (*C* 3913

I3). The ending Yodh is added by analogy to other names.

ʿLYBWL. *Nominal sentence.* ʿBôl is exaltedʾ Arabic ʿalīy. For parallels see Cantineau, *Le Nabatéen*, ii. 131; Ryckmans, i. 243; Nyberg, 'Studien', 337, interprets the name (ad ʿLYBʿL) as ʿAli ist der Baʿal'. This interpretation is inadmissible here, because of the many variants (see below). On the divine name ʿAli see discussion under ʾBLʿLY. See also ʿLYBʿL, ʿLYNʾ, ʿLYŠʾ.

ʿLYBʿL. *Nominal sentence.* 'Baʿal is exalted' For discussion and parallels see under ʿLYBWL.

[ʿ]LYW. *One-word name.* 'Exalted, august' Arabic ʿalīy. Variant of ʿLʾ/Y (see above). The ending Waw has been added to this particular form. The name is very frequent in Nabataean (Cantineau, *Le Nabatéen*, ii. 130).

ʿLYNʾ. *Hypocoristicon.* 'Nabû is exalted'
*ʿly-nbw.
The Greek transcription Alainē is found on a bilingual inscription (*C* 3950). For discussion see under ʿLYBWL.

ʿLYŠʾ. *Hypocoristicon.* 'Šamaš is exalted'
*ʿly-šmš.
The Greek transcription Alaisas is found on a bilingual text (*Inv. X*, 24). For discussion see under ʿLYBWL.

ʿLYT. *One-word name.* 'Exalted'
Arabic ʿaliyat. For parallels see Cantineau, *Le Nabatéen*, ii. 131; 'Hatra', no. 11, with further references.

ʿMBKRʾ. See under ʾMBKRʾ

ʿMLʾ. *One-word name.* 'Worker'
Aramaic ʿamēlāʾ, Arabic ʿamīl. For parallels see Ryckmans, i. 166; Cantineau, *Le Nabatéen*, ii. 132; Wüstenfeld, *Register*, 63, ʿAmal. For similar names see Noth, *IPN*, 231.

ʿMR. *One-word name.* 'Life'
Arabic ʿimr, ʿamr. For parallels see Ryckmans, i. 167; Littmann, *Safaitic Inscriptions*, 336a. Greek transcription: Amros, Wuthnow, 20. ʿAmr, ʿOmar are well-known Arabic names; see Ṭabari, *Index*, 405 ff. The many possible ways of vocalizing Arabic ʿmr make a precise rendering impossible, but the interpretation 'life' is most likely. Variants: ʿMRW, ʿMRʾ. See also under ʿMRT.

ʿMRʾ. See under ʿMR

ʿMRW. See under ʿMR

ʿMRT. *One-word name.* 'Life'
The name is not attested as fem. as Caquot, *RTP*, 177, maintains, basing his conclusion on the reading in *Inv. VIII*, 100. For the correct reading of the same inscription see *CIS*, ii. 4241, and photograph. For parallels see Cantineau, *Le Nabatéen*, ii. 133; Ryckmans, i. 167; Littmann, *Safaitic Inscriptions*, 336a. Greek transcriptions: Amirathou, Amerathos, Wuthnow, 19.

ʿMT. *Uncertain*
The Greek transcription [Am]mathou is attested on a bilingual inscription (*Inv. X*, 40). It tends to show, that the name is to be derived from the Arabic root ʿamama, 'be perfect, complete'. What kind of a noun form the name would be is unknown. The fem. ending -at on masc. names is quite frequent in Arabic; see Ṭabari, *Index*, 172, ḤLYPT, name with a fem. ending, but used as masc. name.

ʿNBW. *One-word name*, 'Grape'
*ʿnb, 'grape' (Common Semitic, Ugaritic ǵnb).
For parallels see Ryckmans, i. 167, who gives as meaning 'light, brisk'. For Akkadian names of the type: Inib-divine name/Inbu-divine name see *CAD*, I/J, 146b. For similar names see Noth, *IPN*, 230.

ʿNYNY. *One-word name.* 'Cloud' (dimin.)
Quṭail form; cf. Arabic ʿanān, Aram ʿānān. For parallels see Littmann, *Safaitic Inscriptions*, 336b; Wüstenfeld, *Register*, 361, ʿUnayn. Caquot's interpretation, *RTP*, 164, makes little sense.

ʿNMW. *One-word name.* 'Successful, noble' Arabic ǵānim. For parallels see Cantineau, *Le Nabatéen*, ii. 133; Ryckmans, i. 175; Littmann, *Safaitic Inscriptions*, 338a; Wüstenfeld, *Register*, 170, Ǵanm. Ǵānim implies a good quality in the language of the Bedouins.

ʿNN. *One-word name.* 'Cloud'
Aramaic ʿānān. Noth, *IPN*, 184, interprets the O.T. names formed from this root with the help of the Arabic ʿanna, 'appear'. The proposed interpretation seems preferable for the Palmyrene names in view of the explanation given of ʿNYNY (see above). Variants: ʿNNW, ʿNNY.

ʿNNW. See under ʿNN

ʿNNY. For parallels see Cowley, *Papyri*, 10^{20}, 22^{12}; 'Hatra', no. 16^{2}. For discussion see under ʿNN.

ʿSTWRGʾ. *Nominal sentence.* 'Aštar is (my) luck'
Variant of ʿŠTWR. On the change š > ś (s) see Rosenthal, *Sprache*, 25. On the change ă > ō see under ʿBDʿSTWR. In the inscription *C* $4199^{2,13}$ the variants ʿSTWRGʾ and ʿŠTWRGʾ appear side by side. For discussion and parallels see under BʿLTGʾ.

ʿSTY. *Unexplained*
According to the photograph a more likely reading is ʿSTYY or ʿSTYW. Variant: ʿSTYʾ.

ʿSTYʾ. *Unexplained*
Variant of ʿSTY (see above).

ʿQBY. *Hypocoristicon.* ʿN.N. has protected' *ʿqb plus divine name.
The variant ʿQBʾ is found at ʿHatra', no. 3. Greek transcription: Akkabaiou, Wuthnow, 15. At Palmyra so far only the structural type divine name plus ʿqb is attested (see under ʾTʿQB). The type: ʿqb plus divine name is found at ʿHatra', no. 27, ʿQBŠM', and at Elephantine, Cowley, *Papyri*, 54[10].

ʿQYBʾ. *Uncertain*
The name can either be explained as the Aramaic pass. part. of ʿqb, or as the Aramaic word ʿᵃqîbā', ʿheel'. For parallels to the first interpretation see ʿHatra', nos. 185, 200[4], 162; see also no. 16[1], ʿQWBʾ. The name occurs frequently in the Talmud (Jastrow, 1105). For a discussion of the root see under ʾTʿQB.

ʿQRBN. *One-word name.* ʿScorpion'
*ʿqrb, ʿscorpion' (Common Semitic).
For parallels see Cantineau, *Le Nabatéen*, ii. 134; Ryckmans, i. 39; Wüstenfeld, *Register*, 40, ʿAqrab; Dura, *Final Report V, Part I*, 64, Acrabanes, Akarabanēs; Nöldeke, *Beiträge*, 89. On the suffix -ān see Barth, *Nominalbildung*, 337, par. 205; see also under MYŠN.

ʿRBY. *One-word name.* ʿArab'
Nisbe form. For parallels see Cantineau, *Le Nabatéen*, ii. 134. Greek transcription: Arabiou, Wuthnow, 25.

ʿRGʾ. *One-word name.* ʿLameness'
Arabic ʿaraj. For parallels see Ryckmans, i. 170. The Aramaic status emphaticus ending has been added. Possible Greek transcription: Oaregathos, Wuthnow, 85. For similar names see Noth, *IPN*, 227. See also: ʿRGN.

ʿRGN. *One-word name.* ʿLameness'
Arabic ʿaraj. For parallels see Littmann, *Safaitic Inscriptions*, 336b. On the ending -ān see under ʿWTN.

ʿRYMʾ. *One-word name.* ʿShrewd'
Aramaic ʿᵃrîmā'. For similar names see Noth, *IPN*, 228.

ʿŠY. *One-word name.* ʿEvening'
Arabic ʿašīy. Possible parallels are found at ʿHatra', nos. 85, 212.

ʿŠYLT. *One-word name.* ʿHoney' (dimin.)
Quṭail form; cf. Arabic ʿasal. The Greek transcription Osailathous is attested from a bilingual text (*RB*, 39 [1930], 523). See also: ʿŠYLTʾ.

ʿŠYLTʾ. See under ʿŠYLT

ʿŠRʾ. *One-word name.* ʿThe tenth'
Arabic ʿâšir. *ʿśr (Heb., Aram., Syr., Phoen., Arab.). For parallels see Ryckmans, i. 172. Cf. the Latin name Decimus and the Ugaritic name ṯtmnt (Aistleitner, 2955).

ʿŠTWR. *Divine name used as personal name*
See discussion under ʿSTWRG' on the variant spelling Š/S. For parallels to this type of name see under BʿŠMN. Cf. the Talmudic name bar ʿaštôr (Jastrow, 1128).

ʿŠTWRGʾ. *Nominal sentence.* "Aštar is (my) fortune'
For discussion see under ʿSTWRG'.

ʿŠT[RG]ʾ. *Nominal sentence.* "Aštar is (my) fortune'
The name is apparently a defective spelling for ʿŠTWR. The reading, however, is not certain. For discussion see under ʿSTWRG'.

ʿTʾ
The word division is not quite clear in this inscription (*Inv. VIII*, 107). The name can either be read BRʿTʾ (reading accepted in Main List) or br ʿTʾ. In the latter case ʿTʾ would be masc. See discussion under variant ʿTH.

ʿTʾM. *Nominal sentence.* ʿAthe is (my) mother'
For parallels see Tallquist, *APN*, 107, Ištar-ummi-šarrani; Ugar., ʿṯtr-ʾum, *CRAIBL*, 1955, 79. This name would show that ʿTH is a female deity if the proposed interpretation is right.

ʿTD/RN. *Unexplained*

ʿTD/RT. *Unexplained*

ʿTH. *Divine name used as personal name*
For parallels to this type of name see under BʿŠMN. On the deity ʿTH see the discussion in Février, *Religion*, 127–34.

ʿTHZB[D]. *Verbal sentence with the perfect*
ʿAthe has given'
For discussion and parallels see under BWLZBD. The orthography is unusual. In composite names the long end-vowel in ʿTH is always dropped; cf. ʿTNTN, ʿTZBD. On this see Rosenthal, *Sprache*, 19, and note his explanation of the orthography in ʿTYKʾ, ʿTYʿQB. In a different inscription the same man's name is spelled ʿTZBD; see Main List for references.

ʿTW. *Uncertain*
The name is most likely a variant of ʿTY (see below).

ʿTZʾ. *Hypocoristicon.* ʿAthe has given'
*ʿth-zbd.
The long final vowel of ʿTH is dropped in compounds. For exception see ʿTHZB[D]. For discussion and parallels see under BWLZBD.

ʿTZBD. *Verbal sentence with the perfect.*
ʿAthe has given'
See variant ʿTHZB[D]. For discussion and parallels see under BWLZBD.

ʿTḤN. *Verbal sentence with the perfect.*
ʿAthe is gracious'
For discussion see under BLTYḤN.

'TY. *Uncertain*
It could be a shortened form of 'TY'QB or 'TYK' (see below), or a variant spelling of the divine name 'TH. Cf. the O.T. name 'attay and Noth's interpretation in *IPN*, 191. The Greek transcription Aththaia is attested from a bilingual text (*RB*, 39 [1930], 531).

'TYK'. *Nominal sentence.* 'Athe is here'
Aramaic kā'. The final long vowel of 'TH is spelled out here; for a different view see Rosenthal, *Sprache*, 19.

'TY'QB. *Verbal sentence with the perfect.* 'Athe has protected'
On the spelling 'TY see under 'TYK'. For discussion and parallels see under 'T'QB.

'TM'. *Nominal sentence*
For discussion and variants see under 'T'MN.

'TNWR. *Nominal sentence.* 'Athe is light'
For parallels and discussion see under BWLNWR.

'TNWRY. *Nominal sentence.* 'Athe is my light'
For discussion see under BWLNWR.

'TNTN. *Verbal sentence with the perfect.* 'Athe has given'
Structural type: divine name plus verb; for type: verb plus divine name, see under NTNY. For discussion and parallels see Tallquist, *APN*, 296a; Huffmon, *APNMT*, 244; Cantineau, *Le Nabatéen*, ii. 73, 151, B'LNTN, ŠLMNTN; van den Branden, *Inscriptions*, 97, 336, '[L]NTN, ṢLMNTN; Old Aramaic, *CIS*, ii. 177, RMNNTN; Cowley, *Papyri*, 14^{12}, $81^{14,29}$, 55^{7}; Kraeling, *BMAP*, 8^{12}; Harris, *Grammar*, 108; Noth, *IPN*, 170. See also under BLYHB and 'TTN.

'T'Y. *Hypocoristicon.* 'Athe has protected' *'th-'qb.
For discussion and parallels see under 'T'QB.

'T'M. *Nominal sentence*
For discussion and variants see under 'T'MN.

'T'QB. *Verbal sentence with the perfect.* 'Athe has protected'
For discussion and parallels see under 'T'QB.

'TR/DN. *Unexplained*

'TRŠWRY. *Nominal sentence.* 'Attar is my stronghold'
For parallels and discussion see under BLŠWR. On the deity see van den Branden, *Histoire*, 109 f.; Caskel in *Studi Semitici*, i. 100–6; Jamme, 'Panthéon', 85 ff.; Höfner in *Wörterbuch*, 497–501.

'TŠ'. *Hypocoristicon.* 'Athe is (my) stronghold'
For discussion and parallels see under BLŠWR.

'TŠB'. *Uncertain*
The Greek transcription Athēsōba is attested from a bilingual text (*Inv. VIII*, 64). A derivation from Aramaic šᵉbā', 'capture', as proposed by Cantineau, *Grammaire*, 52, is very unlikely in view of the Greek transcription. For a different explanation—but unconvincing—see Caquot, 'Onomastique', 250.

'TŠWR. *Nominal sentence.* 'Athe is (my) stronghold'
For discussion and parallels see under BLŠWR.

'TŠ'T. *Unexplained*
Probably a theophorous name with Athe. But the second element remains unexplained.

'TTN. *Verbal sentence with the perfect.* 'Athe has given'
Probably a contracted form of *'tntn > 'ttn. But it is difficult to say how such a contraction would take place with the Nûn having a full vowel. For parallels see under 'TNTN.

PG'. *One-word name.* 'Fig'
Aramaic paggāh. For similar names see Noth, *IPN*, 230; Goldmann, *Personennamen*, 30.

PZG'. *Unexplained*
The reading may well be wrong. The traces that can be recognized on the photograph do not agree with the reading of the *Corpus*. The only letter that is clear is the Aleph at the end of the word.

PZL. *Uncertain*
Hebrew, Aramaic pāzal, 'turn', do not yield any satisfactory meaning. PZL is attested in north African Arabic with the meaning 'club' (Beaussier, ii. 543).

PṬRQLS. *Greek name*
Patroklos; see Pape, 1148. See Appendix IV, 1.3; 1.6; 1.9; 1.15; 1.18; 1.25.D.

PYL'. *One-word name.* 'Elephant, ivory'
Aramaic pîlā'. For similar names see Goldmann, *Personennamen*, 30. The Greek transcription Pheila is attested from a bilingual inscription (*C* 4160).

PLWYN', PLWYNWS. *Latin name*
Flavianus; see *ILS*, 195b. See Appendix IV, 2.8; 2.10; 2.20; 2.22.A. The Aramaic status emphaticus ending has replaced the Latin ending -us in the first variant.

PLWYNWS. See under PLWYN'

PLYN', PLYNWS, PLNS. *Greek name*
Phileinos, Philinos; see Pape, 1617, 1619. See Appendix IV, 1.13; 1.25.D.

PLYNWS. See under PLYN'

PLNS. See under PLYN'

PLPṬR. *Greek name*
Philopatōr; see Pape, 1628. See Appendix IV, 1.6; 1.9; 1.15; 1.16; 1.18; 1.25.E. ō is sometimes written without mater lectionis; see Rosenthal, *Sprache*, 20.

PLQS. *Latin name*
Felix. See *ILS*, 194 f. See Appendix IV, 2.3; 2.9; 2.22.C; 2.23.A. Unusual spelling for expected PLKS; see Rosenthal, *Sprache*, 37.

PPLWS, PPLYS. *Latin name*
Publius; see *ILS*, 121b, 232b. See Appendix IV, 2.4; 2.5; 2.10; 2.22.A; 2.23.B.

PPLYS. See under PPLWS

PṢ'. *Hypocoristicon*
Shortened form of PṢY'L. For parallels see Cantineau, *Le Nabatéen*, ii. 137; Ryckmans, i. 180; Littmann, 'Nabataean', *BSOAS*, 15 (1953), 19, 'PṢY. See also under PṢY'L. Variant: PṢY'.

PṢGW. *One-word name.* 'Sweat'
Arabic faḍij. For parallels see Ryckmans, i. 180.

PṢY'. See under PṢ'

PṢY'L. *Verbal sentence with the perfect.* 'God has opened (the womb)'
Aramaic pᵉṣā'. For parallels see Cantineau, *Le Nabatéen*, ii. 137; Winnett, *Safaitic Inscriptions*, no. 567. The form is comparable to the O.T. name pᵉtaḥyāh; see Noth, *IPN*, 179, for discussion. See also under PṢ'. Greek transcription: Phasaēlēs, Wuthnow, 162.

PRDŠY. *Persian name*
Firdūsī; see Justi, *Namenbuch*, 100. Internal long vowels in Persian words seem to be written without matres lectionis.

PRṬNKS. *Latin name*
Pertinax; see *ILS*, 224b. See Appendix IV, 2.3; 2.5; 2.7; 2.13; 2.22.D.

[PRYSQWS]. *Latin name*
Priscus; see *ILS*, 230 f. See Appendix IV, 2.2; 2.5; 2.14; 2.20; 2.22.A.

PRMWN. *Uncertain*
Goldmann, *Personennamen*, 26, and others explained the name as the Latin Firmus; see *ILS*, 195b: a Persian origin is more likely. Fermān as name of a poet is mentioned in Justi, *Namenbuch*, 99. It is not known whether the Persian ending -ān became -ôn in Palmyrene, but the spelling prmwn, 'decree', is attested from Syriac (*Thes. Syr.* 3267). Thus there should be no objection to the identification with the Persian Fermān. The Greek transcription Phirmōnos is found in a bilingual text (*C* 3914[4]).

PRN(K). *Persian name*
Pharnak; see Justi, *Namenbuch*, 92. The name occurs in the O.T., parnāk (Noth, *IPN*, 64).

PRŠTN'. *Unexplained*
The name does not seem to be Semitic: it may be Persian.

PTYḤB. *Uncertain*
As the name reads one would have to suppose PTY to be a divine name and ḤB to be a shortened form of ḥbb, 'love', but no deity PTY is known. It is more likely that ḤB is dittography of the following ḤBL, and the correct reading should be PTY, 'youthful'. Cf. Arabic fatīy, Aramaic petî. For parallels see Ryckmans, i. 181; Cowley, *Papyri*, 81[103,106]; Kraeling, *BMAP*, 12[3], PTW.

ṢLM'. *One-word name.* 'Strong man'
Arabic ṣalam. For parallels see Ryckmans, i. 184; Hess, *Beduinennamen*, 35. Variant: ṢLMY.

ṢLMY. See under ṢLM'

ṢM'. *One-word name.* 'Dumb'
Syriac ṣamā' (probably loan-word from the Arabic). The name could also be connected with the Arabic ṣimm, 'strong, courageous; lion'. For parallels to the Arabic interpretation see Littmann, *Safaitic Inscriptions*, 340a; Ryckmans, i. 184. The vocalization of the Palmyrene name is unknown. Thus either interpretation is possible. Variant: ṢMY.

ṢMY. See under ṢM'

[Ṣ'DW]. *Hypocoristicon.* 'N.N. rises'
Arabic ṣa'ida. *ṣ'd plus divine name. For parallels and discussion see Littmann, *Safaitic Inscriptions*, 340a; Ryckmans, i. 185; Wüstenfeld, *Register*, 399. The compound name Ṣ'D'L is attested in Safaitic. The Greek transcription Saedou is found in a bilingual text (Cantineau, *Inscriptions palmyréniennes*, 30, no. 41). Variant: Ṣ'DY.

Ṣ'DY. See under [Ṣ'DW]

ṢPR'. *One-word name.* 'Bird'
Aramaic ṣipprā'. For parallels and discussion see Nöldeke, *Beiträge*, 85. Cf. the O.T. names ṣippōrāh and ṣippôr. The Greek transcription Sephphera is attested from a bilingual text (*C* 3950). Variant: ṢPRY.

ṢPRY
For discussion see under ṢPR'. The Yodh is probably not the first person sing. suffix, but rather the ending Yodh, which with Aleph and Waw can be used interchangeably.

ṢT'. *One-word name.* 'Dirt'
Aramaic ṣā'tā'. The name is probably surname here. An explanation from the Arabic does not yield any satisfactory sense; but see Ryckmans, i. 185, 399.

QBWD'. *Uncertain*
The reading QBWD' is unattested. QBWR'

is found with the meaning 'palm-tree that bears quickly' (Steingass, *Persian*, 953).

Q/MBWRM. *Unexplained*

QWP'. *One-word name.* 'Ape'
Aramaic qôp. For parallels see 'Hatra', nos. 43^2, 57^2. For this and similar names see Goldmann, *Personennamen*, 30. See also under QRD'.

QWPYN. *One-word name.* 'Apes'
The plural form to QWP' (see above); cf. also M'ZYN (same grammatical form). It cannot be a dual form, because the dual-ending -ayn has been contracted throughout in Palmyrene; see Cantineau, *Grammaire*, 119; Brockelmann, *GVG*, i. 458, par. 244.

QWQ'. *One-word name.* 'Pelican'
Aramaic qûq. For semantic parallels see Nöldeke, *Beiträge*, 85f.

QWQḤ. *Unexplained*
The name is also found in Syriac, YWḤNN QWQḤ (*Thes. Syr.* 3558). The meaning and the grammatical form are unknown.

QWŠY. *Uncertain*
The name is most likely to be derived from Aramaic qôšî, 'protracted travailing'. The name is given to the daughter because of a difficult childbirth. Cf. the O.T. name qûšāyāhû (Noth, *IPN*, 32, n. 1). The name could also be connected with Arabic qaus, 'longbow, bow'.

QZB[L]. *Unexplained*
The reading of the name is in both occurrences uncertain.

Q/MZY. *Uncertain*
In Judeo-Arabic qizzay means 'accountant' (Dalman, *Handwörterbuch*, 374). See also under MZY.

QḤZN. *Uncertain*
It is probably a qaṭalān form from Arabic qaḥaz, 'jump'. On the ending -ān see Barth, *Nominalbildung*, 337, par. 205, and also under MYŠN.

QYMW. See under QYMY

QYMY. *One-word name.* 'Precious' valuable'
Arabic qayyim. For parallels see 'Hatra', no. 35^2, QYMY; Cantineau, *Le Nabatéen*, ii. 142, QYMW; Ryckmans, i. 189. The name is attested as fem. in epigraphic Syriac (*MUSJ*, 5 [1911], 77; *ZA*, 27 [1912], 379; *BSOAS*, 22 [1959], 38, no. 9^7, QMY, written defectively).

QYS'. *One-word name.* 'Tree, wood'
Syriac qaysā'. Surname here. For semantic parallels see Noth, *IPN*, 230.

QLWDYS. *Latin name*
Claudius; see *ILS*, 182a. See Appendix IV, 2.2; 2.6; 2.10; 2.17; 2.20; 2.22.A.

QLYBW. *One-word name.* 'Heart' (dimin.)
Quṭail form; cf. Arabic qalb. For parallels see Ryckmans, i. 191; Wüstenfeld, *Register*, 138, Qulayb. See also van den Branden, *Histoire*, 59, on the various parts of the body used as personal names.

QLSṬ'. *Greek name*
Kallistos; see Pape, 605. See Appendix IV, 1.3; 1.9; 1.15; 1.25.D.

QLSṬRṬS. *Greek name*
Kallistratos; see Pape, 605. See Appendix IV, 1.3; 1.9; 1.15; 1.25.D.

QLSTQS. *Latin name*
Celesticus? The reading of the name is uncertain; see Lidzbarski, *Ephemeris*, a, 290–1. See Appendix IV, 2.2; 2.7; 2.22.A; 2.23.C.

QLQYS. *Greek name*
Kilix; see Pape, 659. See Appendix IV, 1.3; 1.16; 1.26.II; 1.25.J. Wrong spelling for *QLYQS (Rosenthal, *Sprache*, 13).

QML'. *One-word name.* 'Louse'
Arabic qaml. For parallels see Ryckmans, i. 191. For similar names see Nöldeke, *Beiträge*, 88–90.

QSYN'. *Latin name*
Cassianus; see *ILS*, 179a. See Appendix IV, 2.2; 2.8; 2.10; 2.13; 2.22.A.

QSM'. *One-word name.* 'The divider'
Act. part. I; cf. Arabic qasama. For parallels see Ryckmans, i. 192; Littmann, *Safaitic Inscriptions*, 341b; Wüstenfeld, *Register*, 120, Qāsim. Greek transcription: Kasem, Wuthnow, 62.

QSPRYNS. *Latin name*
Casperianus (derivative of Casperius). See Appendix IV, 2.2; 2.5; 2.8; 2.10; 2.13; 2.22.A. The Greek form Kasperianou is found on an inscription from Palmyra (*Syria*, 20 [1939], 320).

QRBLWN. *Latin name*
Corbulo; see *ILS*, 183b. See Appendix IV, 2.2; 2.12; 2.15; 2.22.E.

QRD'. *One-word name.* 'Ape'
Arabic qird. For parallels and discussion see Ryckmans, i. 194; Wüstenfeld, *Register*, 375, Qird; Nöldeke, *Beiträge*, 76. See also under QWP'.

QRYN. *One-word name.* 'Horn' (dimin.)
Quṭail form. *qarn, 'horn' (Common Semitic). For parallels see Littmann, *Safaitic Inscriptions*, 342a; Huffmon, *APNMT*, 259. Greek transcription: Korenos, Wuthnow, 65. Cf. the name ḏū 'l qarnayn, 'the two-horned', an epithet given to Alexander the Great. The horn is a symbol of strength. Variant: QRYNW.

QRYNW. See under QRYN

Q[R]SPYNWS. *Latin name*
Crispinus; see *ILS*, 185a. See Appendix IV, 2.2; 2.5; 2.11; 2.20; 2.22.A.

QRQPN. *One-word name.* 'Head'
Aramaic qarqap. For similar names see van den Branden, *Histoire*, 59.

QŠṬ'. *One-word name.* 'Archer'
Aramaic qaššāṭ. Cantineau, *Le Nabatéen*, ii. 144, lists the variant QŠṬW, which he derives from Arabic qāšiṭ, 'just, true'. The variant QŠT' makes the rendering 'bowman' more likely. The change ṭ/t is also found in Syriac: qašāṭā' (*Thes. Syr.* 3771) and qašātā' (*Thes. Syr.* 3772). Milik, *Syria*, 37 (1960), 94–5, supports the meaning 'archer', but as term used to denote a profession, not a personal name. The variants QŠT', QŠṬY, QŠṬW speak for an interpretation as personal name.

QŠṬY. See under QŠṬ'

QŠT'. See under QŠṬ'

R'WM'. *Uncertain*
For discussion see under 'R'WM. The Syriac R'WM', 'foster-son', could be connected with the Palmyrene name. Surname here.

RB'. *Hypcoristicon*
This is a shortened form of RB'L (see below). It is sometimes impossible to say whether it is a personal name or an epithet, e.g. NS' RB', 'ns' rb' or ns' the 'elder', *AAS*, 3 (1953), 151. The variant RBW, however, shows that it is most probably a personal name. For parallels see Ryckmans, i. 196, RBY; Cantineau, *Le Nabatéen*, ii. 145. The name is found in epigraphic Syriac (*BSOAS*, 22 [1959], 30, no. 3[1], RBY). Greek transcription: Rabbos, Wuthnow, 96. RB' itself can also mean 'lord, master'; cf. the Talmudic name Rābbā' (Jastrow, 1439). Ingholt, 'Some Sculptures from the Tomb of Malkû at Palmyra', 472 ff., takes rb' in the sense of 'the elder' and contests its use as a personal name (idem., p. 472, n. 59); cf. also Teixidor's reply in *Syria*, 45 (1968), 379–80.

RB'L. *Verbal sentence with the perfect.* 'Great is god'
*rby, 'be, become large' (Heb., Aram., Akk.; cf. Arab. rbw 'increase, grow').
For parallels see Huffmon, *APNMT*, 260; Cantineau, *Le Nabatéen*, ii. 145; Littmann, *Safaitic Inscriptions*, 342b; Ryckmans, i. 248; 'Hatra', no. 38, RBLH; *PRU*, v. 14[27]; Gröndahl, *Personennamen*, 178–9. Dura, *Final Report V*, *Part I*, 62, Rabbelus. The Greek transcription Rabbēlos is attested from a trilingual text (*Syria*, 27 [1950], 137).

RB'N. *Unexplained*
The Aleph within the word is very troublesome. Long internal a is usually written without vowel letter. It is therefore unlikely that the name is a variant of RBN (see below). See also Ibn Doreid, 314[6], for the different etymologies that he offers for Rabbān.

RBBT. *Unexplained*
It cannot be the fem. form of rb, 'lord, master', in view of the doubling of the Beth. Also the name in question is definitely masc.

RBW. See under RB'

RBWTY. *Unexplained*
A connection with Aramaic r^{e}bûtā, 'dignity', or ribbô', 'myriad', does not yield any satisfactory sense.

RBḤ. *One-word name.* 'Male ape'
Arabic rubbāḥ. For parallels and discussion see Ryckmans, i. 196; Littmann, *Safaitic Inscriptions*, 342b. Both derive the name from the Arabic rabāḥ, 'gain, profit'.

RBN. *One-word name.* 'Teacher'
Aramaic rabbān. For parallels see 'Hatra', no. 146[2], RBN; see also Ryckmans, i. 196.

RBN'. *Hypocoristicon.* 'Great is Nabû'
*rb-nbw.
For discussion and parallels see under RB'L. Another possible interpretation would be to consider the name a variant of RBN (see above) augmented by the Aramaic status emphaticus ending. Greek transcription: Rabbanēs, Wuthnow, 96.

RBT. *Unexplained*
The name is masc. It is therefore very unlikely that RBT is the fem. of rb, 'lord'.

RGYN'. *Latin name*
Regina; see *ILS*, 234b. See Appendix IV, 2.1; 2.9; 2.11; 2.22.B.

RDWN. *Greek name*
Rhodōn; see Pape, 1313. See Appendix IV, 1.21; 1.25.F.

RDM. See under DRM

RWḤ'. *One-word name.* 'Joy, rest'
Arabic rauḥ. For parallels see Cantineau, *Le Nabatéen*, ii. 146; Littmann, *Safaitic Inscriptions*, 343a; Wüstenfeld, *Register*, 382, Rawāḥa. Greek transcription: Raouaos, Wuthnow, 97. The transcription Rouaios belongs to RWYḤW (see Littmann, *BSOAS*, 15 [1953], 25). A Palestinian saint of the seventh century A.D. called himself Rawaḥ the Qurašaite (see *Ana. Bollandiana*, 31 [1912], 410–50). Conceivably, RWḤ' could be a shortened form of RWḤBL (see below).

RWḤBL. *Verbal sentence with the perfect.* 'Bēl gives rest'
Aramaic r^{e}waḥ, 'feel easy'; pa''el, rawwaḥ, 'give rest'. See Caquot, 'Onomastique', 249.

RWMY. *One-word name.* 'Lobe of the ear'
Arabic raum. No other attestations. See Nöldeke, *Beiträge*, 101, for similar names.

RWṢY. *One-word name.* 'Meadow'
Arabic rauḍ. For parallels see Ryckmans, i. 198, who offers a different explanation.

RZYṢYḤ. *Unexplained*
Other possible reading is DZYṢYḤ.

RḤ(..)
The name is not fully spelled out and an interpretation is thus impossible.

RYSQ'. *Uncertain.* 'Elegant, graceful'
Cf. Arabic rašîq. Qaiṭal form. On the qaiṭal form see Brockelmann, *GVG*, i. 344, par. 129. This form is known only in Arabic.

RYṢW. *One-word name.* 'Meadow'
Arabic riyāḍ. See also under RWṢY. Riyāḍ is still used as a personal name in Arabic speaking countries.

RM'. *Hypocoristicon.* 'N.N. is exalted'
*rmy, 'exalt' (Heb., Aram., Syr., Arab., Akk.)
For parallels and discussion see Cantineau, *Le Nabatéen*, ii. 146; 'Hatra', nos. 111, 150, RMW; Ryckmans, i. 200; Cowley, *Papyri*, 34^3; Noth, *IPN*, 145. See also under RMŠ'. Variants: RMY, RMW.

RMW. See under RM'

RMY
See under RM'. The reading DMY is found in Thamudic (van den Branden, *Inscriptions*, 494) and possibly in Syriac (*Syria*, 34 [1957], 321). Arabic damīy, 'bloody'.

[R]MLH'. *Uncertain*
Caquot and Starcky restore [']MLH', following the suggestion of the editor of the *Corpus*. The photograph shows no traces of an Aleph. Starcky, *PNO*, 150, ad no. 17, interprets the name as 'le dieu est mère', while Caquot, *Syria*, 39 (1962), 239, n. 7, sees in the name a contracted form of *'MT'LH = [']MLH'. This last interpretation is untenable. The proposed explanation [R]MLH' = *RM-'LH, 'God is exalted', has the support of semantic parallels (see discussion under RMŠ'). On the elision of the Aleph cf. ZBDLH and see Rosenthal, *Sprache*, 29–30. Disturbing, however, is the status emphaticus ending added to 'lh. This is otherwise unattested when 'lh forms part of a personal name. The ending may have been added by analogy to other names.

RMNWS. *Latin name*
Rōmanus; see *ILS*, 235a. See Appendix IV, 2.8; 2.12; 2.22.A.

RMŠ'. *Hypocoristicon.* 'Šamaš is exalted'
*rm-šmš.
Structural type: verb plus divine name; for type: divine name plus verb, see under ŠMŠRM'. For parallels see Ryckmans, i. 249; Cantineau, *Le Nabatéen*, ii. 146. See also: RM', RMW, RMY, [R]MLH'.

RSTQ'. *Latin name*
Rusticus; see *ILS*, 236b. See Appendix IV, 2.2; 2.7; 2.22A; 2.23.C.

R''. *Hypocoristicon.* 'N.N. delights'
*r'' plus divine name.
*rḍy, 'be content' (Common Semitic, except Akkadian).
Aramaic r^e'ā'; Old Aramaic RQY. For discussion and parallels see Huffmon, *APNMT*, 265; Ryckmans, i. 203, 249; Cantineau, *Le Nabatéen*, ii. 147; Cowley, *Papyri*, 34^3, 15^{39}, 8^{33}; 14^{12}, NBWR'Y; Noth, *IPN*, 153, 229. Caquot's reference, *RTP*, 157, to the Old Aramaic name HDRQY (*sic*) is wrong. The correct reading is HDRQY' (*CIS*, ii. 74). It is rather doubtful whether the second name element is connected with the root *rḍy. Variant: R'Y.

R'Y. See under R''

R'T'. See under D'T'

R'TH. See under D'T'

RP'. *Hypocoristicon.* 'N.N. has healed'
*rp' plus divine name.
*rp', 'heal' (Heb., Phoen., Aram.; cf. Arab., Eth. 'repair').
For parallels and discussion see Huffmon, *APNMT*, 263; Ryckmans, i. 202; Caquot, 'Onomastique', 248; 'Hatra', no. 54^3.

RP'L. *Verbal sentence with the perfect.* 'God has healed'
Structural type: verb plus divine name; for type: divine name plus verb see under BWRP'. For parallels and discussion see Huffmon, *APNMT*, 264; Ryckmans, i. 249; 'Hatra', nos. 141, 128, 83^3; Noth, *IPN*, 179; Nöldeke, *Beiträge*, 100. See also: RP', RPBWL, RPNW.

RPBWL. *Verbal sentence with the perfect.* 'Bôl has healed' *rp'-bwl
Long internal a is always written defectively; see Rosenthal, *Sprache*, 15; Cantineau, *Grammaire*, 52. For discussion and parallels see under RP'L.

RPNW. *Hypocoristicon.* 'Nabû has healed' *rp'-nbw.
The form RP'TY, frequently cited by Caquot, *Syria*, 39 (1962), 248, is based on a wrong reading and a misunderstanding of the grammar in the Palmyrene text. The correct reading should be *dy 'TY* (*C* 4527). For parallels and discussion see under RP'L.

RṢ(..)
The name is not fully written out and therefore an interpretation is impossible.

RŠY. *One-word name.* 'Rain'
Arabic rašš. For parallels see under 'YT'.

RT'. *One-word name.* 'Lungs'
Syriac rātā'. So far no other names are attested from this root.

Š'YL'. *One-word name.* 'Asked for'
Aramaic pass. part. For parallels see Noth, *IPN*, 136; cf. the Talmudic name Šîlā' (Jastrow, 1562). The name occurs in epigraphic Syriac (*BSOAS*, 16 [1954], 17, no. 2^2, šîlā'). Cf. the N.T. name Silas (Acts 15^{22}). The Greek name Silas shows that the Aleph is elided. Only at Palmyra is the Aleph retained, which the Greek transcription Seeila, attested from a bilingual text (*C* 3934^3), clearly shows.

ŠB'. *One-word name.* 'Young man, girl'
Arabic šābb. ŠB' occurs as masc. and fem. It is possible that the Aleph was sometimes considered to be a fem. ending. For parallels see Cantineau, *Le Nabatéen*, ii. 148; Ryckmans, i. 204–5. Variant: ŠBY.

ŠBY. See under ŠB'

ŠBḤY. *Uncertain*
Is this name the fem. imperative of š^ebaḥ, 'praise', or a shortened form of a theophorous name? See Noth, *IPN*, 211, who derives the O.T. name yišbāḥ from an altogether different root. Recently on this, Schult, *Vergleichende Studien*, 127–8.

ŠB''. *One-word name.* 'Lion'
Arabic šabuʿ. For parallels and discussion see Ryckmans, i. 146; Cantineau, *Le Nabatéen*, ii. 148; 'Hatra', no. 18; Nöldeke, *Beiträge*, 77. Greek transcription: Sabaos, Wuthnow, 99. It is also conceivable, though less likely, that ŠB'' is a shortened form of ŠB''L. For discussion see Littmann, *Safaitic Inscriptions*, 330b.

ŠB'T'. *Uncertain*
Rosenthal, *JAOS*, 75 (1955), 200, thinks it is a divine name rather than a personal name and considers the form a true Aramaization of Akkadian Sibitti; cf. Sfire i. A^{11}, SBT. This explanation is rather unlikely. It would be hard to explain the Aiyn and the spelling with Shin in view of the Sfire evidence. Caquot, *RTP*, 159, takes the form to be a verbal sentence, 'Athe has captured'. The interpretation of the name as a genitive compound seems to be preferable; 'lion of Athe'. For discussion see under ŠB''.

ŠBTY. *One-word name.* 'Born on a Sabbath'
Nisbe; Jewish name. For parallels see Cantineau, *Le Nabatéen*, ii. 148; Clay, *BEUP*, x. 62, Ša-ba-ta-ai; Cowley, *Papyri*, 58^3; Noth, *IPN*, 222. Greek transcription: Sabbathaios, Wuthnow, 100.

ŠG'. *One-word name.* 'Teak [Indian tree]'
Aramaic šāgā'. For similar names see Noth, *IPN*, 230.

ŠGD. See under ŠGR'.

ŠGL. *Divine name used as personal name*
For discussion of this type of name see under B'ŠMN. On the deity see Caquot, *Semitica*, 4 (1951–2), 55–8.

ŠG'W. *One-word name.* 'Courageous, valiant'
Arabic šijāʿ. For parallels and discussion see Cantineau, *Le Nabatéen*, ii. 149; Ryckmans, i. 205, 401; Caskel, *Lihyan*, 152; Littmann, *Safaitic Inscriptions*, 344b; Wüstenfeld, *Register*, 419, Shijʿ.

ŠGR'. *One-word name.* 'Pistachio-nut'
Syriac šĕgārā' or šĕgdā'; Arabic šajar. Littmann, *Safaitic Inscriptions*, 344b, accepts Ibn Doreid's explanation (220^{11}) of šajjār as 'spear thruster'. The proposed interpretation is preferable. For similar names see Goldmann, *Personennamen*, 30; Noth, *IPN*, 230. Variant: ŠGRY.

ŠGRY. See under ŠGR'

ŠDD'. *One-word name.* 'Tyrant, oppressor'
Arabic šaddād. For parallels see Ryckmans, i. 206; Littmann, *Safaitic Inscriptions*, 344b. The Aramaic status emphaticus ending has been added.

ŠDY. *Uncertain*
It is a matter of doubt whether the name is to be derived from Arabic sīd, 'wolf'; see Beeston, 'Arabian Sibilants', 227. For parallels, the interpretation of which is doubtful, see Littmann, *Safaitic Inscriptions*, 330b; Caskel, *Lihyan*, 151. See also Nöldeke, *Beiträge*, 79.

ŠH(Y)MW. *One-word name.* 'Arrow' (dimin.)
Quṭail form; cf. Arabic sahm. For parallels see Littmann, *Safaitic Inscriptions*, 330b; Ryckmans, i. 147.

ŠWḤBW. *Unexplained*
No photograph is available to verify the reading, which may well be wrong.

ŠWYR'. *Unexplained*
The Greek transcription Seouira, attested from a bilingual text (*Inv. X*, 44), speaks against the possibility of ŠWYR' being a quṭail form (diminutive).

ŠWQN. *One-word name.* 'Leg'
Aramaic šôqā'. See also under ŠQN.

ŠḤR'. *Uncertain*
Either a one-word name meaning 'dawn', augmented by the ending Aleph, or a hypocoristicon of a name with ŠḤR as divine element. For parallels to either of the two interpretations see Ryckmans, i. 306; Cantineau, *Le Nabatéen*, ii. 149; Noth, *IPN*, 169; Harris, *Grammar*, 149, ŠḤRB'L; van den Branden, *Inscriptions*, 381, sḥrmt; Gordon, *UT*, 308: 19, bn ʿbd šḥr; Gröndahl, *Personennamen*, 192. On the deity see Jamme, 'Panthéon', 99; Höfner, Pope in *Wörterbuch*, 525, 306. Variants: ŠḤRW, ŠḤRY.

ŠḤRW. See under ŠḤR'

ŠḤRY. See under ŠḤR'

ŠṬ'. *One-word name.* 'Acacia tree'
Aramaic šiṭṭā', šîṭṭā'. See Goldmann, *Personennamen*, 30, and Noth, *IPN*, 230, for similar names.

ŠYBY. *One-word name.* 'Grey hair, old age'
Aramaic śeybāh, Arabic šaib. For parallels see Cantineau, *Le Nabatéen*, ii. 149; Ryckmans, i. 208; Wüstenfeld, *Register*, 418, Šaybat. Greek transcription: Saibeou, Wuthnow, 102. The name is also attested as gentilic; see Ryckmans, i. 318.

ŠYDN. *One-word name.* 'Lord, master, chief'
Arabic sayyid. Nominal suffix -ān added; see also under MYŠN. See Goldmann, *Personennamen*, 26.

ŠY'N. *One-word name.* 'Follower'
Arabic šayya'. For parallels see Ryckmans, i. 208; Littmann, *Safaitic Inscriptions*, 345b; Wüstenfeld, *Register*, 418, Šay'. Greek transcription: Saios, Wuthnow, 102. See Ryckmans, i. 374, for a region called ŠY'N. For names composed with šy' see Cantineau, *Le Nabatéen*, ii. 150. Note the divine name ŠY''LQWM.

ŠYQN. *One-word name.* 'Mountain'
Arabic šîq.

ŠYŠT'. *One-word name.* 'Vase'
Syriac šîštā'. For similar names see Noth, *IPN*, 226.

ŠKY. *Hypocoristicon*
Shortened form of ŠKYBL (see below).

ŠKYBL. *Uncertain*
A derivation of the first element from Syriac sûkāyā', 'hope', is possible, 'Bēl is my hope'. However, in view of the names ŠKNY, ŠK'T' it is more likely that the first element of this and the other two names is a verbal form; cf. Aramaic s^{e}kā', 'hope, look out', 'Bēl looks out'. Cf. the O.T. names śākyāh, śēkû. See also Caquot, *RTP*, 178, 156.

ŠKYY. *Hypocoristicon*
Shortened form of ŠKYBL. The Greek transcription Sochaieis is attested from a bilingual text (*C* 4134).

ŠKNY. *Uncertain*
The name can be interpreted as a hypocoristicon of a theophorous name (š^{e}kan, 'dwell'). For parallels and discussion see Noth, *IPN*, 194; Gordon, *UT*, 2014: 38, škny; Gröndahl, *Personennamen*, 192. It is also conceivable that ŠKNY is a one-word name; cf. the Arabic sakn, 'dwelling'. For parallels see Littmann, *Safaitic Inscriptions* 331a; Ryckmans, i. 149. ŠKNY can also be a hypocoristic form of *ŠK-NBW, 'Nabû looks out'. For discussion see under ŠKYBL and see Caquot, *RTP*, 156.

ŠK'T'. *Uncertain*
Probably a verbal sentence with the perfect, 'Athe looks out'. For discussion of the verbal element see ŠKYBL.

ŠL'. *Unexplained*
For a tentative interpretation see Cantineau, *Le Nabatéen*, ii. 150, and Starcky, *MUSJ*, 28 (1949–50), 53–4.

ŠLWM. *One-word name.* 'Peace'
Jewish name. For parallels see Littmann, *Safaitic Inscriptions*, 331b; Cantineau, *Le Nabatéen*, ii. 151, lists a group of names derived from šlm, 'peace'; Ryckmans, i. 150–1. Cf. the Greek name Salōmē (Pape, 1333); on this see also Arndt–Gingrich, 748b.

ŠLM. *Uncertain*
It may be a defective writing for ŠLWM. For a parallel see Kraeling, *BMAP*, 9[24]. It is more probable that ŠLM is a variant of ŠLM', ŠLMY, ŠLMW.

ŠLM'. *Uncertain*
Various interpretations are possible. (1) The name is a hypocoristicon of ŠLMN (see below). (2) A shortened form of ŠLMLT. (3) A one-word name derived from the root šlm. The variants are: ŠLMY, ŠLMW.

ŠLMW. See under ŠLM'

ŠLMWY. *Uncertain*
It appears that a second hypocoristic ending was added to ŠLMW (see above).

ŠLMY. See under ŠLM'

ŠLMLT. *Genitive compound.* 'Safety given by Allat'
A similar name—ŠLM'T'—is attested in epigraphic Syriac; see Segal, *BSOAS*, 22 (1959), 26[12]. The Greek transcription [Salam]allathon is attested from a bilingual text (*C* 3966).

ŠLMN. *Divine name used as personal name*
For parallels to this type of name see under B'ŠMN. For parallels see 'Hatra', no. 130; Cantineau, *Le Nabatéen*, ii. 151.

ŠLMN'. *One-word name.* 'Honest, righteous'
Aramaic šalmānā'. For similar names see Noth, *IPN*, 228.

ŠLMN[Y]
This is the reading suggested by the editor of the *Corpus*. An examination of the photograph shows that the space is too big for a Yodh and the traces do not fit the letter. It is tempting to restore an Aleph, which would fit the space exactly. The traces visible are such that practically any letter of the alphabet could be restored. On the interpretation of the new reading see above.

ŠLMT. *Divine name used as personal name*
The name is attested in epigraphic Syriac (*BSOAS*, 16 [1954], 29, no. 14[3]). The wife of Abgar Ukāmā was named Šalmat; see Phillips, *Doctrine*, 9[5]. See also Cantineau, *Le Nabatéen*, ii. 150.

ŠMW'L. *Jewish name*
For discussion see Noth, *IPN*, 123, 140.

ŠMY. *Uncertain*
Šammay is attested as personal name in the Talmud (Jastrow, 1591). The latter name is assumed to be a shortened form of *ŠM'YH.

ŠM'W'. *Unexplained*
The form could be a hypocoristicon of *ŠM'-WD, 'Wadd has heard', but the reading may well be wrong.

ŠM'WN. *Jewish name*
For discussion see Noth, *IPN*, 185; Caquot, *RTP*, 178.

ŠM'R'. *Hypocoristicon.* 'Arṣû has heard'
*šm'-'rṣw.
For parallels see Noth, *IPN*, 185; Harris, *Grammar*, 151; Ryckmans, i. 239. Variant: ŠM'[R]Y.

ŠM'[R]Y. See under ŠM'R'

Š[M]RP'. *Verbal sentence with the perfect.* 'Šamaš has healed'
*šmš-rp'.
For discussion and parallels see under BWRP'.

ŠMŠGRM. *Verbal sentence with the perfect.* 'Šamaš has decided'
Syriac g^e^ram. For parallels see Cantineau, *Le Nabatéen*, ii. 79; Littmann, *Safaitic Inscriptions*, 306a; Caskel, *Lihyan*, 146, takes the meaning of garama in Ethiopic, 'be the object of veneration, respect'; Dura, *Final Report V, Part I*, 62, Garmelus. ŠMŠGRM is widely attested in Syriac; see Phillips, *Doctrine*, 1^{11}, 17^{10}; Cureton, *Spicilegium Syriacum*, 1^{1}; Sachau, 'Edessenische Inschriften', 158. Greek transcription: Samsigeramos, Wuthnow, 105.

ŠMŠRM'. *Verbal sentence.* "Šamaš is exalted'
Structural type: divine name plus verb; for type: verb plus divine name, see under RMŠ'. The name is augmented by the ending Aleph. For parallels see Galling, 191^{126}; Diringer, *Iscrizioni*, 225, GDRM; Noth, *IPN*, 145; Ryckmans, i. 249; Harris, *Grammar*, 90, B'LRM; Wuthnow, 65, Kosramos.

Š''. *Uncertain*
The name is most likely a hypocoristicon of Š''L, 'servant of god'; cf. Arabic šī'a. For parallels see Littmann, *Safaitic Inscriptions*, 345b, Š''L.

Š'D. *One-word name.* 'Luck'
Arabic sa'd. For parallels see Ryckmans, i. 152; Cantineau, *Le Nabatéen*, ii. 152; Littmann, *Safaitic Inscriptions*, 332b, with further references; Wüstenfeld, *Register*, 397. A Syrian bishop is attested by the name šā'ād. This name is rendered in later Syriac texts sa'd. On the use of š/ś in early epigraphic Syriac where later Syriac has s see Segal, *BSOAS*, 30 (1967), 294, with further references to literature. Greek transcription: Sados, Saedos, Wuthnow, 101. It is also conceivable that Š'D is the name of a deity used as personal name. On this see Höfner in *Wörterbuch*, 464f.

Š'D'. *Hypocoristicon*
For discussion see under Š'D'L. Variants: Š'DW, Š'DY.

Š'D'L. *Genitive compound.* 'Luck from god'
For parallels see Cantineau, *Le Nabatéen*, ii. 153; Ryckmans, i. 239–40. Greek transcription: Saddēlou, Wuthnow, 101. See also: Š'D, Š'D', Š'DW, Š'DY, Š'DLT.

Š'DW. See under Š'D'

Š'DY. See under Š'D'

Š'DLT. *Genitive compound.* 'Luck from Allat'
For parallels see under Š'D'L.

Š'W[D]'. *One-word name.* 'Luck'
Arabic sa'ūd.

Š'WT. *Unexplained*
A bishop of Edessa during the fourth century A.D. bore the same name (*Thes. Syr.* 4253). For a tentative interpretation see Caquot, *RTP*, 166.

Š'YDN. *Uncertain*
It is impossible to determine whether this form represents the diminutive (quṭail) or the Arabic pass. part. (qaṭīl) of the Arabic noun sa'd, 'luck'. On the last form see Brockelmann, *GVG*, i. 354. Both forms are attested as names; see Wüstenfeld, *Register*, 399, 423, Sa'īd, Su'aid. For parallels see Cantineau, *Le Nabatéen*, ii. 153; Ryckmans, i. 307. Greek transcription: Soaidou, Wuthnow, 110.

Š'RWN'. *One-word name.* 'Hairy'
Aramaic śa'ărān. For further names from this root see Ryckmans, i. 211; Littmann, *Safaitic Inscriptions*, 326b, MŠ'R; Wüstenfeld, *Register*, 89, Al-Aš'ar. Variant: Š'RN'.

Š'RN'. See under Š'RWN'

Š[']T. *Uncertain*
Cf. Arabic ša'aṯ, 'unkempt'. The name is attested as a tribal name and as a personal name; see Ryckmans, i. 211, 318. Surname here.

ŠP'. *One-word name*
The meaning is uncertain. Caquot, *RTP*, 165, interprets the name from the Arabic siff and the Syriac šapāpā', 'serpent'. Littmann, *Safaitic Inscriptions*, 333a, refers to Ibn Doreid, who offers different etymologies of the name. One might also tentatively propose a connection with Syriac s^e^pā', 'lip'.

ŠQN. *One-word name.* 'Leg'
Aramaic šāqā'. See also under ŠWQN.

ŠRYKW. *One-word name.* 'Associate, friend'
Quṭail form; cf. Arabic šarīk. The variant spellings SRYKW, SRYK' point to PS ś. For parallels see Ryckmans, i. 212; Ibn Doreid, 215[12]; Wüstenfeld, *Register*, 417, Šarīk, 421, Šurayk. Greek transcription: Soraichos, Wuthnow, 111. Latin transcription: Suricus, Lidzbarski, *Handbuch*, 482, no. 2. The name occurs under the variant ŠRWKW in the Shīmbār inscriptions (*BSOAS*, 27 [1964], 272, no. 2). Variant: ŠRYKY.

ŠRYKY. See under ŠRYKW

TBLL. *Uncertain*
Among the Palmyrene personal names is a group of seven verbal sentence names in the imperfect: TBLL, TBNN, TD'L, TW'L, TMLK, T'YR, TQYM. The forms are all third person fem. sing., and they can all be explained from the Arabic. All of the names refer to a goddess. The root bll means in Aramaic 'crumble, penetrate', and in Arabic II 'moisten', IV 'save'. The Aramaic root does not yield any satisfactory meaning. Grammatically the name can only be the Arabic second form, 'she moistens'. For further attestations of the root see Ryckmans, i. 51; Littmann, *Safaitic Inscriptions*, 302b.

TBNN. *Uncertain*
For discussion see under TBLL. Grammatically the verb can only be the Arabic second form. The meaning for this form, as given in Lane, i. 258a, is not applicable here. For attestations of the root see Ryckmans, i. 52; Littmann, *Safaitic Inscriptions*, 302b.

TB'WT. *Unexplained*
For a rather speculative interpretation see Caquot, *RTP*, 166.

TBR'. *One-word name.* 'Destroyer'
Cf. Arabic ṯabīr. Arabic pass. part. with an active meaning. For parallels see Ryckmans, i. 215; Littmann, *Safaitic Inscriptions*, 346b; Wüstenfeld, *Register*, 447, Ṯabīr. The Aramaic status emphaticus ending has been added.

TD'L. *Verbal sentence in the imperfect*
II form; cf. Arabic da'ala. 'She runs with short steps'. For discussion see under TBLL. For a further attestation of the root see Ryckmans, i. 64.

TDMWR. *One-word name.* 'Tadmor'
The name of the city and also a female personal name; cf. Carthago (Ronzevalle, *Rev. arch* 1902, ii. 36). For a parallel see Cantineau, *Le Nabatéen*, ii. 155 (reading uncertain). The etymology of the name is uncertain. It is not possible, however, to derive the name from tāmār, 'date-palm', as was done in older treatments. The dissimilation of m > dm is nowhere else attested. A derivation of TDMWR from the Syriac tĕdmûrtā' 'wonder, marvel', is highly speculative. It is based on the assumption that at the spring Efca miraculous cures have resulted; see Starcky, *Palmyre*, 30; *Supp. au Dict. de la Bible*, 6, 1960. Albright, *JPOS*, 14 (1934), 130, n. 149, explains the name from the root dmr, 'pierce, penetrate'. In case the word is Semitic, it is best to consider it as a ta- preformative of a root *dmr. The cuneiform spellings Ta-ad-mu-ri-im[ki], Ta-ad-me-er[ki], Ta-ad-mar, tend to show that the second syllable is short; see Eisser–Lewy, 'Alt-assyrische Rechtsurkunden vom Kültepe', III+IV, 1935, no. 303 A[16]; *ARM*, v. 23[16]; Luckenbill, *Ancient Records*, i. 287, 292, 308, 330. One will have to assume *tadmar and not *tadmūr. The change of short a to ō is now well attested from Hatra; cf. NRGWL, NTWN. Variant: TDMR.

TDMR. Variant of TDMWR (see above). Cf. the gentilic names TDMWRY' and TDMRY'.

TDM(R)'
The reading is emended and the interpretation uncertain. It may be a variant spelling of TDMR augmented by the ending Aleph.

TDRŠ. *Uncertain*
It is not very likely that the form represents the Greek name Theodoros. For discussion see Appendix IV, 1.12.

TW'L. *Verbal sentence in the imperfect*
II form; cf. Arabic wa'ala. 'She gives refuge' For discussion see under TBLL. For other attestations of the root see Littmann, *Safaitic Inscriptions*, 310b; Ryckmans, i. 75.

TWP'. *One-word name.* 'Kettle-drum'
Aramaic tôp. Lidzbarski, *Ephemeris*, 3, 136, considers the name to be a shortened form of the Greek name Theophilos. See Noth, *IPN*, 226, for similar names.

TWRY. *One-word name*
Meaning uncertain. The name can be derived from Aramaic tôr, 'turtle-dove', or tôr, 'ox'. Parallels favour only the second meaning; see Cantineau. *Le Nabatéen*, ii. 155; Ryckmans, i. 215; Wüstenfeld, *Register*, 452, Ṯaur; Nöldeke, *Beiträge*, 83. Greek transcription: Taur(e)inos, Wuthnow, 175.

TY(..)
The name is abbreviated and can stand for TY(M') or TY(MY) (see below).

TYBWL. *Genitive compound.* 'Servant of Bôl'
*tym-bwl.
On the distinction between 'bd and tym- see under 'BDBL. For parallels of names composed with tym- plus divine name see Cantineau, *Le Nabatéen*, ii. 155; Ryckmans, i. 213; Wüstenfeld, *Register*, 447; 'Hatra',

nos. 177, 184. Greek transcription: Thembēlos, Wuthnow, 54. For semantic parallels in other languages see Harris, *Grammar*, 111, KLB-; Ryckmans, i. 247, QNN. See also TYM', TYMW, TYMḤ', TYMY, [TY]MY'M[D], TYMLT, TYMN', TYMS', TYM', TYM'', TYM'MD, TYMRṢW, TYMṢ', TYMŠ', TYMŠMŠ, TMRṢW.

TYDWR', TYDRWS. *Greek name*
Theodōros; see Pape, 490. See Appendix IV, 1.7; 1.8; 1.12; 1.14; 1.18; 1.25.D.

TYDRWS. See under TYDWR'

TYKS'
In spite of Cantineau's emphasis upon the correctness of the reading, one will probably have to read TYMS' (see below). The spelling with Kaph instead of Mem may well be a scribal mistake.

TYM'. *Hypocoristicon.* 'Servant of N.N.'
*tym plus divine name.
For discussion see under TYBWL. Greek transcription: Thaimēs, Thaimos, Wuthnow, 52. Variants: TYMW, TYMY.

TYMW. See under TYM'

TYMḤ'. *Hypocoristicon.* 'Servant of Ḥerta'
*tym-ḥrt'.
The editor of the *Corpus* (*C* 4115) explains the name as composed of TYM- and 'Ḥ', 'servant of the brother'. He is followed in this by Caquot, *RTP*, 179. In this case 'Ḥ' would substitute for a divine name, for which, however, no clear example can be found at Palmyra (see discussion under 'B' and 'ḤY'). The proposed interpretation is preferable. The Greek transcription Thaimaē is attested from a bilingual text (*RB*, 39 [1930], 531).

TYMY. See under TYM'

[TY]MY'M[D]
The restoration is questionable. The form is unexplained. It could be a variant of TYM'MD (see below).

TYMLT. *Genitive compound.* 'Servant of Allat'
For parallels see Ryckmans, i. 252; 'Hatra', nos. 177, 184. For discussion see under TYBWL.

TYMN'. *Hypocoristicon.* 'Servant of Nabû'
*tym-nbw.
The name could also be a shortened form of *TYM-NNY, 'servant of Nanai'. The rare occurrences of Nanai make the first proposal more likely. For discussion see under TYBWL.

TYMS'. *Hypocoristicon.* 'Servant of Sa'ad'
*tym-s'd.
For discussion see under TYBWL. On the deity see Höfner in *Wörterbuch*, 464 f.

TYM'. *Uncertain*
Probably a shortened form of TYM'MD, but without hypocoristic ending. See also TYM''.

TYM''. *Hypocoristicon.* 'Servant of 'Amad'
*tym-'md.
For discussion see under TYM'MD.

TYM'MD. *Genitive compound.* 'Servant of 'Amad'
'MD as divine name is not attested. It could be the name of a deified person; see Ryckmans, i. 166. For further discussion see Caquot, *RTP*, 179. For parallels see under TYBWL.

TYMṢ'. See under TYMRṢW.

TYMRṢW. *Genitive compound.* 'Servant of Arṣû'
For discussion and parallels see under TYBWL. See also: TYMṢ' (hypocoristic form).

TYMŠ'. *Hypocoristicon.* 'Servant of Šamaš'
*tym-šmš.
For discussion and parallels see under TYBWL.

TYMŠMŠ. *Genitive compound.* 'Servant of Šamaš'
For discussion and parallels see under TYBWL.

TYPYLS. *Greek name*
Theophilos; see Pape, 495. See Appendix IV, 1.8; 1.12; 1.16; 1.18; 1.25.D.

TYRDT. *Persian name*
Tiridatēs; see Justi, *Namenbuch*, 326. A presbyter in Edessa bore the same name (*Thes. Syr.* 4429). The name occurs in epigraphic Syriac (*BSOAS*, 16 [1954], 17, no. 2[4], with further references).

TLY'. *One-word name.* 'Loop, string'
Aramaic talyā'. Starcky, *BMB*, 12 (1955), 39, explains the name as the pass. part. of Aramaic t^{e}lā', 'suspend, hang'. The Aleph has to be the Aramaic status emphaticus ending. The interpretation seems rather unlikely.

TM'. *One-word name.* (Name of a bird)
Aramaic tēmā', tēymā'. For similar names see Noth, *IPN*, 230. Could it also be a shortened form of Safaitic TM'L (*TYM'L)? On this see Littmann, *Safaitic Inscriptions*, 346b. See also TMRṢW. Variant: TMH.

TMH. See under TM'

TMLK. *Verbal sentence in the imperfect*
II form; cf. Arabic malaka. 'She rules'
For discussion see under TBLL. For a parallel see Ryckmans, i. 127. Greek transcription: Thomalechē, Wuthnow, 54.

TMRṢW
Very unusual writing for TYMRṢW (see above). It could be a scribal mistake. See also under TM'.

T'YR. *Verbal sentence in the imperfect.* 'She will make jealous'
IV form; cf. Arabic ǵāra. For discussion see under TBLL. For a parallel see Ryckmans, i. 174.

TQYM. *Verbal sentence in the imperfect.* 'She will elevate'
IV form; cf. Arabic qāma. For a parallel see Cantineau, *Le Nabatéen*, ii. 142, YQWM.

TŠBB. *Uncertain*
Names from the root šbb are well attested; see Littmann, *Safaitic Inscriptions*, 344a; Ryckmans, i. 204. Arabic šabāb, 'youth'. The Tau can only be explained as noun preformative, because the name is masc.

APPENDIX I

IMPROVED READINGS

THE following list includes only improved readings of personal names, divine names, and year dates.

CaA 1 A^{2}	*read* ḤṬRY	*pro* ṢṬRY
CaA 8^{3}	*read* [TYM']	*pro* [TWM']
CaA 39^{5}	*read* wRMNWS	*pro* br MNWS
CaA 40^{6}	*read* 'NṬ[Y]K[S]	*pro* 'S[. . . .
CaA 45^{2}	*read* ʿbd lh MʿNY	*pro* br LHMʿNY
CaA 86	*read* BWDL'	*pro* BWRP'
CaA 91 B	*read* TBʿWT or ŠʿWT bny šlm rb'	*pro* . . .]ʿWT bny bʿlty rb'
CaA 96 B	*read* ZBDBWL	*pro* ——
CaA 97	*read* SṬM BWN' blty	*pro* SṬM bny blty
CaA 99	*read* nbw 'brykw	*pro* '[. . . .]ʿw
CaA 100	*read* ʿTʿQB	*pro* ʿT[Y]ʿM
CaA 103	*add* YRḤBWL'	*to* nbw
CaA 104	*read* GD MŠḤ'	*pro* GD MŠḤY'
CaB 1^{1}	*read* TYMRṢW	*pro* TWMRṢW
CaB 1^{1}	*read* BWRP'	*pro* BYRP'
CaD 5^{1}	*read* YDʿY	*pro* YDʿW
CaD 5^{1}	*read* ʿWYD'	*pro* 'WYD'
CaD 8^{4}	*read* ʿZYZW	*pro* ʿZWZW
CaD 12 A^{2}	*read* wlʿGYLW	*pro* wʿGYLW
CaD 31^{5}	*read* 'LQWNRʿ	*pro* 'LQWNDʿ
CaD 36 C^{4}	*read* TYMRṢW	*pro* TYMRʿW
Inv. I, 2^{2}	*read* LŠ[MŠ]	*pro* LS[MŠ]
Inv. III, 15^{1}	*read* ṣlm [SLWQWS]	*pro* ṣlm[' dnh dy]
Inv. III, 22^{1}	*read* ZBDL'	*pro* ZBDLH
Inv. III. 22^{7}	*read* [PRYSQWS]	*pro* [PRYSKWS]
Inv. IV, 2^{1}	*read* TYMŠ[']	*pro* TYM[']
Inv. IV, 16	*read* ML[KW]	*pro* ML[KY]
Inv. IV, 17 B	*read* PṢY'L br	*pro* PḤ' br
Inv. IV, 17 C	*read* PṢ'	*pro* PḤ'
Inv. IV, 17 E	*read* PṢ'	*pro* PḤ'
Inv. V, 6^{3}	*read* LŠMŠ	*pro* LŠLŠ
Inv. VI, 3^{1}	*read* ʿY[T']	*pro* ʿT[Y]
Inv. VI, 7^{1}	*read* MLKW	*pro* YMLKW
Inv. VII, 13	*read* wRMNWS	*pro* GRMNWS
Inv. VIII, 9^{1}	*read* ZBDB(W)L	*pro* ZBDBRL
Inv. VIII, 18	*read* YDY ḥ(b)l	*pro* YD/RYḤL
Inv. VIII, 29^{2}	*read* ḥbl	*pro* GYD/RZ
Inv. VIII, 34	*read* MRQY	*pro* QRQY

Inv. VIII, 49[3]	*read* TDM(R)'	*pro* TD/RMW'
Inv. VIII, 78	*read* [BGR]N	*pro* [BGB]N
Inv. VIII, 92	*read* ṣlmt 'BYŠY	*pro* ṣlmt' byšy
Inv. VIII, 130[3]	*read* ʿQYB'	*pro* ʿMYB'
Inv. VIII, 138[8]	*read* RMY	*pro* DMY
Inv. VIII, 162	*read* BʿŠMN br TY[...	*pro* BʿŠMN brt W[...
Inv. VIII, 194 E[1]	*read* ʿTM'	*pro* ʿMM'
Inv. IX, 5 A	*read* ZBD' [br] ʿDL b(r) ZBD[']	*pro* ZBD' [..] ʿR/DLB(.) ZBL
Inv. IX, 28[7]	*read* NRQYS	*pro* NSQYS
Inv. X, 77	*read* 'LPYS	*pro* 'LPVS
Inv. X, 96[3]	*read* [ḤDWDN]	*pro* [ḤDDN]
Inv. XI, 11[4]	*read* ḤD'	*pro* ḤM'
Inv. XI, 50[1]	*read* BRT' brt 'M'	*pro* BRT' 'M'
Inv. XI, 67[2]	*read* ZBDBWL	*pro* ZBDWL
Inv. XI, 73[3, 4]	*restore* [ʿGLBW]L wMLKBL ʿl[hy']	
Inv. XI, 76[2]	*read* MTBWL	*pro* MYK
Inv. XI, 78[2]	*read* [Z]BDBWL	*pro* [.]BRBWL
Inv. XI, 80[3]	*restore* [ʿGLBWL] at end of line	
CIS 3939[1]	*read* QRṬSṬS	*pro* QRṬYSṬS
CIS 3958	*restore* [3]92	*pro* [4]92
CIS 3968[3]	*read* 'NQY br ʿG'	*pro* 'NQYR wʿG'
CIS 3972[2]	*read* TŠBB	*pro* TŠKB[']
CIS 3993[3]	*read* ḤLD'	*pro* ḤLD[.]
CIS 4074[2]	*read* [R]MLH'	*pro* [']MLH'
CIS 4122[2]	*read* ḤWML	*pro* ḤWMY
CIS 4125	*read* [Ṭ]LY'	*pro* ṢLMY'
CIS 4197[2]	*read* ŠLM'	*pro* ŠLŠ'
CIS 4198 B[2]	*read* mn	*pro* ZKN'
CIS 4199[6]	*read* BWLNWR (NWR)ʿTH	*pro* BWLNWRʿTH
CIS 4236	*read* ḤWML	*pro* ḤY'L
CIS 4432[3]	*read* 'BYʿ	*pro* 'SYʿ
Ingh. B, p. 115, line 19 (Pl. XLI[5])	*read* 'TʿQB	*pro* ʿTʿQB
Ingh. B, p. 127, Pl. XLVIII[2]	*read* BTŠMY'	*pro* BTSMY'
Ingh. E (Malê) 78, IV[3]	*read* 535	*pro* 531
Ingh. E (Malê) 82, V[1]	*insert* ML' br *after* rḥq YWLYS 'WRLYS	
Ingh. E (Malkû), 90, I[4]	*read* 432	*pro* 427
Ingh. E (Malkû), 91, II[2]	*read* 'MTŠLM'	*pro* 'MTŠLMN
Ingh. E (Malkû), 93, III[1]	*read* w'QMT	pro w'Q'T
Ingh. E (Malkû), 97, VI[1]	*read* br	*pro* bd
Ingh. E (Malkû), 98, VII[2]	*read* 'PRHṬ	*pro* 'WRHṬ
Ingh. E (Malkû), 100, VIII[2]	*read* 'GTPS	*pro* 'GTPL
Ingh. E (Malkû), 106, XIII[10]	*read* 585	*pro* 590

Ingh. E (Naṣrallat), 110, 11^{2}	*read* YWLY’ ’WRLY’ ’MT’ brt	*pro* YWLYS ’WRLYS ’MT’ br
StaF 38, 4	*read* ZBD‘TH	*pro* ZBD‘T’
StaB p. 153, A 1205^{2}	*read* ’‘PY	*pro* ‘‘PY
‘Iraq’, p. 63, Pl. 5	*read* ŠṬ’	*pro* ŠKW’
RTP 98b	*read* Paix	*pro* Shalam
RTP 778b	*omit* br *and read* ...br MLKW NŠWM	
RTP 884a	*read* ’YYR	*pro* ’YWR
RTP 987a	*read* DDḤLWN	*pro* DDḤYWN
Pal. 60: 5 A^{1}	*read* [B‘L]TG’	*pro* [BL]TG’
Pal. 60: 5 A^{4}	*read* [TY]MRṢW	*pro* [T]MRṢW
Pal. 62: 4^{1}	*read* NḤ’	*pro* LḤ’
PNO 26	*read* [B]R’TY	*pro* [B]G/R’TY
PNO 41^{2}	*read* BRH’	*pro* BRHN
‘IP’ 17 A^{5}	*read* ‘ZYZW br br	*pro* ‘ZYZW br
‘Malkû’, p. 106^{5}	*read* ’GTPWS	*pro* ’GṬPWS
‘Wadi Hauran’, 3^{2}	*read* ’MY/WN	*pro* ’M/TY/WN
‘Wadi Hauran’, 8^{6}	*read* ŠWYR’	*pro* ŠWYD’
‘Wadi Hauran’, 10^{3}	*read* mtqr’	*pro* mhqr’
‘Wadi Hauran’, 11^{5}	*read* TYBWL	*pro* TBWL
‘Wadi Hauran’, 12^{2}	*read* ḤDYDW	*pro* ḤD/RYD/RW
‘Wadi Hauran’, 12^{5}	*read* ‘NNW	*pro* ‘ZZ/BW

APPENDIX II

CONCORDANCES

A. Comparing the numbers of Ingholt's *Studier over Palmyrensk Skulptur* (*PS*) with the numbers of the *Corpus Inscriptionum Semiticarum, pars secunda, tomus tertius* (*CIS*). The following additional abbreviations and sigla have been used in section A:

RES — *Répertoire d'Épigraphie Sémitique.*

F — Forged inscription.

G — Greek inscription.

I — Inscription illegible.

N — No inscription.

M — Fragmentary inscription (not incorporated).

* — It is not known whether the sculpture bears an inscription (unpublished so far or published in journals and catalogues that were not accessible).

** — The inscription has been published and is included in the Main List. For place of publication consult Ingholt, *Studier*, under the *PS* number.

PS	*RES*	*CIS*
1	—	3972
2	—	4129
3**	—	—
4	—	4281
5	1608	4246
6	1607	4257
7	733	4561
8	726	4458
9	1050	4578
10	1080	4251
11	—	4616
12	996	4562
13	758	4261 *bis*
14	1074	4250
15	738	4256
16	757	4263
17	723	4549
18**	—	—
19	1046	4292
20	274	4294
21	1615	4439
22	817	3974
23	1004	4306
24	143	4243
25	381	4302
26	2165	4305
27	371	4308
28**	—	—
29	252	4293
30	—	4354
31	1030	4374
32	—	4374 *bis*
33**	—	—
34	725	4247
35	737	4248
36	515	4249
37	754	4258
38	727	4458 *bis*
39**	—	—
40	987	4268
41	745	4363
42	2172	4453
43	1069	4254
44	144	4255
45	—	4527
46	—	4507
47	156	4526
48	764	4554
49	—	4296
50	385	4300
51	142	4244
52	358	4301
53	370	4307
54	2175	4460
55	753	4571
56	—	4412
57	—	4283
58*	—	—
59[F]	—	—
60*	—	—
61	1070	4231
62[F]	—	—
63	—	4352
64	1051	4579
65	970	4537
66[M]	—	—
67	755	4259
68	2184	4440

PS	*RES*	*CIS*
69	1632	4470
70	—	4353
71*	—	—
72[I]	—	—
73	1058	4501
74	1059	4502
75	—	4494
76	—	4400
77	345	4586
78*	—	—
79	257	4277
80	1645	4520
81*	—	—
82*	—	—
83	2194	4318
84	1003	4591
85	—	4008
86*	—	—
87	992	4319
88	2215	4350
89	—	4492
90	—	4360
91	2197	4332
92*	—	—
93	152	4446
94*	—	—
95	2200	4282
96	2202	4392
97	2198	4389
98	409	4372
99	258	4265
100**	—	—
101*	—	—
102	347	4516
103	1028	4282
104**	—	—
105	151	4445
106**	—	—
107	2173	4454
108	2171	4279
109	997	4600
110*	—	—
111*	—	—
112*	—	—
113[F]	—	—
114	1603	4471
115	—	4457
116*	—	—
117	732	4559
118	—	4371
119	348	4447
120*	—	—
121*	—	—
122*	—	—
123*	—	—
124**	—	—
125*	—	—
126	—	4344
127	378	4423
128[N]	—	—
129*	—	—
130*	—	—
131*	—	—
132*	—	—
133*	—	—
134*	—	—
135*	—	—
136*	—	—
137*	—	—
138*	—	—
139*	—	—
140	1049	4577
141**	—	—
142	2199	4285
143**	—	—
144	1634	4402
145	2206	4395
146	1635	4465
147	2211	4191
148**	—	—
149**	—	—
150*	—	—
151	1624	4118
152*	—	—
153*	—	—
153 A	2174	4456
154	2213	4347
155*	—	—
156*	—	—
157*	—	—
158*	—	—
159*	—	—
160*	—	—
160 A*	—	—
161	1048	4575
162*	—	—
163	—	4545
164	—	4615
165	346	4274
166	343	4515
167**	—	—
168	1035	4405
169	159	4330
170*	—	—
171*	—	—
172	359	4511
173	724	4550
174**	—	—
175	1609	4299
176	—	4390
177	—	4357
178*	—	—
179	—	4432
180*	—	—
181*	—	—
182*	—	—
183	276	4329
184*	—	—
185*	—	—
186*	—	—
187	760	4552
188*	—	—
189*	—	—
190	1000	4602
191[F]	—	—
192**	—	—
193**	—	—
194*	—	—
195	2170	4452
196	743	4420
197*	—	—
198*	—	—
199	1024	4563
200	740	4275

APPENDIX II

PS	RES	CIS
201**	—	—
202	158	4328
203**	—	—
204	160	4117
205**	—	—
206	140	4434
207	145	4435
208	1625	4580
209**	—	—
210**	—	—
211	729 A	4555
212	742	4272
213	1022	4491
214	1657	4334
215**	—	—
216	355	4519
217	372	4314
218	—	4280
219	137	4397
220	969	4536
221	407	4381
222	1001	4264
223	741	4564
224	—	4617
225**	—	—
226	384	4506
227	2214	4348
228	267	4273
229	1658	4333
230	2183	4468
231	—	4499
232**	—	—
233*	—	—
234**	—	—
235*	—	—
236*	—	—
237*	—	—
238*	—	—
239*	—	—
240*	—	—
241*	—	—
242*	—	—
243*	—	—
244*	—	—
244 A*	—	—
245	135	4607
246	—	4323
247*	—	—
248F	—	—
249	—	4324
250*	—	—
251	1029	4288
252	801	4573
253	1067	4497
254	—	4403
255*	—	—
256*	—	—
257*	—	—
258	—	4406
259	1002	4603
260	1005	4604
261	1011	4479
262**	—	—
263	260	4310
264	999	4601
265*	—	—
266*	—	—

PS	RES	CIS
267*	—	—
268	150	4414
269	1025	4565
270*	—	—
271	1085	4245
272	731	4558
273	748	4567
274*	—	—
275	730	4557
276	344	4422
277	342	4514
278*	—	—
279	441	4385
280	139	4253
281*	—	—
282	157	4327
283	759	4551
284**	—	—
285	—	4361
286	—	4337
287	2168	4450
288**	—	—
289	375	4303
290	273	4534
291	265	4543
292*	—	—
293*	—	—
294	259	4430
295	747	4566
296*	—	—
297	148	4473
298	256	4269
299	—	4331
300	1017	4610
301	155	4504
302	406	4298
303	—	4322
304*	—	—
305	—	4364
306*	—	—
307**	—	—
308*	—	—
309*	—	—
310*	—	—
311*	—	—
312*	—	—
313*	—	—
314*	—	—
315*	—	—
316*	—	—
317*	—	—
318*	—	—
319*	—	—
320*	—	—
321*	—	—
322*	—	—
323	1641	4377
324*	—	—
325*	—	—
326*	—	—
327*	—	—
328*	—	—
329**	—	—
330*	—	—
331*	—	—
332*	—	—
333	—	4335

PS	*RES*	*CIS*
334*	—	—
335	2176	4461
336*	—	—
337	1055	4287
338	1032	4321
339*	—	—
340	356	4131
341	2210	4345
342*	—	—
343*	—	—
344	—	4493
345	1023	4593
346	1047	4574
347	750	4570
348	—	4488
349	967	4341
350	352	4419
351*	—	—
352	1008	4606
353*	—	—
354	2181	4466
355	1009	4476
356**	—	—
357	2179	4463
358	153	4448
359	1052	4376
360	—	4614
361	2212	4346
362*	—	—
363	351	4518
364	349	4517
365	—	4433
366	264	4542
367	—	4496
368*	—	—
369*	—	—
370*	—	—
371**	—	—
372	1033	4399
373	735	4572
374*	—	—
375	1780	—
376	—	4508
377**	—	—
378	439	4382
379	2193	4320
380*	—	—
381*	—	—
382*	—	—
383*	—	—
384[F]	—	—
384 A*	—	—
385*	—	—
386*	—	—
387*	—	—
388*	—	—
389*	—	—
390*	—	—
391*	—	—
392*	—	—
393*	—	—
394**	—	—
395**	—	—
396[F]	—	—
397	1647	4407
398	277	4276
399	262	4431
400	—	4325
401	379	4424
402	739	4278
403	1075	4428
404	1626	4581
405*	—	—
406	2196	4388
407*	—	—
408*	—	—
409	1037	4503
410**	—	—
411*	—	—
412	1616	4200
413*	—	—
414*	—	—
415	993	4478
416*	—	—
417*	—	—
418	354	4513
419**	—	—
420	756	4260
421[G]	—	—
422	1637	4620
423	—	4495
424	721	4547
425	263	4541
426	972	4584
427*	—	—
428	1640	4340
429**	—	—
430*	—	—
431	—	4585
432	2180	4443
433	752	4313
434	763	4553
435	1077	—
436	1060	4500
437	2201	4391
438[F]	—	—
439	—	4528
440	410	4373
441*	—	—
442*	—	—
443*	—	—
444	—	4489
445	1036	4408
446	353	4512
447	744	4568
448*	—	—
449*	—	—
450*	—	—
451*	—	—
452*	—	—
453	154	4449
454*	—	—
455*	—	—
456*	—	—
457*	—	—
458*	—	—
459*	—	—
460*	—	—
461*	—	—
462	136	4413
463	1007	4429
464*	—	—
465	2203	4393
466*	—	—

PS	*RES*	*CIS*
467*	—	—
468	377	4421
469*	—	—
470*	—	—
471*	—	—
472*	—	—
473*	—	—
474*	—	—
475	1782	4409
476	2205	4394
477*	—	—
478	1023	4593
479	—	4367
480	—	4546
481	350	4416
482	984	4291
483	—	4326
484[F]	1076	—
485	—	4339
486*	—	—
487*	—	—
488	1639	4338
489*	—	—
490[F]	—	—
491	1084	4442
492*	—	—
493**	—	—
494[N]	—	—
495	—	4462
496	—	4622
497	1057	4411

PS	*RES*	*CIS*
498*	—	—
499[F]	—	—
500*	—	—
501*	—	—
502[N]	—	—
503*	—	—
504*	—	—
505*	—	—
506*	—	—
507*	—	—
508*	—	—
509*	—	—
510*	—	—
511*	—	—
512	1636	4538
513	2178	4459
514	412	4369
514 A*	—	—
515	974	4588
516	1034	4398
517	—	4356
518	728	4133
519	—	4362
520*	—	—
521**	—	—
522	1086	4436
523	1613	4474
524	2177	4462
525	408	4368
526[F]	—	—
527[F]	—	—

B. Comparing the numbers of the *Recueil des Tessères de Palmyre* (*RTP*) with Cantineau's *Inscriptions Palmyréniennes* (CaA) and his *Tadmorea* I (CaD).

CaA	*RTP*	CaD
86	92	—
87	77	—
88	80	—
89	81	—
90	306	—
91	184	—
92	714	—
93	315	—
94	580	—
95	821	—
96	311	—

CaA	*RTP*	CaD
97	752	—
98	247	—
99	303	—
100	996	—
101	1	—
102	39	—
103	289	—
104	131	—
105	15	—
	125	14 (p. 193)

C. Comparing the numbers of the *Recueil des Tessères de Palmyre* (*RTP*) with Starcky's numbers in *Syria*, 26 (1949), 70, Pl. IV, and Cantineau's *Inscriptions Palmyréniennes* (CaA).

Starcky	*RTP*	CaA
1	318	—
2	327	—
3	326	—
4	317	—
5	319	—
6	322	—
6 A	321	—

Starcky	*RTP*	CaA
7	328	—
8	329	—
9	325	—
10	589	—
11	92	86
12	320	—

D. Comparing the numbers of the *Inventaire des Inscriptions de Palmyre* (*Inv.*) and Cantineau's other publications (CaA, CaB, CaC, CaD) with the numbers of the *Corpus Inscriptionum Semiticarum, pars secunda, tomus tertius* (*CIS*).

Inv.	*CIS*	CaA	CaB
I, 2	3959	—	
I, 3	3958	—	
I, 4	3983	—	
I, 5	—	30	
II, 1	3966	—	
II, 2	3930	—	
II, 3	3931	—	
III, 2	—	47	
III, 4	—	48	
III, 6	3943	—	
III, 7	3942	—	
III, 8	3941	—	
III, 9	3940	—	
III, 10	3939	—	
III, 11	3938	—	
III, 12	3937	—	
III, 13	3936	—	
III, 14	3934	—	
III, 15	3935	—	
III, 16	3944	—	—
III, 17	3945	—	—
III, 19	3946	—	—
III, 20	3947	—	—
III, 21	3933	—	—
III, 22	3932	—	—
III, 24	—	52	—
III, 25	—	53	—
III, 28	3948	—	—
III, 29	3949	—	—
IV, 1 a	4206	—	—
IV, 1 b	4207	—	—
IV, 1 c	4208	—	—
IV, 2	4187	—	—
IV, 3	4124	—	—
IV, 4 a	4114	—	—
IV, 5	4121	—	—
IV, 6 a	4123 *bis*	—	—
IV, 6 b	4123	—	—
IV, 7	—	—	4
IV, 8	—	68	—
IV, 9 a	4168	—	—
IV, 9 b	—	12	—
IV, 9 c	—	13	—
IV, 9 d	—	13	—
IV, 9 e	—	17	—
IV, 10	—	69	—
IV, 11	—	70	—
IV, 12	—	—	3
IV, 13	—	40	—
IV, 14	—	41	—
IV, 16	—	59	—
IV, 17	4232	—	—
IV, 18 a	4115	—	—
IV, 18 b	4115 *bis*	—	—
IV, 19	4164	—	—
IV, 21	4216	71	—
IV, 22	4192	—	—
IV, 23	4170	—	—
IV, 27 a	4134	—	—
IV, 27 b	4157	—	—
IV, 27 c	4140	—	—
IV, 27 d	4141	—	—

APPENDIX II

Inv.	*CIS*	CaA	CaB	CaC	CaD
IV, 27 e	4142	—	—		
IV, 27 f	4143	—	—		
IV, 27 g	4144	—	—		
IV, 27 h	4135	—	—		
IV, 27 i	4136	—	—		
IV, 27 j	4137	—	—		
IV, 27 k	4138	—			
IV, 27 l	4139	—			
IV, 27 m	4145	—			
IV, 27 n	4146	—			
IV, 27 o	4147	—			
IV, 27 p	4148	—			
IV, 27 q	4149	—			
IV, 27 r	4150	—			
IV, 27 s	4151	—			
IV, 27 t	4152	—			
IV, 27 u	4153	—			
IV, 27 v	4154	—			
IV, 27 w	4155	—			
IV, 27 x	4156	—			
IV, 27 y	4158	—			
IV, 28	4109	—			
V, 1	3950	—			
V, 2	3951	—			
V, 3	3952	—			
V, 4	3953	—			
V, 5	3954	—			
V, 6	3957	—			
V, 7	3956	—			
V, 8	3955	—			
V, 9	3984	—			
V, 10	—	35	—		
VI, 1	3985	—	—		
VI, 3	3988	—	—		
VI, 5	3998	—	—		
VI, 6	3968	—	—		
VI, 7	3967	—	—		
VI, 9	3989	—	—		
VI, 11	3977	—	—		
VI, 12	4102	—	—		
VII, 1 a	4162	65	2 A/B		
VII, 2	4214	—	—		
VII, 4	4201	—	—		
VII, 5	—	—	1		
VII, 6 a	4122	—	—		
VII, 6 b	4236	—	—		
VII, 7	—	64	—		
VII, 8	4237	—	—		
VII, 9	—	63	—		
VII, 11	4213	—	—		
VII, 13	4212	39	—		
VII, 15	4197	38	—		
VIII, 55	4202	—	—		
VIII, 56	4113	—	—		
VIII, 57	4235	—	—		
VIII, 61	4163	—	—	—	39
VIII, 63	—	—	11	—	—
VIII, 65	—	77	—	—	—
VIII, 68	—	72	—	—	—
VIII, 71	—	—	—	—	12 B
VIII, 93	4525	—	—	—	—
VIII, 100	4241	—	—	—	—
VIII, 109	—	75	—	—	—
VIII, 144	—	24	—	—	—
VIII, 145	—	22	—	—	—
VIII, 159	—	66	—	—	—
VIII, 160	4125	—	—	—	—

Inv.	*CIS*	CaA	CaB	CaC	CaD
VIII, 161 a	4126	—	—	—	—
VIII, 161 b	4127 A	—	—	—	—
VIII, 161 c	4127 B	—	—	—	—
VIII, 169	—	29	—	—	—
VIII, 193	4239	—	—	—	—
VIII, 200	—	45	—	—	—
IX, 1	—	—	—	—	1
IX, 6 a	3924	—	—	—	—
IX, 6 b	3925	—	—	—	—
IX, 8	3923	—	—	—	—
IX, 9	3922	—	—	—	—
IX, 11	—	—	—	4	—
IX, 12	—	—	—	5	—
IX, 13	3915	—	—	—	—
IX, 14 a	3916	—	—	—	—
IX, 14 b	—	—	—	6 *bis*	—
IX, 15	3917	—	—	—	—
IX, 16	—	—	—	7	—
IX, 18	3918	—	—	—	—
IX, 19	3919	—	—	—	—
IX, 25	3914	—	—	—	—
IX, 26	—	—	—	3	—
IX, 28	—	31	—	2	—
IX, 29	—	32	—	1	—
IX, 31	3921	—	—	—	—
IX, 32	3920	—	—	—	—
IX, 33	—	—	—	9	—
IX, 34	—	—	—	10	—
IX, 36	—	—	—	—	2 A
X, 17	3962	—	—	—	—
X, 40	—	7	—	—	—
X, 47	3963	—	—	—	—
X, 39	—	6	—	—	—
X, 78	—	8	—	—	—
X, 87	3960	—	—	—	—
X, 88	3960	—	—	—	—
X, 89	3961	—	—	—	—
X, 105	—	—	—	—	30
X, 107	—	—	—	—	28 A
X, 111	—	—	—	—	28 B
X, 143	3913	—	—	—	—
XI, 7	—	74	—	—	—
XI, 18	4043	—	—	—	—
XI, 23	4010	—	—	—	—
XI, 29	4075	—	—	—	—
XI, 84	3969	—	—	—	—
XI, 87	—	—	—	—	6
—	4001	—	—	15	—
—	4193	—	5	—	—
—	3960	9	—	—	—
—	4486	3	—	—	—
—	4614	2	—	—	—
—	4060	—	—	16	—
—	4613	4	—	—	—
—	4483	1	—	—	—

E. Concordance to Ingholt's text publications (Ingh. A, Ingh. B, Ingh. C, Ingh. D, Ingh. E).

Ingh. A, p. 96	*Inv. VIII*, 200
Ingh. B, Pl. XLII^{3}	*CIS* 4600
Ingh. B, Pl. XLII^{4}	CaA 80
Ingh. B, Pl. XLVI^{3}	*CIS* 4419
Ingh. B, Pl. XLVII^{2}	*CIS* 4421
Ingh. B, Pl. XLVIII^{1}	*CIS* 4422
Ingh. B, Pl. XLVIII^{3}	*PS* 232

Ingh. B, Pl. XLVIII[4]	*CIS* 4478 = *PS* 415	Ingh. C, p. 11, Fig. 5	*CIS* 4382
Ingh. B, Pl. XLIX[1]	*PS* 210	Ingh. C, p. 10, Fig. 3	*CIS* 4318 = *PS* 83
Ingh. C, p. 10, Fig. 4	*CIS* 4320 = *PS* 379	Ingh. D, p. 32, Pl. VIII[1]	*CIS* 4317
		Ingh. E (Malkû), 90, I	*Inv. VIII*, 60

F. Comparing the numbers of the *Inventaire des Inscriptions de Palmyre* with Starcky's publications.

Inv.	Starcky	*Inv.*	Starcky
X, 144	*Syria*, 26 (1949), 61	*XI*, 99	StaD, p. 516, no. 3
X, 145	*Syria*, 26 (1949), 44–5, nos. 1–6	*XI*, 100	StaD, p. 514, no. 2

G. Comparing the numbers of Ingholt's *Studier over Palmyrensk Skulptur* (*PS*) with his *Palmyrene and Gandharan Sculpture* (*Palmyrene*) and with the numbers of Cantineau's *Inscriptions Palmyréniennes* (CaA) and with those of the *Corpus Inscriptionum Semiticarum, pars secunda, tomus tertius* (*CIS*).

PS	*CIS*	*Palmyrene*	CaA	*Inv.*
33	—	2	—	—
67	4259	6	—	—
—	4327	9	—	—
106	—	—	84	—
215	—	—	85 B	—
410	—	—	—	130

H. The following inscriptions may be identical.

CaA 76	*Inv. VIII*, 19
PS 124	*CIS* 4205
PS 234	*CIS* 4221

I. The following inscriptions, published twice in different places, are identical.

(1) *Sumer*, 18 (1962), 63–5—*Syria*, 40 (1963), 33–46
(2) *Syria*, 26 (1949), 44–5—*CRAIBL*, 1946, 393.
(3) *Syria*, 25 (1946–8), 334–6—StaB, p. 102, A 1167.

APPENDIX III

A. LIST OF GREEK NAMES FOUND IN PALMYRENE INSCRIPTIONS

'GT'	Agathos
'GTGLS	Agathangelos, Agathaggelos
'GTWN'	Agathōn
'GTPS	Agathopous
'GTPWS	Agathopous
[']WṬYK/Q[']	Eutychēs
'WṬK'	Eutychēs
'WTQ'	Eutykēs
'ṬYK'	Antiochos
'LKDRYS	Alexandros
'LKSDRS	Alexandros
'LKSNDRWS	Alexandros
'LKSNDRS	Alexandros
'LQM'	Alkimos
'LQMS	Alkimos
'NṬYWKWS	Antiochos
'NṬYKYS	Antiochos
'NṬYKS	Antiochos
[']SPYDN	Spedianos
'SPDYN	Spedianos
'SPDY[S]	Spedios
'SQLPYD'	Asklēpiadēs
'PYN	Appiōn
'PLNYS	Apollōnios
'QM'	Akmē
'RSṬYDS	Aristeidēs
'RQṬWS	Arktos
'TNDWR'	Athēnodōros
'TNDR[WS]	Athēnodōros
BRBRS	Barbaros
GLNWS	Galēnos
DWR'	(Athēno)dōros
DYGNS	Diogenēs
DYNYS	Dionysios
[DY]NS	Deinis
DMS	Dēmas
HLDRS	Hēliodōros
HLYDWRS	Hēliodōros
HLYDYRS	Hēliodōros
HLYDRWS	Hēliodōros
[HRMYS]	Hermeias
HRMS	Hermēs
HRMSYN'	Hermēsianos
HRQL'	Hēraklēs
HRQLYD'	Hērakleidēs
ṬYMWN	Timōn
ṬMYS	Timaios
ṬMS	Timaios
KRYSTWS	Chrysanthos
MNDRS	Menandros
MRYWN	Mariōn
NYQ'	Nikē
NRQYS	Narkaios
SLWQ'	Seleukos
SLWQWS	Seleukos
SLWQS	Seleukos
PṬRQLS	Patroklos
PLYN'	Phileinos
PLYNWS	Phileinos
PLNS	Phileinos
PLPṬR	Philopatōr
QLSṬ'	Kallistos
QLSṬRṬS	Kallistratos
QLQYS	Kilix
RDWN	Rhodōn
TYDWR'	Theodōros
TYDRWS	Theodōros
TYPYLS	Theophilos

B. LIST OF LATIN NAMES FOUND IN PALMYRENE INSCRIPTIONS

'GRP'	Agrippa
'DRYNWS	Hadrianus
'WR	Aur(elius)
'WRLY'	Aurelius, Aurelia
'WRLYS	Aurelius
'ṬNYNYS	Antoninus
'LYS	Aelius
'LPYS	Ulpius
'LPS	Ulpius
'MLYWS	Aemilius
'NṬWNYS	Antonius
'NYNWS	Annianus
BRS	Burrus
G'YS	Gaius
GBYNS	Gabinius
GY	Gaius
GYN'	Gaianus
GYNWS	Gaianus
GYS	Gaius
GRMNQWS	Germanicus

GRMNQS	Germanicus	SṬṬYLS	Statilius
DWMNYN'	Domnina	SPṬYMY'	Septimia
HDRYN[WS]	Hadrianus	SPṬYMYWS	Septimius
ṬBRYS	Tiberius	SPṬMY'	Septimia
YWL	Jul(ius)	SPṬMYW'	Septimius
YWL'	Julius	SPṬMYWS	Septimius
YWLY'	Julius, Julia	SPṬMYS	Septimius
YWLYWS	Julius	PLWYN'	Flavianus
[LWQY]WS	Lucius	PLWYNWS	Flavianus
LWQYS	Lucius	PLQS	Felix
LWQL'	Lucilla	PPLWS	Publius
LQY	Lucius	PPLYS	Publius
LQYNS	Licinius	PRṬNKS	Pertinax
MKSMWS	Maximus	[PRYSQWS]	Priscus
MKSMS	Maximus	QLWDYS	Claudius
MKŠM	Maximus	QLSTQS	Celesticus
MRYNS	Marinus	QSYN'	Cassianus
MRQWS	Marcus	QSPRYNS	Casperianus
MRQS	Marcus	QRBLWN	Corbulo
MRQYNWS	Marcianus	Q[R]SPYNWS	Crispinus
MRQL'	Marcellus	RGYN'	Regina
SBYN'	Sabinus	RMNWS	Romanus
SBYNS	Sabinus	RSTQ'	Rusticus

C. LIST OF PERSIAN NAMES FOUND IN PALMYRENE INSCRIPTIONS

'PRHṬ	Frahāta	MHRDD	Mithradāta
'RBZ	Orobazos	MHRDT	Mithradāta
'RṬBN	Artabanos	PRDŠY	Firdūsī
HRMZ	Hurmuz	PRN(K)	Pharnak
HRMZD	Hurmazd	PRMWN	Fermān
WRDN	Wardān	TYRDT	Tiridatēs
WRWD	Hurauda		

APPENDIX IV

A. THE TRANSCRIPTION OF GREEK PERSONAL NAMES IN PALMYRENE

1. *The Velars*

1.1. Palmyrene *g* corresponds to Greek *g*.

'GT'	Agathos	'GTPWS	Agathopous
'GTGLS	Agathangelos	GLNWS	Galēnos
'GTWN'	Agathōn	DYGNS	Diogenēs
'GTPS	Agathopous		

1.2. Palmyrene *k* corresponds to Greek *ch*.

[']WṬYK/Q[']	Eutychēs	'NṬYKYS	Antiochos
'WṬK'	Eutychēs	'NṬYKS	Antiochos
'ṬYK'	Antiochos	KRYSTWS	Chrysanthos
'NṬYWKWS	Antiochos		

1.3. Palmyrene *q* corresponds to Greek *k*.

[']WṬYK/Q[']	Eutychēs	NYQ'	Nikē
'WTQ'	Eutykēs	NRQYS	Narkaios
'LQM'	Alkimos	SLWQ'	Seleukos
'LQMS	Alkimos	SLWQWS	Seleukos
'SQLPYD'	Asklēpiadēs	SLWQS	Seleukos
'QM'	Akmē	PṬRQLS	Patroklos
'RQṬWS	Arktos	QLSṬ'	Kallistos
HRQL'	Hēraklēs	QLSṬRṬS	Kallistratos
HRQLYD'	Hērakleidēs	QLQYS	Kilix

1.4. The Greek letter *ksi* is transcribed by *ks* or *qs*.

'LKSDRS	Alexandros	'LKSNDRS	Alexandros
'LKSNDRWS	Alexandros	QLQYS	Kilix

2. *The Bilabials*

1.5. Palmyrene *b* corresponds to Greek *b*.

BRBRS	Barbaros

1.6. Palmyrene *p* corresponds to Greek *p*.

'GTPS	Agathopous	'SPDY[S]	Spedios
'GTPWS	Agathopous	'PYN	Appiōn
'SQLPYD'	Asklēpiadēs	'PLNYS	Apollōnios
[']SPYDN	Spedianos	PṬRQLS	Patroklos
'SPDYN	Spedianos	PLPṬR	Philopatōr

3. *The Dentals*

1.7. Palmyrene *d* corresponds to Greek *d*.

'LKDRYS	Alexandros	'LKSNDRS	Alexandros
'LKSDRS	Alexandros	'SPDY[S]	Spedios
'LKSNDRWS	Alexandros	'SPDYN	Spedianos

[']SPYDN	Spedianos	DMS	Dēmas
'SQLPYD'	Asklēpiadēs	HLDRS	Hēliodōros
'RSṬYDS	Aristeidēs	HLYDWRS	Hēliodōros
'TNDWR'	Athēnodōros	HLYDYRS	Hēliodōros
'TNDR[WS]	Athēnodōros	HLYDRWS	Hēliodōros
DWR'	(Athēno)dōros	RDWN	Rhodōn
DYGNS	Diogenēs	TYDWR'	Theodōros
DYNYS	Dionysios	TYDRWS	Theodōros
[DY]NS	Deinis		

1.8. Palmyrene *t* corresponds to Greek *th*.

'GT'	Agathos	'TNDR[WS]	Athēnodōros
'GTGLS	Agathangelos	KRYSTWS	Chrysanthos
'GTWN'	Agathōn	TYDWR'	Theodōros
'GTPWS	Agathopous	TYDRWS	Theodōros
'GTPS	Agathopous	TYPYLS	Theophilos
'TNDWR'	Athēnodōros		

1.9. Palmyrene *ṭ* corresponds to Greek *t*.

[']WṬYK/Q[']	Eutychēs	ṬMYS	Timaios
'WṬK'	Eutychēs	ṬMS	*see Lexicon*
'ṬYK'	Antiochos	PṬRQLS	Patroklos
'NṬYWKWS	Antiochos	PLPṬR	Philopatōr
'NṬYKYS	Antiochos	QLSṬ'	Kallistos
'NṬYKS	Antiochos	QLSṬRṬS	Kallistratos
'RSṬYDS	Aristeidēs		
'RQṬWS	Arktos	But note:	
ṬYMWN	Timōn	'WTQ'	Eutykēs

4. *The Vowels*

1.10. Long internal *ā* in Greek personal names is never transcribed with a mater lectionis, e.g. in the following names.

HRQL'	Hērāklēs	HRQLYD'	Hērākleidēs

1.11. Long internal *ē* in Greek personal names is never written with a mater lectionis.

'SQLPYD'	Asklēpiadēs	HLYDWRS	Hēliodōros
'TNDWR'	Athēnodōros	HLYDYRS	Hēliodōros
'TNDR[WS]	Athēnodōros	HLYDRWS	Hēliodōros
GLNWS	Galēnos	HRMSYN'	Hermēsianos
DMS	Dēmas	HRQL'	Hēraklēs
HLDRS	Hēliodōros	HRQLYD'	Hērakleidēs

1.12. In the following three names:

TYDWR'	Theodōros	TYPYLS	Theophilos
TYDRWS	Theodōros		

the short internal vowel *e* has been reflected in the spelling by transcribing it with a mater lectionis (yodh) to render a better transcription of the vowel cluster (-eo) in the Greek names. Cf. also the following names where a similar phenomenon can be observed:

'ṬYK'	Antiochos	DYGNS	Diogenēs
'NṬYWKWS	Antiochos	DYNYS	Dionysios
'NṬYKYS	Antiochos	HLYDWRS	Hēliodōros
'NṬYKS	Antiochos	HLYDYRS	Hēliodōros
[']SPYDN	Spedianos	HLYDRWS	Hēliodōros
'SPDYN	Spedianos	HRMSYN'	Hermēsianos
'SPDY[S]	Spedios	But note:	
'SQLPYD'	Asklēpiadēs	HLDRS	Hēliodōros. It might be a scribal mistake (see under 1.26. III)
'PYN	Appiōn		
'PLNYS	Apollōnios		

1.13. Long internal *ī* (*ei*), *ȳ* in Greek personal names is mostly written with a mater lectionis.

'RSṬYDS	Aristeidēs	KRYSTWS	Chrȳsanthos
DYGNS	Dīogenēs	NYQ'	Nīkē
DYNYS	Dionȳsios	PLYN'	Phileinos, Philīnos
[DY]NS	Deinis	PLYNWS	Phileinos, Philīnos
[HRMYS]	Hermeias	But note:	
HRQLYD'	Hērakleidēs	PLNS	Phileinos, Philīnos
ṬYMWN	Teimōn, Tīmōn	ṬMYS	Tīmaios

1.14. Long internal *ō* in Greek personal names is written with and without a mater lectionis.

'PLNYS	Apollōnios	HLYDYRS	Hēliodōros
'TNDWR'	Athēnodōros	HLYDRWS	Hēliodōros
'TNDR[WS]	Athēnodōros	TYDWR'	Theodōros
HLDRS	Hēliodōros	TYDRWS	Theodōros
HLYDWRS	Hēliodōros	DWR'	(Athēno)dōros

1.15. Short internal *a* in Greek personal names is always written without a mater lectionis.

'GT'	Agathos	DMS	Dēmas
'GTGLS	Agathangelos	HRMSYN'	Hermēsianos
'GTWN'	Agathōn	KRYSTWS	Chrysanthos
[']SPYDN	Spedianos	MNDRS	Menandros
'SPDYN	Spedianos	PṬRQLS	Patroklos
'SQLPYD'	Asklēpiadēs	PLPṬR	Philopatōr
BRBRS	Barbaros	QLSṬ'	Kallistos
GLNWS	Galēnos	QLSṬRṬS	Kallistratos

1.16. Short internal *i* in Greek personal names is written with and without a mater lectionis.

'LQM'	Alkimos	QLSṬ'	Kallistos
'LQMS	Alkimos	QLSṬRṬS	Kallistratos
'RSṬYDS	Aristeidēs	QLQYS	Kilix
MRYWN	Mariōn	TYPYLS	Theophilos
PLPṬR	Philopatōr		

1.17. Short internal *y* in Greek personal names is written with and without a mater lectionis (see also Rosenthal, *Sprache*, 15).

[']WṬYK/Q[']	Eutychēs	'WTQ'	Eutykēs
'WṬK'	Eutychēs		

1.18. Short internal *o* in Greek personal names is always written without a mater lectionis.

'GTPWS	Agathopous	HLYDWRS	Hēliodōros
'GTPS	Agathopous	HLYDYRS	Hēliodōros
'ṬYK'	Antiochos	HLYDRWS	Hēliodōros
'NṬYKYS	Antiochos	PṬRQLS	Patroklos
'NṬYKS	Antiochos	PLPṬR	Philopatōr
'PLNYS	Apollōnios	RDWN	Rhodōn
'TNDWR'	Athenodōros	TYDWR'	Theodōros
'TNDR[WS]	Athenodōros	TYDRWS	Theodōros
DYGNS	Diogenēs	TYPYLS	Theophilos
DYNYS	Dionysios	But note:	
HLDRS	Hēliodōros	'NṬYWKWS	Antiochos

5. *The Diphthongs*

1.19. *eu* in Greek personal names is always written with a mater lectionis.

[']WṬYK/Q[']	Eutychēs	SLWQ'	Seleukos
'WṬK'	Eutychēs	SLWQWS	Seleukos
'WTQ'	Eutykēs	SLWQS	Seleukos

1.20. *ai* in Greek personal names is always written with a mater lectionis (see also Rosenthal, *Sprache*, 23; Cantineau, *Grammaire*, 50).

ṬMYS	Timaios	NRQYS	Narkaios

Compare also the explanation given under 1.12., which might be applicable here too.

6. *Miscellaneous Points*

1.21. The Greek spiritus asper is transcribed by *h*.

HLDRS	Hēliodōros	HRMSYN'	Hermēsianos
HLYDWRS	Hēliodōros	HRQL'	Hēraklēs
HLYDYRS	Hēliodōros	HRQLYD'	Hērakleidēs
HLYDRWS	Hēliodōros		
[HRMYS]	Hermeias	But note:	
HRMS	Hermēs	RDWN	Rhodōn

1.22. The Greek spiritus lenis is transcribed by '.

'GT'	Agathos	'LQM'	Alkimos
'GTGLS	Agathangelos	'LQMS	Alkimos
'GTWN'	Agathōn	'NṬYWKWS	Antiochos
'GTPWS	Agathopous	'NṬYKYS	Antiochos
'GTPS	Agathopous	'NṬYKS	Antiochos
[']WṬYK/Q[']	Eutychēs	'SQLPYD'	Asklēpiadēs
'WṬK'	Eutychēs	'PYN	Appiōn
'WTQ'	Eutykēs	'PLNYS	Apollōnios
'ṬYK'	Antiochos	'QM'	Akmē
'LKDRYS	Alexandros	'RSṬYDS	Aristeidēs
'LKSDRS	Alexandros	'RQṬWS	Arktos
'LKSNDRWS	Alexandros	'TNDWR'	Athēnodōros
'LKSNDRS	Alexandros	'TNDR[WS]	Athēnodōros

1.23. A vowel-less *n* in Greek personal names is sometimes left unexpressed.

'GTGLS	Agathangelos	But note:	
'ṬYK'	Antiochos	'LKSNDRWS	Alexandros
'LKSDRS	Alexandros	'LKSNDRS	Alexandros
'LKDRYS	Alexandros	'NṬYWKWS	Antiochos
KRYSTWS	Chrysanthos	'NṬYKYS	Antiochos
MNDRS	Menandros	'NṬYKS	Antiochos

1.24. A consonant cluster at the beginning of Greek personal names is avoided with the help of a prosthetic vowel (Aleph prostheticum) or left unchanged; see Rosenthal, *Sprache*, 31 f.

[']SPYDN	Spedianos	But note:	
'SPDYN	Spedianos	KRYSTWS	Chrysanthos
'SPDY[S]	Spedios		

7. *The Greek Endings*

1.25. The Greek endings on personal names are rendered the following ways:

A.	-ēs	= S
		= ’
B.	-ē	= ’
C.	-ās	= S
D.	-os	= WS
		= S
		= ’
		= -
E.	-ōr/oros	= R
F.	-ōn/ontos	= WN
		= N
G.	-ous/odos	= WS
		= S
H.	-is/idos	= -
I.	-iks/ikos	= -

A.	DYGNS	Diogenēs
	’RSṬYDS	Aristeidēs
	HRMS	Hermēs
	HRQL’	Hēraklēs
	HRQLYD’	Hērakleidēs
	[’]WṬYK/Q[’]	Eutychēs
	’WṬK’	Eutychēs
	’WTQ’	Eutykēs
	’SQLPYD’	Asklēpiadēs
B.	’QM’	Akmē
	NYQ’	Nikē
C.	DMS	Dēmas
	[HRMYS]	Hermeias
D.	’LKDRYS	Alexandros
	’LKSNDRWS	Alexandros
	’NṬYWKWS	Antiochos
	’NṬYKYS	Antiochos
	’RQṬWS	Arktos
	’TNDR[WS]	Athēnodōros
	GLNWS	Galēnos
	HLYDRWS	Hēliodōros
	KRYSTWS	Chrysanthos
	SLWQWS	Seleukos
	PLYNWS	Phileinos
	TYDRWS	Theodōros
	’GTGLS	Agathangelos
	’LKSDRS	Alexandros
	’LKSNDRS	Alexandros
	’LQMS	Alkimos
	’NṬYKS	Antiochos
	’SPDY[S]	Spedios
	’PLNYS	Apollōnios
	BRBRS	Barbaros
	HLDRS	Hēliodōros
	HLYDWRS	Hēliodōros
	HLYDYRS	Hēliodōros
	ṬMYS	Timaios
	ṬMS	*see Lexicon*
	MNDRS	Menandros
	NRQYS	Narkaios
	SLWQS	Seleukos
	PṬRQLS	Patroklos
	PLNS	Phileinos
	QLSṬRṬS	Kallistratos
	TYPYLS	Theophilos
	’GT’	Agathos
	’ṬYK’	Antiochos
	’LQM’	Alkimos
	’TNDWR’	Athēnodōros
	DWR’	(Athēno)dōros
	HRMSYN’	Hermēsianos
	SLWQ’	Seleukos
	PLYN’	Phileinos
	QLSṬ’	Kallistos
	TYDWR’	Theodōros
	[’]SPYDN	Spedianos
	’SPDYN	Spedianos
	DYNYS	Dionysios
E.	PLPṬR	Philopatōr
F.	’GTWN’	Agathōn
	ṬYMWN	Timōn
	MRYWN	Mariōn
	RDWN	Rhodōn
	’PYN	Appiōn
G.	’GTPWS	Agathopous
	’GTPS	Agathopous
H.	[DY]NS	Deinis
I.	QLQYS	Kilix

8. *Orthographic Peculiarities*

1.26. I. Yodh has been written instead of Waw in the following three cases:

’LKDRYS *pro* ’LKDRWS Alexandros
’NṬYKYS *pro* ’NṬYKWS Antiochos
HLYDYRS *pro* HLYDWRS Heliodoros

II. An accidental transposition of letters has occurred in:

QLQYS *pro* QLYQS Kilix

III. A letter has been accidentally left out in:

’LKDRYS *pro* ’LKSDRWS (see also under 1.26.I)
HLDRS *pro* HLYDRS Hēliodōros (see under 1.12)

B. THE TRANSCRIPTION OF LATIN PERSONAL NAMES IN PALMYRENE

1. *The Velars*

2.1. Palmyrene *g* corresponds to Latin *g*.

'GRP'	Agrippa	GYNWS	Gaianus
G'YS	Gaius	GYS	Gaius
GBYNS	Gabinius	GRMNQWS	Germanicus
GY	Gaius	GRMNQS	Germanicus
GYN'	Gaianus	RGYN'	Regina

2.2. Palmyrene *q* corresponds to Latin *c*.

GRMNQWS	Germanicus	MRQL'	Marcellus
GRMNQS	Germanicus	[PRYSQWS]	Priscus
[LWQY]WS	Lucius	QLWDYS	Claudius
LWQYS	Lucius	QLSTQS	Celesticus (?)
LWQL'	Lucilla	QSYN'	Cassianus
LQY	Lucius	QSPRYNS	Casperianus
LQYNS	Licinius	QRBLWN	Corbulo
MRQWS	Marcus	Q[R]SPYNWS	Crispinus
MRQS	Marcus	RSTQ'	Rusticus
MRQYNWS	Marcianus		

2.3. Latin *x* is usually transcribed by *ks*.

MKSMWS	Maximus	But note:	
MKSMS	Maximus	PLQS	Felix (see also 2.23.A)
PRṬNKS	Pertinax	MKŠM	Maximus (see also 2.23.A; 2.22.A)

2. *The Bilabials*

2.4. Palmyrene *b* usually corresponds to Latin *b*.

BRS	Burrus	SBYNS	Sabinus
GBYNS	Gabinius	But note:	
ṬBRYS	Tiberius	PPLWS	Publius (see also 2.23.B)
SBYN'	Sabinus	PPLYS	Publius

2.5. Palmyrene *p* corresponds to Latin *p*.

'GRP'	Agrippa	SPṬMYS	Septimius
'LPYS	Ulpius	PPLWS	Publius (see also 2.4)
'LPS	Ulpius	PPLYS	Publius (see also 2.4)
SPṬYMY'	Septimia	PRṬNKS	Pertinax
SPṬMY'	Septimia	[PRYSQWS]	Priscus
SPṬYMYWS	Septimius	QSPRYNS	Casperianus
SPṬMYW'	Septimius	Q[R]SPYNWS	Crispinus
SPṬMYWS	Septimius		

3. *The Dentals*

2.6. Palmyrene *d* corresponds to Latin *d*.

'DRYNWS	Hadrianus	HDRYN[WS]	Hadrianus
DWMNYN'	Domnina	QLWDYS	Claudius

2.7. Palmyrene *ṭ* usually corresponds to Latin *t*.

'ṬNYNYS	Antoninus
'NṬWNYS	Antonius
ṬBRYS	Tiberius
SṬṬYLS	Statilius
SPṬYMY'	Septimia
SPṬMY'	Septimia
SPṬYMYWS	Septimius
SPṬMYW'	Septimius
SPṬMYWS	Septimius
SPṬMYS	Septimius
PRṬNKS	Pertinax
But note:	
QLSTQS	Celesticus (?) (see also 2.23.C)
RSTQ'	Rusticus (see also 2.23.C)

4. *The Vowels*

2.8. Long internal *ā* in Latin personal names is usually not transcribed with a mater lectionis.

'DRYNWS	Hadriānus
'NYNWS	Anniānus
GY	Gāius
GYN'	Gāiānus
GYNWS	Gāiānus
GYS	Gāius
GRMNQWS	Germānicus
GRMNQS	Germānicus
HDRYN[WS]	Hadriānus
MRQYNWS	Marciānus
PLWYN'	Flāviānus
PLWYNWS	Flāviānus
QSYN'	Cassiānus
QSPRYNS	Casperiānus
RMNWS	Romānus
But note:	
G'YS	Gāius

2.9. Long internal *ē* in Latin personal names is never written with a mater lectionis.

'WRLY'	Aurēlius, Aurēlia
'WRLYS	Aurēlius
PLQS	Fēlix
RGYN'	Rēgina

2.10. In the following names a vowel cluster (-ia, -iu) has been reflected in the spelling by transcribing *i* with a mater lectionis. Gleitlaut (see Rosenthal, *Sprache*, 15).

'DRYNWS	Hadrianus
'WRLY'	Aurelius, Aurelia
'WRLYS	Aurelius
'LYS	Aelius
'LPYS	Ulpius
'MLYWS	Aemilius
'NṬWNYS	Antonius
'NYNWS	Annianus
G'YS	Gaius
GY	Gaius
GYN'	Gaianus
GYNWS	Gaianus
GYS	Gaius
HDRYN[WS]	Hadrianus
ṬBRYS	Tiberius
YWLYWS	Julius
[LWQY]WS	Lucius
LWQYS	Lucius
LQY	Lucius
MRQYNWS	Marcianus
SPṬYMY'	Septimia
SPṬMY'	Septimia
SPṬYMYWS	Septimius
SPṬMYW'	Septimius
SPṬMYWS	Septimius
SPṬMYS	Septimius
PLWYN'	Flavianus
PLWYNWS	Flavianus
PPLYS	Publius
QLWDYS	Claudius
QSYN'	Cassianus
QSPRYNS	Casperianus
But note:	
'LPS	Ulpius
GBYNS	Gabinius
YWL'	Julia
LQYNS	Licinius
SṬṬYLS	Statilius
PPLWS	Publius

2.11. Long internal *ī* in Latin personal names is transcribed with a mater lectionis.

'ṬNYNYS	Antonīnus
GBYNS	Gabīnius
DWMNYN'	Domnīna
MRYNS	Marīnus
SBYN'	Sabīnus
Q[R]SPYNWS	Crispīnus
RGYN'	Regīna

2.12. Long internal $\bar{o}$ is written with and without mater lectionis.

'ṬNYNYS	Antoninus	QRBLWN	Corbulo
'NṬWNYS	Antonius	RMNWS	Romanus

2.13. Short internal *a* is never written with a mater lectionis.

'DRYNWS	Hadrianus	MRQYNWS	Marcianus
GBYNS	Gabinius	MRQL'	Marcellus
HDRYN[WS]	Hadrianus	SBYN'	Sabinus
MKSMWS	Maximus	SBYNS	Sabinus
MKṢMS	Maximus	SṬṬYLS	Statilius
MKŠM	Maximus	PRṬNKS	Pertinax
MRYNS	Marinus	QSYN'	Cassianus
MRQWS	Marcus	QSPRYNS	Casperianus
MRQS	Marcus		

2.14. Short internal *i* is sometimes written plene, e.g. in the following words.

LQYNS	Licinius	SPṬYMYWS	Septimius
SṬṬYLS	Statilius	[PRYSQWS]	Priscus
SPṬYMY'	Septimia		

2.15. Short internal *o* is written with and without a mater lectionis.

DWMNYN'	Domnina	QRBLWN	Corbulo

5. *The Diphthongs*

2.16. The Diphthong *ae* is never written with a mater lectionis.

'LYS	Aelius	'MLYWS	Aemilius

2.17. The Diphthong *au* is always written with a mater lectionis.

'WR	Aur(elius)	'WRLYS	Aurelius
'WRLY'	Aurelius, Aurelia	QLWDYS	Claudius

6. *Miscellaneous Points*

2.18. A vowel at the beginning of a Latin personal name is always rendered by Aleph.

'GRP'	Agrippa	'LPYS	Ulpius
'ṬNYNYS	Antoninus	'NṬWNYS	Antonius
'LPS	Ulpius	'NYNWS	Annianus

2.19. Latin *h* is transcribed by *h*.

HDRYN[WS]	Hadrianus	But note:	
		'DRYNWS	Hadrianus (see also 2.23.D)

2.20. A consonant cluster at the beginning of Latin personal names is left unchanged.

SṬṬYLS	Statilius	[PRYSQWS]	Priscus
PLWYN'	Flavianus	QLWDYS	Claudius
PLWYNWS	Flavianus	Q[R]SPYNWS	Crispinus

2.21. The *n* in the following name has been assimilated to the following emphatic consonant.

'ṬNYNYS Antoninus

7. *The Latin Endings*

2.22. The Latin endings on personal names are rendered as follows:

A.	-us	=	WS
		=	S
		=	’
		=	-
B.	-a	=	’
C.	-ix/icis	=	QS
D.	-ax/acis	=	KS
E.	-o/onis	=	WN

A.	’DRYNWS	Hadrianus
	’MLYWS	Aemilius
	’NYNWS	Annianus
	GYNWS	Gaianus
	GRMNQWS	Germanicus
	HDRYN[WS]	Hadrianus
	YWLYWS	Julius
	[LWQY]WS	Lucius
	MKSMWS	Maximus
	MRQWS	Marcus
	MRQYNWS	Marcianus
	SPṬYMYWS	Septimius
	SPṬMYWS	Septimius
	PLWYNWS	Flavianus
	PPLWS	Publius
	[PRYSQWS]	Priscus
	Q[R]SPYNWS	Crispinus
	RMNWS	Romanus

	’WRLYS	Aurelius
	’ṬNYNYS	Antoninus
	’LYS	Aelius
	’LPYS	Ulpius
	’LPS	Ulpius
	’NṬWNYS	Antonius
	BRS	Burrus
	G’YS	Gaius
	GBYNS	Gabinius
	GYS	Gaius
	GRMNQS	Germanicus
	ṬBRYS	Tiberius
	YWLYS	Julius
	LWQYS	Lucius
	LQYNS	Licinius
	MKSMS	Maximus
	MRYNS	Marinus
	MRQS	Marcus
	SBYNS	Sabinus
	SṬṬYLS	Statilius
	SPṬMYS	Septimius
	PPLYS	Publius
	QLWDYS	Claudius
	QLSTQS	Celesticus (?)
	QSPRYNS	Casperianus

	’WRLY’	Aurelius, Aurelia
	GYN’	Gaianus
	MRQL’	Marcellus
	SBYN’	Sabinus
	SPṬMYW’	Septimius
	PLWYN’	Flavianus
	QSYN’	Cassianus
	RSTQ’	Rusticus

	GY	Gaius
	LQY	Lucius
	MKŠM	Maximus

B.	’GRP’	Agrippa
	’WRLY’	Aurelia, Aurelius
	DWMNYN’	Domnina
	YWL’	Julius
	YWLY’	Julius, Julia
	LWQL’	Lucilla
	SPṬYMY’	Septimia
	SPṬMY’	Septimia
	RGYN’	Regina
C.	PLQS	Felix
D.	PRṬNKS	Pertinax
E.	QRBLWN	Corbulo

8. *Peculiarities*

2.23. A. The transcription of Latin *x* (see also 2.3.).

PLQS Felix — MKŠM Maximus

B. Cases of retrogressive assimilation of voiced bilabial to voiceless bilabial.

PPLWS Publius — PPLYS Publius

C. Cases of dissimilation of the emphatic due to a following emphatic; see also 2.7.

RSTQ’ Rusticus — QLSTQS Celesticus (?)

D. ’ is written for *h*. It is most probably a scribal mistake; see also 2.19.

’DRYNWS Hadrianus

E. Long internal *ā* is written plene; see also Rosenthal, *Sprache*, 20.

G’YS Gaius

APPENDIX V

THE NAMES IN THE PALMYRENE INSCRIPTIONS FROM DURA-EUROPOS

In this Appendix the inscriptional material from Dura-Europos has been assembled. The Palmyrene inscriptions have been partly published in the *Preliminary Reports of the Excavations at Dura-Europos*, edited by M. J. Rostovzeff *et al.*, and partly in Comte du Mesnil du Buisson's *Inventaire des Inscriptions Palmyréniennes de Doura-Europos* (Paris, 1939). Unfortunately, the latter edition of the inscriptions cannot be relied upon too much as no photographs are supplied and the readings are in a number of cases highly suspect. For this reason the names have not been included in the Main List but are grouped together in this Appendix.

Likewise I have offered no lexical explanations to the names. The more common of them will be found already annotated in the Lexicon, the rest can be found with short explanations in du Mesnil du Buisson's *Inventaire*. Because of the highly suspect reading of a great number of the names, an explanation is in those cases merely guess-work.

'B (*m*) **2.** Du Mesnil du Buisson no. 37—'B.

'BBWHY (*m*) **1.** *343*, *Rep. VII*, p. 308 no. 915c—Du Mesnil du Buisson no. 23—'BBWHY.

'BYHN (*m*) **2.** *Rep. VI*, p. 169 no. 683—Du Mesnil du Buisson no. 27—'BYHN.

'HRY' (*f*) **2.** Du Mesnil du Buisson no. 26—'HRY'.

'LHŠMŠ (*m*) **1.** *505*, Du Mesnil du Buisson no. 25^{5}—'LHŠMŠ br ṣlt.

'ŠR (*m*) **2.** Du Mesnil du Buisson no. 21—'ŠR.

'TM (*m*) **2.** Du Mesnil du Buisson no. 8—'TM.

'TPNY (*m*) **1.** *480*, *Rep. VII*, p. 83 no. 845—Du Mesnil du Buisson no. 19—'TPNY br zbd'h.

BB' (*m*) **2.** Du Mesnil du Buisson no. 16—. . .]br BB' br[. . . . *Rep. II*, p. 146—Du Mesnil du Buisson no. 14—. . .]br zbd'th br BB'.

BBW (*m*) **2.** Du Mesnil du Buisson no. 36—BBW.

B[W]LḤZY (*m*) **2.** *Rep. VI*, p. 171 no. 690—Du Mesnil du Buisson no. 24—B[W]LḤZY.

BZ[**2.** Du Mesnil du Buisson no. 22—. . .]br BZ[. . . .

BLḤ' (*m*) **2.** *Rep. VII*, p. 282 no. 912^{4}—'gylw br BLḤ'.

BLY (*m*) **2.** Du Mesnil du Buisson no. 35—b[r]šmš br BLY br br bnkmyn.

BL'M (?) **2.** Du Mesnil du Buisson no. 40^{4}—BL'M (?).

BNY **2.** Du Mesnil du Buisson nos. 7, 8—BNY.

BNYH (*m*) **1.** *505*, Du Mesnil du Buisson no. 25^{6}—t'[m]' BNYH.

BNKMYN (*m*) **2.** Du Mesnil du Buisson no. 35—b[r]šmš br bly br br BNKMYN.

B'YḤW (*m*) **1.** *279*, *Rep. VII*, p. 318 no. 916^{2}—Du Mesnil du Buisson no. 1^{3}—zbdbwl br B'YḤW.

B'LY **2.** *Rep. VI*, p. 170 no. 685—Du Mesnil du Buisson no. 27—B'LY.

BRB'' (*m*) **2.** Du Mesnil du Buisson no. 54—BRB'' kmyn.

BRKH (?) **2.** Du Mesnil du Buisson no. 43—BRKH (?) zb[d]bwl (?).

BR'T' (*m*) **2.** *Rep. VI*, p. 169 no. 682—Du Mesnil du Buisson no. 27—BR'T'.

B[R]'TH (*m*) **1.** *343*, *Rep. VII*, p. 308 no. 915c—Du Mesnil du Buisson no. 23—B[R]'TH br lwqy.

B[R]ŠMŠ (*m*) **2.** Du Mesnil du Buisson no. 35—B[R]ŠMŠ br bly br br bnkmyn.

BT' (*f*?) **2.** Du Mesnil du Buisson no. 26 —BT'.

BT" **2.** *Rep. VI*, p. 170 no. 687—BT".

GD' (*m*) **2.** Du Mesnil du Buisson no. 2—GD' br[. . . *Rep. VI*, p. 170 no. 686—Du Mesnil du Buisson no. 27—GD'.

GPY' **2.** Du Mesnil du Buisson no. 47—'g' GPY'.

DB **2.** Du Mesnil du Buisson no. 55—DB.

HRBZ **2.** Du Mesnil du Buisson no. 48—HRBZ.

WHBLT (*m*) **2.** Du Mesnil du Buisson no. 15—mlkw br WHBLT. *Rep. VII*, p. 282 no. 912[2]—. . .]br WHBLT.

WHBLṬH **2.** Du Mesnil du Buisson no. 49 —WHBLTH.

ZBD' (*m*) **2.** *Rep. VII*, p. 281 no. 910—Du Mesnil du Buisson no. 34—ZBD' br zb(d)l'.

ZBDBWL (*m*) **1.** *279*, *Rep. VII*, p. 318 no. 916[1]—Du Mesnil du Buisson no. 1—ZBDBWL br b'yḥw. **2.** Du Mesnil du Buisson no. 43—brkh (?) ZB[D]BWL(?). Du Mesnil du Buisson no. 41—md/rw ZBD[BW]L.

ZB(D)L' (*m*) **2.** Du Mesnil du Buisson no. 34—zbd' br ZB(D)L'.

ZBD'H (*m*) **1.** *480*, *Rep. VII*, p. 83 no. 845—Du Mesnil du Buisson no. 19—'tpny br ZBD'H.

ZBD'TH (*m*) **2.** *Rep. II*, p. 146—Du Mesnil du Buisson no. 14—ZBD'TH br bb'.

ḤYM̊ (*m*) **2.** Du Mesnil du Buisson no. 9—mqymw br ḤYM̊.

ḤYRN (*m*) **1.** *470*, *Rep. VII*, p. 278 no. 907 —Du Mesnil du Buisson no. 28—ḤYRN br mlkw br nṣwr. *470*, *Rep. VII*, p. 279 no. 908—Du Mesnil du Buisson nos. 28–30—ḤY[RN] br mlkw br nṣwr.

ḤRT' **2.** Du Mesnil du Buisson no. 17—tymrṣw ḤRT' tym'.

YHY[B'] **2.** Du Mesnil du Buisson no. 42[1] —YHY[B'].

YRḤBWL' (*m*) **2.** *Rep. I*, p. 61—Du Mesnil du Buisson no. 13—mqymw br YRḤBWL'.

YRḤY (*m*) **2.** *Rep. VII*, p. 281 no. 911—Du Mesnil du Buisson no. 38—mlkw br YRḤY nṣwr.

KMYN (*m*) **2.** Du Mesnil du Buisson no. 54 —brb" KMYN.

LBN (*m*) **2.** Du Mesnil du Buisson no. 53—. . .]br LBN.

LWQY (*m*) **1.** *343*, *Rep. VII*, p. 308 no. 915c —Du Mesnil du Buisson no. 23—b[r]'th br LWQY.

MD/RW (*m*) **2.** Du Mesnil du Buisson no. 41 —MD/RW zbd[bw]l.

MLWK' (*m*) **1.** *540*, *Rep. I.* p. 62—Du Mesnil du Buisson no. 12—MLWK' br šwdy.

MLKW (*m*) **1.** *279*, *Rep. VII*, p. 318 no. 916[2] —Du Mesnil du Buisson no. 1—MLKW br rmw. *470*, *Rep. VII*, p. 278 no. 907—Du Mesnil du Buisson nos. 28–30—ḥyrn br MLKW br nṣwr. *470*, *Rep. VII*, p. 279 no. 908—Du Mesnil du Buisson nos. 31–2—ḥy[rn] br MLKW br nṣwr. **2.** *Rep. VI*, p. 170 no. 684—Du Mesnil du Buisson no. 27 —MLKW. *Rep. VII*, p. 281 no. 911—Du Mesnil du Buisson no. 38—MLKW br yrḥy nṣwr. Du Mesnil du Buisson no. 15—MLKW br whblt.

MQYMW (*m*) **2.** Du Mesnil du Buisson no. 9—MQYMW br ḥym̊. Du Mesnil du Buisson no. 10—MQYMW. Du Mesnil du Buisson no. 11—MQYMW br tymy. *Rep. I*, p. 61—Du Mesnil du Buisson no. 13 —MQYMW br yrḥbwl'.

NYQṬWR (*m*) **1.** *470*, *Rep. VII*, p. 278 no. 907—Du Mesnil du Buisson nos. 28–30 —slwqws NYQṬWR.

NṢWR (*m*) **1.** *470*, *Rep. VII*, p. 278 no. 907 —Du Mesnil du Buisson nos. 28–30—ḥyrn br mlkw br NṢWR. *470*, *Rep. VII*, p. 279 no. 908—Du Mesnil du Buisson nos. 28–30 —ḥy[rn] br mlkw br NṢWR. **2.** *Rep. VII*, p. 281 no. 911—Du Mesnil du Buisson no. 38 —mlkw br yrḥy NṢWR.

SLWQWS (*m*) **1.** *470*, *Rep. VII*, p. 278 no. 907—Du Mesnil du Buisson nos. 28–30 —SLWQWS nyqṭwr.

'G' (*m*) **2.** Du Mesnil du Buisson no. 47—'G' gpy'.

'GYLW (*m*) **2.** *Rep. VII*, p. 282 no. 912[3]—'GYLW br blḥ'.

'WYDY **2.** Du Mesnil du Buisson nos. 3–6 —'WYDY.

'ZYZ **2.** Du Mesnil du Buisson no. 39—'ZYZ.

'YB **2.** Du Mesnil du Buisson no. 50—'YB.

ṢLT (*m*) **1.** *505*, Du Mesnil du Buisson no. 25[6]—'lhšmš br ṢLT.

RMW (*m*) **1.** *279*, *Rep. VII*, p. 318 no. 916[3] —Du Mesnil du Buisson no. 1—mlkw br RMW.

ŠWDY (*m*) **1.** *540*, *Rep. I*, p. 62—Du Mesnil du Buisson no. 12—mlwk' br ŠWDY.

ŠKM 2. Du Mesnil du Buisson no. 8—ŠKM.

ŠMŠY 2. *Rep. VII*, p. 282 no. 912[5]—ŠMŠY.

ŠPYL' (?) **2.** *Rep. VII*, p. 282 no. 913a—ŠPYL' (?).

T'[M]' (*m*) **1.** *505*, Du Mesnil du Buisson no. 25[6]—T'[M]' bnyh.

TYM' (*m*) **2.** Du Mesnil du Buisson no. 17—tymrṣw ḥrt' TYM'. *Rep. VII*, p. 283 no. 913b—Du Mesnil du Buisson no. 45—TYM' br[. . . .

TYMY (*m*) **2.** Du Mesnil du Buisson no. 11—mqymw br TYMY.

TYMRṢW 2. Du Mesnil du Buisson no. 17—TYMRṢW ḥrt' tym'.

TML' (*f*) **2.** Du Mesnil du Buisson no. 26—TML'. *Rep. VI*, p. 170 no. 688—TML'.

LIST OF DEITIES

'RṢ' 2. Du Mesnil du Buisson no. 2—bl w'RṢ'.

'RṢW 1. *505*, Du Mesnil du Buisson no. 25[4]—bl wyrḥbwl w'glbwl w'RṢW. **2.** Du Mesnil du Buisson no. 47—'RṢW.

'ŠRW 2. Du Mesnil du Buisson no. 20—*Rep. VI*, p. 240—'ŠRW.

BL 1. *279*, *Rep. VII*, p. 318 no. 916—Du Mesnil du Buisson no. 1—BL wyrḥbwl. *505*, Du Mesnil du Buisson no. 25[3]—BL wyrḥbwl w'glbwl w'rṣw. **2.** Du Mesnil du Buisson no. 2—BL w'rṣ'.

B'LŠMYN 1. *343*, *Rep. VII*, p. 308 no. 915c—Du Mesnil du Buisson no. 23—B'LŠMYN.

GD' 1. *470*, *Rep. VII*, p. 278 no. 907—Du Mesnil du Buisson no. 28—GD' dy dwr'. *470*, *Rep. VII*, p. 279 no. 908—Du Mesnil du Buisson nos. 31–2—GD' dy TDMWR. **2.** *Rep. I*. p. 61—Du Mesnil du Buisson no. 13—GD'.

YRḤBWL 1. *279*, *Rep. VII*, p. 318 no. 916[4]—Du Mesnil du Buisson no. 1—bl wYRḤBWL. *505*, Du Mesnil du Buisson no. 25[3]—bl wYRḤBWL w'glbwl w'rṣw. **2.** Du Mesnil du Buisson no. 15—YRḤBWL w['glbwl] wrṣ'. *Rep. VII*, p. 279 no. 909—Du Mesnil du Buisson no. 33—YRḤBWL.

YR(ḤYBWL) 2. Du Mesnil du Buisson no. 49—YR(ḤYBWL).

MRYN 2. Cumont, *Fouilles* p. 448—mrn wmrt wbr MRYN.

MRN 2. Cumont, *Fouilles* p. 448—MRN wmrt wbr mryn.

MRT 2. Cumont, *Fouilles* p. 448—mrn wMRT wbr mryn.

NBW 2. *Rep. VII*, p. 281 no. 910—Du Mesnil du Buisson no. 34—NBW.

NMSYS 1. *540*, *Rep. I*, p. 62—Du Mesnil du Buisson no. 12—NMSYS.

'GLBWL 1. *505*, Du Mesnil du Buisson no. 25[4]—bl wyrḥbwl w'GLBWL w'rṣw. **2.** Du Mesnil du Buisson no. 15—yrḥbwl w['GLBWL] wrṣ'.

RṢ' 2. Du Mesnil du Buisson no. 15—yrḥbwl w['glbwl] wRṢ'.

Š'D 2. *Rep. VI*, p. 240—Du Mesnil du Buisson no. 20—Š'D.

LIST OF TRIBAL NAMES

BNY GDYBWL 1. *279*, *Rep. VII*, p. 318 no. 916[2]—Du Mesnil du Buisson no. 1—BNY GDYBWL.

BNY KMR' 1. *279*, *Rep. VII*, p. 318 no. 916[3]—Du Mesnil du Buisson no. 1—BNY KMR'.

BNY MYT' 2. *Rep. VII*, p. 279 no. 909—Du Mesnil du Buisson no. 33—BNY MYT'.

BNY SMMT' (?) **2.** Du Mesnil du Buisson no. 20—*Rep. VI*, p. 240—BNY SMMT'.

LIST OF WORKS CITED

ABDUL-HAK, S. 'L'hypogée de Tai à Palmyre', *AAS*, 2 (1952), 193–251.

AISTLEITNER, J. *Wörterbuch der ugaritischen Sprache*, ed. O. Eissfeldt (Berichte über die Verhandlungen der sächsischen Akademie der Wissenschaften zu Leipzig, Phil.-hist. Klasse, 106/3; Berlin, 1967).

ALBRIGHT, W. F. *Archaeology and the Religion of Israel*, 3rd edn. (Baltimore, 1953).

—— 'The Proto-Sinaitic Inscriptions and their Decipherment', *Harvard Theological Studies*, xxii (Cambridge, Massachusetts, 1966).

—— 'Notes on Ammonite history', in *Miscellanea B. Ubach*, ed. Dom. Romualdo Diaz, Scripta et Documenta, 1 (Montserrat, 1953).

ANDRAE, W. *Hatra II. Einzelbeschreibung der Ruinen* (21. Wissenschaftliche Veröffentlichung der Deutschen Orient-Gesellschaft; Leipzig, 1912).

—— and JENSEN, P. 'Aramäische Inschriften aus Assur und Hatra aus der Partherzeit', *MDOG*, 60 (1920), 1–51.

ARNDT, W. F., and GINGRICH, F. W. *A Greek–English Lexicon of the New Testament and other early Christian Literature* (Cambridge, 1963).

ASSEMANUS, J. S. *Bibliotheca Orientalis Clementino Vaticana*. 4 vols. (Rome, 1719–28).

ASTOUR, M. 'Benê-Iamina et Jéricho', *Semitica*, 9 (1959), 5–20.

AVIGAD, N. 'An early Aramaic seal', *IEJ*, 8 (1958), 228–30.

BARTH, J. *Die Nominalbildung in den semitischen Sprachen* (Leipzig, 1894).

BARTHÉLEMY, A. *Dictionnaire arabe–français* (Publication entreprise sous les auspices du Haut-Commissariat de France en Syrie et au Liban; Paris, 1935–54).

BAUER, H. 'Die hebräischen Eigennamen als sprachliche Erkenntnisquelle', *ZAW*, 48/n.f. 7 (1930), 73–80.

BAUER, Th. *Die Ostkanaanäer. Eine philologisch-historische Untersuchung über die Wanderschicht der sogenannten 'Amoriter' in Babylonien* (Leipzig, 1926).

BAUMSTARK, A. *Geschichte der syrischen Literatur* (Bonn, 1922).

BEAUSSIER, M. *Dictionnaire pratique arabe–français*, rev. edn. (Algiers, 1931).

BEESTON, A. F. L. 'Arabian sibilants', *Journal of Semitic Studies*, 7 (1962), 222–33.

—— 'Phonology of the epigraphic south Arabian unvoiced sibilants', *Transactions of the Philological Society* (1951), 1–26.

BEN-HAYYIM, Z. 'Palmyrene inscriptions', *BJPES*, 13 (1947), 141–8.

BIVAR, A. D. H., and SHAKED, S. 'The inscriptions at Shīmbār', *BSOAS*, 27 (1964), 265–90.

BÖHL, F. M. Th. *Opera Minora* (Groningen, 1953).

BOTTÉRO, J. 'Les divinités sémitiques anciennes en Mésopotamie', in *Le antiche divinità semitiche*, ed. S. Moscati (Studi Semitici, 1; Rome, 1958), 17–63.

BOUNNI, A. 'Nouveaux bas-reliefs religieux de la Palmyrène', in *Mélanges offerts à K. Michalowski* (Warsaw, 1966), 313–20.

—— 'Inscriptions palmyréniennes inédites', *AAS*, 11 (1961), 145–62.

—— 'Note sur un nouveau bas-relief palmyrénien', ibid. 15 (1965), 87–98.

—— and SALIBY, N. 'Six nouveaux emplacements fouillés à Palmyre (1963–4)', ibid. 15 (1965), 121–38.

VAN DEN BRANDEN, A. *Histoire de Thamoud* (Publications de l'Université Libanaise, Section des études historiques, vi; Beirut, 1960).

—— *Les inscriptions dédanites* (Publications de l'Université Libanaise, Section des études historiques, viii; Beirut, 1962).

—— *Les inscriptions thamoudéennes* (Bibliothèque du Muséon, 25; Louvain, 1950).

van den Branden, A. 'La divinité thamoudéenne ʿA', *Le Muséon*, 67 (1954), 349–54.

Bräu, H. 'Die altnordarabischen kultischen Namen', *WZKM*, 32 (1925), 31–59, 85–115.

Bresciani, E., and Kamil, M. 'Le lettere aramaiche di Hermopoli', in *Atti della Accademia Nazionale dei Lincei, Memorie, Classe di Scienze morali, storiche e filologiche*, Serie 8, vol. xii/5 (Rome, 1966), 360–428.

Brockelmann, C. *Arabische Grammatik* (Leipzig, 1960).

—— *Grundriss der vergleichenden Grammatik der semitischen Sprachen*, 2 vols. (Berlin, 1908–13).

—— *Lexicon Syriacum*, 2nd edn. (Halle, 1928).

—— *Syrische Grammatik*, 8th edn. (Leipzig, 1960).

Cantineau, J. *Le dialecte arabe de Palmyre* (Mémoires de l'Institut Français de Damas; Beirut, 1934).

—— 'Inscriptions palmyréniennes', *RA*, 27 (1930), 27–51, nos. 1–36; and also separately Damascus, 1930, nos. 1–105.

—— *Inventaire des Inscriptions de Palmyre* (Fasc. 1–9, Damascus, 1930–6; fasc. 10 by J. Starcky, Damascus, 1949; fasc. 11 by J. Teixidor, Beirut, 1965).

—— *Grammaire du palmyrénien épigraphique* (Cairo, 1935).

—— *Le Nabatéen*. 2 vols. (Paris, 1930–2).

—— 'Un Restitutor Orientis dans les inscriptions de Palmyre', *Journal asiatique*, 222 (1933), 217–33.

—— 'La Susiane dans une inscription palmyrénienne', in *Mélanges syriens offerts à M. René Dussaud* (BAH, xxx; Paris, 1939), i. 277–9.

—— 'Tadmorea', *Syria*, 14 (1933), 169–202 (nos. 1–16).

—— 'Tadmorea', ibid. 17 (1936), 267–82, 346–55 (nos. 17–27).

—— 'Tadmorea', ibid. 19 (1938), 72–82, 153–71 (nos. 28–46).

—— 'Textes funéraires palmyréniens', *RB*, 39 (1930), 520–49.

—— 'Textes palmyréniens provenant de la fouille du temple de Bēl', *Syria*, 12 (1931), 116–41.

Caquot, A. 'La déesse Šegal', *Semitica*, 4 (1951–2), 55–8.

—— 'Nouvelles inscriptions de Hatra', *Syria*, 29 (1952), 89–118; ibid. 30 (1953), 234–46; ibid. 32 (1955), 49–69, 261–72; ibid. 40 (1963), 1–16; ibid. 41 (1964), 251–72.

—— 'Quelques nouvelles données palmyréniennes', *GLECS*, 7 (1956), 77–8.

—— 'Remarques linguistiques sur les tessères de Palmyre', in *Recueil des tessères de Palmyre* (BAH, lviii; Paris, 1955).

—— 'Sur l'onomastique religieuse de Palmyre', *Syria*, 39 (1962), 231–56.

Caskel, W. *Lihyan und Lihyanisch* (Arbeitsgemeinschaft für Forschung des Landes Nordrhein-Westfalen, Geisteswissenschaften, Heft 4; Köln, 1954).

Cassirer, M. 'A Fragmentary Palmyrene Inscription', *PEQ*, 84 (1952), 52.

Chabot, J.-B. *Choix des inscriptions de Palmyre* (Paris, 1922).

—— 'Glanures palmyréniennes', *Journal asiatique*, 12 (1918), 277–301.

—— 'Notes palmyréniennes', *CRAIBL*, 1941, 109–15.

—— 'Nouvelle inscription palmyrénienne d'Afrique', ibid. (1932), 265–9.

Chwolson, D. *Die Ssabier und der Ssabismus*, 2 vols. (St. Petersburg, 1856; reprint, New York, 1965).

Clay, A. T. *Business Documents of Murashû Sons of Nippur* (The Babylonian expedition of the University of Pennsylvania, Series A, vol. x; Philadelphia, 1904).

Clermont-Ganneau, Ch. *Recueil d'archéologie orientale*, 8 vols. (Paris, 1888–1924).

Collart, P. 'Le sanctuaire de Baal-Shamim à Palmyre', *AAS*, 7 (1957), 67–90.

—— 'Nouveau monument palmyrénien de Shadrafa', *Museum Helveticum*, 13 (1956), 209–15.

Conti Rossini, C. *Storia d'Etiopia*, Africa Italiana, iii (Bergamo, 1928).

Cooke, G. A. *A textbook of north-Semitic inscriptions* (Oxford, 1903).

Cowley, A. E. *Aramaic papyri of the fifth century* B.C. (Oxford, 1923).

CUMONT, F. *Fouilles de Doura-Europos (1922–1923)* (BAH, ix, Paris, 1926).
CURETON, W. *Ancient Syriac documents* (London and Edinburgh, 1864).
—— Spicilegium Syriacum, 1855 (inaccessible).
DAHOOD, M. J. 'Ancient Semitic Deities in Syria and Palestine', in *Le antiche divinità semitiche*, ed. S. Moscati (Studi Semitici, 1; Rome, 1958), 65–94.
—— 'The divine name ʿēlî in the Psalms', *Theological Studies*, 14 (1953), 452–7.
DALMAN, G. H. *Aramäisch-Neuhebräisches Handwörterbuch* (Frankfurt am Main, 1922).
—— *Grammatik des jüdisch-palästinischen Aramäisch* (Leipzig, 1905).
DESSAU, H. *Inscriptiones Latinae Selectae.* 3 vols. (Berlin, 1892–1916).
DE VAUX, R. *Ancient Israel. Its life and institutions* (London, 1961).
DHORME, E. 'Le dieu parent et le dieu maître dans la religion des Hébreux', *RHR*, 105 (1932), 229–44.
DIRINGER, D. *Le iscrizioni antico-ebraiche palestinesi* (Florence, 1934).
DONNER, H., and RÖLLIG, W. *Kanaanäische und Aramäische Inschriften*, 3 vols. (Wiesbaden, 1962–4).
DOSSIN, G. 'Mention de Palmyre dans les textes de Mari', *Comptes rendus de la première recontre assyriologique (Paris, 26–28 juin 1950)* (Leiden, 1951), 20–1.
DOZY, R. *Supplément aux dictionnaires arabes*, 2 vols. (Leiden, 1881).
DRIVER, G. R. *Aramaic documents of the fifth century B.C.* (Oxford, 1954; abridged edition, Oxford, 1957).
DROWER, E. S., and MACUCH, R. *A Mandaic dictionary* (Oxford, 1963).
DU MESNIL DU BUISSON, R. *Inventaire des inscriptions palmyréniennes de Doura-Europos* (Paris, 1939).
—— 'A propos des inscriptions palmyréniennes de Doura-Europos', *RES* (1938), 95–6.
DUNANT, Ch. 'Nouvelles tessères de Palmyre', *Syria*, 36 (1959), 102–10.
—— 'Nouvelle inscription caravanière de Palmyre', *Museum Helveticum*, 13 (1956), 216–25.
DUPONT-SOMMER, A. 'Un buste palmyrénien inédit', *Syria*, 23 (1942–3), 78–85.
—— '"Bēl et Nabû, Šamaš et Nergal" sur un ostracon araméen inédit d'Éléphantine', *RHR*, 128 (1944), 28–39.
—— 'Un ostracon araméen inédit d'Éléphantine adressé à Aḥuṭab', *Revue des Études Sémitiques et Babyloniaca* (1945), 65–75.
—— 'Une inscription araméenne inédite de l'Ouâdi Hammâmât', *RA*, 41 (1947), 105–10.
DUSSAUD, R. *Les Arabes en Syrie avant l'Islam* (Paris, 1907).
—— *La pénétration des Arabes en Syrie avant l'Islam* (BAH, lix; Paris, 1955).
EDZARD, D. O. '^{m}Ningal-gāmil, ^{f}Ištar-damqat. Die Genuskongruenz im akkadischen theophoren Personennamen', *ZA*, 55/n.f. 21 (1963), 113–30.
EILERS, W. 'Eine Büste mit Inschrift aus Palmyra', *AfO*, 16 (1952–3), 311–15.
EISSER, G., and LEWY, J. *Die altassyrischen Rechtsurkunden vom Kültepe, MVÄG*, 33, 35 (Leipzig, 1930, 1935).
EISSFELDT, O. 'Götternamen und Gottesvorstellungen bei den Semiten', *ZDMG*, 83 (1929), 21–36. Reprinted in *Kleine Schriften*, i (1962), 194–205.
—— '"Gut Glück" in semitischer Namengebung', *JBL*, 82 (1963), 195–200. Reprinted in *Kleine Schriften*, iv (1968), 73–8.
—— 'Ugaritica und Palmyrenica', *ZDMG*, 105 (1955), 37*–8*.
EUTING, J. 'Epigraphische Miscellen', *SBAW* (1885), 669–88, (1887), 407–22.
—— *Nabatäische Inschriften aus Arabien* (Berlin, 1885).
FÉVRIER, J. G. *La religion des Palmyréniens* (Paris, 1931).
FITZMYER, J. *The Aramaic Inscriptions of Sfire*, Biblica et Orientalia, 19 (Rome, 1967).
FLEISCH, H. 'L'arabe classique. Esquisse d'une structure linguistique', *MUSJ*, 33 (1956), 1–151.

FRAENKEL, S. *Die aramäischen Fremdwörter im Arabischen* (Hildesheim, 1962 (reprint)).

GALLING, K. 'Beschriftete Bildsiegel des ersten Jahrhunderts v. Chr. vornehmlich aus Syrien und Palästina', *ZDPV*, 64 (1941), 121–202.

GARBINI, G. 'L'aramaico antico', in *Atti della Accademia Nazionale dei Lincei, Memorie, Classe di Scienze morali, storiche e filologiche*, Serie 8, vol. vii/5 (Rome, 1956), 235–85.

GIRON, N. 'Notes épigraphiques', *MUSJ*, 5 (1911), 71–8.

GOLDMANN, W. *Die palmyrenischen Personennamen* (Leipzig, 1935).

GÓMEZ, G. E. 'Hipocorísticos Árabes y patronímicos Hispánicos', *Arabia*, 1 (1954), 129–35.

GORDON, C. H. Ugaritic Textbook, *AnOr*, 38 (Rome, 1965).

GRÖNDAHL, F. *Die Personennamen der Texte aus Ugarit.* Studia Pohl, 1 (Rome, 1967).

GUSTAVS, A. 'Die Personennamen in den Tontafeln von Tell Ta'annek', *ZDPV*, 51 (1928), 169–218.

HAMMOND, PH. C. 'An Ammonite Stamp Seal from 'Amman', *BASOR*, 160 (1960), 38–41.

HARRIS, Z. *A Grammar of the Phoenician Language* (American Oriental Series, 8; New Haven, 1936).

HESS, J. J. *Beduinennamen aus Zentralarabien* (Sitzungsberichte der Heidelberger Akademie der Wissenschaften, Phil.-hist. Klasse, 19; Heidelberg, 1912).

HÖFNER, M. 'Die Stammesgruppen Nord- und Zentralarabiens in vorislamischer Zeit', in *Wörterbuch der Mythologie, I.1: Die alten Kulturvölker, Vorderer Orient*, ed. H. W. Haussig (Stuttgart, 1965), 407–81 (with E. Merkel).

—— 'Südarabien', in *Wörterbuch der Mythologie, I.1: Die alten Kulturvölker, Vorderer Orient*, ed. H. W. Haussig (Stuttgart, 1965), 483–552.

HUFFMON, H. B. *Amorite Personal Names in the Mari Texts: A Structural and Lexical Study* (Baltimore, 1965).

INGHOLT, H. 'Deux inscriptions bilingues de Palmyre', *Syria*, 13 (1932), 278–92.

—— 'Five dated tombs from Palmyra', *Berytus*, 2 (1935), 57–120.

—— 'Inscriptions and sculptures from Palmyra', ibid. 3 (1936), 83–127.

—— 'Inscriptions and sculptures from Palmyra—II', ibid. 5 (1938), 93–140.

—— 'Some sculptures from the tomb of Malkû at Palmyra', in *Mélanges offerts à K. Michalowski* (Warsaw, 1966), 457–76.

—— 'Un nouveau thiase à Palmyre', *Syria*, 7 (1926), 128–41.

—— 'The oldest known grave-relief from Palmyra', *Acta Archaeologica*, 1 (1930), 191–4.

—— 'Palmyrene sculptures in Beirut', *Berytus*, 1 (1934), 32–43.

—— 'Palmyrene inscription from the tomb of Malkû', *MUSJ*, 38 (1962), 101–19.

—— *Palmyrene and Gandharan sculpture* (Yale University Art Gallery; 1954).

—— 'Quatre bustes palmyréniens', *Syria*, 11 (1930), 242–4.

—— 'Parthian sculptures from Hatra, Orient and Hellas in art and religion', Memoirs of the Connecticut Academy of Arts and Science, xii. 17–27 (New Haven, 1954).

—— 'Quelques fresques récemment découvertes à Palmyre', *Acta Archaeologica*, 3 (1932), 1–20.

—— *Studier over Palmyrensk Skulptur* (Copenhagen, 1928).

INGHOLT, H., SEYRIG, H., and STARCKY, J. 'Recueil des Tessères de Palmyre', BAH lviii (Paris, 1955).

JAMME, A. 'Le panthéon sud-arabe préislamique d'après les sources épigraphiques', *Le Muséon*, 60 (1947), 57–147.

JASTROW, M. *A dictionary of the Targumim, the Talmud Babli and Yerushalmi, and the Midrashic literature* (London, 1903; reprinted New York, 1950).

JAUSSEN, A. J., and SAVIGNAC, R. *Mission archéologique en Arabie*, 2 vols. (Paris, 1909–14).

JEAN, CH.-F., and HOFTIJZER, J. (eds.) *Dictionnaire des inscriptions sémitiques de l'ouest* (Leiden, 1965).
JEFFERY, A. *The foreign vocabulary of the Qur'ān* (Oriental Institute Baroda; 1938).
JUSTI, F. *Iranisches Namenbuch* (Marburg, 1895; reprinted Hildesheim, 1963).
KIRSTE, J. *Orabazes* ('Sitzungsberichte der kaiserlichen Akademie der Wissenschaften zu Wien, Phil.-hist. Klasse', 182/2; Wien, 1917).
KOEHLER, L. 'Jod als hebräisches Nominalpräfix', *WO* (1950), 404–5.
—— and BAUMGARTNER, W. (eds.) *Lexicon in Veteris Testamenti Libros* (Leiden, 1953).
KOPF, L. 'Arabische Etymologien und Parallelen zum Bibelwörterbuch', *VT*, 8 (1958), 161–215.
KRAELING, E. G. *The Brooklyn Museum Aramaic papyri* (New Haven, 1953).
LANE, E. W. *An Arabic–English lexicon* (London, 1863–93).
LANKESTER HARDING, G. *Some Thamudic inscriptions from the Hashimite kingdom of the Jordan* (Leiden, 1952).
LECERF, J. 'Noms propres palmyréniens', *GLECS* (1935), 29–30.
LEDRAIN, E. *Dictionnaire des noms propres palmyréniens* (Paris, 1887).
LEGRAIN, L. 'Tomb sculptures from Palmyra', *The Museum Journal*, 18 (1927), 325–50.
LEROY, J. 'Mosaïques funéraires d'Edesse', *Syria*, 34 (1957), 306–42.
LEVI DELLA VIDA, G. 'Une bilingue gréco-palmyrénienne à Cos', in *Mélanges syriens offerts à M. René Dussaud* (BAH, xxx; Paris, 1939), ii. 883–6.
LEVY, J. *Neuhebräisches und chaldäisches Wörterbuch über die Talmudim und Midraschim* (Leipzig, 1876–89).
LEWY, J. 'The old west Semitic sun-god Ḥammu', *HUCA*, 18 (1943–4), 429–88.
LIDZBARSKI, M. 'Altaramäische Urkunden aus Assur', *WVDOG*, 38 (1921).
—— *Ephemeris für semitische Epigraphik*, 3 vols. (Giessen, 1902–15).
—— *Handbuch der nordsemitischen Epigraphik nebst ausgewählten Inschriften.* 2 vols. (Weimar, 1898).
—— *Phönizische und aramäische Krugaufschriften aus Elephantine* (Abhandlungen der königlich Preussischen Akademie der Wissenschaften, Phil.-hist. Klasse, Anhang; Berlin, 1912).
LITTMAN, E. 'Eine altsyrische Inschrift', *ZA*, 27 (1912), 379–82.
—— *Nabataean inscriptions* ('Publications of the Princeton University Archaeological Expeditions to Syria in 1904–1905 and 1909, Division IV, Section A'). Leiden, 1914.
—— 'Nabataean Inscriptions from Egypt', *BSOAS*, 15 (1953), 1–28.
—— 'Nabataean Inscriptions from Egypt—II', *BSOAS*, 16 (1954), 211–46.
—— *Safaitic inscriptions* ('Publications of the Princeton University Archaeological Expeditions to Syria in 1904–1905 and 1909, Division IV, Section C'; Leiden, 1943).
—— 'Zwei seltenere arabische Nominalbildungen', *ZS*, 4 (1926), 24–41.
—— *Semitic inscriptions* (Part IV of the Publications of an American Expedition to Syria in 1899–1900; New York, 1904).
—— 'Arabische Hypokoristica', in *Studia Orientalia Ioanni Pedersen . . . dicata*, 193–9 (Hauniae, 1953).
LUCKENBILL, D. D. *Ancient Records of Assyria and Babylonia.* 2 vols. (Chicago, 1926).
MACKAY, D. 'The jewellery of Palmyra and its significance', *Iraq*, 11 (1949), 160–87.
MAZAR (MAISLER), B. 'The excavations at Sheikh Ibreiq (Beth Sheʿarīm) 1936/7', *JPOS*, 18 (1938), 41–8.
—— *Beth Sheʿarīm. Report on the Excavations during 1936–40. Volume One: The Catacombs I–IV* (Jerusalem, 1957).
MARGOLIOUTH, J. P. *Supplement to the Thesaurus Syriacus of R. Payne-Smith* (Oxford, 1927).

MARICQ, A. 'Classica et Orientalia', ed. by J. Pirenne, *Syria*, 39 (1962), 88–105.
MARTIN. F. 'Discours de Jacques de Saroug sur la chute des idoles', *ZDMG*, 29 (1876), 107–47.
MICHALOWSKI, K. *Palmyre. Fouilles polonaises 1959–62*, 4 vols. (Paris, 1960–4).
—— *Mélanges offerts à K. Michalowski* (Warsaw, 1966).
MILIK, J. T. 'Notes d'épigraphie orientale', *Syria*, 37 (1960), 94–8.
—— 'Nouvelles inscriptions nabatéennes', *Syria*, 35 (1958), 227–51.
—— 'A propos d'un atélier monétaire d'Adiabène: Natounia', *Revue numismatique*, iv (1962), 51–8.
MORAN, W. L. 'The Hebrew Language in its northwest Semitic background', in *The Bible and the Ancient Near East* (*Essays in honor of William Foxwell Albright*), ed. G. E. Wright (Garden City, 1961), 54–72.
MORDTMANN, J. H. *Palmyrenisches* (*MVÄG*, 4 (1899), Heft 1; Berlin, 1899).
MORITZ, B. 'Syrische Inschriften', in *Inschriften aus Syrien, Mesopotamien und Kleinasien gesammelt im Jahr 1899 von Max Freiherr von Oppenheim*, Beiträge zur Assyriologie und semitischen Sprachwissenschaft, vol. vii (Leipzig, 1909).
Mouterde, R. and Jalabert, L. *Inscriptions grecques et latines de la Syrie*, 5 vols. BAH XII, XXXII, XLVI, LXI, LXVI, (Paris, 1929–59).
NODELMAN, SH. A. 'A Preliminary History of Characene', *Berytus*, 13 (1960), 83–121.
NÖLDEKE, TH. *Beiträge zur semitischen Sprachwissenschaft* (Strassburg, 1904).
—— 'Kleinigkeiten zur semitischen Onomatologie', *WZKM*, 6 (1892), 307–16.
—— *Kurzgefasste syrische Grammatik.* 2nd edn. (Leipzig, 1898).
—— 'Über Orthographie und Sprache der Palmyrener', *ZDMG*, 24 (1870), 85–109.
NÖTSCHER, F. 'Zum emphatischen Lamed', *VT*, 3 (1953), 372–80.
NOTH, M. 'Gemeinsemitische Erscheinungen in der israelitischen Namengebung', *ZDMG*, 81 (1927), 1–45.
—— *Die israelitischen Personennamen im Rahmen der gemeinsemitischen Namengebung*, Beiträge zur Wissenschaft vom Alten und Neuen Testament, 46/iii. 10 (Stuttgart, 1928; reprinted Hildesheim, 1966).
NOUGAYROL, J. *Le Palais royal d'Ugarit, III: Textes accadiens et hourrites des Archives Est, Ouest et Centrales*, 2 vols., *MRS*, tome vi (Paris, 1955).
—— *Le Palais royal d'Ugarit, IV: Textes accadiens des Archives Sud.* 2 vols., *MRS*, tome ix (Paris, 1956).
NYBERG, H. S. 'Studien zum Religionskampf im Alten Testament: I. Der Gott ʿAl: Belege und Bedeutung des Namens, II. Geschichte des Gottes ʿAl im Alten Testament', *Archiv für Religionswissenschaft vereint mit den Beiträgen zur Religionswissenschaft der religionswissenschaftlichen Gesellschaft zu Stockholm*, 35 (1938), 329–87.
OPPENHEIM, A. L., *et al.* (eds.). *The Assyrian dictionary of the Oriental Institute of the University of Chicago* (Chicago, 1956–).
OPPENHEIM, M. FREIHERR VON. *Inschriften aus Syrien, Mesopotamien und Kleinasien.* Beiträge zur Assyriologie und semitischen Sprachwissenschaft, vii/1 (Leipzig, 1909).
PAPE, W. *Wörterbuch der griechischen Eigennamen* (Braunschweig, 1875).
PAYNE-SMITH, R. *Thesaurus Syriacus* (Oxford, 1879–97).
PHILLIPS, G. *The Doctrine of Addai the Apostle* (London, 1876).
POPE, M. 'Syrien. Die Mythologie der Ugariter und Phönizier', in *Wörterbuch der Mythologie, I.1: Die alten Kulturvölker, Vorderer Orient*, ed. H. W. Haussig (Stuttgart, 1965), 217–312 (with W. Röllig).
PRAETORIUS, F. 'Über einige Arten hebräischer Eigennamen', *ZDMG*, 57 (1903), 773–82.
PREISIGKE, F. *Namenbuch, enthaltend alle griechischen, lateinischen, ägyptischen, hebräischen, arabischen und sonstigen semitischen und nichtsemitischen Menschennamen, soweit sie in griechischen Urkunden (Papyri, Ostraka, Inschriften, Mumienschildern usw) Ägyptens sich vorfinden* (Heidelberg, 1922).

PRITCHARD, J. B. *Ancient Near Eastern Texts relating to the Old Testament.* 2nd edn. (Princeton, 1955).
RODINSON, M. 'Une inscription trilingue de Palmyre', *Syria*, 27 (1950), 137–42.
RONZEVALLE, S. 'Monuments palmyréniens', *Mélanges de la Faculté orientale de Beyrouth*, 4 (1910), 145–80.
ROSENTHAL, F. *Die aramaistische Forschung seit Th. Nöldeke's Veröffentlichungen* (Leiden, 1939; reprinted Leiden, 1966).
—— *Die Sprache der palmyrenischen Inschriften, MVÄG*, 41 (1936), 1–114.
ROSMARIN, T. W. 'Aribi und Arabien in den babylonisch-assyrischen Quellen', *JSOR*, 16 (1932), 1–37.
ROSTOVZEFF, M. J. *et al.* (eds.). *The excavations at Dura-Europos conducted by Yale University and the French Academy of Inscriptions and Letters. Preliminary reports 1–9* (New Haven, 1929–46).
RYCKMANS, G. *Les noms propres sud-sémitiques.* 3 vols., Bibliothèque du Muséon, 2 (Louvain, 1934–5).
—— *Les religions arabes préislamiques.* Bibliothèque du Muséon, 26, 2nd edn. (Louvain, 1951).
—— 'Inscriptions safaïtiques', *Le Muséon*, 64 (1951), 83–91.
SABEH, J. 'Sculptures palmyréniennes inédites du Musée de Damas', *AAS*, 3 (1953), 17–26.
SACHAU, ED. 'Edessenische Inschriften', *ZDMG*, 36 (1882), 142–67.
SAFAR, F. 'Inscriptions from Wadi Hauran', *Sumer*, 20 (1964), 9–27.
SCHLUMBERGER, D. *La Palmyrène du Nord-Ouest* (BAH, 49; Paris, 1951).
SCHOTTROFF, W. *'Gedenken' im Alten Orient und im Alten Testament*, Wissenschaftliche Monographien zum Alten und Neuen Testament, 15 (Neukirchen, 1964).
SCHULT, H. *Vergleichende Studien zur alttestamentlichen Namenkunde.* Diss. (Bonn, 1967).
SEGAL, J. B. 'An Aramaic ostracon from Nimrud', *Iraq*, 19 (1957), 139–45.
—— 'New Syriac inscriptions from Edessa', *BSOAS*, 22 (1959), 23–40.
—— 'Pagan Syriac monuments in the Vilayet of Urfa', *Ana. Studies*, 3 (1953), 97–119.
—— 'A Syriac seal inscription', *Iraq*, 29 (1967), 6–15.
—— 'Two Syriac inscriptions from Harran', *BSOAS*, 20 (1957), 513–22.
—— 'Four Syriac inscriptions', *BSOAS*, 30 (1967), 293–304.
SEYRIG, H. 'Notes archéologiques', *Berytus*, 2 (1935), 42–50.
SIGGEL, A. *Arabisch–Deutsches Wörterbuch der Stoffe* (Deutsche Akademie der Wissenschaften zu Berlin, Institut für Orientforschung, 1; Berlin, 1950).
SOBERNHEIM, M. *Palmyrenische Inschriften, MVÄG*, 10/2 (Berlin, 1905).
VON SODEN, W. (ed.). *Akkadisches Handwörterbuch, Unter Benutzung des lexikalischen Nachlasses von Bruno Meissner (1869–1947)* (Wiesbaden, 1959–).
STAMM, J. J. *Die akkadische Namengebung* (*MVÄG*, 44 (1939); reprinted Darmstadt, 1968).
STARCKY, J. 'Autour d'une dédicace palmyrénienne à Šadrafa et à Duʿanat', *Syria*, 26 (1949), 43–85.
—— 'Bas-relief palmyrénien inédit, dédié aux génies Šalman et 'RGYʿ', *Semitica*, 3 (1950), 45–52.
—— 'Deux inscriptions palmyréniennes', *MUSJ*, 38 (1961), 121–39.
—— 'Trois inscriptions palmyréniennes', *MUSJ*, 28 (1949–50), 45–58.
—— 'Inscriptions archaïques de Palmyre', in *Studi orientalistici in onore di G. Levi della Vida*, ii. 509–29 (Rome, 1956).
—— 'Inscriptions palmyréniennes conservées au Musée de Beyrouth', *BMB*, 12 (1955), 29–44.
—— 'Les inscriptions palmyréniennes les plus anciennes', *Actes du 21ème Congrès international des orientalistes*, 111–14 (Paris, 1949).
—— 'Les inscriptions', *Syria*, 26 (1949), 35–41.

STARCKY, J. 'Une inscription palmyrénienne trouvée près de l'Euphrate', *Syria*, 40 (1963), 47–55.
—— 'L'ostracon araméen du sabbat', *Semitica*, 2 (1949), 29–39.
—— *Palmyre*. L'orient ancien illustré, 7 (Paris, 1952).
—— 'Palmyre', in *Supplement au Dictionnaire de la Bible*, 6, 1066–1103 (Paris, 1960).
—— 'Récentes découvertes à Palmyre', *Syria*, 25 (1946–8), 334–6.
—— 'Relief palmyrénien dédié au dieu Ilahay', in *Mélanges bibliques A. Robert*, 370–80 (no date).
—— 'Deux textes religieux de Palmyre', *CRAIBL* (1946), 391–5.
STARCKY, J., and AL-HASSANI, D. 'Autels palmyréniens découverts près de la source Efca', *AAS*, 3 (1953), 145–64; 7 (1957), 95–122.
STEINGASS, F. *Persian–English dictionary* (London, 1963).
ṬABARI, *Annales*, ed. J. de. Goeje (Leiden, 1879–81).
TALLQUIST, K. *Akkadische Götterepitheta*. Studia Orientalia, 7 (Helsingfors, 1938).
—— *Assyrian Personal Names*. *Acta Societatis Scientiarum Fennicae*, xliii/1 (Helsingfors, 1914; reprinted Hildesheim, 1966).
—— *Neubabylonisches Namenbuch*. *Acta Societatis Scientiarum Fennicae*, xxxii/2 (Helsingfors, 1905).
TEIXIDOR, J. 'Aramaic Inscriptions of Hatra', *Sumer*, 20 (1964), 77–80.
—— 'Deux inscriptions palmyréniennes du Musée de Bagdad', *Syria*, 40 (1963), 33–46.
—— 'Bulletin d'Épigraphie sémitique', ibid. 44 (1967), 163–95; ibid. 45 (1968), 353–89.
—— 'Three Inscriptions in the Iraq Museum', *Sumer*, 18 (1962), 63–5.
—— 'Monuments palmyréniens divers', *MUSJ*, 42 (1966), 175–9.
TORREY, CH. C. 'A Syriac Parchment from Edessa of the year 243 A.D.', *ZS*, 10 (1935), 33–45.
TSEVAT, M. 'The Canaanite God Šälaḥ', *VT*, 4 (1954), 41–9.
VINCENT, A. 'Jéricho. Une hypothèse', *MUSJ*, 37 (1960–1), 79–90.
VIROLLEAUD, CH. *Le Palais royal d'Ugarit, II: Textes en cunéiformes alphabétiques des Archives Est, Ouest et Centrales*. MRS, tome vii (Paris, 1957).
WADDINGTON, W. H. *Index alphabétique et analytique des inscriptions grecques et latines de la Syrie*, rédigé par J. B. Chabot. Extrait de la *Revue archéologique* (1896).
WAHRMUND, A. *Handwörterbuch der arabischen und deutschen Sprache*, 2 vols. (Giessen, 1877).
WALKER, J. 'A Palmyrene tessera', in *Studi orientalistici in onore di G. Levi della Vida*, ii. 601–2 (Rome, 1956).
WEHR, H. *A dictionary of modern written Arabic*, ed. J. M. Cowan (Ithaca, N.Y., 1966).
WELLES, C. BRADFORD, *et al.* (eds.) *The excavations at Dura-Europos. Final report V, Part I. The parchments and papyri* (New Haven, 1959).
WELLHAUSEN, J. *Reste arabischen Heidentums* (Berlin, 1897).
WINNETT, F. V. *Safaitic inscriptions from Jordan*. Near and Middle East Series, 2 (Toronto, 1957).
WRIGHT, W. *A grammar of the Arabic language*. 3rd edn. rev. by W. Robertson Smith and M. J. de Goeje, 2 vols. (Cambridge, 1955).
WÜSTENFELD, F. *Abu Bekr Muhammed ben el-Hassan Ibn Doreid's genealogisch-etymologisches Handbuch* (Göttingen, 1854).
—— *Register zu den genealogischen Tabellen der arabischen Stämme und Familien* (Göttingen, 1853).
WUTHNOW, H. 'Eine palmyrenische Büste', in *Orientalistische Studien Enno Littmann . . . überreicht*, 63–9 (Leiden, 1935).
—— *Die semitischen Menschennamen in griechischen Inschriften und Papyri des vorderen Orients*. Studien zur Epigraphik und Papyruskunde, i/4 (Leipzig, 1930).
YADIN, Y. 'Expedition D—The cave of the letters', *IEJ*, 12 (1962), 227–57.